INTERPRETING THE NEW TESTAMENT

Essays on Methods and Issues

David Alan Black & David S. Dockery

BROADMAN
& HOLMAN
PUBLISHERS

NASHVILLE, TENNESSEE

0–8054–1850–4

Published by Broadman & Holman Publishers, Nashville, Tennessee

Dewey Decimal Classification: 225
Subject Heading: NEW TESTAMENT

Library of Congress Cataloging-in-Publication Data

Interpreting the New Testament : essays on methods and issues / edited by David Alan Black and David S. Dockery.
    p. cm.
    Rev. ed. of: New Testament criticism and interpretation. 1991.
    Includes bibliographical references and index.
    ISBN 0–8054–1850–4 (pbk.)
    1. Bible. N.T.—Criticism, interpretation, etc. 2. Bible. N.T.—Hermeneutics. I. Black, David Alan, 1952– II. Dockery, David S. III. New Testament criticism and interpretation.

BS2361.3 .I58 2001
225.6—dc21

00–046804

1 2 3 4 5 6 7 8 9 10   05 04 03 02 01

In Loving Memory

of

Thomas D. Lea

and

John P. Newport

Contents

Preface

One of the world's best-known and most influential bodies of literature, the New Testament is also one of the least understood. If this is partly due to sloth on the part of the modern reader (and who has never been guilty of laziness when it comes to the study of the Bible?), it is also due in no small part to the proliferation of modern approaches to New Testament interpretation in the late twentieth century. Bewildered by this plethora of methodologies, the modern reader may well hesitate to go beyond a cursory reading (and understanding) of the New Testament writings. Even if one has the desire to teach or preach from the New Testament with authority and credibility, who has the time or courage to study it in depth and to proclaim it without fear or favor?

The purpose of *Interpreting the New Testament* is to enhance New Testament interpretation, teaching, and preaching by providing a useful means of learning what the New Testament is all about and—whenever possible—the historical reasons why it speaks the way it does. It endeavors not only to acquaint readers with the scope and trends of modern New Testament scholarship but also to enable them to have a clearer and more enjoyable experience when reading and applying these twenty-seven inspired books.

The present volume is a sequel to our earlier work titled *New Testament Criticism and Interpretation*. It includes many of the previous essays (updated and in some instances completely rewritten) as well as a few new contributions. Together, these essays comprise a representative cross section of current evangelical New Testament scholarship that seeks to be responsible to the supernatural revelation of the New Testament while at the same time keeping abreast of current issues, trends, and methodologies. The editors hope that the essays will serve as a useful overview of current New Testament studies as well as a basis and stimulus for further study. We have prepared this book primarily for students of the New Testament in colleges and seminaries, but we cherish the hope that pastors and lay people will also find the book useful as a means of becoming better acquainted with the various lines of investigation that are germane to the study of the New Testament. No claim to completeness is made, for the field is too vast. The student who wishes to go more deeply into the various subjects should, however, find the brief bibliographies at the end of the chapters useful.

The book is divided into three parts. The first deals with various introductory matters; the second with current methods in New Testament interpretation; and the third with several vital issues that will be of interest to students and pastors. This volume is not an introduction to the New Testament per se, but it does offer some orientation to the task of setting New Testament studies in its contemporary framework. Hopefully it will lay a foundation on which the reader can build in later years.

There are signs today of a revival of interest in the serious study of the New Testament. What is now needed is a revival of authoritative, relevant, and passionate preaching from the New Testament that will enhance the growth of the body of Christ. If this book stimulates such a revival, the editors and contributors will be grateful indeed.

Soli Deo Gloria
David Alan Black
David S. Dockery

Part I

Introduction

Chapter 1

Authority, Hermeneutics, and Criticism

Peter H. Davids
Innsbruck, Austria

As I grew up, I was in a church that stressed that they were a "New Testament church," meeting according to "biblical principles of gathering," having no creed or procedural handbook other than the Bible. For me it was clear that the Bible taught our form of church polity, although I recognized that many otherwise good Christians (whose churches I visited and sometimes even helped out in) apparently were ignorant of such "biblical principles." But then I left home for Wheaton College and for the first time in my life had to *live with* good Christian fellows who went to different churches than I did (mainly Baptist and Free Church) and who were not persuaded by my arguments that our particular style of meeting was the one sanctioned by Scripture. This created a crisis in my life, for here were Christians reading the same Bible and claiming it as their authority and yet interpreting it differently. This was a crisis in hermeneutics, for we were differing not on the authority of the text or on what it said but on what we understood the text to mean for us today.

In the same college were many students who were critical of the church. Their argument was that the evangelical church talked a lot about biblical authority but actually did little to obey the commands of Scripture. It was, they argued, a faith of "cheap grace" without works. Other students had given up their faith entirely and did not see the relevance of Scripture to their lives. For them it was a historic book, the shaper of parts of their culture, but something to be left behind in their parental home. These two groups of students, I noticed, were having a crisis in authority, the one group calling their elders to take the authority of Scripture more seriously and the other group having lost any belief in the authority of Scripture.

Finally, when I left college and went on to seminary and then graduate school, I had to face the variety of critical methodologies discussed in this

2

book. I personally found this challenging, for I believed that through my study I was learning to interpret Scripture more accurately and therefore was becoming more able to obey it. For me, criticism was an aid to biblical authority.

There were two other responses to this same challenge in the same institutions. Some of my friends felt that in giving up their old interpretations of Scripture they also had to give up the authority of Scripture. For them biblical criticism relativized Scripture. Other friends argued that if these tools were needed to understand Scripture then the layperson was in a hopeless state when it came to obeying Scripture. They felt hostile toward critical methodologies; to them these tools were distancing Scripture from them and thus making them dependent on scholars. They resented this removal of biblical meaning from their grasp. These are the issues we will address in this essay, setting the stage for the following discussions in this book.

The Meaning of Biblical Authority

First, what does it mean that Scripture has authority? Although there are several ways of describing authority, for our purposes there are two types of authority, intrinsic and extrinsic. Intrinsic authority is that which something or someone possesses due to what they are. A person with a gun has such authority, for he or she can enforce their demands. A law of nature has similar authority in that, if accurate, life will operate according to it whether anyone knows about it or believes in it.

Extrinsic authority, on the other hand, is the authority that someone or something possesses because people ascribe such authority to them. A president or prime minister has this type of authority in that the minute people refuse to grant them authority they are powerless. Likewise the laws of a government have only extrinsic authority, as one observes in places where the speed limit is set at one speed and police will only enforce a higher limit because the people are all driving faster than the legal limit.

When we are writing about scriptural authority, we are not talking about its intrinsic authority. That topic would turn this into an essay on the doctrine of Scripture. Rather, we assume with 2 Timothy 3:16 that all Scripture[1] is "God breathed" and thus has intrinsic authority.[2] What Scripture says, God says. This truth stands whether anyone ever obeys Scripture, for it does not gain its (intrinsic) authority due to the consensus of a religious community but due to the fact that God has put into the volume a description of reality (i.e., his will) as it is.

Given, then, that Scripture has God's authority, there is still the issue of extrinsic authority. That is, from the human point of view, we first must recognize that Scripture is authoritative and then must understand and respond to it appropriately—with obedience. At this point the issues of criticism and hermeneutic come into play. As readers we may or may not understand the message, which is where hermeneutic comes in, or critical studies may either obscure or clarify the reality of the authority.

The real issue is whether the authority—God's message through Scripture—is received by human beings and is then translated into obedience. If there is no obedience, then all the discussions about authority are no more than abstractions. While we assume that due to its intrinsic authority Scripture will "have the last say" in the day of judgment, as far as today is concerned, it is not functioning in an authoritative way unless we human beings respond to it.

Authority and Hermeneutics

The first issue, then, is hermeneutics. God did not dictate the New Testament from heaven in some sort of timeless, divine language, just as Jesus did not appear in his full glory. Rather, God chose to preserve some of the letters of Paul as he struggled with correcting problems in the churches he founded (apparently totally unconscious that people two thousand years later would be reading his letters), he inspired Luke (how he did so we have no idea, or whether Luke was aware the impulse was divine) to write a two-volume history of the Christian movement, and he chose John on Patmos to receive an extraordinary vision and to communicate it to seven Asian churches.[3]

These differing ways of writing Scripture point out to us that God produced Scripture within the process of daily life. Just as no one noticed Jesus' growing up or differentiated him from other young carpenters they knew, so also scriptural revelation (and in this book our interest is in New Testament revelation) was "incarnate" within the process of human life. No one noticed it being produced.

Even its authors, for the most part, were not aware that they were writing Scripture. At times they were aware of writing divine commands to this or that community,[4] but that is a long way from having any idea that one is writing Scripture, the basic document of the church of God around the world. Only in 2 Peter 3:16 do we catch a glimmer that already, late in the New Testament period, some of Paul's writings (how many we do not know) were beginning to be spoken of in the same breath as the Hebrew Scriptures. We may object to this apparently haphazard method of production, but we might as well object that the gospel was announced to the world through human means, not through angelic voices from heaven. God being God chose to give revelation in his own way and did not consult human beings to discover if we had better ideas.

While Scripture's form may at first appear problematic, it has profound implications for hermeneutics, the science of interpretation. The New Testament is human speech, human beings writing to other human beings. Therefore it needs to be understood as human speech. This is helpful to us, for we constantly interpret human speech; it would be problematic if we had to learn some divine language to understand God's communication. But at the same time there are problems involved in our interpretation. We human beings take our thoughts and encode them in a series of symbols (either oral sounds or written symbols for those sounds) that we share in common with others in our community. A different community will assign different meanings to the same symbols. For example, the English word *hell* means something quite different than the German *hell* (that means "light" as in *hell braun* meaning "light brown"); in this case both the vocal and written symbols are identical in the two languages, but they have very different meanings.

What is more, the same symbol may have a different meaning depending on what other symbols it is combined with. For example, *green* means something different in "The house was green" from "It was a greenhouse" and in "He turned green as the ship pitched on the waves." Therefore, to understand Scripture we need to know how the author and his community used their symbols; and there are multiple authors and at least as many community contexts.

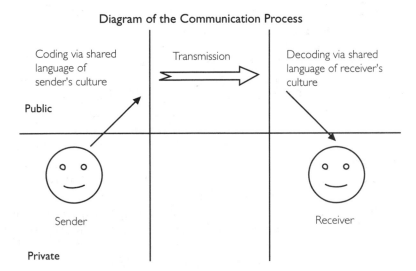

Diagram of the Communication Process

Coding via shared language of sender's culture

Transmission

Decoding via shared language of receiver's culture

Public

Sender

Receiver

Private

At this point one is already involved in discussion of hermeneutics, for, on the one hand, some people have tended to see the symbols of Scripture (i.e., the words of Greek or, in translation, English) as taking on a life of their own separate from the author's culture. It disturbs them when one suggests that as we come to understand the author's thought-world better, we must change our understanding of what appears to be a word with a clear meaning. Thus if one argues that in 1 Timothy 2:9–15 the Greek term *gunē* meant within that cultural context "wife," not "woman,"[5] some folk will feel threatened because it has "always" been understood as "woman" (at least in English translations), while others will respond, "Let's see if this is new and correct information which does in fact assist us in understanding and obeying the message of Scripture more accurately." In each case a different hermeneutical stance has been taken, in this case a hermeneutical stance about the relevance of new exegetical information.[6]

We have argued that the second position is more in keeping with the nature of language (that written or verbal symbols only have meaning within a cultural context); it also allows one to accept new information and change interpretation without losing a sense of the authority of Scripture. But to the former group, those taking the second position may appear to be rejecting biblical authority, for that is what *they* would have to do to change their response to the text. The groundwork is thus laid for a discussion about interpretation to become (falsely) a discussion about authority with charges and counter charges.

The issue of hermeneutics becomes more complicated when we move beyond the understanding of a single text (which itself is not always easy) to the understanding of Scripture as a whole. For example, since the Reformation the adherents of the Lutheran and Reformed traditions have tended to view Paul (particularly Galatians and Romans) as the center of the New Testament with all other biblical material being interpreted in the light of his writings.

This has also been true of Dispensationalist hermeneutics. But the Anabaptist tradition (and to a large degree the Roman Catholic tradition) has tended to put the Gospels in the center with Paul being interpreted in that light. Furthermore, partly based on this difference, there has been an ongoing argument as to whether the Old Testament directions to Israel should be fulfilled in the secular state or instead obeyed in a spiritual form within the community of believers.

These differences in hermeneutics came to a head in the Reformation period with each group calling the other disobedient to Scripture and condemning the other to hell (and at times to prison, torture, and execution). Yet each group was attempting to be obedient to Scripture, and each Scripture was fully authoritative. Unfortunately, they did not discuss hermeneutics but theology, and because these underlying issues were not addressed, they ended up in a dialogue of the deaf. A similar impasse often occurs today when evangelicals discuss such issues as capital punishment, participation in war, or the role of women in ministry.[7]

Some (usually referred to as postmodern or reader-response interpreters)[8] argue that in trying to understand what the original author wanted to communicate we are looking at the wrong end of the communication process. Since the original author is long dead and there are no living representatives of his culture (i.e., his reference group for coding his thoughts into language), we cannot know what he really wanted to communicate.

We really have only the right half of the diagram above, our cultural reference group, and its reading of the text. This means that a text has many meanings, not a single meaning, for there are many possible cultural settings within which a person might read the same text. Thus while the text ma y be viewed as authoritative, the real locus of authority is in the reading community, not in the unrecoverable thought the original author may have wanted to communicate. Such a view does radically change the idea of biblical authority, for then there are multiple true meanings of any text. The problem they had in the Reformation was simply that they did not understand this and so could not recognize that Catholic, Magisterial Reformation, and Anabaptist each read in the context of a different community.

This position describes how most people actually read Scripture. Thus my church community taught me to read it so that some things were "obvious" that were not "obvious" to someone in another church community. It also points to the fact that we often do not know enough to reconstruct fully the intention of the original author, especially when an author, such as Paul, is giving us only half of a dialogue with a church and thus assumes their situation, communication, and cultural context. However, while teaching us humility in our interpretation and describing how most people do read the Bible, it does ignore at least three factors.

First, the methodology was developed for poetry and fiction,[9] not for communications with a high degree of intentionality (e.g., letters or prophecy). Thus Paul does feel that he has a point to communicate and explains it again when people do not get it (e.g., 1 Cor. 5:9–11). This makes application to letters and similar communication experientially questionable.

Second, the methodology, if applied to history, would make us skeptical about any historical writing from a period in which the subjects were already dead. Yet both the Old Testament and the New refer to historical events as the foundation of their message. If taken to the point of historical skepticism, it cuts at the heart of the Christian message.

Third, in its more extreme forms this makes us unable to dialogue about our differences other than to point out that we have different reference groups with different assumptions. For some this is no problem, but for those who feel Scripture and its authority should be the focal point of ecumenical discussion, this is a problem indeed.

Finally, there is yet another set of hermeneutical problems when one attempts to translate obedience in the New Testament period into obedience in our culture. That is, assuming (over against some postmodern positions) that we understand the first-century communication, we still need to discuss how to bring it into a different culture. If some postmoderns lack the left side of the diagram, some interpreters lack the right and so argue that we should simply imitate the first century. For example, in 1 Corinthians 11:2–16, Paul discusses what appears to be the wearing of veils by women when they prayed or prophesied in church.[10] For some Christians this means that Christian women should wear a veil (usually reduced to a hat) in church today, despite the fact that such items are now either archaic curiosities or elements of fashion rather than carrying any of the possible meanings they had in Paul's day. Cultural differences in meaning are irrelevant for these Christians.

Other Christians observe that the veil in Paul's day was probably a sign of marriage.[11] In western culture the sign of marriage is a wedding ring. Thus a cultural translation might be made that Christian women should wear their wedding rings when ministering, or, by extension (since rings are less likely to be thrown aside than veils) they should not dishonor their marriage by the manner in which they minister. This is consistent with Paul's usual order of putting marriage (and other forms of holiness) before ministry.

The first group sees themselves as obeying Scripture and all others as disobedient to a clear command (although in many cases their women neither pray nor prophesy in church, which is presumed by Paul as the context in which the style was relevant). The second group, however, also sees themselves as obeying Scripture and might accuse the first group of failing to obey Paul's meaning in trying to obey the letter of the text. Again, there is no difference between the two groups about the authority of Scripture, but there is a lot of difference about hermeneutics and in particular how one is to apply Scripture in a different culture. And while this particular issue may appear a trivial interest of a small section of the church, the same principles apply to a much wider spectrum of issues.

The upshot of this discussion is that differences in exegesis (the understanding of what the original author was trying to say) and hermeneutics (the understanding of the relevance of a text for today) are not necessarily differences in ascribing authority to Scripture. If the mistake is made of confusing the two issues, then there will be no way of solving the problem. Rather, hermeneutic refinement and its discussion are part of an ongoing process among many evangelicals to understand what John or Paul or Luke really meant (and therefore what God meant)[12] and then to obey it more carefully.

Authority and Criticism

Turning to the issue of criticism, we face a more difficult situation. Some types of critical study will hardly disturb one interested in the issue of authority. For example, the goal of textual criticism is to provide the text most like what the original author actually wrote. Not only are the findings relatively inoffensive, but the goals are in line with the interests of those committed to biblical authority.[13]

On the other hand, tradition criticism (a term that covers some aspects of both form and redaction criticism), which looks at the Gospel tradition as something that changed considerably within the oral period (approximately A.D. 30–60) before the Gospels were written, can be quite threatening. There is a real issue of how to respond. This article is not the place to give a detailed critique of tradition criticism and related methodologies, for that is the job of other authors in this book, but we can discuss the appropriate attitude that enables one to come to terms with such areas of study.

First, it is necessary to separate the methodology from the skeptical presuppositions of some of its practitioners (including in many cases its originators). Luke claims that he used sources (Luke 1:1–4), so it is no surprise to discover that the other evangelists did as well (source criticism). It is clear that a miracle story "looks" different from a proverb of Jesus, and a study of the forms in which such materials circulated does not have to imply that one is less genuine than the other (form criticism). The fact that Paul apparently quotes a hymn in Philippians 2:6–11 does not make him less inspired (or the hymn any less a part of Scripture) any more than does his quotation of pagan poets in Acts 17:28. It may shock a person to discover Paul's methodology, and for some it may indicate the presence of "more primitive pre-Pauline" material; but, whatever our reaction, Paul presumably quotes what any author would quote—material he agrees with that says well what he wants to say (source and redaction criticism).

The truth is that many of these methodologies have been used by people who did have skeptical assumptions, for whom sayings of Jesus were creations of the later church unless proved to be genuine or for whom material that was not actually created by Paul was in some way to be discounted. One does not have to hold such assumptions, however, to profit from the methodology. We can work from a basis of faith and piety as well as from a basis of skepticism and doubt. Indeed, the same tools that some have used to support their doubt will be used by other scholars to support their faith. And scholars on both sides can make good and poor use of their tools. Some are blinded by their personal beliefs and engage in circular reasoning and special pleading. Others can bracket their beliefs and come to conclusions that all applaud, whatever their position of belief or doubt. Those committed to the authority of Scripture need to be able to separate the facts scholars observe from the faith positions they may have mixed with them (and that may distort some of their data). This is what good scholarship is all about.

Second, we must again think about hermeneutic when we consider the issue of criticism. If the authority of Scripture rests in what the original author intended to communicate to his or her first readers, namely, in the message in its original cultural context,[14] then anything that clarifies the author's intentions is desirable. Let us take a series of examples.

Not one of the Gospels names its author (even the fourth Gospel does not name its author, although in chapter 21 it does indicate, without naming him, the disciple who was either the author or the source of at least the second half of the Gospel). Thus there is no *biblical* authority at stake in arguing who wrote what, although there may be a lot of *traditional* authority at risk. On the other hand, in the Epistles (except Hebrews and the Johannine Epistles) the author does identify himself by name, so there is an issue of biblical authority at stake in the authorship issue, unless one can show that in the ancient world pseudonymity was in fact accepted and thus that no deception was intended. In that (hypothetical) case we moderns would be wrongly assuming that the apparent claim of authorship was a true claim of authorship, but the ancient writer and reader would have read it as something like "in the spirit of _____."[15] If that could be proved, then no biblical authority would rest in the claim of authorship (even though for centuries the church has read it as a true claim). On the other hand, if that cannot be proved, then biblical authority is truly at stake.

Moving one step beyond the authorship issue, we know from the ancient world that authorship does not imply actually writing the document. Paul, for example, claims he followed normal practice and actually wrote only the last few lines of his letters (2 Thess. 3:17, which is probably what Gal. 6:11 also indicates). The rest was dictated. Did Paul give any freedom to his secretaries (who were often trusted co-workers)? That should not bother us so long as the author "signed the letter."[16] Were some works, for example James, written after the death of the author from materials he had composed during his lifetime?[17] That would not be surprising in either the ancient or the modern world (although the modern world tends to acknowledge the process more clearly), and James' sayings and sermons were *his* message, not that of whoever might have put them together.

Furthermore, we must read the documents in the context of the accepted canons of writing in the ancient world. Surely Peter did not deliver a five-minute sermon on Pentecost (Acts 2). Every educated ancient reader (and most who could read were educated) knew that the standard practice of historians was to summarize what a speaker said. It was not expected that the author of Acts would have either received or given a verbatim account. It was quite acceptable to put the speaker's thoughts into one's own words (much like the abstract of a book or article today). Indeed, it was even acceptable to make up a speech from the types of things the speaker was known to have said on other occasions! While none of this might be acceptable historical procedure today, the author of Acts lived then and not today; he appears to have been a rather conservative historian within the context of his day.

Similar things can be said about the Gospels. In each of the cases the words of Jesus at some point (whether by the evangelist or by someone who passed the tradition on to him) had to be translated from Aramaic into Greek. At times they also needed to be edited or expanded to make sense in a different culture. For example, Mark 10:12 has the clause, "If she (a wife) divorces her husband and marries another man, she commits adultery." This carried Jesus' thought into the Roman world, where Mark was written, but it was an impossible idea in a Palestinian context, where women could not divorce.[18] Thus Matthew omits the sentence altogether, and Luke changes it to a passive ("The woman who has been divorced by her husband").

Did Mark accurately communicate Jesus' message of no divorce to the Roman world, where women could and did divorce their husbands, expanding Jesus' saying to make it clear that it applied to women as well as men? Did Matthew and Luke shorten Mark to make it more true to a Palestinian context, or did they independently know the original form of the saying? This article is not the place for that discussion. Our point is that the ancient reader would never have raised such issues. So long as Mark (or Matthew) communicated the significance of what Jesus meant, they were satisfied.

From our modern point of view, we might want more careful translation and delineation of exactly how much was an expansion. But the evangelists never went to our schools or wrote in our culture.[19] Their intentions need to be read within the context of their culture. Here critical study can be a help, for it shows what the evangelists (and others) actually did intend. And we can thereby get a clearer idea of what meaning is actually blessed with biblical authority (as differentiated from meanings we happen to read into the text).

Third, we have to remember that biblical authority rests in the canonical form of Scripture, not in real or hypothetical original forms. Certainly Scripture deserves the detailed study that it has been given. After all, if it is authoritative, especially if *God's* authority rests in it, it is of supreme importance. In that case exploring the total way in which it was produced, its historical and cultural background, and all that is involved with it is worthwhile. But that does not mean that if we can discover the earlier forms of this or that work we have something more authoritative. For example, suppose the Q source (the term used for the material that Matthew and Luke have in common but that is not in Mark; this material is mostly sayings of Jesus) turned out to be a written document and was discovered by an archaeologist. This would not be more authoritative than Matthew and Luke. It would not even be Scripture.[20]

How much more true is it that the hypothetical reconstructions of such sources or the original form of sayings (to the degree we are now capable of discovering them) or the Aramaic form of words of Jesus (created through a back translation of Gospel texts in an attempt to obtain what he actually said) are not Scripture. The same is true whether we are considering Gospels, Acts (e.g., if a transcript of Paul's trial in Caesarea were found), or Epistles (e.g., Paul's lost letters or the letter of the church in Corinth to Paul). None of these are Scripture. We do not come to something more authoritative by delineating them.

What, then, is the use of such study? What it does is to reveal the method used by the scriptural author. The more we know about their sources, the better we can state what the authors of Scripture were intending to communicate. And it is in that communication that biblical authority lies. There is an antiquarian interest in some phases of the study of the development of texts and traditions, but the goal of the biblical scholar is, in the end, to understand better the meaning of the text.

Something similar can be said about historical and sociological study. For example, Robert Banks wrote *Going to Church in the First Century*,[21] an excellent example of taking what can be discovered about first-century house churches and turning it into an imaginative narrative. This illustrates two things. First, church in the first century was quite different from church today. Second, there is a lot of information about his social circumstances, which Paul never intended to communicate but which can be teased out of what he does say by those who know about the social and historical context of the ancient world.

We note, on the one hand, that this information is very useful. The more we know about the context of Paul, or any other New Testament author, and his readers (with whose lifestyle and social situation Paul was undoubtedly in touch), the better we are able to understand the communication between them. Knowing that the churches were house churches, for example, explains why the "elect lady" of 2 John (probably a church) is not to receive false teachers "into (her) house" (2 John 10). This is not referring to allowing false teachers to enter someone's home but to receiving them into the gathering of the church where they could do damage. But, on the other hand, this sociological and cultural information is not Scripture. We have not added to biblical authority by discovering this information, but we may have clarified what it was that the author was trying to communicate (and what his first readers probably instantly understood) and therefore what message the authority of the Bible stands behind.

This distinction becomes important in that at times there is a tendency to try to imitate the social and cultural situation of the early church. That the early church met in houses is information that we now know. But because we know this does not mean that the Bible teaches that churches should meet in houses. That the early church celebrated the Lord's Supper as a full communal meal we also know (in fact, it was the mid-fourth century [i.e., A.D.350] before the final shift to a symbolic meal was made), but because the Scripture makes no point of this means that there is no biblical command to return to this practice.

Something similar might be said about baptismal practices. In other words, just because Scripture gives incidental evidence that the church did something in a certain way or that a person held a certain attitude does not mean that the author was making any attempt to communicate that information or that we must imitate it. It would certainly be permissible to meet in houses and celebrate communion as a communal meal; it might even be advisable for any number of reasons; but the most we can claim biblical authority for is that the Scripture gives evidence that this or that was done in the early church, not that it teaches that this should be done.[22]

Fourth, when doing scholarly research, there is a need to maintain firmly in mind the categories of suspended judgment and paradox. God did choose to create Scripture through human processes, namely, in an incarnational manner. Paul, as we noted above, wrote his letters to answer problems in the churches he was addressing. The Gospels were likewise written to meet the needs of certain individuals or communities. The works themselves were written in locations stretching from at least Jerusalem to Rome and at dates ranging from perhaps A.D. 50 to A.D. 96. This means first of all that there are many gaps in information we would like to fill in. We would love a detailed description of a single baptismal service, for example. We would like to know what Paul thought about abortion. We would also like him to explain how 1 Corinthians 15 (which looks forward to transformation at the return of Christ) fits with 2 Corinthians 5 (which appears to speak of transformation at death) or tell us exactly what he had explained to the Thessalonians (2 Thess. 2:5). The fact is, we do not have this information. That does not injure biblical authority, for the authority is in what is, not in what does not exist. But it does mean that we need to be careful that we do not "fill in the gaps" and claim biblical authority for the resulting teaching.

At the same time there are places in which teachings appear to clash. One example from Paul has been cited. Another would be the order of appearances of Jesus after the resurrection. One approach to such problems is to force a reconciliation, however improbable it may seem. To such people a forced harmony is at least better than ambiguity. Another approach would be to point quickly to as many of these problems as possible without attempting any reconciliation in order to relativize biblical authority.[23]

Both of these approaches have their value. There are times when harmonizing accounts comes naturally and is appropriate. Yet when the harmonization is forced and seems a desperate resort, such an approach would appear to come more from an insecurity about biblical authority than a commitment to it. It is also important to be open to the possibility of contradiction in Scripture, for it is a poor defense of biblical authority to take a stance that no data, however well established, could ever convince us to abandon our position. Yet a quick resort to contradiction appears to stem as much from prejudice or a fear of biblical authority as from dispassionate scholarly research.

Once we realize that our data are incomplete, however, we realize that we do not necessarily have to select either of the approaches above. We can suspend judgment, realizing that we do not have complete data. That could be an approach to the resurrection appearances. The basic facts of the resurrection are clear in all accounts. Yet we may have to suspend judgment about to whom Jesus appeared and in what order. We cannot at this distance fill in the gaps and cross-examine the witnesses. But our experience with similar unique and shocking events in modern life (e.g., traffic accidents) should convince us that a variety of difficult-if-not-impossible-to-reconcile reports is precisely what we might expect to receive from honest witnesses reporting on such an event.

In the case of Paul, we might resort to paradox. Is it possible that the transformation of human beings occurs at their death and at the Second Coming of Christ, yet there is only one transformation? Yes, it is possible. We might not be able to figure out how to work it out, but they are not necessarily self-contradictory. They are, however, paradoxical. So are a number of teachings in Paul. No wonder 2 Peter found Paul "hard to understand" (2 Pet. 3:16). We are in good company if we have the same problem.

The New Testament did not come to us as a code of Christian behavior (like a new Mosaic law) or a systematic theology. Nor is there an exhaustive history of either Jesus or the early church within the corpus. If we expect these, we will be disappointed, and critical studies will likely shake us severely. But if we accept the Scripture as it was written, as occasional writings through which God wishes to communicate what we *need* to know, not necessarily what we would *like* to know, then we can hold both biblical authority and critical methodology.

The sum of this discussion is that the critical study of Scripture can clarify the message that the authors were trying to communicate either by showing how the author came to produce his work (through examining sources) or by clarifying the context in which the message was communicated. But it cannot increase the authority of Scripture or find new material of the same level of authority. And while critical methodologies have undoubtedly led to a doubting of biblical authority by some, that is not their necessary conclusion but one resulting from assumptions connected to them or perhaps even from a misuse of the method.

Authority and Functional Canon

Yet one more issue needs to be discussed. There is a tendency—and this postmodern interpreters have done well to point out—for each church community to respond selectively to Scripture. In critical scholarship this is referred to as the "canon within the canon," the part of Scripture that really functions as Scripture for a given scholar or group. The fact that German scholarship in particular has not been shaken by the criticism of the historicity of the Gospels or the authorship of most Epistles other than Paul's main letters (his *Hauptbriefe*, Romans–2 Corinthians) is no surprise in that, as was mentioned above, the center of the Lutheran and Reformed canon has tended to be exactly those main letters of Paul (especially Romans and Galatians). The real center of authority has been preserved for such scholars even if little of the historical Jesus or the later letters of the New Testament are left.

We have rejected such an approach on two grounds. First, we do not believe that this is the necessary conclusion of the critical methodologies. Second, we do not believe that one has any real authority if he or she removes material from its context. To snatch a few paragraphs from this chapter and read them out of the context of the whole would be to distort their meaning. To look at Paul in isolation from the teaching of Jesus is to distort his message and thus not to draw from biblical authority at all. But before we quickly condemn a particular school of thought, it is important to realize that for each community some such canon-within-a-canon is probably functioning. The difference is that some are conscious of it and others are not.

One example of this is found in how a particular tradition uses various biblical genres. For example, if a tradition's canon centered on Paul, one might find that Gospel texts were rarely preached, and when they were used in sermons they functioned mainly as illustrations of an underlying Pauline text. That would mean that the teaching of the Gospels themselves would rarely if ever be heard in that community.[24] The church might assert that the Gospels were fully authoritative, but the Gospels would not function as authorities in its preaching.

Another example would be the use a church makes of certain books or parts of books. The Epistle of James is a case in point; because it is difficult to reconcile with Paul, it has tended to be sidelined and ignored in many churches. But within that book some passages are even more thoroughly ignored. For example, James 5:14–18 instructs that if a person in a church is ill they should call the elders to come and pray and that this prayer of faith will heal the sick individual. Furthermore, Christians are to confess their sins to one another and pray for one another that they may be healed.

A year or so after I completed a doctoral thesis on James, it occurred to me that I had never in more than twenty years in the church heard of an instance in which James 5:14 and the verses following had been followed, although there was no lack of sick people in the churches I had known. In other words, while the text in James was in the Bibles that the hundreds of Christians and dozens of elders I had known had in their homes (and as often as not in their hands every Sunday), it had apparently not functioned as an authoritative text for them. It was not that anyone had chosen to disobey the text. It was simply that it had been ignored in teaching and preaching. When the Scripture was read, it simply was not seen. For all practical purposes it was not in the canon.

While we have given a single example above, each tradition has its own group of "texts to ignore." This is never stated explicitly, for if it were, the texts would not be ignored. Rather, the focus of the community or the tradition is such that some texts are never read, or if they are read, they appear irrelevant and are passed over quickly. The texts have their own intrinsic authority, but in that community they have in practice no extrinsic authority.

This forms an argument, not for giving up traditions and church fellowships (for any other tradition or denomination or even a "nondenominational fellowship" would have the same problem in a different area), but for hermeneutic reflection and critical study. Hermeneutic discussion assists one in discovering how one is interpreting Scripture and thus what one might be filtering out of Scripture. Interaction with the full world of critical scholarship means that one is looking at Scripture from a variety of angles and traditions, many of which will be quite different from one's own. The result will be a tendency to see one's own blind spots and correct the shortcomings of one's theology. Even if one disagrees with a position, if the disagreement is expressed carefully and thoughtfully, he or she has learned and exposed possible areas of ignorance.

Yet one further aid to biblical authority is helpful, and that is working with Christians in a variety of churches and cultures. To return to the example above, while teaching in Germany, I learned that African elders in Tanzania were teaching the missionaries to pray for the sick in obedience to James 5. Those elders had come from a different culture without the same set of blinders (they surely had others), and when they came to that passage, it seemed natural to them to see and obey it. They were in turn able to assist their German teachers in widening their sphere of practical biblical obedience. Our Two-Thirds World brothers and sisters have much to teach us, as we have much to teach them. Something similar happens, although to a lesser degree, when we work closely with Christians in traditions quite different from ours. We may never adopt their theology or practice as a whole, but such ongoing experiences will assist in revealing to us texts we have not been reading and give us new perspectives on texts we have been reading.

This topic, then, brings our discussion full circle. The New Testament is authoritative. This intrinsic authority is an assumption of our whole discussion. The issue under discussion has been how we recognize this authority (i.e., extrinsic authority) and the contribution of hermeneutics and criticism to this process. While noting the dangers, we have tried to argue that in fact both hermeneutical reflection and critical study can assist us in more accurately understanding the Scripture and thus set the stage for the recognition of its authority in obedience. But that is precisely the issue. No study of Scripture can of itself produce obedience. And unless Scripture is obeyed, it has in practice no present authority to those individuals or communities that are not obeying it. It is for a heart set to obey and the carrying out of understanding in obedience that we have implicitly argued. Only when that happens will biblical authority be a truly meaningful category in our lives.

Bibliography

Barton, J., ed. *The Cambridge Companion to Biblical Interpretation.* Cambridge: Cambridge University Press, 1998.

Bray, G. *Biblical Interpretation, Past and Present.* Downers Grove, Ill.: InterVarsity, 1996.

Carson, D. A. *Hermeneutics, Authority and Canon.* Downers Grove, Ill.: InterVarsity Press, 1986.

Carson, D. A. and J. D. Woodbridge, eds. *Scripture and Truth.* Grand Rapids: Zondervan, 1983.

Dockery, D. S. *Biblical Interpretation Then and Now.* Grand Rapids: Baker Book House, 1992.

Farrow, D. *The Word of Truth and Disputes about Words.* Winona Lake, Ind.: Carpenter Books, 1987.

Fee, G. D. *Gospel and Spirit: Issues in New Testament Hermeneutics.* Peabody, Mass.: Hendrickson, 1991.

Fee, G. D., and Stuart, D., *How to Read the Bible for All Its Worth.* Grand Rapids: Zondervan, 1984.

Garrett, D. A. and R. R. Melick, eds. *Authority and Interpretation: A Baptist Perspective.* Grand Rapids: Baker, 1987.

Gnuse, R. *The Authority of the Bible.* New York: Paulist Press, 1985.

Kaiser, W. C., Jr., and M. Silva. *An Introduction to Biblical Hermeneutics.* Grand Rapids: Zondervan, 1994.

Marshall, I. H. *Biblical Inspiration.* Grand Rapids: Wm. B. Eerdmans, 1982.

Morris, L. *I Believe in Revelation.* Grand Rapids: Wm. B. Eerdmans, 1976.

Nixon, R. "The Authority of the New Testament." In I. H. Marshall, ed. *New Testament Interpretation: Essays on Principles and Methods.* Grand Rapids: Eerdmans, 1977. Pages 334–351. The rest of this symposium volume is also relevant.

Osborne, G. R. *The Hermeneutical Spiral: A Comprehensive Introduction to Biblical Interpretation.* Downers Grove, Ill.: InterVarsity, 1991.

Pinnock, C. H. *The Scripture Principle.* San Francisco: Harper and Row, 1984.

Radmacher, E. D. and R. D. Preus, eds. *Hermeneutics, Inerrancy, and the Bible.* Grand Rapids: Academie Books, 1984.

Silva, M. *God, Language and Scripture.* Grand Rapids: Zondervan, 1990.

Thiselton, A. C. *New Horizons in Hermeneutics.* Carlisle: Paternoster, 1995.

Vanhoozer, Kevin J. *Is There a Meaning in This Text?* Grand Rapids: Zondervan, 1998.

Yoder, P. B. *Toward Understanding the Bible.* Newton, Kan.: Faith and Life Press, 1978.

Zehr, P. M. *Biblical Criticism in the Life of the Church.* Scottsdale, Penn.: Herald Press, 1986.

Notes

1. By "Scripture" 2 Timothy is referring to the Hebrew Scriptures that Timothy was brought up with, although in the canonical context in which it now stands this may be widened to include the New Testament of which it is a part. See the article on canonical criticism.

2. For further information on the issue of the intrinsic authority of Scripture, see L. Morris, *I Believe in Revelation* (Grand Rapids: Eerdmans, 1976); C. H. Pinnock, "The Inspiration of Scripture and the Authority of Jesus Christ," in J. W. Montgomery, ed., *God's Inerrant Word* (Minneapolis: Bethany Fellowship, 1974), 201–18; or C. H. Pinnock, *The Scripture Principle* (San Francisco: Harper and Row, 1984), especially 3–82. See also W. Grudem, *Systematic Theology: An Introduction to Biblical Doctrine* (Grand Rapids: Zondervan, 1994), part 1.

3. Numerous visions and related phenomena are reported in the New Testament, but John's was extraordinary in (1) the command to send it to a group of churches, (2) its

extent, and (3) its significance. It is more comparable to the experience Paul refers to in 2 Corinthians 12 than to the visions of Acts.

4. John in Revelation is the closest to being conscious that he is writing Scripture, but the only command he reports is that what he was writing was a divine message for seven churches in the Roman province of Asia. He does not show any awareness that his message was for the whole church of his day, let alone for the whole church down through the ages.

5. As R. Remin did in "1 Timothy 2:12: Woman or Wife?" *His Dominion* 14:3 (1988): 2–14, E. E. Ellis takes a similar position in *Pauline Theology: Ministry and Society* (Grand Rapids: Eerdmans, 1989). In none of the examples in this article does this writer intend to take sides, although the examples chosen are ones that have intrinsic attractiveness and should be taken seriously as a basis for further research.

6. The exegetical part is whether in fact the Greek symbol meant this or that in its original context (place and time of writing). The hermeneutic part is whether this information should make any difference today or whether "received" interpretations (including those in beloved translations) are all that matter.

7. For a careful study of the hermeneutic differences involved in these arguments, see W. M. Swartley, *Slavery, Sabbath, War, and Women: Case Issues in Biblical Interpretation* (Scottsdale, Penn.: Herald Press, 1983), which is still useful despite the fact that the exegetical discussion (and the political rhetoric) has moved on in the last fifteen years. See also R. K. Johnston, *Evangelicals at an Impasse: Biblical Authority in Practice* (Atlanta: John Knox Press, 1979), although this book goes beyond purely hermeneutic concerns.

8. See, for example, D. Jasper, "Literary Readings of the Bible," in John Barton, ed., *The Cambridge Companion to Biblical Interpretation* (Cambridge: Cambridge University Press, 1998), 21–34, and R. P. Carroll, "Poststructuralist Approaches: New Historicism and Postmodernism," in the same work, 50–66. Some political and feminist readings of Scripture (e.g., some of the work of Phyllis Trible) have a similar theoretical base, although others would argue that their reading is the *only* correct one.

9. Stanley Fish's famous work *Is There a Text in This Class? The Authority of Interpretive Communities* (Cambridge: Harvard University Press, 1980) has a title referring to a question in a poetry class. Artists, literary and otherwise, are often relatively obscure about their intended communication and may deny that there is any intention other than art. While this could have some relevance for the Psalms and similar more artistic parts of Scripture, it is quite different from the high intentionality of at least some biblical writers.

10. A number of interpretations have been given for this passage. Some argue that the Greek *katakaluptō* and its related terms refer to a veil, while others believe it referred to a particular hairstyle, i.e. the hair braided and put up on the head. See J. B. Hurley, *Man and Woman in Biblical Perspective* (Grand Rapids: Zondervan, 1981), 168–171 for the evidence for this latter position, while G. D. Fee, *The First Epistle to the Corinthians* (NICNT; Grand Rapids: Eerdmans, 1987) covers a broader spectrum of positions. But for the purposes of this article the term *veil* is accurate enough to indicate a way of covering the head which indicated that a woman was married, whether the covering was with cloth or with hair.

11. Fee believes the difference in clothing was a sign that differentiated the sexes rather than differentiated married from unmarried women. Even if accepted, however, this does not change the principle of our illustration, for men and women are not distinguished in Western culture today by the presence or absence of head covering.

12. Or, for a postmodern interpreter, what Paul or Luke means to us and our group, and thus what God is saying to us. I have no intention of denying a sense of textual authority to the postmodern interpreter, even if the authority is only binding on the interpretive community. See further Kevin J. Vanhoozer, *Is There a Meaning in This Text?* (Grand Rapids: Zondervan, 1998).

13. The major battles of textual criticism were fought over the issue of whether 1 John 5:7b, Mark 16:9–20, and John 7:53–8:11 were part of the original texts of their respective works. In each case textual scholars from a variety of perspectives have argued uniformly in the negative. No other large blocks of text are similarly in doubt, so for the most part textual criticism is dealing with the details of a word or a phrase, which rarely upset people, although differing schools of textual criticism may argue heatedly and even be used by some as indicating whether or not one is committed to biblical authority. Naturally, the fact that a given passage did not occur in the autograph of a document does not mean it is not canonical or inspired in that, while it may not have been in the autograph, it may have been in that form of the document generally recognized as canon by the church. But that is an issue of canonical criticism, not of textual criticism.

14. While a postmodern interpreter might not agree with this statement, even for such a person the text provides a control on what can be claimed as authoritative, and thus deeper understanding of the text is desirable.

15. For example, R. Bauckham, *Jude–2 Peter* (WBC 50; Waco: Word Books, 1983), 131–135, 158–162, argues that 2 Peter is a testament of Peter and was recognizable as such when it first appeared. Thus no right-thinking original reader would have thought it was actually by Peter. It is only later centuries that misread the form as an actual ascription of authorship. While we may dispute Bauckham's evidence for his position (his exegesis), his position is compatible with a high view of biblical authority, for there is no deception intended or originally perceived.

16. In the case of 1 Peter, at least the totality of the Greek style of the letter must be attributed to a secretary if one argues that 2 Peter is also a product of Simon Peter. Cf. P. H. Davids, *The Epistle of 1 Peter* (NICNT; Grand Rapids: Eerdmans, 1990).

17. Cf. P. H. Davids, *James* (NIBC; Peabody, Mass.: Hendrickson Publishers, 1989) or *The Epistle of James* (NIGTC; Grand Rapids: Eerdmans, 1982).

18. In Palestine, even in cases in which the wife needed to initiate a divorce (e.g., if the husband went to sea and did not return and it could be assumed that he had either abandoned his wife or died on the journey), she could not. What she had to do was to petition the court to divorce her in the name of her husband. Thus, even if he were not present, he did the divorcing.

19. For example, in John 3 the author never indicates where the words of Jesus leave off and his begin. His culture did not use quotation marks, just as James did not use them in James 5:12 where he quotes what we know from Matthew 5:33–37 to have been a saying of Jesus. The concern for exact quotation was not part of that culture. Of course for the modern evangelical both what the evangelist wrote and what Jesus said in John 3 are equally inspired since we argue that God inspired the book, not necessarily the sources. Likewise, both the form of the saying in James 5:12 and that in Matthew 5:33–37 are inspired.

20. That is, it would not automatically be Scripture. In theory the whole church might recognize the genuineness of the text and might note the hand of the inspiriting Holy Spirit upon it and thus decide that the document did belong in the canon. In practice this would at least take decades and probably has about the same chance of happening as that of penguins learning to fly.

21. R. Banks, *Going to Church in the First Century* (Chipping Norton, NSW, Australia: Hexagon Press, 1980). The church in question is Priscilla and Aquilla's house church in Rome because it was the easiest social context to describe.

22. Cf. the chapter on Acts and historical precedent in G. D. Fee and D. Stuart, *How to Read the Bible for All Its Worth* (Grand Rapids: Zondervan, 1982).

23. An example of this would be J. T. Sanders, *Ethics in the New Testament* (Philadelphia: Fortress Press, 1975), who, after arguing that the New Testament contains several contradictory ethical stances, chooses a humanistic ethic on the basis of James 2.

24. This is a real example, but we avoid naming the interpretive tradition so as not to appear to be attacking a particular school of thought.

Chapter 2

New Testament Interpretation: A Historical Survey

David S. Dockery
Union University

New Testament interpretation has had as its goal the discovery of the meaning of the writings of the New Testament. Throughout the history of the church, different people or schools have offered different ways to interpret the biblical texts and convey that interpretation to their contemporaries. Even for those in the early centuries of the church, and especially for twentieth-century interpreters, the New Testament has posed a considerable challenge because it was written in languages and cultures quite different from those of the respective generations. Too often these differences have been neglected, and thus, at various times, interpreters have made the New Testament sound more like a medieval document or a contemporary political statement.

Our purpose in this chapter is to reflect on these different interpretations in order to recognize that we stand on the shoulders of numerous others who have gone before us when we attempt to interpret the New Testament. There are many strengths and brilliant insights from which we can learn as well as weaknesses and pitfalls to be avoided from studying the history of interpretation. We shall begin with Scripture's own interpretation of itself, then move to examine the interpretations during successive periods of church history. While we will offer some analysis and evaluation along the way, our purposes are primarily descriptive.

The Background and Beginnings of New Testament Interpretation

Christian interpretation of Scripture has inherited, from its birth, the approaches to interpretation found in the writings of intertestamental

21

Judaism as well as those of the contemporary Graeco-Roman world. From this dual heritage Christian interpretation has adopted characteristics of extreme literalism and extreme fancifulness. The first resulted from an unquestioning belief in the divine origin, nature, and authority of the Scripture, word by word. The latter developed from a desire to discover a deeper meaning hidden in the Bible or to sanction certain practices either not mentioned or even contradicted by the written word. Because of this heritage there was an observable continuity with the hermeneutical methods of the rabbis and Philo as well as the followers of Plato and Aristotle. Yet there was also a discontinuity as Christianity attempted to break with Judaism and surrounding Graeco-Roman religions to establish its uniqueness.

The New Testament's interpretation of the old was primarily typological and Christocentric. As F. F. Bruce has rightly noted, "The interpretation of the Old Testament in the New is a subject on which books are still being written and examination candidates still questioned."[1] There are few examples for our purposes regarding the way the latter parts of the New Testament interpreted the earlier sections.[2] Examples, however, include the way the church principles of 1 Corinthians were reset in Ephesians and reapplied in another way in the Pastoral Epistles. Second Peter mentions those who twisted the letters of Paul (3:16). An important passage in 2 Peter 1:20 (NASB) reads, "No prophecy of Scripture is a matter of one's own interpretation." This appears to recognize that an informal rule of faith served as the proper guide to interpret the Bible. Certainly in light of the following verse (v. 21), we learn the apostolic church recognized that the doctrine of inspiration did not guarantee that the Scriptures were easily or rightly understood.

INTERPRETATION IN THE POSTAPOSTOLIC PERIOD

The Apostolic Fathers in the second century found the true understanding of the Bible in the teaching of the apostles. The rise of Gnosticism and other challenges to accepted orthodoxy caused a hermeneutical shift. The result was a contextual development that sought to wrestle with the hermeneutical confusion and ambiguity in the struggle for orthodoxy.[3]

In order to demonstrate the unity of Scripture and its message, an authoritative framework was implemented by Irenaeus (ca. A.D. 30–200) and Tertullian (ca. A.D. 155–225) to handle such matters. Irenaeus has been described by R. M. Grant as "the father of authoritative exegesis in the church."[4] With Irenaeus we discover the first clear evidence of a Christian Bible and also a framework of interpretation in the church's rule of faith.[5] Continuing the Christological emphasis of the apostles, these early exegetes also emphasized that the rule of faith outlined the theological story that found its focus in the incarnate Lord.

Problematically, with his defensive posture Tertullian shifted the issue from a right understanding of Scripture to the more sharply stated issue of whether the heretics even had a right to read Holy Scripture.[6] Moreover, interpreting Scripture through this theological grid often forced the New Testament text into a preconceived set of theological convictions. The authoritative framework tended to divorce the text from its literary or historical context. Yet in light of the challenges faced by the second-century church, this hermeneutical approach was the only proper response. Included in this approach was a continuity with the typological-Christological method of the apostles and Justin Martyr (ca. A.D. 100–165?).[7] The authoritative response resulted in a hermeneutical circle that safeguarded the church's message but reduced the possibility of creativity among individual interpreters.

THE SCHOOLS OF ALEXANDRIA AND ANTIOCH

With the rise of the Alexandrian school in the third century, an obvious innovational development arose in the church as scriptural exegesis reached new heights. The innovation of allegorical interpretation grew out of its own context. Adapting the allegorical interpretation of Philo and the philosophical framework of Platonism, biblical hermeneutics in Clement (ca. A.D. 150–215) and Origen (ca. A.D. 185–254) moved beyond the defensive posture of Irenaeus and Tertullian.[8] Clement's work initiated the allegorical method, but Origen was the premier exegete of the period. While several Christian writers of the second and third centuries engaged in biblical interpretation, Origen brought the touch of a master to what had been nothing much more than the exercise of amateurs.[9]

Origen created a threefold hermeneutical methodology that emphasized the spiritual sense.[10] He thought Scripture had three different yet complementary meanings: (1) literal or physical sense, (2) a moral or psychical sense, and (3) an allegorical or intellectual sense. In his spiritualization of Scripture, he often "out Philo-ed Philo." The spiritual sense served an apologetic purpose against the Gnostic and other challenges, but primarily it served a pastoral purpose to mature the souls of the faithful.[11] While Origen rejected the authoritative framework of Irenaeus, he nevertheless sought to remain faithful to the church's rule of faith.[12] Origen's genius and allegorical hermeneutic occasionally led him down wrongheaded paths. Yet the allegorical method, at a critical moment in church history, made it possible to uphold the rationality of the Christian faith. Origen's total worldview brought the Alexandrian hermeneutic to new heights, not only in its methodology but also in its spirit.[13] Alexandrian hermeneutics was primarily practical, and its interpretation of Scripture cannot be understood until this is realized.

The successors of Origen were challenged by the school of Antioch and its emphasis on a literal and historical interpretation. The development that brought about the Antiochene school took place within the context of the maturing church's Christological debates.[14] The Antiochenes emphasized a theology and a hermeneutic that focused on the human and the historical, informed by an Aristotelian philosophy. In reaction to the Platonism and allegorical hermeneutics of the Alexandrians, the Antiochenes responded with a mature understanding of grammatical, historical, and contextual hermeneutics.[15]

If hermeneutics is both an art and science, the Alexandrians emphasized the aspect of art while the Antiochenes raised interpretation to the level of a science. The mature interpretation of Theodore of Mopsuestia (ca. A.D. 350–428)[16] and John Chrysostom (ca. A.D. 354–407),[17] while literal, was not a crude or wooden literalism that failed to recognize figures of speech in the biblical text. Their emphasis on the human element of the text allowed for a critical reading that accounted for doctrinal development within the New Testament text, even within a single author.[18] The author-oriented perspective of the Antiochenes' objective hermeneutic represented a new advancement in patristic exegesis.

Both Alexandrians and Antiochenes recognized a plenary sense in Scripture.[19] The difference between their understanding of the fuller sense rested in their view of its scope and purpose. The Antiochenes limited the plenary sense to historical correspondences while the Alexandrians' limitations were generally their own creativity. The Alexandrian allegorical approach led the soul into a realm of true knowledge where the vision of truth could be discovered.[20] The Antiochene purpose led humans into a truly moral life developing in goodness and maturity that would continue into eternity.[21]

TOWARD A THEOLOGICAL HERMENEUTIC

As the church moved into the fifth century, eclectic and multifaceted hermeneutical practice developed that sometimes emphasized the literal and historical, and sometimes the allegorical, but always the canonical and theological. The consensus began to develop because of the dominating Christological controversies of the fifth century.[22] With Jerome (ca. A.D. 341–420) and Augustine (A.D. 354–430) in the West and Theodoret of Cyrrhus (ca. A.D. 393–466) in the East, a convergence emerged toward a textual, canonical, and theological interpretation of the Old and New Testaments. The contribution of this period was the emphasis on the biblical canon whereby a text was interpreted in its larger context, understood as the biblical canon.[23]

The canon established parameters for validating spiritualized interpretations so that the historical meaning remained primary. Especially in the interpretive work of Augustine and Theodoret the rule of faith and Catholic tradition played a dominant role.[24] Neither the allegorical practices of Alexandria nor the historical emphases of Antioch dominated. A balanced hermeneutic emerged that impacted hermeneutical practices in the Middle Ages as well as in post-Reformation times. The eclectic fifth-century hermeneutic was shaped by (1) pastoral and theological concerns, (2) presuppositions that viewed the text from the standpoint of faith, and (3) interpretations that produced edification among the saints (Jerome),[25] love toward God and neighbor (Augustine),[26] and benefit and blessing for the church (Theodoret).[27]

THE MIDDLE AGES

From the time of Augustine, the church, following the lead of John Cassian (d. ca. 433), subscribed to a theory of the fourfold Scripture.[28] These four senses were (1) literal, (2) allegorical, (3) tropological or moral, and (4) anagogical.[29] The literal sense of Scripture could and usually did nurture the virtues of faith, hope, and love; but when it did not, the interpreter could appeal to three additional virtues, each sense corresponding to one of the virtues. The allegorical sense referred to the church and its faith, what it was to believe. The tropological sense referred to individuals and what they should do, corresponding to love. The anagogical sense pointed to the church's future expectation, corresponding to hope.

Bernard of Clairvaux (1090–1153) clearly explicated this fourfold approach. In the fourteenth century Nicholas of Lyra (1265–1349) summarized this medieval hermeneutical approach in a much-quoted rhyme:

> Littera gesta doucet
> > (The letter teaches facts)
> Quid credas allegoria
> > (allegory what one should believe)
> Moralis quid ages
> > (tropology what one should do)
> Quo tendas anagogia
> > (anagogy where one should aspire).

For example, the city of Jerusalem, in all of its appearances in Scripture was understood literally as a Jewish city, allegorically as the church of Christ, tropologically as the souls of women and men, and anagogically as the heavenly city.[30]

Thomas Aquinas (1224–1274) wanted to establish the spiritual sense more securely in the literal sense than it had been grounded in earlier medieval thought. He returned to the distinction between things and signs as in Augustine, but because of his Aristotelianism he preferred "things" and "words."[31] In Scripture, the things designated by words can themselves have the character of a sign. He maintained that the literal sense of Scripture has to do with the sign-character of things. Thus, he was able to demonstrate that the spiritual sense of Scripture was always based on the literal sense and derived from it.[32] Also, he equated the literal sense as the meaning of the text intended by the author.[33] The medieval exegetes and theologians admitted that the words of Scripture contained a meaning in the historical situation in which they were first uttered, but overall they denied that the final and full meaning of those words was restricted to what the first audience thought or heard.

Reformation Hermeneutics

Martin Luther (1483–1546), the great Reformer, started his career as a biblical interpreter by employing the allegorical method but later abandoned it.[34] Yet it was Desiderius Erasmus (1466–1536), more so than Luther, who through the influence of John Colet (1466–1519) rediscovered the priority of the literal sense.[35] As the chief founder of modern biblical criticism and hermeneutics, he must always hold a cherished position among interpreters of the New Testament. Erasmus exemplified the finest in renaissance scholarship that emphasized the original sources. The ultimate source to which he returned was the Greek New Testament. Coupled with the return to the sources was a truly historical understanding of ancient texts, but he also desired that the texts bring edification to the readers through the spiritual sense as well.[36] His hermeneutical approach developed toward a more critical-historical and philological approach as his method matured, though he always, following his hero, Origen, emphasized the spiritual sense as well.

Erasmus recognized the need for a Greek Testament as early as 1507, and from 1511 onward he carefully studied and collated more Greek manuscripts of the New Testament than has been generally realized. He produced successive editions of the Greek New Testament in 1516, 1519, 1522, 1527, and 1535. In 1516, he published a revised Vulgate alongside his Greek text. His own fresh Latin translation appeared in 1519. From 1517 onward, he produced several editions of his own paraphrases of the New Testament Epistles and Gospels.[37]

As significant and innovative as Erasmus's works were, the pivotal figures in New Testament studies during the Reformation period were Martin Luther and John Calvin (1509–1564). Calvin was the greatest exegete of the Reformation. He developed the grammatical-historical exegetical method as revived by Erasmus, focusing the place of meaning in the historical interpretation and developing the spiritual message from the text.[38] In his commentary on Romans, he inscribed a dedication that read:

> Since it is almost the interpreter's only task to unfold the mind of the writer whom he has undertaken to expound, he misses his mark, or at least strays outside his limits, by the extent to which he leads his readers away from the meaning of his author. . . . It is presumptuous and almost blasphemous to turn the meaning of scripture around without due care, as though it were some game that we were playing. And yet many scholars have done this at one time.[39]

While Erasmus and Luther broke tradition to establish a new Protestant hermeneutic, Calvin exemplified it with his touch of genius. Where Luther was bold, sweeping, and prophetic, Calvin was more scholarly and painstaking. Luther was a prophet, a preacher; Calvin a scholarly lecturer. Indeed in the eyes of some he is regarded as the greatest interpreter in the history of the Christian church.[40]

Luther wrote important commentaries on Romans and Galatians. He failed to find equal value in all the writings of the New Testament, judging those that most clearly conveyed the biblical gospel to be superior. He observed:

> In short, St. John's Gospel and his first Epistle; St. Paul's Epistles, especially those to the Romans, Galatians and Ephesians; and St. Peter's first Epistle— these are the books which show you Christ and teach everything which is necessary and blessed for you to know, even if you never see or hear any other book or teaching. Therefore in comparison with them St. James's Epistle is a right strawy epistle, for it has no evangelical quality about it.[41]

Calvin wrote commentaries on every book in the New Testament except Revelation and 2 and 3 John. His works evidence an applied theological exegesis. Always insisting that Scripture interprets Scripture, Calvin rejected allegorical interpretation and emphasized the necessity of examining the historical and literary context while comparing Scriptures which treated common subjects.[42]

Post-Reformation Interpretation

SCHOLASTICISM, PIETISM, AND RATIONALISM

It is commonly believed that the followers of the Reformers shrank from the exegetical creativity and freedom employed by Luther and Calvin. They instead produced their expositions along newly established theological boundaries, which resulted in a Protestant scholasticism. Yet as F. F. Bruce has noted, there were several independent thinkers during this period including Matthias Flacius Illyricus (1520–1575), Joachim Camerarius (1500–1574), Hugo Grotius (1583–1645), John Lightfoot (1602–1675), Christian Schöttgen (1687–1751), and Johann Jakob Wettstein (1693–1754).[43]

It is true, however, that the followers of Luther and Calvin tended to systematize their exegesis into an Aristotelian mold.[44] Primarily this approach was exemplified on the Lutheran side in Philip Melanchthon (1497–1560) and on the Calvinist side by Francis Turretin (1623–1687). This new form of scholasticism exercised an authoritative and dogmatic hermeneutic. The new scholasticism coupled with the rise of the Enlightenment, which rejected both authoritative and dogmatic approaches, issued in two reactions: (1) a newfound pietism in Philipp Jakob Spener (1635–1705) and August Herman Franke (1663–1727),[45] and (2) a historical-critical method that stressed the importance of the historical over against the theological interpretation of the New Testament pioneered by Johann Salamo Semler (1725–1791) and Johann David Michaelis (1717–1791).[46]

The most valuable contribution for New Testament studies from the Pietist tradition came from Johann Albert Bengel (1687–1752). He was the first scholar to classify the New Testament Greek manuscripts into families on the basis of various similarities. His commentary, the well-known *Gnomon of the New Testament* (1742), served as a model for its combination of historical roots, explanation of figures of speech, and suggestions for devotional applications.[47]

Philosophical and theological rationalism provided much of the foundation for the rise of historical criticism. The rationalism of R. Descartes (1506–1560), T. Hobbes (1588–1679), B. Spinoza (1632–1677), and J. Locke (1632–1704) greatly influenced biblical and theological studies. H. S. Reimarus (1694–1768) and G. E. Lessing (1729–1781) subsumed biblical revelation under the role of reason. F. D. E. Schleiermacher (1768–1834) combined aspects of pietism (experience) with rationalism and developed new hermeneutical concerns. Schleiermacher granted that the historical-critical approach helped disclose the intention of the biblical writers in the context of their day, but he also raised the question of what their message might mean to readers and hearers in a different age and culture. In so doing he became not only the "Father of Theological Liberalism," but also the "Father of Modern Hermeneutics."[48]

The Modern Period

HISTORICAL CRITICISM

A new approach to New Testament interpretation was introduced by J. Semler, who approached the New Testament text only on a historical basis. Unsatisfied with the pietist tradition, Semler made a distinction between the "Word of God," which has abiding authority unto salvation, and the "Scriptures," which contain information important only for the times in which they were written. Inspiration had given way to "objective" history.[49] A contemporary, Johann A. Ernesti, in his *Institutio Interpretis Novi Testamenti* (1761), applied to the New Testament the philological-historical method he had successfully used earlier in editing classical texts. Though F. Lau has considered Ernesti as "the father of the profane scientific interpretation of the Bible," it is Semler who is the father of historical-critical study. Ernesti did not divorce historical study from biblical inspiration and continued to affirm the complete truthfulness of the Bible.[50] J. D. Michaelis introduced a new discipline, "Introduction to the New Testament," seeking to interpret the New Testament without dogmatic presuppositions.

In the seventeenth century B. Spinoza argued the importance of asking questions about the authorship, date, and purpose of the writings. Michaelis tackled these questions and determined that those New Testament books not actually written by apostles were neither inspired nor canonical. Semler and Michaelis approached the New Testament apart from confessional or theological concerns. Together they should be acknowledged as the pioneers of historical-critical interpretation of the New Testament.[51] Historical criticism is used as a comprehensive term designating several techniques to discover the historical situation, the sources behind the writings, the literary style and relationships, the date, authorship, approach to composition, destination, and recipients. In contrast to textual criticism, which was known as "lower criticism," historical criticism was called "higher criticism," but this term is now virtually obsolete.

GOSPEL STUDIES

Johann Jakob Griesbach (1745–1812), the pupil of Semler, refused to harmonize the Synoptic Gospels and separated John's Gospel from the Synoptics, thus advancing beyond the historical issues of his mentors to a focus on literary relationships in the New Testament. Griesbach was not the first to raise these issues. Tatian (ca. A.D. 170) developed his *Diatessaron*, a harmony of all four Gospels. The Reformers recognized the harmony of Matthew, Mark, and Luke. Griesbach, however, marked the transition in an obvious way from the Reformation approach to the modern period by his treatment of the Gospels. He proposed that Matthew was written first and Mark last, positing that it was a digest of the other Synoptics.[52] His work was published as *Synopsis Evangeliorum* (1776). G. E. Lessing proposed in *Neue Hypothese über die Evangelisten als bloss menschliche Geschichtsschreiber* (1778) that the Gospels were different translations or fragments of an older Aramaic *Gospel of the Nazarenes*. J. G. Eichhorn (1752–1827), a pupil of Michaelis, advanced Lessing's idea by proposing nine different gospels developed from the Aramaic *Gospel*. He suggested that the Synoptics were the final results of this complicated literary process.[53]

The Tübingen scholar G. C. Storr (1746–1804), a supernaturalist, convincingly explained the absence of large portions of material from Mark's Gospel by suggesting that Mark was the initial Gospel penned. This Marcan priority hypothesis was advanced by K. Lachmann (1793–1851) and H. J. Holtzmann (1832–1910).[54] Although it has been challenged in recent years by W. R. Farmer, J. B. Orchard, and several of their followers, the priority of Mark is the prominent position among most New Testament scholars today. These issues are clearly and carefully explained and evaluated by Scot McKnight and Robert Stein in their chapters later in this book.[55]

UNITY AND DIVERSITY

During this period near the end of the eighteenth century, biblical theology, distinct from dogmatic theology, was introduced by J. P. Gabler (1753–1826). In his inaugural speech as professor of theology at the University of Altdorf in 1787, he outlined his understanding of biblical theology. He indicated that the New Testament authors must be interpreted in the light of their own historical contexts and that in comparing these writings with one another their differences must be acknowledged. Gabler, a rationalist, disavowed New Testament miracles. Similarly he failed to acknowledge a unity in diversity in the theology of the New Testament, instead focusing on irreconcilable differences. The result was a New Testament that included only kernels of confessional truth that were not limited by historical conditioning.[56]

This line of thought was developed significantly in the epoch-making work of Ferdinand Christian Baur (1792–1860). Baur was convinced that a deep gulf existed in early Christianity between the Jerusalem church and the Pauline mission. He and other members of the infamous Tübingen School reconstructed the history of the apostolic and subapostolic age by postulating a major antithesis between Peter and Paul. The solution for Baur came in his suggested synthesis that the New Testament writings were not first-century apostolic documents but second-century works that presented a developing catholicism. This "tendency criticism" came to dominate New Testament research and still strongly influences various schools of thought. Further research has shown that there is greater unity than allowed for by either Gabler or Baur.

The Tübingen school exaggerated the antithesis, failed to recognize Peter's role as a reconciler, and miscalculated the time involved in the advancement and development of early Christianity. The turning point in this research came from J. B. Lightfoot (1829–1889), who demonstrated the early date of the writings of the Apostolic Fathers.[57] Biblical theology has moved in different directions, reflecting various nuances, each wrestling with the theological contributions of the biblical writers, the unity, diversity, and development in the New Testament.[58] Important works in this regard are W. Bauer's *Orthodoxy and Heresy in Earliest Christianity* (1934); H. Koester and J. Robinson, *Trajectories Through Earliest Christianity* (1971); and J. D. G. Dunn, *Unity and Diversity in the New Testament* (1977). Brad Green examines these themes in greater detail in his chapter in this volume.

Quest for the Historical Jesus

Simultaneous with Baur's work and building on the work of Gospel criticism, several scholars began a quest for the "historical Jesus." The purpose of the quest was to reconstruct the Gospels and the sources behind the Gospels to understand and interpret Jesus in purely historical and human categories. The phrase achieved widespread usage from the title of Albert Schweitzer's (1875–1965) volume, *The Quest for the Historical Jesus* (1906). Originally published as *From Reimarus to Wrede,* Schweitzer summarized more than 250 authors who, from the end of the eighteenth century to the beginning of the twentieth, investigated the life of Jesus.[59]

The primary scholars examined were H. S. Reimarus (1694–1768), H. E. G. Paulus (1761–1851), F. D. E. Schleiermacher (1768–1834), D. F. Strauss (1801–1874), and W. Wrede (1859–1906). Reimarus separated the teachings of Jesus from what the apostles taught about him, suggesting that the apostles' teaching was a fabrication of their own theology. Paulus continued this line of thinking and rejected the miraculous events in the life of Jesus, claiming that the observers of those events misunderstood natural events as "miracles." Paulus generally distrusted anything outside of rational thought.

Schleiermacher's *Leben Jesu* was published posthumously in 1864 based on lecture notes transcribed by a student. Schleiermacher differentiated between the Jesus of history in the Synoptics and the Christ of faith in the Fourth Gospel. Strauss, perhaps as radical as any "questor," rejected the idea that God could intervene in this world. He thus rejected the idea of incarnation and reconstructed the gospel story in mythological fashion. What was created by Schleiermacher and Strauss was a false either/or choice: either Jesus was historical or supernatural; either he was the Jesus of the Synoptic presentation or of the Johannine picture.

Wrede argued that the Gospels were not intended to be historical works but were written as biased theology; thus the historical Jesus could not be discovered in the Gospels. Schweitzer reviewed all of these and with J. Weiss (1863–1914) concluded that the kingdom proclamation of Jesus should be understood from a thoroughgoing eschatological perspective.[60] R. Bultmann (1884–1976) declared that the historical Jesus was inaccessible to the historian.[61] Most nineteenth- and early twentieth-century New Testament scholars felt the importance of interacting with this movement. T. W. Manson's infamous words point to this seeming necessity: "Indeed, it may be said of all theological schools of thought: By their lives of Jesus ye shall know them."[62] The problems were created by either/or choices when the Gospel picture is both/and. Jesus is historical (man) and supernatural (God), and the portraits in the Synoptics and John are complementary not contradictory. Jesus inaugurated the kingdom, but the kingdom yet awaits a consummation.

The psychological quest closed with Bultmann but was reopened with Bultmann's students, J. Robinson and E. Käsemann. They began an existential quest that was little more profitable than the previous one. What was important about this new exploration was that Bultmann's disciples were rejecting the teaching of their mentor. Outside the Bultmannian circle, J. Jeremias, C. H. Dodd, T. W. Manson, and V. Taylor raised opposition to the old quest and the new one.[63] Craig Blomberg's chapter amplifies on these important issues.

AMERICAN PROTESTANT EXEGESIS

While these innovative questions were pursued, primarily in Europe, we must not neglect the able exegesis being carried out in North America during these centuries. America's greatest theologian, Jonathan Edwards (1703–1758), undertook two major exegetical projects seeking to advance a

Reformed theological exegesis, though he was open to multiple levels of meaning in the biblical text. He was not bound to the literal sense but assumed that every passage held the possibility of multiple interpretations. In the same passage he often found a literal meaning, a statement about Christ, the church, and last things (heaven/hell). Edwards' spiritual approach has greatly influenced American pulpits for more than two centuries.[64]

A more consistent echo of the Calvinist tradition's grammatical-historical exegesis was advanced at Princeton Seminary in the nineteenth century. Charles Hodge (1797–1878) published masterful volumes on Romans, Ephesians, 1 and 2 Corinthians from 1835 to 1859. Other Princetonians, J. A. Alexander, A. A. Hodge, and B. B. Warfield, also contributed to the advancement of the theological exposition of the New Testament, which so influenced the work of J. G. Machen and N. B. Stonehouse.[65] This approach combined with the British evangelical tradition has greatly shaped the contemporary American evangelical understanding of New Testament interpretation.

Baptists in America have also made significant contributions to New Testament studies. Moses Stuart, the great Andover scholar, primarily concentrated his work in Old Testament but also wrote important New Testament commentaries that interacted with critical European scholarship. His commentary on Romans served as a model for handling difficult textual and grammatical issues. A. T. Robertson, a prolific scholar, wrote commentaries, grammatical works, and textual studies. His *Word Pictures* remains a standard for pastors and teachers. His massive grammar continues to serve as a valuable resource for New Testament scholars, even though linguistic research has reversed some of his findings. Robertson's father-in-law, John A. Broadus, contributed significant studies in New Testament and preaching. Chief among these was his commentary on Matthew in the important *American Commentary* series edited by A. Hovey. George E. Ladd stands at the forefront of American Baptist and evangelical scholarship with his first-rate New Testament theology, his studies on the kingdom in the New Testament, and his pioneering efforts in New Testament criticism. A new generation of scholars is shaping the American landscape carrying on this important tradition in major new commentary series such as: *Word Biblical Commentary, Baker Exegetical Commentary, Zondervan Application* series, the *New American Commentary*, and IVP *Biblical Commentary*.

BRITISH CONTRIBUTIONS

British scholarship at this time advanced a historical-critical interpretation of the New Testament, but generally the Cambridge trio of J. B. Lightfoot (1828–1889), B. F. Westcott (1825–1901), and J. A. Hort (1828–1892) reached different conclusions from their German counterparts. As previously noted, Lightfoot refuted the Tübingen school's unwarranted conclusions regarding the supposed conflict between Pauline and Petrine movements in the apostolic church. He also wrote exemplary commentaries on several Pauline Epistles including Galatians, Philippians, and Colossians.

Westcott and Hort are best known for their 1881 critical edition of the Greek New Testament. They also made other significant contributions, including Hort's commentaries on 1 Peter, James, and Revelation. Westcott produced a major survey of the New Testament canon (1855) and outstanding commentaries on John's Gospel, John's Epistles, and Hebrews. These three masterful exegetes modeled an exacting scholarship that brilliantly influenced men like C. H. Dodd, T. W. Manson, and more recent New Testament scholars such as F. F. Bruce and I. Howard Marshall.

FORM CRITICISM

All twentieth-century New Testament scholarship has had to reckon with the influential Marburg scholar Rudolf Bultmann. His form-critical approach advanced what had been proposed by source-critical and tradition-critical approaches via his existential hermeneutic. Tradition criticism moved the concerns of source criticism beyond the written sources, endeavoring to trace the course of the transmission of these oral or written traditions. Form criticism attempts to reconstruct the various New Testament "forms" of the preliminary tradition by classifying the principal forms such as legal, poetic, legends, parables, etc. The process includes examining these to discover the contents of the forms, how they were handed down, and what their successive life settings were until they assumed their present shape and position. Some scholars have undertaken to recover the exact words of Jesus by removing the so-called additions attached to the sayings in the course of transmission. The threefold interpretation task works back from (1) interpretation of the present Gospels through (2) interpretation of the tradition lying behind them to (3) reconstruction of the proclamation of Jesus. This framework was applied to the Gospels almost independently by K. L. Schmidt in *The Framework of the Story of Jesus* (1919); M. Diebelius in *From Tradition to Gospel* (1919), and Bultmann in *History of the Synoptic Tradition* (1921). Further exposition and evaluation will be offered by Darrell L. Bock in the chapter on form criticism.

When this approach is applied to New Testament Epistles, form criticism of another type seeks to recognize the form of a forensic argument or rhetorical situation, which also incorporates the concerns of rhetorical criticism. H. D. Betz has pioneered this approach by applying form criticism to Galatians.[66] Likewise, the work of George Kennedy in this field is worthy of special mention.

REDACTION CRITICISM

Redaction criticism moved beyond the findings of form criticism as the limits of form criticism became apparent. Redaction criticism developed out of a concern to see the relationship of authors to written sources. This approach has four basic concerns: (1) the original situation of the Gospel event or saying, (2) the tradition and process of transmission, (3) the situation in the early church, and (4) the situation and purpose of the writer/editor. Basic to redaction criticism is the theological motivation of the author/redactor. Redaction criticism is concerned with the entire framework, not individual units of material. Pioneering studies using this method included H. Conzelmann's *The Theology of Luke* (1954); W. Marxen's *Mark the Evangelist* (1959); and G. Bornkamm, G. Barth, and H. J. Held's *Tradition and Interpretation in Matthew* (1960). Grant Osborne treats this subject in the present volume, including a thorough analysis and evaluation.

GENRE CRITICISM

Genre criticism seeks to identify the genre of the New Testament writing by the interrelation of the form, style, and content. Writings grouped together by content may belong to the same genre, but similarity of content alone is not a sufficient criterion. One of the chief criteria is how the writings function. Thus the classification of genres is really not so much to classify as to clarify. The four major genres of the New Testament, according to style, content, form, and function, are Gospels, letters/epistles, Acts, and apocalyptic. These four overlap at times, and all include numerous subcategories such as parable, hymn, poetry, rhetoric, diatribe, sermon, prophecy, liturgy, and other figures of speech and literary devices.[67] Craig Blomberg ably tackles these issues in the second section of this book.

Contemporary Hermeneutics

Foundational hermeneutical theories have grown up alongside the specific interests and methods outlined in the previous pages. These contemporary hermeneutical concerns have produced new approaches in recent years. In order to understand the background of these approaches, we will outline the major hermeneutical discussions of the past two centuries. A. Thiselton has performed an invaluable service for New Testament studies with his monumental works on contemporary hermeneutics titled *Two Horizons* (1980) and *New Horizons in Hermeneutics* (1992).

The critical methods we have noted are generally built on an author-oriented hermeneutical perspective. Advocates of this position such as K. Stendahl and J. L. McKenzie writing in the *Journal of Biblical Literature* (1958) defined interpretation as determining the meaning intended by the human author and understood by the original readers.[68] This approach considered the meaning of texts to be stable and univocal, and its meaning in the original setting to be where meaning is located. Such an understanding can be traced to J. A. Ernesti and Friedrich Schleiermacher.

Schleiermacher contended for a preunderstanding that must take place before interpretation can happen.[69] Understanding, for Schleiermacher, was related to the author's intention. The early Schleiermacher in his section on grammatical interpretation articulated some of the most incisive statements found in all hermeneutical literature on the principles for grasping what an author willed to communicate. The ultimate aim, however, was to get through to an author's unique individuality, a psychological interpretation. Interpretation required a knowledge of grammatical concerns but also a divinatory intuition through empathy with and imagination of the author's experience. The interpreter must attempt to divine the author so that one transforms oneself into another and seeks an immediate knowledge of the author's individuality.[70]

But this was not enough for Schleiermacher. He argued that the interpreter can potentially understand the author's work as well as or even better than the author.[71] W. Dilthey carried on this tradition by making the goal of interpretation that of inducing in oneself an imitation of life that is not native to him or her. He postulated the idea of a universal human nature that could make this possible, yet he conceded that an author's personality could not be fully grasped.[72] The most notable theorist of an author-oriented approach in the contemporary discussion is E. D. Hirsch.[73] He works in the Schleiermacher tradition but has modified it by moving toward a more grammatical and, therefore, more objective direction. In many ways these insights reflect the best of the Antiochene school, Erasmus, Calvin, the Princetonians, the Cambridge trio, and the historical-critical tradition.

Yet the author-oriented approach moved from an emphasis on epistemology in Schleiermacher to an existential emphasis with M. Heidegger (1889–1976) and Bultmann. With Heidegger came an increasing skepticism toward the possibility of achieving determinate meaning in textual interpretation. In his classic works, *Being and Time* (E.T. 1962) and *On the Way to Language* (E.T. 1971), Heidegger shifted the emphasis away from historical concerns of the text to a priori concerns of the interpreter.[74] Indeed, understanding was generated from the interpreter's existential awareness of human possibilities. From this level of awareness, understanding moved from cognition to expression in the use of language. He affirmed that what came to expression in discourse was the projection of an understanding of the possibility of human being.[75] The interpreter became the source of meaning as emphasis shifted from the author to the reader and even to the core of the reader's being.

It is well-known that Bultmann was primarily responsible for Heidegger's views entering the field of New Testament studies.[76] Bultmann's concern was not the objectifying language of the New Testament, but the existential possibilities of human being projected through it. One such possibility obviously rested in the New Testament concept of faith. He noted the New Testament was written from the vantage point of faith and called for a faith response from its readers.[77] Denying any coherent doctrinal norm in the New Testament, Bultmann claimed that by faith, New Testament doctrine, couched in the objectifying mode of language, which he called "myth," was to be interpreted in terms of the primordial possibilities of human being.[78] His program of demythologizing was not intended to remove myth from the New Testament but to existentialize it. Understanding occurs when the existential possibilities of the language of faith are appropriated by faith and result in a new self-understanding.

Bultmann thought biblical exegesis without prior understanding an impossibility.[79] By de-emphasizing the cognitive aspects of the biblical text and shifting the notion of interpretation to existential encounter, Bultmann redirected the focus of New Testament interpretation in the twentieth century.

The discussion has been refined and redirected by Hans-Georg Gadamer, a student of the Marburg scholars. His classic work, *Truth and Method* (E.T. 1975), stressed the distance that separates contemporary readers from ancient texts, like the New Testament, in terms of time, culture, and language. He also emphasized the prejudgments interpreters bring to the text as well as the way tradition impinges on how they read texts. The goal is not to understand the author's intention or the text's historical meaning but to focus on what the text says to present readers. Interpretation is best pictured as a conversation in which two people try to come to a common understanding about some matter which is of interest to both.

Gadamer also contends that an ancient text is not a fixed depository of univocal language but an exposition of something whose meaning exceeds the text.[80] Language, he maintains, is always polyvalent and analogical. The text contains a fullness of meaning by which its very nature can never be exhausted. Meaning, then, always exceeds the conscious intention of the author.[81]

Paul Ricoeur (1913–), in some ways, theoretically combines the concerns of author-oriented hermeneutics and reader-oriented hermeneutics.[82] While Ricoeur agrees that a text has intentionality, he stresses that when reading texts the author generally is not present to be questioned about ambiguous meaning in the text. In contrast to Gadamer, Ricoeur posits that a text's meaning is intelligible across historical and cultural distance. Because of the nature of writing, the text opens up the text world to the interpreter. The interpreter may then enter that world and appropriate the possibilities that it offers. What is understood or appropriated, then, is not necessarily the author's intended meaning or the historical situation of the original author or readers but the text itself.[83] It is in this sense that Ricoeur can claim that Romans, Galatians, 1 Peter, or John's Gospel can be addressed to contemporary readers as much as to original readers. Building on the shift in hermeneutics from finding meaning[84] in the author's intention or author's results to uncovering meaning in the text itself or the reader via existential encounter or shared conversation, current New Testament methods and approaches also have shifted the idea of interpretation away from the author. The final section of our survey will briefly note these recent developments.

Recent Developments

Though historical criticism continues to be immensely productive in some circles, there is a wide-ranging outlook suggesting that it has seen its best days.[85] Several chapters in this volume focus on these new ideas. One thing that has happened with these recent approaches is different questions have been asked and new insights have emerged.

Sociological criticism recognizes that conditioning factors helped to shape and focus the religious aspiration of the New Testament period.[86] The sociological approach is also interested in the New Testament's value for religious goals today. Several liberation[87] and feminist[88] models have come to the forefront asking how the New Testament was influenced by societal pressures and prejudices and how, if at all, similar pressures and prejudices can be understood and addressed today. Though interesting, these approaches are of little value in helping us understand the meaning and significance of Holy Scripture for the church today.

Structuralism, based on the findings of C. Levi-Strauss, *Structural Anthropology* (1960), and F. de Saussure, *Course on General Linguistics* (1966), is concerned not with the formal structure of a unit of tradition but with the deep structure of human self-expression. Daniel Patte, more than any other scholar, has advocated the possibilities of structuralism for New Testament studies.[89] One of the issues involved in this approach, as well as the other recent contributions, revolves around the value or lack of value of historical issues. There is even a strong contention by some for an anti-historicism, believing that historical criticism is illegitimate and without value. George Guthrie's chapter in this volume demonstrates the right usage of a related discipline, "Discourse Analysis" or "Text-linguistics." His insights show the value of such an approach for careful New Testament interpretation.

Closely related, and at times indistinguishable, are new classifications of literary criticism called narrative criticism, compositional criticism, or rhetorical criticism. These models seek to understand not the history behind the text or the historical situation of the original authors or readers or even their understanding of themselves as human beings but the text itself. Two Johannine scholars have been prominent in the employment of this perspective: R. Alan Culpepper, *Anatomy of the Fourth Gospel* (Philadelphia: Fortress, 1983) and Paul Duke, *Irony in the Fourth Gospel* (Atlanta: John Knox, 1985). Their work follows in the path of Frank Kermode. Fresh ground is being plowed in many areas of the New Testament, particularly in the Gospels, such as Jack Dean Kingsbury's works on Matthew and Mark. The goal of such an approach is to discover the intertextual keys that allow the text to reveal itself. A similar approach which affirms the historicity of the Gospel accounts is found in David Garland's work on Matthew (Crossroad) and Mark (Zondervan).

A final observation about canonical criticism closes our survey. Originally voiced as a protest against preoccupation with the authenticity and forms of the Jesus tradition, canonical criticism has shifted the emphasis in interpretation back to the existing text in its canonical framework. Initially developed as an Old Testament discipline by J. A. Sanders, *Torah and Canon* (1972) and *Canon and Community* (1984), and B. S. Childs, *Introduction to the Old Testament as Scripture* (1979), the approach has expanded the concerns of redaction criticism to see how the canonical shape and the place of the book in the canon also impact interpretation. Childs' work has pioneered the entrance of this discipline into New Testament studies.[90]

Studies in canonical criticism have developed alongside parallel concerns in the area of New Testament canon. Questions addressed in these recent works include the traditional concerns of canon as well as the matters of authorship and inspiration, pseudonymity, and the place of tradition. Four works, among others, are worthy of special notice: D. G. Meade's *Pseudonymity and Canon*, Bruce Metzger's *The New Testament Canon*, Lee M. McDonald's *The Formation of the Christian Biblical Canon*, and F. F. Bruce's *The Canon of Scripture*. The answers to issues addressed above have received various responses in these volumes, indicating that much work still remains to be done in this area.

The space limitation of our chapter will not permit us to note interpretation issues in particular books. A fine survey of these matters can be found in the new three-volume Dictionary on the New Testament by InterVarsity Press.[91] Obviously the current state of New Testament studies is as diverse and varied as is its history. As someone has well said, "The field of New Testament studies is an inch wide and a mile deep." We have not come close to exploring the width or depth in this overview. I hope, however, that the survey introduces the reader to issues that will be addressed in the remainder of this volume. It is important to recognize that the articles in this volume are written by men and women who accept the New Testament as God's inspired Word written by human authors.[92] Each recognizes the importance of the Holy Spirit's illuminating work in the process of interpretation. Our goal is to build on the initial chapters, which affirm the full inspiration and authority of the New Testament and acknowledge the diversity of our past. We therefore approach our God-called task as interpreters and theologians with a simultaneous confidence in the Scripture illumined by the Spirit that points us to Christ and a sanctified tolerance and humility, recognizing that all interpretation is open to further correction and revision.

Bibliography

Ackroyd, P. R., and C. F. Evans, eds. *Cambridge History of the Bible*. 3 vols. Cambridge: Cambridge University Press, 1970.

Bray, Gerald. *Biblical Interpretation: Past and Present*. Downers Grove: InterVarsity, 1996.

Bruce, F. F. "The History of New Testament Study." In *New Testament Interpretation: Essays on Principles and Methods*. Ed. by I. Howard Marshall. Grand Rapids: Eerdmans, 1977.

Dockery, David S. *Biblical Interpretation Then and Now*. Grand Rapids: Baker, 1991.

Dockery, David S., Kenneth A. Matthews, and Robert B. Sloan. *Foundations for Biblical Interpretation*. Nashville: Broadman and Holman, 1994.

Goldingay, John. *Models for Interpretation of Scripture*. Grand Rapids: Eerdmans, 1995.

Grant, Robert M., and David Tracey. A *Short History of the Interpretation of the Bible*. Philadelphia: Fortress, 1984.

Hayes, John H., ed. *Dictionary of Biblical Interpretation*. 2 vols. Nashville: Abingdon, 1999.

Klein, William W., Craig L. Blomberg, and Robert L. Hubbard Jr. *Introduction to Biblical Interpretation*. Dallas: Word, 1993.

Kugel, James L., and Rowan A. Greer. *Early Biblical Interpretation*. Philadelphia: Westminster, 1986.

Kümmel, W. G. *The New Testament: The History of the Investigation of Its Problems*. Trans. S. M. Gilmour and H. C. Keel. Nashville: Abingdon, 1972.

McKim, Donald K. *Historical Handbook of Major Biblical Interpreters*. Downers Grove: InterVarsity, 1998.

Neill, Stephen and T. Wright. *The Interpretation of the New Testament 1861–1986*. 2d ed. New York: Oxford, 1988.

Rogerson, John, Christopher Rowland, and Barnabas Lindars SSF. *The Study and Use of the Bible*. Grand Rapids: Eerdmans, 1988.

Silva, Moises. *Has the Church Misread the Bible?* Grand Rapids: Zondervan, 1987.

Thiselton, Anthony. *New Horizons in Hermeneutics*. Grand Rapids: Zondervan, 1992.

_____. *Two Horizons: New Testament Hermeneutics and Philosophical Description*. Grand Rapids: Eerdmans, 1980.

Notes

1. F. F. Bruce, "The History of New Testament Study," in *New Testament Interpretation: Essays on Principles and Methods,* ed. I. Howard Marshall (Grand Rapids: Eerdmans, 1977), 21; also see the chapter in this book by Klyne Snodgrass.

2. Chapter 6, "Redaction Criticism" by Grant Osborne touches on these matters.

3. Cf. Walter Bauer, *Orthodoxy and Heresy in Earliest* Christianity, ed. Robert Kraft and Gerhard Krodel (Philadelphia: Fortress, 1971), 61–194; Harold O. J. Brown, *Heresies* (Garden City, N.Y.: Doubleday, 1984), 38–94.

4. Robert M. Grant with David Tracy, *A Short History of the Interpretation of the Bible*, rev. ed. (Philadelphia: Fortress, 1984), 55.

5. Irenaeus, *Against Heresies* 1.10, 22; 2.25; 3.4; cf. Rowan A. Greer, "The Dog and the Mushrooms: Irenaeus' View of the Valentinians Assessed," in *The Rediscovery of Gnosticism*, vol. 1 of *The School of Valentine*, ed. Bentley Layton (Leiden: Brill, 1980), 146–75.

6. Karlfried Froehlich, trans. and ed., *Biblical Interpretation in the Early Church* (Philadelphia: Fortress, 1984), 13–15.

7. Cf. Oskar Skarsaune, *Proof from Prophecy: A Study in Justin Martyr's Proof-Text Tradition* (Leiden: Brill, 1987); also Willis A. Shotwell, *The Biblical Exegesis of Justin Martyr* (London: SPCK, 1965).

8. Cf. James L. Kugel and Rowan A. Greer, *Early Biblical Interpretation* (Philadelphia: Westminster, 1986), 177–99.

9. R. P. C. Hanson, *Allegory and Event: A Study of the Sources and Significance of Origen's Interpretation of Scripture* (London: SCM, 1959), 360.

10. Origen, *De Principiis* 4.2.4–17; cf. J. N. D. Kelly, *Early Christian Doctrines* (New York: Harper, 1960), 70–75. Origen built his model on his translation of Proverbs 22:20, "Write them in a threefold way."

11. Cf. Karen J. Torjesen, "Hermeneutical Procedure and Theological Structure in Origen's Exegesis" (Ph.D. dissertation, Claremont Graduate School, 1982).

12. See R. P. C. Hanson, *Origen's Doctrine of Tradition* (London: SPCK, 1954); also Albert C. Outler, "Origen and the Regulae Fidei," in *Church History* 8 (1939): 212–21.

13. Joseph Wilson Trigg, *Origen: The Bible and Philosophy in the Third Century Church* (Atlanta: John Knox, 1983), 31–75; Dan G. McCartney, "Literal and Allegorical Interpretation in Origen's *Contra Celsum*," in *Westminster Theological Journal* 48 (1986): 281–301.

14. Cf. F. A. Sullivan, *The Christology of Theodore of Mopsuestia* (Rome: Gregorian University Press, 1956); also R. A. Norris, *Manhood and Christ: A Study in the Christology of Theodore of Mopseustia* (Oxford: Clarendon, 1963).

15. Jacques Guillet, "Les exegeses d'Alexandrie et d'Antioche: conflit ou Malentendu?" in *Recherches de science religieuse* 34 (1957): 275–302, is incorrect in concluding that the differences between the two schools were caused only by a fundamental misunderstanding of each other.

16. Cf. Rowan A. Greer, *Theodore of Mopsuestia: Exegete and Theologian* (London: Faith, 1961).

17. Cf. Donald Attwater, *St. John Chrysostom: Pastor and Preacher* (London: Harvill, 1959).

18. See the discussion concerning the Antiochene treatment of the apostle Paul in Maurice F. Wiles, *The Divine Apostle: The Interpretation of St. Paul's Epistles in the Early Church* (Cambridge: Cambridge University Press, 1967).

19. Raymond E. Brown, *The Sensus Plenior of Holy Scripture* (Baltimore: St. Mary's University Press, 1955), 46.

20. Cf. Origen, *Contra Celsum* 4.19. He contended that if the biblical text is divine, it must bear allegorical meaning. If a text cannot be interpreted allegorically, it must then be relegated to a state of unimportance.

21. Cf. Chrysostom, *Expositions in the Psalms* 46.1.

22. R. L. Wilken, "Tradition, Exegesis and the Christological Controversies," *Church History* 34 (1965): 123–45.

23. See the discussion on Jerome and Augustine in H. F. D. Sparks, "Jerome as Biblical Scholar," and Gerald Bonner, "Augustine as Biblical Scholar" in *Cambridge History of the Bible*, eds. P. R. Ackroyd and C. F. Evans, 3 vols. (Cambridge: Cambridge University Press, 1970), 510–63.

24. Augustine, *On Christian Doctrine* 3.2. In 3.5, he referred to the *praescriptio fidei*.

25. See J. N. D. Kelly, *Jerome: His Life, Writings and Controversies* (London: Duckworth, 1975), 264–73.

26. Augustine, *On Christian Doctrine* 3.15.

27. Theodoret, *Letters* 16.

28. Beryl Smalley, *The Study of the Bible in the Middle Ages* (2nd ed., Oxford: Blackwell, 1952), 26–36; cf. Gillian R. Evans, *The Language and Logic of the Bible: The Earlier Middle Ages* (Cambridge: Cambridge University Press, 1984).

29. Robert E. McNally, *The Bible in the Early Middle Ages* (Westminster, Md.: Newman, 1959), 50–54.

30. See James Houston's introduction in Bernard of Clairvaux, *The Love of God and Spiritual Friendship,* ed. with an extended introduction by J. Houston (Portland: Multnomah, 1983), 32–33; Beryl Smalley, "The Bible in the Middle Ages," in *The Church's Use of the Bible Past and Present,* ed. D. E. Nineham (London: Macmillan, 1963), 60; John Rogerson, Christopher Rowland, Barnabas Lindars SSF, *The Study and Use of the Bible* (Grand Rapids: Eerdmans, 1988), 274–94.

31. David C. Steinmetz, "The Superiority of Precritical Exegesis," *Theology Today* 27 (1980): 31–32; cf. F. Van Steenberghen, *Aristotle in the West: The Origins of Latin Aristotelianism,* trans. Leonard Johnston (Louvain: E. Nauwelaerts, 1955), 62–63.

32. Cf. Thomas Aquinas, *On Interpretation,* trans. J. T. Oesterle (Milwaukee: Marquette University Press, 1962).

33. Cf. B. Moeller, "Scripture, Tradition, and Sacrament in the Middle Ages and in Luther," in *Holy Book and Holy Tradition,* ed. F. F. Bruce and E. G. Rupp (Manchester: Manchester University Press, 1968), 120–22; also E. Gilson, *The Christian Philosophy of St. Thomas Aquinas,* trans. L. K. Shook (London: Victor Gollancz, 1957), 20–21.

34. Cf. Raymond Barry Shelton, "Martin Luther's Concept of Biblical Interpretation in Historical Perspective" (Ph.D. dissertation Fuller Theological Seminary, 1974); also Jaroslav Pelikan, *Luther the Expositor* (St. Louis: Concordia, 1959). Also see David S. Dockery, "The Christological Hermeneutics of Martin Luther," in *Grace Theological Journal* 4 (1983): 189–203.

35. A. Rabil, *Erasmus and the New Testament: The Mind of a Christian Humanist* (San Antonio: Trinity University Press, 1972), 43–45; cf. J. H. Bentley, *Humanist and Holy Writ* (Princeton: Princeton University Press, 1983), 115–26.

36. Cf. J. W. Aldridge, *The Hermeneutics of Erasmus* (Richmond: John Knox, 1966); also J. B. Payne, *Erasmus: His Theology of the Sacraments* (New York: Bratcher, 1970), 54–70.

37. Traditionally negative evaluations have been given to Erasmus' work, e.g., A. T. Robertson, *An Introduction to the Textual Criticism of the New Testament* (New York: Doubleday, 1925), 19–20; Bruce M. Metzger, *The Text of the New Testament* (Oxford: Oxford University Press, 1968), 97–103. Recently more balanced and positive renderings have been offered by Bentley, *Humanist and Holy Writ,* 114ff., and Henk Jan DeJonge, "The Character of Erasmus' Translation of the New Testament as Reflected in His Translation of Hebrews 9," in *The Journal of Medieval and Renaissance Studies* 14 (1984): 81–87; idem, *"Novum Testamentum a Nobis Versum:* The Essence of Erasmus' Edition of the New Testament," in *Journal of Theological Studies* 35 (1984): 394–413.

38. Hans-Joachim Kraus, "Calvin's Exegetical Principles," in *Interpretation* 31 (1977): 8–18; cf. Timothy George, *Theology of the Reformers* (Nashville: Broadman, 1988).

39. John Calvin, *The Epistles of Paul the Apostle to the Romans and to the Thessalonians,* ed. D. W. Torrance and T. F. Torrance (Grand Rapids: Eerdmans, 1961), 1.4.

40. Even a rival like J. Arminius said Calvin's interpretation of Scripture was incomparable, saying, "He stands above others, above most, indeed, above all." Cited by C. Bangs, *Arminius: A Study in the Dutch Reformation* (Nashville: Abingdon, 1971), 287–88.

41. Martin Luther, *Luther's Works,* ed. J. Pelikan (St. Louis: Concordia, 1955), 35:361–62.

42. Cf. P. A. Verhoef, "Luther and Calvin's Exegetical Library," in *Calvin Theological Journal* 3 (1968): 5–20; also B. A. Gerrish, *The Old Protestantism and the New: Essays on the Reformation Heritage* (Chicago: University of Chicago, 1982), 51–68.

43. Bruce, "History of New Testament Study," 34–37; also see W. G. Kümmel, *The New Testament: The History of the Investigation of Its Problems,* trans. S. M. Gilmour and H. C. Kee (Nashville: Abingdon, 1972), 27–28.

44. Cf. J. P. Donnelly, "Calvinist Thomism," in *Victor* 7 (1976): 441–51; also J. K. S. Reid, *The Authority of Scripture: A Study of Reformation and Post-Reformation Understanding of the Bible* (London: Methuen, 1962).

45. Spener, in *Pia Desideria* (1675) offered six proposals for reform that became a short summary of pietism. Chief among these proposals was the appeal for a more extensive use of the Word of God among us. The Bible must be the chief means for reform. See J. O. Duke, "Pietism versus Establishment: The Halle Phase," in *Classical Quarterly* 72 (1978): 3–16; K. J. Stein, "Philip Jacob Spener's Hope for Better Times: Contribution in Controversy," in *Classical Quarterly* 73 (1979): 3–20.

46. Edgar Krentz, *The Historical-Critical Method* (Philadelphia: Fortress, 1975), 16–23.

47. Johann Albert Bengel, *Gnomon of the New Testament,* ed. Andrew R. Fausset, 5 vols. (Edinburgh: T. & T. Clark, 1857–1858); cf. W. C. Kaiser Jr., *Toward an Exegetical Theology* (Grand Rapids: Baker, 1981), 60–63.

48. F. D. E. Schleiermacher, *Hermeneutics: The Handwritten Manuscripts,* ed. H. Kimmerle, trans. James Duke and H. J. Forstman (Missoula, Mont.: Scholar's, 1977).

49. Kümmel, *The New Testament,* 19; Stephen Neill, *The Interpretation of the New Testament 1861–1961* (London: Oxford, 1966), 65.

50. F. Lau, *Neue Deutsche Biographie* (Berlin: Duncker & Humbolt, 1959), 4:605.

51. Cf. Hans W. Frei, *The Eclipse of Biblical Narrative* (New Haven: Yale, 1974), 111–12; Craig Blomberg, *The Historical Reliability of the Gospels* (Downers Grove, Ill.: InterVarsity, 1987), 5–7.

52. Cf. W. R. Farmer, *The Synoptic Problem* (New York: Macmillan, 1964); for a concise overview of the history of this issue, see D. Guthrie, *New Testament Introduction* (Downers Grove, Ill.: InterVarsity, 1990), 121–87; and Robert Stein's chapter in this volume.

53. Kümmel, *The New Testament,* 77–79.

54. Ibid., 75–77.

55. See also Scot McKnight, *Interpreting the Synoptic Gospels* (Grand Rapids: Baker, 1989); cf. C. M. Tuckett, *The Revival of the Griesbach Hypothesis* (Cambridge: University Press, 1983).

56. Kümmel, *The New Testament,* 98–104.

57. Neill, *Interpretation of the New Testament,* 18–28, 33–57. Also see Carey C. Newman, "Images of the Church in Acts," *People of God,* ed. P. Basden and D. Dockery (Nashville: Broadman, 1991).

58. Important theologians, among many, include J. von Hoffman (1810–1877); A. Schlatter (1852–1938); K. Barth (1886–1968); R. Bultmann (1884–1976); C. H. Dodd (1884–1973); J. Jeremias (1900–1979); O. Cullmann (1902–1999); G. E. Ladd (1911–1982); and D. Guthrie (b. 1916).

59. See D. E. Nineham, "Schweitzer Revisited," in *Explorations* in *Theology* 1 (London: SCM, 1977), 112–33.

60. D. Luhrmann, *An Itinerary for New Testament Study,* trans. l. Bowden (Philadelphia: Trinity, 1989), 67–69.

6l. R. Bultmann, *The History of the Synoptic Tradition* (New York: Harper, 1968).

62. T. W. Manson, "The Failure of Liberalism to Interpret the Bible as the Word of God," in *The Interpretation of the Bible,* ed. C. W. Dugmore (London: SPCK, 1944), 92.

63. See I. H. Marshall, *I Believe in the Historical Jesus* (Grand Rapids: Eerdmans, 1977).

64. Stephen J. Stein, "The Quest for the Spiritual Sense: The Biblical Hermeneutics of Jonathan Edwards," in *Harvard Theological Review* 70 (1977): 99–113.

65. See M. Silva, "Old Princeton, Westminster, and Inerrancy," in *Inerrancy and Hermeneutic* (Grand Rapids: Baker, 1988), 67–80.

66. H. D. Betz, *Galatians* (Philadelphia: Fortress, 1979).

67. R. P. Martin, "Approaches to New Testament Exegesis," *New Testament Interpretation,* 229–47.

68. K. Stendahl, "Implications of Form Criticism and Tradition Criticism for Biblical Interpretation," in *Journal of Biblical Literature* 77 (1958): 33–38; J. L. McKenzie, "Problems of Hermeneutics in Roman Catholic Exegesis," in *Journal of Biblical Literature* 77 (1958): 197–204.

69. Schleiermacher, *Hermeneutics,* 141; cf. Hans-Georg Gadamer, "The Problem of Language in Schleiermacher's Hermeneutic," in *Journal for Theology and Church* 7 (1970): 70–76.

70. Anthony Thiselton, *Two Horizons: New Testament Hermeneutics and Philosophical Description* (Grand Rapids: Eerdmans, 1980), 103–106.

71. Cf. R. E. Palmer, *Hermeneutics* (Evanston: Northwestern University Press, 1969), 98–113.

72. W. Dilthey, "Die Entstehung der Hermeneutik," *Gesammelte Schriften* (Stuttgart: Teubner, 1964), 5:324–30.

73. Cf. E. D. Hirsch, *Validity in Interpretation* (New Haven: Yale, 1967); idem, *The Aims of Interpretation* (Chicago: University of Chicago, 1976).

74. Cf. Thiselton, *Two Horizons,* 143–204.

75. See W. Pannenberg, "Hermeneutics and Universal History," in *History and Hermeneutics,* ed. R. W. Funk (Tübingen: Mohr, 1967), 132.

76. M. Silva, *Has the Church Misread the Bible?* (Grand Rapids: Zondervan, 1987), 115–17.

77. R. Bultmann, *Theology of the New Testament,* trans. K. Grobel, 2 vols. (New York: Scribner's, 1955), 2:130–35.

78. R. Bultmann, *Kerygma and Myth,* ed. H. W. Bartsch (London: SCM, 1953); idem, *Jesus Christ and Mythology* (London: SCM, 1960).

79. So he brilliantly articulated in his classic article, "Is Exegesis without Presuppositions Possible?" in *Existence and Faith,* ed. S. Ogden (London: Hodder and Stoughton, 1961), 289–96.

80. Gadamer, "Problem of Language," 90–92; also cf. Thiselton, *Two Horizons,* 304–19.

8l. See the fuller discussion in David S. Dockery, "Author? Reader? Text? Toward a Hermeneutical Synthesis," in *Theological Educator* (1988): 7–16.

82. Cf. P. Ricoeur, *Interpretation Theory: Discourse and the Surplus of Meaning* (Fort Worth: Texas Christian University Press, 1976); idem, *Essays in Biblical Interpretation* (Philadelphia: Fortress, 1980).

83. Cf. Peter Cotterell and Max Turner, *Linguistics and Biblical Interpretation* (Downers Grove, Ill.: InterVarsity, 1989); also R. E. Longacre, *The Grammar of Discourse* (New York: Plenum, 1983).

84. G. B. Caird, *The Language and Imagery of the Bible* (Philadelphia: Westminster, 1980), 61, has discussed the difficulty of defining or identifying meaning. As carefully as anyone, Caird has detailed the concept of "meaning" and discovering "meaning" (see pp. 32–61). He distinguishes between meaning R (referent), meaning S (sense), meaning V (value), meaning E (entailment), and meaning I (intention).

85. See Gerhard Maier, *The End of the Historical-Critical Method* (St. Louis: Concordia, 1977); Peter Stuhlmacher, *Historical Criticism and Theological Interpretation: Towards a Hermeneutics of Consent,* trans. R. A. Harrisville (Philadelphia: Fortress, 1977); and David C. Steinmetz, "The Superiority of Precritical Exegesis," 27–38.

86. One of the finest examples of sociological interpretation can be found in W. A. Meeks, *The First Urban Christians: The Social Work of the Apostle Paul* (New Haven: Yale, 1983). See Robert Mulholland's chapter in this book.

87. E.g., J. M. Bonino, *Doing Theology in a Revolutionary Situation* (Philadelphia: Fortress, 1975).

88. E.g., E. S. Fiorenza, *In Memory of Her: A Feminist Theological Reconstruction of Christian Origins* (New York: Crossroad, 1983).

89. See D. M. Patte, *The Gospel According to Matthew: A Structural Commentary on Matthew's Faith* (Philadelphia: Fortress, 1987); and idem, *Structural Exegesis: From Theory to Practice* (Philadelphia: Fortress, 1978).

90. B. S. Childs, *The New Testament as Canon: An Introduction* (Philadelphia: Westminster, 1984); also see the discussion in F. F. Bruce, "Canon, Criticism, and Interpretation," in *The Canon of Scripture* (Downers Grove, Ill.: InterVarsity, 1988), 284–97.

91. See *Dictionary of Jesus and the Gospels, Dictionary of Paul and His Letters,* and *Dictionary of the Later New Testament* (Downers Grove, IVP).

92. See David S. Dockery, *Christian Scripture* (Nashville: Broadman & Holman, 1995).

Part II

Basic Methods in New Testament Interpretation

Chapter 3

Textual Criticism

Michael W. Holmes
Bethel College

In an age of mass-produced books and copy machines that enable us to obtain virtually on-demand, perfect copies of almost anything, it is difficult to imagine just how hard it was to obtain a reliable copy of a book before the invention of printing. All copying was done by hand (thus books produced in this way are called *manuscripts*), and this slow, laborious, and expensive[1] process was subject to all the vagaries and corrupting influences and effects of the human mind and body. Consequently no two copies of a book were identical, and neither perfectly represented the exemplar (model) from which they were copied.[2] This means, among other things, that all surviving manuscripts of the New Testament differ (sometimes widely) among themselves.

This would be, of course, of no great significance if the originals were available; one could then ignore the imperfect copies and simply consult the original to determine exactly what an author wrote. But this is not possible, since no autograph of any classical, biblical, or early patristic writer is extant today. This means that our only access to any of these writers is via the surviving imperfect copies. These two circumstances make *textual criticism*—the art and science of recovering the original text of a document—a necessary and foundational step in the study of any ancient author or book. It is, after all, somewhat difficult to study or interpret a document accurately unless one first knows exactly what that document says.

New Testament textual criticism involves three major tasks: (1) the gathering and organization of evidence, including especially the collation (comparison) of manuscripts (= MSS) with one another to ascertain where errors and alterations have produced variations in the text, and the study of how and why these variations happened; (2) the evaluation and assessment of the significance and implications of the evidence with a view to determining which of the variant readings most likely represents the original text; and (3) the reconstruction of the history of the transmission of the text, to the extent allowed by the available evidence.

This chapter will focus primarily on the first two areas, though there will be opportunity to say something about the third area as well. After discussing in greater detail the causes of variation in MSS and surveying the available resources for recovering the original text, we will consider the methodological approaches and practical guidelines textual critics use to reconstruct, with a very high degree of confidence, the original text of the New Testament from the mass of variations and errors among the extant copies.

Causes of Error

Both the format of books and the mechanics of the copying process facilitated the commission of errors when copying a book. Books were written in *scriptio continua* (i.e., without breaks between words) with minimal punctuation or other aids for the reader, generally in either one wide column or several narrow ones per page.[3] Thus it was not difficult to misread the text or lose one's place while copying. Scribes would often inadvertently skip between words or syllables with similar beginnings or endings,[4] the result being either the loss or duplication of material.[5] The steps involved in the copying process itself—reading the text, remembering it, and writing it down[6]—offered easy opportunity to misread the text, rearrange word order, or substitute a more familiar word or better remembered phrase for a less common or unusual one.[7] Fatigue,[8] poor eyesight or hearing, or simple stupidity could also contribute to errors in copying.

Not all alterations, however, were inadvertent. Harmonization, for example, could be deliberate as well as unintentional; and as Greek grammar, syntax, and style changed over the centuries, scribes often "updated" the text to conform to current standards or substituted a more refined or literary term for a colloquial one.[9] Sometimes a scribe would venture to correct what appeared to him to be an error or difficulty in his exemplar; if done unskillfully, this not infrequently resulted in the replacement of one error by another or a compounding of the initial problem. Occasionally the text was altered for doctrinal reasons.[10] Orthodox and heretics alike leveled this charge against their opponents; the surviving evidence suggests that the charges had some basis in reality.

These, then, are some of the reasons why there are variations in all extant copies of the New Testament and thus textual criticism is a necessary and foundational step in the interpretation of the New Testament. In a sense, textual criticism involves the *reversal* of the process of corruption described above. That is, the textual critic seeks to understand the transmission process and the causes and effects of corruption that produced imperfect copies from the originals in order to reverse the process and thus work back from these surviving imperfect copies to reconstruct the lost originals.

Sources of Information About the Text

New Testament textual criticism enjoys an embarrassment of riches with regard to sources of information about the New Testament text. Unlike many classical or patristic texts, which have been preserved in only a few late copies or, in extreme cases, only a single, now-destroyed copy, there exist today thousands of copies of the New Testament in several ancient languages. In addition, almost all of the Greek New Testament could be reconstructed on the basis of quotations by ancient writers. For ease of reference scholars have grouped these sources under three headings: Greek manuscripts, ancient versions, and patristic citations.

GREEK MANUSCRIPTS

The Greek manuscripts are categorized, somewhat arbitrarily, on the basis of either writing material, style, or format. First are the *papyri,* manuscripts of the Greek New Testament written on papyrus, an ancient paperlike writing material. These MSS, which include some of the oldest surviving copies,[11] are designated by a Gothic "p" followed by a superscript Arabic numeral (e.g., $\mathfrak{p}^{46}$). As of late 1998 the remains of about 115 papyri are known, most of which are extremely fragmentary. Some of the better preserved and more important witnesses in this category include $\mathfrak{p}^{45}$ (third century; substantial parts of Gospels and Acts), $\mathfrak{p}^{46}$ (ca. 200; Pauline Epistles), $\mathfrak{p}^{66}$ (ca. 200; large parts of John), $\mathfrak{p}^{72}$ (third/fourth centuries; parts of 1–2 Peter, Jude), and $\mathfrak{p}^{75}$ (early third century; over half of Luke and John).[12]

Continuous-text Greek MSS written on material other than papyrus (usually parchment, though after the twelfth century increasingly on paper) are subdivided on the basis of writing style. *Majuscules* (more often called uncials)[13] are MSS written in a formal literary style of unconnected capital letters. They were initially designated by letters of the alphabet; when these proved insufficient, the Greek and then Hebrew alphabets were used. Because of the resulting confusion, numbers prefixed with a zero (e.g., 01, 02) were eventually assigned to these MSS. Today only the most famous of the majuscules/uncials continue to be known by their original letters; these include codices Sinaiticus (‭א‬/01; mid-fourth century), Alexandrinus (A/02; early fifth century), Vaticanus (B/03; early fourth century), Bezae (D/05; fifth century), Washingtonianus (W/032; fourth/fifth centuries), and Koridethi (Θ/038; ninth century). Today about 270 majuscule MSS are recognized.[14]

Minuscules are MSS written in a smaller cursive style that was developed in the eighth or ninth century. As this style was faster to write and more space efficient than the majuscule, it enabled books to be produced more cheaply. Minuscule MSS are identified by a simple Arabic numeral; the list now runs through at least 2862.[15] Some of the more significant minuscules include groups or "families" headed by 1 and 13 (symbols: f^1 and f^{13}), and 28, 33, 81, 323, 565, 614, 700, 892, 1241, 1424, 1739, and 2495.

Lectionaries are books containing selections from Scripture for use in worship and other services. These comprise the final category of Greek witnesses and are identified by an Arabic number preceded by a script ell (e.g., 132). More than twenty-two hundred lectionary MSS are known to exist today.

In all, something over five thousand witnesses to the Greek New Testament are extant today. Many (if not most) of these, it should be noted, are fragmentary or incomplete. Only 3 majuscules (ℵ/01, A/02, and C/04) and fifty-six minuscules contain the entire New Testament; another 2 majuscules and 147 minuscules lack only Revelation.[16] As for content, the Gospels are found in just over 2,300 MSS, the Acts and Catholic letters in about 655, the Pauline letters in about 780, and Revelation in about 290. With regard to date, over 65 percent are from the eleventh through fourteenth centuries, while less than 2.5 percent are from the first five centuries.[17]

Ancient Versions

As Christianity spread into regions and social strata where Greek was not understood, the need for translations of the New Testament arose. By about A.D. 180 the process of translating the New Testament into Latin, Syriac, and Coptic was underway. The Latin eventually developed into at least two major forms, the Old Latin or Itala and the Vulgate (of which more than eight thousand MSS are known), while the Syriac and Coptic exist in a number of versions and dialects. Later translations include Armenian, Georgian, Ethiopic, Gothic, and Old Church Slavonic. In several instances these translations were the first literary work in that particular language, and occasionally, as in the case of the Gothic, an alphabet first had to be created.[18]

Because the roots of some of these early versions antedate the vast majority of the Greek MSS, they are valuable historical witnesses to the transmission of the New Testament text, particularly regarding the form of the text in various regions or provinces. Limitations, however, in the ability of these languages to represent aspects of Greek grammar and syntax (Latin, e.g., has no definite article) restrict their value at some points.[19]

Patristic Citations

Early Christian writers frequently quoted the New Testament in their writings and sermons, often at length, and many wrote commentaries on it. Together these constitute another important source of information about the New Testament text. "Indeed, so extensive are these citations that if all other sources for our knowledge of the text of the New Testament were destroyed, they would be sufficient alone for the reconstruction of practically the entire New Testament."[20] Their particular value lies in the help they provide in dating and localizing variant readings and text-types. Like the versions, however, their value is sometimes limited, in this case by a tendency to cite from memory or adapt a quotation to its context. Thus it can be difficult to determine if a reading represents a genuine Greek variant or merely the author's adaptation of the text.[21] Nevertheless these citations represent an important additional source of information.

The sheer volume of the information available to the New Testament textual critic makes it practically certain that the original text has been preserved somewhere among the surviving witnesses.[22] Thus only occasionally is it necessary to consider the possibility of textual emendation (the proposal of a reading not found in any extant witness). This is in sharp contrast to the textual criticism of the Old Testament, classical, and patristic texts where textual emendation is routinely necessary.

Classification and Genealogical Relationships of MSS

The volume of information also means that at times textual questions can become quite technical and difficult. To be sure, computer applications have eliminated some of the drudgery involved; even so, simply gathering all the evidence for a particular problem, not to mention analyzing and evaluating it, can be a formidable challenge.

The phenomenon of genealogical relationships and the classification of MSS into certain broad textual traditions (text-types) do, however, alleviate the problem significantly. In normal circumstances, MSS copied from a distinctive model will themselves exhibit those distinctive elements. Because they share these elements by virtue of a common parent, they may be said to be genetically related or to have a genealogical relationship.

Now in the case of the New Testament, as it was being copied throughout the Roman Empire, distinctive variations that arose in one region or area and which came to characterize MSS copied in that region would not, except by occasional sheer coincidence, occur in the same way or pattern in MSS copied elsewhere from different exemplars. On the basis of these particular patterns it is possible to group most MSS into one of three broad text-types, the Alexandrian, the Western, and the Byzantine.[23] Each of these text-types, identified on the basis of a high degree of agreement between certain MSS over both a set of readings peculiar to a text-type and the total area of variation, has a distinctive character and history.

The Alexandrian text-type, so named because most of the MSS belonging to it have come from Egypt, at one time was thought to be a carefully edited, late third-century recension (edition), a product of Alexandrian classical scholarship applied to the New Testament. But new discoveries, especially $\mathfrak{p}^{75}$ and $\mathfrak{p}^{46}$, have demonstrated that this text-type was already in existence well before the end of the second century. Thus it appears to represent the result of a carefully controlled and supervised process of copying and transmission. Primary representatives include $\mathfrak{p}^{46}$, $\mathfrak{p}^{66}$, $\mathfrak{p}^{75}$, $\aleph$, B, and Origen; secondary[24] witnesses include C L W 33 892 1739 and later Alexandrian fathers like Didymus.[25]

The Western[26] text-type, equally as old as the Alexandrian, is more widely attested geographically; major witnesses derive from North Africa, Italy, Gaul, Syria, and Egypt. But it lacks the homogeneity and consistency of relationships characteristic of the other two texts. It appears to represent a tradition of uncontrolled copying, editing, and translation; it is typified by harmonistic tendencies, paraphrasing, and substitution of synonyms, additions (sometimes quite long[27]), and a small but theologically significant group of omissions.[28] Major representatives include Codex Bezae (D/05); $\mathfrak{p}^{45}$ $\aleph$ W in the Gospels (all in part only), D/06 F G in the Pauline Epistles, the Old Latin and Old Syriac versions, and Tatian, Irenaeus, Cyprian, and Tertullian among the fathers.

The Byzantine text-type, also known as the Koine, Syrian, or Majority text, comprises about 80 percent of all known MSS. While scattered, individual Byzantine readings are known to be ancient, the Byzantine text-type as such—that is, as an identifiable pattern of distinctive variants and agreements—first appears only in the mid-fourth century among a group of fathers associated with Antioch. Thus it is the largest and latest of the three major text-types and, in view of the obvious secondary character of many of its distinctive readings,[29] also the least valuable for recovering the original text.

The phenomenon of genealogical relationships is important not only for classifying MSS but for evaluating them as well. When evaluating witnesses and text-types, the genealogical principle means that *MSS must be weighed rather than counted*. The total number of MSS supporting a particular variant *in and of itself* is of little significance. Consider the following diagram, in which the first level (X) represents the now-lost original reading of a document and the second level represents copies of it (each letter stands for one copy):

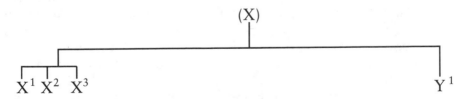

Of the four surviving copies in this hypothetical case, three read X and one reads Y. If one were to decide the original reading by simply counting MSS, one would conclude, in this case correctly, that the original read X.

But suppose that X^3 was destroyed during a persecution and that Y^1 was used by a scriptorium as an exemplar for several additional copies. The diagram would now look like this:

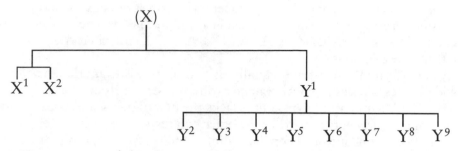

Here a count of the eleven surviving MSS would lead one to conclude, on the basis of the nine Y versus two X tally, that the original reading was Y. But in this case that conclusion would be wrong! Because Y^2 through Y^9 are all copies of Y^1, they add nothing to the weight or significance of Y^1.

In short, since even ten thousand copies of a mistake are still a mistake, the number of MSS in a given text-type or supporting a particular reading is of little intrinsic significance. Manuscript readings and text-types must be evaluated on the basis of their probable origin, character, and other considerations. This explains why the Byzantine text-type is of lesser importance than the other two, even though it comprises over 80 percent of all known MSS. Its distinctive readings consistently betray themselves, on the basis of historically verifiable criteria,[30] as secondary and derivitive, rather than original, despite their numerical preponderance.

The Recovery of the Text of the New Testament

Almost as soon as there were multiple copies of the books of the New Testament, people were aware that there were differences among the MSS.[31] But while early Christians (and some pagans, as well) were quite aware of variations between MSS of the New Testament, it was not until the late Renaissance that there were any systematic efforts to attempt to recover the original text of the New Testament.

Erasmus of Rotterdam, the man primarily responsible for the first published edition of the Greek New Testament,[32] reveals in his *Annotations* on the New Testament a well-developed critical sense of the causes of errors and variations in New Testament MSS and of criteria for discerning the original reading. He uses, at least in embryonic form, many of the analytic tools developed by later scholars.[33]

The text he edited was not, however, equal in quality to his methods, largely because of the severely limited manuscript resources with which he had to work.[34] Consequently his text ended up representing in printed form a late, corrupt form of the Byzantine text-type. Because it was first on the market and because of its low price, Erasmus' Greek New Testament was widely influential and often reprinted without authorization. Even the later editions of such notable scholars as Robert Estienne (Stephanus) and Theodore Beza were essentially reprints of Erasmus. So dominant was this form of text that in 1633 a printer could boast that this was "the text which is now received by all" (*textum . . . nunc ab omnibus receptum*), from which arose the now common designation for this text, the "Textus Receptus," or TR. It was the basis of all the major European Protestant translations prior to 1881, including especially the King James of 1611, and unwarrantedly dominated the scholarly scene for more than three hundred years.

Indeed, "so superstitious has been the reverence accorded the Textus Receptus that in some cases attempts to criticize or emend it have been regarded as akin to sacrilege;"[35] those who dared to change the TR were vehemently attacked as heretics. As a result, scholars tended to relegate new manuscript discoveries or advances in methodology to the margins, the critical apparatus, or long appendices to their editions of the TR, and it is here that we must look for signs of progress beyond Erasmus.

Notable among those who advanced the discipline of textual criticism is J. A. Bengel (1687–1752). He recognized that many MSS could, on the basis of a shared pattern of variant readings, be classified into families or groups and that MSS must therefore be weighed rather than merely counted. He also expressed in classical form a still-fundamental principle for evaluating readings first used by Erasmus: the difficult reading is to be preferred to the easy one.[36] Other notable figures during this era include Richard Simon (1638–1712), John Mill (1645–1707), Richard Bentley (1662–1742), and J. J. Wettstein (1693–1754).[37]

The next fundamental advance was made by J. J. Griesbach (1745–1812), also known for his investigations of the Synoptic Problem. Further developing Bengel's system of classifying MSS, he divided them into three major groups, which he termed Alexandrian, Western, and Byzantine. He also set out in substantial detail fifteen canons or criteria of textual criticism which continue, often in only slightly altered form, to be used today. Finally, he printed editions of the Greek New Testament in which he abandoned the text of the TR in many places and printed instead the form of text which his research had convinced him was closer to the original. His text, widely reprinted, was influential in England, Scotland, America, and on the Continent, and marks an important step away from the stultifying dominance of the TR. His influence upon the discipline, as Metzger notes, "can scarcely be overestimated."[38]

The first to make a clean break from the TR was Karl Lachmann (1793–1851), who in 1831 published an edition based solely upon the evidence of the earlier uncials, the Old Latin and Vulgate, and early patristic citations. In other words, rather than modifying the TR, as Bengel had done, Lachmann bypassed it entirely in favor of the oldest available evidence, and thus brought to fruition a proposal first set out by Bentley in 1716.

A weakness of Lachmann's edition was the still slender manuscript basis upon which it rested at points. That this is no longer the case for modern critics is due primarily to the tireless labors of Constantin Tischendorf (1815–1874). Best known for his dramatic discovery of Codex Sinaiticus,[39] his enduring contribution was the discovery (he published twenty-two volumes of biblical texts) and assembling of textual evidence.[40] The critical apparatus of the eighth edition of his Greek New Testament, published in two large volumes,[41] remains an indispensable source of information even today.

The work of Lachmann, Tischendorf, and their predecessors set the stage for an epochal event in the history of New Testament textual criticism, the publication in 1881 of *The New Testament in the Original Greek*, by B. F. Westcott and F. J. A. Hort.[42] They contributed, in addition to a new edition of the Greek text, a fundamental statement of methodological principles upon which it was based and a reconstruction of the history of the text.[43] While new discoveries (especially the papyri) have led contemporary textual critics to lay aside Westcott and Hort's historical reconstruction, their methodology was so sound and insightful that these same discoveries have essentially confirmed their edition of the text.[44] So significant was their work that whereas it overshadows all previous efforts to recover the original text, almost all[45] fundamental progress since then has in some way been built upon or in relation to their foundation.[46]

Among the editions since Westcott and Hort, perhaps the most widely used for several decades was Eberhard Nestle's *Novum Testamentum Graece*, first published in 1898.[47] A handy pocket edition, the Nestle text was based upon the editions of Westcott and Hort, Tischendorf, and (after 1901) Bernhard Weiss; it thus represented the consensus of nineteenth-century scholarship. Under the successive editorship of Erwin Nestle, Kurt Aland, and now Barbara Aland, and with the assistance of the Institut für neutestamentliche Textforschung, it has evolved into a critical text based no longer upon previous editions but solely upon manuscript evidence, which is presented along with numerous variant readings (over ten thousand) in a highly useful critical apparatus. Currently in its twenty-seventh edition,[48] "Nestle-Aland" (= NA^{27}) is one of two forms of the standard critical text in use today.

The other is *The Greek New Testament* published by the United Bible Societies (= UBS^4).[49] Intended for the use of translators, and edited by the same committee responsible for NA^{27}, it presents a much fuller apparatus for a smaller number of variants (ca. 1500). While differing with regard to punctuation, orthography, format, etc.,[50] the two editions present an identical text, and thus represent, in general if not in detail, the consensus of contemporary scholarship and research.[51]

Contemporary Methodological Approaches

The work of Lachmann and his predecessors marked a watershed in the application of a classical method of textual criticism, one that (for both the

New Testament and the classics) relied heavily on a stemmatic or genealogical approach. This approach sought to reconstruct a *stemma* or family tree of surviving MSS and then by working backward through the branches of the tradition to determine the most reliable or "best manuscript" upon which to base an edition.

But the work of Westcott and Hort and new discoveries and developments since their time have made it abundantly clear that this classical approach is unworkable in the case of the New Testament. Except in the case of certain small subgroups of MSS (e.g., "Family 1" [f^1] or "Family 13" [f^{13}]), it has not been possible to reconstruct a stemma for the textual tradition as a whole. This is because of (1) the relatively large number of MSS involved and (2) the widespread presence of mixture (or "cross-pollination") within the textual tradition.[52] That is, when copying, a scribe might use two exemplars, following now one and then the other, or he might correct his new copy against a different exemplar, which could be either older or more recent than the initial exemplar. Thus the lines of descent of a particular MS often may be said to be mixed or contaminated.

In practical terms this means that at any given point even the most reliable MS or group of MSS may be wrong and conversely (at least in theory) even a MS of very poor quality may occasionally preserve a true reading. Consequently there has emerged an approach that is best described as a *reasoned eclecticism*.[53] This approach seeks to apply to the New Testament all the tools and criteria developed by the classical method on a passage-by-passage basis. No one rule or principle can be applied or any one MS (no matter how reliable) or group of MSS (no matter how large) followed in a mechanical or across-the-board fashion; each variation unit must be approached on its own merits and as possibly unique.

Differences in method today are largely a matter of differing judgments as to the relative weight to be given to "external" evidence (i.e., the MSS themselves) over against "internal" evidence (i.e., considerations having to do with the habits, mistakes, and tendencies of scribes or the style and thought of an author).[54] There are, however, two notable exceptions. One is the so-called "rigorous eclecticism,"[55] which relies virtually exclusively on internal considerations and places little if any weight on external evidence; it treats the MSS as little more than a storehouse of readings to be evaluated on other grounds.[56] On the other extreme is the "Majority text method," embodied in *The Greek New Testament According to the Majority Text*.[57] This approach seeks to eliminate entirely any appeal to internal evidence, arguing instead that at any given point a variant which is supported by a majority of the MSS ought to be accepted as original.[58] But this essentially substitutes counting for reasoned criticism, and fails to realize that, as was pointed out above, MSS must be weighed, not simply counted, since ten thousand copies of a mistake do not make it any less a mistake.[59]

What the Majority text and the rigorous eclectic approaches have in common is a disregard for the history of the textual tradition. If, however, one takes the history of the text seriously, it becomes impossible to rely entirely upon either external or internal criteria alone. Instead, depending upon the facts in any given instance, a reasoned eclecticism applies a combination of internal and external considerations, evaluating the character of the variants in light of the manuscript evidence and vice versa in order to obtain a balanced view of the matter and as a check upon purely subjective tendencies.[60] This is the method and approach most widely practiced today and that lies behind, for example, recent translations such as the NRSV, REB, NASB, NIV, and HCSB.

Evaluating Variant Readings: The Method in Practice

A reasoned eclecticism seeks to follow one fundamental guideline that governs all other considerations: *the variant most likely to be original is the one that best accounts for the existence of the others*. That is, when confronted with two or more variant readings at some point in the text, it asks, "Which one best explains, in terms of both external and internal evidence, the origin of the others?" It is important to emphasize that "best accounts for" is here defined in terms of both external and internal considerations, because *prerequisite to reaching a judgment about a variant is the reconstruction of its history*. This is where both the Majority text and rigorous eclectic approaches fall short, in that they repeatedly contend for the originality of readings that cannot account for the historical (i.e., manuscript) evidence. Only the variant that can best account for *all* the evidence can seriously be considered as original.

Within the framework established by this fundamental guideline, several factors must be taken into consideration. Exactly which ones ought to be considered and how much weight is to be given to each depends upon the particular facts and circumstances in any given case. It may be helpful, therefore, to list the basic criteria for evaluating variant readings along with the various considerations that must be taken into account. We will then illustrate their application and use by means of some examples.

EXTERNAL EVIDENCE

Four basic factors to consider when evaluating external evidence (i.e., the evidence provided by the MSS and other witnesses themselves) are: (1) the relative date of the witnesses (Does the earlier[61] evidence support one variant more than the others? Are some variants without any early support? Or do all the readings have early support?); (2) the geographic distribution of the witnesses (generally, the broader the geographic distribution of the supporting witnesses, the higher the probability that the variant may be original, assuming that remote witnesses are not otherwise related);[62] (3) the genealogical relationships among the MSS (one must determine whether the

MSS supporting a variant represent a variety of text-types or are all from a single one, in which case it may be that a variant represents only a peculiarity of that text-type; also, once the reading of the text-type has been established, the addition of large numbers of additional witnesses of the same text-type does not appreciably affect matters); and (4) the relative quality of the witnesses.[63]

INTERNAL EVIDENCE

Internal evidence is of two kinds, *transcriptional* (having to do with the habits and practices of scribes) and *intrinsic* (having to do with the author's style and vocabulary). Each must be considered separately.

In evaluating transcriptional factors, it is a matter of asking whether any of the readings may be the result of slips, errors, or alterations in the copying process. In addition to the causes of error discussed above, one must take into account scribal tendencies to smooth over or resolve difficulties rather than create them, to harmonize passages, and to add rather than omit material.

As for intrinsic factors, the aim is to evaluate readings in light of what an author is most likely to have written. Factors to consider include the author's vocabulary and style, the flow of thought and logic of the immediate context (here exegesis may be decisive for the textual decision), congruence with the author's ideas or teachings, whether traditional material is being used, and, in the Gospels, the Aramaic background of Jesus' teachings.[64]

Not all these factors will apply in every case, of course, and it is not uncommon for two or more of them to conflict. This is why none of them can be applied or followed in a mechanical or thoughtless fashion and why the fundamental guideline must always be kept in mind: the variant most likely to be original is the one that best accounts for, in terms of both external and internal considerations, the origin of the others.

SUMMARY

By now it should be clear that textual criticism is an art as well as a science. Like other historical disciplines it resists being reduced to a mechanical application of any one rule or set of rules. Each new variant confronts the critic with a potentially unique set of circumstances and data and must be approached on that basis. Thus it is no surprise that two instances of variation may offer variants having identical external attestation and yet be evaluated quite differently on the basis of other considerations. As A. E. Housman so aptly and colorfully expressed it, textual criticism

> is not a branch of mathematics, nor indeed an exact science at all. It deals with
> . . . the frailties and aberrations of the human mind, and of its insubordinate
> servants, the human fingers. It therefore is not susceptible of hard-and-fast
> rules. It would be much easier if it were; and that is why people try to pretend
> that it is . . . . Of course you can have hard-and-fast rules if you like, but then
> you will have false rules, and they will lead you wrong; because their simplicity

will render them inapplicable to problems which are not simple, but complicated by the play of personality. . . . A textual critic engaged upon his business is not at all like Newton investigating the motions of the planets: he is much more like a dog hunting for fleas. If a dog hunted for fleas on mathematical principles, basing his researches on statistics of area and population, he would never catch a flea except by accident. They require to be treated as individuals; and every problem which presents itself to the textual critic must be regarded as possibly unique.[65]

Selected Examples

The following section attempts to illustrate by means of a discussion of selected variant readings some of the principles outlined above. Not every point touched on earlier can be mentioned here, of course, but the range and variety of the chosen examples should serve to give one a feel for how textual critics go about the business of applying these general considerations to specific problems.

It is customary to present the data of the Greek MSS, early versions and early church fathers in the format of a *critical apparatus* (in Latin, *apparatus criticus*) to the passage under discussion. This offers a concise and precise way to present the mass of data available for most passages. To further save space numerous abbreviations are used. To the uninitiated, a critical apparatus can appear intimidating. But with a little practice and some knowledge of the abbreviations used, it is possible to unpack the information presented in a critical apparatus without too much difficulty. Some common abbreviations and symbols used below include the following:

Byz	=	the reading of the majority of the Byzantine MSS
f^1, f^{13}	=	the "Family 1" or "Family 13" group of MSS
it	=	the Itala or Old Latin version (superscript letters indicate individual MSS)
vg	=	the Vulgate
sy^s	=	Sinaitic Syriac version
sy^c	=	Curetonian Syriac version
sy^p	=	Peshitta Syriac version
sy^h	=	Harclean Syriac version
sy^{pal}	=	Palestinian Syriac version
cop	=	Coptic version (the united witness of the dialects)
cop^{sa}	=	Coptic version, Sahidic dialect
cop^{bo}	=	Coptic version, Bohairic dialect
cop^{pbo}	=	Coptic version, Proto-Bohairic dialect
cop^{ac2}	=	Coptic version, Sub-Achmimic dialect
pc	=	a few (*pauci*)
pt	=	in part
marg	=	an alternate reading in the margin of a MS
*	=	reading of the original scribe of a MS (e.g., ℵ*)

^c   = reading of the corrector of a MS (e.g., ℵ^c)
_{2,3,4} = readings of successive correctors of a MS

The first example will provide both a critical apparatus and a narrative listing of the evidence; successive examples will provide only a critical apparatus.

LUKE 11:2, 4

What are the opening and closing words of the Lord's Prayer in the Gospel according to Luke?[66] The MSS offer the following possibilities:

11:2   *Father* 𝔭⁷⁵ ℵ B *f*¹ 700 *pc* vg sy^s Marcion Origen
        Our Father L *pc*
        Our Father in heaven A C D K P W X Δ Θ Π Ψ *f*¹³ 28
        565 892 1010 1071 1241 *Byz* it sy^{c,p,h} cop

11:4   *temptation* 𝔭⁷⁵ ℵ^{*,2} B L *f*¹ 700 *pc* vg sy^s cop^{sa,bo(pt)}
        Marcion Tertullian Origen
        temptation but deliver us from the evil one ℵ¹ A C D K W
        X Δ Θ Π Ψ *f*¹³ 28 33 565 892 1010 1071 1241
        Byz it sy^{c,p,h}cop^{bo(pt)}

When we unpack this apparatus, we find the following information: In Luke 11:2, the prayer opens with the single word "Father" in Greek manuscripts 𝔭⁷⁵, ℵ, B, Family 1 (*f*¹), 700, and a few others, in the Latin Vulgate and Sinaitic Syriac among the versions, and Marcion and Origen among the early church fathers. It opens with "Our Father" in Greek manuscript L and a few others, while the opening line is "Our Father in heaven" in manuscripts A, C, D, K, P, W, X, Δ, Θ, Π, Ψ, Family 13 (*f*¹³), 28, 565, 892, 1010, 1071, 1241, and the rest of the Byzantine text-type, and in the Old Latin, the Curetonian, Peshitta, and Harclean Syriac, and the Coptic versions.

In 11:4, the prayer ends with "lead us not into temptation" in 𝔭⁷⁵, both the original reading and the second corrector of Codex Sinaiticus (ℵ^{*,2}), B, L, Family 1, 700, and a few other Greek MSS, in the Vulgate, the Siniatic Syriac, the Sahidic Coptic, and part of the Bohairic Coptic among the versions, and Marcion, Tertullian, and Origen among the early fathers. It ends with "lead us not into temptation but deliver us from the evil one" according to the first corrector of Sinaiticus (ℵ¹), A, C, D, K, W, X, Δ, Θ, Π, Ψ, Family 13, 28, 33, 565, 892, 1010, 1071, 1241, and the rest of the Byzantine text-type, and in the Old Latin, the Curetonian, Peshitta, and Harclean Syriac, and part of the Bohairic Coptic versions.

Now that we have unpacked the apparatus and found out what the external evidence (i.e., the actual readings of the Greek manuscripts, the versions, and the church fathers) is, we are now in a position to evaluate it. In this instance the support for the two sets[67] of variants is so similar that they may be evaluated together.

The first thing to evaluate is external evidence: date, geographical distribution, genealogical relationships, and relative quality. In purely numerical terms the support for the longer reading is overwhelming. When the evidence is weighed, however, rather than counted, the situation is rather different. In view of the conjunction of Western (e.g., D it sy^c) and Byzantine support (A, most uncial and almost all minuscule MSS) the longer reading clearly is an early one,[68] but 𝔭^{75} (early third century) and the patristic citations, especially Marcion (ca. 140), show that the shorter reading is even earlier. The longer reading is broadly supported by representatives of the secondary Alexandrian (e.g., C 33 892 cop^{sa,bo}), Western (D it sy^c), and Byzantine (A K W Δ Π most uncials and minuscules) textual traditions, the shorter largely by primary Alexandrian witnesses (𝔭^{75} ℵ B Origen) and, significantly, the Vulgate and Sinaitic Syriac. The geographic distribution of the witnesses for each is roughly similar; the shorter reading, however, has the edge in terms of relative quality.[69] Overall, then, the external evidence favors the shorter reading.

Internal evidence, it will be recalled, is of two kinds, transcriptional (having to do with the habits and practices of scribes) and intrinsic (having to do with the author's style and vocabulary). Since both the longer and shorter forms of the prayer are consistent with the style and teaching of Jesus, the key considerations in this instance are transcriptional in nature. As is the case today, in the ancient church the Matthean version of the Lord's prayer (Matt. 6:9–13) was best known, memorized, and used in worship. In light of this fact, the fundamental guideline given above (the variant most likely to be original is the one that bests accounts for the existence of the others) may be applied by asking this question: Which of the readings best explains the rise of the others? Specifically, in this instance is a scribe more likely to have shortened the longer Lucan reading (thereby creating a discrepency between Matthew and Luke), or added to the shorter Lucan form in order to harmonize it to the much more familiar Matthean version? The answer is clear: if the longer reading were original, it is virtually inconceivable that a scribe would cut out such well-known phrases, whereas if the shorter reading is original, it is easy to account for the rise of the longer reading as the result of inadvertant or deliberate assimilation to the better known Matthean form of the prayer. In short, the shorter reading can account for the rise of the longer, but not vice versa.

Note how in this case both external and internal considerations favor the shorter reading. This convergence of evidence demonstrates conclusively that it represents the original text of the Lucan form of the Lord's Prayer.

JOHN 6:69

The difference between the New King James Version and the New International Version of John 6:69—"You are the Christ, the Son of the living God" versus "You are the Holy One of God"—only hints at the extent of variation in this text. The textual evidence reads as follows:

(1)   *the Christ the Son of the living God* K (Δ) Θ^c Π Ψ 0250 *f* ^{13} 28 700 892 1071 1241 *Byz* it^{pt} sy^{p,h} cop$^{bo(pt)}$

(2)   *the Christ the Son of God* C^3 Θ* *f* ^{1} 33 565 *pc* it^{pt} sys

(3)   *the Son of God* it^b sy^c

(4)   *the Christ* Tertullian

(5)   *the Christ the Holy One of God* 𝔭^{66} cop$^{sa(pt),ac2,bo}$

(6)   *the Holy One of God* 𝔭^{75} ℵ B C* D L W cop$^{sa(1ms),pbo}$

An initial assessment suggests (barring some consideration to the contrary) that readings 2, 3, 4, and 5 should probably be set aside on the basis of their slim external support. With regard to internal considerations, these readings appear upon further investigation to be the result of harmonization to or conflation with parallel passages (John 11:27; 1:49; and Mark 8:29 respectively), an observation that clinches the case against them. Reading 1, which has good Byzantine (K Δ Π 700 *Byz*) and some versional (it^{pt} sy^{p,h}) and secondary Alexandrian (892 cop$^{bo(pt)}$) support, and 6, which has support from Alexandrian (𝔭^{75} B C L W) and Western (ℵ [in John 1:1–8:38] D) witnesses, require further attention.

Both readings have parallels elsewhere in the Gospel accounts: 1 parallels Matthew 16:16, the disciples' confession at Caesarea Philippi (the Synoptic episode parallel to John 6:60–71), while 6 parallels Mark 1:24/Luke 4:34, where an unclean spirit about to be cast out acknowledges that Jesus is "the Holy One of God!" Conceivably either reading could be explained as the result of assimilation to the parallel passage. It seems far more likely, however, that scribes would harmonize 6 to Matthew 16:16, and thereby remove a discrepancy between the two parallel episodes, than that they would create a discrepancy by replacing 1 with words spoken elsewhere only by an unclean spirit. Thus one may conclude that transcriptional considerations clearly favor 6.

The same may be said for intrinsic considerations. In verse 69, Peter says, "We have come to know," or "We have recognized the truth" (*pepisteukamen*), implying a new depth of insight on the part of the disciples. Yet the essence of the other variants here—that Jesus is Messiah and Son of God—was already confessed as early as 1:41 and 1:49. Variant (6), however—"the Holy One [*hagios*] of God"—is appropriate as the disciples' response to the events recorded in John 6. Furthermore, it also sets up, in a typically Johannine way, 10:36 (the Father sanctified [*hēgiasen*] and sent Jesus into the world) and 17:19 (Jesus sanctifies [*hagiazō*] himself for the disciples' sake). Of all the variants it best fits both the immediate context and the structural development of the book as a whole.

Thus all three lines of evidence—external, transcriptional, and intrinsic—come together in support of variant 6 as the reading that best meets our basic guideline. We may in this case be virtually certain that "the Holy One of God" represents the original text of John 6:69.

JOHN 5:44

Though much less complex than the last example, this variant is of interest because of the similar alignment of the MS evidence. Consideration of other factors, however, leads to a different conclusion. In the phrase "yet you do not seek the praise that comes from the only God," one finds these variants:

> *the only One [tou monou]* $\mathfrak{p}^{66}$ $\mathfrak{p}^{75}$ B W it^{a,b} cop$^{sa,ac2,pbo,bo(pt)}$
>
> *the only God [tou monou theou]* ℵ A D K L Δ Θ Ψ 063 0210 *f* $^{1.13}$ 28 33 565 700 892 1071 1241 *Byz* it vg sy$^{c.p.h.pal}$ cop$^{bo(pt)}$

While the Alexandrian support ($\mathfrak{p}^{66}$ $\mathfrak{p}^{75}$ B W cop^{sa,bo}) for the shorter reading is early and very impressive, internal considerations suggest that in this instance it is also wrong. First, *God* (*theou*) appears to be required by the context, a point confirmed by the observation that John nowhere else calls God "the only One." Second, the accidental omission of $\overline{\Theta Y}$ (*theta upsilon*, the customary Greek contraction of *theou* [God]) from the sequence ΤΟΥΜΟΝΟΥ$\overline{\Theta Y}$ΟΥ (TOUMONOUTHUOU, remembering that the earliest manuscripts were written in continuous capitals) seems more likely than its insertion. Thus both intrinsic and transcriptional considerations favor the inclusion of *theou*, which in addition has substantial external support (secondary Alexandrian [L 33 892 cop$^{bo(pt)}$], Western [ℵ D it sy^c], and Byzantine [A K Δ Π *Byz*]). It seems relatively certain, therefore, that here the longer reading is original, rather than the shorter.

MATTHEW 22:13

Three forms of the king's instructions to his servants are found in the MSS at this point:

(1) *binding [deō] him hand and foot, toss [ekballō] him* . . . ℵ B L Θ 085 *f* ^{1} (*f* ^{13}) 700 892 *pc* (sy^p) cop

(2) *seize [airō] him hand and foot and throw [ballō] him* . . . D it (sy^{s,c}) Irenaeus Lucifer of Calaris

(3) *binding [deō] him hand and foot, seize [airō] him and toss [ekballō] him* . . . C (M) W (Φ) 0138 (565 1241 1424) *Byz* it^f (sy^h)

Variant 3, the Byzantine reading, is easily accounted for as a combination of 1 and 2, whereas it is not possible to derive both 1 and 2 from 3, as a little experimentation will demonstrate. Hence it may be set aside as a clever (but obviously secondary) conflation of the other two variants.

The differences between 1 and 2 are (a) *deō* ("bind") versus *airō* ("seize"); (b) *ekballō* ("toss") versus *ballō* ("throw"); and (c) subordination (participle + verb) versus parataxis (two verbs joined by "and"). In this instance transcriptional considerations are of little help in choosing between the two variants, since the differences are obviously not accidental. It is just possible that *airō* has been deliberately substituted for *deō* because it was thought to be more suited to the setting (Why bind someone just to toss him out of the banquet hall?), but this is too slim a point to carry much weight. Intrinsic factors are also indecisive. On the basis of usage, all four verbs under evaluation may be said to be equally Matthean (*deō* occurs ten times, *airō* nineteen, *ballō* thirty-four, and *ekballō* twenty-eight times in Matthew), and while Matthew generally prefers subordination to parataxis (a point in favor of the first reading), this can be turned around to favor 2 as the more unusual construction (and thus more likely to be altered). In short, in this instance internal considerations either cancel each other out or are indecisive.

Hence it is necessary to make the decision solely on external grounds. Here Westcott and Hort's dictum—knowledge of documents should precede judgment upon readings[70]—comes into play. For the Western textual tradition, and particularly D, its leading witness, exhibits a decided tendency towards substitutions and revisions (of which the above variant is typical), which almost always prove to be secondary rather than original. The Alexandrian text-type, on the other hand, manifests a consistent freedom from these types of secondary alterations. In instances like this, therefore, when a decision must be made on purely external grounds, one is justified in preferring the Alexandrian reading and adopting 1 as the text of 22:13.

The preceding examples should serve to (1) illustrate the application of the primary guideline given above, (2) demonstrate that no one manuscript or textual tradition is always right, and (3) make clear that no one rule, consideration, group of MSS, etc., can be followed or applied to textual problems in a mechanical or thoughtless fashion. Every textual problem must be approached on its own terms; all the critics can learn about MSS, about scribes, about the author, must be brought to bear on it. Above all, the fundamental guideline must be kept in mind: Which variant best accounts for the origin of the others? The variant that, after thoughtful consideration of all the evidence, best satisfies this question will almost invariably best represent the original text.

The Significance of Textual Criticism for Exegesis

Before one can understand an author, one must know what the author wrote. Thus textual criticism is foundational to all study of the New Testament; one cannot hope to produce fruitful work without a reliable textual basis. Moreover, for many of the methods and approaches described elsewhere in this book, textual criticism is critically important. Source and redaction criticism, for example, involve the close study of sometimes small details and differences among the Gospels, details, and differences that frequently involve textual variants. The textual choices one makes on this level often have a noticeable impact upon one's results.[71]

In practical terms, obtaining a reliable text means for most students using one of the two excellent critical editions available today, either UBS[4] or NA[27]. But the availability of reliable critical editions produced by a committee of experts should not lull the student into thinking that textual criticism is an avoidable technicality, or that textual variants and their accompanying apparatus may be safely ignored. There are two reasons for this.

First, even so distinguished a group as the editorial committee responsible for the UBS[4] and NA[27] editions slips occasionally, and its work is sometimes capable of being improved. The student should always work through any variants in a passage being exegeted. In most cases she or he will find the committee's work convincing. At times, however, good reasons may be found for adopting another reading as more likely to be original,[72] and such decisions will of course affect one's exegesis.[73]

Second, the doing of textual criticism often leads to exegetical insights that might otherwise be missed. Textual decisions often require the closest attention to an author's style, thought, and argument, which are all in turn crucial to sound exegesis. The reverse also happens, as the exegesis of a passage may be decisive for the resolution of a textual difficulty within it.[74] Either way, attention to textual difficulties lays the basis for good exegesis. In a fundamental sense, therefore, textual criticism is not just preparatory to exegesis, but part and parcel of it.

Bibliography

BASIC WORKS

Aland, Kurt, and Barbara Aland. *The Text of the New Testament. An Introduction to the Critical Editions and to the Theory and Practice of Modern Textual Criticism.* 2d ed., rev. and enlarged. Trans. by E. F. Rhodes. Leiden/Grand Rapids: Brill/Eerdmans, 1989.

Elliott, Keith, and Ian Moir. *Manuscripts and the Text of the New Testament: An Introduction for English Readers.* Edinburgh: T. & T. Clark, 1995.

Fee, Gordon D. "The Textual Criticism of the New Testament." In *The Expositor's Bible Commentary*, vol. 1. Ed. by F. E. Gaebelein. Grand Rapids: Zondervan, 1979. Pages 419–33.

Finegan, Jack. *Encountering New Testament Manuscripts: A Working Introduction to Textual Criticism.* Grand Rapids: Eerdmans, 1974.

Metzger, Bruce M. *The Text of the New Testament: Its Transmission, Corruption, and Restoration.* 3d, enlarged ed. New York/Oxford: Oxford University Press, 1992.

──────. *A Textual Commentary on the Greek New Testament*, 2d ed.: *A Companion Volume to the United Bible Societies' Greek New Testament (fourth revised edition)*. Stuttgart: Deutsche Bibelgesellschaft/United Bible Societies, 1994.

Parker, D. C. *The Living Text of the Gospels*. Cambridge: Cambridge University Press, 1997.

For Further Reading

Aland, Kurt. *Studien zur Überlieferung des Neuen Testaments und seines Textes*. Berlin: de Gruyter, 1967.

Birdsall, J. Neville. "The New Testament Text." In *The Cambridge History of the Bible*. Vol. 1: *From the Beginnings to Jerome*. Ed. P. R. Ackroyd and C. F. Evans. Cambridge: University Press, 1970. Pages 308–77.

──────. "The Recent History of New Testament Textual Criticism (from Westcott and Hort, 1881, to the present)." In *Aufstieg und Niedergang der Römischen Welt*, 2.26.1 Ed. H. Temporini and W. Haase. Berlin/New York: de Gruyter, 1992. Pages 99–197.

Colwell, Ernest C. *Studies in Methodology in Textual Criticism of the New Testament*. Leiden: Brill, 1969.

Ehrman, Bart D., and Michael W. Holmes, eds. *The Text of the New Testament in Contemporary Research: Essays on the* Status Quaestionis. Studies and Documents, 46. Grand Rapids: Eerdmans, 1995.

Epp, Eldon J., and Gordon D. Fee. *Studies in the Theory and Method of New Testament Textual Criticism*. Studies and Documents, 45. Grand Rapids: Eerdmans, 1993.

Kenyon, F. G. *The Text of the Greek Bible*. 3d ed. revised and augmented by A. W. Adams. London: Duckworth, 1975.

Lagrange, M. J. *Critique textuelle*. II. *La Critique rationnelle*. 2d ed. Paris: Gabalda, 1935.

Metzger, Bruce M. *The Early Versions of the New Testament: Their Origin, Transmission, and Limitations*. Oxford: Clarendon, 1977.

──────. *Manuscripts of the Greek Bible: An Introduction to Palaeography*. New York/Oxford: Oxford University Press, 1981.

Reynolds, L. D., and Wilson, N. G. *Scribes and Scholars: A Guide to the Transmission of Greek and Latin Literature*. 2d ed. Oxford: Clarendon, 1974.

Westcott, B. F., and Hort, F. J. A. *The New Testament in the Original Greek*, [ii] *Introduction* [and] *Appendix*. Cambridge: Macmillan, 1881; 2d ed. 1896.

Zuntz, G. *The Text of the Epistles: A Disquisition upon the Corpus Paulinum*. London: The British Academy, 1953.

Notes

1. Codex Sinaiticus, for example, a parchment manuscript that originally contained the entire Greek Bible, is estimated to have required the hides of approximately 360 sheep and goats.

2. A professional scriptorium, or copy center, employed people to correct the work of the scribes and was capable of turning out very high quality work. But with regard to New Testament manuscripts, production under such careful control appears to have been the exception rather than the rule.

3. In the second century Christians seem to have been among the first to abandon the scroll for the less expensive and more convenient codex or book format. For example, out of a group of 476 non-Christian second-century papyri from Egypt, over 97 percent

are scrolls, while all the Christian papyri from the same period and area are in codex form (J. Finegan, *Encountering New Testament Manuscripts* [Grand Rapids: Eerdmans, 1974], 29). See further the fundamental study by Harry Y. Gamble, *Books and Readers in the Early Church* (New Haven and London: Yale University Press, 1995); also Eldon Jay Epp, "The Codex and Literacy in Early Christianity and at Oxyrhynchus: Issues Raised by Harry Y. Gamble's *Books and Readers in the Early Church*," in *Critical Review of Books in Religion* 10 (1997), 15–37.

4. This phenomenon is termed *homoioarcton, homoiomeson,* or *homoioteleuton,* depending on whether the beginning, middle, or end of a word is involved.

5. In Matthew 5:19–20, e.g., the phrase "the kingdom of heaven" occurs at the end of verses 19a, 19b, and 20. A few scribes have skipped from the first occurrence to the second, thus eliminating 19b; one has skipped from the first to the third, thereby eliminating all of 19b and 20.

6. The use of dictation, common in scriptoria, added another step and opportunity for error, particularly in the case of homonyms. The well-known variation in Romans 5:1 between "let us have peace" (*echōmen*) and "we have peace" (*echomen*; both words were pronounced alike) exemplifies this problem.

7. The substitution of the frequently repeated Matthean form of the Lord's prayer for the less-familiar Lucan form in Luke 11 (see the first example below) is a good example of the latter phenomenon.

8. A scribe's note in an Armenian MS (cited by B. M. Metzger, *The Text of the New Testament: Its Transmission, Corruption, and Restoration,* 3d enlarged ed. [New York and Oxford: Oxford University Press, 1992], 18) mentions that it is snowing heavily outside, the ink is frozen, and his hand is numb. Others complain of the physical discomfort involved in copying for six or more hours a day. Little wonder that copies were less than perfect!

9. An ancient historian records an incident around A.D. 350 in which a man was publicly rebuked for substituting the more refined Attic word *skimpous* for the colloquial Koine *krabbatos* ("pallet") in John 5:8 (cited by Metzger, *Text,* 196).

10. As in Luke 3:22, where "You are my son; today I have begotten you" (as in NRSV^margin and REB^margin; cf. Ps. 2:7) has been replaced by the less problematic "You are my beloved son; with you I am well pleased" (as in NRSV, NIV, NASB, REB; cf. Mark 1:11). On the subject of doctrinally motivated changes, see Bart D. Ehrman, *The Orthodox Corruption of Scripture: The Effect of Early Christological Controversies on the Text of the New Testament* (New York and Oxford: Oxford University Press, 1993).

11. ₱⁵² (ca. 125, containing John 18:31–33, 37–38) is the earliest known MS of any part of the New Testament thus far identified. Claims that portions of Mark have been identified among the manuscript fragments of the Dead Sea Scrolls from Qumran are quite unconvincing (see Graham Stanton, *Gospel Truth? New Light on Jesus and the Gospels* [Valley Forge, Pa.: Trinity Press International, 1995], 20–32; Metzger, *Text,* 264–65). The proposal by Y. K. Kim ("Palaeographical Dating of ₱⁴⁶ to the Later First Century," *Biblica* 69 [1988]: 248–257) that p⁴⁶ (widely dated to ca. 200) should be dated prior to the end of the first century has not proven to be persuasive (see Metzger, *Text,* 265–66). The claim by C. P. Thiede that fragments of Matthew should be dated to "c. A.D. 66" is based on a rat's nest of fanciful hypotheses and unsubstantiated assertions (for a brief overview and response, see Stanton, *Gospel Truth?* 11–19).

12. For a descriptive list of the papyri, see K. Aland and B. Aland, *The Text of the New Testament. An Introduction to the Critical Editions and to the Theory and Practice*

of Modern Textual Criticism, 2d ed. rev. and enlarged (Grand Rapids: Eerdmans, 1989), 96–102 [through 𝔭⁹⁶].

13. Whereas *uncial* is the more common term by which this category of MSS has traditionally been designated, palaeographical specialists are increasingly using "uncial" to describe only a specific style of Latin majuscule script, with "majuscule" the preferred term for the larger category.

14. Although the majuscule numbers now run up to 309, for a number of reasons only about 270 different MSS are recognized; see Aland and Aland, *Text*, 106. For a descriptive list see Aland and Aland, *Text*, 107–28, and for greater detail on selected majuscules see Metzger, *Text*, 42–61.

15. For a descriptive list of selected minuscules see Aland and Aland, *Text*, 129–40, and Metzger, *Text*, 61–66.

16. According to Aland and Aland, *Text*, 78. Strictly speaking, A and C are now incomplete, although they do contain at least part of every New Testament book.

17. For the basis of these and other statistics, see Aland and Aland, *Text*, 78–83.

18. See B. M. Metzger, *The Early Versions of the New Testament: Their Origin, Transmission, and Limitations* (Oxford: Clarendon, 1977); this may be supplemented by the relevant chapters in Bart D. Ehrman and Michael W. Holmes, eds., *The Text of the New Testament in Contemporary Research: Essays on the* Status Quaestionis (Studies and Documents 46; Grand Rapids: Eerdmans, 1995). For briefer treatments see Metzger, *Text*, 67–86, and Aland and Aland, *Text*, 185–214.

19. See especially the sections on limitations in Metzger, *Early Versions*.

20. Metzger, *Text*, 86.

21. See Metzger, *Text*, 86–88. For a useful annotated list of early Church Fathers, see Aland and Aland, *Text*, 215–21.

22. Indeed, in view of the attention that is rightly focused on the places where the evidence differs, it is worth noting just how much of the New Testament is well established. A survey by the Alands reveals that of the 7,947 verses in the Greek New Testament, seven major editions are in complete agreement regarding 4,999, or 62.9 percent (Aland and Aland, *Text*, 28–29). If one were to leave aside certain idiosyncracies and minor differences between these editions, it may be estimated that the number of verses about which there is substantial agreement approaches 90 percent of the total. To be sure, the remaining differences can be substantial and important and fully merit the attention given to them over the centuries by textual critics. One should not neglect, however, to keep them in perspective, especially as people unacquainted with textual matters are sometimes shocked to encounter statements to the effect that "there are over 30,000 errors in the New Testament." The intended implication is that the New Testament is unreliable. Such statements are uninformed and inaccurate. If one defines error broadly enough, to include, e.g., spelling mistakes or differences, then it is true that there are tens if not hundreds of thousands of "errors" among the 5,000+ MSS of the New Testament. But this hardly affects the reliability of the New Testament itself, since wherever some MSS are in error, others have accurately preserved the text.

23. The so-called Caesarean text was for several decades thought to comprise a fourth text-type of the Gospels (the classic expression of this view is by B. H. Streeter, *The Four Gospels: A Study in Origins*. 5th impression [London: Macmillan, 1936]). This has recently been shown not to be the case. See B. M. Metzger, "The Caesarean Text of the Gospels," *Chapters in the History of New Testament Textual Criticism* (Leiden/Grand Rapids: Brill/Eerdmans, 1963), 42–72; and L. W. Hurtado, *Text-Critical*

Methodology and the Pre-Caesarean Text: Codex W in the Gospel of Mark (Grand Rapids: Eerdmans, 1981).

24. Labels used by other writers for the two subdivisions of this text-type ("primary" and "secondary") include "neutral" and "Alexandrian" (Westcott and Hort); "Proto-Alexandrian" and "Later Alexandrian"; and "Alexandrian" and "Egyptian" (Aland and Aland, *Text*).

25. For a more detailed listing of witnesses in all three text-types, as well as other important witnesses, categorized according to Gospels, Acts, Pauline Epistles, Catholic Epistles, and Revelation, see Tables 1–5 in M. W. Holmes, "New Testament Textual Criticism," in *Introducing New Testament Interpretation*, ed. Scot McKnight (Grand Rapids: Baker, 1989), 53–74, or Bruce M. Metzger, *A Textual Commentary on the Greek New Testament*, 2d ed. (Stuttgart: Deutsche Bibelgesellschaft and United Bible Societies, 1994), 14–16.

26. The term *Western* is somewhat misleading. It was first applied to this particular textual tradition at a time when the only witnesses to it had ties to the West, i.e., Rome, North Africa, and Gaul. Discoveries since then, however, have made clear that this early textual tradition was widely disseminated throughout the Roman Empire and may have originated in the East, perhaps in Egypt. The continued use of the term today is largely a matter of custom and convenience.

27. The Western text of Acts, for example, is over 8 percent longer than the Alexandrian text of the same book.

28. For examples and discussion of these features in the Matthean text of Codex Bezae, see Michael W. Holmes, "Codex Bezae as a Recension of the Gospels," *in Codex Bezae: Studies from the Lunel Colloquium*, ed. D. C. Parker and C. B. Amphoux (Leiden: Brill, 1996), 123–60, esp. 128–42.

29. These betray decided tendencies towards smoothing out grammar, supplying assumed words or pronouns, harmonization, removal of ambiguity, and conflation (combination) of readings found in the Alexandrian and Western text-types.

30. For selected examples see G. D. Fee, "Modern Textual Criticism and the Revival of the Textus Receptus," *JETS* 21 (1978): 31–33.

31. Already Irenaeus (ca. 175), for example, reports that while some copies read "616" at Revelation 13:18, "all good and ancient copies" read "666" (Irenaeus, *Against Heresies* 5.30.1). Scholars such as Origen (ca. 185–253) and Jerome (ca. 342–420) noted and discussed variances between MSS (see Bruce M. Metzger, "Explicit References in the Works of Origen to Variant Readings in New Testament Manuscripts," in *Biblical and Patristic Studies in Memory of Robert Pierce Casey*, ed. by J. N. Birdsall and R. W. Thomson [Freiburg: Herder, 1963], 78–95, repr. in Metzger, *Historical and Literary Studies* [Leiden/Grand Rapids: Brill/Eerdmans, 1968], 88–103; and "St. Jerome's Explicit References to Variant Readings in Manuscripts of the New Testament," in *Text and Interpretation. Studies in the New Testament Presented to Matthew Black,* ed. by E. Best and R. McL. Wilson [Cambridge: Cambridge University Press, 1979], 179–90), and marginal and/or interlinear notes and comments remain as testimony to the occasional concern of now-anonymous editors to recover a "good and ancient" form of the text. Overall, however, there is little evidence of any sustained effort to choose between variant readings.

32. The first *printed* edition of the Greek New Testament (part of a multilingual edition of the entire Bible known as the Complutensian Polyglot) was the product of a group of Spanish scholars at the University of Alcala (= Complutum in Latin), who finished

their work in 1514. But it was not until 1520 that they were able to obtain permission to release it.

33. See Jerry H. Bentley, *Humanists and Holy Writ: New Testament Scholarship in the Renaissance* (Princeton: Princeton University Press, 1983), 112–61.

34. For the first edition he relied primarily upon MS 2 of the Gospels and MS 2 of the Acts and Catholic Epistles; his sources of corrections were MS 817 (Gospels) and MS 4 (Acts and Catholic Epistles). His main source for the Pauline Epistles was MS 7 (Bentley, *Humanists*, 127–29). His only source for Revelation, MS 1, was missing the last six verses. Erasmus filled in the gap by translating from the Vulgate back into Greek; his self-made text includes readings not found in any known Greek MS. He did make numerous corrections in later editions (including the definitive fourth) on the basis of later collations of a substantial number of MSS, but these were not enough to affect the basic character of his original edition.

35. Metzger, *Text*, 106.

36. This principle recognizes that a scribe is far more likely to make a difficult reading easier than he is to create a difficult or awkward reading out of one that presents no difficulty. Thus, e.g., in Mark 1:2 (which cites Malachi 3:1 and then Isaiah 40:3) the original reading is certainly "in Isaiah the prophet" and not "in the prophets." The former is the "harder reading," in that it raises a question or difficulty for the reader, while the latter does not.

37. On Mill, Bentley, and Wettstein, see Metzger, *Text*, 107–15, and for the often-neglected Simon, L. D. Reynolds, and N. G. Wilson, *Scribes and Scholars. A Guide to the Transmission of Greek and Latin Literature*, 2d ed. (Oxford: Clarendon, 1974), 169–70, 244.

38. Metzger, *Text*, 121.

39. For details of this fascinating story, see Metzger, *Text*, 42–45, and for more recent developments J. H. Charlesworth, *The New Discoveries in St. Catherine's Monastery: A Preliminary Report on the Manuscripts* (American Schools of Oriental Research, 1981).

40. Somewhat overshadowed by Tischendorf's fame is the work of his English colleague, S. P. Tregelles (1813–1875). A careful and systematic worker, his examination of nearly all the then-known uncials and most of the leading minuscules contributed greatly to an accurate knowledge of the evidence. Unlike Tischendorf, who rushed out a new edition almost every time he discovered a new manuscript, Tregelles focused his effort upon a single definitive edition, which, preceded by a statement of his own critical principles (*An Account of the Printed Text of the Greek New Testament ...* [London, 1854]), appeared between 1857 and 1872. Cf. Metzger, *Text*, 127–28.

41. Constantinus Tischendorf, *Novum Testamentum Graece . . . Editio octava critica maior*, 2 vols. (Leipzig, 1869–1872). A third volume of *Prolegomena* was edited by the American scholar C. R. Gregory (Leipzig, 1884, 1890, 1894); it later appeared in a German translation, with additions and corrections, under the title *Textkritik des Neuen Testamentes* (Leipzig, 1900–1909).

42. B. F. Westcott and F. J. A. Hort, *The New Testament in the Original Greek*, 2 vols. (Cambridge, 1881–1882). Volume 1 contains the Greek text, while volume 2 contains an *Introduction* setting out their method and principles and an *Appendix* of notes on select readings.

43. For a brief survey and assessment see Metzger, *Text*, 129–35.

44. E.g., the text of the two most recent and widely used editions, NA[27] and UBS[4], stands closer to the text of Westcott and Hort than it does to any other text published since Tischendorf.

45. A notable exception is the industrious, idiosyncratic, and ultimately misdirected efforts of H. F. von Soden (*Die Schriften des Neuen Testaments in ihrer ältesten erreichbaren Textgestalt hergestellt auf Grund ihrer Textgeschichte*), which appeared in three large parts between 1902 and 1913. Cf. Metzger, *Text*, 139–43.

46. Cf. on this point the important article by E. J. Epp, "Textual Criticism," in *The New Testament and Its Modern Interpreters*, ed. by E. J. Epp and G. W. MacRae (Atlanta: Scholars, 1989), 75–126 (reprinted as "Decision Points in Past, Present, and Future New Testament Textual Criticism," in Eldon J. Epp and Gordon D. Fee, *Studies in the Theory and Method of New Testament Textual Criticism* [Grand Rapids: Eerdmans, 1993], 17–44), and his earlier articles to which he there refers. A different view is offered by Kurt Aland, "The Twentieth-Century Interlude in New Testament Textual Criticism," in Best and Wilson, *Text and Interpretation*, 1–14.

47. See Aland and Aland, *Text*, 19–22, or Metzger, *Text*, 144.

48. Nestle-Aland, *Novum Testamentum Graece*, 27th ed. (Stuttgart: Deutsche Bibelstiftung, 1993).

49. First edition, 1966; fourth revised edition, 1993.

50. For a discussion of their distinctive features and aims, and an introduction to their use and textual symbols, see Aland and Aland, *Text*, 30–36, 43–47, 218–62.

51. And, it may be added, the essential basis of nearly every recent major translation, including the NASB, TEV, NIV, NAB, NRSV, and HCSB. In fact, the Westcott and Hort/Nestle-Aland/UBS textual tradition underlies virtually all major European and American Protestant translations of the last century, beginning with the Revised Version of 1881 (which used materials supplied by Westcott and Hort during the translation process). The sole significant exception among English translations is the NKJV, which continues to be based on the Textus Receptus, which was essentially the textual basis of the KJV. But whereas in their day the KJV translators used the best—and only—Greek text available to them, the NKJV follows what is now the worst text available. Even proponents of the Majority text recognize that the TR is a corrupt representative of the Majority text-type, differing from it in more than 1,800 instances. As a consequence of following the TR, the NKJV both includes words, phrases, and even sentences (cf. Acts 8:37) that never were part of the original text of Scripture and also omits parts that are original (cf. 1 John 3:1).

52. A related factor is the circumstance that almost all of the extant MSS are "orphans," without a parent, offspring, or siblings. Thus many of the genealogical links helpful in constructing a stemma are missing. As Metzger observes, "Instances of a known copy of another manuscript are exceedingly rare, which suggests that only a very small percentage of manuscripts have survived" (Metzger, *Manuscripts*, 54).

53. Sometimes refered to as "rational criticism" (M.-J. Lagrange) or the "local-genealogical" method (Aland and Aland, *Text*, 34, 286).

54. To give just two illustrations: the editors of the United Bible Societies' *The Greek New Testament* (UBS[4]) tend to follow, when all other criteria are equal, the reading of the Alexandrian witnesses; the editors of the NIV appear to have a tendency to prefer the reading that best harmonizes with other passages.

55. Exemplified most notably by G. D. Kilpatrick and J. K. Elliott; see J. Keith Elliott, "Thoroughgoing Eclecticism in New Testament Textual Criticism," in Ehrman and Holmes, *The Text of the New Testament in Contemporary Research*, 321–35; idem, "Keeping up with Recent Studies XV. New Testament Textual Criticism," *Expository Times* 99 (1987): 40–45, esp. 43–44.

56. Cf. Elliott ("Keeping Up," 43): "I think it is perfectly feasible to try to reconstruct the original text by applying only internal criteria. . . . According to this method . . . the manuscripts are of importance primarily as bearers of readings. . . . (The number or age of the manuscripts supporting the readings are of little significance.)." A slightly more nuanced position is offered in Elliott, "Thoroughgoing Eclecticism," 330. For a detailed critique see G. D. Fee, "Rigorous or Reasoned Eclecticism—Which?" in *Studies in New Testament Language and Text*, ed. by J. K. Elliott (Leiden: Brill, 1976), 174–97 (reprinted in Epp and Fee, *Studies*, 124–40).

57. Zane C. Hodges and A. L. Farstad, eds., *The Greek New Testament According to the Majority Text* (Nashville, Camden, and New York: Nelson, 1982; 2d ed., 1985). A similar text, but based on different principles, is presented in Maurice A. Robinson and William G. Pierpont, eds., *The New Testament in the Original Greek According to the Byzantine/Majority Textform* (Atlanta: Original Word, 1991). See Maurice A. Robinson, "Investigating Text-Critical Dichotomy: A Critique of Modern Eclectic Praxis from a Byzantine-Priority Perspective," *Faith and Mission* 16(1999): 16–31.

58. As Hodges puts it:

> Under normal circumstances the older a text is than its rivals, the greater are its chances to survive in a plurality or a majority of the texts extant at any subsequent period. But the *oldest* text of all is the autograph. Thus it ought to be taken for granted that, barring some radical dislocation in the history of transmission, a majority of texts will be far more likely to represent correctly the character of the original than a small minority of texts. This is especially true when the ratio is an overwhelming 8:2. Under any reasonably normal transmissional conditions, it would be for all practical purposes quite impossible for a later text-form to secure so one-sided a preponderance of extant witnesses. (Zane C. Hodges, "A Defense of the Majority Text" [printed syllabus notes, Dallas Theological Seminary, n.d.], 4).

In short, acceptance of modern critical texts "constitutes nothing less than a wholesale rejection of probabilities on a sweeping scale!" (Hodges, "Defense," 9). His entire case, however, rests upon a single assumption—that the transmission of the New Testament has occurred under "reasonably normal" conditions, that there has been no "radical dislocation in the history of transmission"—and that assumption is false. The history of transmission has been radically dislocated; examples include the destruction of MSS and entire libraries during times of persecution and the Muslim conquests. Thus readings once known to be in the minority are today dominant, and vice versa; this fact alone rules out any attempt to do textual criticism by counting or statistical means. See further the critique and bibliography in M. W. Holmes, "The 'Majority text debate': new form of an old issue," *Themelios* 8 (1983): 13–19; Metzger, *Text*, 290–93; Gordon D. Fee, "The Majority Text and the Original Text of the New Testament," in Epp and Fee, *Studies*, 184–89.

59. Moreover, in practice this "method" suffers from an internal contradiction. Hodges and Farstad place a great deal of importance upon the construction of a genealogical stemma of MSS, one result being a text that in numerous places is supported by only a *minority* of MSS. Cf. Daniel B. Wallace, "Some Second Thoughts on the Majority Text," *Bibliotheca Sacra* 146 (1989): 270–90, especially 279–85; *idem*, "The Majority Text Theory: History, Methods, and Critique," in Ehrman and Holmes, *The Text of the New Testament in Contemporary Research*, 297–320; and Holmes, "The 'Majority text debate'," 18.

60. The best introductory (and now classic) treatment of this approach is still that of Metzger, *Text*, 207–46.

61. It must be remembered, of course, that a late MS or witness may preserve a very early form of the text; e.g., MS 1739 (tenth century) preserves a text closely related to p^{46} (ca. 200).

62. It is also true, however, as in linguistics, that change often affects remote areas last, if at all; hence a true reading may be preserved in only a few witnesses from the fringes of the MSS tradition.

63. This may well be the most difficult of the four external factors to ascertain, and perhaps the most subjective. But it is an observable fact that certain MSS display fewer readings that are obviously secondary (conflations, stylistic improvements, harmonizations, etc.) or scribal slips than do other MSS, which suggests that they are the product of a more controlled copying process, and therefore may be judged more likely to preserve an uncontaminated form of the text.

64. Intrinsic considerations are often the most subjective kind of evidence the text critic must take into account, since at any particular point an author may have deviated from his usual style or lexical preference for the sake of variety, if nothing else. At times, however, it can be decisive in judging between readings and for this reason must never be neglected.

65. A. E. Housman, "The Application of Thought to Textual Criticism," in *Selected Prose*, ed. by John Carter (Cambridge: Cambridge University Press, 1961), 132–33.

66. There are also several other variations of a very similar character within the prayer, but due to considerations of space and clarity we will focus on only these two places.

67. Given that the third reading in 11:2 (*Our Father*) has very slim external attestation (L *pc*) and that the addition of "our" is almost certainly due to the influence of Matthew 6:9, it may be confidently set aside as a secondary or corrupt reading.

68. Since these two textual traditions began to go their separate ways by the end of the second century, a reading broadly attested by both text-types likely antedates the split, and hence must be reckoned as a very old reading.

69. This based upon the demonstrable fact that at those places where the original text is established beyond doubt, the Alexandrian text-type preserves the original reading far more frequently than do either of the other two text-types combined. But since at any particular point any of the text-types or MSS may be in error, this consideration of relative quality generally comes into play only in those cases where there are no other more weighty considerations upon which to base a decision, or when the other evidence is so evenly balanced that a decision is difficult. In these circumstances one will most likely pick the original text if one picks the Alexandrian reading. Cf. the discussion of Matthew 22:13 following in the text.

70. Westcott and Hort, *Introduction*, 30.

71. And, on occasion, vice versa: for some scholars, a particular view of the Synoptic Problem has a decisive effect upon their textual decisions. Thus while textual decisions can affect one's view of the Synoptic Problem, one's view of the Synoptic Problem can affect one's textual choices. The danger of circular reasoning is apparent.

72. Examples include Matthew 5:11 and 19:9, Mark 14:70, and 1 Corinthians 2:1. On Matthew 5:11, see M. W. Holmes, "The Text of Matthew 5.11" *NTS* 32 (1986): 283–86, and on 19:9 and Mark 14:70 see idem, "The Text of the Matthean Divorce Passages: A Comment on the Appeal to Harmonization in Textual Decisions," *JBL* 109 (1990): 651–64. On 1 Corinthians 2:1 see G. D. Fee, *The First Epistle to the Corinthians* (NICNT; Grand Rapids: Eerdmans, 1987), 88, 91.

73. Compare, for example, the textual variants in Matthew 17:21 and Mark 9:29 (see the marginal notes in the NRSV, NIV, NASB, or NKJV for details), which impact both one's interpretation and view of the Synoptic Problem, or the variants in John 7:1: in place of "did not wish," some MSS read Jesus "did not have the authority" to go to Galilee. Clearly one's choice here is crucial to one's interpretation.

74. See the discussion of John 6:69 above, for example, or the discussion of 1 Thessalonians 2:7 in either Metzger, *Text*, 230–33, or Holmes, "Textual Criticism," 69–70.

Chapter 4

Source Criticism

Scot McKnight
North Park University

In the spring of my senior year in college I pulled a book from one of my shelves; and knowing that the requirements for graduation were fulfilled and that I could now read simply for the pleasure of learning, I read the book from cover to cover. That book was R. P. Martin's *New Testament Foundations: A Guide for Christian Students, Volume 1: The Four Gospels.*[1] The book raised what were, for me at least, some disturbing questions, and it answered these same questions in ways and with methods with which I was completely unfamiliar. The eleventh chapter, however, captivated me; that chapter covered "The Synoptic Problem."[2] Here Martin assessed the literary relationship of the Synoptic Gospels and concluded that Mark, along with the hypothetical source Q, were the sources used by Matthew and Luke (along with other sources) when they composed their Gospels. I found this conclusion theoretically (at least) confirmed by Luke's statement of procedure (Luke 1:1–4) but also found myself dismayed for I had never thought of the Evangelists proceeding in such a manner. Frankly, I had a fuzzy dictation theory of inspiration and had never really entertained any "historical thinking" on the origin of the Synoptic Gospels.

Though at the time I could not foresee it, that book set the agenda for the interests in scholarship that remain with me to this day. I entered seminary with a host of questions about the Gospels, many of which were first raised by Martin, and I used that time to work through many fundamental issues about the Gospels—questions about historical reliability, about sources and about the editorial activity of the Evangelists. Not long thereafter, I underlined an entire synopsis and read the major books in the discussion, including Sanday, Streeter, and Farmer. But my own view of the Synoptic Problem was shaped more by underlining the relationships I there discovered than by the current voices in the discussion. In fact, I am frequently surprised by the scholars who tell me they have never underlined an *entire* synopsis, even though they might take strong positions on the matter.

This chapter is concerned with one of those questions, namely, did the Evangelists use written sources when they wrote their Gospels?[3] And, if so (and I conclude they did), what is the relationship of the Synoptic Gospels to one another? For many these are disturbing questions.[4] However, they must be asked and a reasonable answer ought to be given if we are to do our Gospel study with any sense of integrity.

The Phenomena of the Synoptic Gospels

I begin with observing that our Synoptic Gospels (Matthew, Mark, and Luke), when carefully compared in a synopsis,[5] show some remarkable signs of *similarity*. Thus, if one compares the *wording* of Matthew 3:7–10 and Luke 3:7–9 in parallel columns, one observes substantial similarity. (Similarity appears as single underscore; dissimilarity as a double underscore.)

Matthew 3:7–10	Luke 3:7–9
But when he saw many of the Pharisees and Sadducees coming for baptism, he said to them, "You brood of vipers, who warned you to flee from the wrath to come? Therefore bring forth fruit in keeping with *your* repentance; and do not suppose that you can say to yourselves, 'We have Abraham for our father'; for I say to you, that God is able from these stones to raise up children to Abraham. "And the axe is already laid at the root of the trees; every tree therefore that does not bear good fruit is cut down and thrown into the fire."	He therefore began saying to the multitudes who were going out to be baptized by him, "You brood of vipers, who warned you to flee from the wrath to come? Therefore bring forth fruits in keeping with your repentance, and do not begin to say to yourselves, 'We have Abraham for our father'; for I say to you, that God is able from these stones to raise up children to Abraham. And also the axe is already laid at the root of the trees; every tree therefore that does not bear good fruit is cut down and thrown into the fire."

(Translation adapted from the NASB.)

Observe how this statement by John (Matt. 3:7b–10; Luke 3:7b–9) is repeated by two authors in nearly identical language. The Greek text, apart from the introductory statements, shows only three variations, indicated by a double underscore: (1) whereas Matthew has the singular "fruit" (3:8), Luke has "fruits" (3:8); (2) whereas Matthew has "do not suppose that you can . . ." (3:9), Luke has "do not begin to" (3:8); (3) Luke has added "Indeed" at Luke 3:9. Now these differences do not count for much. Substantial similarities are evident, and it can be easily seen that one could be the source for the other or that each copied another source.

Yet we cannot stop there. The Gospels also demonstrate significant *dissimilarity* as can be seen in the introductory statements of each Evangelist.

Apparently, each Evangelist prepared his readers for the statements of John in a different way. Whereas Matthew has John addressing many of the Pharisees and Sadducees (3:7a), Luke records that John spoke to the crowds (3:7a).

What has been observed so far pertains to the *phenomenon of wording,* one of three phenomena (empirically observable facts) involved in the Synoptic Problem. The phenomenon of wording is recognized by anyone who reads the Synoptic Gospels and observes that different Evangelists record the same events often with the same words. A second is the *phenomenon of content,* namely, that the Evangelists record similar events and sayings of Jesus. In fact, approximately 90 percent of Mark is found in Matthew and approximately 50 percent of Mark is found in Luke. Furthermore, approximately 235 verses, mostly sayings of Jesus, are common to Matthew and Luke but are not found in Mark.[6] The *phenomenon of order* describes the simple fact that at least two of the Evangelists agree almost all the time on the order of the events in the life of Jesus. This may be observed by anyone who will begin at Matthew 17:22–23; Mark 9:30–32 and Luke 9:43b–45. The next event is found only in Matthew (17:24–27). Then a common order is resumed: Matthew 18:1–5; Mark 9:33–37; Luke 9:46–48. Though Matthew does not record the next incident, both Mark and Luke do (cf. Mark 9:38–41; Luke 9:49–50). Again, two are united on the next event (Matt. 18:6–9; Mark 9:42–50). The point is simple: two Evangelists almost always agree on the matter of order. These three phenomena (wording, content, and order) form the basis for the Synoptic Problem.

The study of these phenomena in the Synoptic Gospels is called *source criticism,* and source criticism "attempts to identify the written traditions behind the Gospels in order to determine the relationship of the Synoptics."[7] The precise relationship of the Synoptics to one another, a problem that naturally arises from the observations illustrated above, is called "the Synoptic Problem."[8]

The Importance of Source Criticism

It may be asked, "What significance does source criticism have for understanding the Gospels?" This is an important question, for if the discipline has no usefulness, we may discard it as "an interesting, but irrelevant, historical method." But the method is quite significant and is an assumption of most New Testament studies today.

For instance, one of the standard editions of the Greek NT used by many students and scholars today is the United Bible Societies' text (UBS, 4th rev. ed.). The editors of that text clearly state that they assume that the Gospel writers were dependent on one another and they use what I will describe as the Oxford Hypothesis. The editor of a recent anthology of treatments on the Synoptic Problem has clearly expressed the crucial significance one's solution to the Synoptic Problem plays in NT studies, stating that:

> The Synoptic Problem lies at the heart of so many issues of New Testament scholarship that a change in our model of synoptic relationships affects meaningfully such other areas of New Testament research as form criticism, textual criticism, the quest of the historical Jesus, etc. The history of Christian theology, of early Christian sacraments, and of church institutions and government is affected significantly by our answer to the question of the order of composition of the Synoptic Gospels and the matter of their literary relationship. *Since Markan priority is an assumption of so much of the research of the last century, many of the conclusions of that research would have to be redrawn and much of the literature rewritten if the consensus of scholarship were suddenly to shift.*[9]

In light of the significance of source criticism and the manifold implications it has for interpretation, it is not surprising that the particular conclusion one takes as to the precise relationship has generated great debate today. In fact, though the Oxford Hypothesis (see below) dominated Gospel scholarship for at least two generations, that theory has been under fire for nearly thirty-five years though discussion has of late taken a new turn toward an acceptance of the Oxford Hypothesis, toward intricate analysis of how the traditions developed, and toward a resurgence of Q studies. Not surprisingly, the revival of historical Jesus studies finds itself banking on one theory of the Synoptic Problem.[10]

THE HISTORY AND DEVELOPMENT OF SOURCE CRITICISM

In the broadest of terms one can say that the story about source criticism has four chapters: (1) earliest Christianity seems to have preferred the Augustinian Hypothesis, that Matthew was first, Mark second, and Luke third; (2) in the middle of the eighteenth century some scholars were moved by J. J. Griesbach to accept what we now call the Griesbach Hypothesis, that Matthew wrote first, that Luke used Matthew, and that Mark, conflating both Matthew and Luke into a briefer Gospel, wrote third; (3) at the end of the nineteenth century and in the first quarter of the twentieth, scholars converted *en masse* to the Oxford Hypothesis, a view that states that Mark and Q were used independently by both Matthew and Luke and that Matthew and Luke both had access to at least one other source or sources (called "M" and "L" respectively); (4) since the middle of the twentieth century, the discussion over the precise relationship of the Synoptic Gospels has been renewed with vigorous debate. This discussion, though at times heated, shows no prospect of resolution, but there is a growing awareness of the role both presuppositions and methodologies play as well as a developing attention to precise details of significance in the debate.

A theory of long-standing tradition, though with few actual practicing proponents today, is that the Gospels are the result only of oral tradition finally come home to roost in Gospels which were independently written. Some of these theories are extremely complex, if not ingenious, but they are also rooted in sound historical methodology and a critical awareness of how ancient Jews passed on their stories, traditions, and beliefs.[11] This chapter will not analyze such approaches to the issues swirling around the Synoptic source criticism.

Augustinian Hypothesis[12]

The earliest comment in the earliest churches about the Gospels is from Papias, as found in Eusebius (*Church History* 3.39. 15–16), and is worthy of repetition. According to Papias (c. 60–138), Mark is an interpreter (or translator) of Peter, though Papias adds that Mark's design was not in "order" (*ou mentoi taxei*). Following his comments on Mark, Papias says that Matthew "composed the logia" (*ta logia sunetaxato*) in a Hebraic style and that each person had to interpret (or translate) them as he was able.

Following Papias there is a widespread if uncritical tradition regarding the origins of the Synoptic Gospels.[13] The general consensus was that Matthew wrote his Gospel "among the Jews in their own tongue, when Peter and Paul were preaching the gospel at Rome and founding the Church."[14] After Matthew came Mark, the disciple and recorder of Peter. After Mark, Luke, a follower of Paul, wrote his Gospel. Thus, the consensus of the early Church seems to have been Matthew, Mark, Luke; that is, the canonical order is the chronological order.

This understanding received its definitive form in Augustine and, because of his stature, was bequeathed to the Church as authoritative. Augustine's major statement follows: "Now, those four evangelists . . . are believed to have written in the order which follows: first Matthew, then Mark, thirdly, Luke, lastly John" (*Harmony* 1.2.3; cf. also 1.2.4; 4.10.11). Thus, the *Augustinian Hypothesis* affirms the canonical order as the chronological order.

This view of Augustine was the dominant view of the relationships of the Synoptics for nearly a millennium and a half though it needs to be said that Christian writers of this period were not seriously interested in the Synoptic Problem and simply repeated what tradition they had come to know. It must not be supposed that even Augustine was interested in this as a theoretical and historical problem: his concerns were with chronology, historical reliability, and theological presentation.[15] A recent advocate of this position, in a nuanced form, is J. W. Wenham, who combines the oral and written use of traditions, dates the Gospels unusually early, and argues for the general reliability of the early church traditions.[16]

Griesbach Hypothesis: Two-Gospel Hypothesis

J. J. Griesbach (1745–1812) published two essays in Latin that both called into the question the Augustinian Hypothesis as well as the then developing view of Markan priority and an Ur-Gospel theory.[17] He then formulated an entirely different theory as to how the Synoptic Gospels were related.[18] In brief, the Griesbach Hypothesis is that Matthew was written first; Luke, using Matthew, was second; and Mark, conflating both Matthew and Luke, was third.

At the time of Griesbach, few scholars accepted his theory.[19] However, in recent times, especially since the works of B. C. Butler and W. R. Farmer, the Griesbach Hypothesis has attracted a great deal of attention both to the problems in the Oxford Hypothesis and the plausibility of Griesbach's formulations.

Oxford Hypothesis: Two- or Four-Source Hypothesis

Contemporary with, though independent of, the Griesbach Hypothesis, the theory of Markan priority developed in Europe until it was fully expounded at Oxford under the direction of W. Sanday, receiving its most complete exposition in the famous work of B. H. Streeter.[20]

When William Sanday organized his famous seminar on the Synoptic Problem in 1894, which convened three times per term until 1910, the dominant solution to the Synoptic Problem in England seems to have been the so-called "oral hypothesis."[21] For approximately fifteen years students and friends of Sanday, including Sir J. C. Hawkins,[22] B. H. Streeter, and W. C. Allen,[23] gathered periodically to go through a synopsis paragraph by paragraph. The discussions were eventually brought to fruition in an influential volume entitled *Studies in the Synoptic Problem by Members of the University of Oxford*.[24]

The singularly most influential source critic of Sanday's Oxford Seminar is B. H. Streeter who, thirteen years after Sanday's *Studies* were published and upon further reflection, completed the definitive work that expounded the Oxford Hypothesis.[25] Though scholars have criticized Streeter and modified his views here and there, it cannot be said that any one work on the Synoptic Problem has had more influence than his. In brief, Streeter contended that there were four sources involved in the making of the Synoptic Gospels; and, he maintained, both their dates and provenance can be discerned: (1) Q, those verses common to Matthew and Luke, but not in Mark, was composed in Antioch in approximately 50 A.D.; (2) L, the original source for Luke's Gospel was written in approximately 60 A.D. in Caesarea; (3) M, the source for the special material in Matthew, was written in Jerusalem in approximately 60 A.D.; (4) Mark was written in 66 A.D. in Rome; (5) the combination of Q and L was made by Luke, a companion of Paul, and the resultant document Streeter called "Proto-Luke"; (6) our canonical Luke is the result of conflating Proto-Luke with a special source for Luke 1–2 and the Gospel of Mark; this was accomplished in approximately 80 A.D., perhaps in Corinth; (7) Matthew wrote his Gospel in approximately 85 A.D. in Antioch; and he did so by combining Mark, Q, M, and what Streeter called the "Antiochene Tradition."[26]

What has survived from this complex hypothesis, admittedly with dimensions that are from time to time challenged,[27] is more accurately called the Oxford Hypothesis, which states that there were at least two written sources: Q and Mark. Few today would contend that there was a written source M or L; fewer still adhere to the Proto-Luke hypothesis.[28] Nonetheless, in spite of its weaknesses, the essential theory of B. H. Streeter won the day and to this day holds the majority of scholars. The theory, no matter how deeply rooted it is in German scholarship, owes its definitive form to the work of Sanday's seminar.[29]

The Modern Debate

Of the more notable recent developments in the Synoptic Problem, four deserve mention. The first is a salty essay by A. M. Farrer that contests the necessity of Q. Instead, he maintains, it must be seriously queried whether it might be more useful (and accurate) to consider that Luke used Matthew, thus "dispensing with Q,"[30] and this position has recently been thoroughly defended by M. Goulder.[31]

A second development, though now significantly abating, is the revival of the Griesbach Hypothesis, largely due to the pressing and persistent questions of W. R. Farmer. Because of the persuasive and administrative designs of Farmer (and other Griesbach proponents), there have been five major international conferences that have taken up the Synoptic Problem in a serious forum.[32] However, the revival of the Griesbach Hypothesis has not been unchallenged. In 1979, C. M. Tuckett successfully defended a Ph.D. dissertation on the Griesbach revival and an abbreviated version of this dissertation followed (*The Revival of the Griesbach Hypothesis: An Analysis and Appraisal*).[33] Tuckett concludes that the Griesbach Hypothesis is not as satisfactory a solution to the Synoptic Problem as the Oxford Hypothesis.

A third area, the most significant in intensity today, is "Q research" which got its impetus from the works of H. E. Tödt and D. Lührmann.[34] At the annual meetings of the Society of Biblical Literature, major papers are read to discuss the original shape, order, and the redactions of different Q texts. Alongside this official seminar, and the foundation for some of it, has been the publication of two books which seek to provide a Q text (with apparatus!) in light of these modern discussions. These two texts have been composed by A. Polag[35] and J. S. Kloppenborg.[36] Even if some scholars doubt the existence of Q and are unsure as to its original language (Aramaic, Greek, or both), vast amounts of research have gone into the Q discussion and its proper methodology,[37] and the debate shows no signs of abating. Two examples will suffice.[38]

John Kloppenborg, it can be justly said, leads the contemporary discussion about Q in North America. In brief, as a result of decades of study of Q, Kloppenborg argues that Q emerges into the canonical Gospels as a result of three phases of evolution: (1) the sapiential stage during which stage the Q1 was largely a set of instructions; (2) the polemical stage during which stage Q1 combined with especially prophetic traditions to form Q2, a kind of "chreia collection"; (3) and then in its last phase the Q tradition picks up some narrative material, most notably the temptation narrative to become a "proto-biography." Though at one time a nonbeliever in the evolutionary theories for Q, recently D. C. Allison Jr. has laid out an intricate and believable theory on the evolution of Q. The document as we have reconstructed it began in the 30s and was largely completed by the 40s (maybe 50s) but was at first probably Semitic (Q1). Its two later stages, Q2 and Q3, were probably Greek in nature. Allison also argues that Q1 is both a good source for Jesus and what Papias was referring to when he described Matthew as writing "Logia." Such brief descriptions do not do justice to either Kloppenborg or Allison, but enough detail has been given to reveal what is going on in current Q scholarship.

A final discussion, though not vigorous, concerns a recent attempt to revive the older oral traditions hypothesis by Bo Reicke.[39] In a careful analysis of the data, along with both a solid awareness of the origins of the discussions in eighteenth and nineteenth century Germany as well as the earliest church traditions, Reicke argues for a greater contribution of oral traditions as well as smaller, fragmented traditions that came together to form our canonical Gospels. Further, Reicke argues for distinct geographical locations for these traditions and Gospels, a connection to apostles, specific church contexts as a decisive impetus for the rise of the traditions and Gospels, as well as early dates for the Gospels. While few are likely to agree with most, or many, of Reicke's conclusions, the independence of mind and courage to address hitherto neglected issues only gives to this work a promise to improve the current discussion.

EVALUATION OF TWO HYPOTHESES

Because nearly all of contemporary discussions revolve around the Griesbach and Oxford Hypotheses, the Augustinian view will not be evaluated here. Because of the intensity of the debate, at many points it will be needful to have a synopsis at hand.

An Evaluation of the Griesbach Hypothesis

It is not remotely possible to do justice to this position in such short space. I will simply mention two strengths and a few weaknesses of the Griesbach Hypothesis.

The Strengths of the Griesbach Hypothesis

Perhaps the greatest strength of the Griesbach proponents is their calling into question the sloppy logic of the Oxford Hypothesis, a position that had become by the middle of this century so dominant that most any argument went unchallenged. In particular, it has been pointed out that the argument from order actually proves nothing. Here is the classic statement of B. H. Streeter: "The relative order of incidents and sections in Mark is in general supported by both Matthew and Luke; where either of them deserts Mark, the other is usually found supporting him."[40] Now this statement is patently circular, for it concludes (a little later) exactly what it assumes: that Mark was used by Matthew and Luke.[41] Accordingly, a Griesbach proponent might describe the phenomenon of order like this: "Mark follows the order of Matthew and Luke, and whenever Matthew's or Luke's order diverge, Mark follows either one or the other."[42] This restates the phenomenon in a way that is just as unambiguous. A major contribution of modern Griesbach proponents is this: they have demonstrated that the phenomena of wording, contents, and order are nothing more than phenomena which are subject to several explanations.[43]

Another strength of this view is its careful attention to early Christian statements. To my knowledge, no one in the history of the Church has written as careful an analysis of early Church testimony on the relationships of the Gospels as that by B. Orchard.[44] The Oxford proponents cannot simply dismiss early Church traditions as pious and sentimental legends.[45]

Problems for the Griesbach Hypothesis

Though Griesbach proponents continually trumpet their successes (and there are some),[46] the majority of Gospel scholarship still holds tenaciously, though not now so naively, to the Oxford Hypothesis. Several arguments, therefore, have been lodged against the Griesbach Hypothesis.

First, far too frequently the Griesbach proponents do not seem to recognize the logical difference between an *explanation* and a *proof*. This is noticed most frequently when Griesbach proponents seek to show that the Griesbach Hypothesis makes most sense of the phenomenon of order simply because *its proponents can explain the order in light of their hypothesis*. I will illustrate this with only one example, but many others could be given.[47] I will pick on a statement of W. R. Farmer and show the inconclusive logic that is so typical of the Griesbach argumentation. In his article on how certain results of J. C. Hawkins and C. F. Burney would be more readily explicable on the basis of the Griesbach Hypothesis, Farmer makes this statement: "This [his careful explanation of how Luke used Matthew 24:1–17] is a perfectly comprehensible literary device, and *lends support to the hypothesis that Luke was using Matthew as his source*."[48] The first statement, beginning with "This" is acceptable, for it is true that, *if Luke did use Matthew*, what he did to Matthew is a reasonable procedure. However, this does not *"lend support* to the hypothesis that Luke was using Matthew as his source" *because it assumes that Luke used Matthew*. In other words, Farmer (1) assumes that Luke used Matthew, (2) *explains* Luke's use of Matthew in light of his assumption, and then (3) concludes that this shows that Luke used Matthew. The point I am making is simple but very important: an explanation is not necessarily a proof.[49] A conclusion of one's assumptions because of the "explanation" is nothing more than a triumph of circular reasoning.

Second, the assumed purpose of Mark in conflating Matthew and Luke goes contrary to clear evidence of what Mark did. It is laid down as an observable feature of Mark's redactional practice (assuming the Griesbach Hypothesis), that Mark recorded in his Gospel that "which deviated in no significant sense from the narrative to which the texts of Matthew and Luke 'bore concurrent testimony.'"[50] Now it is an easily demonstrable *fact* that this is not how Mark proceeded, and because this is not how Mark worked, a serious blow is dealt to the Griesbach Hypothesis. A careful comparison, for instance, of Matthew 13:31–32 and Luke 13:18–19 with Mark 4:30–32 yields just the opposite conclusion. In the words of C. M. Tuckett, "For the overall picture, if Mark is using Matthew and Luke as his sources [at Mark 4:30–32], is that *Mark has carefully and systematically avoided everything that is common to Matthew and Luke: where they agree, Mark disagrees, and where Matthew disagrees with Luke, Mark follows Matthew closely.* Thus, Mark appears to have taken an intense dislike to Luke . . . , and to have gone through Matthew's text, changing it where Matthew and Luke agree, but leaving it alone where they differ. Moreover, the result is, in places, grammatical chaos."[51] If Mark avoids everything in common, then his procedure is not as Farmer says it is.[52]

Third, F. G. Downing has ably demonstrated that there are no contemporary parallels to the complicated kind of conflation assumed to have been performed by Mark by Griesbach proponents. The procedure for Mark, assuming the Griesbach Hypothesis, would have been a tedious and exacting process—sometimes lifting a word from Matthew, then one from Luke, and then a phrase from Matthew, and then back to Luke, and so forth. In some recent work Downing has shown that when we have clear instances of ancient historians using different sources covering the same material and were compelled to conflate, the procedure was simple. Instead of working through the different sources carefully and adding one word from one source and another phrase from another source, producing a truly conflated text, the authors took one source as primary and then supplemented that source with larger conflated blocks. The Griesbach Hypothesis, he contends, goes contrary to everything we know about how historians thought of their procedure and how they actually practiced their historiography.[53] Downing's work deserves careful reading.

Fourth, so far as I can see, the Griesbach proponents have not dealt with the most decisive argument favoring the Oxford Hypothesis, namely, the argument from primitive language.[54] The most telling argument against the Griesbach Hypothesis is the accumulated answers to this question: which reading most likely gave rise to the other readings? Put differently, given Matthew's (or Luke's) rendering of a saying or event, is it likely that Mark is a later rendition of Matthew or Luke (or both), or is it more likely that Mark is the source for the others?[55] The answers so consistently move in the direction of Markan priority that one is compelled either to adopt the Oxford Hypothesis or jettison text-critical procedures in use by all scholars today.[56] In fact, the recent analysis of the text-critical argument by M. C. Williams establishes such an argument. After analyzing the Markan apparatus to establish the kinds of features that characterize posteriority in variant readings, Williams then compares Mark to Matthew to see if the same kinds of changes characterize Matthew's relationship to Mark. His conclusions are threefold: (1) the kinds of readings in Mark's apparatus are the kinds of readings in Matthew when compared to Mark; (2) text-critical arguments clearly and consistently support Markan priority and Matthean posteriority; and (3) those who use the Nestle-Aland text should also, to maintain consistency, conclude for Markan priority when compared to Matthew.[57]

At this point I need to give but one specific example. At Mark 7:31, Mark records what is, by all accounts, a trip of Jesus: "And again, Jesus left the regions of Tyre and went through Sidon to the Sea of Galilee through the middle of the regions of the Decapolis." Now on any reading of this text, a strange route has been followed: a trip southeast begins by going north, and one gets to this southeast destination, the Sea of Galilee, through a region of cities even farther southeast than the sea itself. What is noteworthy here is that Matthew's account of this trip is much easier to follow: "And departing from there [the regions of Tyre and Sidon], Jesus came to the Sea of Galilee" (Matt. 15:29). For the purposes of the Synoptic Problem, we can ask a simple text-critical question: "Which reading most likely gave rise to the other?" And the answer, *for all text-critics,* would be that it is more likely that Mark gave rise to Matthew's clarification than for Mark to take this perfectly sensible statement of Matthew and make it obscure. What is at least more difficult to understand in Mark is easier to understand in Matthew. Mark is, therefore, more primitive and therefore probably prior to Matthew. Full analysis of the texts of Mark and Matthew show that Matthew is consistently secondary when compared to Mark.

An Evaluation of the Oxford Hypothesis

In this section I want to explain the traditional arguments for the Oxford Hypothesis and then proceed to list a few of the problems that have been pointed out regarding the adequacy of this solution. The Oxford Hypothesis, it will be remembered, argues that Matthew and Luke used the Gospel of Mark, the source Q, and that both Evangelists also had access to other material, conveniently dubbed "M" and "L."

What are the arguments in favor of this hypothesis? The arguments reduce themselves naturally into two issues: the priority of Mark and the existence of Q. I begin with the arguments that favor Markan priority.

Arguments for Markan Priority

First, the Oxford Hypothesis is more probable because of the *linguistic phenomena*. Since I have mentioned this in the fourth criticism of the Griesbach Hypothesis, I will restate the argument and then give a couple more examples. Put simply, the linguistic phenomena of the Synoptic Gospels can be more easily explained if Mark is seen as prior to both Matthew and Luke than if Mark is seen as a later conflation of Luke and Matthew.[58]

At Mark 14:3, we find an unusual concurrence of two genitive absolutes in the same sentence; Matthew has a genitive absolute and then a finite verb (26:6). It is more likely that Matthew "corrected" Mark than that Mark took a perfectly normal expression and made it irregular.

A second example can be found at Mark 4:31 (par. Matt. 13:31–32; Luke 13:18–19). Mark has a peculiar opening "as clause" that assumes some verb; this is followed by a masculine gender relative clause with a passive verb, and then Mark breaks all normal rules of grammar by turning the previous masculine relative pronoun into a neuter gender. Now my point is not that this is incompetent grammar; it is, however, peculiar. Matthew and Luke, on the other hand, have perfectly normal and simple grammatical constructions. It is much more likely that Matthew and Luke have "corrected" Mark than that Mark has taken normal constructions and created a gaffe. In the infamous words of B. H. Streeter, when commenting on the cumulative effect of the linguistic phenomena when examining a synopsis, "How any one who has worked through those pages with a synopsis of the Greek text can retain the slightest doubt of the original and primitive character of Mark I am unable to comprehend."[59]

Second, the Oxford Hypothesis is more probable because of the *theological phenomena*;[60] this is the same logic of the first argument but now looked at from the angle of theology and its development. One example will illustrate the point. At Mark 6:5–6, it is stated that Jesus was amazed at the unbelief of the Nazareth crowd and that Jesus was *unable* to do any miracles there. Early Christians may very well have been bothered by this statement since it could suggest the inability of Jesus, God incarnate, to do something. Such an impression, however, will not be given by Matthew. When he reports this narrative, in nearly identical terms, he states that Jesus "did not do many miracles there" (13:58). Now on the Griesbach Hypothesis one has to come up with an explanation for why Mark would have taken a statement that in no way casts doubts on Jesus' ability (Matt. 13:58) and created a theological problem, whereas the Oxford Hypothesis has a more probable account of the event. Matthew eliminated a theological difficulty. It is more probable that Matthew erased a theological problem than that Mark created one. This kind of observation when comparing

Matthew, Mark, and Luke not only lends support to the Oxford Hypothesis; it makes it the most probable hypothesis.

Third, the Oxford Hypothesis is more probable because of the *redactional phenomena*. Once again this argument is a variant of combining arguments one and two. It is often argued that the consistency that has been found in either Matthew's or Luke's treatment of Mark is an argument in favor of Markan priority. In other words the coherency of the theory is an argument in its favor.[61] This is an important point, but the limitations of this argument need to be noted before an illustration is given. This argument is really nothing more than an explanation that makes good sense of the data; it is not, however, a decisive proof for Markan priority. I quote from G. N. Stanton: "As far as Matthean scholarship is concerned, it has yet to be shown that any of the alternatives to the assumption that Matthew has used Mark and Q provide a more plausible and coherent account of Matthean redaction than the generally accepted view [Oxford Hypothesis]."[62]

One example of redactional activity from Matthew will illustrate the nature of this argument. No one who reads Matthew will fail to miss the importance he attaches to the term *righteousness*. It is found seven times in Matthew (3:15; 5:6, 10, 20; 6:1, 33; 21:32). In addition, if one examines each of these in a synopsis, one observes that each is unparalleled. Thus, it appears that Matthew has consistently added the term to his sources because that term expresses what he wants to emphasize. One would have to ask then, on the Griesbach or Augustinian Hypothesis, why neither Luke nor Mark ever had any reason to use this term when using Matthew as a source. (It is simply not the case that Mark and Luke do not record traditions about doing God's will.) Further, one would have to provide reasons for Mark's or Luke's omission in each instance. These regular omissions of Matthew's particular emphases count very heavily in favor of Matthew's having added them. Furthermore, the notion of doing God's will (i.e., being righteous) is a dominant and consistent feature of Matthew's redactional presentation of discipleship.[63] In light of the absence of this Matthean theme in Mark and Luke and the pervasiveness of this theme in Matthew, it can be concluded that righteousness is a part of Matthew's redactional scheme. Accordingly, if one assumes Markan priority (and the existence of Q) and then examines Matthew's emphasis on righteousness and doing God's will, one finds a consistent redactional tendency on the part of Matthew. This, it is argued, lends support to the Oxford Hypothesis; the hypothesis is coherent. Again, however, such an "explanation" is not a "proof."

These two arguments, along with a coherent explanation, demonstrate with a high degree of probability that Mark is prior to either Matthew or Luke. This is the first argument for the Oxford Hypothesis—Mark is prior to Matthew and Luke.

Arguments for the Existence of Q

The Oxford Hypothesis is more probable because *it is unlikely that Luke used Matthew and therefore it is likely that they independently used another source* (Q). A fact that needs to be noted here is that Matthew and Luke contain approximately 235 verses, mostly comprised of sayings of Jesus, that are not found in Mark. Most of these sayings are similar in wording— so much so that most would agree literary dependence is well-nigh certain. However, Matthew and Luke almost never record the same Q saying in the same location or order, though most scholars have concluded that Luke best preserved the original order of Q.[64] Thus, if one looks up Matthew 23:37–39 in a synopsis, one finds a parallel at Luke 13:34–35. Two things can be observed for our purposes: (1) the saying of Jesus is recorded in almost identical Greek wording and (2) each Evangelist records this saying in a different context. What I have been labeling Q in the present discussion is sometimes considered to be Luke's copying of Matthew.[65] But there is suf- ficient evidence to suggest that Luke and Matthew are independent and that therefore a Q hypothesis is probable.[66] I turn now to these.

1. When Matthew and Luke are recording the same event or saying that is also found in Mark, Luke never picks up the material that Matthew adds to Mark.[67] Thus, it can be argued that Matthew and Luke are independent. For instance, both Matthew and Luke used Mark to record the baptism of Jesus (Mark 1:9–11; Matt. 3:13–17; Luke 3:21–22). But none of the addi- tions to Mark by Matthew (e.g., Matt. 3:14–15) are added to Mark by Luke. If Luke is dependent on Matthew, then Luke made a conscious choice (almost) never to record Matthew's additions to Mark.

This observation can be extended: Luke also never included what we now call the *M* traditions, those incidents and sayings of Jesus found now only in Matthew. On first glance this could be taken as a logical error: Luke never records *M* traditions; *M* traditions are those traditions found only in Matthew; therefore, Luke by definition could not have included *M* tradi- tions because then they would be classed as Q traditions. This is a fair observation. However, there is still an important observation here. Namely, Luke chose consistently not to include any narrative material added by Matthew to Mark (e.g., Matt. 1:1–2:23; 27:62–66; 28:11–15) and seems regularly not to have included, for instance, parables not paralleled in Mark (e.g., Matt. 13:24–30, 36–43, 44–46, 47–50, 51–52; 18:23–35; 20:1–16; 21:28–32)—several of which are right to the heart of Luke's favorite themes: reversal of this world's values and the salvation of the unlikely. It is more probable that Luke did not know these traditions (and was therefore independent of Matthew) than that Luke did know them but chose not to include them. Even though this argument can easily turn into nonsensical circularity, it does have some value. Luke seems not to have known of these traditions (else he would have used them) and, thus, was independent of

Matthew. Thus, this suggests the independence as well as the use of a common source (Q).

2. After the temptation of Jesus, Luke and Matthew never place their common material in the same setting, though each occasionally uses what appear to be "blocks" of similar tradition. The fact that similar placement would almost certainly occur if Luke were using Matthew suggests that Matthew and Luke are independent and that they each used a common source (Q). Argument here of Lukan dependence on Matthew would require that Luke used Mark in one manner consistently but that he used Matthew in a completely different manner, an argument that could be sustained though with little conviction.

The examples here could be easily multiplied. It is a known fact that Matthew has five discourses (5:1–7:29; 9:35–11:1; 13:1–52; 18:1–19:2; 23:1–26:2) and that the parallels to the sayings of Jesus found in Matthew's discourses are scattered throughout Luke (especially in Luke 6:20–8:3 and 9:51–18:14). That Luke did not place one of these sayings in the same setting that Matthew did suggests, if it does not prove, that Luke and Matthew are independent. The early observation of B. H. Streeter is worthy of repetition: "A theory which would make the author capable of such a proceeding [Luke's treatment of Matthew's ordering of this non-Markan material] would only be tenable if, on other grounds, we had reason to believe that he was a crank."[68]

3. When Matthew and Luke contain material not found in Mark, sometimes it is Matthew and sometimes it is Luke that appears to be the more primitive. Again, this suggests that they are independent of each other and using a common source (Q). However subjective a factor "more primitive" might appear, interpretation always involves a certain measure of subjectivity so that one ought not to discard this observation casually. Sometimes primitivity relates to theological understanding, but then turns on which saying of Jesus is more Semitic than the other. Two examples, one showing Matthew to be more primitive and the other Luke, will be given.

Matthew 7:9–11 records Jesus' statements on the goodness of God that can be trusted in prayer. The final statement is, "How much more will your Father who is in the heavens give *good things* to those who ask Him?" Luke, who also composed the Acts of the Apostles which details the power of the Holy Spirit in the earliest churches, has a parallel to Matthew 7:9–11, which reads in this last line: "How much more will your Father who is from heaven give *the Holy Spirit* to those who ask Him?" (Luke 11:13). By all accounts, Matthew's account is the more primitive (theologically speaking) than Luke's. Apparently, for Luke the "good things" of Matthew could be summarized (because they were focused) in the Holy Spirit—the essence of all good things.

On the other hand, Luke 14:26 seems to be more primitive than Matthew 10:37. Luke 14:26 reads, "If anyone comes to me and does not *hate* his father and mother and wife and children and brothers and sisters, and even his own soul, is not able to be my disciple." Matthew, on the other hand, showing a sensitivity to potential misunderstandings, edits out the Semitic idiom and writes, "The one who *loves* father or mother *more than* me is not worthy of me" (Matt. 10:37). The more primitive Semitic idiom of Luke has been reexpressed by Matthew in both a historically reliable manner and in a way that cannot be misunderstood. This suggests that Luke's account is more primitive.

These two examples, one from Matthew and one from Luke, illustrate the argument being made for the independence of Matthew and Luke. If, say, Luke were dependent on Matthew, then one would expect that Matthew would have a monopoly on the more primitive, in both theology and language. In fact, neither Evangelist gets the consistent nod on primitivity, and the concluding inference is that this demonstrates that neither is more primitive because each Evangelist drew independently on a common source that was itself more primitive.

4. It appears that at times Matthew or Luke record one saying of Jesus two different times in their Gospels.[69] On these occasions, one time there is a parallel in Mark, and the other time there is a parallel in Matthew or Luke. These sayings are called "doublets," and these doublets suggest that Matthew and Luke are independently drawing from two sources (Mark and Q). J. C. Hawkins listed twenty-two doublets in Matthew, one in Mark, and eleven in Luke.[70] Our concern is with those doublets in Matthew or Luke that have parallels in Mark and the other Gospel. A listing of these doublets follows:[71]

Markan Tradition	Q Tradition
Mark 4:25, cf. Matthew 13.12; Luke 8:18	Matthew 25:29; Luke 19:26
Mark 8:34–35, cf. Matthew 16:24–25; Luke 9:23–24	Matthew 10:38–39; Luke 14:27; 17:33
Mark 8:38, cf. Matthew 16:27; Luke 9:26	Matthew 10:32–33; Luke 12:8–9
Mark 13:9, 13, cf. Matthew 24:9, 13; Luke 21:12, 17, 19	Matthew 10:19–20, 22; Luke 12:11–12

The presence of doublets suggests that Matthew and Luke both used Mark and another source—from which they drew the second instance of the saying.[72]

5. If Luke used Matthew, it is almost impossible to propose a reasonable motive for what Luke would have had to do to Matthew. Thus, on the grounds of coherency, a Q hypothesis is more coherent than a Griesbach theory. This argument is subject to the same, if not even more, weaknesses that we encountered in the argument from order in the Griesbach Hypothesis. It is a fact that one could find, I suppose, sufficient motives for

anything Luke would have done to Matthew. Granted the explanatory nature of this argument, we still need to recognize the problems that need to be dealt with by anyone who denies the independence of Matthew and Luke. If Luke is dependent on Matthew, then it is difficult for us to understand why he took beautiful structures, structures that have appealed to Christians since the beginning of the Church, structures like the birth narratives of Matthew and the Sermon on the Mount, broke them into separate pieces and then placed the pieces in much less pleasing places.[73] The argument, though not a proof, tends to favor the independence of Matthew and Luke, and therefore Q, and so deserves being mentioned.

For these five reasons it is highly improbable that Luke and Matthew are interdependent, and it is highly probable that Matthew and Luke independently used a source of the sayings of Jesus, now called Q. However, in light of the fact that Matthew and Luke almost never use the same material in the same location (with the exception of "blocks"—which themselves might be explained as use of the same material in the same location if the individual elements of the blocks are to be understood as separate traditions in Q), it is more probable, in my opinion, that Q is to be understood not so much as a "book" as it is a "collection" of disparate sayings of Jesus. Therefore, the variety of content, context, form, and function suggest to me that Q was (1) not a single document, (2) more likely a set of traditions, and (3) a set of traditions that have an evolution prior to their incorporation into the canonical Gospels. Thus, the theories of Kloppenborg and Allison are more likely to be realities than the theories of Streeter.

Problems for the Oxford Hypothesis

It must not be thought, however, that the Oxford Hypothesis is without its problems. Certainly it is the foremost theory for explaining the origins and the relationship of the Synoptic Gospels, but the critique of the Oxford Hypothesis in the last generation by Griesbach proponents has caused some important revisions, many of which are reflected in our previous discussion. What are the weaknesses of the Oxford Hypothesis? Three major problems need to be mentioned.

First, the Oxford Hypothesis has not sufficiently struggled with the early Christian evidence on the origins of the Gospels. It is a noticeable feature that W. Sanday's Seminar, so far as I know, did not deal with the patristic evidence with sufficient rigor. It will just not do for Oxford proponents to dismiss patristic evidence as tendentious or, worse yet, precritical and therefore naive. Examination of this evidence may lead to the conclusion that the patristic evidence is mistaken, but such a conclusion ought not to be drawn unless careful attention is given to the matter.

Second, the major criticism of the Oxford Hypothesis has been the observation of so-called "minor agreements of Matthew and Luke against Mark." What are these? An "agreement of Matthew and Luke against

Mark" is a term, expression, or entire incident in the life of Jesus that is related one way by Mark and in a different but identical way by both Matthew and Luke—and, assuming the Oxford Hypothesis, when Matthew and Luke are supposed to be unaware of each other's work. Thus, these are "coincidental, independent but identical alterations" to Mark.

For example, I include a synopsis of Mark 1:41–43; Matthew 8:3, and Luke 5:13. Mark is in the middle to make the problem more visible.

Matthew 8:3	Mark 1:41–43	"Luke 5:13
And................................	And <u>displaying compassion</u>	And................................
he stretched out <u>the</u> hand	he stretched out his hand	he stretched out <u>the</u> hand
and touched him, <u>saying</u>	and touched him <u>and</u> <u>said</u>	he touched him, <u>saying</u>
....	to him	....
I will, be cleansed	I will, be cleansed	I will, be cleansed
And <u>immediately</u> his	And <u>immediately</u> his	And <u>immediately</u> his
leprosy	leprosy departed from him	leprosy departed from him.
was cleansed.	and he was cleansed.	
....	And warning him sternly,	....
....	immediately he sent him	....
....	away.	....

From this synopsis several "minor agreements" can be observed. (1) Matthew and Luke agree against Mark in omitting "displaying compassion." (2) They both omit "his" from "his hand." (3) They both alter "and said" to "saying." (4) Though not seen in English, when Mark records "immediately," both Matthew and Luke have another form of the word "immediately": Mark has *euthus,* and Matthew and Luke have *eutheos.* (5) Both Matthew and Luke omit the emotional charge of Jesus. Seen individually, one would not take notice of such minor changes, for changing Mark's typical "and said" to "saying" is typical both for Matthew and Luke (assuming the Oxford Hypothesis). But the insignificance of such a minor change becomes altogether more important when it is observed that within the space of three verses of Mark five independent but identical changes occur. This is more than a minor agreement. And it must be admitted that these "minor agreements" work against the Oxford Hypothesis because they suggest a literary relationship between Matthew and Luke. Griesbach proponents explain these as Markan alterations of Matthew and Luke where Luke has followed Matthew identically.

Thus, the "minor agreements" are not "minor" and deserve careful attention by Oxford proponents. One recent study by an Oxford proponent, C. M. Tuckett, has tackled the issue of the "minor agreements," and his work is worthy of careful attention.[74] Tuckett contends that the "minor agreements," are not more easily explained by the Griesbach Hypothesis than by the Oxford Hypothesis. One of his examples will suffice. Matthew

21:23 and Luke 20:1 both describe Jesus as "teaching"; Mark 11:27, the parallel, and according to the Griesbach Hypothesis the conflation of the two, does not have "teaching." Griesbach proponents point to the "agreement" between Matthew and Luke against Mark and infer that the Oxford Hypothesis cannot make sense of this phenomenon. Tuckett, however, shows that Mark's plan—according to Griesbach—is to use the concurrent testimony (in this case, Matthew and Luke agreeing that Jesus was teaching) and does not do so. Further, since Mark often stresses the fact that Jesus was teaching, its absence is even less explicable. After presenting a coherent explanation in light of the Oxford Hypothesis, Tuckett concludes: "On the theory of Markan priority this agreement can be explained as due to independent editing, whilst on the GH [Griesbach Hypothesis], the text is very difficult to explain."[75] After examining a sufficient number of these "minor agreements," Tuckett concludes his chapter with the following statement: "Whilst the minor agreements all present some difficulties for the 2DH (Two Document Hypothesis = Oxford Hypothesis), and whilst some of Streeter's own arguments were suspect (e.g. his stress on textual corruption), overall, the 2DH can often give a more coherent explanation of these agreements than can the GH."[76] If this is just a beginning for the Oxford Hypothesis on the road to serious working on the minor agreements, that future is bright because Tuckett has offered a serious challenge and a reasonable explanation for a great number of the minor agreements.

A final problem for the Oxford Hypothesis revolves around the difficulties encountered in Q studies. In particular, three problems stand out: (1) problems with the original wording, (2) problems with the original contents, and (3) problems with speculative theories. I begin with the last. It goes without saying that some of the most fertile and imaginative theories of Synoptic studies have been raised by Q scholars.[77] Scholars have inferred a Q tradition to a Q document to a Q genre, from a Q document to a Q author and his community, from a Q author and his community to redactional layers and theological ideas of the Q author(s) and his (their) community/communities, even to the point that some scholars have convinced themselves that the Q community moved several times. The problem is with probability—and the multiplication of theories on the basis of a document that is already hypothetical does not increase one's chances of being accurate. The opposite is the case! In fact, I suspect that many Gospel students are put off by the speculative nature of Q scholarship.[78] I am, for one, quite convinced that there was at least a Q tradition that can be reasonably separated from our present Synoptic Gospels, but I am greatly suspicious of any theories that go much beyond the level of identifying the general contents and wording of such a tradition. To speak then of a Q redactor or a Q community strikes me as too speculative to be of use. Granted, these things are not impossibilities, but they are so highly speculative that we are best left with suggestions.

And further problems arise when we try to determine the original wording of Q—did Q have "finger" or "Spirit" of God (cf. Matt. 12:28; Luke 11:20)? Not only is wording a problem. Will it ever be possible for modern scholars to approach probability on the original contents and even order of this hypothetical document? Connected to this is the problem that many find in Q scholarship: a theme or a formal feature (prophetic utterance, narrative) is equated with a layer, and absolute consistency in a theme marks a layer. The question many of us have asked is this: was any ancient Jewish or Christian writer absolutely consistent in this manner with themes? And cannot different themes be used together and in different ways by one author? Thus, cannot the earliest edition of Q have had a complex relationship of wisdom and eschatology just as it did at the final layer?

For these reasons it is impossible to determine with certainty and high probability the original contents, wording, and order[79] of Q. In spite of these problems, scholars of the Oxford Hypothesis have come to a fairly unanimous conclusion regarding the probable shape and contents of Q. It must not be supposed that it is all up for grabs. Rather, though the general contents are fairly agreed upon, it is when we need precision that we must admit we do not have certain results.

It is not possible to evaluate carefully the other theories mentioned. Virtually all scholars today fit either into the Griesbach or Oxford Hypothesis. And arguments for either of these are arguments contrary to the other theories. It remains for us now to apply the one theory, the Oxford Hypothesis, to one passage. Our goal here is simply to show how an Oxford proponent would examine this text source-critically.[80] And our procedure will be to show how an Oxford proponent would explain what Luke has done to Mark.

EXEMPLAR: PETER'S CONFESSION AND THE MESSIAH'S RESPONSE

An introductory comment is necessary at this point. A source critic's work is a preliminary matter. A source critic is looking at the Synoptic passages in order to determine the sources of the Evangelist and, through that determination, to discern what is traditional and what is redactional. The historian will use the source critic's conclusions to write a "history of the tradition" of that event or saying; the redaction critic will use that information to examine why the Evangelist did what he did to his sources in order to explain that Evangelist's theology and church setting. Accordingly, the task below is preliminary. I will look at this one passage in light of the Oxford Hypothesis to show the source pattern. A subsequent chapter on redaction criticism by G. R. Osborne will then expound the significance of these findings for exegesis.

The passage to be examined is Peter's confession and the Messiah's response to Peter. The passage, in general, contains these elements, with the Lukan references: The Situation and Question (Luke 9:18); The General Responses (9:19); Peter's Response (9:20); Jesus' Response to Peter (9:21); The Implications of the Confession (9:22–27); For Jesus (9:22); and For the Disciples (9:23–27). These five elements will provide the structure for our source-critical observations.

A source critic looks at a given passage and, through tedious examination, asks, "Where did the Evangelist get this word or idea?" Sometimes the source critic discovers an amazing pattern of alteration; more frequently this is not the case. In the following source-critical observations I will at times point out a pattern of alteration. Most of our observations are little more than comparative remarks.

We have discussed above the phenomenon of order, and it needs to be illustrated here. Whereas Mark's order and Matthew's order are virtually identical to Mark 6:14–8:21 (Matt. 14:1–16:12), with only one omission (Mark 8:14–21), Luke's order diverges markedly at this point. Luke joins the confession of Peter and the response of the Messiah to Peter to the feeding of five thousand (Luke 9:10–17 and 9:18–27). In effect, Luke "omits" Mark 6:45–8:26.[81] Thus, though the Evangelists do join the responses of Jesus to Peter's confession in identical fashion, the exact placement of the unit differs. According to the Griesbach Hypothesis, Mark has preferred Matthew here; according to the Oxford Hypothesis, Matthew witnesses to Mark's order when Luke does not. Both can explain the phenomena; neither proves the solution.

Luke's Redaction of Mark

THE SITUATION AND QUESTION (MARK 8:27; LUKE 9:18)

Because Luke has placed this pericope in a different location, he provides some "glue" to put his sections together. Taking Mark's "and," Luke composes a transition that emphasizes Jesus' prayer life.[82] This is a fact not known in Mark and has evidently been discovered by Luke. Luke takes over Mark's verb, agreeing with Mark when Matthew does not; and, though Matthew agrees with Mark on "men," Luke alters this to "the crowds."

THE GENERAL RESPONSES (MARK 8:19; LUKE 9:19)

Luke changes Mark's "said, saying" (*eipan, legontes*) to "saying, said" (*apokrithentes, eipan*). Though Luke alone follows Mark in two words in this sentence ("others," "that"), Matthew and Luke both dropped "and" and changed it to "but." Mark's phrase "one of the prophets" is altered by Luke to "a certain prophet of old has arisen."[83]

PETER'S RESPONSE (MARK 8:29; LUKE 9:20)

Though Luke has taken Mark as his source here, Luke adds (1) "but he said";[84] (2) puts the confession in the accusative case—a grammatical nicety since technically "the Messiah of God" is the predicate of "I" and "I" is in the accusative case; and (3) Luke adds "of God" to "the Messiah." Furthermore, there are four "minor agreements" here: both Matthew and Luke (1) alter the accusative "them" to the dative "them,"[85] (2) begin the response of Peter with a similarly added "but,"[86] (3) change Mark's historical present ("he says") to an aorist indicative ("he said"), and (4) add "of God" to the Messiah, though Matthew's is part of a larger addition.

JESUS' RESPONSE TO PETER (MARK 8:30; LUKE 9:21)

Luke betrays no awareness of Matthew's insertion of the revelation to Peter and thus moves directly to Jesus' demand not to make him known. And here we see the phenomenon of alternating agreement again: though Matthew diverges substantially in wording, Luke does not diverge as widely. In common, Luke follows Mark in (1) the verb used,[87] (2) the object, (3) the negative, and (4) the verb "say." However, Luke reshapes the saying by altering "and" to "but," by adding the verb "ordered" (cf. 5:14; 8:29, 56), and by using "this" for Mark's "concerning him." Here Mark is Luke's source, but Luke prefers his own diction.

THE IMPLICATIONS OF THE CONFESSION (MARK 8:31–9:1; LUKE 9:22–27)

This section has every appearance of being dependent on Mark. Here we have some evidence of Luke following Mark when Matthew diverges (cf. Luke 9:22, 26–27). Overall, Luke's presentation is tidier and neater than Mark's.[88]

FOR JESUS (MARK 8:31–33; LUKE 9:22)

Luke chooses to make this verse subordinate to the previous command of silence, bringing the passion prediction into the very heart of the messianic secret; he does this by using "saying" as the introductory words to the prediction of the passion. This is a substitute for Mark's "and he began to teach them." Then Luke follows Mark for ten consecutive words[89] and apart from some "minor agreements" follows Mark for the next twelve words.

At this point Mark continues with Peter's rebuke and Jesus' counter rebuke; Luke drops this material altogether. Notice, however, that Matthew continues with this material, evincing proof for Mark as the "middle factor." A plausible motive for Luke's omission is his desire to avoid the unflattering aspects of Peter.

For the Disciples (Mark 8:34–9:1; Luke 9:23–27)

Luke, having omitted the firm interchange between Jesus and Peter, joins the passion prediction to the prediction of discipleship passion by adding "but he was saying to all" (Luke 9:23).[90] Luke betrays an awareness of Mark's larger audience and makes this explicit with "to all." In the rest of Luke 9:23 and all of Luke 9:24, we find only the following changes to Mark: (1) Luke uses the present tense of "come" (*erchesthai*) for Mark's "follow"; (2) drops Mark's intensifying preposition (Mark: *aparnesasthō*; Luke: *arnesasthō*); (3) adds "daily" (cf. 11:3; 16:19; 19:47; 22:53) to Mark's "let him take up the cross;"[91] (4) alters, along with Matthew, Mark's incorrect future to a subjunctive; (5) drops, along with Matthew, Mark's "and the Gospel"; and (6) adds "this" before the verb "will save."[92]

Luke changes Mark's grammar at Luke 9:25 by (1) putting Mark's object as the subject and turning the verb into a present middle-passive, (2) turning Mark's infinitives into participles, and (3) clarifying Mark's "forfeit his soul" with "destroying or forfeiting himself." Luke then drops Mark 8:37, apparently because of its redundancy. But it ought to be noticed that Matthew retained this element (Matt. 16:26b); Mark is shown again to be the middle factor.

Luke 9:26 is based on Mark 8:38. Apart from Luke's "correction" of Mark's conditional particle (*ean*), changing it to an indefinite (*an*), the first third of Luke 9:26 is identical to its Markan parallel. Improving Mark's grammar, Luke drops Mark's "in this adulterous and sinful generation" and Mark's unnecessary "and."[93] Luke's alteration of Mark 8:38b is peculiar: he follows Mark for the first five words and then changes Mark's "glory of his father with his holy angels" to "his glory, and the Father's glory, and the glory of the holy angel."[94]

Luke again improves the grammar of Mark 9:1 (Luke 9:27) by omitting "and he was saying to them" and adding "but." Luke's use of "truly" (*alethōs*) is a grecized form of the Hebrew "truly" (*amen*)(cf. 12:44; 21:3), evincing a later development than Mark's form. Luke's use of "here" (*autou*) is a legitimate (cf. Acts 18:19; 21:4), though unpredictable, substitute for Mark's "here" (*hōde*), and his substitute of the simpler relative "who" (*hoi*) is a slight refinement of Mark's indefinite "whoever" (*hoitines*). Luke then follows Mark until Luke drops Mark's final "having come in power."

In summary, the changes made by Luke to Mark are typical and generally characteristic of his editorial procedures elsewhere. Second, his changes are frequently in the way of improving Mark's grammar and diction. This counts in favor of the Oxford Hypothesis. Third, many of the changes are attributable to observable theological tendencies for this author—as seen, for instance, in Luke's emphasis on prayer (Luke 9:18).

Conclusion
Source criticism involves the tedious procedure of going through the Gospels word-by-word looking for potential clues for priority and sources. The conclusions to such quests are merely historical. It remains for the redaction critic and interpreter to pick up these conclusions and explore them for their significance and motivation. Some of these have been suggested throughout this paper; an exposition of these awaits the following chapters.

Bibliography

Farmer, W. R. *The Synoptic Problem*. London: Collier-Macmillan, 1964.

Guthrie, Donald. *New Testament Introduction*. Downers Grove, Ill.: InterVarsity, rev. 1989.

Kümmel, W. G. *New Testament Introduction*. Nashville, Abingdon, 1975.

Longstaff, Thomas R. W. and Page A. Thomas, eds. *The Synoptic Problem: A Bibliography 1716–1988*. Macon, Ga.: Mercer, 1988.

McKnight, Scot. *Interpreting the Synoptic Gospels*. Grand Rapids: Baker, 1988.

Stein, Robert H. *The Synoptic Problem: An Introduction*. Grand Rapids: Baker, 1987.

Stonehouse, Ned B. *Origins of the Synoptic Gospels*. Grand Rapids: Eerdmans, 1963.

Streeter, B. H. *The Four Gospels: A Study of Origins*. London: Macmillan, 1924.

Tuckett, C. M. *The Revival of the Griesbach Hypothesis*. Philadelphia: Fortress, 1983.

Notes

1. R. P. Martin, *New Testament Foundations: A Guide for Christian Students*, Vol. 1: *The Four Gospels* (Grand Rapids: Eerdmans, 1975).

2. Ibid., 139–60.

3. This chapter covers source criticism for the Synoptic Gospels only; on John's Gospel, see G. M. Burge, *Interpreting the Gospel of John* (Grand Rapids: Baker, 1992), 57–83.

4. See the overreaction of Eta Linnemann to her own heritage which, though perhaps a part of German pedagogy, hardly applies in an American or British setting. See her *Is There a Synoptic Problem? Rethinking the Literary Dependence of the First Three Gospels*, trans. R. W. Yarbrough (Grand Rapids: Baker, 1992). Linnemann argues that the Synoptics were originally independent of one another.

5. There are several good synopses available. The standard, critical synopsis of the Gospels is K. Aland, *Synopsis Quattuor Evangeliorum*, 10th ed. (Stuttgart: Deutsche Bibelgesellschaft, 1978). Because this synopsis contains no English translation, many students prefer K. Aland, *Synopsis of the Four Gospels*, 7th ed. (New York: United Bible Societies, 1984). Other good synopses include A. Huck, H. Greeven, *Synopsis of the First Three Gospels* (Tübingen: J. C. B. Mohr, 1981; available from Eerdmans); B. Orchard, *A Synopsis of the Four Gospels in Greek: Arranged According to the Two-Gospel Hypothesis* (Macon, Ga.: Mercer University Press, 1983).

English synopses include K. Aland, *Synopsis of the Four Gospels*, 7th ed. (New York: United Bible Societies, 1984); B. Orchard, *A Synopsis of the Four Gospels in Greek: Arranged According to the Two-Gospel Hypothesis* (Macon, Ga.: Mercer University Press, 1983); R. W. Funk, *New Gospel Parallels*, 2 vols. (Philadelphia: Fortress, 1985).

For a survey of the history of making synopses, cf. R. H. Stein, *The Synoptic Problem: An Introduction* (Grand Rapids: Baker, 1987), 16–25.

6. This is commonly referred to as Q, the first letter of the German word Quelle, meaning "sayings source."

7. S. McKnight, *Interpreting the Synoptic Gospels* (Grand Rapids: Baker, 1988), 34.

8. See Stein, *Synoptic Problem*.

9. A.J. Bellinzoni, Jr., *The Two-Source Hypothesis: A Critical Appraisal* (Macon, Ga.: Mercer University Press, 1985), 9 (emphasis added).

10. A good analysis of this issue, though from the angle of the Griesbach Hypothesis, is W. R. Farmer, *The Gospel of Jesus: The Pastoral Relevance of the Synoptic Problem* (Louisville: WJKP, 1994). One might consult, for a good discussion of methodology, J. P. Meier, *A Marginal Jew: Rethinking the Historical Jesus*, ABRL (New York: Doubleday, 1991), 21–195.

11. Good examples may be seen in B. D. Chilton, *Profiles of a Rabbi: Synoptic Opportunities in Reading about Jesus* (Atlanta: Scholars Press, 1989); B. Reicke, *The Roots of the Synoptic Gospels* (Philadelphia: Fortress, 1986); J. W. Wenham, *Redating Matthew, Mark & Luke: A Fresh Assault on the Synoptic Problem* (Downers Grove: IVP, 1992), deserves to be mentioned here though he does not lean as heavily as the others on oral traditions.

12. A convenient collection of the early Christian comments (in their original language) on the origins of the Gospels is found in Aland, *Synopsis Quattuor*, 531–48. For discussion, cf. esp. B. Orchard, H. Riley, *The Order of the Synoptics: Why Three Synoptic Gospels?* (Macon, Ga.: Mercer University Press, 1987), 111–226.

13. It must not be thought, however, that the early Christians were oblivious to chronological and historical problems. Tertullian, for instance, states, "It matters not that the arrangement of their narratives varies, so long as there is agreement on the essentials of the Faith" (*Against Marcion* 4.2.2; trans. Orchard, *Order*, 134). See also especially Augustine, *Harmony*.

14. The wording is that of Irenaeus (*Against Heresies* 3.1.1; trans. Orchard, *Order*, 128). It is a known fact that Peter and Paul did not "found" the Church at Rome though this statement could be taken to mean "establishing through teaching subsequent to its genesis as a church." Clement of Alexandria argues that Mark was written while Peter was alive (cf. his *Adumbrationes in epistolas canonicas*; text and trans. in Orchard, *Order*, 131; see also Eusebius, *Church History* 2.15). Irenaeus most likely suggests that Mark was not written until after the death of Peter and Paul (*Against Heresies* 3.1.1; trans. Orchard, *Order*, 128 and note "b." on p. 129).

15. A more recent defense of the Augustinian Hypothesis may be seen in B. C. Butler, *The Originality of St. Matthew: A Critique of the Two-Document Hypothesis* (Cambridge: Cambridge University Press, 1951).

16. See J. W. Wenham, *Redating Matthew, Mark & Luke*. Wenham is attracted to some form of written dependence because of the issues of genre and order of pericopes.

17. "Ur" means "original" in German. This "Ur-Gospel," it was argued, is not extant.

18. The first essay, published in Jena in 1783, was *Inquiritur in fontes, unde Evangelistae suas de resurrectione Domini narrationes hauserint*, Jena, 1783 [*An Inquiry into the Sources from which the Evangelists drew their Narratives of the Resurrection of the Lord*]; the second, more substantial essay, published also in Jena in 1789 and enlarged in 1794 was *Commentatio, qua Marci Evangelium totum e Matthaei et Lucae*

commentariis decerptum esse monstratur, Jena, 1789, 1794 [*The Theory in which it is proven that the whole of Mark's Gospel is derived from the works of Matthew and Luke*]. The Latin text and translation of the second work can be found in B. Reicke and B. Orchard, "Commentatio" and "Demonstration," *J. J. Griesbach: Synoptic and Text-critical Studies 1776–1976*, SNTSMS 34; ed. B. Orchard, T. R. W. Longstaff (Cambridge: Cambridge University Press, 1978), 68–102, 103–35.

19. A few useful studies about the history of the Griesbach hypothesis are G. Delling, "Johann Jakob Griesbach: His Life, Work and Times," and B. Reicke, "Griesbach's Answer to the Synoptic Question," both in *J. J. Griesbach: Synoptic and Text-Critical Studies 1776–1976*, SNTSMS 34; ed. B. Orchard, T. R. W. Longstaff (Cambridge: Cambridge University Press, 1978), 5–21 and 50–67; C. M. Tuckett, "The Griesbach Hypothesis in the 19th Century," *JSNT* 3 (1979): 29–60; Farmer, *Synoptic Problem*, 1–198; H. H. Stoldt, *History and Criticism of the Marcan Hypothesis* (Macon, Ga.: Mercer University Press, 1980); C. M. Tuckett, *The Revival of the Griesbach Hypothesis: An Analysis and Appraisal* (SNTSMS 44; Cambridge: Cambridge University Press, 1983).

20. For this reason I choose to call this theory the "Oxford Hypothesis." All historians recognize that the roots of the movement are in Germany and not England; however, no one will contest the fact that the view that became dominant was most clearly articulated by B. H. Streeter.

21. For example, one can consult the standard work of B. F. Westcott, *An Introduction to the Study of the Gospels*, 8th ed. (London: Macmillan, 1895), 165–212, esp. 192–212, where Westcott puts each current theory to the test. It is clear that Sanday himself was dependent on the German scholar H. J. Holtzmann; cf. e.g., Farmer, *Synoptic Problem*, 51–63. (I must add that Farmer is unduly hard on Sanday and explores too many unknowable psychological motivations on Sanday's part—motivations which are all but impossible for historians to discern.)

22. See especially his *Horae Synopticae: Contributions to the Study of the Synoptic Problem*, 2d ed.; reprinted. (Grand Rapids: Baker, 1968 [=1909]). On Hawkins, see the statements of Neill, *Interpretation*, 126–27.

23. Famous for his ICC volume on Matthew, a commentary singularly concerned with source-critical matters; cf. *A Critical and Exegetical Commentary on the Gospel according to S. Matthew*, 3d ed. Edinburgh: T & T Clark, 1912).

24. Edited by W. Sanday (Oxford: Clarendon, 1911).

25. Streeter, *Four Gospels*. For further details about Streeter, cf. Neill, *Interpretation*, 131–36.

26. Streeter's famous chart can be found on p. 150.

27. Streeter was hit hardest for suggesting order and date for these hypothetical sources. In short, he "knew too much" because he inferred more than the evidence allowed.

28. See Martin, *NT Foundations* 1:152–56 for a sympathetic discussion.

29. It is a criticism of both B. Reicke, *Roots*, and E. Linnemann, *Problem?* that they too narrowly describe the Two-Source Hypothesis (Oxford Hypothesis) from its German roots.

30. A. M. Farrer, "On Dispensing with Q," *Studies in the Gospels: Essays in Memory of R. H. Lightfoot*, ed. D. E. Nineham (Oxford: Basil Blackwell, 1955), 55–88.

31. See esp. his *Luke—A New Paradigm* (JSNTSS 20; Sheffield: Sheffield Academic Press, 1989).

32. A survey of these conferences, with listings of major papers and participants, can be found in W. R. Farmer, ed., *New Synoptic Studies: The Cambridge Conference and Beyond* (Macon, Ga.: Mercer University Press, 1983), vii–xxiii.

33. SNTSMS 44 (Cambridge: Cambridge University Press, 1983).

34. A massive bibliographical undertaking can be found under the able direction of the bibliophile, D. M. Scholer, which is published annually in the Society of Biblical Literature Seminar Papers. See H. E. Tödt, *The Son of Man in the Synoptic Tradition*, trans. D. M. Barton (London: SCM, 1965); D. Lührmann, *Die Redaktion der Logienquelle*, WMANT 33 (Neukirchen-Vluyn: Neukirchener, 1969).

35. A. Polag, *Fragmenta Q: Textheft zur Logienquelle*, 2d. ed. (Neukirchen-Vluyn: Neukirchener Verlag, 1982). In spite of the German title, this book can be used easily by those who cannot read German but who can read Greek. There is an English introduction and key.

36. J. S. Kloppenborg, *Q Parallels: Synopsis, Critical Notes, & Concordance*, Foundations & Facets, Reference Series (Sonoma, Calif.: Polebridge, 1988). This is the most complete Q text available and has a number of useful features: (1) the Greek and English texts for the parallels in question are given with the Greek words in common in boldface; (2) other parallels are provided with English translations; (3) a brief discussion of modern scholarship on the Q text is given; (4) a Greek concordance is found; and (5) a useful bibliography is added.

37. See esp. C. Tuckett, *Q and the History of Early Christianity: Studies on Q* (Peabody, Mass.: Hendrickson, 1996), 41–82.

38. J. Kloppenborg, *The Formation of Q: Trajectories in Ancient Wisdom Collections*, SAC (Philadelphia: Fortress, 1987); D. C. Allison Jr., *The Jesus Tradition in Q* (Harrisburg, Pa.: Trinity Press International, 1997).

39. See his *Roots*.

40. Streeter, *Four Gospels*, 151 (cf. 161–62). The quotation is from Streeter's introductory précis; pp. 161–62 further expound this point, and they do not show any sign of being aware of the circular nature of his argument.

41. This is usually referred to as the Lachmann fallacy. A good critique of the Lachmann fallacy was made originally by Butler, *Originality*, 62–71.

42. It is probably impossible to state the phenomenon of order in a way that is completely neutral. The most neutral statement I have seen is offered by Tuckett: "Whenever Matthew's order and Mark's order differ, Mark's order and Luke's order agree; and whenever Luke's order and Mark's order differ, Matthew's order and Mark's order agree." See "Arguments from Order," 198.

43. The odd thing about the Griesbach proponents is that they, too, have committed a kind of Lachmann fallacy. Frequently, too frequently in fact, Griesbach theorists have concluded that the Griesbach Hypothesis is the only credible explanation of the phenomenon of order. But this is no more the case for the Griesbach Hypothesis than for the Oxford Hypothesis since either hypothesis can readily explain the phenomenon of order. See e.g., W. R. Farmer, "Modern Developments of Griesbach's Hypothesis," *NTS* 23 (1977), 275–95, esp. 293-5. "Farmer's fallacy" has been ably exposed by Tuckett, "Arguments from Order," 205–06. The same critique can be applied to H. Riley, *Order*, 3–18. The fallacy, simply stated, is to argue that a given hypothesis is the only hypothesis that can explain the phenomenon of order.

However, it needs to be observed that the phenomenon of order may have as its best explanation the Griesbach point of view. It is a notable feature that, as they put it, Mark "zigzags" in that he moves back and forth from Matthew to Luke, never retracing his steps. And, as Riley has stated of the Oxford Hypothesis, "at every point where Matthew ceases to follow Mark's order, whether for a short or longer period, Luke continues it; and wherever Luke ceases to follow Mark's order, Matthew in his turn continues it. There is surely an inescapable conclusion to be drawn from this. If Matthew and Luke were dependent on Mark for the order of events, they must have agreed together that they would do this. Without constant collaboration, the result would be quite impossible." From H. Riley, B. Orchard, *Order*, 7 (italics added). What Riley states is important and, I think, probably favors the Griesbach Hypothesis. However, as Tuckett has pointed out, the frequency of this phenomenon is "statistically insignificant" and ought not to be given the importance that it is by Griesbach proponents; cf. Tuckett, "Arguments from Order," 202–05.

44. B. Orchard, *Order*, 111–221.

45. See this kind of procedure in W. G. Kümmel, *Introduction to the New Testament*, rev. ed. (Nashville: Abingdon, 1975), 53–55.

46. In a recent survey of the literature in preparation for this essay, I was amazed at the frequency of this self-congratulation. I will restrict the notations to four. W. R. Farmer, "Introduction," *New Synoptic Studies: The Cambridge Conference and Beyond*, ed. W.R. Farmer (Macon, Ga.: Mercer University Press, 1983), xx (here he cites statistics of those invited, but one might ask, "Was it a fair sampling?"); xxi ("The old consensus about Markan Priority has gone. We can now recognize that we have entered a new era in Synoptic studies."); xxviii (here he seems to assume that active writing on the Synoptic Problem is somehow a measure of statistics); in the same volume, the essay by O. L. Cope is entitled "The Argument Revolves: The Pivotal Evidence for Markan Priority Is Reversing Itself," 143–59; Dungan, "Abridgement," 87 (speaks of the "death-knell").

The most grievous statement of this sort is by Farmer, "Certain Results," 79–80, who states, "I take the situation to be this. Since Austin Farrer wrote 'On Dispensing with Q', those who have followed his counsel to read Luke through carefully, to test whether there was any need to appeal to 'Q', have uniformly, so far as I know, come to the same conclusion: there is no need for 'Q'." Now this statement is inaccurate and a tendentious statement of the worst kind.

47. For example, observe the explanatory nature of the proof given, or a simple assumption, and then the conclusion in favor of the Griesbach Hypothesis in the following sampling: it begins with J. J. Griesbach, "Demonstration," 108–13, 123–33 (observe, however, his apparent awareness of this kind of an assumption as a problem on p. 120), trans. Orchard, "Demonstration"; H. Riley, B. Orchard, *Order*, 3–99, 229–74.

48. "Certain Results," 91. Italics added.

49. I do not wish to deny the importance of overall coherence for any theory being proposed. What I do want to point out is that explanations are not necessarily proofs. A similar, but consciously aware, procedure is found in Tuckett, "Arguments from Order," 206–13; outlined originally in idem, *Revival*, 9–15, and used throughout his book.

50. Farmer, *Synoptic Problem*, 79; cf. also 83, 217, 264.

51. Tuckett, *Revival*, 80; italics added; see pp. 78–85 for the complete discussion.

52. Another careful demonstration of the same kind of phenomenon can be found in F. G. Downing, "Towards the Rehabilitation of Q," *NTS* 11 (1964–65): 169–81; reprinted in Bellinzoni, *Two-Source Hypothesis*, 269–85.

53. F. G. Downing, "Compositional Conventions and the Synoptic Problem," *JBL* 107 (1988): 69–85; "Redaction Criticism: Josephus' Antiquities and the Synoptic Problem, I, II," *JSNT* 8 (1980): 46–65; 9 (1980): 29–48.

54. The most careful linguistic work to date from a Griesbach Hypothesis viewpoint is that of Farmer's student, D. Peabody, *Mark as Composer*, NGS 1 (Macon, Ga.: Mercer University Press, 1988). But Peabody's work is surprisingly disappointing in conclusions regarding the Synoptic Problem. I know of no thorough response to the kind of linguistic phenomena pointed out by Hawkins, *Horae Synopticae*, 114–53. Consequently, the language factor remains the Achilles' heel for the Griesbach Hypothesis.

55. This is the classical argument put forward in convincing fashion by J. Fitzmyer. Cf. his "The Priority of Mark and the 'Q' Source in Luke," *Jesus and Man's Hope* (Pittsburgh: Pittsburgh Theological Seminary, 1970), 1.131–70, esp. 134–47.

56. See D. R. Catchpole, *The Quest for Q* (Edinburgh: T & T Clark, 1993), 4. This has been thoroughly researched by a student of mine, Matthew C. Williams, in his dissertation, *Is Matthew a Scribe? An Examination of the Text-Critical Argument for the Synoptic Problem* (Ph.D. dissertation, Trinity Evangelical Divinity School, 1996).

57. See his *Is Matthew a Scribe?*

58. The best listing of these can be found in Hawkins, *Horae Synopticae*, 131–38, and deals with odd Markan elements that are not found in the parallels in Matthew and Luke; these include unusual words and constructions (33 examples), incomplete sentences (13 examples), and omission of conjunctions (21 examples).

59. Streeter, *Four Gospels*, 164. The next sentence, from the same page, is perhaps more frequently quoted: "But since there are, from time to time, ingenious persons who rush into print with theories to the contrary, I can only suppose, either that they have not been at pains to do this, or else that—like some of the highly cultivated people who think Bacon wrote Shakespeare, or that the British are the Lost Ten Tribes—they have eccentric views of what constitutes evidence." In spite of the rhetoric one hears here, it cannot be denied that the grammatical argument is the most important argument for the Oxford Hypothesis. And it remains a fact that the Griesbach proponents simply have not dealt with the phenomenon squarely.

In 1992, at the SBL Annual Meeting in San Francisco, David Alan Black (an editor of this book) and I engaged in a public discussion about this kind of argument. David's piece was published later as "Discourse Analysis, Synoptic Criticism, and Markan Grammar: Some Methodological Considerations," in *Linguistics and New Testament Interpretation: Essays on Discourse Analysis*, ed. D. A. Black, K. Barnwell, S. Levinsohn; (Nashville: Broadman Press, 1992), 90–98. In brief, my argument against David's paper is that whereas I take his point that the argument I make in this paper about Mark's grammar being "corrected" by Matthew or Luke do not point to the impossibility of Mark's grammar making sense, I would argue that such features, when run through the mill of text-critical arguments, more likely are primitive when compared to Matthew's and Luke's grammar. The issue is one of which is more likely to be primitive if one asks the question that a textual critic would ask. For further analysis, I point the reader back again to M. C. Williams, *Is Matthew a Scribe?*

60. A good listing can be found in Hawkins, *Horae Synopticae*, 117–25.

61. This has been a major criterion for a solution to the Synoptic Problem for C. M. Tuckett; cf. his *Revival*, 9–15; "Arguments from Order," 205–13. See also J. M. Robinson, "On the Gattung of Mark (and John)," *Jesus and Man's Hope* (Pittsburgh: Pittsburgh Theological Seminary, 1970), 99–129, esp. 101–02: "In a generation in which

the Synoptic problem has been largely dominant, the success of Redaktionsgeschichte ["redaction criticism"] in clarifying the theologies of Matthew and Luke on the assumption of dependence on Mark is perhaps the most important new argument for Marcan priority, just as perhaps the main ingredient lacking in William R. Farmer's argument for Marcan dependence on the other written Gospels is a convincing Redaktionsgeschichte of Mark based on that assumption." The same point is made by G. N. Stanton in his masterful survey of Matthean research; cf. "The Origin and Purpose of Matthew's Gospel: Matthean Scholarship from 1945 to 1980," *Austieg und Niedergang der Römischen Welt*, 2.25.3; ed. H. Temporini, W. Haase (Berlin: de Gruyter, 1984), 1899–1903.

62. G. N. Stanton, "Origin," 1902.

63. Cf. e.g., B. Przybylski, *Righteousness in Matthew and His World of Thought*, SNTSMS 41 (Cambridge: Cambridge University Press, 1980); R. Mohrlang, *Matthew and Paul: A Comparison of Ethical Perspectives*, SNTSMS 48 (Cambridge: Cambridge University Press, 1984), 7–26; S. McKnight, "Justice, Righteousness," *DJG* 411–16.

64. A useful survey may be found in J. S. Kloppenborg, *The Formation of Q: Trajectories in Ancient Wisdom Collections*, SA&C (Philadelphia: Fortress, 1987), 64–80.

65. See again M. Goulder, *Luke—A New Paradigm*; see also C. Tuckett, *Q and the History of Early Christianity*, 16–31, for an incisive critique of Goulder.

66. A lucid defense of the Q hypothesis by an evangelical scholar can be seen in Stein, *Synoptic Problem*, 89–112. The classic defenses can be found in J. C. Hawkins, "Probabilities as to the So-called Double Tradition of St. Matthew and St. Luke," *Studies in the Synoptic Problem by Members of the University of Oxford*, ed. W. Sanday (Oxford: Clarendon, 1911), 95–138; Streeter, *Four Gospels*, 182–86. A useful commentary on Q is T. W. Manson, *The Sayings of Jesus* (London: SCM, 1949 [=1937]).

67. See here D. R. Catchpole, *The Quest for Q*; see also C. Tuckett, *Q and the History of Early Christianity*, 1–39.

68. B. H. Streeter, *Four Gospels*, 183.

69. A doublet by definition is a single saying of Jesus that was then reported by Mark and also found its way into the "Q material." The Evangelists Matthew and Luke then picked the saying both from Mark and Q. Calling something a doublet does not necessarily mean that Jesus did not repeat the saying more than once. Calling something a doublet, however, speaks of the Evangelists drawing the same saying of Jesus from two different sources.

70. Hawkins, *Horae Synopticae*, 80–107.

71. From Martin, *New Testament Foundations*, 1.145.

72. Evangelicals often appeal here to Jesus' repeating his own sayings. This is an altogether natural response and too often neglected by critical scholars. However, a fundamental question here is not, "Did Jesus repeat himself?" for the answer is, "Of course he did." Rather, the question here is, "Are the Evangelists obtaining their information from Mark or Q?" In other words, Jesus may have repeated himself, but the saying remains a doublet because Matthew or Luke have taken a saying from Mark and Q, and therefore that one-time saying has appeared twice.

73. Critics of the Griesbach and Augustinian hypotheses continue to ask this question. Cf. e.g., Fitzmyer, "Priority," 149.

74. Tuckett, *Revival*, 61–75. Streeter's solution to these was "to divide and conquer." What Streeter did was isolate the various kinds of "minor agreements" and examine

them separately. By doing this he avoided the serious accumulation of agreements in a single location. Cf. Streeter, *Four Gospels*, 293–331, and the telling criticisms of Farmer, *Synoptic Problem*, 118–52 (though Farmer's tone is not productive).

75. Ibid., 67.

76. Ibid., 75.

77. Recently, E. P. Meadors has taken Q scholarship to task for assuming too great a difference between the theology of Mark and "Q"; see his *Jesus the Messianic Herald of Salvation* (Peabody, Mass.: Hendrickson, 1997).

78. A brief survey of Q studies can be found in Kloppenborg, *Formation of Q*, 8–40. What will strike most readers is that some of the studies on Q are solid pieces whereas others are too speculative to be probable.

79. Since Streeter there have been several major treatments of the original order of Q. These have been surveyed by Kloppenborg, *Formation of Q*, 64–80.

80. Students will need to have a synopsis to follow the next section.

81. This omission was discussed intensively in the early Oxford school. Cf. esp. J. C. Hawkins, "Three Limitations to St. Luke's Use of St. Mark's Gospel," *Studies in the Synoptic Problem by Members of the University of Oxford*, ed. W. Sanday (Oxford: Clarendon, 1911), 27–94, who argued that Luke intentionally omitted this section. On the other hand, Streeter, *Four Gospels*, 172–79, tentatively suggested that Luke's copy of Mark was mutilated at this point. Others have suggested an Ur-Gospel theory. Most Oxford proponents today seem to favor deliberate omission; cf. e.g., Fitzmyer, *Luke*, 1: 770–71.

82. The style of the verse is Lukan. Cf. I. H. Marshall, *The Gospel of Luke: A Commentary on the Greek Text*, NIGTC (Grand Rapids: Eerdmans, 1978), 366; J. A. Fitzmyer, *The Gospel according to Luke*, 2 vols. AB 28, 28A (Garden City, N.Y.: Doubleday, 1981, 1985), 1:773–74.

83. The language here is reminiscent of Luke 9:7–8 and shows Lukan style.

84. This is a substitute for Mark's wordy "and he was asking them," and the change of verbs may be to avoid repetition (cf. Mark 8:27 with Luke 9:18).

85. The case, of course, is dictated by the verb *used*. Both have used "say" though Matthew uses the historical present and Luke the aorist indicative.

86. Mark's answer is asyndeton; this may give sufficient reason for both Matthew and Luke to insert a conjunction.

87. However, Luke uses a participle; Mark uses a finite verb.

88. See Fitzmyer, *Luke*, 1.783–84.

89. Six of these words are singular agreements between Mark and Luke and are not the words of Matthew.

90. Though Luke alters Mark's aorist to an imperfect, Matthew has the aorist, confirming again Mark's middle status.

91. That Luke is concerned with a daily denial is also seen in the present tense "to come" at the beginning of 9:23.

92. Such a word is not strictly necessary since it creates a "suspended subject clause" but such a grammatical feature is common to NT writers.

93. Mark has, "For whoever is ashamed of me" and then, "and the Son of Man will be ashamed of him," leaving the first clause grammatically incomplete. Luke improves this by placing "this person" at the head of the second clause, even though Luke here leaves a very typical suspended subject clause. Luke's grammar, though not stylistically "pure," is better than Mark's, suggesting that Mark is prior. Furthermore, this is the

second case of a "doublet" in this section; cf. Mark 8:38 and Luke 9:26 with Matthew 10:33 and Luke 12:9. Cf. above at Matthew's use of Mark 8:35.

94. On the Oxford Hypothesis, this is difficult to explain since Luke, in effect, tones down the christology of Mark 8:38 by giving the angels a glory separate from the Son of Man's. On the other hand, only in Luke does the Son of Man have a separate glory. Further, the Griesbach Hypothesis has just as much trouble with Luke's redaction since he has performed a similar operation on Matthew's saying, a saying that is quite similar to Mark's in the wording that concerns us here.

Chapter 5

Form Criticism

Darrell L. Bock
Dallas Theological Seminary

When I was a child, there was a special moment when the teacher said, "Once upon a time." I knew it was time to hear a fairy tale. I also could count on the last words bringing joy and being something like, "And they lived happily ever after." Such is the nature of form. In a set format, stories or events are told in certain ways, with certain stylistic or programmatic indicators that let the reader know the type of account that is present.

The five-minute newscast seeks a succinct presentation of the news, while a news commentary expresses opinion more overtly than a news report does. Both forms do have perspective (which is why news can be a subtle form of commentary!), but when commentary is explicitly present, one automatically knows the author is speaking his or her mind. News presentations will take on a certain form in order to get in as many details in as short a space as possible. Commentary tends to focus more on cause, effect, and significance. Such differences are differences of form and can help orient the audience to the content of what is presented.

In New Testament studies, especially in the Gospels, one often hears about issues of form. Pericopes appear with certain titles like "pronouncement story," "miracle story," "saying," "tale," "legend," "parable," "proverb," or "controversy account." The different titles indicate different concerns in the account. These are designed to be descriptive titles that help the interpreter understand the account, its structure, and its emphasis. But beyond description, form criticism has often moved into determining the historicity of an account by an appeal to "form" and *Sitz im Leben* (setting in life). What guides such analyses? Can one move from form to setting? Is form criticism helpful to New Testament study? What presuppositions produced it and are they valid? These are some of the questions this essay seeks to probe.

We shall pursue our topic in several parts. First, I will define the task of form criticism and briefly overview its axioms and history, including major categories form criticism has developed. Then I will evaluate these categories. Within this section evaluation will be made of the various groupings. Finally, I will summarize the benefits and limitations of the discipline with an illustration.

Definition, Axioms, and History of Form Criticism

DEFINITION

In 1919, form criticism burst on the New Testament scene as the rising star of New Testament analysis.[1] It offered hope that this method would aid the interpreter to get at the thrust of what a passage's message was, especially since source criticism had, in the judgment of most, established the order and nature of written sources.[2] Form criticism also sought to get behind the written sources by studying the form of the individual units of the Gospels; it intended to be both descriptive and historical. Descriptively, it sought to specify the characteristics of existing forms in the New Testament and then attempted to investigate how those forms emerged in the history of the oral transmission of the church. The fundamental presupposition of the discipline is that stories about Jesus circulated in individual oral units before being fixed in written form. These forms had a certain structure or consisted of certain motif elements that made the story memorable. Thus, whether a passage was an account about a key pronouncement of Jesus or a miracle, each kind of story had a likely structure.

The accounts about Jesus were passed on as "popular" literature. The Gospel writers served more as collectors, to use Dibelius' metaphor, than as "authors." Certain motives drove the accounts to be fixed in form, and those motives rested primarily in the edification and instruction of the early church community. It was these later communities that gave the stories their final shaping before they were fixed in the Gospels. In fact, when one thinks of the tradition, one should not think of the activity of an individual mind but of the activity of a community as the tradition is passed along.

The individual accounts in the Gospels are but the last step in this developing tradition. Yet one can understand both the text and the history of the tradition better by analyzing what is present in the text.[3] The emphasis on community formation over historical concerns about Jesus is one of the weaknesses of form criticism. It is likely that what is remembered about Jesus is chosen in part because it spoke to the needs of the community, but that does not rule out the corresponding likelihood that the text was recalled because Jesus did teach to those concerns or an event in his life addressed it. The choice between community need and historical concern is a false one.

How then does one define *form criticism*? Bultmann, in analyzing his own work and that of Dibelius, explains it this way:

> I am entirely in agreement with M. Dibelius when he maintains that form-criticism is not simply an exercise in aesthetics nor yet simply a process of description and classification, that is to say, it does not consist of identifying the individual units of the tradition according to their aesthetic or other characteristics and placing them in their various categories. It is much rather "to discover the origin and the history of the particular units and thereby to throw some light on the history of the tradition before it took literary form." The proper understanding of form-criticism rests upon the judgment that the literature in which the life of a given community, even the primitive Christian community, has taken shape, springs out of the quite definite conditions and wants of life from which grows up a quite definite style and quite specific forms and categories. Thus every literary category has its "life situation" (*Sitz im Leben,* Gunkel), whether it be worship in its different forms, or work, or hunting, or war. The *Sitz im Leben* is not, however, an individual historical event, but a typical situation or occupation in the life of a community.[4]

The citation shows clearly that Bultmann is not interested merely in descriptive classification. Rather, he wishes to use this classification of form as a means to determine what general social setting in the church allowed for the preservation and perpetuation of a given account. In short, form criticism, as originally formulated, is both descriptive and historical in its concerns. Form deals with description, and *Sitz im Leben* deals with history. In addition, the tracing of the form's history is really an aspect of tradition criticism. So in its comprehensive sense form criticism deals with literary questions (the forms), historical questions (the community setting), and theological development questions (the tradition history of the form's development).

A simple definition comes from F. F. Bruce: "Form criticism (Ger. *Formgeschichte,* 'form history') represents an endeavor to determine the oral prehistory of written documents or sources, and to classify the material according to the various 'forms or categories or narrative, discourse, and so forth.'"[5] Now when practitioners speak of the setting in the church, they usually are thinking of forms that are used in preaching or have settings in the liturgy, instruction, or ordinances of the church. Often a form is said to have value because it contributed to exhortation to the body, to the defense of the gospel, to instruction for baptism, or other such corporate concerns. Early form criticism tended to deny that the individual units were preserved simply because people were interested in knowing about the historical Jesus, though it is not clear why one should insist that such interest did not exist in the early church.

AXIOMS

The basic axioms of form criticism can be briefly stated, since the definitions have already raised many of the basic points.[6]

1. The Gospels are "popular" or "folk" literature. They are not primarily the work of one person or one mind. They belong to the community. The stories passed through the communities, where their shape was determined by the shared needs of the group. The accounts moved from being fluid in wording and detail to fixed in this process. Many form critics argued that many texts received their details and teaching from the church, which put teaching into Jesus' mouth. It was this dimension of form criticism that made many conservatives nervous about it.

2. The material circulated for at least twenty years in oral form and in individual units. The only exception to this rule was the Passion material, which became a large unit fairly quickly because of apologetic needs. Often a citation like that of Papias, as recorded in Eusebius's *Ecclesiastical History* 3.39.4, is noted to show the ancient's love of the oral word. Papias said, "I supposed that things out of books did not profit me so much as the utterances of a voice which lives and abides."

3. Units were used as the occasion required, and it was their usefulness that caused them to be retained. Occasionally stories were grouped together because they shared the same form or terms, but these instances were few.

4. As the materials were used in the same types of settings, they took on a particular form according to the function they had in the community, which is why the form can help surface the account's concern and thus be useful for analysis. Here is where *Sitz im Leben* enters the discussion. One could even speak of various settings such as the *Sitz im Leben Jesu* (a setting in Jesus' life) or the *Sitz im Leben Kirche* (a setting in the church). Early form criticism tended to look first for the setting in the church, as the various axioms show. The tradition is the servant of the church's needs according to these earliest expressions of the approach.

5. One can assume that the Gospels, as we now have them, had the following sources: Mark, Q, special Matthean material (M), and special Lukan material (L). In other words, the results of source criticism in terms of Marcan priority were and are a given for most form critics. However, it is not a requirement that form criticism accept a given source view. One can consider form, even if one thinks the order of the Gospels began with Matthew or views them as independent. The one difference will be that those who see the Gospels as independent will not speak about how the tradition was consciously changed. Nonetheless, the differences between the parallels remain and thus should be the subject of study.

6. Alongside form criticism came criteria by which to look for secondary elements, that is, elements the church added later to the Jesus accounts. These criteria of authenticity are really a part of tradition historical analysis, but they indicate how far-reaching the task of form criticism was.[7] Three criteria were key: (1) The *criterion of dissimilarity* argues that a saying was authentic when it could not emerge either from Judaism or from the early church. Skeptics of this criterion rightly said that this gave us only the distinctive or

minimalist Jesus. It also was a "guilty until innocent" approach. (2) The *criterion of multiple attestation* said that those sayings that appear in a variety of distinct sources or forms are more likely to be authentic. The argument here is that such distribution is evidence of an early and widespread tradition. This category can be helpful, though it tends to suggest wrongly that an individual witness is not enough. (3) The *criterion of coherence is* the most subjective category. It argues that the other sayings that fit together or cohere with already demonstrated authentic sayings are most likely to be authentic as well.

In addition, form critics tended to assume that accounts expanded as they got older. Dibelius's treatment of the forms tended to suggest that forms became more complicated. So additions to the parallels were looked on with historical skepticism. It is precisely this type of particular stylistic criterion that Sanders examined and found wanting.[8] In other words, some of the so-called "rules" of the early form critics did not work when considered by the evidence of the text.

HISTORY

The foundations of form criticism lie in biblical studies as it emerged in the eighteenth and nineteenth centuries. Johann Gottfried Herder (1796) studied folk poetry and applied what he learned about such popular literature to biblical studies. His work argued for viewing the texts as popularly developed literature that passed through a community.[9] Franz Overbeck (1899) distinguished biblical literature from patristic texts and raised the issue of forms, while Hermann Jordan (1911) attempted to come up with a list of the various forms within the history of the canonical and postcanonical ancient churches.[10] Jordan's list included narratives and historical books such as the Gospels and Acts, letters, apocalypses, speeches and sermons, apologies, dialogues, controversy writings, tracts, church ordinances, rules of faith, hermeneutical literature such as commentaries, and translations.[11]

Finally Hermann Gunkel, especially influenced by Herder, applied his work to the investigation of the Old Testament, especially Genesis and the Psalms, and also emphasized the *Sitz im Leben*.[12] What all of this ignored was a careful consideration of the nearest historical parallel of the handling of tradition, namely, how the rabbinic tradition worked as well as how the biblical tradition was passed on within Judaism. Later form critics would supply this badly needed corrective (Gerhardsson, Ellis, 1975, 1999).[13] It would temper the results of earlier form critics by showing the tradition was not as fluid as the early critics argued.

Clearly by the time Dibelius and Schmidt wrote, the study of form was on the rise. Those responsible for developing form criticism simply applied the ongoing discussion to their disciplines. The attention form criticism received was partially because the originators were so thorough in treating all the text. For example, Bultmann's study attempted to classify and discuss every Synoptic Gospel text. The new tool created great interest.

Eventually the high interest waned. The work of Bultmann was so thorough it implied that little else was left to do. On the other hand, some frustration set in with going behind the text. Most importantly, very early on, some key questions were raised about the fundamental suppositions of the method.

Vincent Taylor expressed some important reservations about the historical results of form criticism, while analyzing its presuppositions.[14] He particularly criticized form criticism's ignoring of the role of eyewitnesses and refusing to see some basic structure in the various units of the tradition. Speaking of form criticism and eyewitnesses, he says, "It is on the question of eyewitnesses that form criticism presents a very vulnerable front. If the Form-Critics are right, the disciples must have been translated to heaven immediately after the Resurrection. As Bultmann sees it, the primitive community exists *in vacuo,* cut off from its founders by the walls of inexplicable ignorance. Like Robinson Crusoe it must do the best it can."[15] Later he says, "All this is absurd."

Taylor represented a more conservative approach to form criticism. He did not doubt the existence of oral tradition or the influence of the community on the tradition. He simply did not see the tradition as floating out at sea without any anchor in the original setting. Taylor did not see a need to divorce community concerns from the historical Jesus. He contended for a better definition of the method early in the history of the approach.

The rise of redaction criticism in the 1950s brought the Gospel writers again to the fore as theologians and editors who helped shape and present Gospel material.[16] The image of the evangelists as collectors was forever lost as examination of the text revealed the Synoptic writers had presented their material with their own emphases about Jesus as reflected in what they chose to discuss and how they expressed those choices. One can think here of the different order in the temptation accounts, which shows either Matthew or Luke has presented the material in a distinct order to make a point (Matt. 4:1–11—kingdom temptation last; Luke 4:1–13—temple temptation last).

In addition, the rules of oral tradition were evaluated and found wanting, while the Jewish parallels for handling oral tradition showed that tradition could be passed on and remain relatively fixed.[17] The idea that the tradition was extremely fluid came under severe challenge. So serious is the damage that some today regard as questionable many of the essential elements of the historical quest of the old form criticism in which community rules over concerns about Jesus.[18]

But efforts to focus on the more literary aspects of the discipline have not died. Klaus Berger has tried to classify most of the New Testament through comparison with other ancient writings and has been the most prolific writer in attempting to speak of the "new" form criticism.[19] His emphasis has still tended to fall on examples from Greek literature, whereas a setting within Judaism needs more attention given the Jewish roots of the Gospel writers. So the scope of the value of form criticism is still to be decided, though aspects of the old form criticism are probably a relic of the past, especially those elements that represent a severe challenge to historicity.[20]

The Basic Forms Described

We begin with the five basic categories that originally emerged from the discipline. Then we will briefly consider the new form criticism and its approach to classification. The value of identifying the basic forms is that they help one see the structure of a passage and thus trace its argument.

PARADIGMS / APOPHTHEGMS / PRONOUNCEMENT STORIES

These accounts have five characteristics according to Dibelius.[21] First, they are stories that are rounded off. By this Dibelius means that the high point comes toward the end, either through a word or deed of Jesus. This is the reason Taylor preferred the name "pronouncement story," which certainly is a better title.[22] The key to the account is the final pronouncement in the unit. Bultmann had a different name for these accounts and divided them into "controversy" dialogues when opponents were present, "scholastic dialogues" when disciples were present, and biographical apophthegms where there is much more narrative detail present and where there is simply an event in which Jesus participates.[23] It should be noted that Bultmann regarded the controversy and scholastic texts as similar in that they treated some issue which is in dispute and which the pronouncement addresses.

The second characteristic is that the narrative is brief and simple. There is little extra detail. Third, there is religious coloring in the account. This means that expressions describing actions have a religious tone to them, like "he preached to them" (Mark 2:2) or "he was grieved at their hardness of heart" (Mark 3:5). Fourth, the goal of the narrative is the didactic point that concludes or summarizes the account. It is the final word from Jesus that counts. In short, it is a story with a punch line. Fifth, the account is useful for preaching purposes. Here one crosses from descriptive into historical categories. This is why the accounts are preserved. For Bultmann, the origin of these accounts is in the polemic atmosphere of the church (controversy dialogues) or in the desire simply to teach (scholastic dialogues) or for preaching (biographical apophthegms). The problem with the final point is that many of the disputes recorded were remembered because the dispute dated back to Jesus' life or involve issues that were not in dispute in the later church, showing that they were preserved for historical memory.

Some illustrations of such accounts are Controversy Dialogue: Mark 2:23–28 *(Plucking Corn on the Sabbath);* Scholastic Dialogue: Mark 10:17–31 *(The Rich Young Man);* and Biographical Apophthegm: Luke

10:38–42 *(Mary and Martha)*. Each account ends with a punch line and drives toward it. In some cases, the punch line consists of several arguments placed together as in the "plucking grain" incident. In other words, the final pronouncement need not be just one remark. In the controversy, inherent conflict is resolved in Jesus' remark. The tension in the scholastic dialogue is more a probe into what is so or how one should view something. The biographical account simply tells something that happened to Jesus that elicited a key saying. It is easy to see how the category, though broad, is a helpful description of the kind of account and its emphasis.

It can be extremely helpful to identify accounts by their subform. In Mark 2:1–3:6, a sequence of five controversies in a row end in the Jewish leadership's reaction "to destroy" Jesus (Mark 3:6; Luke also keeps this structure, while the same controversies are more spread out in Matthew). The recognition of the form helps one see the running sequence of disputes covering topics as diverse as forgiveness of sins, association, fasting, work on the Sabbath, and healing on the Sabbath. Jesus' differences with the leaders on issues of law and piety were a major reason the leadership rejected him. Mark has succinctly grouped these controversies in one place to present the roots of these differences.

TALES / NOVELLEN / MIRACLE STORIES

These accounts are slightly more complex. The accounts are complete units in themselves and also have clear characteristics.[24] Bultmann again has subgroupings like exorcisms, healings, raisings from the dead, and nature miracles. The basis of the names for these subgroupings are not really the form but the nature of the miracle. A more recent attempt at such analysis is that of Gerd Theissen.[25] Theissen speaks of exorcisms, healings, epiphanies (appearances), rescue miracles, gift miracles, and rule miracles. Again the nature of the miracle dictates the title and is helpful in focusing on the key act in the passage.

The issue of the name of this category and several that follow it needs notation. Names like tales or myth have a connotation in English that suggest fictitious. To the extent that such names are attempts to be prescriptive in relationship to historicity, they represent a serious flaw in the approach. For many critics the name simply refers to an account exalting or embellishing the key figure, yet it also has the suggestion that the account is somehow untrue. This is why the name *miracle story* is far better. It is descriptive of the passage content without judging its historical character in the naming. The term *miracle story* does not prejudge the question of whether God does act in these direct ways. The name *miracle story* is old, going back to Taylor's work.

The characteristics are that the accounts are self-contained as they possess a clear beginning and end. They also are descriptive, telling details of the story with a note of pleasure. The malady in such accounts is specified, as opposed to a summary account, where sicknesses are merely noted as a broad category. Finally, there is a note of the healing's success, often accompanied with a note about the reaction to the healing. There is a lack of devotion in the account in that religious language is lacking and often there is an absence of teaching by Jesus, which makes this category distinct from the previous category of paradigm. Part of the pleasure in the account is the detail given to the nature of the malady, the means of healing, and the public reaction to the miracle.

Numerous examples exist: The Leper of Mark 1:40–45 (healing); The Stilling of the Storm in Mark 4:35–41 (nature miracle); The Healing of Jairus' Daughter and the Stilling of the Flow of Blood in Mark 5:21–43 (healing and raising from the dead); and The Demons and the Swine in Mark 5:1–20 (exorcism). One can look at any of these accounts and trace the sequence of the traits. But it is interesting also to note how fluid the form can be. In Mark 5:1–20, the account is full of detail leading up to the miracle; while in Luke 11:14–23 the entire miracle is covered in a verse, and the emphasis is on the reaction to the miracle, which comprises the bulk of the unit. This kind of proportionality difference shows that for Luke 11, it is the commentary about the miracle that is key. Its very deviation from the normal form marks this text as having exceptional importance. A study sensitive to form will make such differences more evident, showing the value of the approach at a literary level.

SAYINGS / PARENESIS OR EXHORTATIONS / PARABLES

Here is the most varied category. This group of accounts deals with the individual teachings of Jesus that are not tied to a controversy or a simple event. In other words, this category covers the range of his discourse.[26] Again, there are subgroupings. Dibelius had maxims (Matt. 12:34b: Out of the Abundance of the Heart; also called proverb or gnome); metaphor (Mark 4:21: Is a Lamp Put under a Bushel?); parable (Luke 15:1–7: Lost Sheep); prophetic call (Matt. 5:3–12: Beatitudes); short command (Matt. 18:10: Do Not Despise Little Ones); and extended command (Luke 6:27–49: Sermon on the Plain).[27] Most of these names are straightforward. The most difficult is the prophetic call, which is really a word of blessing or warning that comes from God through a prophet about what God will do or what will happen. It is quite possible for a saying to reflect a few of these categories at the same time, as some of them overlap versus being totally distinct. In other words, one might have a maxim or a wisdom saying embedded in a longer discourse. This overlapping can explain why sometimes different names are attached to the same saying by different form critics. It does not always denote disagreement about form.

Bultmann's names differ but represent similar categories. First, he has logia (or wisdom), which equals Dibelius's maxims (Mark 3:24–26: A Kingdom Divided Against Itself). Second, he speaks of prophetic or apocalyptic sayings, which equal the prophetic call as well as including parable and metaphor. This category is further subdivided into preaching of salvation (Luke 7:22–23: The Blind See, etc.); minatory sayings, which are threats of judgment or woe (Luke 6:24–26: Woes to the Rich); and admonitions, which are warnings. Admonitions include many parables where there is a warning about response (Luke 12:42–48: Parable of the Stewards). Finally, apocalyptic predictions belong here (Mark 13:5–27: Olivet Discourse). As one can see, some material in this grouping is short, while other material is much longer, reflecting the range within Jesus' own teaching style.

Third, Bultmann speaks of legal sayings and church rules. Some of these are metaphors or prophetic sayings as well. These are sayings that set down limits on life or that indicate where authority lies. Here he includes The Sin Against the Spirit in Luke 12:10; the Instruction on Reconciliation in Matthew 6:14–15; and the Divorce Pericope of Matthew 5:31–32.

Fourth, he speaks of "I sayings." These are mission statements about why Jesus has come or has been sent or how he acts. They usually start with "I have come" (Mark 2:17: Not to Call the Righteous but Sinners); or "I am sent" (Luke 4:43: To Preach the Kingdom); or "I have given/made" (Mark 1:17: You Fishers of Men). Any saying where Jesus speaks of his activity belongs here. Again the separation of sayings into such groupings is helpful.

The fifth and final subunit under sayings is the similitudes. It is sometimes hard to see the difference between these and parables. In fact, some critics do not distinguish the categories. For those who do distinguish, a similitude is a comparison between two unlike objects using present tense verbs (Kingdom like Leaven), while a parable is a complete story with some type of metaphorical significance (The Prodigal Son). Some add to this the category of example story, a narrative in the past tense with no metaphorical meaning.[28]

The example is the lesson of the story (Good Samaritan). There is a wide variety in this subunit. Here appear hyperbole (Matt. 5:29–30: Plucking Out the Eye); paradox (Mark 10:39: The One Who Seeks His Life Will Lose It); metaphor (Matt. 7:13–14: The Narrow Gate); and similitudes proper, which are the extended metaphors (Luke 18:1–8: The Nagging Widow). Such comparisons to life can be short (Matt. 13:33: The Leaven) or long (Luke 15:11–32: The Prodigal Son). Through such descriptive and distinguishing categories, form criticism shows its strength and its value for study. The categories are an analytical and descriptive aid to the interpreter.[29] They help the interpreter ask the right kinds of questions about the content of the text and look for its high points in the commonality of the structure of the form or the deviations from it.

LEGENDS / STORIES ABOUT JESUS

In this category the story is told to exalt a saint or great figure.[30] It will be distinguished from the next category, myth, in that the figure's greatness in a legend does not include divine qualities. Bultmann used the title "Historical Stories and Legends." The name "legend" is unfortunate because in English it suggests that the accounts are false. This situation with the names here is like that with tales in miracle stories. To comment necessarily on historicity is not the intent of the title, though it is true that for many form critics most of the accounts in this category are embellished beyond the historical realities. The name denotes that the key figure's stature is elevated by the account.

Bultmann's alternate name, "Historical Stories," is also a problem since he does not mean to suggest by that title that the stories are true historically. Either title is simply intended to describe an account that is interested in the life and adventures of Jesus for its own sake, without being concerned to recount his sayings or other such things. The problem of title caused Taylor to prefer the simple "Stories of Jesus." It is the best title for the category.

These accounts are interested in revealing the person of Jesus or those around him. They underline how God has marked the life of these individuals. These accounts are told simply to enhance the respect for the main character. The story of Jesus as a twelve-year-old in Luke 2:41–52 is an example of such an account, though here the saying of Luke 2:49 also has an important role to play.[31] Bultmann lacks Dibelius's category of myth, which is an account that has explicit supernatural elements in it, so his section combines Dibelius's categories of legend and myth. Thus, The Voice at the Baptism (Mark 1:9–11 and parallels), The Triumphal Entry (Mark 11:1–10 and parallels), Peter's Confession (Mark 8:27–30 and parallels), and The Transfiguration (Mark 9:2–8 and parallels) are among the accounts that fall into this category for Bultmann. Apparently, Bultmann found it difficult to sort out when "supernatural elements" were present or else he decided a distinction in these two categories was not possible because so many of the accounts had supernatural touches. In contrast, Dibelius placed the baptism with its heavenly voice and the transfiguration, with its transformation of Jesus, in the next category to be discussed, myth.

In fact, this category of legend is the most elusive of all because in many cases the texts could be put elsewhere as well. Dibelius puts the Synagogue Speech of Luke 4:16–21 here, but is this not a prophetic call and a mission account? One senses that accounts end up in this category because they are too supernaturally charged, even if only implicitly so. Nonetheless, the category, rightly understood, is helpful in pointing out that the person of Jesus is the issue in these accounts. Usually something about his person, something marvelous, is revealed in these accounts and is the focal point of the unit.

However, a problem with this classification points to a warning about form that needs attention. Sometimes there is the complaint that one should not classify texts by content.[32] The value of the complaint depends on what is meant by "content." Guthrie is disturbed that some classifications look at the supernatural content in the account and call the result legend or myth as a result, when in fact the account differs little otherwise from a pronouncement story, a miracle story, or a saying.

The complaint at this level is certainly valid. Form cannot be used to determine historicity unless a clear set of genuine literary, formal characteristics are present and clearly established as part of the form, such as in the case of a parable or a metaphor. Only then can a textual element be marked off as nonhistorical and strictly a literary element present in the passage. In fact, the claim about these categories was that legend and myth theoretically could contain historical material, but often that was not in reality assessed to be the case.

Thus, Guthrie's warning is a real one. The terms *legend* and *myth* cannot be used to indicate historicity. Nor should they be so used, as if a form classification based on how exalted a figure is portrayed to be can settle issues about historicity. If embellishment is what a critic's use of a descriptive term intends to communicate, then other terms might be better and clearer, such as "embellished accounts." This is why Taylor's "Stories about Jesus" is the best title for this category. All titles should be clear or at least historically neutral, as descriptive categories of literary emphasis and focus. Issues of historicity have to be tackled at other levels by other approaches. Here is a case where form criticism can attempt to do too much with too little. It is better not to suggest form criticism can settle these more historical, worldview questions as if they were merely literary questions.

On the other hand, the classification of form by content can be helpful in determining subcategories within a larger category and can be helpful in describing the point of focus in an account. So the subclassifications of miracle stories and parables are helped when this procedure is applied. As always, defining terms and procedures carefully is the key, and generalizations should be examined carefully to see whether they have been established rather than asserted. In addition, categories should be carefully evaluated to see if they conceal worldview judgments as opposed to being neutral names.

MYTHS

The last category is Dibelius's alone.[33] These accounts, considered as a literary classification, deal with the "many sided doings of the gods." These accounts contain the explicit presence of the divine or of supernatural agents. Here we move from Jesus the teacher to Jesus the divine figure. Again, the intent of the title is not necessarily to make a historical judgment, but the name is unfortunate in that it suggests the account is false when normal English usage is applied to the meaning of the term. In fact, many form critics do believe these accounts are embellishments about Jesus, since their worldview excludes being able to assess how God acts in history. However, that was not the intent of the title as a literary description of form. It is really a way of saying that God or Satan deals directly with Jesus in these accounts and that these encounters, in turn, point to the mystery of his person.

Dibelius has only a few events here. For him the baptism, the temptation, and the transfiguration belong here. Once again, if the category name were not a problem, the description would prove helpful, for it points to the presence of supernatural forces in an explicit way that is lacking from other accounts. Perhaps the name *direct supernatural encounter stories* is a better, more neutral name to suggest for this category.

THE NEW FORM CRITICISM: FORMS AND MULTIPLE SUBFORMS

When one turns to the treatment of Berger, many of the old categories are gone, though most have really only received new names or new subcategories.[34] In addition, Berger covers the passages of the entire New Testament. He does not limit himself to the Synoptic Gospels. He also is clear that his version of the discipline is distinct from tradition history. This separation is positive, though it means that the concerns of the "new" form criticism represent the emasculation of much of what was form criticism for Dibelius and Bultmann. No longer does a seeking out of *Sitz im Leben* drive the approach as it did for the German originators of the approach. This is something Berger is aware of and welcomes, even as he continues to practice the approach.[35] In short, the literary features of form criticism remain, but the issues of history and tradition are largely removed. This surgery on form criticism probably strikes some as no longer being form criticism, but what it represents is a slimmed-down version that allows the tool to do what it does best, which is to describe.

Berger has four basic categories. The first is *Sammelgattungen* ("Collected Forms").[36] This is largely discourse material. Here he has pictorial texts, which include metaphors and parables, sentences, speeches, apophthegm, and argumentation, which are the controversial texts, whether apologetic, instructive, or diatribe. Second comes the *Symbuleutische Gattungen* ("Behavior Forms").[37] Here are found, among many others, parenesis, warnings, house rules, martyr warnings, blessings, woes, and community rules. Third come the *Epideiktische Gattungen* ("Demonstration Texts").[38] These are texts about things, persons, or events that are to lead the reader to admiration or repulsion. Here we find acclamations ("you are worthy," "this one is"), hymns, doxologies, prayers, proclamation, judgments, "I sayings," visions, apocalyptic genres, miracle accounts, travel accounts, martyr accounts, conflict accounts, example accounts from the disciples, and summaries. We move into events or their significance in these accounts. Finally are the *Dikanische Gattungen* ("Decision Texts").[39] These are apologetic texts in one way or another that explain why something is done or how one should look at a matter. It should be noted that individual texts for Berger can fall into many categories at the same time, another departure from the older version of form criticism, which tended to hunt for the "pure" form and regarded most mixed forms as evidence of a position later in the given tradition's historical development. The possibility of fixed forms not being the sign of early church accretion is a positive development for the approach.

What Berger gave up in leaving history behind he added by introducing numerous new categories on the literary side. Such detailed and thorough analysis is to be appreciated, but one wonders whether the simplicity of the old classifications has been lost in the plethora of options now provided and in the multiplied categories within which a text can function. Nonetheless, here is form criticism at its descriptive level carried out to its logical and detailed end. Only time will tell whether the pursuit of this degree of detail is helpful or whether a retreat to more general categories is advisable.

An Example: Luke 5:1–11

Such a vast discipline with its many subcategories makes difficult the choice of an example that is representative. Luke 5:1–11 has the advantage of a rich history of discussion about its form that reveals both the strengths and the weaknesses of the discipline. In examining this passage, we shall note the history of this discussion and show how the discipline wrestles with itself to understand a given text. We will do this by tracing the position of a variety of interpreters about the form of this passage and note the strengths and weaknesses of their approach.

Dibelius called the account a "legend."[40] The major reason for the choice appears to be the miraculous catch, along with the detail about Peter's view of himself. This classification means that the story enhances how one sees Jesus. Now source criticism had suggested that John 21:1–14 and Luke 5:1–11 were related to each other, a point that others dispute. Dibelius picks up on this and argues that John 21 is the later account, since Peter in Luke 5:8 does not confess his specific sin (and thus would be alluding to his denials); rather, he speaks of sin in general terms. He notes the passage is really a call word and that it might in reality have been tied to a real catch of fish. So Dibelius ends up using form criticism to challenge the attempt to link Luke 5 and John 21.

Dibelius's denial that Luke 5 comes from John 21 is a good example of careful observation that is frequent in form criticism. However, the tendency otherwise simply to assume the results of source criticism is not always good. Another assumption crippling the analysis at both a source and form level is that similar events mean originally unified traditions. The possibility that Luke 5 and John 21 were distinct is not raised despite numerous differences in the events. Differences such as timing, the setting of the fishing, the role of the participants, and the contents of what Jesus says do not count sufficiently to overcome the belief that similarity is really identity or that accounts about Jesus originated in one example of a kind only (i.e., there is only one originating fish catch story, and there is no possibility of a similar miracle taking place on more than one occasion). Dibelius's treatment also tends to assume that accounts move from simple to more complex forms, since he seems to suggest a basic call and event were expanded into a more miraculous form.[41]

Bultmann discussed the account as a nature miracle, though he argued that it really is a legend.[42] The reason for this distinction is not made clear. What the struggle to classify shows is that the text both has a point at the level of the picture in the miracle performed as well as in showing Jesus in an exalted light. The passage evidences how difficult it is to keep categories distinct if only supernatural contents create a shift in category. He argues that the original tradition was the saying of Luke 5:10, which has been expanded into its "symbolic actualization," that is, the miracle of Luke 5:4–8. He sees John 21 as the earlier account, though why this is so is not made clear. Perhaps the confession and christology are considered to be more appropriate in the post-resurrection setting. But possessing fear because a holy man has revealed himself as present is all Peter's action suggests. The christology of the text does not demand a postresurrection appreciation of who Jesus is, something Peter and the disciples are still sorting out at this point in Jesus' life (see Luke 8:22–25).

The category of nature miracle is an appropriate description of what Jesus does here. But again old assumptions crowd in. The movement from simple to complex accounts fuels the suggestion that originally the simplest form of the tradition had only a saying. In addition, like the previous effort, there is no attempt to deal with the possibility that Luke 5 is distinct from John 21. Despite any superficial similarities, differences are treated as the work of the evangelists rather than reckoning with the possibility that they are older or even signs of distinct traditions. Others have criticized the choice of *legend* for the account, noting that Peter's person and piety are not the focus of the account.[43] If "legend" is in view, it is because of what the text suggests about Jesus, not Peter. However, it would be hard to read this passage and not see Peter's character and example of humility as a major part of the teaching point, since the passage seems to suggest that one of the reasons Jesus can call for Peter to join him is that Peter appreciates the limitations he has in the light of Jesus' presence.

Theissen called the account a "gift miracle."[44] This is another way to refer in more detail to a nature miracle. The gift miracle has three basic characteristics: (1) The miracle is spontaneous and surprising. This means the miracle worker initiates the miracle. There is no request for it. (2) The miracle is unobtrusive, which means the "how" of the miracle or the actions associated with it are absent. (3) The final demonstration of the miracle is stressed. This means that the consequences are detailed. All of these observations are true of Luke 5:1–11. Jesus does the miracle without lifting a finger. He simply says go out and toss the nets. The fishermen are left to deal with the (too great!) consequences in order to avoid the tragedy of sinking under the weight of the catch. The point of the miracle is that a situation of want is overcome. Theissen does not mention John 21 in his treatment. His handling of the text is reflective of more recent form criticism, distancing itself from historical judgment. His descriptive approach is helpful.

Fitzmyer calls the account a pronouncement story (Luke 5:10b) plus a miracle story.[45] The miracle serves the saying, which is why the emphasis is on the pronouncement part of the account. The combination was Luke's doing. This classification highlights how the miracle leads into the pronouncement, which itself issues a promise that Peter and others will join Jesus in a task to "catch people for God." Again strengths and weaknesses exist. The assumption that there is no such thing as a mixed form appears to force the conclusion that Luke has taken Mark 1:16–20 and joined it to another tradition to form this unit. This is not helpful. However, of more value is the observation, which certainly is correct, that the key to the account is the saying, which in turn is set up by the miracle. In other words, Fitzmyer's double classification and description nicely prioritizes the elements within the story and notes that the punch line of Luke 5:10 is pivotal. It correctly prioritizes the contribution of the account's elements.

Talbert discusses the form of this text in great detail.[46] He argues that the text is a commission account, not a call. A commission account has an introduction (Luke 5:2), a confrontation (5:3), a commission (5:4), a protest (5:5), a reaction (5:8–9) and a reassurance (5:10), and a response (5:11). This is in contrast to the call that has Jesus coming, seeing, calling, and then the person(s) leaving and following.

This classification looks good on the surface, but it seems to suffer from overanalysis and shows that any classification should be examined carefully. For example, to call Luke 5:5 a protest is to undermine the very point of the verse. The verse really concerns Peter's faith, which despite appearances leads him to *obey* Jesus. Peter's remark is not a protest but the expression of great faith. In addition, Luke 5:3 is hardly a confrontation. Finally, to distinguish between a call and a commission seems artificial.

Nonetheless, one of the values of form criticism or thinking about it can come from critically interacting with the suggestions of critics. For in seeing where a proposal might have problems, the text itself becomes clearer for what it is and is not doing.

Tiede briefly handles the passage with some sharp observations.[47] He speaks of an "epiphany-call," by which he means that the passage evidences a divine presence and makes a call to the fisherman to be a disciple. He compares the account in form to Exodus 3, Judges 6, and Isaiah 6. The center of the passage is Peter's faith, which leads to the manifestation of divine presence, which in turn is the basis of a call. The miracle is less crucial except to set up the call, since the miracle's material success is totally ignored. In other words, the men leave behind their nets as well as the great catch and take up a vocation based on a new call. The action of the account reinforces the point of the story and the priorities in it.

Here is helpful form critical work. The form is defined; it is related to other similar types of biblical material, and the parts are placed in order of priority. In addition, parallels are noted to show other examples of the form within Scripture.

Finally we look at Berger's handling of the text.[48] He complains that the title *miracle story* is a modern category and that often miracles can be placed in other categories more easily. Again such a complaint depends on what one wishes to do with the account once it is placed in the category. If *miracle story* is a way to deny historicity, then his complaint has merit. It also is true that miracle accounts can often fit elsewhere. However, it also is the case that the category *miracle stories* and their subclassifications can be descriptively helpful, as Theissen's work shows.

Berger argues that the issue of an account like Luke 5 is Jesus' spiritual power and evinces the fellowship that he had with the disciples. The text also shows the prominence of Peter. He speaks of a *mandatio*, or mandate account, and also speaks of a "call history." Berger, unlike his predecessors, will use several categories at once. The mandate is an account in which there is an order by a superior to an inferior that is to be obeyed. Here is the call to cast the nets and the call to commission. The mandate is but a small part of the total text, but the point is well taken that a passage consists of several subunits and spotting each portion helps us appreciate the whole passage. The call history has precedent in 1 Kings 19:19–20 and is like Mark 1:19. Again biblical parallels are noted. Berger argues that the miracle is less important than the call and also speaks of subforms within the account, such as dialogue and "religious self witness," the latter describing Peter's exclamation that he is a sinner (Luke 5:8).

Many strengths are seen here. There is an absence of traditional form critical historical speculation. The account is related in terms of form to other similar biblical texts. There is a willingness to recognize mixed types or many types within a passage. Berger prioritizes the parts to one another. He recognized the problem with the title *miracle story*, though there may be an overreaction here. He surfaces much here to work with in terms of exegesis.

One sees in the example a certain flexibility of category and a playing around with category titles. This is inevitable in a descriptive process where one is searching to be more precise.

But what of the historical-applicational question? Can it be pursued in this text at all? What could be the *Sitz im Leben* of such an account that would cause it to be recorded and passed down? How would it function in the church? Two motives seem clear and do not require a subjective filling of gaps for the text.

First, the account would explain the roots of the early disciples' involvement in the church, especially that of one of its key figures, Peter. How did they come to be called? What did they see in Jesus? The account shows the knowledge and authority of the one whom the church confesses as Savior.

Second, the account vividly articulates the church's mission. The disciples are to be "fishers of humanity." They are to cast nets into the world and seek to rescue people from death. In this perspective Peter is not just the first disciple; he is the exemplary disciple. All disciples share his call and can identify with his mission. The account suggests these two emphases. As long as one does not deny that the origins of the tradition go back to the participants, this search for the *Sitz im Leben* in the church need not be a problem and in fact can help show the way to methods one might use to teach the account today.

In this limited sense, the pursuit of a setting in Jesus' life that also matches that in the church can be a benefit to those who are contemplating the message of this passage. One might well come to such conclusions without form criticism, but asking the question in this focused way, as form criticism does, might help one see these teaching points more easily.

Summary

Form criticism is not the center of New Testament exegesis. It is but one humble tool among many. It has the potential to be a blunt instrument that is not helpful in the exegetical task when it is used for things for which it was not designed. It should not be designed to help us determine the historicity of the events it analyzes. On the other hand, the descriptive features of the discipline and the hunting for parallels can be helpful in describing the focus, elements, and structure of a text's argument. In the hands of a skilled exegete who uses the tools of interpretation in a way that fits what they are capable of, form criticism can be a fruitful aid to understanding and to exposition.

Bibliography

Beasley-Murray, George R. *Preaching the Gospel from the Gospels.* London: Lutterworth, 1965.

Blomberg, Craig. *Interpreting the Parables.* Downers Grove, Ill.: InterVarsity, 1990, esp. pp. 71–99.

Bultmann, Rudolf. *The History of the Synoptic Tradition.* Oxford: Blackwell, 1968.

Doty, W. G. "The Discipline and Literature of New Testament Form Criticism." *Anglican Theological Review* 51 (1969): 257–321.

Ellis, E. E. "New Directions in Form Criticism." *Jesus Christus in Historie und Theologie.* Ed. G. Strecker. Tübingen: Mohr, 1975, 299–315.

_____. "The Synoptic Gospels and History." *Authenticating the Activities of Jesus.* Ed. Bruce Chilton and Craig A. Evans. Boston: Brill, 1999, 49–57 (esp. 53–56).

France, R. T. "The Authenticity of the Sayings of Jesus." *History, Criticism, and Faith.* Ed. Colin Brown. Downers Grove, Ill.: InterVarsity, 1977.

Gerhardsson, Birger. *Memory and Manuscript: Oral Tradition and Written Transmission in Rabbinic Judaism and Early Christianity.* Trans. E. J. Sharpe. Lund: Gleerup, 1961.

McKnight, E. V. *What Is Form Criticism?* Philadelphia: Fortress, 1969.
Manson, T. W. *The Teachings of Jesus: Studies of Its Form and Content.* Cambridge: Cambridge University Press, 1931.
Taylor, Vincent. *The Formation of the Gospel Tradition.* London: Macmillan, 1949. Reprint of 1935 2d ed.

Notes

1. Though we will refer to updated, translated editions, the key studies were in German. Martin Dibelius, *Die Formgeschichte des Evangeliums,* and K. L. Schmidt, *Der Rahmen der Geschichte Jesu,* were both released in 1919. Two years later came the comprehensive and influential study by R. Bultmann, *Die Geschichte der synoptischen Tradition.*

2. The history and nature of source criticism is the topic of the previous essay.

3. Early in this study, Dibelius described his aim this way: "The right to read the Gospels from the standpoint of their form is the objective of the present volume." Later he says, "Further, the categories allow us to draw a conclusion as to what is called the *Sitz im Leben,* i.e., the historical and social stratum in which precisely these literary forms were developed." Finally, Dibelius again states, "The ultimate origin of the Form is the primitive Christian life itself." The English title of Dibelius's work, *From Tradition to Gospel,* summarizes the discipline's concern nicely. The quotations are from pp. 6, 7, and 8 of Dibelius, *From Tradition to Gospel,* 2d ed., trans. B. L. Woolf (London: James Clarke & Co., 1971 trans. of 1933 ed.). The Dibelius metaphor of the evangelists as "collectors" can be found on pp. 3 and 59. The emphasis on the Gospel pericopes as "sociological" products, not as individual creations, can be found on p. 7.

4. Bultmann, *The History of the Synoptic Tradition,* 3d ed., trans. J. Marsh (New York: Harper, 1963 trans. of 1958 ed.), 3–4. Note the assumption of division between history and application in this citation.

5. Bruce, "Criticism," *ISBE* 1:822.

6. Such axioms are rarely listed in the early works. Rather, they are introduced in the opening remarks. So Dibelius, *From Tradition to Gospel,* 1–36, where he stresses the role of preaching as a major formative factor. Cf. Bultmann, *History of the Synoptic Tradition,* 1–7. Bultmann has one sentence on p. 3 that summarizes the approach: "The following investigation therefore sets out to give an account of the history of the *individual units of the tradition,* and how the tradition passed from a fluid state to the fixed form in which it meets us in the Synoptics and in some instances even outside of them."

7. For this list, see David Catchpole, "Tradition History," in *New Testament Interpretation,* ed. by I. H. Marshall (Grand Rapids: Eerdmans, 1977), 174–77. A detailed article noting some eleven criteria is Robert Stein, "Criteria for Authenticity," in *Gospel Perspectives 1,* ed. R. T. France and David Wenham (Sheffield: *JSOT,* 1980). The article is excellent for its scope, though it fails to distinguish when a criterion authenticates the exact wording of a saying versus only the conceptual thrust of the saying.

8. E. P. Sanders, *The Tendencies of the Synoptic Tradition,* SNTSMS 9 (Cambridge: Cambridge University, 1969).

9. K. Berger, *Einführung in die Formgeschichte,* UTB 144 (Tübingen: Franke, 1987), 63–67, traces Herder's influence.

10. Ibid., 33–34, 56.

11. Jordan, *Geschichte der altchristlichen Literatur* (Leipzig, 1911).

12. E. Güttgemanns, *Candid Questions Concerning Gospel Form Criticism,* trans. W. Doty (Pittsburgh: Pickwick, 1979, trans. of 1971 ed. with author's additions in

1978), 235–48, evaluates Gunkel's role. His prolific work was 1901–1932. Gunkel's work on Genesis was published in 1901.

13. Ellis, "The Synoptic Gospels and History," *Authenticating the Activities of Jesus,* ed. Bruce Chilton and Craig A. Evans (Boston: Brill, 1999), 53–56, notes how findings at Qumran and a greater appreciation for the literacy of first-century Jews have countered the attempt to compare oral transmission to that of other later, less literate, folk culture. Jewish tradition was passed on with great care. He also notes that the presence of eyewitnesses served as a check on any fluidity in the tradition. He also stresses that putting key events down in writing would not have required a long passing of time and that the basic outline of the chronological-geographical flow of Jesus' ministry would have been remembered.

14. V. Taylor, *The Formation of the Gospel Tradition* (London: Macmillan, 1949 reprint of 1935 ed). The original volume was published in 1933 and came from lectures given in 1932.

15. Ibid., 41. On the other hand, he says on p. 20, "I have no doubt that the value of form criticism is considerable." He speaks of a "tool with limited powers" here. If one may play with this picture a bit, one thinks of a standard screwdriver that has been made into a Phillips screwdriver and is no longer able to work with normal screws as a result. In this sense, the critics have argued that form criticism overstepped what the texts were capable of yielding. Form criticism as an historical tool often is not a very good fit. The search for a community *Sitz im Leben* is fraught with subjective difficulties and the lack of an adequate evidentiary base for the judgments made.

16. See the essay on redaction criticism that follows in this volume.

17. Here one can mention the study of E. Güttgemanns and E. P. Sanders, *The Tendencies of the Synoptic Tradition,* SNTSMS 9 (Cambridge: Cambridge University Press, 1969) for the issue of the rules of transmission. Sanders especially showed that accounts both get simpler and more complex with time. There is no "rule" that applies. In addition, the examination of oral tradition in Judaism revealed the potential for very stable tradition; so H. Reisenfeld, *The Gospel Tradition and Its Beginnings: A Study in the Limits of Form Criticism* (London: Mowbray, 1957) and B. Gerhardsson, *Memory and Manuscript: Oral and Written Transmission in Rabbinic Judaism and Early Christianity* (Lund: Gleerup, 1961).

18. K. Müller, "Neutestamentlicher Literaturüberlick (1)," *Pastoral-Theologie* 78 (1989): 278. This article is an overview by a German New Testament scholar reviewing developments in New Testament study for pastors. He speaks of the form criticism of Bultmann and Dibelius as past, at least in terms of reconstructing the oral tradition; the assumption about the makeup of the Christian community; and the pursuit of *Sitz im Leben.* He notes that form criticism today is more interested in rhetorical issues and synchronic comparison than with diachronic study, by which he means they engage in contemporary comparison with other New Testament works and outside sources rather than reaching back through the tradition history. In other words, form criticism is moving in a descriptive, literary direction. Its role as a historical tool is significantly reduced.

19. K. Berger, *Formgeschichte des Neuen Testaments* (Heidelberg: Quelle & Meyer, 1984).

20. Many treatments of form criticism in discussing the history of the movement also launch into a discussion of the New Quest for the historical Jesus, a movement started in Germany by Bultmann's students in the fifties. They thought he was too negative on issues of historicity. This movement is now known as the second quest for the historical Jesus, since it predates the third quest, an even more recent development of the eighties that seeks to understand Jesus in terms of his Jewish background and often sees more

historical information in the Gospels than second questers do. The second quest also evidences some frustration with form criticism as a historical tool, though most second questers still give an emphasis to the later community, which means they tend to doubt historicity in many places of the tradition. This is not a function of form criticism *per se* as much as the suppositions by which the forms are handled.

21. Dibelius, *From Tradition to Gospel*, 37–58.

22. Taylor, *The Formation of the Gospel Tradition*, 30.

23. Bultmann, *The History of the Synoptic Tradition*, 11–69.

24. Dibelius, *From Tradition to Gospel*, 70–103; Bultmann, *The History of the Synoptic Tradition*, 209–44. Bultmann preferred the name "miracle story," as did Taylor, *The Formation of the Gospel Tradition*, 119–41.

25. Gerd Theissen, *The Miracle Stories of the Early Christian Tradition*, trans. Francis McDonaugh, ed. John Riches (Philadelphia: Fortress, 1983 ed. of 1974 German ed.).

26. Dibelius, *From Tradition to Gospel*, 233–65. He called them "Exhortation" or "Parenesis." Bultmann, *The History of the Synoptic Tradition*, 69–205. He spoke of "Dominical Sayings." Often the material in this category was also described as present in the source Q.

27. The list of example passages here is mostly ours, since Dibelius does not supply a clear list for each category.

28. Blomberg, *Interpreting the Parables* (Downers Grove, Ill.: InterVarsity, 1990), esp. pp. 71–99.

29. Many have also attempted to subject the parables to a more comprehensive examination of form. By far the most famous attempts are: C. H. Dodd, *The Parables of the Kingdom*, rev. ed. (New York: Scribner's, 1961 ed. of original ed. in 1935) and J. Jeremias, *The Parables of Jesus*, 2d rev. ed., trans. S. H. Hooke (New York: Scribner's, 1972, ed. of 1954 original). Here one can speak of kingdom parables, parables of the return, parables of discipleship, parables of mission, or parables about God. Again the subcategories are determined by the topic at hand within the parable.

30. Dibelius, *From Tradition to Gospel*, 104–32. Bultmann, *The History of the Synoptic Tradition*, 244–317.

31. This raises the problem of "mixed forms," which will be addressed in a following example. Some passages combine forms to make their point. Spotting mixed forms can help one appreciate the complexity of an account's argument.

32. So D. Guthrie, *New Testament Introduction* (Downers Grove, Ill.: InterVarsity, 1970 ed.), 211, point 1.

33. Dibelius, *From Tradition to Gospel*, 266–86.

34. Berger, *Formgeschichte des Neuen Testaments*.

35. Ibid., 11–13.

36. This category as well as the subsequent ones come from Berger, *Formgeschichte des Neuen Testaments*. The subgenres of this category are described on pp. 25–116. The translation of his titles are my own, since his work is currently available only in German.

37. This is a rough translation of a difficult German term. Berger is clear on p. 18 of his work that behavior, injunction, or advice is the issue here. The subgenres are discussed on pp. 117–220.

38. Another difficult term is present. The name comes from the Greek *epideiknymi*, which means "to point out something to someone" or "to show, demonstrate." Berger's description is on p. 18. The subgenres are on pp. 221–359.

39. Again Berger's choice of terms makes translation difficult. The burden of these texts is to lead the reader to a decision about a disputed matter. See pp. 18–19. In fact, Berger spends little time here, pp. 360–65.

40. Dibelius, *From Tradition to Gospel,* 113.

41. What Dibelius may be doing here is arguing that the call Mark 1:16–20 records has been "transformed" and expanded here. See the treatment of Fitzmyer below. The possibility that this catch reinforced that call by repeating its imagery is not even considered.

42. Bultmann, *The History of the Synoptic Tradition,* 217–18, 230.

43. Schurmann, *Das Lukasevangelium,* Erster Teil, Herders theologischer Kommentar zum Neuen Testament, Band 111 (Freiburg: Herder, 1984 printing of 1968 ed.), 273, n. 79.

44. Theissen, *The Miracle Stories of the Early Christian Tradition,* 104, 161–62, and esp. 321.

45. Fitzmyer, *The Gospel according to Luke I–LX,* Anchor Bible 28 (Garden City, N.Y.: Doubleday, 1981), 562.

46. C. Talbert, *Reading Luke* (New York: Crossroad, 1984), 60–61. His work is built on that of Hubbard, "Commissioning Stories in Luke-Acts: Their Antecedents, Form and Content," *Semeia* 8 (1977), 103–26.

47. D. Tiede, *Luke,* Augsburg Commentary on the New Testament (Minneapolis: Augsburg, 1988), 115.

48. Berger, *Formgeschichte des Neuen Testaments,* 305–06, 309–10, 316, 255, and 278.

Chapter 6

Redaction Criticism

Grant R. Osborne
Trinity Evangelical Divinity School

Four disciplines have been developed in this century that have special relevance for Gospel studies—form criticism, tradition criticism (usually considered not so much a "school" as a "method" used by form and redaction criticism), redaction criticism, and narrative or literary criticism. Each discipline presupposes the validity of and builds upon its predecessor, yet each also has originated partly because of inherent weaknesses in the preceding approaches. Form criticism assumes that the Gospel authors were mere "scissors and paste" editors who artificially strung together the traditions of Jesus, while tradition criticism concludes that since the traditions themselves were the product of a long period of oral development and often had little connection with the historical Jesus, the scholar has to remove those later additions to get at the "true" meaning of the stories. Both disciplines ignore the author (or "redactor"), considering that author of little value for the task of interpreting the Gospels. Redaction criticism arose in the 1950s to correct this erroneous omission.

Redaction criticism may be defined as a historical discipline that seeks to uncover the theology and setting of a writing by studying the ways the redactor or editor changed the traditions he inherited and the seams or transitions that the redactor used to link those traditions together. The creative force shifts from Jesus (the traditional view) and the early church (form criticism) to the author (redaction criticism).[1] There are two foci for the discipline: (1) the editorial alterations of the traditions (this is the primary concern of earlier redaction critics) and (2) the process by which the authors combined the traditions into a holistic work (this is called composition criticism and is the goal of later redaction critics). Critics today use the two approaches together.

There are several elements in the process of redactional inquiry. First, redaction criticism builds upon the results of source criticism, which assumes that written or oral sources lay behind the Gospels, and studies the interdependence between those sources.[2] The general consensus[3] (called the two- or four-document hypothesis) is that there were two primary sources, Mark and Q (either a written or oral source containing sayings of Jesus and accounting for 235 verses common to Matthew and Luke but missing from Mark). In addition, both Matthew and Luke used their own sources (M and L) in constructing their Gospels. Redaction critics take this data and study the editorial alterations made to their sources by the individual Evangelists. For instance, they will ask why Luke has added three sayings of Jesus in his crucifixion scene: "Father, forgive these people, for they don't know what they are doing" (23:34); "today you will be with me in paradise" (23:43); and "Father, I commit my spirit to you"(23:46)—while omitting Mark's and Matthew's, "My God, my God, why have you forsaken me" (Mark 15:34; Matt. 27:46).

Second, redaction criticism works with the results of form and tradition criticism. Form critics seek the original or authentic tradition behind the final Gospel form, while tradition critics try to discover the history or development of that tradition from the earliest to the final form in the Gospels. Redaction critics center upon the final stage of the editorial process, the Evangelist's changes, believing that these are the clue to the intentions of the author and the situation of his community.[4] For instance, they would inquire about which of the sayings may have been added earlier in the tradition-history of the crucifixion narratives and which might be Luke's own contributions. The latter would provide the data for determining Luke's distinctive emphases.

Third, the primary goal of redaction criticism is to discern the theological message of each Evangelist. This is accomplished both by asking why the changes were introduced into the final form of the traditions and by looking for consistent patterns in the ongoing composition of that Gospel. The alterations introduced in a Gospel begin to fall into certain categories or patterns, and these patterns denote redactional interests or theological tendencies that characterize that Gospel.[5] In Luke's crucifixion narrative, two such theological tendencies have emerged: (1) Jesus is portrayed as the quintessential innocent righteous martyr (seen in Luke's version of the centurion's cry, "Surely, this man is innocent," and in the Christological focus of the entire account); and (2) Luke's version is altered into an awesome scene of worship (two of the last sayings in Luke are prayers, and the negative elements of Mark and Matthew have been omitted). Furthermore, both of these emphases are part of larger patterns in Luke's Gospel.

Fourth, the setting or situation of the Lukan church is often surmised on the basis of these redactional tendencies. This is a highly controversial aspect of redaction criticism because of its speculative nature, but the majority of scholars continue to seek such conclusions in their studies. They believe that the changes were introduced by particular problems in the church behind each Gospel and that by looking at the sociological factors hinted at in the text one can surmise the pastoral concerns that led to the final form. Thus the redaction critic elucidates not only the theological interests but also the ecclesiastical situation behind the editorial alterations. The portrayal of Jesus as the righteous martyr is said to be addressed to a church undergoing persecution, and the emphasis on worship presupposes a liturgical setting.

The Origins of Redaction Criticism

There were several precursors to redaction criticism, including Wilhelm Wrede's "messianic secret," Ned Stonehouse's study of the Christological emphases of the Synoptic Gospels, and R. H. Lightfoot's Bampton Lectures of 1934, which traced theological nuances in Mark's treatment of his sources.[6] In ways remarkably similar to the founding of form criticism in post-World War I Germany (via three scholars working independently— K. L. Schmidt, Martin Dibelius, and Rudolf Bultmann), redaction criticism began in post-World War II Germany with three scholars working independently—Gunther Bornkamm, Willi Marxsen, and Hans Conzelmann.

Bornkamm launched the movement with his 1948 article on "The Stifling of the Storm" in Matthew, which was later combined with similar essays by two of his students in *Tradition and Interpretation in Matthew.*[7] By comparing Matthew 8:23–27 with Mark 4:35–41, Bornkamm argued that Matthew not only altered but reinterpreted the stilling of the storm scene in the direction of discipleship. While in Mark the miracle is predominant, for Bornkamm the central element in Matthew is the "little faith" of the disciples, which designates the difficult journey of the "little ship of the church." Thus Bornkamm concludes, "Matthew is not only a hander-on of the narrative, but also its oldest exegete."[8] In a 1954 article entitled "End Expectation and Church in Matthew,"[9] Bornkamm expands his horizons to consider Matthew's Gospel as a whole, stating that for Matthew ecclesiology must be understood via eschatology; the church defines itself and its mission on the basis of the coming judgment that applies to believers as well as unbelievers. For instance, John the Baptist, with his message, "Repent for the kingdom of heaven is at hand" (3:2; 4:17), becomes a proclaimer of the Christian gospel by anticipating Jesus' denunciation of false teachers in 3:2 and 7:15–23 (both messages for Matthew address the church in the "end times"). This article even more than the earlier one led to a flood of redaction-critical studies of Matthew, for it demonstrated the contribution that such an approach could make to an understanding of the theology of the first Gospel as a whole.

Hans Conzelmann first published his study of Luke in a 1952 article, "Zur Lukasanalyse,"[10] and later expanded it in 1954 into a monograph with the English title, *The Theology of St. Luke.*[11] Perrin writes, "If Gunther

Bornkamm is the first of the true redaction critics, Hans Conzelmann is certainly the most important."[12] Conzelmann challenges the prevalent approach to Luke by arguing that he is self-consciously a theologian rather than a historian. Accepting the priority of Mark and studying Luke's editorial alterations of his Marcan source,[13] Conzelmann traces Luke's theological interests in a series of areas, beginning with geography and eschatology. The basic thesis is that the delay of the parousia led Luke to replace the imminent eschatology of his predecessors with a salvation historical framework centered upon a three-stage view of history: the time of Israel, which moved from the law and the prophets to John the Baptist; the time of Jesus, in which Satan is silent (4:13; 22:3) and salvation is present in "the center of time" (the original title of the book); and the time of the church, from the exaltation of Jesus to his return, characterized by persecution and temptation and overcome by the church as the messenger of salvation.

According to Conzelmann, the central stage predominates, and in it eschatology reinterpreted as salvation history has caused Luke to redefine the ministry of Jesus. The kingdom has become a timeless entity, and the parousia is no longer the focus. The brief interim of Mark has become an indefinite period, and the church is prepared by Jesus for a prolonged conflict in the world. Luke does this by positing three periods in Jesus' life and ministry: the ministry in Galilee (3:21–9:50), centering upon the gathering of the disciples; the travel narrative (9:51–19:27), in which the disciples are prepared for suffering; and the final events (19:28–23:49), in which suffering is actualized. In each section Jesus is seen as preparing the church to be the true Israel in the lengthy period before the final judgment.

Willi Marxsen in 1956 was the first to use the term *Redaktionsgeschichte* to describe the new movement, and the first and most influential portion of his *Mark the Evangelist*[14] is devoted to describing the differences between form and redaction criticism. He argues that form criticism has missed a third *Sitz im Leben* behind the Gospels (in addition to the situation of Jesus and of the early church), namely that of the Evangelist. In this way the Gospels are commentaries written backward in that they interpret the life of Jesus from the perspective of the Evangelist and read each pericope or story from the standpoint of those episodes preceding it. Marxsen then applies this methodology to a study of Mark's Gospel, concluding that Mark emphasizes Galilee over Jerusalem due to the desperate situation of his community during the Jewish War of A.D. 66. Four separate but connected studies make up this second half of the book: John the Baptist, geography, the concept of "gospel," and Mark 13. His thesis is that, unlike Luke, Mark believed in an imminent parousia, and his Gospel is a call to the church to flee the serious persecution and go to Galilee where the parousia would occur. Details like the Baptist tradition or geographical references do not have independent historical value but function rather as theological pointers to Jesus and this message. Marxsen's thesis has been the least accepted of the three pioneers, but he was the first to develop a redaction critical methodology; and his introduction of the third *Sitz im Leben* has made a lasting contribution to the discipline.[15]

The Methodology of Redaction Criticism

The challenge of redaction criticism is ascertaining with a fair degree of probability that one has discovered a redactional nuance. The discipline is prone to highly speculative theories because the conclusions depend entirely upon how one chooses and organizes the data. If the search is not complete and if the changes are not studied carefully, virtually opposite theories can be promulgated. For instance, Marxsen has argued that Mark was written to call Jewish Christians to the parousia in Galilee, while Theodore Weeden has theorized that Mark wrote to confront a Hellenistic "divine-man" heresy by casting himself and his opponents in the form of a dramatic conflict between Jesus and his disciples. When Jesus is portrayed as castigating the disciples so thoroughly in Mark's Gospel, it is actually Mark castigating his opponents.[16] In both cases the evidence was not examined thoroughly, and few interpreters have followed either theory. Yet this sample demonstrates the necessity of a developed methodology to protect against such excesses.

The key to Gospel research is a good Greek synopsis (Kurt Aland's *Synopsis* is the best). One begins by underlining the pericopes and noting which elements are found in one (Mark, M, or L source), two (Q, Mark, and M against L, or Mark, and L against M), three (the Synoptics), or all four Gospels. When this step is completed, the interpreter evaluates the data by using tradition-critical, form-critical, and redaction-critical techniques.

Tradition-Critical Analysis

The historical aspect is evaluated by applying the "criteria for authenticity" in order to determine the development of the tradition from Jesus through the early church to the Evangelist. These criteria originated within form criticism but are universally accepted by redaction critics. For the most part they have been controlled by a "hermeneutics of suspicion" that places the burden of proof upon those who affirm the historicity of the pericope. Perrin says, "The burden of proof must lay on the claim to authenticity, and the difficulties of establishing that claim become very great—very great indeed but not impossible."[17] On the other hand, there has been a strong reaction to such implications, with many arguing that the text should be presumed innocent until proved guilty and that the burden should be upon the skeptic,[18] while others assert that the scholar should at least be neutral and let the evidence decide.[19] Peter Davids lists four grounds for taking a more positive approach to the criteria: (1) the post-Easter church was intensely interested in what Jesus taught and did. (2) Since Jesus was a first-century Jewish teacher, his followers would naturally have learned and passed on his precepts. (3) There is evidence that his disciples not only memorized but wrote down his teachings. (4) Within Judaism there were highly developed models for transmitting tradition with great accuracy.[20] I will organize the criteria somewhat historically, beginning with the "big three" mentioned in Perrin and Fuller and then proceeding loosely to others used by the critics.

CRITERION OF DISSIMILARITY

This is the most negative criterion. It assumes that whenever a saying can be paralleled in either Judaism or the early church it cannot be affirmed as authentic because it could have been derived from Jewish teaching or read back onto Jesus' lips by the early church. As such this criterion has come under severe criticism for its overly skeptical nature since it assumes that the historical Jesus had no ties with Judaism and no influence upon the church. But the kerygma hardly arose in a vacuum, and it is erroneous to shift the creative genius behind the Christian movement from Jesus to the early church. The resultant "critically assured minimum" ignores large amounts of authentic material.[21] Yet at the same time this criterion, when used positively (i.e., to authenticate rather than to disprove a pericope), does have value, for those passages that do meet the criterion are certainly trustworthy.[22]

CRITERION OF MULTIPLE ATTESTATION

Called the "cross-section method" by Fuller,[23] this criterion states that a saying (or pericope) is authentic if it is repeated in several or all of the primary sources behind the Gospels. For instance, if a saying is found in Mark, Q, M, L, and John, it is considered a reliable tradition. Perrin uses this criterion to authenticate Jesus' concern for "tax collectors and sinners" (found in several of the sources), and Stein uses it to support the view that Jesus said that the kingdom of God was realized in his own person (Mark 2:21–22; Q=Luke 11:20; M=Matt 5:17; L=Luke 17:20–21; John 12:31).[24] Another version of this criterion asserts that if a saying appears in more than one form (e.g., parable, aphorism, or pronouncement story) it is verified.[25]

CRITERION OF COHERENCE

In actuality this criterion should be last, for it logically assumes that any pericope that is consistent or coheres with a passage already authenticated on the basis of the other criteria is itself acceptable. This means that such investigations do not have to be repeated whenever a saying is part of a larger pattern of sayings that have already been judged reliable. Of course, it is a secondary proof, for the passage depends for its validity upon the quality of argumentation used for the primary passage. Nevertheless, this criterion is widely accepted by scholars.

CRITERION OF DIVERGENT PATTERN

C. F. D. Moule has said, "It would appear that there are certain features in the story of Jesus, the retention of which can scarcely be explained except by their genuineness and durable quality, since everything else was hostile to their survival."[26] The well-known "pillar" sayings are an example, e.g.,

Mark 3:21 (Jesus' relatives think him insane), 10:18 ("Why do you call me good?"), or 13:32 (Jesus' ignorance regarding the coming of the end of the ages). Since these sayings are contrary to emphases of the early church, they at least were so firmly embedded in the tradition that the Evangelist decided to include them.

CRITERION OF "UNINTENTIONAL" SIGNS OF HISTORY

When a story contains details that would suggest an eyewitness account and that demonstrate accurate knowledge of the environment surrounding the original event, it is more likely to be reliable. Mark and John have such details, and scholars have argued viably for their basic historicity. Of course, such could be simply the product of a good storyteller adding details to heighten the realism,[27] but when such Palestinian features and customs betray a real knowledge of the original scene, the details are less likely to be fictional additions and more likely to be authentic.

CRITERION OF PALESTINIAN ENVIRONMENT OR ARAMAIC LINGUISTIC FEATURES

Joachim Jeremias and Matthew Black have especially stressed the presence of Aramaisms (since Jesus undoubtedly spoke Aramaic) as proof of authenticity. Jeremias for instance attempts to uncover an Aramaic original behind the Lord's Prayer as well as Aramaisms that prove the validity of Mark's account of the Lord's Supper.[28] Two basic criticisms have been leveled against this view: (1) Aramaic features could be the product of septuagintal influence, and (2) the presence of Semitic features demonstrates only that the saying stems from the Aramaic church; that is, it does not prove that the saying comes from Jesus himself. Hence, while such criteria cannot "prove" that a saying or story is authentic, they do give it greater reliability and point to the probability of a valid tradition.

CRITERION OF CONTRADICTION

Calvert and Stein[29] discuss the possibility that any saying or story that could not have occurred in the life of Jesus or that contradicts an existing authentic saying is invalid. The difficulty, of course, is in the application of this criterion. For instance, Matthew 22:7 (since the destruction and burning of the offending city could reflect a post-70 A.D. Gentile setting) and Mark 10:12 (since Jewish women could not divorce their husbands) are denied on these grounds. Yet the Matthew saying fits Old Testament and Near Eastern practices, and the Marcan divorce logion could actually stem from Herodias's divorce of her husband. Moreover, contradictions (e.g., Luke 14:26 on "hating" one's family vs. Luke 6:27 on "honoring" parents) are often such in appearance only. In short, this criterion could be valid only if such contradictions could be proved; however, the scholar must move with extreme caution lest such a "contradiction" exist more in the mind than in the ancient setting.

Tradition-critical analysis has more benefits than just anchoring stories in history. It also enables the scholar to detect how the traditions have been handled by the Evangelists, and it provides the data for the form-critical and redaction-critical stages to follow. Nevertheless, demonstrating the reliability of the material is an important step in itself, for it anchors interpreters in history and helps them to realize they are not simply studying the ideas of Mark or Matthew (one danger of a redaction-critical approach) but the teachings of Jesus himself.

Form-Critical Analysis

Before one can begin a detailed study of a pericope, it is important to decide what form the story takes—pronouncement story (in which the details prepare for the climactic saying of Jesus); controversy narrative (similar to the pronouncement story but centering upon Jesus' conflict with the Jewish authorities); miracle story (of which there are several types, some centering upon discipleship, others upon Christology, still others upon cosmic conflict or the presence of the kingdom); dominical saying (short maxims, often without specific context; Bultmann further classifies these into wisdom logia, prophetic or apocalyptic sayings, legal sayings or church rules, "I" sayings, and similitudes); parable (often classified into similitudes or brief comparisons, example stories centering upon moral paradigms to be imitated, and one-, two-, or three-point parables depending upon the number of characters involved[30]); event or historical story (episodes in Jesus' life like the baptism or transfiguration—called "legends" by many form critics because of the predominance of the supernatural); and passion stories (considered a separate set of traditions though containing a variety of actual "forms").[31]

Identifying the form is important because each subgenre has its own set of hermeneutical principles to guide the interpreter.[32] For the scholar there are technical works on each of these formal types like pronouncement stories, miracles, or parables. In the final analysis the formal features help more in composition criticism than in redaction criticism, but these are two aspects of a larger whole, and therefore formal analysis is critical for a redactional understanding of the pericope.

Redaction-Critical Analysis

This is the most detailed aspect and the one in which the Greek synopsis is the most critical. Each alteration of the source should be examined to see whether it is a redactional or stylistic change, that is, whether the alteration has a theological purpose or is merely cosmetic, part of the Evangelist's normal style. One complication is that redaction criticism is more easily done in Matthew and Luke (if one accepts Marcan priority) since identification of sources in Mark is highly speculative and since the Gospel of John is so independent of the Synoptics. Yet it is not impossible to analyze Mark and

John in this way (though obviously the source-critical techniques do not readily apply). The following principles are intended to guide the student through the process as it applies to all four Gospels. There are two stages to the redaction-critical process: (1) the individual analysis of a single pericope, and (2) the holistic analysis of the entire Gospel. These are interdependent steps, for the material from the pericopes form the building blocks for the study of the whole, and the repetition of themes throughout the book is a critical control against an overzealous attempt to see every change as theologically motivated.

INDIVIDUAL ANALYSIS

McKnight provides an excellent approach for underlining a pericope in the synopsis in order to delineate the particular emphases of each Gospel. There are six steps[33]: (1) Determine whether a true parallel exists, that is, whether the accounts are independent (e.g., Matt 22:1–14 and Luke 14:16–24, which have few words in common and occur in separate places in the narrative); do not underline. (2) If the accounts are parallel, note those words that are not paralleled in the others that are peculiar to that Gospel, and either do not underline them or underline them in brown. (3) Underline terms or phrases that are common to all three Synoptic Gospels in blue. (4) Where Mark and Matthew agree against Luke, underline in yellow or black. (5) Where Mark and Luke agree against Matthew, underline in green. (6) Material found in Matthew and Luke but not Mark (mostly Q sayings) should be underlined in red.[34] This procedure provides the raw data for the following analysis.

Noting the various relationships within the pericope on the basis of the underlining, the student evaluates the account from the standpoint of the Evangelist and his sources. For Matthew and Luke, steps two and six will tell the interpreter how each altered Mark or Q. By grouping the changes, one can begin to see a pattern emerging and can detect certain theological nuances developing within the larger matrix of the story as a whole. For instance, Luke's version of the centurion's cry (23:47) says, "Surely, this man was innocent *(dikaios),*" while both Matthew and Mark have, "Surely this was the Son of God." The alteration in Luke is in keeping with his stress throughout his passion narrative upon Jesus as the righteous martyr and is undoubtedly a redactional emphasis.[35]

HOLISTIC ANALYSIS

The preceding step is primarily used for Matthean and Lukan studies (for those who accept Marcan priority). The present step can be used in analyzing any of the four Gospels since it is not dependent upon a source-critical theory.[36] Here we would note again that the analysis of the individual pericopes becomes the building blocks for the larger study of the Gospel as a whole. Edgar McKnight calls this "the principle of comprehensiveness," quoting Schreiber: "All verses of Mark that are to be ascribed to the redaction of Mark with the help of the methods of analytical research provide the point of departure for establishing his theology, to the extent that in these verses scattered over the whole gospel a unified theological conception becomes visible."[37]

1. *Study the Seams.* The "seams" in a Gospel are the transitions (introductions and conclusions) that link episodes together and provide the setting and often the theological emphases for the passage. Since K. L. Schmidt's influential form-critical study of the Marcan seams,[38] scholars have realized the importance of these units for critical research. One might note the synagogue ministry of Jesus in Mark 1:21 and 3:1, in which Jesus confronts the Jews via his authority in word and deed. Marcan Christology becomes apparent in the two seams by providing the setting for Jesus' ministry of confrontation.

2. *Note the Summaries.* Where an Evangelist has summarized material, redactional emphases are particularly apparent. The recurrent themes of these passages provide clues to major theological overtones in the Gospel. One example might be Matthew 4:23 and 9:35, which are virtually identical in wording, which summarize Jesus' itinerant missionary activity, and which lead into the Sermon on the Mount and the missionary discourse respectively. The combination of teaching, preaching, and healing is a major theological emphasis of Matthew.[39]

3. *Note Editorial Asides and Insertions.* Comments that are peculiar to a particular Evangelist become invaluable guides to the direction the stories are taking. Mark often introduces such comments with *gar* ("for"), as in 1:16 ("for he was teaching them as one with authority, not like the scribes") or 2:15 ("for there were many like this [tax-collectors and sinners] who followed him"). In both instances the editorial aside points to the major emphasis of the passage. One of the better known examples is the series of editorial comments by John, as in 3:16–21, which is most likely the Evangelist's commentary on the soteriological significance of the Nicodemus dialogue (3:1–15).[40]

4. *Note Repeated or Favorite Words/Phrases.* The repetition of a word or phrase is indicative of emphasis and functions at both the micro- (individual pericope) and macro- (whole Gospel) levels. For instance, in the healing of the demon-possessed child in Mark 9:14–29, the attempt of the demon to destroy the child is repeated four times (vv. 18, 20, 22, 26, none of which are found in the Matthean parallel [17:14–21]). Obviously Mark wants the reader to note the cosmic conflict taking place (a major Marcan theme). John, of course, is the master of this technique. Every term he favors is found nearly as often in his Gospel as in the rest of the New Testament together: *pisteuein* (ninety-eight times in John versus thirty-four total in the other Gospels); *zōē* (66 of the 135 New Testament uses); *kosmos* (105 of the 185 New Testament uses); *alētheia* (85 of the 163 New Testament uses). Each term is also a primary source of Johannine theology.

Composition-Critical Analysis

The task of delineating the theology of the Evangelist is incomplete if one considers only the redactional changes, for the Evangelist obviously intended that the tradition he decided to include be part of his theological message as well. This step reverses the tradition-critical approach above; instead of removing the tradition in order to identify the redactional changes, we now study the tradition as well as redaction to see how the whole fits together to produce the theological message. Here redaction criticism shades over into literary or narrative criticism, for the interpreter now looks at the whole product as the source of theological emphases.[41]

NOTE THE STRUCTURE

Rearrangement of the inherited tradition usually points to theological emphases. For instance, in the temptation narrative, Matthew (4:5–10) and Luke (4:5–12) reverse the order of the last two temptations, Matthew ending with the mountaintop temptation and Luke with the temple temptation. Most believe that Matthew has preserved the original order and that Luke places the temple scene last in order to conclude with Jesus at the temple in Jerusalem (a major thrust in Luke-Acts), although it could also be true that Matthew decided to conclude with a mountain scene (cf. Matt 5:1; 8:1; 14:23; 15:29; 17:1). Rearrangement may also occur at the macro level. Mark and Luke do different things with Jesus' early Capernaum-based ministry. Mark places the call of the disciples at the beginning (1:16–20) in order to focus at the start on the issue of discipleship and only then goes into the Capernaum ministry, reserving the rejection at Nazareth for 6:1–6. Luke, however, starts with Jesus' inaugural address and rejection at Nazareth (4:16–30), reserving the call of the disciples for 5:1–11. Thus Luke begins with Christology rather than discipleship.

STUDY INTERTEXTUAL DEVELOPMENT

As the Gospel narrative unfolds, the Evangelist arranges his stories so that they interact with one another to produce the intended message. A primary maxim of narrative criticism is that this intertextual arrangement is not haphazard. In fact, intertextuality at the macro level is the literary counterpart of redaction criticism at the macro level, for the writer uses the same principles of selection, omission, and expansion to develop the narrative as a whole. This can be seen, for instance, in the strategic placement of the pericope of the healing of the blind man in Mark 8:22–26 (found only in Mark). At one level the pericope forms an inclusion with the healing of the deaf man in 7:31–37, thus framing the feeding of the four thousand and discipleship failure scenes (8:1–21) and stressing the need for spiritual healing on the part of the disciples. On a second level, as a two-stage miracle it leads into the two-stage healing of the disciples' misunderstanding via Peter's confession at Caesarea Philippa (8:27–33, in which Peter metaphorically sees

Jesus' messianic status in "blurred" fashion) and the transfiguration (9:1–10, in which the disciples glimpse the true nature of Jesus). In this sense the miracle of 8:22–26 links together the discipleship emphases of Mark's middle section.

STUDY THE PLOT

This also is done at both the micro and macro levels. Plot refers to an interconnected sequence of events that centers on conflict and follows a cause-effect order. In studying plot we note the lines of causality, that is, how the characters interact and how the interplay of opposing forces builds to a climax. To discover this we chart the actantial units (the individual events and actions) and study the ebb and flow of the story line. Within redaction criticism the key is to compare the differing plots of the Evangelists in order to determine their distinctive approaches and theological purposes in writing. The differences are often striking. Consider the resurrection narratives as an example. Mark has a linear flow centering upon discipleship failure and concluding with the women's failure to witness in 16:8; this is countered by Jesus' enigmatic promise to meet them in Galilee (14:28; 16:7), where they apparently will be reinstated (14:28 following v. 27). Matthew, on the other hand, centers upon the power of God overcoming the double attempt by the priests to thwart his ordained purpose (27:62–66; 27:11–15) via supernatural intervention (28:2–4) and by the universal authority of the Son passed on to the church in mission (28:18–20).[42]

NOTE THE SETTING AND STYLE

These are also redactional peculiarities that enable the scholar to detect the theological message of the Evangelist. The setting is the textual context within which the action occurs. As Rhoads and Michie state, this setting can have several functions: "generating atmosphere, determining conflict, revealing traits in the characters who must deal with problems or threats caused by the settings, offering commentary (sometimes ironic) on the action, and evoking associations and nuances of meaning present in the culture of the readers."[43] The Evangelists, by giving the same or similar episode a different setting, can evoke various nuances of meaning. For instance, the parable of the lost sheep in Matthew is delivered to the disciples and church (18:12–14) and apparently refers to "straying" members, while in Luke 15:3–7 it is addressed to the Pharisees and scribes and refers to those outside the kingdom.[44] Style refers to the way the material has been arranged in the individual Gospels. There can be inclusion or chiasma, a repetition, gaps, or omissions that draw the reader into the story in order to complete its meaning, antitheses, irony, or poetic parallelism. All these stylistic devices are used by the authors and should be carefully scrutinized by the reader as important clues to the theological message.

Dangers of Redaction Criticism

Redaction criticism has found a firm place in the list of hermeneutical tools, but by no means has it won universal acceptance. Evangelical and nonevangelical scholars alike have criticized its excesses, and some have argued that it should be discarded as an unworkable tool. This is stated most strongly in *The Jesus Crisis*[45] in which Robert Thomas[46] argues that any evangelical using redaction criticism must accept the premises of its founders: (1) the Evangelists are theologians, not historians; (2) the Gospel stories originate not in the actual historical event but in the faith and preaching needs of the early church; (3) the Gospels are the creation of the authors and not sources for the life of Christ; (4) the writers embellished the sayings and stories with their own ideas; (5) the subjective bias of the critics leads them to read their own ideas into the stories; (6) critics are biased toward nonhistoricity in deciding about the historical veracity of the Gospel material. The arguments below will seek to demonstrate that these assumptions are false. Redaction criticism can be used without the negative bias of radical critics, and it becomes the friend of a high view of Scripture when used without these presuppositions.[47] The major problems must be considered carefully before we can evaluate its usefulness.

DEPENDENCE ON THE FOUR-DOCUMENT HYPOTHESIS

This is primarily a problem for those who doubt the Streeter solution accepted above. It is true that the issue of sources will never be settled with certainty, but it is also a fact that anyone studying the Gospels seriously must adopt some theory regarding the relationship between these Gospels, and the four-document hypothesis is clearly the best of the alternatives (see McKnight's article in this volume). Therefore we can proceed with confidence that Marcan priority is basically correct.

HISTORICAL SKEPTICISM

Many critics proceed with the assumption that every redactional change is by definition a creation and thus cannot be historical. Yet this is a presupposition and by no means carries the day. Addition and omission are not criteria for historicity, but for style, selection, and emphasis. As Caird says, "Redaction criticism treat[s] the Evangelists as interpreters, but all too often with the tacit assumption that to interpret is to misinterpret. Considering that they are themselves professional interpreters, it might seem wiser to allow for the possibility that an interpreter should occasionally be right."[48] Some Evangelists have argued that this skepticism is inherent in the tool itself and that redaction criticism should therefore be discarded.[49] This pessimism is as unwarranted as is the historical skepticism above. Antihistorical tendencies are not inherent in redaction critical methodology, and many studies have proceeded with a positive outlook toward the historicity of the pericopes.[50]

REJECTION OF HARMONIZATION

Due to the excesses of some who answer all historical discrepancies by shallow harmonization, modern critics have too often refused any attempt to harmonize accounts. At the same time these scholars assume that any sayings, parables, or stories that are somewhat similar are variations of the same account, and their so-called "contradictions" are often just as shallow as the aforementioned harmonizations. Jesus was certainly an itinerant preacher-teacher who used variations of the same story or saying on more than one occasion, and it is often erroneous to assume that one is "more authentic" than the other.[51]

TENDENCY TOWARD FRAGMENTATION

Form criticism with its assumption that each pericope was an independent unit was certainly more guilty of fragmenting rather than unifying the Gospels, but redaction criticism has a similar problem when it studies only the additions to the tradition. Many have called this the "disintegration" process, and McKnight labels it the "problem of interpretative priority"[52] since the critic seeks meaning in the redaction rather than the tradition. The movement toward composition criticism has provided a good solution from within this school. Scholars now realize that theology comes from the pericope as a whole and not just from the alterations.

OVERSTATEMENT

Many proponents of redaction criticism assume that every jot and tittle of the author's changes carry theological weight. They seem to forget that many changes are stylistic rather than theological and that the Evangelists were often paraphrasing rather than quoting their sources verbatim. Again, composition criticism provides a corrective, for it demands that theological emphases be part of a larger pattern rather than be read into every individual change.

SUBJECTIVISM

The bewildering multiplicity of theories coming from redactional studies belies any pretence that the method leads to assured results. Carson goes so far as to claim that "the tools are incapable of providing an entirely neutral and agreed judgment as to what is authentic."[53] There is a great deal of truth to this charge, for each scholar seems to produce different results from the same data, results that suspiciously resemble the thesis with which the scholar began! This tendency is counteracted only by a judicious use of *all* the hermeneutical tools mentioned above in such a way that they challenge and correct excesses.

THE SPECULATIVE NATURE OF "SITZ IM LEBEN" DETERMINATIONS

The preoccupation of many with the situation behind the Evangelist's redactional changes provides probably the best evidence for the subjective nature of the whole enterprise. Attempts to describe the church behind Matthew's Gospel as Gentile or upper middle class or Jewish have established little except the academic morass behind such attempts. In fact, there is an implicit negativism within such an enterprise, for it assumes that redactional emphases are always due to problems in the Evangelist's church and ignores the fact that many of the changes are the result of Christological or worship or historical interests. The solution is to recognize that the true place of a life-situation approach lies not in the speculative reconstruction of the church behind a Gospel but in the delineation of the Evangelist's message to that church.

The Value and Place of Redaction Criticism

One could assume from these difficulties that redaction criticism is more trouble than it is worth. Such would be an unfortunate mistake. A careful methodology can remove or control most of these potential problems, and the values far outweigh the dangers. In fact, I would go so far as to say that any responsible study of the Gospels must proceed from a redaction- (and literary-) critical perspective. It can be claimed with virtual certainty that the Gospel writers were led by God to use sources in the production of their Gospels. Moreover, these sources (most likely Mark and Q behind Matthew and Luke as well as the special sources M and L) can be detected and should be used in any attempt to understand the Gospels more deeply. At the same time, the message is found in the pericope as a whole and not just in the redactional changes so the next step is to trace the message through a combination of tradition and redaction in the unified story and finally through the Gospel as a whole.

The values of such an approach are obvious. Redaction criticism enables us to understand as never before how the process of inspiration took place in the production of the Gospels. Heretofore the authors of every book of the Bible were regarded as inspired, but the authors of the Gospels were ignored because these books contained the stories of Jesus. Now we can see how God inspired the Evangelists to select, highlight, and emphasize certain aspects of the life of Jesus in order to speak to their readers. For the first time these writings have actually become "Gospels," not just biographical accounts but "history with a message." These inspired authors did not just chronicle historical events but produced historical sermons, as God inspired the Evangelists to take virtually the same set of stories and weave out of them individual tapestries of theological truth.

Until this school developed, most of us turned to the Epistles for theology because they were the didactic tools of the early church. Redactional studies have demonstrated that the Gospels are also theological; and in many ways this theology is even more exciting than that stemming from the Epistles, for it is presented through living relationships and enacted in dynamic events, thus producing a sort of case study workbook for theological understanding.

In other words, the Gospels are not just theology taught but theology lived. As a result we have an exciting "new" source for the relevant presentation of God's truths.

Redaction criticism enables the modern interpreter to reconstruct the theology of each Evangelist by detecting how he used his sources to produce that intended message. While the theology comes out of the unified (tradition and redaction) product, redactional analysis provides a control that leads to greater precision and less subjectivism in uncovering the intended message. By itself, of course, a new subjectivism could arise, exemplified in those early studies (e.g., Conzelmann or Marxsen) that drew erroneous conclusions by studying only part of the evidence. However, composition analysis interacts with redaction criticism in such a way that the whole and the parts correct one another, with the redactional study providing the data and the compositional study analyzing it all together before making final conclusions.

Furthermore, the reader can appreciate the twofold thrust of the Gospels better: they present the events and sayings of the historical Jesus (the historical component) in such a way that the stories speak to the church (the kerygmatic component). We dare not forget that the life and teachings of the historical Jesus are also an assured result of the study of the Gospels. We cannot trace with certainty the "footsteps of Jesus," since no Gospel gives a chronological (i.e., day-by-day or even month-by-month) account of Jesus' ministry; and we can seldom detect the *ipsissima verba* (exact words) of Jesus. But we can know the broad contours of his life and certainly the *ipsissima vox* (exact understanding) of his teaching.[54] In short, the Gospels are historical records that tell us about Jesus and about his life and teachings. While redaction criticism as a discipline centers upon the theological aspect, it does not neglect the historical factor. By its very nature it studies only the diverse theologies of the four Evangelists, and in fact this diversity is what God inspired. However, it is valid and in some ways obligatory for us to put these diverse accounts together to produce a unified account of the life and teachings of Jesus,[55] so long as we recognize that we cannot do so with precision. For instance, we cannot harmonize the chronologies of John and the Synoptics in such a way as to know the precise order of events in Jesus' life, but we can know the broad contours, and that is sufficient. The way we must do this is not to ignore the results of redaction criticism but to work with them by harmonizing the diverse accounts and theologies of the separate Gospels into a unified record of Jesus' life and teaching.

Finally, redaction criticism is a preaching and not just an academic tool. When we contextualize the Gospels for our contemporary audiences, we must realize that the Evangelists have already done so; they contextualized the life of Jesus for their own churches and thus provided a model to guide our own homiletical process. The Gospels have been shown to be inspired sermons (*gospel* means "a good news sermon") using the person and impact of Jesus upon three groups (the disciples, the crowds, and the Jewish leaders) to speak to their own contemporary world (evangelism) and church (exhortation). Therefore it is in keeping with the very nature of the Gospels to use them as a source for preaching. It is here that the true value of the *Sitz im Leben* (life-situation) approach to the Gospels can be found, not in determining the exact nature of the church behind, say, Matthew's Gospel, but in discovering Matthew's message to that church. As Stein says, "If one attributes divine authority to the Evangelists, we often possess not only a divine word from Jesus himself, but an authoritative interpretation of that word. We are doubly enriched in such instances."[56] In fact, one could argue that the true intention of the Gospels is incomplete until they are indeed preached. The true goal of hermeneutics is not so much the learned monograph as it is the sermon. The gospel (and Gospels) is not just the good news probed but the good news proclaimed.

Redaction criticism is not an end in itself. It must be used along with other hermeneutical tools if it is to be effective. For instance, it should not be done without the historical-grammatical exegesis of the text itself, for exegesis will yield that detailed understanding of the pericope that redaction criticism by itself can never provide. On the other hand, redactional study will deepen one's knowledge regarding the Evangelists' emphases. In other words, the two work together in the study of biblical narrative. Background study is another essential, for this draws the interpreter back into the historical dimensions of the text and protects the scholar from reading the story with a twentieth-century literary bias. When redaction criticism is placed within this larger hermeneutical paradigm, it is not only a valuable but an essential tool for understanding the God-inspired meaning that each Evangelist gave to the story of Jesus the Christ in his Gospel.

Bibliography

Bornkamm, G., G. Barth, and H. J. Held. *Tradition and Interpretation in Matthew.* Philadelphia: Westminster, 1963.

Conzelmann, Hans. *The Theology of St. Luke.* New York: Harper, 1961.

Marshall, I. Howard. *Luke: Historian and Theologian.* Grand Rapids: Zondervan, 1971.

Marxsen, W. *Mark the Evangelist: Studies on the Redaction History of the Gospel.* Nashville: Abingdon, 1969.

Osborne, Grant. *The Resurrection Narratives: A Redaction Study.* Grand Rapids: Baker, 1984.

Perrin, Norman. *What Is Redaction Criticism?* Philadelphia: Fortress, 1970.

Stein, R. H. "What Is Redaktionsgeschichte?" *Journal of Biblical Literature* 88 (1969): 45–56.

Notes

1. One should note here that in neither form nor redaction criticism is Jesus the creative force. Both assume the negative results of tradition criticism, which concludes that the historical Jesus is an elusive presence in the Gospels.

2. See the chapter "Source Criticism" in this volume. Robert H. Stein, *The Synoptic Problem: An Introduction* (Grand Rapids: Baker, 1987), 143, calls source criticism "the single most important tool of the redaction critic" because the changes the Evangelists chose to introduce into their sources guide the interpreter to their theological interests (see pp. 143–51).

3. This has been challenged in recent years by the Griesbach Hypothesis, rejuvenated recently by Farmer and Orchard and arguing for Matthean priority. As McKnight shows in his article on source criticism, however, this has far more problems than does the four-document hypothesis presented here. For the independence of the Gospel writers from one another, see Eta Linnemann, *Is There a Synoptic Problem?* trans. R. Yarbrough (Grand Rapids: Baker, 1992).

4. See the fine discussion of this in E. P. Sanders and Margaret Davies, *Studying the Synoptic Gospels* (Philadelphia: Trinity Press International, 1989), 201–02. They state that redaction criticism began when Bultmann's disciples reworked the final section on his *History of the Synoptic Tradition*, entitled "The Editing (*Redaktion*) of the Traditional Material."

5. Scot McKnight, *Interpreting the Synoptic Gospels* (Grand Rapids: Baker, 1988), 85, notes the developing interest of critics as they move "from minute alterations unique to an Evangelist as compared with his inherited traditions to larger patterns (including literary strategies)." There are three successive stages: the process moves from (1) the detection of individual changes to (2) the discovery of patterns that indicate theological interest and finally to (3) noting the overall literary strategy of the author that led to those alterations. These three levels are obviously interdependent.

6. Wilhelm Wrede, *The Messianic Secret*, trans. J. C. G. Greig (Cambridge: James Clarke, 1971, originally 1901); Ned B. Stonehouse, *The Witness of the Synoptic Gospels to Christ* (Grand Rapids: Baker, 1979, originally 1951); R. H. Lightfoot, *History and Interpretation in the Gospels* (New York: Harper, n.d.). On the history of redaction criticism, see also Norman Perrin, *What Is Redaction Criticism?* (Philadelphia: Fortress, 1969), 7–13, 21–24; McKnight, *Interpreting*, 87; and Moises Silva, "Ned B. Stonehouse and Redaction Criticism, Part 1: The Witness of the Synoptic Evangelists to Christ," *Westminster Theological Journal* 40 (1977): 77–88. For an interesting recent survey, see J. R. Donahue, "Redaction Criticism: New Testament," in *Dictionary of Biblical Interpretation*, ed. John Hayes, 2 vols. (Nashville: Abingdon, 1999), 2:376–79.

7. Gunther Bornkamm, Gerhard Barth, and H. J. Held, *Tradition and Interpretation in Matthew*, trans. P. Scott (Philadelphia: Westminster, 1963).

8. Bornkamm, *Tradition*, 55. Joachim Rohde, *Rediscovering the Teaching of the Evangelists*, trans. D. M. Barton (Philadelphia: Westminster, 1968), 13, summarizes Bornkamm's conclusions: "By its connection with the sayings about discipleship, the stilling of the storm has become *kerygma* and a paradigm of the danger and glory of discipleship."

9. Originally presented at a conference in 1954 under the title, "Matthew as Interpreter of the Words of the Lord" but expanded into the form found in *Tradition and Interpretation*, 15–51. There are four parts to the article dealing with eschatology, the law, Christology, and ecclesiology.

10. Hans Conzelmann, "Zur Lukasanlyse," *Zeitschrift für Theologie und Kirche* 49 (1952): 16–33.

11. Hans Conzelmann, *The Theology of St. Luke*, trans. G. Buswell (New York: Harper, 1960, German 1954).

12. Perrin, *Redaction Criticism*, 28. Perrin believes that Conzelmann's work ranks with Bultmann's *History of the Synoptic Tradition* and Jeremias' *The Parables of Jesus* as one of the most important New Testament studies of our time.

13. Conzelmann speaks of Luke's "critical attitude to tradition" as seen in his "positive formation of a new picture of history out of those already current, like stones used as parts of a new mosaic" (*Theology*, 12).

14. Willi Marxsen, *Mark the Evangelist: Studies on the Redaction History of the Gospel*, trans. J. Boyce, D. Juel, W. Poehlmann, and R. A. Harrisville (New York: Abingdon, 1969, German 1956).

15. For others who have used redaction criticism, see Rohde, *Rediscovering,* passim; and for an updated discussion, see Edgar V. McKnight, "Form and Redaction Criticism," in *The New Testament and Its Modern Interpreters*, ed. Eldon J. Epp and George W. McRae (Philadelphia: Fortress, 1989), 157–63; and Donahue, "Redaction Criticism," 376–79. For Old Testament redaction criticism, see M. E. Biddle in the same volume, 373–76.

16. Theodore J. Weeden, *Mark—Traditions in Conflict* (Philadelphia: Fortress, 1971).

17. Perrin, *Redaction Criticism*, 79.

18. See Stewart C. Goetz and Craig L. Blomberg, "The Burden of Proof," *Journal of the Study of the New Testament* 11 (1981): 39–63; Grant R. Osborne, *The Resurrection Narratives: A Redactional Study* (Grand Rapids: Baker, 1984), 195–96.

19. See Morna Hooker, "Christology and Methodology," *New Testament Studies* 17 (1970–71): 485. While accepting the reliability of the tradition, R. T. France, "The Authenticity of the Sayings of Jesus," *History, Criticism, and Faith*, ed. Colin Brown (Downers Grove, Ill.: InterVarsity, 1977), 117, says of the negative and positive burdens of proof that "both views are assumptions" and that "what we must both do is to examine our assumptions in the light of the available evidence." On the other hand, scholars on both sides are skeptical of the viability of any such "neutral" position. See from the skeptical side E. P. Sanders, *Jesus and Judaism* (Philadelphia: Fortress, 1985), 13–14; from the positive side see Craig L. Blomberg, *The Historical Reliability of the Gospels* (Downers Grove, Ill.: InterVarsity, 1987), 241–42. Both believe that it is necessary to take a studied position while remaining open to the evidence.

20. Peter H. Davids, "Tradition Criticism," in *Dictionary of Jesus and the Gospels*, ed. J. B. Green and S. McKnight (Downers Grove, Ill.: InterVarsity Press, 1992), 833.

21. See Morna Hooker, "On Using the Wrong Tool," *Theology* 75 (1972): 570–81; and her "Christology," 481–85; cf. R. S. Barbour, *Traditio-Historical Criticism of the Gospels* (London: SPCK, 1972), 19–22.

22. See Grant R. Osborne, "The Evangelical and *Tradionsgeschichte*," *Journal of the Evangelical Theological Society* 21/2 (1978): 122–23; and Robert H. Stein, "The 'Criteria' for Authenticity," *Gospel Perspectives*, vol. 1, ed. R. T. France and David Wenham (Sheffield: JSOT, 1980), 244–45.

23. Reginald H. Fuller, *The Foundations of New Testament Christology* (New York: Scribner's, 1965), 96–97.

24. Perrin, *Redaction Criticism*, 71; Stein, "Authenticity," 230.

25. See Stein, "Authenticity," 232–33, who considers this a separate criterion ("of multiple forms"). However, it is so closely connected with the source-critical form that the two become one. Moreover, in most instances the two blend into a single criterion, as in the realized kingdom passages above that take the form of aphorisms or sayings (Matt. 5:17; John 12:31), pronouncement stories (Mark 2:18–22; Luke 11:14–22), and parables (Matt. 25).

26. C. F. D. Moule, *The Phenomenon of the New Testament* (London: SCM, 1967), 62–63. See also Richard N. Longenecker, "Literary Criteria in the Life of Jesus Research," *Current Issues in Biblical and Patristic Interpretation*, ed. G. F. Hawthorne (Grand Rapids: Eerdmans, 1975), 227–28. R. S. A. Calvert, "An Examination of the Criteria for Distinguishing the Authentic Words of Jesus," *New Testament Studies* 18 (1972): 215; and Stein, "Authenticity," 247, extend this to material that does not fit the Evangelist's purposes—for instance, positive statements about the disciples in Mark (contrary to Mark's stress on discipleship failure) or Matthew 11:13, "the prophets and the law prophesied until John" (contrary to Matthew's emphasis on the permanence of the law).

27. S. Hugh Anderson, *The Gospel of Mark* (London: Oliphants, 1979), 22.

28. Joachim Jeremias, *New Testament Theology*, trans. J. Bowden (New York: Scribner's, 1971), 193–96, 288–92.

29. Calvert, "Criteria," 212–13; Stein, "Authenticity," 248–50.

30. See the excellent discussion in Craig L. Blomberg, *Interpreting the Parables* (Downers Grove, Ill.: InterVarsity, 1990).

31. See chapter on form criticism in this volume, the summary in McKnight, *Synoptic*, 74–76, and Craig Blomberg, "Form Criticism," in *Dictionary of Jesus and the Gospels*, 243–50.

32. For the best work on genre analysis from a practical perspective, see Gordon D. Fee and Douglas Stuart, *How to Read the Bible for All Its Worth* (Grand Rapids: Zondervan, 1981), especially chapters 7–8 on Gospel and parable.

33. McKnight, *Synoptic*, 41–44. He builds upon similar suggestions in Farmer (*Synopticon*) and Stein (*Synoptic Problem*). The colors mentioned are suggested by all three authors.

34. These steps are directed only to the Synoptics and take no account of John. McKnight suggests highlighting agreements with John in yellow (if black is used for step four). While this does not indicate which Gospel John agrees with, a simple look across the synopsis will quickly provide that information.

35. Luke also adds that the centurion was "stricken with awe before God," which adds an atmosphere of worship to the scene (the other Lukan emphasis in his crucifixion narrative).

36. The following material is dependent largely upon Grant R. Osborne, "The Evangelical and Redaction Criticism: Critique and Methodology," *Journal of the Evangelical Theological Society* 22/4 (1979): 316–18; and Stein, *Synoptic Problem*, 251–58.

37. McKnight, "Form and Redaction," 163, quoting Johannes Schreiber, "Die Christologie des Markusevangeliums: Beobachtungen zur Theologie and Komposition des zweiten Evangeliums," *Zeitschrift für Theologie and Kirche* 58 (1961): 154.

38. Karl Ludwig Schmidt, *Der Rahmen der Geschichte Jesu: Literarkritische Untersuchungen zur ältesten Jesusüberlieferung* (Berlin: Trowitzsch und Sohn, 1919). Schmidt was another precursor of redaction criticism. He presupposed that the seams were nonhistorical and purely theological. Recently, however, studies in audience criticism among other disciplines have shown that the seams blend tradition and redaction.

39. For a more detailed discussion of Matthean theological emphases, see D. A. Carson, "Matthew," *The Expositor's Bible Commentary*, vol. 8, ed. Frank E. Gaebelein (Grand Rapids: Zondervan, 1984), 120–21; and Donald A. Hagner, *Matthew 1–13*, WBC 33A (Dallas: Word Books, 1993), lix–lxiv. For other Matthean summaries, see 7:28–29; 11:1; 15:30–31; for Marcan summaries, see 1:14–15, 28, 39; 2:13; 3:7–12; 6:53–56; 9:30–32; 10:32–34.

40. See Merrill F. Tenney, "The Footnotes of John's Gospel," *Bibliothecra Sacra* 117 (1960): 350–64.

41. McKnight, *Synoptic*, 135, goes so far as to say that "much of the good in literary criticism has already been exposed through redaction criticism in its 'composition criticism' emphases." While this is overstated, there is some truth in it, for composition criticism uses many of the tools (though not such perspectives as plot, characterization, or intended author). For an introduction to literary criticism, see R. A. Culpepper, *Anatomy of the Fourth Gospel* (Philadelphia: Fortress, 1983); and Rhoads and Michie (note 42). For an evangelical response, see Tremper Longman III, *Literary Approaches to Biblical Interpretation* (Grand Rapids: Zondervan, 1987).

42. For details on these and other resurrection narratives, see my *Resurrection Narratives*, passim.

43. David Rhoads and Donald Michie, *Mark as Story: An Introduction to the Narrative of a Gospel* (Philadelphia: Fortress, 1982), 63.

44. See the excellent discussion in Stein, *Synoptic Problem*, 247–51, who argues strongly for the parable's historical veracity whether it was spoken on one occasion by Jesus or two. Stein and Blomberg, *Parables*, 83, prefer to see it as more likely a single parable placed in different settings "due to the amount of verbal and conceptual parallelism" (Blomberg), while Carson, "Matthew," 400, argues that it was a similar parable within the bounds of repetition expected in an itinerant ministry. Either way, biblical authority is upheld.

45. Robert L. Thomas and David Farnell, eds., *The Jesus Crisis: The Inroads of Historical Criticism into Evangelical Scholarship* (Grand Rapids: Kregel, 1998).

46. Thomas, "Redaction Criticism," in *Jesus Crisis*, 253–57.

47. Also, see Grant R. Osborne, "Historical Criticism and the Evangelical," *JETS* 42/2 (1999), 193–210.

48. George B. Caird, "Study of the Gospels. III. Redaction Criticism," *Expository Times* 87 (1976): 172.

49. See John Warwick Montgomery, "Why Has God Incarnate Suddenly Become Mythical?" in *Perspectives on Evangelical Theology*, ed. K. Kantzer and S. N. Gundry (Grand Rapids: Baker, 1979), 57–65; and Robert L. Thomas, "The Hermeneutics of Evangelical Redaction Criticism," *Journal of the Evangelical Theological Society* 29/4 (1986): 447–59.

50. For articles chronicling this debate but with a more positive assessment of the discipline, see David L. Turner, "Evangelicals, Redaction Criticism, and the Current Inerrancy Crisis," *Grace Theological Journal* 4 (1982): 263–88; idem, "Evangelicals, Redaction Criticism and Innerancy: The Debate Continues," *Grace Theological Journal* 5 (1984): 37–45; and Grant R. Osborne, "Round Four: The Redaction Debate Continues," *Journal of the Evangelical Theological Society* 28/4 (1985): 399–410. For an excellent example of the use of redaction-critical tools to support the historicity of a Gospel pericope, see Eckhard J. Schnabel, "The Silence of Jesus: The Galilean Rabbi Who Was More Than a Prophet," in *Authenticating the Word of Jesus*, ed. B. D. Chilton and C. A. Evans (Leidon: Brill, 1999), 203–57.

51. An excellent and balanced introduction to harmonization can be found in Craig L. Blomberg, "The Legitimacy and Limits of Harmonization," in *Hermeneutics, Authority, and Canon*, ed. D. A. Carson and John D. Woodbridge (Grand Rapids: Zondervan, 1986), 139–74.

52. McKnight, *Synoptic*, 90.

53. D. A. Carson, "Redaction Criticism: On the Legitimacy and Illegitimacy of a Literary Tool," in *Scripture and Truth*, ed. D. A. Carson and John D. Woodbridge

(Grand Rapids: Zondervan, 1983), 126. He quotes Hooker, "Wrong Tool," 577: "Of course, NT scholars recognize the inadequacy of their tools; when different people look at the same passage, and all get different answers, the inadequacy is obvious, even to NT scholars! But they do not draw the logical deduction from this fact."

54. Paul Feinberg, "The Meaning of Inerrancy," in *Inerrancy*, ed. Norman L. Geisler (Grand Rapids: Zondervan, 1979), 301, says, "*Inerrancy does not demand that the logia Jesu (the sayings of Jesus) contain the ipsissima verba (the exact words) of Jesus, only the ipsissima vox (the exact voice)*. . . . When a New Testament writer cites the sayings of Jesus, it need not be the case that Jesus said those exact words. Undoubtedly the exact words of Jesus are to be found in the New Testament, but they need not be so in every instance. . . . With regard to the sayings of Jesus, what would count against inerrancy? The words in the sense of *ipsissima vox* were not uttered by Jesus, or the *ipsissima verba* were spoken by our Lord but so used by the writer that the meaning given by the writer is inconsistent with the intended meaning of Jesus" (italics his). For an interesting article on the words of Jesus in the Gospels, see Darrell Bock, "The Words of Jesus in the Gospels: Live, Jive, or Memorex," in *Jesus Under Fire*, ed. M. J. Wilkins and J. P. Moreland (Grand Rapids: Zondervan, 1995), 77–80.

55. A good book in this respect is Robert H. Stein, *The Method and Message of Jesus' Teachings* (Philadelphia: Westminster, 1978).

56. Stein, *Synoptic Problem*, 270. See also Grant R. Osborne, "Preaching the Gospels: Methodology and Contextualization," *Journal of the Evangelical Theological Society* 27/1 (1984): 27–42.

Chapter 7

Literary Criticism

Jeffrey A. D. Weima
Calvin Theological Seminary

The past few decades have witnessed a paradigm shift taking place in biblical studies. The old perspective that viewed Scripture as primarily a historical or theological document has been replaced by a new conviction that the Bible is literature and as such ought to be interpreted from a literary perspective. The traditional methods of higher criticism—that is, source criticism, form criticism, and redaction criticism—which dominated New Testament studies for so long have given way to a new criticism that emphasizes the literary character of the biblical text and finds the key to meaning in the form and structure of the writing rather than in its use of possible sources, the reconstruction of its hypothetical historical context, or the perceived intention of its author.[1] It is common today, therefore, to find not just specialized monographs but also commentaries, general introductions, and other popular guides to the Bible that advertise themselves as offering a "literary approach."

But while biblical scholars have been using the term *literary criticism* with increasing frequency over the past thirty years, until recent times they did not define this method in the same way that literary scholars in the humanities did. Many biblical scholars early on used the term *literary criticism* simply as another way to refer to traditional debates about authorship, dating, sources, and so on. This older view can be seen, for example, in George Ladd's statement that "literary criticism is the study of such questions as the authorship, date, place of writing, recipients, sources, integrity, and purpose of any piece of literature."[2] That literary scholars in the humanities did not share this understanding is evident from Amos Wilder's "astonishment that the term 'literary criticism' should have such different connotations for biblical scholars as for students of literature generally," noting specifically the preoccupation of biblical scholars with authorship,

150

sources, dating, and purpose as opposed to "those appreciative and interpretive questions which are the goal of criticism everywhere else."[3]

Today the gap between biblical scholars and nonbiblical literary scholars has been largely bridged as both communities share a number of convictions about what literary criticism involves: an appreciation for the sophisticated artistry and aesthetic quality of biblical texts; a concern with the diverse literary genres (e.g., narrative, poetry, gospel, letter, apocalypse) found in the Bible; a preoccupation with formal features of the text and the function that these formal features have in communicating information; a commitment to treat texts as finished wholes rather than as patchwork collections or originally independent sources; and a growing awareness that the Bible is a work of literature and that the methods of literary scholarship are thus a valid and necessary part of the interpretation process.

But even though these convictions are held by many, they by no means fully define the term *literary criticism* or wholly explain what a literary approach to Scripture involves. This is due to the fact that there is no single literary-critical method of interpretation. Instead, a wide variety of interpretative approaches have been forwarded, each under the banner of "literary criticism" and vying for its preeminent place in the critical marketplace. The plethora of proposed literary theories has caused one observer to note the following:

> There is no longer any such thing as a "working majority" in literary studies . . . Marxists, Freudians, Jungians, Semioticians, Structuralists, Formalists, myth critics, deconstructionalists, Lacanians, Foucauldians, Neo-Aristotelians, feminists, subjectivists, historical critics, rhetorical critics, old New Critics, and humanists of every kind and stripe, have laid before us a smorgasbord of interpretations and interpretative principles that if we are wise we can pick and choose from to reach *our own* critical method.[4]

In order not to overindulge ourselves in the veritable feast of interpretative theories currently available, we limit our appetite in the first and major part of this chapter to an overview of those literary methods that have had the greatest impact upon biblical studies. For dessert, we offer in the second part of this chapter a brief literary analysis of the letter of Jude that illustrates the exegetical payoff of a literary approach to Scripture.

An Overview of Literary Criticism: Major Methods of Interpretation

A helpful way to survey the various literary methods of interpretation is to make use of the linguistic communication model of Roman Jakobson.[5] In any act of communication, one can distinguish between the sender, the message which that person conveys, and the recipient of the message. When this model is applied to literary texts, these three components become (1) the author, (2) the text, and (3) the reader. The communication itself takes place in a historical or social context that may be called the universe. The following diagram visually depicts the major elements of this communication model:

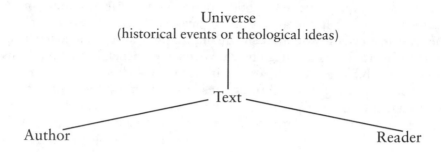

Each of the major literary methods of interpretation typically focuses on one of these three components: the author, the text, or the reader. In other words, the center of authority that is appealed to in order to arbitrate matters of interpretative debate about any given text is either the author, the text, or the reader. Thus, it is possible to survey the various literary methods according to the following tripartite schema: author-centered approaches, text-centered approaches, and reader-centered approaches.

AUTHOR-CENTERED APPROACHES

The approach that concentrates on the author as the center of authority for interpreting texts is typically referred to as Traditional Criticism. This approach is associated with the romantic-humanist tradition and predates the rise of the various literary methods that have been part of the paradigm shift taking place in biblical studies during the past few decades. The underlying belief of traditional criticism is that one understands a text best by learning as much as possible about the author who composed it and the specific historical circumstances that gave rise to it. Thus, for example, if one is going to interpret properly Keats' sonnet "Bright Star," in which this English Romantic poet pairs the themes of death and love, it is important to know that Keats wrote this poem at the same time as he was caring for his brother Tom who was dying of tuberculosis and also when he was hopelessly in love with a young neighbor girl named Fanny Brawne.[6]

Biblical scholars have long concentrated on the author as the key to interpreting Old and New Testament texts. This method of investigation, however, is usually not identified with the nomenclature of traditional criticism but that of higher criticism. Biblical scholars also differed somewhat from secular literary critics in that they went beyond a probe into the life of a particular author to investigate also what sources the author may have used (source criticism), the original form and setting of these sources (form criticism), and how the author shaped or arranged these sources in creating the final form of the text (redaction criticism). Although evangelicals have been somewhat hesitant to make full use of various methods of higher criticism, they have for the most part also assumed that the meaning of a text resides in the author's intention and that an understanding of the author's historical context is a crucial part of the interpretive process.

The author-centered approach of traditional criticism came under attack with the rise of "new criticism" (see below) in the 1940s. Some became frustrated with certain traditional critics who expended so much energy and effort in investigating the lives of the authors that they ended up either ignoring the actual literary text before them or offering psychoanalyzed readings of the text that were unconvincing. Others questioned whether it is even possible to discern an author's intention, since a writer is not always fully aware of his or her own motives. Still others wondered how contemporary readers can get back into the mind of an author, especially in ancient texts that were written in a time and culture quite different from that of our own. Concerns such as these spawned a variety of new interpretative approaches where the focus was no longer on the author but on either the text itself or the reader.[7]

TEXT-CENTERED APPROACHES

Modern literary criticism has rejected the author as the center of authority in the interpretive process and looked primarily to the text itself to determine meaning. This dramatic shift away from authorial intent to the text alone as the primary or even sole guide for understanding literary works can be witnessed in the landmark essay, "The Intentional Fallacy," written by the American literary critics William Wimsatt and Monroe Beardsley.[8] The intentional fallacy claims that "whether the author has expressly stated what his intention was in writing a poem, or whether it is merely inferred from what we know about his life and opinions, his intention is irrelevant to the literary critic, because meaning and value reside within the text of the finished, free-standing, and public work of literature itself."[9] This new focus on the text as the locus of authority in the interpretative process gave rise to a variety of literary approaches, the three most important ones being New Criticism (also known as Formalism), Structuralism, and Poststructuralism (also known as Deconstruction).

New Criticism (or Formalism)

New Criticism[10] (or Formalism)[11] has been by far the most important literary approach in the field of New Testament studies. Indeed, this approach is often equated with literary criticism.[12] The fundamental tenet of new criticism has already been described above: the text is sufficient in and of itself for the process of interpretation. There is little or no need for a historical investigation of the author and his circumstances or a psychological analysis of any development in his thinking. The text itself is sufficient to guide the contemporary reader to an understanding that more or less corresponds to that of the author. This self-sufficiency of the text in turn demands that the text be subjected to a detailed analysis. Since meaning resides in the text itself, that meaning can be discovered only through a careful study of the literary document. In this close study of the text, one needs to distinguish between content (*what* a text says—the events, character, and settings that make up a story) and form (*how* a text says it—the formal features of a story and especially the function that these formal features have in communicating information). Although content and form are ultimately inseparable, they may be analyzed and assessed separately. One other important aspect of form involves the issue of genre—the kind of writing to which the text belongs.

The dominance of the New Criticism among secular literary critics did not last long, as this approach was soon superseded by Structuralism and Poststructuralism (or Deconstruction). Among biblical scholars, however, New Criticism continued to enjoy much support. It was a welcome alternative for many New Testament practitioners who were frustrated with the traditional approach of higher criticism that seemed to raise more questions about the text than it answered and that tended to focus less on the final form of the text than on the hypothetical reconstruction of the text in its precanonical form. Many were also attracted by an approach that took seriously the sophisticated artistry and high aesthetic quality of the biblical text. Thus the appeal of New Criticism, as Stanley Porter notes, is clear: "It exalts the aesthetic qualities of the biblical text to the point of critical respectability, appears to provide an objective method of analysis and grounds for assessment and evaluation of critical readings, does not get entangled with historical issues, and is compatible with a theology that is concerned with the biblical story."[13]

One of the more important works to have successfully applied the insights of New Criticism to the New Testament text is David Rhoads and Donald Michie's *Mark as Story*.[14] This volume is unique in that it is cowritten by both a New Testament scholar and a secular literary critic—an English literature specialist. This work is also noteworthy, however, for its brief introduction which, despite numbering a mere five pages, illustrates well many of the basic principles of new criticism:

1. An appreciation of the complex, yet aesthetic, quality of the biblical text:

> The author has used sophisticated literary techniques, developed the characters and the conflicts, and built suspense with deliberateness, telling the story in such a way as to generate certain emotions and insights in the reader (p. 1).

2. A commitment to modern methods of literary criticism as the interpretive key to analyze the text:

> We have drawn extensively on the work of contemporary literary criticism. Literary critics have developed methods to analyze the formal features of narrative, such as the role of the narrator, point of view, style, plot, settings, and characters. Although these methods were developed primarily in the study of

modern novels and short stories, most ancient narratives share the same formal features, and the use of these methods greatly aids students in their study of ancient literature such as the Gospel of Mark (p. 2).

3. An emphasis on the text as a whole in its final form:

We seldom experience the total impact of Mark's gospel because we seldom hear or read the story in its entirety. We usually encounter Mark's gospel in bits and pieces. . . . Such an experience of Mark's story is similar to hearing quotations from different Shakespearean plays without ever having read or seen one of those plays in its entirety (p. 2). The study of narrative emphasizes the unity of the final text. Such a study of the formal features of Mark's gospel tends to reveal the narrative as whole cloth . . . Although scholars know little about the origin of this gospel, a literary study of its formal features suggests that the author has succeeded in creating a unified narrative (p. 3).

4. A downplaying of the traditional methods of source, form, and redaction criticism:

Many of the modern methodologies for studying Mark's gospel have differentiated the sources from the author's editorial additions and the traditions from the author's arrangement of them. As necessary as these methods are to investigating the history and to understand the author's intention, they do not help us see this gospel as a unified narrative (p. 2).

5. A belief in the self-sufficiency and autonomous character of the text in the interpretative process:

Mark's story is complete in itself. . . . We cannot legitimately use the other gospels to "fill out" or to "fill in" some unclear passage in Mark's story. Rather we need to read Mark's gospel more carefully as a self-sufficient story. To interpret Mark's gospel in its autonomous integrity we bracket what other sources or later generations have said or believed about Jesus. . . . Thus, Mark's narrative contains a closed and self-sufficient world with its own integrity (pp. 3–4).

6. A distinction between content (what is said) and form (how it is said):

We will look at rhetoric, or "how" the author of the Gospel of Mark presents his story in the narrative: the role of the narrator, point of view, standards of judgment, style, narrative patterns, and other rhetorical devices. Then in subsequent chapters, we will explore the story or "what" the narrative is about (p. 5).

Structuralism

A second text-centered approach that has had a prominent role in literary criticism is Structuralism.[15] This approach is difficult to define since it involves much more than just a method of literary study; it is a philosophy of reality that has been applied to such diverse fields as linguistics, anthropology, psychology, philosophy, history, sociology, and literature—including biblical studies. Structuralism began in the area of linguistics with the work of the Swiss scholar, Ferdianand de Saussure (1857–1913), whose posthumously published treatise, *Course in General Linguistics*,[16] forms the basis of twentieth-century linguistics and has ultimately influenced much in literary criticism. Claude Lévi-Strauss pioneered the use of structuralism in the field of anthropology, especially in his work on myths from various world cultures.[17] A. J. Greimas applied the insights of structuralism to narrative texts[18] and thus paved the way for the use of structuralism in the analysis of biblical texts.

Structuralism contends that the most profound meaning of any form of communication, including written documents, is not to be found at the surface level of words or in the plain meaning conveyed by an author or in a text's intended purpose. The structuralist interpreter looks instead to the "deep structure" of the text—a hidden or underlying structure that offers some explanation for the more or less visible or obvious pattern seen at the surface level of the text. The word *structure* in this approach does not, then, refer to the author's outline, pattern, or internal organization of his writing. It rather denotes the deep, underlying structure that exists below the surface level of the text—a structure that, unlike a surface outline or pattern, is not obvious to the casual reader. In fact, even the author himself was not likely aware of the many underlying factors that gave rise to the creation of the text. The deep structures beneath the text are claimed to be self-sufficient and independent of outside forces such as the cultural context or theological perspective of the speaker or writer. Consequently, structuralists reject the author as the center of authority in comprehending texts and look to the text itself as the sole arbitrator in the interpretative process.

A deep structure consists of a system or network of abstract elements that exist in a logical relationship to one another and that collectively generate the surface structure—the text as we see it—and account for its meaning in some way. In order to discern what these hidden, abstract elements are and the nature of their interrelationship, structuralists make use of three key distinctions introduced by Saussure. The first is a distinction between *langue*, language as a whole consisting of a set of fixed rules and norms, and *parole*, language as it specifically comes to expression in light of these established rules. The second is a distinction between the *signifier* and the *signified* in which the former term refers to a specific word used in a text while the latter term refers to the meaning or concept which that word evokes. The third is a distinction between a *diachronic* approach that examines the evolutionary growth and developments of a language as they occur over time (the traditional method of biblical criticism) and a *synchronic* approach that studies language as a fixed system whose constituent elements belong to the same system or structure, regardless of their chronological order or diachronic relationship (the competing approach of structuralism).

Although structuralism has had a significant impact in secular literary studies, its importance for biblical studies has been rather limited and short-lived. Many scholars quickly became frustrated with its high level of complexity, esoteric language, and ubiquitous grids and charts. Joseph

Cahill, for example, marvels that anyone would enter the "minefield" of structuralism without some "professional constraint" or "inexplicable compulsion."[19] Others have criticized the meager payoff this approach has produced for understanding the text. James Barr speaks for many when he observes that structuralism has "produced no large body of profound and convincing exegesis," that its results are "paltry and insubstantial," and that its proponents "express themselves in a new way but have essentially banal things to say."[20] Still others believe that the structuralist attempt to move from the surface level of the biblical text back to its hidden, underlying deep structure only serves to distance the text even further from the contemporary reader. These are a few of the reasons structuralism today is virtually ignored by biblical commentators. In fact, a recent essay that surveys various literary approaches to the New Testament chooses not to treat structuralism on the grounds that it is "a moribund sub-discipline of New Testament studies (and only tangentially related to literary criticism)."[21]

Poststructuralism (or Deconstruction)

A third text-centered approach that has had a limited but noteworthy impact in literary criticism is that of poststructuralism.[22] Like structuralism, it too is not merely a method of interpretation but a philosophical movement that has been applied to several disciplines. The term *deconstruction* is often used as a synonym for *poststructuralism,* although this former term more properly refers to the work by and patterned after the French philosopher Jacques Derrida whose writings in the mid-1970s began a new critical movement.[23]

Derrida claims that any kind of text can be interpreted to mean something quite different from what it appears to be saying. In fact, any text can be read in such a way that its alternate meaning is at variance with, contrary to, and subversive of what is widely considered to be—at least, according to traditional literary approaches—its single, fixed meaning. Thus, a text may "betray" itself. And since a text may possess a multiplicity of differing meanings, this in turn implies that a text cannot have one stable meaning. Poststructuralism or deconstruction, therefore, is a literary approach that possesses a radical skepticism about the possibility of deriving any kind of fixed or constant meaning from texts.

At the heart of Derrida's thinking is his breaking the connection between the signifier and what is signified in a language system—a connection fundamental to the structuralist language-system of Saussure. The text does not have a meaning as a reference to something that is signified. Poststructuralists reject the author, the deep structure of the text, or the reader as a determinative authority of meaning. All they have is the text itself (hence Derrida's motto: "There is nothing outside of the text"[24]) and this text is open to divergent meanings.

It did not take long for insights of Derrida and other key figures in the poststructuralist camp (Michel Foucault, Harold Bloom, Paul de Man, Jacques Lacan)[25] to be applied to the biblical text. The deconstructive project not only resulted in the overthrow of old, established interpretations of Scripture but also opened the door for novel, innovative readings of the biblical text. These fresh readings are typically accomplished "through the use of complicated word-plays, innuendoes (often sexual), interlinguistic etymologies (often in reverse chronological order), and outright re-writing of the text."[26] All these features are well illustrated in the following selection taken from the work of Stephen Moore, the most prolific producer of poststructuralist readings of the New Testament:[27]

> Mark's theology is commonly said to be a theology of the cross, a theology in which life and death crisscross. . . . In Mark, the signature of the disciple can only ever be that of a crisscross or Christcross, which my dictionary defines as "the figure or mark of a cross in general; esp. that made in signing his name by a person that cannot write" (*OED*). But a person unable to write is generally unable to read, and in Mark, the disciples, generally at cross-purposes with Jesus, are singularly unable to read. Jesus must speak cross words to his puzzled disciples (8:33; cf. 8:17–21).
>
> A cross is also a chiasmus, a crosswise fusion in which the order established in the first instance (whoever would *save* their life will *lose* it) is inverted in the second instance (and whoever *loses* their life will *save* it). Central to Mark is the fact of the crucifiction (*sic*), a fiction structured like a cross or chiasmus.
>
> Chiasmus comes from the Greek verb *chiazein*, "to mark with the letter x," pronounced *chi*. And *chi* is an anagram of *ich*, which is German for the personal pronoun *I*, and the technical term in Freud that English translators render as *ego*. And Jesus, who identifies himself to his terrified disciples in Mark 6.50 with the words *egō eimi* ("I am," or "it is I"), himself possesses a name that is an echo of the French *Je suis* ("I am"), the single superfluous letter being the *I* (or ego), which is thus marked out for deletion: "Father, not what I [*egō*] want, but what you want" (14.36).
>
> To be marked with the x, the cross, is painful, for *chiazein* also means "to cut." Another meaning of *chiasma* is "piece of wood." And the *chiasma* on which Jesus writ(h)es is a lectern as well as a writing desk. Dying, he opens up the book to Psalm 22 and reads the opening verse: "My God, my God, why have you forsaken me?" *Chi*, the first letter of *Christos* ("Christ"), is also the twenty-second letter of the Greek alphabet.[28]

This lengthy quotation shows the clever and creative way poststructuralists often handle the biblical text—an approach that proponents often refer to as "playing with texts."[29] But as inventive and ingenious as such deconstructive readings are, only a handful of contemporary scholars embrace this literary approach. The radical skepticism concerning the coherence of linguistic communication that makes deconstructive readings possible also serves to undermine the impact that this approach has. Indeed, most today question whether the deconstructive methodology will produce anything of lasting value in New Testament studies.[30]

READER-CENTERED APPROACHES

A third broad literary approach that turns its attention away from the author and the text and concentrates instead on the reader as the center of authority for interpretation is reader-response criticism (also identified as reader-orientated criticism).[31] This approach deals with the relationship between text and reader and reader and text, with the emphasis on the different ways in which a reader participates in the course of reading a text and the different perspectives that arise in that relationship. In essence, reader-response criticism examines the reader's contribution to a text and thus challenges to varying degrees the text-orientated approach of New Criticism (along with its methodological cousin Formalism) and Structuralism that tend to ignore or, at least, underestimate the reader's role.

The reader-response approach operates on the assumption that any text—whether it is a poem, short story, essay, or scientific exposition—has no real existence until it is read. A text has unrealized meaning potential but requires a reader to actualize this potential meaning. Thus, the reader does not have, as has been traditionally thought and accepted, a passive role. Quite the opposite, the reader is an active agent in shaping or even creating meaning. The key role of the reader in determining meaning in any given text is highlighted in the following quote from Robert Fowler, one of the more prolific New Testament scholars to embrace this literary approach:

> The reader-response critic argues that whatever meaning is and wherever it is found the reader is ultimately responsible for determining meaning. In reader-response criticism, meaning is no longer considered a given. It is not something ready-made, buried in the text, and just waiting to be uncovered. Rather, it is something produced in the act of reading through the unique interaction of the text and the particular reader doing the reading, at a particular moment, from a particular slant. Instead of *What* determines the meaning of a text? reader-response critics prefer the question, *Who* determines the meaning? The immediate answer is "the reader."[32]

Two versions of reader-response criticism have emerged: a more conservative approach in which the reader shapes the meaning of the text but to varying degrees is controlled by the text; and a more radical approach in which the reader is wholly determinative in creating meaning for a text. The earlier and more conservative version is represented in the work of Wolfgang Iser,[33] one of the founders of the reader-response approach. Iser argues that all literary texts have "gaps" that the reader needs to fill in so that the potential meaning of the text can be actualized.

Although the gaps can be completed in a variety of ways by the reader, there are limits established by the text. The reader must participate, but the nature of this participating is governed by the text. Thus, Iser speaks of the "implied reader," a hypothetical or ideal reader established by the boundaries of the text. This conservative reader-response approach has been adopted by a number of biblical scholars, as a recent commentary on Romans well illustrates: "By mentally placing ourselves in the position of the implied reader(s) of the text and making the responses that the process of reading or listening to it demands or requires, we hope to experience more precisely and fully what this Epistle is meant to communicate."[34] In other words, if the actual reader of today plays the role of the implied or ideal reader, he or she will actualize or decode the text as the author intended.

The later and more radical version of reader-response criticism is represented in the work of Stanley Fish[35] who claims that the reader is wholly determinative in creating meaning: "The text as an entity independent of interpretation and (ideally) responsible for its career drops out and is replaced by the texts that emerge as the consequence of our interpretative activities."[36] In other words, the only "text in the class" (to borrow Fish's phrase) and the only meaning in this text is the text and the meaning that readers produce through their interpretive practices. Thus, it is no longer the author who is the historical cause of the text and creator of its meaning, but the reader. Whereas in the conservative reader-response approach the reader is somewhat limited or bound by the text,[37] here in the more radical reader-response approach the reader is free to give to the text whatever unique meaning he or she might offer. The notion of an "ideal reader" is replaced by an "autonomous reader" whose ideological concerns are free to play a key role in the creation of a new meaning(s) for the text.

CONCLUSION

It is difficult to define in narrow terms what it meant by the term *literary criticism*. The problem lies in the fact that there is no single literary-critical method of interpretation. Instead, as illustrated above, a wide variety of interpretative methods have been forwarded, each one claiming to present a literary approach to Scripture. Nevertheless, one can identify a set of convictions that are widely held by literary critics and that serve to distinguish a literary reading of the Bible from the historical and theological readings that have traditionally been employed.

First, literary criticism involves an appreciation for the sophisticated artistry and aesthetic quality of the text. It recognizes that the Bible is the result of conscious composition, careful patterning, and the strategic use of literary conventions prevalent in its day. This appreciation for the literary features of the Bible means that the methods of literary scholarship are a valid and necessary part of the interpretative process.

Second, literary criticism exhibits a preoccupation with the form of the text. Literary critics focus no longer just on the content of the text (*what* is said) but also on the form of the text (*how* it is said). As Leland Ryken notes: "We cannot fully comprehend the 'what' of New Testament writings (their religious content) without first paying attention to the 'how' (the literary modes in which the content is embodied."[38] This preoccupation with form manifests itself in the attempt of literary critics to identify the various literary conventions used by a biblical author and to understand the function that these conventions have in the text. This concern with form also shows itself in the great attention given the diverse genres found in the Bible and how an awareness of genre impacts interpretation.

Third, literary criticism is committed to treat texts as finished wholes. Before the rise of literary criticism, liberal scholars concentrated on the various sources lying behind the text and how the biblical author arranged and redacted these sources. Conservative scholars, on the basis of their belief in the verbal inspiration of Scripture, concentrated on individual words in the text and also highlighted individual verses that could serve as proof texts for certain theological positions. Both procedures ended up dividing the biblical text into fragments, as evident in the verse-by-verse commentary that has become such a staple of biblical scholarship. A literary approach, by contrast, accepts the biblical text in its final form and is committed to a holistic reading of a particular passage or book.

Fourth, literary criticism exhibits an ahistorical orientation. Literary critics frequently have very little interest and even outright antipathy to historical considerations. They do not wish to deal with the historical uncertainties surrounding the author, context, and readers and so frequently bracket out questions of history in order to concentrate on the literary features of a text. Literary criticism, therefore, is largely ahistorical in theoretical or methodological orientation and does not usually ask or answer the historical questions that play such a crucial role in the traditional methods of higher criticism.

An Example of Literary Criticism: The Letter of Jude

The letter of Jude suffers from neglect, partly because it is so brief and partly because it is perceived to have very little "doctrinal content." What is worse than this neglect, however, is the all too common way that this letter has been wrongly interpreted and applied to the mission of the church for today.

It is clear that the central theme of the letter is found in verse 4. Although Jude had originally planned to write to his readers about "our common salvation," the specific circumstance that this church faced caused him, instead, to issue the following appeal: "Contend for the faith which was once and for all delivered to the saints." What does Jude have in mind with this exhortation? How should believers fight for the faith?

Many have answered this question by wrongly looking to the lengthy denunciation of false teachers that makes up the largest section of the letter body. This extended word of condemnation all too often becomes the justification for calling the church today to similarly root out and denounce false teachers. In other words, the primary way for believers to "contend for the faith" is supposedly to identify and proclaim judgment on all those who are perceived to be a threat to the true teaching of the gospel.

This interpretation, however, misses the main message of the letter. For when one reads Jude from a literary perspective and pays careful attention to the overall structure of this ancient letter, it becomes clear that its primary point is to be found not in the negative judgment of the false teachers given in the first and lengthiest part of the document (vv. 5–19) but in the positive exhortation to believers given in the concluding section of the document (vv. 20–23). In other words, the principal means by which believers contend for the faith is not to proclaim judgment on their enemies but to "keep yourselves in the love of God" (v. 21) and to "have mercy on others with fear" (v. 23).

The key to this interpretation is to recognize the chiastic structure found in the letter body. A "chiasmus" is a literary device where the various elements of a text are arranged in a balanced structure: the elements are first presented in a series (A, B, C, . . .) and then the same elements are repeated but in an inverted order (. . . , C', B', A'). Although there is no maximum number of elements in a chiasmus, this literary device must have a minimum of four elements to make inversion of order possible. In fact, the four-element chiasmus (A B B' A') is the form that occurs most frequently and the form from which the name of this literary device is ultimately derived.[39] In light of the very frequent use of chiasmus in the Old Testament, especially in Hebrew poetry, one can readily understand why New Testament authors, familiar as they were with the Scriptures, similarly employed this literary device in their own writings. It is not at all surprising, therefore, that Jude structures his letter according to a chiastic pattern that can be outlined as follows:

A   The Appeal (General): Believers must contend for the faith (v. 3)
B   The Reason for the Appeal (General): Danger of false teachers (v. 4)
B' The Reason for the Appeal (Specific): Judgment of false teachers (vv. 5–19)
A' The Appeal (Specific): How believers must contend for the faith (vv. 20–23)

This chiastic structure is supported by a variety of literary elements in the letter, as the following discussion will clearly demonstrate. The reader is strongly encouraged to have the text of Jude available so that the literary elements identified and described below may be visually observed.

THE APPEAL (GENERAL): BELIEVERS MUST CONTEND FOR THE FAITH (V. 3)

The opening of the first section (Unit A) is identified by two epistolary conventions typically used to indicate transition. The first is the vocative form of address "beloved" (*agapētoi*) that serves to mark the end of the letter opening (vv. 1–2) and the beginning of the letter body (vv. 4–23). This term also identifies the readers as belonging to the first group of people, who throughout the letter will be referred to as the "beloved," in contrast to the second group of people, who are most often referred to as the "ungodly" (*asebeis*). The use of the term *beloved* here also recalls the identification of the readers in the letter opening as "those who are *beloved* in God the Father" (v. 1) as well as the opening greeting or benediction in which Jude wishes that "mercy, peace and *love* may be multiplied to you" (v. 2). The second epistolary convention used in verse 3 to indicate the transition from the letter opening to Unit A of the letter body is the "appeal formula" given here in the simplified form "appealing . . ." (*parakalōn*). This epistolary formula typically indicates a major transition in the text, either to the beginning of the letter body (1 Cor. 1:10; Philem. 8–9) as it does here, or, as more typically happens, to a new literary unit within the letter body (e.g., Rom. 12:1; 15:30; 16:7; 1 Cor. 16:15; 2 Cor. 10:1; Phil. 4:2; 1 Thess. 4:1; Eph. 4:1). Finally, it is important to observe the lexical link or inclusio between the general appeal here in Unit A ("contend for the *faith* [*pistei*] which was once and for all delivered to the *holy ones* [*hagiois*]": v. 3) and the opening words of the specific appeal in Unit A' ("building yourselves up on your most *holy faith* [*hagiōtatē pistei*]": v. 20).

THE REASON FOR THE APPEAL (GENERAL): DANGER OF FALSE TEACHERS (V. 4)

The conjunction "for" (*gar*) introduces the second section (Unit B), which gives the reason Jude had to change his original plan of writing to his audience about "our common salvation" and write instead an appeal to "contend for the faith." Whereas Unit A identifies the readers with the key term *beloved*, Unit B describes the false teachers with five terms or phrases that are simply placed in apposition to each other: "certain men, the ones who long ago were destined for this judgment, ungodly ones, those who transform the grace of our God into licentiousness, and who deny our only Master and Lord, Jesus Christ." The term *ungodly* (*asebeis*), heightened somewhat by its location at the center of the fivefold description of the false teachers, is a catchword in the letter, linking this statement forward to the specific judgment of the false teachers in Unit B' (the root form of the word *ungodly* occurs six times in the letter [vv. 4, 15 [4x], 18], more than in any other New Testament writing).

THE REASON FOR THE APPEAL (SPECIFIC): JUDGMENT OF FALSE TEACHERS (VV. 5–19)

The beginning of the third section (Unit B') is marked by the presence of a modified "disclosure formula" in verse 5: "I want to remind you, because you know . . ." The disclosure formula makes use of a verb of knowing and derives its name from the fact that the letter writer wishes to make known to the recipient(s) some information. Like the appeal formula, the disclosure formula is a transitionary marker, indicating a shift from one major section of the letter to another (see, e.g., Rom. 1:13; 2 Cor. 1:8; Gal. 1:11; Phil. 1:12; 1 Thess. 2:1; etc). The presence of this epistolary convention here, therefore, functions to introduce the third major section of the letter body— Unit B'—which gives an expanded description of the "ungodly" and the judgment that they face.

Unit B' is further identified by the repeated use of the demonstrative pronoun "these ones" (*houtoi*) to identify the false teachers (vv. 8, 10, 12, 16, 19), thereby giving the verses that make up this unit (vv. 5–19) lexical coherence. The demonstrative pronoun "these ones" is part of a consistent pattern found in verses 5–19 where Jude first presents evidence from authoritative sources (the Old Testament, Enoch, and the apostles), which is then followed by an interpretation introduced with either "these ones" (*houtoi*) or the slightly fuller expression "these ones are" (*houtoi eisin*):[40]

vv. 5–7	(1)	Three Old Testament Types
vv. 8–10		plus interpretation ("these ones": 2x)
v. 11	(2)	Three More Old Testament Types
vv. 12–13		plus interpretation ("these ones are . . .")
vv. 14–15	(3)	Prophecy of Enoch
v. 16		plus interpretation ("these ones are . . .")
vv. 17–18	(4)	Prophecy of the Apostles
v. 19		plus interpretation ("these ones are . . .")

A number of commentators want to begin a new major section in verse 17, appealing to the presence of the vocative "beloved," which elsewhere in the letter marks a transition. The shift in verse 17, however, is a minor one and intended to highlight the contrast between the preceding prophecy of Enoch and its accompanying interpretation (vv. 14–16) and the subsequent prophecy of the apostles and its interpretation (vv. 17–19). The presence of the catchword *ungodly* (*asebeis*) in verse 18 and the key phrase *these ones are* (*houtoi eisin*) in verse 19 as part of the literary pattern identified above (i.e., an appeal to an authoritative source followed by its accompanying interpretation) provide compelling grounds that verses 17–19 do not constitute a new major section in the letter body but belong to the preceding verses that make up Unit B'.

This conclusion is confirmed by two lexical links between the material of verses 17–19 and the preceding verses of Units B and B'. First, there is an inclusio between the command of verse 17 that the readers "remember" (*mnēsthēte*) and the statement of verse 5 where Jude wants to "remind" (*hypomnēsai*) his readers. Second, the idea that the coming of false teachers was "prophesied" beforehand by both Enoch (v. 14: *proephēteusen*) and the apostles (v. 17: *proeirēmenōn*) looks back to the claim of verse 4 that the judgment of these false teachers had been "prophesied" (*progegrammenoi*) long ago.

The Appeal (Specific): How believers must contend for the faith (vv. 20–23)

The fourth and final section of the letter body (Unit A') is introduced in verse 20 by two means. The first is the vocative "beloved," which commonly serves in letters as a transitionary marker. The second is the personal pronoun "you" (*hymeis*), located here in the emphatic position at the head of the sentence, where it serves to highlight the contrast between the following verses (vv. 19–23) that deal with "you" (i.e., the "beloved" letter recipients) and the preceding verses (vv. 5–19) that deal with the oft-repeated "these ones" (i.e., the false or "ungodly" teachers). As noted above, there is an important lexical link or inclusio between the opening words of the specific appeal here in Unit A' ("building yourselves up on your most *holy faith* [*hagiōtatē pistei*]": v. 20) and the general appeal given earlier in Unit A ("contend for the *faith* [*pistei*] which was once and for all delivered to the *holy ones* [*hagiois*]": v. 3).

Conclusion

Our analysis of the literary features of Jude demonstrates quite clearly its chiastic structure. This A B B' A' pattern indicates that the primary purpose of the letter is not to be found in the lengthy denunciation of the false teachers in Units B (v. 4) and B' (vv. 5–19) but rather in the general appeal to the "beloved" readers to "contend for the faith" in Unit A (v. 3) and the fuller explanation of that appeal in Unit A' (vv. 20–23). The exhortations in verses 20–23, therefore, are in no way a mere appendix or afterthought but rather the key passage in the whole letter. As Richard Bauckham observes:

> The structure of the letter is most important for establishing what Jude intended his readers to do to continue the fight for the faith. What this appeal means he spells out in vv. 20–23, which contain entirely positive exhortations. The common mistake of supposing that, for Jude, contending for the faith means denouncing opponents, arises from a misunderstanding of the significance of vv. 5–19. Those verses are intended to awaken Jude's readers to the dangerous reality of their situation which makes Jude's appeal necessary, but it is only when he has done this that Jude goes on (in vv. 20–23) to explain how they must continue the fight for the faith.[41]

How then ought believers to "contend for the faith"? The specific appeal of Unit A' consists of two parts: (1) verses 20–21, which focus on the conduct of believers toward themselves (note the twofold occurrence of the reflexive pronoun *yourselves* [*heautous*]); and (2) verses 22–23, which focus on the conduct of believers toward others (note the threefold occurrence of the relative pronoun *whom* [*hous*]). The first part of the specific appeal that focuses on the conduct of believers toward themselves (vv. 20–21) consists of a single command ("Keep yourselves in the love of God") and three participial clauses that give the means by which this command can be accomplished ("by building yourselves up on your most holy faith, by praying in the Holy Spirit, by waiting for the mercy of our Lord Jesus Christ unto eternal life").[42] Therefore, the first and foremost way in which believers ought to contend for the faith is to stand squarely and securely in the love of God, and they ought to do this through much study of God's Word (the place where our "most holy faith" is recorded), much time in prayer, and much anticipation and preparation for Christ's glorious return.

The second part of the specific appeal that focuses on the conduct of believers toward others (vv. 22–23) is complicated by the fact that the Greek text "is uncertain at several points" (see NRSV footnote). In fact, the baffling variety of readings found in the manuscripts has led one scholar to identify verses 22–23 as "undoubtedly one of the most corrupt passages in New Testament literature."[43] Among the many variant readings, however, there is one phrase that is consistently found: "have mercy with fear." The text originally said more than this, but it at least minimally included the command for believers to "have mercy with fear."[44] Therefore, the second way in which believers ought to fight for the faith is to deal with false teachers and others who threaten the faith with a combination of mercy and fear: a mercy that reflects the gracious character of the God who has dealt mercifully with his chosen people, and a fear that reflects the serious nature of the threat to the faith that has been once and for all delivered to the saints.

Our analysis of Jude has demonstrated how crucial an awareness of literary features is for a proper interpretation of the letter. The primary way for believers to "contend for the faith" is not, as is so often supposed, by denouncing false teachers but rather by following the positive appeal in verses 20–23, namely, to "keep yourselves in the love of God" and to "have mercy on others with fear." This analysis of Jude is but one small example of numerous and diverse ways in which a literary approach to Scripture can yield a rich exegetical reward.

Bibliography

Longman III, Tremper. *Literary Approaches to Biblical Interpretation*. Grand Rapids: Zondervan, 1987.

McKnight, Scott. "An Appendix: Literatry Criticism," *Interpreting the Synoptic Gospels*. Grande Rapids: Baker, 1988. 121–37.

Pearson, Brook W. R. "New Testament Literary Criticism," *Handbook of Exegesis of the New Testament*, ed. S. E. Porter (Leiden: Brill, 1997), 241–66.

Peterson, Norman R. *Literary Criticm for New Testament Critics*. Philadelphia: Fortress Press, 1978.

Porter, Stanley E. "Literary Approaches to the New Testament: From Formalism to Deconstruction and Back," *Approaches to New Testament Study*, S. E. Porter and D. Tombs, eds. (JSNTSup 120; Sheffield: Sheffield Academic Press, 1995), 77–128.

Ryken, Leland and Tremper Longman III, eds. *A Complete Literary Guide to the Bible*. Grand Rapids: Zondervan, 1993.

Walhout, Clarence and Leland Ryken, eds., *Contemporary Literary Theory: A Christian Appraisal*. Grand Rapids: Eerdmans, 1991.

Notes

1. Although there existed a long-standing interest in the literary nature of the Bible, much of the current interest in biblical literary criticism stems from the 1969 presidential address by James Muilenburg to the Society of Biblical Literature. This seminal essay challenged biblical scholars to move beyond form criticism and consider literary aspects of the text such as structure and aesthetics (J. Muilenburg, "Form Criticism and Beyond," *Journal of Biblical Literature* 88 [1969]: 1–18).

2. G. E. Ladd, *The New Testament and Criticism* (Grand Rapids: Eerdmans, 1967), 112.

3. A. Wilder, *Early Christian Rhetoric: The Language of the Gospel* (Cambridge, Mass.: Harvard University Press, 1971), xxii.

4. R. Crosman, "Is There Such a Thing as Misreading?" *Criticism and Critical Theory,* ed., J. Hawthorn (London: Edward Arnold, 1984), 11; cited in K. A. Mathews, "Literary Criticism of the Old Testament," *Foundations for Biblical Interpretation,* eds. D. S. Dockery, K. A. Mathews, and R. B. Sloan (Nashville: Broadman & Holman, 1994), 208.

5. R. Jakobson, "Closing Statement: Linguistic and Poetics," *Style in Language,* ed., T. A. Sebeok (New York: Wiley; Cambridge, Mass.: MIT Press, 1960), 350–77, esp., p. 353. Jakobson's model is frequently cited in introductions to literary criticism.

6. This example is cited by T. Longman III, *Literary Approaches to Biblical Interpretation* (Grand Rapids: Zondervan, 1987), 19.

7. A notable exception to contemporary literary critics who reject authorial intention is E. D. Hirsch. Although his views have undergone some development, Hirsch has remained firm in his emphasis on the crucial role of the author in determining meaning. Texts may well have multiple interpretations, but the author's position is the one that dictates which of these interpretations is correct. See E. D. Hirsch Jr., *Validity in Interpretation* (New Haven: Yale University Press, 1967) and also his *The Aims of Interpretation* (Chicago: University of Chicago Press, 1976).

8. Reprinted in W. K. Wimsatt, *The Verbal Icon: Studies in the Meaning of Poetry* (Lexington: University Press of Kentucky, 1954), 3–18.

9. M. H. Abrams, *A Glossary of Literary Terms* (New York: Holt, Rinehard and Winston, 1981), 83.

10. The name apparently derives from the title of John Crowe Ransom's 1941 book on literary criticism, *The New Criticism* (Norfolk, Conn.: New Directions, 1941). Among the vast list of sources dealing with New Criticism, the following works are especially important: R. Wellek and A. Warren, *Theory of Literature* (New York: Harcourt, Brace & World, 1956[3] [1942]); R. P. Blackmur, *Form and Value in Modern Poetry* (Garden City, N.Y.: Doubleday, 1957); F. R. Leavis, *The Great Tradition* (New York: New York University Press, 1960); W. S. Scott, *Five Approaches of Literary Criticism* (New York: Collier, 1962); K. R. R. Gos Louis, J. Ackerman and T. Warshaw, eds., *Literary Interpretation of Biblical Narratives,* 2 vols. (Nashville: Abingdon, 1974, 1982).

11. Formalism, or as it is more properly identified, Russian Formalism, is a literary theory that developed in Russia in the early 1920s well before the rise of New Criticism. This movement was not very influential outside of Russia until a couple of decades later when several leading figures fled the Soviet Union for the West. While some elements of Russian Formalism overlap with that of New Criticism (hence the frequent interchangeability of the terms "New Criticism" and "Formalism"), it brought a sociological dimension to interpretation that has not been incorporated by New Critics, especially those engaged in biblical studies.

12. See, e.g., C. Tuckett, *Reading the New Testament: Methods of Interpretation* (London: SPCK, 1987), 174–75; S. McKnight, "Appendix: Literary Criticism," *Interpreting the Synoptic Gospels* (Grand Rapids: Baker, 1988), 121–37.

13. S. Porter, "Literary Approaches," *Approaches to New Testament Study,* eds., S. E. Porter and D. Tombs (Sheffield: Sheffield Academic Press, 1995), 97.

14. D. Rhoads and D. Michie, *Mark as Story: An Introduction to the Narrative of a Gospel* (Philadelphia: Fortress Press, 1982).

15. See J. Culler, *Structuralist Poetics: Structuralism, Linguistics, and the Study of Literature* (Ithaca, N.Y.: Cornell University Press, 1975); J. Calloud, *Structural Analysis of Narrative* (Philadelphia: Fortress, 1976); Robert M. Polzin, *Biblical Structuralism* (Missoula, Mont.: Scholars Press, 1977); D. Patte, *What is Structural Exegesis?* (Philadelphia: Fortress, 1976); idem, *Paul's Faith and the Power of the Gospel: A Structural Introduction to the Pauline Letters* (Philadelphia: Fortress, 1983); idem, *The Gospel according to Matthew: A Structural Commentary on Matthew's Gospel* (Philadelphia: Fortress, 1987); idem, *Structural Exegesis for New Testament Critics* (Minneapolis: Fortress, 1990).

16. F. de Saussure, *Course in General Linguistics* (New York: McGraw-Hill, 1959).

17. C. Lévi-Strauss, *Structural Anthropology,* trans. Claire Jacobson and Brooke Grundfest Schoepf (New York: Basic Books, 1963).

18. A. J. Greimas, *Sémantique structurale* (Paris: Larousse, 1967). Translated and published as *Structural Semantics: An Attempt at a Method,* trans. D. McDowell, R. Schleifer, and A. Velie (Lincoln: University of Nebraska Press, 1983).

19. J. Cahill, "A House Half Built," *Religious Studies Bulletin* (September 1982): 143.

20. J. Barr, "Biblical Language and Exegesis—How Far Does Structuralism Help Us?" *King's Theological Review* 7 (1984): 50.

21. Porter, "Literary Approaches," 83, n. 21.

22. See, e.g., M. Foucault, *The Order of Things: An Archaeology of the Human Sciences* (New York: Random House, 1970); idem, *The Archaeology of Knowledge and the Discourse on Language* (New York: Random House, 1972); H. Bloom, *A Map of Misreading* (Oxford: Oxford University Press, 1975); J. Lacan, *Ecrits,* trans. A. Sheridan (New York: Norton, 1977); J. Culler, *On Deconstruction: Theory and Criticism after Structuralism* (Ithaca, N.Y.: Cornell University Press, 1982); C. Norris, *Deconstruction: Theory and Practice* (London: Methuen, 1982); P. de Man, *Blindness and Insight: Essays in the Rhetoric of Contemporary Criticism* (Minneapolis: University of Minneapolis Press, 1983).

23. Among Derrida's many publications, the most influential is *Of Grammatology,* trans. G. C. Spivak (Baltimore: Johns Hopkins University Press, 1976).

24. Ibid., 158.

25. See the works cited in note 22.

26. B. W. R. Pearson, "New Testament Literary Criticism," *Handbook to Exegesis of the New Testament,* ed., S. E. Porter (Leiden: Brill, 1997), 246.

27. Moore's major works on poststructuralism include the following: *Literary Criticism and the Gospels: The Theoretical Challenge* (New Haven: Yale University Press, 1989); *Mark and Luke in Poststructuralist Perspectives: Jesus Begins to Write* (New Haven: Yale University Press, 1989); "Deconstructive Criticism: The Gospel of Mark," *Mark and Method: New Approaches in Biblical Studies,* eds., J. C. Anderson and S. D. Moore (Minneapolis: Fortress, 1992), 84–102; *Poststructuralism and the New Testament: Derrida and Foucault at the Foot of the Cross* (Minneapolis: Fortress, 1994).

28. Moore, "Deconstructive Criticism," 95–96. This passage is cited by Pearson, "Literary Criticism," 246–47.

29. The metaphor of play is a favorite one among those in the poststructuralist and deconstructionist camp: see, e.g., P. D. Jubl, "Playing with Texts: Can Deconstruction Account for Critical Practice?" *Criticism and Critical Theory,* 59–72. Derrida states: "I do not 'concentrate' in my reading . . . , either exclusively or primarily on those points that appear to be most 'important,' 'central,' 'crucial.' Rather, I de-concentrate, and it is the secondary, eccentric, lateral, marginal, parasitic, borderline cases which are 'important' to me and are a source of many things, such as pleasure, but also insight into the general functioning of a textual system" (cited twice in the main text of Moore, "Deconstructive Criticism," 85, 95).

30. See, e.g., the comments of Pearson, "Literary Criticism," 247.

31. See, e.g., Jane P. Tompkins, ed., *Reader-Response Criticism: From Formalism to Post-Structuralism* (Baltimore: Johns Hopkins University Press, 1980); S. R. Suleiman and I. Crosman, eds., *The Reader in the Text: Essays on Audience and Interpretation* (Princeton: Princeton University Press, 1980); Robert Detweiler, ed., *Reader Response Approaches to Biblical and Secular Texts,* Semeia 31 (Decatur, Ga.: Scholars Press, 1985); Edgar V. McKnight, ed., *Reader Perspectives on the New Testament,* Semeia 48 (Atlanta: Scholars Press, 1989).

32. R. F. Fowler, "Reader-Response Criticism: Figuring Mark's Reader," *Mark and Method. New Approaches in Biblical Studies,* eds., J. C. Anderson and S. D. Moore (Minneapolis: Fortress Press, 1992), 51–52.

33. Wolfgang Iser, "The Reading Process: A Phenomenological Approach," *New Literary History* 3 (1972): 279–99; ibid., *The Implied Reader* (Baltimore and London: Johns Hopkins University Press, 1974); ibid., *The Act of Reading: A Theory of Aesthetic Response* (Baltimore and London: Johns Hopkins University Press, 1978).

34. John Paul Heil, *Paul's Letter to the Romans: A Reader-Response Commentary* (New York: Paulist, 1987), 1.

35. S. E. Fish, *Is There a Text in This Class? The Authority of Interpretative Communities* (Cambridge and London: Harvard University Press, 1980).

36. Ibid., 13.

37. This leads more radical reader-response critics to complain that the more conservative readings "invariably disempower the reader. They circumscribe and limit . . ." (Temma F. Berg, "Reading in/to Mark," *Semeia* 48 [1989]: 197).

38. L. Ryken, "The Literature of the New Testament," *A Complete Literary Guide to the Bible,* eds., L. Ryken and T. Longman (Grand Rapids: Zondervan, 1993), 367.

39. The term *chiasmus* originates from the Greek letter *chi,* which looks like an English "x."

40. See Richard J. Bauckham, *Jude, 2 Peter* (Waco, Tex.: Word, 1983), 4–6.

41. Ibid., 32.

42. Most contemporary translations turn the subordinate participial phrases into independent clauses: e.g., the NIV has three independent commands and one subordinate participial clause; the RSV, NRSV and NASB have four independent commands. Although this makes for an easier or smoother reading, it fails to reflect the emphasis in the original Greek on the primary command to "keep yourselves in the love of God."

43. C. D. Osburn, "The Text of Jude 22–23," *Zeitschrift für die neutestamentliche Wissenschaft* 63 (1972): 139.

44. See A. J. Bandstra, "Onward Christian Soldiers—Praying in Love, with Mercy: Preaching on the Epistle of Jude," *Calvin Theological Journal* 32 (1997): 139.

Chapter 8

Sociological Criticism

M. Robert Mulholland, Jr.
Asbury Theological Seminary

Incarnation is the mystery at the heart of Christianity. "The Word became flesh and dwelt among us" (John 1:14) not only encapsulates the reality of the incarnation, it also establishes the primary context for the interpretation of Scripture. The revelation of God takes place within the particularities of historical human existence. In Jesus, God became enfleshed in a Jewish man whose life was set within the social, political, economic, religious, and cultural contexts of the Judaisms of first-century Palestine. Those defining contexts were further influenced by the larger reality of the Roman world whose presence brought another set of sociological dynamics to the mix. For God, in Jesus, to communicate with those in whose midst the incarnation took place, the communication necessitated using the varied matrices of the sociological world in which Jesus lived.

For example, when Jesus lifted up the radical nature of the kingdom of God above all other loyalties, he said, "I have come to set a man against his father, and a daughter against her mother, and a daughter-in-law against her mother-in-law" (Matt. 10:35 NRSV). Jesus was resonating with the basic relationships of the family in his day: a father and mother, unmarried daughters, and sons with their wives (daughters-in-law). Married daughters would have been living with their husbands' families (thus no "sons-in-law"). Furthermore, the family was *the* primary loyalty in the culture, making Jesus' word radically disturbing to his hearers.

Again, we miss the powerful thrust of the crowd's response to Jesus' teaching in the synagogue of Capernaum—"He taught them as one having authority, and not as the scribes" (Mark 1:22 NRSV)—unless we realize that the scribes were *the* authority figures in the religious community of Jesus' day.

When the writers of the New Testament sought to convey the ongoing reality of the incarnational God to their worlds or, in a manner of speaking, to make the Word become text, their only option, like God's, was to clothe the proclamation with the sociologically conditioned language and experience of their worlds. For example, we miss the import of Luke's account of the burning of magic books in Ephesus (Acts 19:19) unless we understand the role of magic within the worldview of the first century. Magic was what gave people control over those spiritual powers that determined human life. When they came to faith in Christ as Lord, they were liberated from those powers and made a powerful public witness to this reality by burning their magic books.

The New Testament writers operate within the sociological fabric of the first-century Roman-Hellenistic world. Without a comprehension of the sociological dynamics of that world, our understanding of the New Testament and the early Christian movement is terribly superficial at best and woefully mistaken at the worst.

History and Development[1]

In the latter half of the twentieth century, a growing number of New Testament scholars have chafed under what has been perceived to be the restrictive and inadequate paradigm of historical-critical methodologies. Some have prematurely announced the demise of the historical-critical method.[2] One new methodology, structuralism, which is built upon the structuralist anthropology of Claude Lévi-Strauss, the linguistic studies of A. J. Greimas, and especially the structural linguistics of Ferdinand de Saussure, has largely chosen to ignore the sweep of historical-critical methodologies and to inaugurate a new paradigm that claims to disclose the deep meaning of texts.[3] Still others, however, have chosen to build upon the positive contribution of historical-critical methodologies but to move beyond the restrictions and inadequacies of the method by developing new dimensions of the paradigm. Sociological criticism is one such effort.

Since the latter part of the nineteenth century, scholars have realized that understanding the New Testament on theological grounds alone is woefully inadequate. The social setting of the New Testament and early Christianity has been seen as an indispensable ingredient in holistic interpretation. Even many of the most conservative scholars, who relied almost totally upon linguistic and grammatical methods of interpretation, have come to realize that language and grammar operate within a social matrix that shapes their usage and meaning.

Realization of the significance of social setting for New Testament interpretation led, in the twentieth century, to a wealth of resources that aim to put the flesh of social data upon the skeleton of New Testament history.[4] Much of this work is, however, descriptive rather than analytical. It tends to describe the characteristics of the New Testament world without using social theory to analyze the dynamics of the Roman-Hellenistic world in general and its religious movements in particular. It is this weakness in historical-critical methodology that sociological criticism seeks to correct.

As early as 1960, but especially since 1970, there has been a virtual explosion of studies on the sociological dimensions of the New Testament. E. A. Judge's *The Social Pattern of Christian Groups in the First Century*[5] was one of the earliest attempts to use social description to understand early Christianity. Judge sought to clarify the social situation of the original readers of the New Testament writings by an analysis of the different groups within which Christianity emerged, both in Palestine and in the larger Roman world, and the interaction of these groups within their larger culture. More recently Derek Tidball has provided a similar study[6] with an excellent synopsis and evaluation of the ways social theories have been used to study the New Testament together with his own study of the Christian community as a sect and its social status. Judge and Tidball, along with numerous other scholars, have worked more along the lines of social description.

A large number of scholars have begun to apply various sociological theories to the study of the New Testament and early Christianity. One of the pioneers in this endeavor is Gerd Theissen. His *Sociology of Early Palestinian Christianity*[7] studied the role of the charismatic leader in religious communities with a focus upon the role of Jesus in the early Christian community and the role Jesus assigned to the disciples. While this study did not move strongly into social theory, his work *The Social Setting of Pauline Christianity*[8] did, looking at the leadership dynamics and community organizational structure of the Pauline churches.

Anthony Saldarini has moved even more strongly into the use of sociological theory. Building upon the work of Eisentadt and Lenski on social stratification and differentiation,[9] he analyzes the roles of the Pharisees, scribes, and Sadducees in Palestinian Judaism of the New Testament period in order to illuminate the conflicts both Jesus and the early Christians encountered with these groups.[10] Along similar lines, Richard Horsley and John Hanson have built upon sociological studies of conflict within peasant societies to analyze those groups whom Josephus and the New Testament called "brigands," conflict that caused social and political instability in Palestine in the first century.[11] Scholars such as Saldarini, Horsley, and Hanson build upon work in the field of social theory and use many of the hypothetical models that have been developed to assist in the analysis of the sociological dynamics of a culture.

The work of such social scientists as Max Weber,[12] Emile Durkheim,[13] Louis Kriesberg,[14] and Clifford Geertz[15] have provided the foundation of sociological theory upon which New Testament scholars have built. In addition to theories of social stratification and social conflict noted above, sociological theories of group development, group self-identity, religious dynamics, religious communities, and organizational structures have been used, along with a wide diversity of sociological hypotheses, to study the first-century Jewish and Roman Hellenistic world and the Christian communities that emerged within that diverse sociological matrix.

Of particular interest from an anthropological frame of reference are the studies of the origins and growth of millenarian groups. These studies analyze marginalized groups formed by prophetic/charismatic leaders that expect a divine intervention that will vindicate the group's perspective and ethos and inaugurate a utopian era of divine rule in which the group will have a focal place. Early studies of these phenomena were conducted by Leon Festinger,[16] Norman Cohn,[17] and Peter Worsley.[18]

Such studies have provided the inspiration for analyzing the early Christian movement as a millenarian movement. John Gager[19] and Howard Kee[20] are two New Testament scholars who have undertaken such study.

A somewhat faulty use of cultural anthropology for sociological analysis of the New Testament has been employed by Bruce Malina. In *The New Testament World: Insights from Cultural Anthropology,*[21] Malina uses helpful insights from cultural anthropology but fails to discern the tremendous diversity of social and cultural dynamics that constituted the Roman world in the first century. In a later work, *Christian Origins and Cultural Anthropology: Practical Models for Biblical Interpretation,*[22] he employs rather uncritically and inappropriately the group/grid scheme of Mary Douglas. Malina applies Douglas's scheme as a means of classification of data into sociological categories rather than using the scheme as a means of sensitization to sociological dynamics as Douglas intended.[23]

Another area of sociological criticism that has gained significance in New Testament study is the field of sociolinguistics. Scholars have come to realize that language not only provides the linguistic symbol system of a culture but is itself an integral part of the sociological matrix of the culture in which it is used. Language provides the symbolic world of a linguistic community by which that community orders and maintains its "world" as well as confirms and communicates it. A simplistic example: consider the perceptual/experiential cultural matrix that operates when the word *gay* is used in the first years of the twenty-first century as opposed to the closing years of the nineteenth century.

The philosophical work of Gadamer[24] and Wittgenstein[25] has established the foundations for sociolinguistics. One of Gadamer's formative insights is that language operates within a particular sociological "horizon" that encompasses the worldview of the community and the symbol system employed the community to describe and communicate its worldview. Linguistic communication across horizons becomes difficult because language does not function in the same way within every horizon. Wittgenstein developed the ideas of the "language game." By this he implied that in any given community and at any given point in time there is an agreed-upon set of assumptions (the "rules" of the language game) within which communication (the "game") takes place.

One of the best applications of the work of Wittgenstein and Gadamer to the study of the New Testament is by Anthony Thiselton,[26] who uses Gadamer's two horizons to illustrate how modern interpreters "hear" the language of the New Testament from within the culturally shaped horizon of their own sociological matrix and must learn to discern the sociological/cultural horizon of the original writers/readers if hermeneutical fusion of horizons is to be accomplished, a fusion that is essential to any adequate understanding of a text. Thiselton also builds upon Wittgenstein's "language game" to emphasize the necessity of understanding the "language game" of the writer and original readers if accurate interpretation is to take place.

As a witness to the significance of sociolinguistics, Eugene Nida, one of the fathers of the field, produced a new type of lexicon that enables interpreters and exegetes to access the insights of sociolinguistics in their work with the New Testament.[27] This resource organizes the vocabulary of the New Testament in ninety-three semantic domains and provides the interpreter an entree into the perceptual framework of the writer whose work is being studied.

Postmodern biblical interpretation has developed its own nuances of sociological criticism. In the words of Thiselton, "*Sociocritical hermeneutics* may be defined as an approach to texts . . . which seeks to penetrate beneath their surface function *to expose their role as instruments of power, domination, or social manipulation.*"[28] Such an approach is employed, for example, by feminist interpretations that view the biblical text as an instrument written within a male dominant culture to further entrench that male domination. Sociocritical approaches lead to the kind of sociopragmatic interpretation espoused by Rorty in which interpreters impose upon the text their own sociological frame of reference and develop support for that frame of reference from the text.[29] These postmodern approaches start with the sociological context of the text, but then move toward reader-response theories of interpretation that decenter the text from its original context in order to read it as a vehicle for the expression of the reader's own sociological agendas.

Principles of Sociological Criticism

Five general levels operate interactively in the use of sociological criticism in New Testament interpretation.

First, the preliminary level is the study of the social setting of the New Testament. This level is almost entirely descriptive, using textual, archaeological, and inscriptional evidence to define the political, economic, cultural, religious, social, educational, and communal structures of the New Testament period. An example is the role of the scribes as *the* premier authority figures in first-century Judaism as noted in the introduction.

Second, and more analytical, is the description of the sociological dynamics of the New Testament world, understanding the interactions between the various social structures that either maintain the balance of the status quo or bring about disequilibrium and subsequent change (growth, decline, or the emergence of new social structures). Care must be taken to avoid neatly packaged descriptions that avoid the anomalous realities of any human social matrix. Balance and disequilibrium, growth and decline, old established structures and new emergent structures can and often do exist in the same sociological matrix. The economic disequilibrium in Ephesus as a result of the Christian movement is a good example (Acts 19:23–27).

Third, and both descriptive and analytical, is the use of sociological models to help define and analyze the ways in which groups and individuals exist and function within the multifaceted sociological matrix of their world. These models help to analyze such sociological characteristics as the relationships between individuals, the relationships between individuals and groups, the relationships between groups, the structures of groups (definition, formation, ethos and discipline, support structures, rituals, worldview and its symbol system, conflict and resolution, differentiation and stratification, leadership and authority, mechanisms for change), and the social stratification of the culture. As we will see in the illustration at the close of this chapter, Christians in Philippi who emerged from within an outcast group, who were founded by an itinerant teacher that was arrested, beaten, and banished by the city authorities, who were centered in the house of a foreign woman, could be a case study in the dynamics of a marginalized group.

Fourth, as part of the process of coming to some grasp of the sociological matrix of the New Testament world and the dynamics of the Christian movement within that matrix, the text of the New Testament is studied within the sociological context of the Christian communities in the Roman world of the first century. Meaning of the words and symbols of the text are sought within the sociological matrix of the New Testament world and not in a set of "external, unchanging meanings" inherent in the terms and symbols themselves. For example, Paul's use of "mystery" terminology throughout his writings[30] can only be understood within the pervasive presence of mystery religions in the Roman world.[31]

Fifth, throughout the process of sociological criticism, a careful distinction must be maintained between the sociological horizon of the interpreter and that of the text. The interpreter, through sociological criticism, seeks to enter into the life-matrix of the text and its community of faith and to draw out the meaning of the text within that life-matrix. Once this has been accomplished, even during the process of its accomplishment, the analogues in the interpreter's own sociological matrix can begin to be perceived, and the transfer of meaning from the sociological matrix of the text to that of the interpreter can begin. In Colossians 2:20, Paul asks his readers, "If you died with Christ from the structural principles of the world, why are your lives still controlled by them?"[32] Paul uses a phrase here, *tōn stoicheiōn tou kosmou* ("the structural principles of the world") that, for his readers, denoted those forces and powers, structures and dynamics of the world that shaped their lives in that world. Today we would speak of prevailing cultural perspectives, values, and structures that shape human living in our "world."

While these principles can be helpful in and of themselves, they operate best within a developed sensitivity to sociological dimensions of inter- and cross-cultural communication and comprehension. This becomes especially significant in helping the interpreter's awareness of when the New Testament writers are being countercultural, that is, "turning the world upside down," like Jesus' use of the family as noted in the introduction or his parable of the tax collector and the Pharisee. In that parable Jesus' hearers would have been siding with the Pharisee, a model of Jewish holiness, and appalled by the tax collector defiling the temple with his unholy presence. Then in the "punch line" Jesus radically decenters their world.

As can be seen from this brief survey of the history and principles of sociological criticism, the field is teeming with life and vitality. The discipline has great potential for enhancing our ability to enter more fully into the matrix of life that shaped the life and perception of the early church, thus enriching our understanding of the New Testament and its significance for Christian discipleship in our own matrix of experience. As with any scholarly discipline, however, there are benefits to be gained and pitfalls to be avoided in the use of the methodology in the interpretation of the New Testament.

Strengths of Sociological Criticism

One strength of sociological criticism is its ability to help us distinguish between our own sociological matrix and that of the New Testament. Without this ability we are likely to succumb to the eisegesis of reading the New Testament through the eyes of our own life-matrix and interpreting it in the light of our own frames of reference. Another obvious strength is the ability to clarify the sociological matrix of the New Testament world and the life and activities of the Christian communities within that world. These strengths confront us, however, at one of the major areas of weakness in the study of the New Testament—the tendency to read the New Testament as a text from our own life-matrix. It is much easier simply to presume that the New Testament's frame of reference is the same as ours and to interpret it from within that matrix. Such interpretation results in the cultural captivity of the Scripture.

At this point someone is bound to ask, "But if we read the New Testament from within the sociological matrix of the first-century Roman world, are we not making it captive to that culture?" Not any more than God's incarnation in Jesus is captive to the sociological matrix of first-century Palestinian

Judaism. "But," you will say, "Jesus brought something transformingly new to that cultural matrix. He transcended the cultural matrix, 'broke out' of the sociological 'box' of Palestinian Judaism." That may be true, but we can understand the true dimensions of these aspects of the incarnation only if we first comprehend the sociological matrix from within which the incarnation broke forth into the world.

The same is true of the New Testament's account of the primitive Christian movement. While God was definitely doing a "new thing" in the formation of the Christian movement, the movement was formed, developed, and grew within the sociological matrix of the first-century world. Its radical experience can best be understood only when the sociological matrix of its life and witness is understood.

Another important strength is sociological criticism's insights into the essentially sociological dimension of language. This was illustrated above by the term *gay* as used at the end of the nineteenth century as opposed to its use at the beginning of the twenty-first century. As a New Testament example, take the term *gospel*.

The term *gospel* is one that gives us extreme difficulty from a sociological perspective. Our first problem is that we hear the term from within our own well-established sociological frame of reference. The term has a variety of particular religious denotations, each of which may carry an additional number of connotations within our own particular subculture. It can mean, variously, "Scripture," "preaching," a biblical book, something "true," a type of music, and so forth.[33] No matter what our individual frame of reference for understanding *gospel* may be, it bears little relationship to the frame of reference in which Paul used it.

Gospel was a term that carried significant sociological dynamics in the Roman world. These dynamics clustered around the emperor. The emperor's birthday was celebrated throughout the empire as a "gospel" (Greek *euangelion,* "good news"). The anniversary of his accession to the throne occasioned an empire-wide celebration of a "gospel." Commemoration of the crucial victories of the emperor's legions were also celebrated as a "gospel." Thus "gospel" was intimately associated with the emperor as the one in whom the welfare, stability, and preservation of the status quo resided. The entire complex of sociological dynamics that shaped the Roman Empire were inseparably linked to the emperor in the worldview of the Roman world.

It becomes apparent that when Paul used *gospel* it carried far different dimensions for his first-century hearers than it does for us. We will look at some of those dimensions in the illustration of sociological criticism that closes this chapter.

Perhaps the greatest strength of sociological criticism is its focus upon the incarnational reality of human life. Sociological criticism awakens us to the reality that all human existence is lived within specific, even if tremendously multifaceted and confusingly interactive, sociological matrices. This means that Christian life is not lived in some kind of spiritual cocoon but in the full-orbed sociological matrix of any given age with all the ebb and flow of its political, economic, social, religious, educational, institutional, and cultural dynamics. Human experiences with God take place within and are informed by the sociological matrices within which they occur.

Here again we see the mystery of incarnation. God chooses to indwell human communities of faith that are clothed in the sociological dynamics of their world. In a sense God chooses to submit to the shaping of human sociological dynamics. While there is a body of divine reality beneath the sociological clothing of any human community of faith, we must be careful not to mistake the clothing for the body or isolate the body from the clothing as an abstraction that captures God within our own conceptualization.

Sociological criticism can be an effective means of radical encounter with God by enabling us to enter into the life-matrix of the community of faith, to understand the reality of God's incarnation in that particular sociological milieu, and to open ourselves and our community of faith to the same kind of relationship with God in our own life-matrix. Ultimately, the meaning of a biblical text is not a "truth" to be learned but a reality of relationship with God to be incarnated again in the sociological matrix of a human community of faith. The purpose of the Scripture is not information but transformation, an encounter with God that is fully known only incarnationally within a specific sociological matrix.

Weaknesses of Sociological Criticism

One of the primary weaknesses of any behavioral methodology applied to the Scriptures is the almost overpowering tendency to view the realities of spiritual experience from within a human-centered frame of reference. If, for instance, some aspect of the Christian community as portrayed in the New Testament has its parallels in the sociological dynamics of the Roman-Hellenistic world, it is a great temptation to presume that this feature is simply a common sociological phenomenon of the time and to explain away any claims of unique spiritual experience as simply the theologizing of the Christian community.

Take as an example Paul's use of terminology drawn from the mystery religions of the Roman world.[34] The mystery religions, with their dying and rising redeemer figures, with their promise of salvation in this world and the next, with their clearly defined rites of passage into the community of the redeemed that separated "insiders" from "outsiders," with their regular calendar of liturgy and even daily office constantly to reinforce the worldview and ethos of the mystery in the lives of the adherents, provide a sociological phenomenon with strong parallels to the life of the Christian communities. From a sociological perspective, it would be easy to conclude that Christianity was simply another Hellenistic mystery religion with its roots in

Jewish messianism rather than Greek mythology. But Paul signifies something more than this. His use of mystery terminology breaks the pattern of its use and meaning in the Roman world. Paul speaks of the mystery that has been revealed, and he proclaims the mystery to *all*, something that would have been anathema to the mystery religions. Further, the center of this mystery is not some ancient deity encrusted with ages of mythological clothing, but a historical figure of the time, a man who had lived in Palestine and whose life, death, and resurrection inaugurated a new community of people who have experienced the reality of God's transforming presence in their lives. To be sure, the incarnation of this experience in human community follows something of the sociological pattern of the mystery religions. But to understand the phenomenon only within the limits of the sociological pattern is to miss the radically different reality that is incarnate in the pattern.

Another potential weakness in sociological criticism is to apply to the world of the New Testament sociological paradigms developed in the present world whose social, political, economic, and cultural dynamics are radically if not totally alien to the Roman world of the first century. This practice can sometimes be found in the work of liberation theologians when they impose the sociological paradigms of their *Sitz im Leben* (life setting) upon the text of the Bible in ways that overlook the sociological matrix of the text and violate the integrity of that matrix for interpretation of the text.

Another weakness, as noted in reference to the work of Malina,[35] is to employ sociological models and/or methods in a Procrustian manner that trims the evidence to fit the parameters of the model/method, often casting aside evidence whose presence is crucial for an accurate understanding of the sociological dynamics so necessary for a full understanding of the text.

The weakness of the postmodern sociocritical and sociopragmatic approaches lies at two levels. The sociocritical approach starts with a presupposition that the text manifests and plays a role in the power games of the sociological context of the text. Such an approach imposes an interpretive grid upon the text which predetermines what sociological context will be seen. The sociopragmatic approach then uses reader-response theories of interpretation which decenter the text from its original context in order to read it as a vehicle for the expression of the reader's own sociological agenda.

Perhaps the most subtle weakness in sociological criticism, implicit in all that has been said, is the tendency toward sociological reductionism. It is possible for the process of sociological criticism to be employed wisely, sensitively, accurately, and with care to avoid the weaknesses noted above but to arrive at conclusions that leave the reality of God's presence, power, and purpose out of the interpretive equation. The witness of the text is understood as a sociological phenomenon only, and even if the reality of a supernatural element is acknowledged, it is subordinated to sociological phenomena.

For example, in his excellent survey of sociological criticism, Kee applies Berger's analysis of the sociology of knowledge as a pattern of social appropriation relevant to the New Testament. After sketching Mark's portrayal of Jesus' understanding of his role, Kee states, "To the extent that his followers commit themselves to this understanding, it becomes the motivation for their lives. And as a group they have a new mode of social identity, which they pass on by preaching and teaching."[36] While such an understanding is sociologically sound, it omits the presence and work of God in the lives of the followers. They do not simply commit themselves to an understanding; they commit themselves to a transforming relationship with God.

Understanding of the relationship is secondary to the relationship itself, and it is the reality of the relationship that becomes the motivation of their lives, not simply their understanding of it. They do indeed have a new mode of social identity, but one whose sociological dimensions are subordinate to the profound reality of their experience of God as the one who has bonded them together in this new community. Preaching and teaching are not merely sociological methods for promulgating an understanding, but vehicles for inviting others into the fellowship of this relationship with God.

Illustration of Sociological Criticism

Philippians 1:27–28 provides an excellent insight into the need for and the contribution of sociological criticism. Translations vary somewhat, but none do justice to the sociological dimensions of this brief passage. A faithful rendering of the Greek text would be:

> Live as worthy citizens of the gospel of Christ so that whether I am present or absent I will hear things about you that indicate you are standing in one spirit, striving together with one soul for the faith of the gospel, and not frightened in anything by those who oppose you, which is proof to them of their destruction but your salvation, and this from God.

Even this translation, however, cannot begin to convey the tremendous significance of what Paul is saying to the Philippians in this brief passage. A number of meaningful sociological factors must be introduced to provide the full weight of Paul's exhortation.

First, the social setting of Philippi is crucial, as are the sociological dynamics of the setting that shaped the daily life of the Philippians. Philippi became a Roman colony in 42 B.C., established by Mark Antony after the victorious battle he and Octavian (who later became the Caesar Augustus of Luke 2:1) waged against Brutus and Cassius on the plains of Philippi following the assassination of Julius Caesar. As one of the first cities in the eastern Mediterranean to receive this prized status, Philippi would have been proud of this privileged bond with Rome and careful to protect this highly prized status that exempted it from taxes, tribute, and duties and allowed it to have the Roman polity. For the first eighty-eight years of its life as a colony, Philippi was the last military outpost between the Roman

Empire and the incursions of the restless and warlike peoples of Thrace, who were not subdued and made a Roman province until A.D. 46. As such, Philippi had a long history of standing united against those who threatened the Roman way of life.

Those fortunate enough to be citizens of a colony, either by birth to parents who possessed citizenship or in recognition of meritorious service to the colony or empire, were also extended members of one of the tribes that constituted the citizenship of the city of Rome. As such, the welfare of Rome and the welfare of the colony were one and the same. Colonies were extremely careful to follow Rome's lead in all matters of life whether political, social, economic, religious, or cultural. Whatever Rome did, the colony followed suit lest it be seen as fractious if not seditious.

This probably accounts for the strange fact that Paul finds the Jewish community of Philippi worshiping "outside the gate at the riverside" (Acts 16:13). The only gate in Philippi near a river was the triumphal arch of Antony that marked the western boundary of the pomerium, the sacred precinct that constituted a Roman colony. Only licit religions were allowed to worship within the pomerium. What is puzzling in this case is that Judaism was a licit religion in the Roman Empire. Paul does not have to go outside the pomerium of the colonies of Pisidian Antioch or Corinth to find the synagogue. Why in Philippi? Chronologically, Paul appears to arrive in Philippi sometime in the latter part of A.D. 49, the year in which the emperor Claudius expelled the Jews from Rome.[37] Rome, historically, took such action against the Jews whenever there were disturbances of the social order usually caused by proselytizing.[38] It is significant that the charges against Paul and Silas in Philippi were: "These men are *Jews*, they are *disturbing the city*, they are *advocating customs* that are not lawful for us Romans to practice" (Acts 16:20–21). It would appear that Philippi had followed Rome's lead and expelled the Jewish community from the sacred precincts of the colony.

To be a colony was to be a microcosm of the sociological dynamics that shaped the life of the city of Rome. A number of those sociological dynamics inform Paul's exhortation to the Philippians.

The phrase "live as worthy citizens" translates a term that, for Paul, related to life lived as faithful members of God's covenant community,[39] and that for the Philippians who lived in a Roman military colony would also have indicated a life conformed to the full range of sociological dynamics that shaped the Roman worldview and lifestyle. It means to be thoroughly Roman in thought, word, and deed; to have every aspect of one's life shaped by the ethos of the Roman culture: political, economic, religious, educational, even linguistic (all the official inscriptions at Philippi are in Latin rather than Greek!). When Paul uses the term in addressing the Philippians, this is the larger sociological context within which they would hear it.

We have already seen that the word *gospel* operated in a totally different sociological milieu in Paul's world than in ours. Can you begin to understand the radical dimensions of Paul's exhortation to the Philippians to "live as worthy citizens of the gospel of Christ"? When informed by sociological analysis, Paul's call is radically and ultimately seditious in the setting of the Roman world. He is implying that Christ is the embodiment of a new order of being, a new context of life, a new matrix of existence, and that the Christians of Philippi should live lives shaped by the ethos of this new realm. Paul's exhortation is profoundly countercultural when its sociological dimensions are clear.

Paul further highlights the countercultural nature of Christian existence in the world in Philippians 3:20, when he reminds the Philippians that their citizenship[40] is in heaven from where they await a Savior, the Lord Jesus Christ. Here the Christians' matrix of existence is clearly alternative to that of the Roman world whose savior and lord was the emperor.[41]

In the remainder of our passage (1:27–28), Paul indicates that the Philippians' posture toward the Roman world is not simply one of an alternative lifestyle. He again employs terminology that creates for his readers images that are rooted in the sociological dynamics of the Roman world. Paul's military images ("standing in one spirit," "striving together with one soul," "not frightened by those who oppose you") play upon the community spirit and solidarity that would have energized a Roman military colony in the face of a threat to its way of life. The myth of Roman invincibility in the first century might well have alleviated fear in the face of opposition. For the Christians of Philippi, however, their reliance was to be upon the invincibility of a new order of being in which the Spirit of God established a new matrix of existence for community solidarity.

Perhaps the most radical portion of Paul's exhortation is his affirmation of the "destruction" of the opponents. The word Paul uses for "destruction" *(apōleias)* means, literally, to be uncitied, to experience the loss of that matrix of life that gives meaning, value, identity, and purpose to the community and the individual. Paul is implying that the entire sociological matrix of the Roman world is doomed to fail but that the Christian matrix of existence will endure. What an impact this would have on Christians living in a Roman colony in the golden age of Rome's glory!

Discerning the sociological dimensions within which Paul is working to convey meaning to his readers is only half of the role of sociological criticism. Another sociological aspect relates to the community to which Paul writes. How does that community identify itself within the larger community of Philippi? How does it understand its role in the midst of the Roman matrix? What is its worldview, its ethos?

We must remember that this community was formed within a context of ostracism and persecution. As Jews, they appear to have been expelled from the colony as far as their worship was concerned and, as Paul's trial in

Philippi reveals, the political leadership of the colony couldn't distinguish between Jews and Christians. The fact that their "founder" had been beaten, imprisoned, and subsequently banished from the colony certainly would not enhance their status as a community within the colony. The fact that they operated out of the house of a foreign woman would not serve to allay suspicions. It appears, then, that the Christian community in Philippi found itself at least marginalized within the sociological matrix of the colony if not alienated from that matrix. In such a situation it is easy for a group to feel isolated, alone, and powerless in the face of what appears to be the overwhelming superiority of the surrounding community.

It is no wonder that Paul describes his own imprisonment in more detail in Philippians than in any of the other imprisonment Epistles and calls the readers his partners in his imprisonment and the defense and confirmation of the gospel (1:7). Paul reminds them that they are engaged in the same conflict they saw (Paul's imprisonment in Philippi) and now hear to be his (his present imprisonment in Ephesus). Paul is especially careful to note the Roman context of his imprisonment (the praetorian guard) and that it is a witness for Christ in the midst of Roman power (1:13). It is in this context that he calls them to be worthy citizens of the gospel of Christ.

Paul is reminding the Philippians of the new matrix of their existence in Christ that provides them with their identity as a community in the midst of a Roman military colony. They are citizens of a new order of being whose reality will endure while Rome's will crumble. Their role in the midst of the Roman order is to live as worthy citizens of the new order, and the bulk of Paul's letter provides them the worldview and ethos of citizenship in this new order.

The space of this chapter prohibits a more in-depth analysis of this portion of Paul's letter to the Philippians, to say nothing of how it relates to other sociological dynamics that inform the rest of the letter. What we have looked at, however, should provide an introduction to the need for and the value of sociological criticism for the interpretation of the New Testament.

Bibliography

Elliott, John H. *A Home for the Homeless: A Sociological Exegesis of 1 Peter*. Philadelphia: Fortress, 1981.

———. *Social-scientific Criticism of the New Testament and Its Social World*. Semeia 35. Decatur, Ga.: Scholars Press, 1986.

Esler, Philip F., ed., *Modelling Early Christianity: Social-scientific Studies of the New Testament in Its Context*. New York: Routledge, 1995.

Gager, John C. *Kingdom and Community: The Social World of Early Christianity*. Englewood Cliffs, N.J.: Prentice-Hall, 1975.

Kee, Howard Clark. *Knowing the Truth: A Sociological Approach to New Testament Interpretation*. Philadelphia: Fortress, 1989.

Malherbe, Abraham J. *Social Aspects of Early Christianity*. Philadelphia: Fortress, 1983.

Malina, Bruce. *The New Testament World: Insights from Cultural Anthropology.* Atlanta: John Knox, 1981.

Meeks, Wayne A. *The First Urban Christians: The Social World of the Apostle Paul.* New Haven: Yale University Press, 1983.

———. *The Moral World of the First Christians.* Philadelphia: Westminster, 1986.

Neyrey, Jerome H. *Paul in Other Worlds: A Cultural Reading of His Letters.* Louisville: Westminster/John Knox, 1991.

———, ed. *The Social World of Luke-Acts: Models for Interpretation.* Peabody: Hendrickson, 1991.

Theissen, Gerd. *The Sociology of Early Palestinian Christianity.* Philadelphia: Fortress, 1978.

———. *The Gospels in Context: Social and Political History in the Synoptic Tradition.* Minneapolis: Fortress, 1991

Tidball, Derek. *The Social Context of the New Testament.* Grand Rapids: Zondervan, 1984.

Notes

1. For a succinct yet comprehensive synopsis of the development of sociological criticism, see Howard Clark Kee, *Knowing the Truth: A Sociological Approach to New Testament Interpretation* (Minneapolis: Augsburg Fortress, 1989). For an earlier survey, see Robin Scroggs, "The Sociological Interpretation of the New Testament: The Present State of Research," *New Testament Studies* 26, No. 2 (1980): 164–79.

2. Gerhard Meier, *The End of the Historical-Critical Method* (St. Louis: Concordia, 1977).

3. Cf. Robert M. Polzin, *Biblical Structuralism: Method and Subjectivity in the Study of Ancient Texts* (Philadelphia: Fortress, 1977); Roland Barthes, et. al., *Structural Analysis and Biblical Exegesis,* Pittsburgh Theological Monograph Series, 3 (Pittsburgh: Pickwick, 1974); Daniel Patte, *What Is Structural Exegesis?* Guides to Biblical Scholarship (Philadelphia: Fortress, 1976); for a succinct overview of structuralism, see Raymond F. Collins, *Introduction to the New Testament* (Garden City, N.Y.: Doubleday, 1983), chapter 7.

4. Cf. such works as Bo Reicke, *The New Testament Era* (Philadelphia: Fortress, 1968); F. F. Bruce, *New Testament History* (London: Nelson, 1969); Joachim Jeremias, *Jerusalem in the Time of Jesus* (Philadelphia: Fortress, 1975); Eduard Lohse, *The New Testament Environment* (Nashville: Abingdon, 1976); Helmut Koester, *Introduction to the New Testament,* Vol. 1, *History, Culture, and Religion of the Hellenistic Age* (Philadelphia: Fortress, 1982); Everett Ferguson, *Backgrounds of Early Christianity*, 2d ed. (Grand Rapids: Eerdmans, 1993).

5. London: Tyndale, 1960.

6. Derek Tidball, *The Social Context of the New Testament* (Grand Rapids: Zondervan, 1984).

7. Philadelphia: Fortress, 1978.

8. Trans. John H. Schuetz (Philadelphia: Fortress, 1982).

9. S. N. Eisenstadt, *Social Differentiation and Stratification* (Glenview, Ill.: 1971); Gerhard E. Lenski, *Power and Privilege: A Theory of Social Stratification* (New York: McGraw-Hill, 1966).

10. Anthony Saldarini, *Pharisees, Scribes and Sadducees in Palestinian Society: A Sociological Approach* (Wilmington: Michael Glazier, 1988).

11. Richard A. Horsley and John S. Hanson, *Bandits, Prophets and Messiahs: Popular Movements at the Time of Jesus* (Minneapolis: Winston Press, 1985).

12. *The Methodology of the Social Sciences,* trans. F. R. Shils and H. A. Finch (New York: Free Press of Glencoe, 1949).

13. *The Elementary Forms of the Religious Life* (New York: Free Press of Glencoe, 1965).

14. *The Sociology of Social Conflict* (Englewood Cliffs, N.J.: Prentice-Hall, 1973).

15. *The Interpretation of Cultures* (New York: Basic Books, 1973).

16. Leon Festinger, Henry W. Reicken, Stanley Schachter, *When Prophecy Fails: A Social and Psychological Study of a Modern Group that Predicted the Destruction of the World* (New York: Harper, 1956).

17. *Pursuit of the Millennium: Revolutionary Millenarians and Mystical Anarchists of the Middle Ages* (New York: Oxford University Press, 1970).

18. *The Trumpet Shall Sound* (New York: Schocken Books, 1968).

19. John G. Gager, *Kingdom and Community: The Social World of Early Christianity* (Englewood Cliffs, N.J.: Prentice-Hall, 1975).

20. Howard Clark Kee, *Community of the New Age: Studies in Mark's Gospel* (Philadelphia: Westminster, 1977).

21. Atlanta: John Knox, 1981.

22. Atlanta: John Knox, 1986.

23. Douglas sees two dynamics of social structure: group and grid. Group relates to the level of individual commitment to the social matrix; grid relates to the level of control of the individual by the group. For example, a low-group/low-grid community would be characterized by a high level of individualism, whereas a high-group/high-grid community would be characterized by a strong hierarchical structure in which loyalty is paramount. Douglas sees this analytical method as a means for discerning the sociological matrix within which a group lives out its worldview but not as a means for establishing categories by which phenomena are classified. Cf. Mary Tew Douglas, *Natural Symbols: Explorations in Cosmology* (London: Barrie and Jenkins, 1973); Mary Douglas, ed., *Essays in the Sociology of Perception* (London: Routledge and Kegan Paul, 1976).

24. Hans Gadamer, *Truth and Method,* trans./ed., Garrett Barden and John Cumming (New York: Seabury, 1975); *Philosophical Hermeneutics,* trans. and ed., David E. Linge (Berkeley: University of California Press, 1976).

25. Ludwig Wittgenstein, *On Certainty,* ed. Anscome and Wright, trans. Paul and Anscome (Oxford: Blackwell, 1969); *Philosophical Investigations,* trans. G. E. M. Anscome (New York: Macmillan, 1968).

26. Anthony Thiselton, *The Two Horizons: New Testament Hermeneutics and Philosophical Description* (Grand Rapids: Eerdmans, 1980).

27. Eugene A. Nida and Johannes P. Louw, eds., *Greek-English Lexicon of the New Testament Based on Semantic Domains,* 2 vols. (New York: United Bible Societies, 1988). See also J. P. Louw, ed., *Sociolinguistics and Communication,* UBS Monograph Series 1 (New York: United Bible Societies, 1986).

28. Anthony Thiselton, *New Horizons in Hermeneutics* (Grand Rapids: Zondervan, 1992), 379 (emphasis his).

29. Cf. Richard Rorty, *Philosophy and the Mirror of Nature* (Princeton: Princeton University Press, 1979 and 1980).

30. Paul writes of the revelation of the mystery (Rom. 16:25) and the proclamation of the mystery (1 Cor. 2:1; Eph. 6:19; Col. 1:27; 4:3), ideas that would be shocking to a world in which mystery religions jealously safeguarded their "mysteries" from all but the

initiates. In 1 Cor. 4:1, Paul describes himself and Apollos by using the technical term for functionaries in the mystery religions.

31. Cf. Marvin W. Meyer, ed. *The Ancient Mysteries: A Sourcebook* (New York: Harper and Row, 1987); Joscelyn Godwin, *Mystery Religions in the Ancient World* (San Francisco: Harper and Row, 1981).

32. This is a dynamic equivalent translation of the Greek.

33. "And so forth" is itself a phrase that indicates the writer presumes the hearers share a common sociological frame of reference within which they can fill out what is implied.

34. Paul repeatedly speaks of the "mystery" (Rom. 16:25; 1 Cor. 2:7, 4:1, 13:2(?); Eph. 1:9, 3:3–4, 9; 6:19; Col. 1:26–27, 2:2, 4:3; 1 Tim. 3:9, 16), especially the mystery revealed (Rom. 16:25–26; 1 Cor. 2:7–10; Eph. 1:9, 3:3–4, 6:19; Col. 1:26-27), which is now proclaimed to all (Rom. 16:26; Eph. 3:9, 6:19) and of which Paul is a "steward" (1 Cor. 4:1)—a technical phrase used of the chief functionaries of the Hellenistic mystery religions.

35. See notes 21 and 22.

36. Howard Clark Kee, *Knowing the Truth: A Sociological Approach to New Testament Interpretation* (Minneapolis: Augsburg Fortress, 1989), 52.

37. Suetonius, *Claudius* 24.5; cf. Acts 18:2.

38. In about 139 B.C., there appears to have been an expulsion of Jews from Rome due to the spread of Judaism through proselytizing (The Epitome of Paris, *Valerius Maximus* i, 3.3). In A.D. 19 Jews were again expelled from Rome. Although the accounts of Tacitus (*Annals ii*, 85, 5), Suetonius (*Tiberius* 36.1), Dio (lvli, 18, Sa), and Josephus (*Antiquities* xviii, 65–84) vary, they agree that proselytizing lay at the heart of the problem. (For a full development of this Roman posture toward the Jews, see M. Robert Mulholland Jr., *Revelation: Holy Living in an Unholy World* [Grand Rapids: Zondervan, 1990], Appendix.)

39. Ernest C. Miller, Jr., "*Politeuesthe* in Philippians 1:27: Some Philological and Thematic Observations," *Journal for the Study of the New Testament* 15 (1982): 86–96. Note also Paul's use of *politeuma* in 3:20. Only in Philippians does Paul use these two terms that would have carried added significance for people living in a Roman colony.

40. *Politeuma* = the full matrix of sociological factors that structured community life.

41. In fact, the term *savior* represented one who either established, maintained, and defended or reestablished the sociological matrix within which the community and individuals found meaning, value, purpose, identity, and welfare.

Part III

Special Issues in New Testament Interpretation

Chapter 9

Background Studies And
New Testament Interpretation

Paul Norman Jackson
Union University

Phenomenal growth, unprecedented unity, selfless charity, powerful proclamation of the resurrection of Jesus Christ, and the saturation of God's grace characterized the first-century church, according to Luke's summary narrative in Acts 4:32–35.[1] What could possibly sidetrack such a dynamic fellowship of God's people? Textually, the first indication of trouble is the initial word in chapter 5—"but" (NASB). The story that unfolds is quite shocking. In successive scenes, an early church couple named Ananias and Sapphira are suddenly struck dead for what appears to be a "white lie." One would think the God of grace portrayed so clearly in the opening chapters of Acts could have dealt with the erring pair less harshly. Why did they have to die?

At the conclusion of the third missionary journey, the warnings Paul received about going to Jerusalem painfully came true as he was arrested, cruelly mistreated, and remained imprisoned for the remainder of his story in Acts. When some unbelieving Jews from the province of Asia saw Paul at the temple, they seized him with murderous intentions. Paul triggered this riot because these enraged Jews were thoroughly convinced he had taken Trophimus, a Gentile seen earlier in his company, into the temple (Acts 22:1–21). Why did they react so violently? What did the Jews mean by shouting, throwing off their cloaks, and flinging dust into the air in response to Paul's echoing God's love for the Gentiles (22:23)? Claudius Lysias, the Roman commander, intervened in order to discover why the crowd suddenly turned bloodthirsty. Although Paul faced certain death by remaining in the hands of the Jews, Claudius's design was no great consolation as he intended to torture Paul with the scourge (*flagellum*) for information. "The

188

scourge was a fearful instrument of torture, consisting of leather thongs, weighted with rough pieces of metal or bone, and attached to a stout wooden handle. If a man did not actually die under the scourge (which frequently happened), he would certainly be crippled for life."[2] With Paul stretched out in whipping position, what caused Claudius and his soldiers to withdraw abruptly and fearfully? From the meaning of the Greek text, one can picture Claudius throwing the whip down as if he were holding a poisonous viper and were immediately gripped with fear!

In the textually questionable story of Jesus and the adulterous woman (*pericope de adultera*, John 7:53–8:11), Jesus responded initially to a loaded question posed by some headstrong religious authorities by writing something in the dirt.[3] In addition he uttered, "If any one of you is without sin, let him be the first to throw a stone at her" (John 8:7). Beginning with the older ones first, the men departed one by one until only the accused woman and Jesus remained. Jesus then exhorted the undoubtedly surprised woman to walk away from her life of sin. The age-old question every interpreter wants to know is, "What did Jesus write in the dirt?"

In the unique Lukan account of Jesus' *via dolorosa* in the passion narrative, the Lord addresses the "daughters of Jerusalem" who were following and mourning bitterly for him:

> "Daughters of Jerusalem, do not weep for me; weep for yourselves and for your children. For the time will come when you will say, 'Blessed are the barren women, the wombs that never bore and the breasts that never nursed!'
> Then they will say to the mountains, 'Fall on us!' and to the hills, 'Cover us!'
> For if men do these things when the tree is green, what will happen when it is dry?" (Luke 23:28–31).

T. W. Manson perceptively described this episode: "They raise the death-wail over Him in anticipation. He in His turn raises, as it were, the death-wail over Jerusalem in anticipation."[4] In anticipation of what? What does this cryptic saying mean? Why would Jesus utter it at this particular time? Historically and extrabiblically, did something happen that would help in the interpretation of its meaning?

Heretic! The simple utterance of this word stirs up many negative connotations. Branding someone as heretical carries with it the idea of biblical or doctrinal treason. Our meaning, though, is not the biblical meaning usually. The adjective translated "heretical" occurs only once in the New Testament. In Titus 3:10, Paul described a man who should be rejected as heretical after two warnings. Have Christians, regardless of intention, misinterpreted the concept of heresy throughout church history? What did Paul really mean by the term *hairetikon*?

The denouement of the "Book of Signs" emerges in John 11 with the story of the death and resuscitation of Jesus' friend Lazarus. This culminating sign not only served as a harbinger of Jesus' quickly approaching passion, but also John marked it as the religious authorities' overarching reason for issuing death warrants on him and Lazarus. The point of interest here, however, is the puzzling exchange between Jesus and the mourners at Lazarus' tomb. In verse 33, John described a raw emotional discharge: "When Jesus saw her weeping, and the Jews who had come along with her also weeping, *he was deeply moved in spirit and troubled*." After seeing the resting spot of Lazarus, weeping himself, and hearing some harsh criticism, "Jesus, once more, *was deeply moved*" (V. 38). Typically, this passage has been preached and taught as an example of Jesus' deep compassion for people mourning the death of a loved one. Could there not be another emotion Jesus communicated instead? Is there any textual support for the idea that Jesus vented anger because of the mourners' collective and individual display of hopelessness and lack of faith in the face of death? When one chooses to interpret the passage as an example of deep compassion, does that reflect a Christological bias over clear textual evidence?

One of the keys to interpreting successfully each of the previous examples is to consult various background tools that in turn shed important light on its cultural-historical situation. The interpreter needs to frame the text with the available rich background sources. Meaning is only then properly gleaned from a proper consultation of the background in which the text is couched.

Context Is King: Framing the Text

Surely every responsible interpreter would agree that no text is an island. Even one word requires some contextual bedding for meaning to emerge. ESPN, the most widely recognized sports reporting network in America today, frequently provides examples of the vivid and creative use of words, which are understood accurately only in context. During the evening postgame coverage of a baseball game, Stuart Scott described a massive home run off the bat of Boston Red Sox cleanup hitter Mo Vaughn as "it's going *back*, way *back*; it hit somebody in the *back*; it's not coming *back*!" The simple word *back* appeared four times with three different meanings, understood only within the dynamic triangular relationship of author, text, and subject matter.

Semantic versatility in any language (verbal or concept delivery system) exists in words, phrases, sentences, and paragraphs. More information, however, is actually present in the sports illustration than meets the eye. If you were reading or hearing Scott's description and knew little or nothing about baseball (let's say you abhorred sports but loved operas, the symphony, and mathematics), your ability to comprehend the event would be severely hampered. Granted, seeing the film footage simultaneously with the verbal description could clear some possible ambiguities and therefore enhance your mental grasp of the situation.

Pictorial replays of events provide a dimension not afforded to words. Imagine how much more difficult the task for understanding a text becomes when mere wooden descriptions are intermingled with sarcasm, irony, plays on words, jargon, or some other rhetorical device. Some of these devices tend to be highly cultural or governed by time. I remember watching a baseball game at Union University during which a player on the opposing team commented that the "bases were drunk." Baseball jargon describing the situation when every base is occupied is technically, "the bases are loaded." *Getting loaded* is a synonymous phrase for getting drunk. The word *loaded* has multiple meanings, thus allowing for some creative humor employed to describe something understandable to those knowledgeable of baseball terminology.

Scott's report connected because his words described a real, antecedent event, not because he happened to find some background footage to match his words. And he depended on his audience to have some functional pre-understanding, not to have to consult a dictionary or an interpreter to make sense of his utterance. Proper background information, though, is necessary to make the report more enjoyable, memorable, but, and more importantly, understandable. Some questions need to be answered: Who is Stuart Scott? Why does he comment on sports events? Who is Mo Vaughn, and why is he the cleanup hitter? What is a cleanup hitter? What is a home run? Does Mr. Vaughn have a distinct penchant for hitting them? What kind of an instrument is a bat? Who are the Boston Red Sox? What is baseball, and what are the rules for playing it? Having played high school and college baseball, and now enjoying baseball as a fan, I know the answers to all the previous questions. On the other hand, someone who has never encountered that specific culture would have an extremely difficult time answering those questions and certainly could not comprehend an oral or written report about an event emerging from that genre. Some pertinent background information is necessary. Specific background coloring affords the hearer or reader with the indispensable context responsible for generating meaning.

So it is with the New Testament. The words of the text alone do not provide enough information to complete the entire process of biblical interpretation. While determining the best available Greek text is crucial and figures in heavily as the primary step in the overall exegetical procedure, the interpreter needs further assistance for moving to the intended goal—the personal application of the text.[5] With respect to the Book of Revelation for instance, Bruce Metzger offered an insightful axiom for interpreting its particular genre by stressing the urgency of background assistance: "A text does not mean what it says, it means what it means."[6]

To go a step further, a text can never mean what it never meant. Discovering what the text meant can be tedious and time-consuming. R. H. Charles, Ray Summers, Robert Mounce, and David Aune, just to name a few, provide good examples of individuals who present the background material necessary for proper exegesis of the Apocalypse.[7] A lot of unfruitful ink, however, has proceeded form the pens of those who chose rather to minimize this step. Grappling with the historical, cultural milieu of the text is an absolute must. "Since Christianity is a historical religion, the interpreter must recognize that an understanding of the history and culture within which the passage was produced is an indispensable tool for uncovering the meaning of that passage."[8]

Each semester during the opening session of my hermeneutics class entitled, "Introduction to Bible Study and Interpretation," I illustrate this point by making several students try to set up, play, and explain a game they have never heard of or played. What game you use is arbitrary, but I use Stratego, touted as the classic game of battlefield strategy. The students usually can figure out a few basic guidelines of the game. For instance, there are two sets of playing pieces, blue and red, each distinguishable by a discernible military ranking system. Both sets of pieces also include a flag and several bombs. So the students preliminarily deduce there are two opposing teams and, in some way, each one must protect its hidden flag with bombs while trying to capture the other team's flag. Even though my human guinea pigs usually make several correct judgments, they nevertheless do not know how to play the game correctly and clearly according to the rules. I then come to the rescue by explaining the rules in great detail. I, in effect, frame the game for them so they can play (interpret).

New Testament interpretation is a similar venture. Each genre must be interpreted according to its own set of rules. But one of the huge problems for the interpreter (player) is that the rules are not so easily accessed. Facing the text, four basic classes of exegetical problems exist: (1) the problem of semantics; (2) the problem of cultural distance; (3) the problem of context; and (4) the problem of genre.[9] The author (designer) has deliberately encoded the text (game) for the purpose of addressing a target group; in other words, the encoder created "shareability" so understanding could occur. As an interpreter I must attempt to gain historical consciousness of that previously shared experience. "Hermeneutics is cousin to historical consciousness; the realization that we do not know things directly and immediately suggests that knowledge is the result of interpretation. Reality is a text to be interpreted, mediated by language, history, culture, and tradition."[10] Therefore, I should approach New Testament documents and texts purposefully, knowing that they are not coincidental but highly occasional. For example, in A.D. 57, the apostle Paul did not arise one wintry morning in Corinth and decide to fire off a quick letter to the Romans. Something tangible and real precipitated this profound theological treatise. Making the right kinds of background assessments, one enters into a contextual window which provides an informative way to engage a text.[11]

Tools of the Trade

In recent years numerous new sources have been published to aid interpreters in the task of illuminating New Testament texts through background inquiries. The following is an annotated list of some important background tools yielding rich information I have found extremely useful in interpreting the New Testament. A number of these sources were used in the exegesis of passages in this chapter. This list is far from exhaustive but is intended to be representative of the kinds of excellent background helps one should consult regularly if satisfactory exegesis is desired.

1. Ceslas Spicq. *Theological Lexicon of the NT*, 3 vols. Ed. and trans. James D. Ernest. Peabody, Mass.: Hendrickson, 1994.

   Gives an in-depth explanation of New Testament terms through an examination of their meaning in classical writings, epigraphical texts, papyri, and other background sources. Useful for understanding Greek words and concepts in their original contexts.

2. Leland Ryken, et al., ed., *Dictionary of Biblical Imagery*. Downers Grove, Ill.: IVP, 1998.

   Discusses a variety of biblical images, giving concise and useful explanations of metaphors, symbols, motifs, figures of speech, and literary patterns found in Scripture. Explanations rely on biblical passages and information on background customs and culture to convey the true sense implicit in the biblical images.

3. Craig L. Blomberg. *Jesus and the Gospels*. Nashville: Broadman & Holman, 1997.

   Includes insightful and fresh treatments of the political, religious, and socioeconomic backgrounds related to New Testament studies.

4. Joel B. Green, et al., ed., *Dictionary of Jesus and the Gospels*. Downers Grove, Ill.: IVP, 1992.

   Provides insightful treatments of significant terms, ideas, and events related to Jesus and the Gospels.

5. Gerald F. Hawthorne, et al., ed., *Dictionary of Paul and His Letters*. Downers Grove, Ill.: IVP, 1993.

   Gives thorough topical explanations of concepts, people, and theological terms found in the Pauline Epistles. Entries use extensive background information, past theological studies, and biblical references to explain topics. Useful for a deeper understanding of theological and historical concepts in Paul's writings.

6. Ralph P. Martin and Peter H. Davids, eds. *Dictionary of the Later New Testament and Its Developments*. Downers Grove, Ill.: IVP, 1997.

   Features extensive articles on subjects related to early Christian history, literature, theology, and practice. It also includes full coverage of all New Testament literature outside the Gospels and the Pauline corpus, and full coverage of the apostolic fathers and early Christianity through the middle of the second century.

7. S. R. Llewelyn, ed. *New Documents Illustrating Early Christianity.* Grand Rapids: Eerdmans, 1998.

Reviews and reproduces information gleaned from extrabiblical papyri and inscriptions discovered in recent years. Useful for a better understanding of the life and language of the Greco-Roman world.

8. *Loeb's Classical Library.*

While not new it is an invaluable collection of primary source material from the classical world. Includes works of such prominent figures as Plato, Cicero, and Josephus, as well as any others. Provides ready reference to texts describing firsthand the historical and cultural context of biblical times.

9. Walter C. Kaiser, ed. *Hard Sayings of the Bible.* Downers Grove, Ill.: IVP, 1996.

Provides succinct yet useful explanations of verses which are often troubling to biblical interpreters. Uses knowledge of historical, cultural, and linguistic background to explain the true meaning of these passages in their biblical context.

10. Craig S. Keener, *IVP Bible Background Commentary: New Testament.* Downers Grove, Ill.: IVP, 1993.

Presents a verse-by-verse explanation of the cultural background of the entire New Testament. Gives a useful summary of the basic thrust of a passage in light of its cultural and historical context.

11. LaMoine F. Devries. *Cities of the Biblical World.* Peabody, Mass.: Hendrickson, 1997.

A chronological, city-by-city approach detailing the archaeology, geography, and history of important biblical cities and towns. Highlights the chief importance of locations as they relate to their biblical contexts. Provides a source of quality information and summary without delving into unnecessary detail.

12. W. Bauer, W. F. Arndt, F. W. Gingrich, F. Danker. *Greek-English Lexicon of the New Testament,* 3d rev. ed., Chicago: University of Chicago Press, 2000.

This new revised edition of BAGD, the undisputed leading lexicon of New Testament Greek, is geared toward the beginning student as well as the scholar. It includes the most recent information, research, and analysis with translations in contemporary English. This is an invaluable reference tool for anyone with knowledge of New Testament Greek.

13. Horst Balz and Gerhard Schneider, eds. *Exegetical Dictionary of the New Testament,* 3 vols. Grand Rapids: Eerdmans, 1992.

A complete dictionary of New Testament Greek as well as a guide to the context and usage of every New Testament word. Provides valuable articles and essays for New Testament exegesis and theology.

14. Thomas C. Brisco. *Holman Bible Atlas.* Nashville: Holman Reference, 1998.

    A colorful, informative, and easy-to-use atlas of the ancient Near East. Includes numerous color plates, maps, and textual notes which aid in the understanding of biblical geography. Useful for students and scholars alike.

15. Michael Grant and Rachel Kitzinger, eds. *Civilization of the Ancient Mediterranean,* 3 vols. New York: Scribner's Sons, 1988.

    This three-volume reference work contains ninety-seven original essays canvassing the full range of topics on the people, customs, government, religion, and arts of the ancient world, from 2000 B.C. to the fall of Rome, in A.D. 476.

16. Alfred Edersheim. *Sketches of Jewish Social Life,* updated ed. Peabody, Mass.: Hendrickson, 1998.

    Time-honored, updated classic containing relevant citations of Scripture, rabbinic sources, and the works of Philo and Josephus, making bland references come alive and shedding invaluable light on difficult passages so the interpreter might understand better the world of Jesus and his disciples.

17. E. Glenn Hinson. *The Early Church: Origins to the Dawn of the Middle Ages.* Nashville, Abingdon Press, 1996.

    Introduces the history of the early church until approximately A.D. 600. Includes the story of ordinary lay Christians, including women, in this period, as well as information on notable people and events.

18. *Zondervan Image Archives: Bible and Church History Sites and Artifacts.*

    CD-ROM which provides more than five thousand color photographs in a searchable archive. Includes historical and biblical sites, archeological sites, and important artifacts and descriptions.

19. *Ancient Christian Commentary on Scripture.* Downers Grove, Ill.: IVP, 1998 and forthcoming.

    Volumes on Mark, Romans, Galatians, Ephesians, and Philippians already published, with twenty-seven volumes planned. Includes the comments of the patristic fathers on New Testament texts, giving a historical perspective on Scripture and its interpretation. Includes portions of sermons, letters, early commentaries, and newly translated texts.

20. I. Howard Marshall, et al., ed., *New Bible Dictionary,* 3d ed., Downers Grove, Ill.: IVP, 1996.

Features more than two thousand articles on the Bible's documents, people, places, key words, and major doctrines. Provides essential background on the history, geography, and customs of Israel and its Middle Eastern neighbors.

Putting the Tools to Work

At the outset of this chapter, I posed some open-ended questions connected to various New Testament textual scenarios requiring additional background information for adequate understanding. Now I will show how the various background sources are instrumental in the overall exegetical process to give us a firmer grip on its meaning. As will be seen, framing the text with helpful background information renders more accurate interpretations.

AN OMINOUS ECHO FROM AI

The more I study the New Testament, the more I see the essential background role the Old Testament plays for gaining a deeper and clearer grasp of its contents.[12] Proper exegesis of Old Testament background texts along with the assessment of Persian, Greek, Maccabean, and Roman history takes its place for shedding light on the New Testament. Jesus himself used the Old Testament as a rich source for his teaching. Interacting with at least twenty-one different Old Testament books (Deuteronomy and Psalms being his favorites), he quoted directly from them forty times and alluded to them another sixty. Additionally, he made more than a hundred references to Old Testament characters, events, or things. Adequately equipped with a working knowledge of the Old Testament, it is easy to see how it thoroughly saturated the minds of all New Testament authors, even Luke.[13] Responsible and successful interpreters of the New Testament regularly feed upon the rich background of the Old Testament.

How can the Old Testament help us understand the deaths of Ananias and Sapphira in Acts 5? This unfortunate event in the early Christian church sadly had a precursor, one that evidently this first-century couple either chose to ignore or failed to learn. During the conquest of Canaan the Israelites experienced a rare setback due to the sin of one man, Achan. Similar to the pristine church, the people of God enjoyed the benefits of obedience to God outlined clearly in the early chapters of Joshua. It was simple—obey and enjoy the favor of God or disobey and suffer the same consequences as the enemy by being placed under the ban.[14]

After an impressive victory at Jericho, chapter 6 of Joshua closes with a summary statement similar to those found in the Lukan narrative of Acts: "So the LORD was with Joshua, and his fame spread throughout the land" (6:27).[15] Joshua 7, however, begins the same way Acts 5 does—"but" (NASB). Both authors presented the people of God, warts and all. Trouble lurked in the camp of the Israelites and did not surface until they tried to overtake Ai, the next victim on their list. Surprisingly, they suffered a glaring defeat, losing thirty-six men and their courage. "At this the hearts of the people melted and became like water" (7:5b). A stunning reversal occurred as God's people quivered in fear just as the Canaanites had even before the Israelites arrived to conquer the land!

Next the author desires the reader to flashback to the Exodus with the accusatory response of Joshua in 7:6–9. Reminiscent of the grumbling, mumbling mob of Moses-led defectors in the desert, Joshua blamed God for their sudden misfortune. God quickly apprised Joshua that the defeat and now impending doom of the whole nation were due to what was buried under Achan's tent. In time Achan admitted to his sin, and shockingly he and his entire family were stoned to death.

What was so terrible about the actions of Achan, Ananias, and Sapphira can be seen in a discussion of the application of both incidents. Acts 5:2 uses the rare Greek verb *nosphizomai* to describe Ananias' embezzlement of funds.

> Significantly, the same rare verb occurs in the Greek version of Joshua 7:1–26, the story of Achan, who took from Jericho some of the booty 'devoted' (i.e., set aside for God) for sacred use. Achan received a judgment of death from God himself, and Luke may well have seen a reminder of his fate in the similar divine judgment that came upon Ananias and Sapphira. They too had embezzled what was sacred, what belonged to the community in whom the Holy Spirit resided.[16]

First, deliberate deception ruled the hearts of all three as they kept what was devoted to God. Integrity, not honesty, was the prime issue at stake. The people of God in any age must be holy because God is holy. Being "separate" from the world is a key component of kingdom citizenry. If not, God's mission will not succeed. In Canaan and Jerusalem God had begun a new work to establish his people at critical junctures in his overall plan of salvation history. Timing was important. Longenecker is correct in pointing out that by the use of the rare verb *nosphizomai* Luke intended to draw a parallel between the sin of Achan as the Israelites began their conquest of Canaan and the sin of Ananias and Sapphira as the church began its mission—both incidents coming under the immediate and drastic judgment of God and teaching a sobering lesson. And this is very likely how the early church saw the incident as well.[17]

Second, failure to recognize God's claim creates a rupture in the community of faith in any age. Thus an individual problem is automatically a body problem. Disobedience on behalf of one has the potential to affect the whole group. It is interesting that Joshua 7:1 reads, "But the *Israelites* acted unfaithfully in regard to the devoted things." The emphasis is clearly placed on community culpability, and therefore the sin is ultimately against God who created that community for himself, regardless of which covenant was in effect.

First Corinthians 3:16–17 is another illustration that shows the importance of understanding the Old Testament background of the New Testament for proper exegesis and interpretation. After employing agricultural and architectural metaphors to instruct about how one builds on the sole foundation of Jesus Christ, Paul used the metaphor of the temple to issue a strong warning: "Don't *you* know that *you yourselves* are God's temple and that God's Spirit lives in *you*? If anyone destroys God's temple, God will destroy him; for God's temple is sacred, and *you* are that temple."[18] Some Corinthian believers traipsed dangerously near disaster because of their divisive, disruptive behavior within the fellowship. That it was a body issue can be seen in the fact that all the italicized words in the text above are plural in the Greek text. This might be the most stringent warning issued in all of Paul's letters.

A similar kind of urgency is seen in 1 Corinthians 5 and 11. Paul calls for the dismissal of a sexually aberrant member four times in just thirteen verses in chapter 5. One of the reasons offered by Paul for the seemingly harsh discipline was that unchecked sin is exceedingly pervasive and therefore has the power to infect every member (5:6). Some believe Paul's instruction to "hand this man over to Satan, so that the sinful nature may be destroyed and his spirit saved on the day of the Lord" (5:5) means that he died.[19] In chapter 11, we are told that some church members had evidently died because they profaned the sacredness of the Lord's Supper with gluttony and drunkenness. So the common threat God dealt with in each situation is the potential fracturing of God's people and, thus, his purpose.

The second lesson transitions naturally to the last. In light of clear scriptural attestation, the church is compelled to exercise discipline among its members. Even though discipline is an unsavory action to be carried out, Scripture warrants it. Historically, the church committed itself to the extremes of hard-nosed pugilism or soft-handed passivity. "The church has tended to oscillate in this area between extreme offenses and extreme laxity."[20] Scripture categorically disallows both. The question is not, "Should we discipline?" but "How should we discipline?" Certainly, the church making effective advances in the world is the gospel, but the world run amuck in the church is a disaster and a direct invitation for God's judgment. With respect to discipline, sometimes the hardest road is the best road to travel. We must deal with sin seriously because God does.

DIPLOMATIC IMMUNITY

During his second missionary campaign, Paul along with Silas, had been arrested, stripped, beaten, and thrown into prison in Philippi, thus directly violating their Roman citizenship (Acts 16:16–40). Once the authorities discovered their mistake, they were alarmed. But without apology, the officials escorted them from prison, probably to the city limits, and asked them to leave town quietly. What were they worried about? The same thing

Claudius feared—severe punishment as a result of wrongful abuse of a Roman citizen. Some of the benefits afforded a Roman citizen were: (1) the right to appeal after trial, (2) exemption from imperial duty such as military service, (3) the right to choose local or Roman trial, and (4) usually being exempt from flogging.[21]

In the dialogue with Claudius found in Acts 22:22–29, one can see a haughty, heavy-handed soldier about to inflict some dire punishment on a troublemaker. The centurion responded sarcastically to Paul's question concerning the legitimacy of flogging a Roman citizen without a guilty verdict: "I had to pay a big price for my citizenship" (v. 28). Larkin says that Claudius was referring to the bribes he paid to intermediaries in the imperial secretariat or provincial administration to ensure that his name would appear on the list of candidates for enfranchisement.[22] At this, Paul probably showed his birth certificate or certificate of citizenship as evidence and said: "But I was born a [Roman] citizen" (Acts 22:28b). Most Roman citizens who traveled carried these credentials. The mood changed suddenly as the centurion understood his error.

> Paul is at least the tribune's social equal, if not his slight superior by longevity of Roman citizenship in his family. The declaration of citizenship has its desired effect. The military inquisitors withdrew immediately. Alarm or fear grips the tribune as he realizes that he violated one of the basic rights of a Roman citizen when he put Paul in chains (21:33).[23]

Wrong treatment of a social or legal inferior had lesser punishment than wrong treatment of a superior. Claudius was startled to hear Paul had superior citizenship because it threatened his person and his career much more. Caesar had imprisoned people for similar legal mistakes.[24] The exclamation of Cicero captures the centurion's dread: "To bind a Roman is a crime, to flog him is an abomination, to slay him is almost an act of murder."[25]

DOODLING IN THE DIRT

How can a knowledge of background information give us insight into Jesus' "doodling in the dirt" in John 8? According to some scholars, Arabic literature reveals the common Semitic custom of "doodling when distraught."[26] In this view Jesus was simply writing in the dirt in order to calm his anger and have time to think. While this explanation initially seems feasible, it fails to account for the accusation inherent in Jesus' doodling. A closer examination of the Greek text reveals parallel structure which seems to support the idea that both Jesus' words and his writings accused his audience. The contrasting wordplay appears in the author's commentary in verse 6 and serves as a watershed in the passage: "They were using this question as a trap, in order to have *a basis for accusing [katagorein]* him. But Jesus bent down and *started to write [kategraphen]* on the ground with his finger." Perhaps the author attempted to demonstrate that although the teachers of the law and the Pharisees desired to trap Jesus he effectively turned the tables on them by his accusation. A sure cure for hypocrisy is an exposed conscience.

Background information supported by this insight is offered by J. D. M. Derrett, who proposes that Jesus was writing either the sins of his accusers or a passage from the Torah.[27] According to his study, the Torah was not properly spoken aloud except when read, so writing it would have been more readily acceptable. A knowledge of customs and writing in Jesus' day reveals that he could have written only sixteen Hebrew characters from a sitting position. While no scholar can claim sure knowledge of these characters, the comparable apocryphal story of Susanna quotes Exodus 23:1b and 23:7, which according to Derrett would fit the contextual and (length) requirements. Perhaps Jesus wrote a few lines from the law to show his audience the source of his potential judgment and make them anxious to hear his words. His doodling may have reminded them of Jeremiah 17:13, "Those who turn away from you will be written in the dust."[28] No matter the exact words, it is clear from an examination of the text and its background that something jolted them into an immediate abortion of their plans.

YOU HAVEN'T SEEN ANYTHING YET!

Jesus provided the disciples with provocative death forecasts during his teaching and preaching ministry. The disciples, however, shied away from accepting any scenario involving the death of their Messiah (see Matt. 16:21–28). Unfortunately, their messianic expectation had been molded greatly by the heroics of Judas Maccabeus, whose successes included expunging Jerusalem of Roman domination and rededicating the temple in 164 B.C.[29] The Messiah would accordingly follow in Judas's previous mode of operation by physically squelching the foreign dominators and simultaneously ushering in the kingdom in which they would assume important roles. So the disciples shunned this repeated death talk, probably by attributing Jesus' sentiments to his unfortunate misunderstanding of his own mission. But he desperately wanted them to understand the reason for and the reality of his quickly approaching death.

With the commencement of Jesus' execution fully unfolding, not many of the followers could be found in the vicinity of Golgotha. Most likely they feared suffering a similar fate for mere association. While Jesus was being led to the place of execution, he addressed the mourning female inhabitants of Jerusalem with a chilling but caring note of sadness. These women were not necessarily disciples but were devout and sympathetic nonetheless.[30] Having probably seen numerous executions and thus being all too aware of the attendant cruelty, they came to bewail him as well. Their lamentation, though, is redirected to an unforeseen and unexpected day of unbelievable suffering for them. Barrenness was taken as a sign of disfavor from God (see Luke 11:27), but Jesus uttered a strange beatitude, blessing those in the coming days who would be childless (Luke 23:29). Not having children, they will be spared the horror of seeing them executed. Evidently, the suffering will be so great that they will welcome death with cries of utter despair (v. 30).[31] In the next verse Jesus concluded his remarks with a comparative proverb emphasizing further their impending doom: "For if men do these things when the tree is green, what will happen when it is dry?" Interpretations vary, but I agree with Fitzmyer that Jesus was basically contrasting his own execution with the coming destruction of Jerusalem.[32] If God allows the innocent Jesus (likened to a green tree) to suffer such cruelty meted out by Jerusalem (likened to a dry tree), what will happen to Jerusalem? The contrast is driven deeper between the wood on which Jesus is crucified (not consumed by fire) and the wood of Jerusalem (consumed by fire).[33] Dry wood burns better!

Did these atrocities come true? Yes. Titus's egregious destruction of Jerusalem is graphically recounted by Josephus. One must read it in its entirety to feel the full force, but one excerpt will sufficiently capture the horror the inhabitants of Jerusalem suffered at the hands of Titus and his brutal army.

> They were accordingly scourged and subjected to torture of every description, before being killed, and then crucified opposite the walls. Titus indeed commiserated their fate, five hundred or sometimes more being captured daily; on the other hand, he recognized the risk of dismissing prisoners of war, and that the custody of such numbers would amount to the imprisonment of their custodians; but his main reason for not stopping the crucifixions was the hope that the spectacle might perhaps induce the Jews to surrender, for fear that continued resistance would involve them in a similar fate. The soldiers out of rage and hatred amused themselves by nailing their prisoners in different postures; and so great was their number, that space could not be found for the crosses nor crosses for the bodies.[34]

Now we can see the stark contrast Jesus alluded to during his trek to the cross. From Josephus's account we can deduce that due to the lack of crosses caused by the sheer number of prisoners and the rapidity of execution, the soldiers most likely crucified multiple victims on the same cross. How different this unimaginable horror was from the execution of Jesus and the two thieves some forty years before.

PRACTICING AND PREACHING

Historically, *hairesis* had an interesting career. The noun occurs nine times in the New Testament. Of these occurrences, six are found in Acts where they refer to Sadducees (5:17), Pharisees (15:5, 26:5), Nazarenes (24:5), and "sect" (24:14; 28:22).[35] No negative connotations are connected to these usages as the word is translated variously as "doctrine," "school," or "religious party." Extrabiblical citations with corresponding meanings can be found in the writings of Josephus.[36] Jewish parties voluntarily formed alliances, according to Acts, as the verbal form (*haireomai*) designates. Finer designations took the shape of a more zealous adherence to the law within the people of God, such as the Hasidim and the Essenes of the Qumran community.[37] Luke clearly stated in Acts that Christianity did not come into existence under the umbrella of the synagogue as another Jewish "heresy." Neither did Paul consider the church of God as a parallel Jewish party since he employed the *hairesis* twice in a harshly negative manner: (1) in association with the deadly, disruptive behavior of gluttony and drunkenness during the observation of the Lord's Supper at Corinth (1 Cor. 11:18–34), and (2) in a list of fellowship-debilitating vices in Galatians 5:19–21. Heresy, for Paul, was dissension issuing from false teachings or inappropriate behavior among God's people.

In the postapostolic era, *hairesis* was always set in diametric opposition to correct doctrine.[38] This probably had a direct influence on why the King James Version of the Bible translates *hairesis* as "heretic" in Titus 3:10. It is translated in other versions as "divisive," "factious," and "anyone who causes divisions." Assessing Paul's purpose for Titus in Crete is the key to interpreting this passage: "The reason I left you in Crete was that you might straighten out what was left unfinished" (1:5). Paul dealt with the inimical influence of the Judaizers by including two warning passages against false teachers (Tit. 1:10–16; 3:9–11). The important "household code" section of 2:1–3:8 served to provide God's new society with moral rules of behavior.[39] Beginning in 3:9, Paul advised Titus to avoid the evil works existing in direct conflict with the good deeds referred to in 3:8. Therefore, not only the theological inadequacies of the false teachers were to be avoided (1:10–16) but also their unprofitable behavior as well. The command to reject a *hairetikon* man in 3:10 is based on his behavior, not his theology. An important implication needs to be learned from this passage. Sometimes the so-called *orthodox* are not so *orthoprax* when it comes to the task of ridding the church of "heretics." Due to their own caustic, unruly behavior, they have in fact become the "heretics." Sadly, right conduct is an early casualty in the midst of the battle, for who has the right doctrine? Thinking differently from another does not necessarily make one a heretic. But correct thinking and correct behavior should embrace each other in a Christian's life.

ANGER, COMPASSION, OR BOTH?

In order to understand the high emotions exhibited in the exchange between Jesus and Mary, the interpreter must deal with the clause translated "he was deeply moved in spirit and troubled" in John 11:33. The problem arises at the point of rendering this difficult Greek phrase into English. G. R. Beasley-Murray underscores an unusual disagreement between English and German translations of the clause.[40] The translation, "He groaned in the spirit, and was troubled," found in the KJV and RV, set a definite pattern among interpreters. The NEB has, "He sighed heavily and was deeply moved." The RSV, in similar tone, renders it, "He was deeply moved in spirit and troubled."

In contrast German interpretation has been governed largely by Luther's Bible, which translated into English is basically, "He was angry in the spirit and distressed." Upon further investigation, the German interpretation presents itself as closer to the true meaning of the difficult phrase. It appears that the English translation of the original German edition of Walter Bauer's Greek lexicon rendered the phrase "to be deeply moved" instead of "to be inwardly angered or disgusted."[41] The evidence continues to stack up in favor of the German rendition when one considers the Old Testament background of this word.[42] A correct interpretation, therefore, reflecting this evidence and accurately capturing Jesus' mood is offered by Gustav Stählin: "He is provoked by unbelieving Jews who in His presence give away to unrestricted grief even though He proclaims Himself to be the resurrection and the life (11:33), and He makes severe remarks about their lack of faith and understanding."[43]

If Jesus were angry in verse 33, how can his tears be explained in verse 35? This can best be explained by the content of the following verse. Upon seeing the tears of Jesus, the Jews took note of his deep love for Lazarus. Schnackenburg recognizes the tears as a genuine display of sympathy in light of human suffering and summarizes: "The weeping here has no connection with the surge of anger."[44] He compares this verse with Revelation 7:17 and 21:4, thus attributing the tears as response to the sadness and darkness of the world.

Arriving at verse 38, the anger of Jesus is kindled again as some of the Jews criticized him for not preventing Lazarus's death. Here again, the translation, and therefore the interpretation of *embrimaomai* is missed by most English translations. The continued expressions of disbelief had to be frustrating for Jesus. Martha is alarmed that Jesus wanted to remove the stone because of the malodorous air that would exude from the already decomposing body. But Jesus, ultimately echoing verse 4, reminded Martha that the glory of God was about to be manifested before her eyes. Thus, Jesus situated the whole narrative in the framework of God's revelatory action in him.

By allowing Jesus to be angry, the interpreter does no violence to the nature of Christ. He was angry and did not sin, but he was angry nonetheless. He also became visibly sad. He loved the people for whom he would die, and he resonated with their feelings of grief. But I think his sentiments in the face of death were the same as Paul's in 1 Thessalonians 4:13: "Brothers, we do not want you to be ignorant about those who fall asleep, or to grieve like the rest of men, who have no hope." Jesus addressed this same hopelessness. It is interesting to note that one of the most recent modern Bible translations, *The New Living Translation* published by Tyndale

House, renders the part of verse 33 under consideration here as, "He was moved with indignation and was deeply troubled."

Summary

At the conclusion of each semester, I ask my Introduction to Bible Study class, "What did you learn about Bible study?" Each time someone says something to the effect, "It's harder than I thought!" Another frequently used answer is, "There is more to the biblical text than meets the eye." I happily and quickly agree with them that responsible and successful interpreters devote themselves to arduous study which requires them to read many sources beyond the biblical text.

To help illustrate the importance of background study and biblical interpretation I have the class view the excellent movie, *The Spitfire Grill*. This is a brilliant feature depicting a young woman named Percy (short for Perchance), who attempts to restart her life in the small tight-knit town of Gilead, Maine, after a brief stint in prison for manslaughter. The story is saturated with biblical imagery, serving as a commentary to the Lord's question in Jeremiah 8:22: "Is there no balm in Gilead? Is there no physician there? Why then is there no healing for the wound of my people?" At first, the students do not know a great deal about this passage until they see the movie that functions basically as a commentary on it. Then the next step is to read some background information on Jeremiah and the passage under consideration. The ensuing class session is boiling over with informed and excited discussion because that text was framed with written and color commentary helping them understand it properly from a parallel, contemporary view. They could see the biblical story in the movie, and it made sense. Although their names did not run in the credits, various biblical figures manifested themselves in story.

Once the background work is accomplished, the rest of the work can follow. Interpretation alone does not dictate how one is to apply the text. New Testament interpretation requires probing detective work. The biblical text provides clues which will lead into a multitude of investigative arenas including: the Old Testament corpus; archaeological discoveries; geographical concerns; numismatics (the study of coins); the sources connected to second temple Judaism including Aramaic targums, the Dead Sea scrolls, Babylonian and Palestinian Talmuds, and rabbinic midrash; early church father assessments; extrabiblical Greek papyrological evidence; memorial inscriptions and epitaphs; sepulchral art; lexicography; pseudepigraphy; linguistics; and the ancient histories of Josephus, Philo, and Eusebius. Reading between and behind the lines of the text is required. I can ensure myself of better applications of the text if I am willing to pay the price for arriving at the proper interpretations of the text first. Because the story of the New Testament did not unfold in a vacuum, it is expedient for the interpreter to discover all the background information possible to uncover its true meaning so one may apply it responsibly.

Bibliography

Blomberg, Craig. *Jesus and the Gospels*. Nashville: Broadman & Holman, 1997.

Borgen, Peder. *Early Christianity and Hellenistic Judaism*. Edinburgh: T. & T. Clark, 1998.

Brisco, Thomas C. *Holman Bible Atlas: A Complete Guide to the Expansive Geography of Biblical History*. Nashville: Holman Reference, 1998.

Brown, Raymond. *An Introduction to the New Testament*. The Anchor Bible Reference Library. New York: Doubleday, 1997.

Collins, J. J. *The Scepter and the Star: The Messiahs of the Dead Sea Scrolls*. The Anchor Bible Reference Library. New York: Doubleday, 1995.

Corley, Bruce, Steve LeMarke, and Grant Lovejoy, eds. *Biblical Hermeneutics: A Comprehensive Introduction to Interpreting the Scriptures*. Nashville: Broadman & Holman, 1996.

Danker, Frederick. *Multipurpose Tools for Bible Study*. Philadelphia: Fortress, 1993.

DeVries, LaMoine. *Cities of the Biblical World*. Peabody, Mass.: Hendrickson, 1997.

Frend, William H. C. *Archaeology of Early Christianity*. Philadelphia: Fortress, 1996.

Ferguson, Everett. *Backgrounds of Early Christianity*. Grand Rapids: Eerdmans, 1993.

Fitzmyer, Joseph A. *The Semitic Background of the New Testament: Essays on the Semitic Background of the New Testament and a Wandering Aramean*. Grand Rapids: Eerdmans, 1997.

Freyne, Sean. *Galilee: From Alexander the Great to Hadrian, 323 BCE to 135 CE—A Study of Second Temple Judaism*. Edinburgh: T. & T. Clark, 1998.

Grant, Michael and Rachel Kitzinger, eds. *Civilization of the Ancient Mediterranean*. 3 vols. New York: Charles Scribner's Sons, 1988.

Green, Joel B., Scot McKnight, and I. Howard Marshall, eds. *Dictionary of Jesus and the Gospels*. Downers Grove, Ill.: IVP, 1992.

Hawthorne, Gerald F., Ralph P. Martin, and Daniel G. Reid, eds. *Dictionary of Paul and His Letters*. Downers Grove, Ill.: IVP, 1993.

Johnson, Luke Timothy. *Religious Experience in Earliest Christianity: A Missing Dimension in New Testament Studies*. Philadelphia: Fortress, 1992.

Keener, Craig S. *The IVP Bible Background Commentary*. Downers Grove, Ill.: IVP, 1993.

Martin, Ralph P. and Peter H. Davids, eds. *Dictionary of the Later New Testament and Its Developments*. Downers Grove, Ill.: IVP, 1997.

McCartney, Dan and Charles Clayton. *Let the Reader Understand: A Guide to Interpreting and Applying the Bible*. Wheaton, Ill.: Victor Books, 1994.

Osborne, Grant R. *The Hermeneutical Spiral: A Comprehensive Introduction to Biblical Interpretation*. Downers Grove: IVP, 1991.

Ryken, Leland, James C. Wilhoit, and Tremper Longman III, eds. *Dictionary of Biblical Imagery*. Downers Grove, Ill.: IVP, 1998.

Scott, Jr., J. Julius. *Customs and Controversies: Intertestamental Jewish Backgrounds of the New Testament*. Grand Rapids: Baker, 1995.

Stein, Robert H. *A Basic Guide to Interpreting the Bible: Playing by the Rules*. Grand Rapids: Baker Books, 1994.

Vanhoozer, Kevin J. *Is There Meaning in This Text?: The Bible, the Reader, and the Morality of Literary Knowledge*. Grand Rapids: Zondervan, 1998.

Witherington, III, Ben. *The Jesus Quest: The Search for the Jew of Nazareth*. Downers Grove: Ill.: IVP, 1995.

———. *The Paul Quest: The Renewed Search for the Jew of Tarsus*. Downers Grove, Ill.: IVP, 1998.

Notes

1. Also see Acts 2:42–47.

2. F. F. Bruce, *The Book of Acts*, NICNT (Grand Rapids: Eerdmans, 1954), 445.

3. Although this text is not found in the best Greek manuscripts available and is probably one of the most corrupt texts in the New Testament, Bart Ehrman provides a plausible background scenario explaining its late entry into the textual tradition in "Jesus and the Adulteress," *New Testament Studies* 34 (1988): 24–44.

4. T. W. Manson, *The Sayings of Jesus as Recorded in the Gospels according to St. Matthew and St. Luke Arranged with Introduction and Commentary* (London: SCM Press, 1971), 343.

5. See the chapter on textual criticism in this book. For a brief, yet insightful introduction to this skill, see David Alan Black, *New Testament Textual Criticism: A Concise Guide* (Grand Rapids: Baker, 1994). For full treatments consult the standards, Bruce M. Metzger, *The Text of the New Testament: Its Transmission, Corruption, and Restoration*, 2d ed., (Oxford: Oxford University Press, 1968); Kurt and Barabara Aland, *The Text of the New Testament: An Introduction to the Critical Editions and to the Theory and Practice of Modern Textual Criticism*, 2d rev. ed. (Grand Rapids: Eerdmans, 1995); and most recently, Paul D. Wegner, *The Journey from Texts to Translations: The Origin and Development of the Bible* (Grand Rapids: Baker, 1999).

6. Bruce Metzger, *Breaking the Code* (Nashville: Abingdon Press, 1995), 12.

7. Consult R. H. Charles, *The Revelation of St. John*, 2 vols., The International Critical Commentary (New York: Scribner's Sons, 1920); Ray Summers, *Worthy Is the Lamb* (Nashville: Broadman Press, 1951); Robert Mounce, *The Book of Revelation*, rev. ed., NICOT (Grand Rapids: Eerdmans, 1997); and David Aune, *Revelation*, 3 vols. (Dallas: Word Books, 1997, 1998).

8. Grant R. Osborne, *The Hermeneutical Spiral: A Comprehensive Introduction to Biblical Interpretation* (Downer's Grove, Ill.: IVP, 1991), 127.

9. See the extended discussion of these issues in Dan McCartney and Charles Clayton, *Let the Reader Understand: A Guide to Interpreting and Applying the Bible* (Wheaton, Ill.: Victor Books, 1994), 112–49.

10. Kevin J. Vanhoozer, *Is There Meaning in This Text?: The Bible, the Reader, and the Morality of Literary Knowledge* (Grand Rapids: Zondervan, 1998), 20.

11. See Silva's excellent discussion of "Reading the New Testament Letters Historically" in Walter C. Kaiser and Moisés Silva, *An Introduction to Biblical Hermeneutics: The Search for Meaning* (Grand Rapids: Zondervan, 1994), 124–29.

12. See E. Earle Ellis, *Paul's Use of the Old Testament* (Grand Rapids: Baker, 1957), for a good example of the importance of the relationship of the two testaments for New Testament interpretation.

13. Comparing his and Matthew's genealogies, both used the Old Testament to support different theological emphases. While Matthew desired to connect Jesus to weighty Jewish stock by beginning with Abraham, the father of the Jews, Luke reaches back to connect Jesus with the first man, Adam. In addition to presenting Jesus as the Savior of the world, he positions Jesus' temptation account (ch. 4) immediately on the heels of the genealogy (ch. 3). With the name of Adam fresh on the reader's mind, Luke intended to

highlight the contrasting success of Jesus in his own temptation ordeal. And during Satan's assault, Jesus answered each temptation with a quote from the wilderness wandering passages in Deuteronomy 6–8, during which the Israelites faced temptation and failed.

14. See Joshua 7:12. Alarmingly, the Israelites were placed under the same ban of destruction executed against the inhabitants of Jericho.

15. See H. Alan Brehm, "The Significance of the Summaries for Interpreting Acts," *Southwestern Journal of Theology* 33.3 (1990): 33, which cites Acts 6:7, 9:31, 12:24, 16:5, and 19:20 as "summary statements."

16. John B. Polhill, *Acts*, The New American Commentary, vol. 26, ed. David S. Dockery (Nashville: Broadman, 1992), 156.

17. Richard N. Longenecker, *Acts*, The Expositor's Bible Commentary (Grand Rapids: Zondervan, 1995): 110. See Titus 2:10 for the only other use of the verb *nosphizomai* in the New Testament, where it is translated "steal."

18. See the discussion of F. F. Bruce in *The Book of Acts*, The New International Commentary on the New Testament (Grand Rapids: Eerdmans, 1954), 112.

19. Ernst Käsemann, "Satze Heiligen Rechts im Neuen Testament," *New Testament Studies* 1 (1954/55): 71. Käsemann seems to agree with the majority of commentators, who feel that this "obviously entails the death of the guilty." For a different opinion, see William Barclay, *The Letters to the Corinthians*, The Daily Study Bible (Philadelphia: Westminster, 1954), 49–51, which states that the man's punishment was excommunication.

20. John R. W. Stott, *The Message of Acts*, The Bible Speaks Today (Downers Grove, Ill.: IVP, 1990), 112.

21. M. Reasoner, "Citizenship, Roman and Heavenly," in *The Dictionary of Paul and His Letters* (Downers Grove, Ill.: IVP, 1993), 140.

22. William J. Larkin, *Acts*, IVP New Testament Commentary Series, ed. Grant R. Osborne, (Downers Grove, Ill.: InterVarsity, 1995), 324–25.

23. Ibid.

24. Brian Rapske, *The Book of Acts in Its First Century Setting*, vol. 3: *Paul in Roman Custody*, Bruce W. Winter, ed. (Grand Rapids: Eerdmans, 1994), 143–45.

25. *Against Verres* 2.5.66, quoted in Larkin, *Acts*, 325.

26. R. E. Brown, *The Commentary of the Beloved Disciple* (New York: Paulist Press, 1979), 334.

27. J. D. M. Derrett, "Law in the New Testament: The Story of the Woman Taken in Adultery," *New Testament Studies* 10 (1963–64): 23.

28. Ibid., 24.

29. See 1 Maccabees 3–5.

30. Joseph A. Fitzmyer, *The Gospel According to Luke X–XXIV*, The Anchor Bible (New York: Doubleday & Co., 1985), 1497.

31. Cf. Hosea 10:8 and Revelation 6:16 for the same phraseology.

32. Fitzmyer, 1498–99.

33. Ibid.

34. Josephus, *Wars* 5.447–53.

35. G. Baumbach, "*hairesis, hairetikos*," in *Exegetical Dictionary of the New Testament*, eds. Horst Balz and Gerhard Schneider (Grand Rapids: Eerdmans, 1990), 40.

36. For example, see *Wars of the Jews* ii.118, 122, 137 and *Antiquities* vii.347, xiii.171, 288, 293.

37. Ibid. A plurality of opinion existed within the ranks of Judaism. Also consult H. Schlier, "*haireomai*, et al.," in *Theological Dictionary of the New Testament*, vol. 1, ed.

Gerhard Friedrich and trans. Geoffrey W. Bromiley (Grand Rapids: Eerdmans, 1971), 181–82.

38. Hans Dieter Betz, "Heresy and Orthodoxy in the New Testament," in *Anchor Bible Dictionary*, vol. 3, ed. David Noel Freedman (New York: Doubleday, 1992), 144. For example, see Ignatius *Eph.* 6:2, *Trall.* 6:1, *1 Clem.* 14:2.

39. P. H. Towner, "Households and Household Codes," in *Dictionary of Paul and His Letters*, eds. Gerald F. Hawthorne and Ralph P. Martin (Downers Grove, Ill.: IVP, 1993), 418–19.

40. *John,* Word Biblical Commentary (Dallas: Word Books, 1987), 192–93. At this point it is necessary to check as many translations as possible.

41. Walter Bauer, ed., *A Greek-English Lexicon of the New Testament and Other Early Christian Literature*, 2d ed., trans. W. F. Arndt and F. W. Gingrich, rev. and aug. F. W. Gingrich and F. W. Danker (Chicago: University of Chicago Press, 1979), s.v. *"embrimaomai."*

42. Isaiah 13:5 renders the word, "wrath," Zephaniah 3:8, "fierce anger," and Lamentations 2:6, "fierce indignation" (NRSV). Jesus' attitude was described with this same word that is harsh in tone and usually employed in connection with judgment. The underlying Hebrew term is *za'am.* An Arabic equivalent was used to describe the roar of a camel or angry speech (Francis Brown, et al, *A Hebrew and English Lexicon of the Old Testament* [Oxford: The Clarendon Press, 1979], 276). For a full listing of the Old Testament examples, see Gerhard Lisowsky, *Konkordanz zum Hebräischen Alten Testament*, 2d ed. (Stuttgart: Württembergische Bibelanstalt, 1958), 450.

43. "*Orgē*, 3. The Revelation of Divine Wrath," *TDNT*, vol. 5 (Grand Rapids: Eerdmans, 1964), 428.

44. *The Gospel according to John*, Herder's Theological Commentary, trans. Cecily Hastings (New York: Seabury Press, 1980), 336–37.

Chapter 10

The Use of the Old Testament in the New

Klyne Snodgrass
North Park Theological Seminary

No subject is perhaps more important for the understanding of the Christian faith than the use of the Old Testament in the New Testament. The Hebrew and Aramaic Scriptures were, of course, the only Bible the early Christian thinkers and writers had. Many of these Christians were transformed Jews and would have known Hebrew. Other early Christians would have known the Jewish Scriptures only in Greek translation. Regardless of their language, however, all Christians would have been engaged in relating the two most important realities of their lives—the Scriptures and Jesus Christ.

At every point early Christians attempted to understand their Scriptures in the new light of the ministry, death, and resurrection of Jesus Christ. They used the Old Testament to prove their Christian theology and to solve Christian problems. The Old Testament provided the substructure of New Testament theology.[1] The Old Testament also provided the language and imagery for much of New Testament thought, although this is not always obvious to a casual reader. Therefore, New Testament concepts must be understood from Old Testament passages. Virtually every New Testament subject must be approached through the contribution of the Old Testament. As Augustine observed, "The New Testament is in the Old concealed; the Old Testament is in the New revealed."[2]

However, not everything in the Old Testament is brought into the new faith. There is both continuity and discontinuity between the Old Testament and the New Testament. That is, while some parts of the New Testament are direct extensions of the Old Testament message, some parts of the Old Testament message have been superseded. Even so, none of the New

209

Testament writers ever suggests that the Old Testament is less than fully the Word of God.

The analysis of this continuity and discontinuity is a much more fascinating and intriguing study than many people have realized. Too often Old Testament texts are considered as only so many prophecies to be calculated and at which to marvel. Any serious reading will show that the way the New Testament uses the Old Testament is far different from what we expected or have been led to believe. The New Testament writers have been disturbingly creative in their use of the Old Testament. Not only do New Testament quotations of the Old Testament sometimes differ from the Hebrew and Aramaic Scriptures on which our translations are based, the New Testament writers also have applied texts in surprising ways. For example, why does Matthew 2:18 view Jeremiah 31:15 as a prophecy of Herod's slaying of innocent babies, while Jeremiah's words obviously relate to the Babylonian invasion of Judea? Do the New Testament writers twist the Old Testament Scriptures, as some have charged?[3]

In addition to being fascinating, the study of the use of the Old Testament in the New Testament is comprehensive and demanding. To enter this arena is to be engaged in studies on the history of the text. Serious study requires the knowledge of Hebrew, Greek, and Aramaic because one has to compare the New Testament wording with the Masoretic Hebrew text, the Septuagint (the translation of the Old Testament into Greek), information from the Dead Sea Scrolls, the targums (Aramaic paraphrases of the Old Testament), and other Jewish or Christian uses of the Old Testament.

Do not think that this is an exercise in tedium, however, for the use of the Old Testament in the New Testament also engages a person in hermeneutics, exegesis, and theology, study that in many cases will require adjustment of previous conclusions. How the Old Testament is viewed is *the* theological issue dividing many Christians. Dispensational theology, which views God as operating in different ways in different eras, and covenant theology, which emphasizes the unity of God's action throughout history, divide from each other and also from other approaches specifically over this issue.[4]

Our subject also has the potential of being a troublesome one. There are issues here that have not been treated adequately. We often proclaim our theories about Scripture in the abstract, but the use of the Old Testament by New Testament writers raises questions about our theories. Are all the discussions about inerrancy or other labels irrelevant in view of the selectivity by which the New Testament writers use the Old Testament? Obviously there are numerous Old Testament texts that were and are ignored by Christians, and we would argue that many are not to be implemented.[5] Why?

Brief Historical Considerations

The question of how the Old Testament should be appropriated exists already with the teaching of Jesus. His way of reading the Old Testament angered the religious authorities, for he did not focus on Sabbath keeping and laws of purity as they did. In fact, according to the Gospels, Jesus appeared to flaunt violation of the purity code by touching lepers, a woman with an issue of blood, and corpses, and by eating with defiled people (note especially Matt. 8–9 in contrast with Lev. 13; 15:19f. and Ezra 10:11). He argued that *sin* defiled a person, not eating with unclean hands (Matt. 15:10–20). Mark 7:19 extends Jesus' teaching so that all foods are clean.[6] So much for dietary laws!

Jesus focused on the intent of the law in the love commands and on the theme of mercy. Still, he claimed that none of the Scripture was set aside (Matt. 5:17–20) and complained that the Jewish authorities substituted human traditions for the commands of God (Matt. 15:3).[7] In Luke 24:44–45 the risen Christ claimed that all three sections of the Hebrew Scriptures (law, prophets, and writings) find their fulfillment in him. He then opened the mind of his disciples to understand the Scriptures. Clearly the issue both for the earthly and risen Christ is *how* the Hebrew Scriptures are to be interpreted correctly. The usual reading of the religious authorities was not sufficient.

The same question dominated the life of the early church. When asked whether he understood the text from Isaiah 53, the Ethiopian eunuch replied, "How am I able unless someone should guide me?" Beginning from that text, Philip then proclaimed Christ to him (Acts 8:26–35). This account points both to the Christological way in which the early church interpreted the Old Testament and to the need of guidance in understanding.

One crucial issue for the early church was the question of how to treat the Old Testament commands on circumcision. At the "Jerusalem Council," surprisingly, explicit Old Testament commands on circumcision were set aside because of Christian experience *and other Old Testament texts* focusing on the inclusion of the Gentiles (Acts 15). One can well ask how Paul could say, "Circumcision is nothing and uncircumcision is nothing, but keeping the commands of God is what counts" (1 Cor. 7:19), when circumcision was obviously an Old Testament command. Clearly it was no longer a relevant command for him. Still, the discussions of law in the Epistles to the Galatians and to the Romans show how much the debate continued over the right use of the Old Testament. However, even when conclusions were drawn that a command was not binding, they were made from the Old Testament itself and with no thought of nullifying the Word of God.

In the second century a radical solution to the problem of the Old Testament emerged. Marcion of Sinope, influenced by Gnosticism, argued that the whole Old Testament should be rejected, even though he found value in some sections of the Old Testament. Marcion repudiated the God of the Old Testament as the creator of evil and sought to separate Christianity from anything Jewish. Consequently, he accepted as canonical only Paul's Epistles (excluding the Pastorals) and the Gospel of Luke. In addition, he expurgated sections of these books that he felt were influenced too much by the Old Testament.[8] Unfortunately, there are still those around who are essentially Marcionite in their approach.

Most Christians, thankfully, did not follow Marcion. Instead, they sought to extend the interpretive practices of the New Testament writers and appropriate the Old Testament for Christian purposes in new ways. The Old Testament was combed for passages that could be understood of Christ and his church. Christians used the Old Testament to teach morality, to explain who Jesus was, and to provide illustrations of Christian thought. Unfortunately, however, usually there was little historical sensitivity or treatment of extended texts. Instead, the Old Testament was viewed as prophecy about Christ, as providing types of Christ, or as holding hidden ideas and symbols that may be spiritually understood through allegory.[9] Justin Martyr, for example, and numerous others found references to Christ in places most of us could hardly imagine. The stone cut out without hands in Daniel 2:45 was understood as a reference to the virgin birth. Nearly every stick, piece of wood, or tree was understood as pointing to the crucifixion.[10]

In the centuries that followed, the Old Testament and New Testament were interpreted along two divergent New Testament paths. The Antiochean School, represented by John Chrysostom and Theodore of Mopsuestia, argued against allegorizing and engaged in fairly straightforward exegesis. Far more influential, but far more unacceptable from a modern viewpoint, was the Alexandrian School represented by Origen and Augustine. This school engaged in allegorical exegesis, by which a spiritual meaning could be assigned to a text, especially if that text were troublesome.[11]

Allegorizing made it easy to read Christian theology into Old Testament texts. Allegorical exegesis was dominant until the Reformation and is still encountered today as pastors read into texts spiritual meanings that have nothing to do with the original purposes of the authors.

The Protestant reformers turned away from allegorical exegesis to focus on the plain meaning of the text, although Martin Luther on occasion still allegorized. Both Luther and John Calvin were aware of the unity and the differences between the Testaments. Luther stressed the discontinuity between the Testaments because of his distinction between law and gospel. Calvin, on the other hand, focused on continuity between the Testaments and argued for a "third use" of the law.[12] By this he argued what Luther was not ready to accept, that the law still has a role in guiding Christian morality. These differences in understanding the Old Testament have characterized the followers of Luther and Calvin to the present day.

How the Old Testament should be viewed in relation to the New Testament is still a matter of debate. In his *Two Testaments: One Bible,* D. L. Baker presented eight modern solutions to the problem of the relation of the Testaments.[13] Some of these solutions, such as that by A. A. Van Ruler, place priority on the Old Testament.[14] Some are much more negative in the assessment of the Old Testament, such as the view of Rudolf Bultmann, for whom the Old Testament is the necessary presupposition of the New Testament, but in actuality is only a history of Israel's *failure*.[15] The other solutions all view both Testaments positively but vary in the degree to which they see the Old Testament as Christological, how they deal with Old Testament history, and how they balance continuity and discontinuity.

The main problem for modern readers in the New Testament use of the Old Testament is the tendency of New Testament writers to use Old Testament texts in ways different from their original intention. A particular expression came into use to provide a solution. *Sensus plenior* is a Latin term popular among Roman Catholics and also among some evangelicals. It refers to the "fuller sense" God intended for a text beyond the human author's intention. The New Testament writers are viewed as inspired by the Spirit to understand and apply this fuller sense.[16] For some this is a solution; for others it is an obfuscation.

The questions that emerge from this historical overview cannot be neglected. Is the Old Testament really revelation for Christians? Can it be appropriated without being violated? To what degree does it tell of Jesus Christ? How do we deal with the discontinuity?

Distribution and Frequency of the Use of the Old Testament in the New Testament

Interesting results derive from an examination of Old Testament quotations and allusions printed in bold print in the United Bible Society's first edition of *The Greek New Testament*.[17] Three-fourths of the 401 quotations and allusions appear in the Gospels, Acts, Romans, and Hebrews. Of those 401 uses of the Old Testament, 195 have some type of accompanying formula such as "it is written" to inform the reader that a Scripture text is being cited.[18] In the remaining uses the only way the reader would know the Old Testament was being cited is by knowing the wording from the Old Testament text.

How and where the Old Testament is used depends on the author's purposes. Whereas Matthew focused on Jesus as the fulfillment of the Old Testament, Paul did not use this language, even though he believed it (Rom. 1:2). Paul's use of the Old Testament is clearly circumstantial. When he discussed the relation of Jews to salvation in Christ in the Epistle to the Romans, he quoted the Old Testament fifty-four times. But in several of his letters he makes little or no reference to the Old Testament. Colossians, for example, does not have any explicit reference to the Old Testament. The author of Revelation never quotes the Old Testament, but he uses wording of the Old Testament as much as any other writer. He merely reuses Old Testament language and images to make his point. The more an author attempts to explain the identity of Jesus or to address Jews, the more likely the Old Testament will be used. To the degree that the identity of Jesus is assumed or that Gentiles are addressed, there is usually less use of the Old Testament.[19] The New Testament books with the most dependence on the Old Testament are Hebrews, Revelation, and 1 Peter.

Methods and Hermeneutical Assumptions

The fascinating aspect of this subject is the *way* in which Old Testament texts are used. As is clear already, not all New Testament writers use the Old Testament in what we would consider straightforward ways. Straightforward uses do occur, of course. Old Testament texts are used as direct prophecy (Matt. 2:5–6) or as direct logical proof of an argument (Matt. 4:4f.; Rom. 4). New Testament writers adapt the words of the Old Testament for new purposes in easily understood ways. Analogies to the ministry of Jesus are found in Old Testament events (John 3:14). Words of judgment in Hosea 13:14 become words of victory in 1 Corinthians 15:54–55.[20] Such uses are easily justified as merely the rhetorical adaptation of familiar language. It is easy to understand the use of an Old Testament text as an illustration (1 Cor. 10:7f.). It is not so easy to understand how a text that was not intended as messianic (Deut. 18:15) becomes understood as messianic (Acts 3:22–23).[21] This is not a straightforward use. It is also not easy to see how Hosea 11:1, which refers to the exodus of Israel from Egypt, can be fulfilled by Joseph's taking Jesus and Mary to Egypt (Matt. 2:15). Nor is it easy to see how words clearly addressed to Isaiah (6:9–10) are seen as fulfilled in Jesus (John 12:39–41). Such examples of unexpected uses of the Old Testament could be multiplied easily.

The key to understanding the New Testament writers' use of the Old Testament is in understanding the presuppositions and exegetical methods by which they operated. Most of this necessary framework can be gleaned from the New Testament itself, but the discovery of the Qumran Scrolls has provided helpful insight and parallels to the practices of the New Testament writers.

The first presupposition about which we need to know is *corporate solidarity*.[22] This expression refers to the oscillation or reciprocal relation between the individual and the community that existed in the Semitic mind. The act of the individual is not merely an individual act, for it affects the community and vice versa. The individual is often representative of the community and vice versa. Achan sinned, and the nation suffered (Josh. 7). An individual speaks in Psalm 118:10, but almost certainly he is representative of the nation. The "servant" is a collective term for the nation (Isa. 44:1), but it also refers to the remnant (Isa. 49:5) and probably also to an individual. Corporate solidarity should not be viewed as strange, for it is the basis for Paul's understanding of the atonement: "One died for all; therefore all died" (2 Cor. 5:14 NASB).

The representative character of Jesus' ministry, which is closely related to corporate solidarity, is one of the most important keys in understanding him and the way Old Testament texts are applied to him. The Christological titles "Servant," "Son of Man," and "Son of God" were all representative titles that were applied to Israel first. Jesus took on these titles because he had taken Israel's task.[23] He was representative of Israel and in solidarity with her. God's purposes for Israel were now taken up in his ministry. If this were true, what had been used to describe Israel could legitimately be used of him.

The second presupposition is *correspondence in history*, which is sometimes referred to as "typology."[24] Correspondence in history is actually a conviction about God and the way he works. The presupposition is that the way God worked in the past is mirrored in the way he works in the present and future. There is a correspondence between what happened to God's people in the past and what happens now or in the future. Climactic events in Israel's history become the paradigms by which new events are explained. For example, the Exodus was the climactic event by which God saved his people. Later writers use exodus terminology to describe God's saving his people from Assyria (Isa. 11:6) or salvation generally. The suffering of a righteous person (Ps. 22) finds correspondence in the crucifixion of Jesus (Matt. 22:39–46).[25]

The important point about correspondence in history is that the text is not used up by a single event. Isaiah 40:3 was understood as a classic expression of God's salvation from Babylon. Malachi 3:1 reused the language to express the promise of future salvation. The New Testament writers saw John the Baptist as the one in whom this verse finds its climax.[26] He was the voice crying in the wilderness to prepare the way before the Lord for ultimate salvation (Luke 3:4–6). Still, Luke 9:52 can adapt the words of Isaiah 40:3 to the disciples who prepare the way for Jesus as he goes to Jerusalem.[27] Those same words from Isaiah can even be applied to others who prepare the way.[28] Often words that find their climax in Jesus find further correspondence in his followers. If Jesus is the fulfillment of Isaiah 49:6 as the light to the Gentiles (Luke 2:32), the words can still be applied to Paul (Acts 13:47). If Jesus is a living stone, partly on the basis of Isaiah 28:16 and Psalm 118:22, his followers are living stones (l Pet. 2:4–5). If he is the Anointed One, they too are anointed (2 Cor. 1:21). If 2 Samuel 7:14 can be interpreted of Jesus in Hebrews 1:5, it can also be applied to Christians in 2 Corinthians 6:18. We have not interpreted a text appropriately until we have determined how it corresponds or does not correspond with our present situation.

A third presupposition of the early church is that they lived in the days of *eschatological fulfillment*.[29] They believed that the end time had dawned upon them (1 Cor. 10:11). This presupposition has a near parallel in the beliefs of the people of the Qumran community. They and many other Jews had an eschatological focus in their reading of the Hebrew Scriptures. Whereas for some Jews the end time belonged to an unknown future, the people at Qumran believed they were an end-time community from whose gates God would break out very soon in victorious conquest over his enemies. The early Christians viewed themselves as an end-time community as well, but there are major differences. For Christians, the end time was not just soon to appear. It had *already* appeared in the ministry of Jesus and especially in his resurrection and the pouring out of the Spirit. They could look at these events and know that God's kingdom had broken into their midst, even though its full realization was yet to come.

Old Testament texts that were viewed eschatologically were, therefore, texts that were descriptive of the reality they experienced. This presupposition can be seen clearly in a text like 1 Peter 1:12, where the author states that it was revealed to Old Testament prophets that, not to themselves but to his readers, they were ministering their prophecies. If the Scriptures find their *climax* in Christ, surely what is written there is especially for his followers. Similar expressions of this hermeneutical presupposition are seen in Romans 15:4; 1 Corinthians 9:10, and especially 10:11 ("These things happened to those people as an example, and they were written for our admonition upon whom the ends of the ages has come").[30]

The fourth presupposition is actually inherent in the third but needs to be made explicit. The early church, like most of Judaism, assumed that the Scriptures were *Christological*. Texts that may have been general statements about the nation, prophets, priests, or kings were often *idealized* in anticipation of God's end-time deliverer who would fill the categories as no one else had. David had been the king *par excellence*, but one day there would be a king like him, only better.[31] The early church applied such texts to Jesus because of their conviction about his identity. The conviction about his identity did *not* derive from the Old Testament. They did not find texts and then find Jesus. They found Jesus and then saw how the Scriptures fit with him. They were not *proving* his identity in the technical sense so much as they were demonstrating how the Scriptures fit with him. Often they were merely following his lead in pointing to texts that summarized his ministry.[32]

Before examples of how these presuppositions are evidenced in specific New Testament quotations of Old Testament texts, another point needs to be made. Too often people look only at Old Testament texts and New Testament quotations without asking what those Old Testament texts had become in the history of Judaism. Specifically because of Christological or eschatological concerns, texts had a "life" in Judaism that led to their being understood in specific ways. These traditional interpretations have influenced the way Jesus and the early church adapted texts. Many times they are only picking up or adapting common understandings so as to make their point. They were only entering into the conversation of their hearers. The Dead Sea Scrolls have been particularly helpful in showing how texts were understood in the time of Jesus.

With these presuppositions, and with the awareness that there were traditional interpretations, we can understand why Old Testament texts were adapted the way they were. The presuppositions of corporate solidarity and correspondence in history are both at work in the application to Jesus of Hosea 11:1 ("Out of Egypt I called my son," Matt. 2:15). Since Jesus, like Israel, is Son of God, there is parallelism between what happens to these two "sons." The application of Jeremiah 31:15 to the slaying of babies by Herod is also understandable. This is not merely correspondence between two sets of mothers who cry. Jeremiah 31 is an eschatological text, and the words immediately following 31:15 are words of comfort and hope for salvation that climax in 31:31–34 with the focus on the new covenant. Matthew and his readers know that Jesus has ushered in that eschatological time.[33] There is both correspondence and fulfillment.

The application of Isaiah 6:9–10 to the ministry of Jesus is another example of correspondence in history. This Old Testament text was spoken specifically to Isaiah about the hardness of heart of his hearers. Other Old Testament prophets picked up the language of Isaiah 6:9–10 so that these words became the classic expression of hardness of heart (cf. Jer. 5:21; Ezek. 12:2). In the Synoptic Gospels the words are applied to Jesus' ministry as evidence of the hardness of heart of Jews in not responding to his teaching in parables (Matt. 13:14–15/Mark 4:12/Luke 8:10). They are applied in a similar way in John 12:39–40 as a summary statement marking the rejection of Jesus by the Jews. Interestingly, these words are also addressed to the *disciples* in Mark 8:18 to ask whether they have hardened hearts, Isaiah 6:9–10 finds further correspondence as a description of the rejection of the Jews in Paul's ministry (Acts 28:26–27).[34]

Such examples suggest that the statement "Jesus is the fulfillment of the Scriptures" might be more adequately expressed as "Jesus is the *climax* of the Scriptures." His identity and ministry are mirrored there in unique ways, but "fulfillment" suggests a singularity and a focus on predictive prophecy that does justice only to some texts. Many Old Testament texts had other initial referents and also found later referents after Jesus. They find their coherence and true brilliance in him. This suggestion is not an effort to diminish the importance of predictive prophecy. It is merely a recognition that other uses of the Old Testament are common in the New Testament.

The use of Deuteronomy 18:15–19 is a good example of a text that had a life in Judaism. This text was not messianic originally, but the promise of a prophet like Moses became idealized (possibly because of Deut. 34:10) so that hope emerged for an eschatological prophet. In both the Samaritan

Pentateuch and in 4Q Testimonia of the Dead Sea Scrolls, Deuteronomy 18:18 is understood messianically. This expectation of an eschatological prophet is obvious in John 1:21, where John the Baptist is asked whether he is *the* prophet, and in 6:14, where people exclaim that Jesus is "truly *the* prophet, the one coming into the world." In Acts 3:22, Peter uses this expectation to define the identity of Jesus for his hearers.[35] Such usage arises from a context where certain assumptions were held about a text and where those assumptions become the tools to describe something else.

Pesher and Midrash

In addition to the Jewish presuppositions we have mentioned, an interpreter of the New Testament's use of the Old Testament needs to be aware of other Jewish methods of treating the Scriptures. One method of appropriating Scripture for some Jews, particularly Jews from Qumran, was *pesher*. This practice does not seek to explain a text so much as it seeks to show where a text fits. The word *pesher* derives from an Aramaic root meaning "solution." The presupposition is that the text contains a mystery communicated by God that is not understood until the solution is made known by an inspired interpreter. With *pesher*, the starting point for understanding is not the Old Testament text but a historical event or person. By viewing a text in the framework of an event, a *pesher* interpretation provides a solution to the mystery involved in understanding. In effect, *pesher* says, "This [event or person] is that [of which the Scripture speaks]."[36] For example, the Qumran *Pesher* on Habakkuk understands the judgment spoken against Babylon (Hab. 2:7–8) to refer to a wicked priest in Jerusalem who caused trouble for the Qumran community (lQpH 8.13f.).

Pesher also occurs in the New Testament. The most obvious example is Acts 2:17.[37] The event of the pouring out of the Spirit provided a framework for understanding Joel 2:28f. The event is seen as an actualization of the text.

The more common method of interpreting Scripture among Jews, however, was *midrash*. *Midrash* derives from a Hebrew word meaning "to seek" and refers to interpretive exposition. The starting point is the text itself, and the concern is to provide practical instruction so that people may understand God's Word and live accordingly. If *pesher* says, "This is that," *midrash* says "That [Scripture] has relevance to this [aspect of life]." In the earlier rabbinic material, midrashic interpretation is fairly straightforward, but later rabbinic practices often focused more on individual words and even letters. The result is a "creative" exegesis in which the original concern of the text is often lost.[38] Even where the midrashic interpretation is fairly straightforward, the focus with *midrash* is on the application of the text rather than with understanding the text itself. *Midrash* is not usually a commentary on the text.

Still, *midrash* is not arbitrary application of the text. There are rules to guide an interpreter that legitimated an interpretation. The early rabbinic practices were guided by seven rules of exposition, which later were expanded until eventually there were thirty-two.[39] The seven rules are fairly logical and may have derived from Hellenistic rhetoric.[40] Such procedures have frequently been adopted by expositors of texts. These seven rules merit repetition and consideration, for at least some of them are observable in the New Testament.[41]

> *Qal wahomer*—"light and heavy," meaning what applies in a less important case applies also in a more important case and vice versa.
>
> *Gezerah shawa*—"an equivalent regulation," meaning where the same words are applied in two separate cases the same considerations apply.
>
> *Binyan ab mikathub 'ehad*—"constructing a family from one passage," meaning that where texts are similar a principle derived from one of them applies to the others.
>
> *Binyan ab mishene kethubim*—"constructing a family from two texts," meaning that where texts are similar a principle derived from two texts can be applied to the others.
>
> *Kelal uferat*—"general and particular," meaning that a general rule may be applied to a particular situation and vice versa.
>
> *Kayotse bo bemaqom 'aher*—"something similar in another passage," meaning that a text may be interpreted by comparison with a similar text.
>
> *Dabar halamed me'inyano*—"explanation from the context."

Such midrashic techniques are observable in the New Testament. When Jesus argued that if God cared for the birds, surely he cared much more for humans (Matt. 6:26), he was arguing in good rabbinic fashion from the less important case to the more important. Similarly, when Jesus justified his disciples' eating grain on the Sabbath by pointing to the eating of the showbread by David and his men, he was arguing on the basis of an equivalent regulation (or possibly also from a less important case to a more important).[42] When Paul quoted several Old Testament texts with common key words, as he does in Galatians 3:8–14,[43] he was following the midrashic technique of bringing texts together to provide explanation. Such grouping of texts as a method of argumentation occurs often.[44]

Testimonia

One further Jewish practice that must be noted is the use of *testimonia*. If one analyzes the use of Old Testament passages in the New Testament, very quickly one sees that certain Old Testament passages are quoted by several New Testament writers. In addition sometimes the New Testament writers agree in using combinations of texts, and sometimes they even agree in wording that does not agree with the Septuagint or other known texts. The best example of these interesting phenomena is the agreement between 1 Peter 2 and Romans 9. First Peter 2:6–10 uses Isaiah 28:16; Psalm 118:22,

Isaiah 8:14; parts of several other texts; and Hosea 2:23. Romans 9:25–33 uses Hosea 2:23, other texts from Isaiah, and then a conflation of Isaiah 28:16 and 8:14 in the same non-Septuagintal form that 1 Peter has.[45] Should we account for such instances by arguing that one writer copied from the other?[46] Furthermore, there are a few places where Old Testament texts seem to have been joined in unexpected ways. For example, Mark 1:2–3 attributes to Isaiah words that appear to be a combination of Exodus 23:20; Malachi 3:1; and Isaiah 40:3.[47]

An attractive explanation of these phenomena is the argument that early Christians used *testimonia*. That is, they used collections of Old Testament texts that had been grouped thematically for apologetic, liturgical, and catechetical purposes. While it would be easy to overstate the case for *testimonia*[48] their existence and use seem to be beyond doubt. Pre-Christian Jewish *testimonia* have been found at Qumran.[49] Evidence of the continued use and growth of *testimonia* in the patristic period also is without question.[50] For the New Testament itself, the argument that one author copied from the other is often far too simplistic to account for the data.[51] Rather, there were collections of Old Testament texts that were useful to the church in a variety of ways. Such collections would have circulated in *both* written and oral forms and would have offered practical resources for both itinerant preachers and Gentile congregations.

The stone *testimonia*, then, would have been a pre-Christian Jewish collection that was adopted by Christians. The frequent use of Psalm 8 and Psalm 110 in combination reflects Christological *testimonia* brought together by the church.[52] The most common uses of *testimonia* were Christological and apologetic, but catechetical and liturgical uses are present as well. Romans 3:10–18 possibly is a grouping of *testimonia* on sin.[53] Romans 15:9–12 may reflect *testimonia* thematically arranged around the subject of the Gentiles.

Testimonia provide a window into the way the early church did its theology and ministry. They also provide insight into Old Testament quotations that are otherwise anomalies. Therefore, when an Old Testament quotation occurs, one must inquire about its use and textual form elsewhere in the New Testament and, if possible, in Judaism and the patristic period as well.

EXAMPLE ONE—AN IMPORTANT ALLUSION
JOHN 1:14–18

John 1:14–18 is a marvelously rich theological text on almost any reading. But a reading that does justice to the Old Testament background increases the significance of this text considerably. There is no Old Testament quotation in these verses, but there is an important allusion. Without an awareness of the Old Testament background on which the author frames his material, not only will much of the theological significance of this passage be lost, but one will not know why the author has chosen these words. There often is argument about whether a New Testament writer is alluding to an Old Testament text,[54] but there is such a constellation of words drawn from Exodus 33:17–34:6 that there can be no doubt that John 1:14–18 is based on this passage.[55]

Exodus 33:17f. is about Moses seeking a revelation of God's glory. Moses was told that neither he nor any other human could see God and live. He was allowed to see all God's goodness pass before him and, as it were, also to see the "back" of God. In this context Moses received the two tables of the law and was told that God is, among other things, full of lovingkindness and truth (*ḥesed veʿemet*). More than any text, this Old Testament passage defined who God was for Israel, and this event was viewed by Jews as the supreme revelation of God.

In John 1:14, the author claims to have seen the glory of the Word *(logos)*, who was full of grace and truth. "Glory" is frequently to be understood as that which makes God visible.[56] Although "grace" *(charis) is* not often used to render the Hebrew word for lovingkindness *(ḥesed)*, clearly the intention in John 1:14 is to say that in the *logos* made flesh we encounter a revelation of God. He is the unique one from the Father in whom we encounter the very character of the Father, grace and truth.

Similarly in John 1:17, the intention of the author is clear with an awareness of the background in Exodus. The law, a valid revelation, was given through Moses. The true revelation of the Father, however, was given through Jesus Christ. There is a contrast with the revelation of Moses, but there is not a rejection of that revelation. In effect, this verse says, "Revelation did take place through Moses, but the supreme revelation of God is to be found in Jesus Christ."

John 1:18 expresses the whole of Johannine theology in a nutshell. The assertion that no human can see God and live is drawn from Exodus 33:20 and is an important theme throughout the gospel.[57] No one, not even Moses, has ever seen God, but the unique God,[58] the one in the bosom of the Father, has revealed him. To see him is to see the Father (John 14:9).

EXAMPLE TWO — AN IMPORTANT QUOTATION
LUKE 4:18–19

Like John, the other Gospel writers use Old Testament quotations early in their writing to establish the identity of Jesus. The reader knows who Jesus is right from the start in every Gospel. In addition, Luke 4:18–19 established the character of Jesus' ministry through the quotation of Isaiah 61:1–2. This Old Testament text was the focus of Jesus' preaching in Nazareth.[59] Luke has placed this incident first in his account of Jesus' ministry to provide a programmatic description of Jesus' task. The importance of Isaiah 61:1–2 for Luke is obvious. He has moved this narrative to the beginning of his account of Jesus' ministry, whereas Matthew and Mark had it much later. Also, many of the main themes of Lukan theology are evidenced in this quotation (the Spirit, proclamation of the good news, the *aphesis*—which is both release and forgiveness, the poor and oppressed, and eschatology).

The words of Isaiah 61 are obviously important, but this text is another example of an Old Testament passage with a life in Judaism. The ideas associated with this text would have made it even more significant for Jesus and his hearers. Isaiah 61, with its focus on the "acceptable year of the Lord," would have alluded both to the "Year of Jubilee" described in Leviticus 25 and to God's end-time salvation.[60] The interpretation of Isaiah 61 in 11Q Melchizedek with reference to the "end of days" is clear proof of the eschatological association this text had. When people heard Isaiah 61, they understood it as a classic text describing end-time salvation. In effect, Jesus proclaimed to his hearers that God's end-time salvation had been fulfilled in their hearing. Their surprise is understandable.[61]

Guidelines

We have looked at a few examples of the significance of the Old Testament quotations in the New Testament. Other examples could be multiplied easily. Given that the use of the Old Testament in the New Testament is one of the most important issues in understanding the New Testament, certain guidelines will be helpful for studying those quotations.

1. Determine the original intention of the Old Testament passage. Close attention must be given to the context and to the theology at work in the Old Testament text.
2. Analyze the form of the text. To the degree that one is able, comparison should be made between the New Testament quotation and the Old Testament text and various witnesses to it. Is the New Testament reference a precise quotation, a quotation from memory, a paraphrase, or an allusion? Does the New Testament agree with the Masoretic text or the Septuagint or some other witness such as a targum? Are any insights to be gained from the form of the quotation? Even when one cannot make an independent comparison of other forms of the text, good commentaries will provide summaries of such comparisons.
3. Determine, if possible, how the Old Testament text was understood and used in Judaism. Again, where personal investigation is not practical, good commentaries will provide such information.
4. Determine the hermeneutical or exegetical assumptions that enabled the use of the Old Testament text. Is the use straightforward from our standpoint, or is there an assumption such as corporate solidarity or correspondence in history that makes the usage possible? Have any rabbinic techniques or wordplays made the Old Testament text attractive?

5. Analyze the *way* the New Testament writer uses the Old Testament text. Is the text being used as divine proof of the validity of his statement? Are words from the Old Testament used to enlighten, but with no thought of providing validation (as John 1:14–18)? Are the words adapted and used for rhetorical effect in the writer's own argument (as in 1 Pet. 1:3)? Is the New Testament writer only using an analogy based on an Old Testament text (John 3:14)?

6. Determine the theological significance and relevance of the use of the Old Testament text. For example, the Christological importance of the adaptation of Isaiah 8:12–13 to Christ in 1 Peter 3:14–15 is enormous. An Old Testament text that was explicitly about "*Yahweh* of hosts" has been applied to Christ without hesitation or any sense of need for explanation. That Paul could interpret Isaiah 49:8 eschatologically of his own ministry (2 Cor. 6:2) is important in understanding both him and our own ministries.

7. Note which Old Testament texts are used in the New Testament and which are not.[62] Most of the New Testament references to the Old Testament come from parts of the Pentateuch, the Psalms, and a few of the prophets, especially Isaiah. Clearly all the Hebrew Scriptures were considered the Word of God, but what theological conclusions should be drawn with regard to texts that were set aside (as the food laws) or ignored? On what ground did Jesus and the New Testament writers find the essence of their gospel in certain texts, especially those that focused on God's promises, love, and mercy rather than those that focused on separation and the exclusiveness of Israel?

Beyond these guidelines a further question must be mentioned. In view of the fact that the New Testament writers use Old Testament passages in ways that we find surprising, should we interpret the Old Testament the same way they did? In other words, can we use their technique to find Christian significance in Old Testament texts, or were they operating from a revelatory stance in ways we cannot?[63] This question is crucial, for the abuse of the Old Testament message is all too common in Christian history. Clearly the proximity of the apostles to the ministry, death, and resurrection of Jesus places them in a unique category. Also, the eschatological significance of Jesus' ministry and his identity have been marked out in ways that, even though they may be enhanced, do not need improvement. We should not expect to see new instances of verses applied to Jesus on the basis of corporate solidarity or eschatological or messianic presuppositions.

With great fear of possible abuse, however, I would not want to argue that the apostles could be creative because of their context but that we are confined to more mundane methods. In terms of approaching the text, whether Old Testament or New Testament, we must be guided by the author's intention. We do also, however, read the Scriptures in light of the person and work of Christ. We must resist superimposing Christian theology on Old Testament texts and should feel no compulsion to give every Old Testament text, or even most of them, a Christological conclusion. But we will have failed if we do not ask how Old Testament texts function in the whole context of Scripture. Without allegorizing the Old Testament, we must seek to understand God's overall purpose with his people. I am not impressed with the concept of *sensus plenior*, but neither am I willing to isolate texts from God's overall purpose.

Specifically, I have become convinced that the concept of correspondence in history is particularly valuable in interpretation. We have not completed the interpretive task until we have determined how a text does or does not correspond with Jesus' ministry or the ministry of the church.[64] The writers of the New Testament seem to have looked for patterns of God's working in the Hebrew Scriptures, in the life of Jesus, and in their own experience. Our reading of the Scriptures should do no less. Noting such patterns is a far cry from the abusive interpretation of allegorizing.

The New Testament writers were immersed in their Scriptures. The Scriptures were the frame of reference for their theology and provided many of the tools for their thinking. The same should be true of us.

Bibliography

Anderson, Bernhard W., ed. *The Old Testament and Christian Faith*. New York: Herder and Herder, 1969.

Baker, D. L. *Two Testaments: One Bible*. Downers Grove, Ill.: InterVarsity, 1976.

Bock, Darrell L. *Proclamation from Prophecy and Pattern*. Sheffield: JSOT, 1987.

Bruce, F. F. *The New Testament Development of Old Testament Themes*. Grand Rapids: Eerdmans, 1968.

Carson, D. A. and H. G. M. Williamson. *It Is Written: Scripture Citing Scripture*. Cambridge: Cambridge University Press, 1988.

Dodd, C. H. *According to the Scriptures*. New York: Scribner's, 1952.

Efird, James M., ed. *The Use of the Old Testament in the New*. Durham, N. C.: Duke University Press, 1972.

Ellis, Earle E. *Paul's Use of the Old Testament*. Grand Rapids: Eerdmans, 1957.

———. *Prophecy and Hermeneutic in Earliest Christianity*. Grand Rapids: Eerdmans, 1978.

Feinberg, John S., ed. *Continuity and Discontinuity: Perspectives on the Relationship Between the Old and New Testaments*. Westchester, Ill.: Crossway, 1988.

France, R. T. *Jesus and the Old Testament*. London: Tyndale, 1971.

Goppelt, Leonhard. *Typos: The Typological Interpretation of the Old Testament in the New*. Trans. Donald H. Madvig. Grand Rapids: Eerdmans, 1982.

Juel, Donald. *Messianic Exegesis: Christological Interpretation of the Old Testament in Early Christianity*. Philadelphia: Fortress, 1988.

Lindars, B. *New Testament Apologetic*. Philadelphia: Westminster, 1961.

Longenecker, Richard N. *Biblical Exegesis in the Apostolic Period*. Grand Rapids: Eerdmans, 1975.

Westermann, Claus, ed. *Essays on Old Testament Hermeneutics*. English trans., ed. James Luther Mays. Richmond: John Knox, 1963.

Notes

1. C. H. Dodd, *According to the Scriptures: The Sub-structure of New Testament Theology* (London: Nisbet, 1952).

2. Augustine, *Quaestionum in Heptateuchum libri Septem* 2.73.

3. See S. Vernon McCasland, "Matthew Twists the Scriptures," *JBL* 80 (1961): 143–8.

4. See the collection of essays edited by John S. Feinberg, *Continuity and Discontinuity: Perspectives on the Relationship Between the Old and the New Testaments* (Westchester, Ill.: Crossway, 1988). The main problem is how promises to the nation of Israel should be treated.

5. No one would argue that we should test a suspected adulteress with "bitter waters" (Num. 11f.) or that we should execute heretics (Deut. 13:6f.) or Sabbath breakers (Exod. 31:15). The number of such texts is not small.

6. See Robert Banks, *Jesus and the Law in the Synoptic Tradition* (Cambridge: Cambridge University Press, 1975), 132–46. Is Jesus' thought from Proverbs 4:23? See also Acts 10:9–16; Romans 14:14; 1 Corinthians 10:26f; and 1 Timothy 4:4, which place Christian conclusions in opposition with dietary restrictions in the Old Testament.

7. On the question of Jesus and the law in Matthew, see my "Matthew and the Law," *Society of Biblical Literature 1988 Seminar Papers,* ed. David J. Lull (Atlanta: Scholars, 1988), 536–54.

8. See Irenaeus, *Against Heresies* 1.27.2; Tertullian, *Against Marcion* 4.5–7 and 5.2–4; Richard N. Longenecker, "Three Ways of Understanding Relations Between the Testaments: Historically and Today," *Tradition and Interpretation in the New Testament,* ed. Gerald F. Hawthorne with Otto Betz (Grand Rapids: Eerdmans, 1987), 22–23; and E. C. Blackman, *Marcion and His Influence* (London: SPCK, 1948), 23f., 42f., and 113–24.

9. For information on the early church's treatment of the Old Testament, see R. P. C. Hanson, "Biblical Exegesis in the Early Church," *The Cambridge History of the Bible*, ed. P. R. Ackroyd and C. F. Evans (Cambridge: Cambridge University Press, 1970), 1: 412–53; Robert M. Grant with David Tracy, *A Short History of the Interpretation of the Bible* (Philadelphia: Fortress, 1984); Karlfried Froehlich, *Biblical Interpretation in the Early Church* (Philadelphia: Fortress, 1984); and James L. Kugel and Rowan A. Greer, *Early Biblical Interpretation* (Philadelphia: Westminster, 1986).

10. See Justin, *Dialogue with Trypho* 70 and 76 (on the stone of Dan. 2) and 86 and 90–91 (on wood and trees and other symbols of the cross).

11. On the Antiochean and Alexandrian schools of interpretation, see Richard N. Longenecker, "Three Ways of Understanding the Relations between the Testaments: Historically and Today," 22–32; and Grant with Tracy, 52–72.

12. For the approaches of Luther and Calvin, see Grant with Tracy, 92–99; Roland Bainton, "The Bible in the Reformation," *The Cambridge History of the Bible*, ed. S. L. Greenslade (Cambridge: Cambridge University Press, 1963), 3: 1–37; Paul Althaus, *The Theology of Martin Luther*, trans. Robert C. Schultz (Philadelphia: Fortress, 1966), 86–102; Wilhelm Niesel, *The Theology of Calvin*, trans. Harold Knight (Philadelphia: Westminster, 1956), 104–09. On the third use of the law, see *Calvin: The Institutes of the Christian Religion*, ed. John T. McNeill; trans. Ford Lewis Battles (Philadelphia: Westminster), 2.7.12.

13. D. L. Baker, *Two Testaments: One Bible* (Downers Grove, Ill.: InterVarsity, 1976).

14. Arnold A. van Ruler, *The Christian Church and the Old Testament*, trans. Geoffrey W. Bromiley (Grand Rapids: Eerdmans, 1971).

15. Rudolf Bultmann, "The Significance of the Old Testament for the Christian Faith," *The Old Testament and Christian Faith*, ed. Bernhard W. Anderson (New York: Herder and Herder, 1969), 8–35, especially 14–15; and "Prophecy and Fulfillment," *Essays on Old Testament Hermeneutics*, ed. Claus Westermann; English trans. ed. James Luther Mays (Richmond: John Knox, 1963), 50–75, especially 75.

16. On *sensus plenior*, see Raymond Edward Brown, *The Sensus Plenior of Sacred Scripture* (Baltimore: St. Mary's University, 1955); "The History and Development of the Theory of a Sensus Plenior," *CBQ* 15 (1953): 141–62; "The *Sensus Plenior* in the Last Ten Years," CBQ 25 (1963): 262–85; William Sanford LaSor, "The *Sensus Plenior* and Biblical Interpretation," *Scripture, Tradition and Interpretation*, ed. W. Ward Gasque and William Sanford LaSor (Grand Rapids: Eerdmans, 1978), 260–77; and Douglas Moo, "The Problem of Sensus Plenior," *Hermeneutics, Authority, and Canon*, ed. D. A. Carson and John D. Woodbridge (Grand Rapids: Zondervan, 1986), 179–211.

17. The first edition UBS Greek New Testament has more passages in bold print and a much better index than later editions.

18. The actual statistics of usage in the first edition UBS text are: Matthew, sixty-two quotations or allusions in bold print with thirty-two of them having an introductory formula; Mark, thirty with eleven having an introductory formula; Luke, thirty-nine with fifteen; John eighteen with fourteen; Acts, thirty-seven with twenty-three; Romans, fifty-four with forty; 1 Corinthians, sixteen with ten; 2 Corinthians, twelve with five; Galatians, eleven with five; Ephesians, ten with one; Philippians, one with zero; Colossians, zero; 1 Thessalonians, one with zero; 2 Thessalonians, four with zero; 1 Timothy, two with one; 2 Timothy, one with zero; Titus, zero; Philemon, zero; Hebrews, fifty-nine with thirty; James, six with four; 1 Peter, fifteen with three; 2 Peter, two with zero; 1 John, zero; 2 John, zero; 3 John, zero; Jude, one with one; Revelation, twenty with zero. There are, of course, other allusions besides the ones in bold print in the UBS text, and other editions will assess quotations differently. There are a variety of introductory formulae. See Joseph A. Fitzmyer, "The Use of Explicit Old Testament Quotations in Qumran Literature and in the New Testament," *NTS* 7 (1960–61): 299–305.

On the extent of the canon in the first century, see Roger Beckwith, *The Old Testament Canon of the New Testament Church* (Grand Rapids: Eerdmans, 1985). It is significant that there are no quotations from the apocryphal and pseudepigraphal writings. There are, however, allusions to these writings.

Helpful treatments of the use of the Old Testament in the New Testament can be found in C. K. Barrett, "The Interpretation of the Old Testament in the New," *The Cambridge History of the Bible*, ed. P. R. Ackroyd and C. F. Evans (Cambridge: Cambridge University Press, 1970), 1: 377–411; E. Earle Ellis, "How the New Testament Uses the Old," *New Testament Interpretation* (Grand Rapids: Eerdmans, 1978), 199–219; and D. Moody Smith, "The Use of the Old Testament in the New," *The Use of the Old Testament in the New and Other Essays*, ed. James M. Efird (Durham: Duke University Press, 1972), 3–65.

19. First Corinthians is an exception.

20. Hosea 13:14 should be translated, as in the New English Bible, with questions and a call for death to bring its plagues. The passage expects judgment.

21. Deuteronomy 18:15f. refers to prophets in general who serve as spokespersons for God to the community. Note that 18:20f. refers to prophets who speak falsely.

22. See Richard N. Longenecker, *Biblical Exegesis in the Apostolic Period* (Grand Rapids: Eerdmans 1975), 93–94; E. Earle Ellis, "Biblical Interpretation in the New Testament Church," *Mikra*, ed. Martin Jan Mulder and Harry Sysling, *Compendia Rerum Iudaicarum ad Novum Testamentum*, sec. 2 pt. 1 (Philadelphia: Fortress, 1988), 716–20; H. Wheeler Robinson, *Corporate Personality in Ancient Israel* (Philadelphia: Fortress, 1964); and Russell Philip Shedd, *Man in Community* (Grand Rapids: Eerdmans, 1964).

23. N. T. Wright, "Jesus, Israel, and the Cross," *Society of Biblical Literature 1985 Seminar Papers*, ed. Kent Harold Richards (Atlanta: Scholars, 1985), 75–96, especially 83f.

24. On correspondence in history see Ellis, "Biblical Interpretation in the New Testament Church," 713–16; Baker, 239–70; Gerhard von Rad, "Typological Interpretation of the Old Testament," *Essays on Old Testament Hermeneutics*, ed. Claus Westermann; English trans. ed. James Luther Mays (Richmond: John Knox, 1963), 17–39; Leonhard Goppelt, *Typos: The Typological Interpretation of the Old Testament in the New*, trans. Donald H. Madvig (Grand Rapids: Eerdmans, 1982). "Correspondence in history" is to be preferred to "typology"; the latter is too restricting and too associated with abuse.

25. Jesus' cry of dereliction no doubt expressed the initial awareness of correspondence with Psalm 22. This psalm must be seen as the lament of a righteous sufferer and not as a prophecy of Jesus' death.

26. In John 1:23, it is John the Baptist himself who uses Isaiah 40:3 as a description of his role.

27. Isaiah 40:3 was also used at Qumran as a description of the role of the community. See my "Streams of Tradition Emerging from Isaiah 40:1–5 and their Adaptation in the New Testament," *JSNT* 8 (1980): 24–45, for a discussion of the use of Isaiah 40:3.

28. Even if they are not applied in the same way.

29. On eschatological fulfillment as a hermeneutical presupposition, see Ellis, "Biblical Interpretation in the New Testament Church," 710–13; Longenecker, *Biblical Exegesis in the Apostolic Period*, 95; Donald Juel, *Messianic Exegesis* (Philadelphia: Fortress, 1988), 49–56; F. F. Bruce, *Biblical Exegesis in the Qumran Texts* (London: Tyndale, 1960), especially 9–19.

30. Romans 4:23–24 is slightly different but also represents an eschatological presupposition.

31. The Jews' expectation of an idealized Davidic king is well known. Note especially Jeremiah 23:5–8; 33:15–18; Psalm 89; and 4Q Florilegium. See Juel, 59–88.

32. Several Old Testament texts seem to have provided the framework for Jesus' understanding of his ministry. Of primary significance are Psalm 118:22–26; Isaiah 61:1–3; Daniel 7:13–14. The impact of Isaiah 53 is debated but seems probable.

33. On the infancy quotations in Matthew, see Longenecker, *Biblical Exegesis in the Apostolic Period*, 140–47; Raymond E. Brown, *The Birth of the Messiah* (Garden City: Doubleday, 1979), 96–116, 143–53, 184–88, and 219–25.

34. See Craig A. Evans, *To See and Not Perceive: Isaiah 6:9–10 in Early Jewish and Christian Interpretation* (Sheffield: JSOT, 1989).

35. See Richard N. Longenecker, *The Christology of the Early Jewish Christianity* (London: SCM, 1970), 32–38; and Howard M. Teeple, *The Mosaic Eschatological Prophet* (Philadelphia: Society of Biblical Literature, 1957). Note also John 7:40.

36. See Bruce, 7–11; and Longenecker, *Biblical Exegesis in the Apostolic Period*, 39–45. On the interpretation of Scripture more generally at Qumran, see Daniel Patte, *Early Jewish Hermeneutic in Palestine* (Missoula, Mont.: Scholars, 1975), 211–314.

37. Note also Acts 4:11 and Luke 4:18–21. Longnecker, *Biblical Exegesis in the Apostolic Period*, 70–75 and 100–101, lists several other passages that he would categorize as New Testament *pesher* interpretations of Old Testament texts.

38. On *midrash*, Rimon Kasher, "The Interpretation of Scripture in Rabbinic Literature," *Mikra* ed. Martin Jan Mulder and Harry Sysling; *Compendia Rerum Iudaicarum ad Novum Testamentum*, sec. 2, pt. 1 (Philadelphia: Fortress, 1988), 560–77; Longenecker, *Biblical Exegesis in the Apostolic Period*, 32–38; Ellis "Biblical Interpretation in the New Testament Church," 702–09.

39. On hermeneutical rules for exposition, see Kasher, 584–94; Ellis, "Biblical Interpretation in the New Testament Church," 699–702; and Hermann L. Strack, *Introduction to the Talmud and Midrash* (Cleveland: World, 1963), 93–98.

40. See David Daube, "Rabbinic Methods of Interpretation and Hellenistic Rhetoric," *HUCA* 22 (1949): 239–64.

41. Ellis, "Biblical Interpretation in the New Testament Church," 700–02, would argue that all seven are used in the New Testament.

42. Matthew 12:1–8; see Ellis, "Biblical Interpretation in the New Testament Church," 700.

43. Note the use of *epikataratos* in Galatians 3:10 (quoting Deut. 27:26) and 3:13 (quoting Deut. 21:23), *poiēsai auta* in 3:10 (from Deut. 27:26) and *poiesas auta* in 3:12 (from Lev. 18:5), and *zēsetai* in 3:11 (quoting Hab. 2:4) and 3:12 (quoting Lev. 18:5).

44. Note Acts 2:25, 30, and 34; 13:34–35; Romans 4:2 and 7; 9:33 and 11:9; 1 Corinthians 15:54–55; and Hebrews 1:5, 6–7.

45. Psalm 118:22 also occurs in Matthew 21:42 and parallels and in Barnabas 6.4.

46. See, for example, C. Leslie Mitton, *The Epistle to the Ephesians* (Oxford: Clarendon Press, 1951), 186–89.

47. Note a similar example in Matthew 27:9–10, where a conflation of Zechariah 11:12–13 and Jeremiah 32:6–9 is attributed to Jeremiah. Such combinations of texts and their attributions to a specific author ought not be considered "errors."

48. As Rendel Harris did with his "testimony book" hypothesis. See Rendel Harris, with the assistance of Vacher Burch, *Testimonies* (Cambridge: Cambridge University Press, 1916–20), 2 vols.

49. Note 4Q Testimonia and 4Q Florilegium. See Joseph A. Fitzmeyer, "'4Q Testimonia' and the New Testament," *TS* 18 (1957): 513–37.

50. See Barnabas 6.2–4 for an example, and cf. Peirre Prigent, *Les Testimonia dans le christianisme primitif: L'Epître de Barnabé I–XVI et ses sources* (Paris: J. Gabalda et Cie, 1961), *passim*. Note also Cyprian, *Treatise 12* ("Three Books of Testimonies against the Jews").

51. See my "I Peter II.1–10: Its Formation and Literary Affinities," *NTS* 24 (1978): 97–106, especially 101–03.

52. Note 1 Corinthians 15:25–27; Ephesians 1:20–22; and Hebrews 1:13 and 2:6–8. Psalm 110:1 is used in several other places, and is used in the New Testament more than any other Old Testament text. On the use of Psalm 110, see David M. Hay, *Glory at the Right Hand* (Nashville: Abingdon, 1973).

53. As several commentators have suggested. See, e.g., Ernst Käsemann, *Commentary on Romans*, trans. Geoffrey W. Bromiley (Grand Rapids: Eerdmans, 1980), 86. Note that this grouping of Old Testament texts on sin is present in the Septuagint version of Psalm 14:2–3. This could be due to Christian influence, but it seems more likely that these verses had earlier been collected in Judaism.

54. What constitutes an allusion? Is one word in common between New Testament and Old Testament texts sufficient? Certainly not unless there is something in the New

Testament context that suggests dependence on the Old Testament text. Does an allusion have to be a conscious allusion? Does it have to be an allusion that one could expect the readers to recognize? Frequently allusions are suggested that require a stretch of the imagination to accept.

55. See Morna Hooker, "The Johannine Prologue and the Messianic Secret," *NTS* 21 (1975): 52–56; and Anthony T. Hanson, "John i.14–18 and Exodus XXXIV," *NTS* 23 (1977): 90–101.

56. S. Aalen, "Glory, Honour," *The New International Dictionary of New Testament Theology*, ed. Colin Brown (Grand Rapids: Zondervan, 1976), 2: 45.

57. Cf. 5:37; 6:46; 12:41; and 14:8–9. Note also 1 John 4:12–20.

58. *Theos*, not *huios*, is the correct reading.

59. Note that while Luke's quotation is basically septuagintal, part of Isaiah 61:1 is omitted, and part of Isaiah 58:6 is inserted.

60. The Jubilee included four elements: (1) return of all property to the original owner; (2) release of all Jewish slaves; (3) cancellation of all debts; (4) allowing the land to lie fallow.

61. See also 4Q/521 and the discussion of Luke 4 in Robert B. Sloan Jr., *The Favorable Year of the Lord* (Austin, Tex.: Scholars Press, 1977); John Howard Yoder, *The Politics of Jesus* (Grand Rapids: Eerdmans, 1972), 34–40, 64–77.

62. Note Dodd's summary, *According to the Scriptures*, 107–08.

63. Note the discussions in Longenecker, *Biblical Exegesis in the Apostolic Period*, 214–20; "Can We Reproduce the Exegesis of the Apostles," *Tyndale Bulletin* 21 (1970): 3–38; and G. K. Beale, "Did Jesus and His Followers Preach the Right Doctrine from the Wrong Texts?" *Themelios* 14 (1989): 89–96.

64. See my "Streams of Tradition Emerging from Isaiah 40:1–5 and Their Adaptation in the New Testament," 39–40. For example, I would argue that the application of Lamentations 1:12 to the ministry of Jesus is legitimate on the basis of correspondence between the suffering of the nation and the suffering of Christ. This is not a text referring to Christ; it is a text applicable to Christ.

Chapter 11

The Study of New Testament Greek in the Light of Ancient and Modern Linguistics

David Alan Black
Southeastern Baptist Theological Seminary

Introduction

Students of the New Testament are generally expected to have a knowledge of the language of the New Testament. Many of these students will find themselves exposed at the same time to the principles and methods of linguistics—the scientific study of language. While several textbooks deal with the application of modern linguistics to the study of New Testament Greek, little is written on the history of language study and how that history influences the study of Greek today. The present essay is a brief synopsis of this subject appraising the historical factors that have led to the present state of New Testament Greek studies and calling attention to issues that both scholars and students will face in the years ahead.[1]

Where It All Started: The Ancient Greeks

Although there is evidence of language study from an earlier time—the oldest extant work of a linguistic nature is the admirable Sanskrit grammar of the Indian Panini (fifth century B.C.)—it was the ancient Greeks who initiated the formal study of language. That the history of grammar can be traced back to the writings of the early Greeks should come as no surprise, for it is a common pattern in the history of Western culture.

Somewhat less well-known is the fact that the earliest works on grammar came not from grammarians but from philosophers who speculated upon a number of subjects, among them the nature of language. Living in an age in which problems were attacked by thinking them through instead of gathering data in a laboratory, the Greeks did not examine their language with the objectivity of a scientist. Instead, they thought about language, and in the course of philosophizing on the subject, they made several important—if at times also inaccurate—observations.

PLATO AND THE PHYSIS-NOMOS CONTROVERSY

One of the earliest philosophical questions about language is still with us today: how do words in particular, and language in general, acquire meaning? Plato (429–347 B.C.) devoted one of his dialogues, the *Cratylus,* to this question. This dialogue, sometimes called Plato's dullest, is actually fascinating because it contains several important insights about language. In *Cratylus* much of the dialogue is carried on by Socrates, who is asked to settle a dispute between Hermogenes and Cratylus. Cratylus believes that the name *(onoma)* of a thing is a consequence of the *nature* of the thing named, and thus that language has meaning "naturally" (*physei,* "by nature"), whereas Hermogenes denies this assumption and holds that names stand for things only through *agreement* among speakers, that is, through "convention" (*nomō,* "by law [of usage]"). In the view of Cratylus, the phonetic composition of a thing named should reflect the composition of the thing itself so that words can be examined as being true or false in themselves. In Hermogenes' view, any word is the correct word so long as there is general agreement among its users about its meaning.

Exactly how Plato himself felt about the controversy is not clear, although he has Socrates champion both sides of the argument with equal vigor. Socrates discusses two sorts of words in the dialogue, those that are compound, and those that are simple, noting that one must use a different method to analyze the two types. A compound word should be examined by first dividing it into its constituent parts. Taking the name of the Greek god Poseidon as an example, Socrates suggests that its constituents could be *posi* ("for the feet," dative plural of *pous,* "*foot*") and *desmos* ("chain"), since the one who first used the name might have contemplated that walking through the water would have been difficult for Poseidon. He notes further that the name is not simply a combination of these two parts since some of the letters have been added or dropped for the sake of euphony (beauty of sound).

In the case of simple words, Socrates says we must ask what the single letters imitate. One can classify letters into consonants, vowels, and semivowels (diphthongs) and then examine their qualities, much like an artist would examine the colors on a pallet. A letter like *r* seems apt to express motion since the tongue moves rapidly when pronouncing it; it would therefore be an appropriate sound to use in a word like *rhoein* ("to flow"). On the other hand, *s, x,* and *ch* are pronounced with a great expenditure of breath and so are well used in *seisthai* ("to shake"), *xeon* ("seething"), and *psychron* ("shivering"). The *l* sound, because of its gliding movements, is aptly used in *leios* ("slippery") and *olisthanei* ("he slips"). Then Socrates cites contrary examples, such as the oddity of finding an *l* in the word for "hardness" *(sklērotēs),* which is complicated when it is discovered that this word in the Eritrean dialect is *sklērotēr,* suggesting an inexplicable equivalence of *s* and *r.*

Socrates concludes that since some names are more accurately descriptive than others, the one who depends on names to learn about the nature of their referents is risking receiving unreliable information. Thus Socrates is portrayed by Plato as taking a middle ground in this popular *nature versus convention* controversy.

Although the physis-nomos controversy seems pointless today, a remnant of the controversy can still be seen. Descendants of the "naturalist" school still argue for the dependence of grammatical distinctions on real distinctions in the human mind, while supporters of the "conventionalist" school deny a resemblance between symbol (word) and referent (object), except in scattered cases of onomatopoeia (words such as *buzz* or *crack*). We should emphasize that the Greeks studied only their own language. To them, all foreigners were *barbaroi*—people who did not talk but merely "babbled." Thus, not having evidence of words with the same meaning but completely different pronunciations in other languages, it was relatively easy for the naturalists to maintain their position. But today, with the linguistic descriptions of many languages available, the natural view is clearly untrue for the great majority of words found in all languages. In nearly every case, the conventional view that the relationship between sound and meaning is arbitrary provides the most valid and accurate position.

A number of other concepts of language that are important in modern grammatical study can also be found in Plato. As we have seen, his discussion of phonology included the breaking of sounds into consonants, vowels, and semivowels. He also distinguished different dialects of Greek, letters from their names, native Greek words from those borrowed from other languages, and a sound sequence as either a word or a combination of words, depending on the accent.

Plato also seems to have been the first person to distinguish between larger constituents that today are called *nouns* and *verbs*. In his *Theatetus,* Plato defines language as a combination of *onomata* and *rhēmata*. The expressions *onomata* (plural of *onoma*) and *rhēmata* (plural of *rhēma*) correspond to expressions used in both ordinary language and the vocabulary of grammar and logic. In ordinary language *onoma* can mean "name," but in the vocabulary of grammar it can mean "noun," "nominal," or "subject," and in logic it corresponds to "logical subject." In ordinary language *rhēma* can mean "phrase" or "saying;" in grammar it may mean "verb," "verbal," or "predicate," and in logic it corresponds to "logical predicate." These definitions come very close to our understanding of "subject" and "predicate" in traditional grammar. The *onoma* and *rhēma* were, in Plato's usage, the basic members of a *logos,* which can mean "nature," "plan," "argument," "clause," "sentence," and "proposition." But Plato did not distinguish the vocabulary of ordinary language, grammar, and logic, so that the translation of *logos* as "sentence" must be viewed with caution.

Plato would hardly have considered himself a linguist. Yet through his writings we catch a first glimpse of the foundations of linguistics and also the first formulations of problems that have been discussed by linguists ever since. Although his studies were designed to be modified and corrected, they remain a helpful revelation of some of the speculation out of which our thinking today on the question of grammar grew.

ARISTOTLE

Aristotle (384–322 B.C.), like his predecessor Plato, was a grammarian only in the sense that philosophers of the time considered language to be a valid object of philosophical inquiry. He wrote no single essay on language but referred to the structure of language in a number of works. In Aristotle's *Poetics, On Interpretation,* and *Rhetoric,* we have the first grammatical sketch of the Greek language known to us. This sketch is mainly an attempt to systematize the observations made on language by Plato and other philosophers. But it had far-reaching consequences. In the centuries following, and especially during the Middle Ages preceding the Renaissance, the works of Aristotle came to be considered second only to the Bible as the final authority on all topics.

Aristotle's *Poetics,* although a treatise on dramatic criticism, includes an analysis of grammar blended with a description of the "virtues" and "barbarisms" of various literary works. Aristotle discussed types of letters, the division of sounds into consonants, vowels, and semivowels, and such categories as gender, number, case, and sentence. These categories represented a major step forward in the systematization of grammar, although it is questionable how much of it is due to Aristotle's original observations.

Another important work of Aristotle was *On Interpretation,* which he wrote as an introduction to and background for his system of logic. It is also the clearest formulation of his general theory of language. In it Aristotle defined noun and verb and discussed noun cases and verb tenses as well as types of sentences. Aristotle defined the *word* as the minimal unit of language, incapable of being divided into smaller parts, a concept that modern morphologists have revealed to be inadequate. He also stated that words, in and of themselves, are not significant but must be used in combination with other words. Although this is related to the modern concept of structural meaning and the need for completeness, it ignores the fact that some utterances are composed of single words only: "Hi"; "John" (in answer to "What's your name?").

The most interesting work of Aristotle for our purposes is the *Rhetoric*. In most other works Aristotle took a conventionalist view of language, emphasizing the role of custom and convention in language usage, but in the *Rhetoric* he tried to correct and improve usage. In describing correctness, Aristotle distinguished the same units as Plato did but added another word class that Plato had discussed (without naming) in *On Interpretation:* the *conjunction (ho syndesmos)*. To Aristotle, conjunctions were all words that are not nouns or verbs. They differ from the latter in that they have no independent meaning but are simply used to tie sentences together. This division of words into those that do and those that do not have lexical (dictionary) meaning represents an early attempt to divide all words into two groups that are known today as *structure* and *content* classes.

THE STOICS

After Plato and Aristotle the first real advances in grammar were made by the Stoics, a group of philosophers and logicians who flourished from about the beginning of the fourth century B.C. until the rule of the Roman Emperor Marcus Aurelius (A.D. 161–180). Known today for their poker-faced attitude toward life, the Stoics were in fact the first real grammarians, producing the earliest purely linguistic monographs we know about in the Greek world. Unfortunately, not a single work of theirs is extant, and what we do have preserved are scattered quotations by other authors, mostly opponents of the Stoic school. But in spite of the scanty material and the problems connected with interpreting it, there is no doubt that the Stoic contribution to the development of linguistics was significant and, in many areas, of fundamental importance.

The Stoics sought to improve on Aristotle's definitions and to add still more to the general knowledge about Greek grammar. They expanded Aristotle's three classes to four (noun, verb, conjunction, article). Within the category of conjunction, the Stoics seem to have differentiated between prepositions and conjunctions and in the article category between pronouns and articles. The Stoics were also the first to study number and agreement in nouns and verbs; to study the case in the noun; and to discuss voice, mood, and tense in the verb. They distinguished five cases: nominative, genitive, dative, accusative, and vocative. The Stoic theory of tenses was fairly elaborate, based for the most part on the principle of opposition. The present and imperfect were "opposed" to the perfect and pluperfect; these four tenses were opposed to the aorist and the future; and the aorist in particular was opposed to the perfect and pluperfect. The present and imperfect were called duratives, the perfect and pluperfect completives, and the aorist and future indeterminates.

We are not particularly concerned here with a complete list of Stoic contributions to Greek grammar. It is sufficient to call attention to the Stoic practice of dividing their data into as many distinguishable parts as they could and of assigning a technical term to each division. Much of their terminology has become a basic part of our linguistic heritage. For instance, Aristotle did not use (and probably did not know about) specific names for different cases. It was the Stoics who gave them the names they have kept to the present day. The Stoics seem further to have established the definite name for the neuter gender of nouns, namely *oudeteron*, "neither [masculine nor feminine]." Aristotle had simply called it *metaxu*, "in the middle."

But the Stoics are probably best known for their contribution in an entirely different area of grammar. Unlike Aristotle the Stoics held that there was, in the remote history of the Greek language, a natural, necessary connection between the sounds of the language and the things for which the sounds stand, although they could see that the present forms of their language did not fully justify their claim. They therefore undertook to search for the original forms, the "roots" or *etyma* of current expressions, thus initiating the study called *etymology*.

THE ALEXANDRIANS AND THE ANALOGY-ANOMALY CONTROVERSY

After the Stoics the center of grammatical thought in the West shifted to the Alexandrian school, founded by Alexander the Great at Alexandria, then the capital of Egypt. The famous library of this school started from the personal collection of Aristotle, teacher of Alexander. Many scholars settled in Alexandria and conducted research in varied fields, including mathematics (Euclid), physics (Archimedes), and astronomy (Ptolemy). From this school also came two of the most famous and influential books in the world: the *Elements* of Euclid and the *Grammar* of Dionysius Thrax. It was during the Alexandrian period that grammar finally gained status as an independent discipline.

An important debate among the Alexandrians concerned the problem of how language is related to logic—a question that had been discussed, in less sophisticated terms, in the older physis-nomos controversy. Some scholars held that language should be *analogous* to logic and that it should be consistent in construction and free from illogical usages such as inconsistent verb endings or irregular noun forms. Examples of consistent patterns in English are the plural forms created by adding s to the singular form, as in *books, maps, characteristics,* and *effects*. Other Greek philosophers believed that language was full of *anomaly,* or irregularity in form. They were less concerned with consistency than with how language was actually spoken. In English, words that do not conform to the general pattern for plural formation include *men, sheep,* and *children*. Those who stressed the regularity of language were known as *analogists,* while those who emphasized the presence of irregularity were called *anomalists*. The analogists felt their duty was to "correct" inconsistencies in language and to make them conform to a logical pattern, whereas the anomalists saw their function as that of students and recorders of language.

In one respect, the Greek interest in regularity and irregularity was extremely fortunate for the study of Greek, since the analogists of Alexandria expended a great deal of effort to construct *kanones,* or lists of regularities in the forms of Greek, thereby establishing a form of grammatical description that survives today. However, because they concentrated on the final, single letter of forms, they were unable to show the complete regularities of noun declensions and verb conjugations, so that their lists were always subject to the attacks of the anomalists. As an example of what the analogists considered an exception, we can give the parallel declension of two Greek nouns—*aspis,* "shield," and *logos,* "word":

Nom.	*aspis*	*logos*
Gen.	*aspidos*	*logou*
Dat.	*aspidi*	*logō*
Acc.	*aspida*	*logon*

Since the nominative of these forms ends in the same letter, *s,* the analogists thought that they should be the "same" form and, therefore, be declined alike. Because of their misguided preference for the nominative case, they were unable to show the regularity of *aspis* (stem *aspid-*). Later on it became obvious that the best selection of the stem of *aspis* is one of its other cases, whereas it makes little difference for *logos.*

The analogist-anomalist controversy was never completely resolved in the ancient world. Today the debate can be seen in the differing approaches of those who would teach correct usage (prescriptive grammar) and those who feel that grammar is a matter of studying language analytically to see how it functions (descriptive grammar).

DIONYSIUS THRAX

Alexandrian scholarship lasted for centuries in the grammatical field, beginning with the work of Xenodotus Philadelphus (284–257 B.C.) and culminating in the work of Apollonius Dyscolus (A.D. 180). The most influential and well-known Alexandrian grammarian was Dionysius Thrax, whose *Grammar* (100 B.C.) became the standard textbook on Greek grammar for the next eighteen hundred years. Although it made no original contributions, it was the most comprehensive treatment of the Greek language to date, classifying and codifying the grammatical thinking of the time. It was largely through Dionysius that the Greek grammar of Plato and Aristotle was transmitted to later generations of students.

The entire text of Thrax's treatise consists of only twenty-five brief paragraphs dealing with what linguists today would call the phonology and morphology of the language. In the section on phonology, Thrax discusses *grammata,* "letters," a terminological confusion that does not explicitly distinguish between the sounds and the symbols used to represent them. The textbook also discusses such topics as a definition of grammar, accenting, punctuation, syllables, parts of speech, and declension and conjugation.

Thrax listed the article and the participle among the eight parts of speech, omitting the adjective and interjection. Otherwise, his classifications are similar to those used in modern grammar texts, except that many of his definitions have become revised.

Originally written in Greek, Thrax's volume was translated into Latin as the *Arts Grammatica* by Remmius Palaemon in the first century A.D. From this work came many of the technical terms currently employed in formal grammar. Thus the *Grammar* of Dionysius Thrax has had an influence in inverse proportion to its brevity. It became the subject of a great number of commentaries, known as scholia, which sometimes contain very valuable linguistic information. Its one great weakness, however, was a lack of information about syntactic constructions, a gap partially filled later by the work of Apollonius Dyscolus.

SUMMARY OF THE GREEK CONTRIBUTION

Before we turn our attention to the Roman grammarians, we may briefly summarize the major characteristics associated with Greek grammatical thought. First, the story of Greek linguistics is identical with the study of the Greek language alone. Aristotle, for example, being at heart a philosopher, examined language to derive "universal" principles. Using the Athenian speech he knew so well, he could not have imagined how limited his sample was. Egyptian and Hebrew were nearby, as were the Greek dialects, but these were largely ignored. It was therefore inevitable that Greek language study became mainly a study of local Greek.

Second, being concerned with the effective use of language, the Greeks were interested in what language "should" be, not what language was. Following Aristotle's lead, the Alexandrian scholars fostered the idea that it is the duty of the grammarian to improve language, to formulate rules by which language usage will become more logical and persuasive. The informal use of language was of no interest to these rhetoricians; they were interested only in literature and oratory.

Finally, this admiration of literature led to the totally unwarranted assumption that the language of literature was somehow "better" or "more pure" than the everyday speech of men and women. Common speech was assumed to be a corrupt form of the language. This unfortunate side effect of Alexandrian scholarship has continued down to our own times.

A Tradition Develops: The Roman Grammarians

The linguistic situation in Italy was in several respects different from that in Greece. Unlike the majority of Greek scholars, the Romans were not philosophers, and as Greek culture gave way to Roman, it was the poets and politicians who were occupied with grammatical studies. Moreover, Italy was a multilingual country with several literary languages besides Latin, including Oscan, Umbrian, and Etruscan. Finally, the widespread knowledge of Greek among educated Romans gave Roman linguistics a comparative perspective unknown to the Greek grammarians.

Nevertheless, these differences had little effect on the Roman linguists, whose basic outlook was no broader than that of their Greek predecessors and contemporaries. The Romans observed what they could scarcely have failed to notice—that their native tongue, Latin, closely resembled Greek. Minor differences there were, but these did not require a complete overhaul of the grammatical system. As a result, the descriptive categories of the Alexandrian grammarians, based on Greek structures, were simply transferred from the Greek language to Latin.

The most influential and well-known Roman grammarians followed the Alexandrian tradition of concentrating on the language of literature instead of describing the Latin used by their contemporaries. They also shared the Greek attitude toward "barbarians"—excluding themselves, of course, from this undesirable category. Roman scholars also used the same terms and forms of description as the Greeks had several centuries before. On the whole, this superimposition of Greek grammar on the structure of Latin worked fairly well, for there are many similarities between the two languages. Perhaps if Latin and Greek had contained major structural differences, the Romans might have been forced to study Latin independently. But because of the affinities between the two languages and because the Romans tended to view Greek culture as foundational, it seemed natural to assume that one system of grammar could serve both languages.

VARRO

Probably the first Roman to study the Latin language as a specific object of inquiry was Marcus Terentius Varro (116–27 B.C.), whose *De Lingua Latina* was published near the middle of the first century B.C. It consisted of twenty-five books on Latin structure, of which only Books V to X have been preserved. Varro dealt with etymology, inflection, the analogy-anomaly controversy, parts of speech, and syntax.

The evaluation of the extant books of *De Lingua Latina* reveals many interesting insights. In Book VIII, for example, Varro divided the words of the Latin language into four classes: those with case forms (nouns), those with tense (verbs), those with neither case nor tense (adverbs), and those with both case and tense (participles). This classification represents an advance over those who defined parts of speech according to meaning, for one can debate the meaning of the terms *noun* and *verb*, but one cannot deny that Latin nouns have case and that verbs have tense.

On the subject of analogy-anomaly, Varro took a middle-of-the-road position. He assumed the presence of some patterns in language but also recognized gaps or anomalies that could not be integrated into any linguistic pattern. He argued, for example, that while the words *nox* ("night") and *mox* ("soon") look alike, they are incompatible, since *nox is* a declinable form and *mox* is invariable. But he then went on to force other words into a regular pattern. An example of this is Varro's wholesale invention of the form *esum* ("I am") to make a regular pattern out of the present active indicative singular of the Latin verb *esse* ("to be"), which is *sum, es, est*.

Varro's grammatical system, if incomplete and inaccurate by today's standards, represented advanced thinking for his time. He attempted to use the structure of a word (inflection) to classify it as to type rather than basing his observations on function alone. He divided verbs into past, present, and future and subdivided these into complete and incompleted action, as well as active and passive. But his discussion of Latin was not intended as a grammar in the same sense as Thrax's, and his work therefore remained outside of the Latin pedagogical tradition.

QUINTILIAN

Marcus Fabius Quintilianus (A. D. 35–97), a famed educator and orator, wrote a treatise on rhetoric entitled *Institutio Oratoria*. Quintilian assumed that grammar, among other things, should be included as part of the orator's training, an assumption that remains unquestioned by many teachers to this day. He also stated that grammar should be based on reason, authority, and usage. Much of his text was therefore devoted to rooting out "barbarisms" (improper uses of a word) and "solecisms" (errors in syntax).

In addition to the elementary teaching of grammar, the *Institutio* included some etymological observations and a few more subtle points belonging to a more advanced analysis of language. For example, Quintilian recommended the admission of a seventh case in Latin and a sixth in Greek, since the Latin ablative and the Greek dative often have an "instrumental" meaning, different from the "usual" meaning of these cases. He also sought to improve the phonetic analysis of vowels and to introduce a classification of the Latin passive forms.

The basis of Quintilian's whole curriculum was an emphasis upon correctness and respect for authority, and his work gave great impetus to the analogist (prescriptive) approach to language. With Rome the center of the civilized world, it was natural that people throughout the Roman Empire would want to acquire a knowledge of educated Latin. The outline for the elementary teaching of grammar given by Quintilian would form the basis for the teaching of grammar up to the present century.

DONATUS AND PRISCIAN

The Roman heritage of Varro and Quintilian was transmitted to us by those grammarians who succeeded them, the most famous of these being Donatus and Priscian. Aelius Donatus was a fourth-century grammarian whose short Latin grammar became a standard text throughout the Middle Ages. As evidence of its influence and popularity, it was the first book to be printed by means of wooden type.

But the most complete and authoritative description of the Latin language to emerge from this period is that of Priscian, a Latin who taught Greeks in Constantinople in the sixth century A.D. Priscian divided his *Institutiones Grammaticae* into eighteen books, of which the first sixteen deal with morphology and the last two with syntax. Along with the shorter grammar of Donatus, Priscian's work became the authority not only for Latin but for the discussion of language in general among scholars of the Middle Ages.

Priscian's work is important for two reasons. First, it is the most complete and accurate description of Latin by a native speaker of the language. Second, his grammatical theory is the foundation of the traditional way of describing language. An examination of Priscian's parts of speech reveals that much of our current grammatical theory was in fact formulated fifteen hundred years ago and that only minor refinements have been added to this basic concept of the classification of words.

While Priscian's work is still a valuable and accurate source of information about Latin, it can be criticized from a linguistic point of view for several reasons. Chief among these is Priscian's use of both semantic and formal criteria in defining parts of speech but never in any consistent way. For example, by denying that the form *vires* ("men") is analyzable into *vir-* and *-es*, Priscian was guilty of one of the grammarian's greatest mistakes, since *vir-* and *-es* are clearly distinguishable morphemes in Latin. The reason for Priscian's error was his insistence that "meaning" is the cardinal criterion of grammatical work. The result of this view is to make the study of language a study of vocabulary rather than the study of those individual units of meaning that make up words. Likewise, Priscian defined the verb as "a part of speech with tense and mood, but without case-inflection, signifying action or being acted upon." This definition begins by examining the *form* of the verb but concludes with its *meaning*. On the other hand, Priscian's sections on syntax, declension of nouns, and conjugations of verbs were highly satisfactory, even though he followed Thrax in defining the word as the minimal unit of utterance.

This survey of the Roman contribution to linguistics has dealt with only the most prominent Latin grammarians among the ancients—and certainly not even all of them, as a glance at one of the larger specialized handbooks will reveal. The Latins followed faithfully the method of analysis marked out by the Greeks. Although we must examine briefly the achievements of the Middle Ages, we shall find little actually new in the study of language until we reach the nineteenth century.

After the Fall:
Medieval and Renaissance Linguistics

After the fall of Rome, grammar became firmly established as one of the major subjects of study during the Middle Ages, the leader of the *trivium* of grammar, rhetoric, and dialectic. The Middle Ages were dominated by Christian theism, respect for authority, tradition, and theology. With Latin firmly established as the language of the church, with monasteries scattered throughout Europe, and with the Christianization of new nations, the teaching of Latin took on renewed importance.

Training of the clergy involved the grammars of Donatus and Priscian, although a textbook written in 1199 by Alexander de Villa Dei entitled *Doctrinale Puerorum* eventually became the standard school grammar of the Middle Ages. Around A.D. 1000, Aelfric, Abbot of Enysham, England, wrote a Latin grammar for English speakers. This text was presumed by the author to be applicable to Old English as well as Latin. Thus the tradition of imposing the grammar of one language on another was carried into English, and as this was one of the earliest grammars for English speakers, it established the basic curriculum for many years of scholarship.

THE MODISTAE

Scholarship in medieval Europe was almost entirely confined to Latin. Greek had all but disappeared—which explains how *Graecum non est legitur,* the forerunner of "It's Greek to me," became a catch phrase among scholars.

About the middle of the twelfth century, however, Greek language and literature were rediscovered and translated. With the study of the classical authors, particularly Aristotle, grammatical thinking throughout Europe became more prescriptive, more logical, and more authoritative as grammarians renewed their search for a universal system. This attempt to formulate a unified theory of human language was part of the dominant thinking of the age, generally known as *scholasticism*. A number of writers of this time wrote commentaries entitled *De Modis Significandi,* from which these scholars became known as the *Modistae*. The Modistae believed that since language is governed by a system of rules, thought and therefore language are also rule-governed. Furthermore, the Modistae concluded that since the universe, including humankind, is everywhere the same; the ways in which humankind attains knowledge are everywhere the same; and language, as a means of expressing this knowledge, must also be universal. The Modistae's interest in a universal theory of language was continued by the rationalistic philosophers of the sixteenth, seventeenth, and eighteenth centuries, and the questions they asked about the nature of language are strikingly similar to those of modern scientific linguists.

THE RENAISSANCE

The Modistae's faith in a universal grammar typified the school of grammatical thought that dominated the late Middle Ages. The Renaissance, however, introduced an age of greater tolerance for divergent ideas as well as an emphasis on humanity rather than on the divine. Hitherto grammar had consisted of the study of Latin, with a system based on Greek, but now other languages were being scrutinized, including Hebrew and Arabic. This new interest in the Semitic tongues helped break the exclusive hold of Latin on the attention of European scholars, and by the sixteenth century studies of vernacular languages were beginning to appear. In 1606, the Frenchman Etienne Guichard compiled an etymological dictionary of Hebrew, Chaldean, Syriac, Greek, Latin, French, Italian, Spanish, German, Flemish, and English. Other scholars produced grammars of their own language. As expanding commerce created rivalries among nations, these grammars came to reflect pride in one's nation and the desire to promote a particular language. Probably the most celebrated linguistic chauvinist was the Swede Andreas Kemke, who maintained that in the Garden of Eden God spoke Swedish, Adam Dutch, and the serpent French.

The Medieval and Renaissance eras—that is, the period until about the end of the eighteenth century—witnessed a tremendous increase in the amount of information about language, even though the methods of analysis were still firmly rooted in the classical tradition. A new school of thought would be required to do what Newton did for physics or what Calvin did for theology; but this linguistic revolution had to wait until the nineteenth century. There were, however, important precursors, and one of these—Sir William Jones—calls for special attention.

SIR WILLIAM JONES

Many people regard the year 1786 as the birth date of modern linguistics. On September 27, British judge Sir William Jones (1749–1794) read a paper to the Royal "Asiatick" Society in Calcutta pointing out that the resemblances of Sanskrit to Greek and Latin are too close to be coincidental and therefore show that all three "have sprung from some common source which, perhaps, no longer exists." This is the first recorded recognition of language kinship as recognized by modern linguistics, and it set off a veritable chain reaction of comparative studies extending throughout the nineteenth century.

Before this time, others had drawn attention to the importance of Sanskrit, but their observations had fallen on infertile soil, like "discoveries" of America prior to Columbus. Attempts to derive one known language from another often produced ludicrous results. Thus, one might have tried to show how Latin was derived from Greek or Greek derived from Sanskrit in some kind of linear order:

Sanskrit ⟶ Greek ⟶ Latin

What Jones proposed is that all three languages evolved more or less independently from a common ancestor, in which case our diagram would look like:

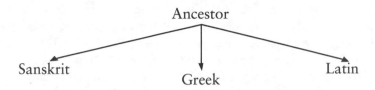

Ancestor

Sanskrit   Greek   Latin

Moreover, Jones suggested that the ancestor "might no longer exist." What he meant was that the ancestor might not be attested or written down. The concept of an unrecorded common ancestor freed language students from having to explain everything in language history exclusively by what is found in written documents.

The Nineteenth Century: Historical and Comparative Linguistics

With Sir William's discovery the way was clear to approach the study of language from a new perspective. Scholars came to understand that language is in a constant state of flux, that it has history, and that its genesis and development can be studied from the historical point of view. For the next hundred years, linguistic thinking was centered largely around historical and comparative "philology" (as it was called), as linguists began to piece together a picture of the evolution of languages—tracing, comparing, and classifying them into families.

INDO-EUROPEAN PHILOLOGY

For the Indo-European languages, the beginning of systematic comparison was Rasmus Rask's *Investigation of the Origin of Old Norse or Icelandic* (1814), which offered a complete classification of Indo-European languages and even a statement of the Germanic consonant shifts that was later more fully formulated by J. Grimm. Franz Bopp's *Ueber das Conjugationssystem der Sanskritsprache* (1816) did for comparative morphology what Rask had done for comparative phonology. Beginning in 1819 and ending in 1840, Jacob Grimm (of fairy tale fame) published a series of editions of his *Deutsche Grammatik*, where he sketched the grammatical structures of the older and modern forms of the Germanic languages. In the second edition Grimm set out clearly the sound correspondences he had noted between Sanskrit, Greek, and Latin and the

Germanic languages. These *Lautverschiebungen,* or "sound shifts," as he called them, came to be known as "Grimm's Law." Grimm's picture of the Germanic correspondences was rounded out by Bopp's *Comparative Grammar of Sanskrit, Zend, Greek, Latin, Lithuanian, Gothic and German* (1833) and by Karl Verner's discovery of the role played by the position of the accent in consonantal development, first made public in an essay entitled "An Exception to the First Consonant Shift" (1875).

Interest in comparative linguistics led to the investigation of other language families and also to the beginning of the linguistic treatment of contemporary languages without regard to history. In 1836, Friedrich Diez produced a comparative grammar of the Romance languages; in 1852, Franz von Miklosich wrote a grammar of the Slavic languages; and in 1853, Johann Kaspar Zeuss began the study of Celtic. But the most impressive achievement of comparative linguistic scholarship was the monumental *Outline of the Comparative Grammar of the Indo-European Languages* by Karl Brugmann and Berthold Delbruck, first published in 1886. Although later studies have disclosed errors in it, the second edition of this massive work is still quoted today.

THE NEO-GRAMMARIANS

The emphasis on language change eventually led to a major theoretical advance. In the last quarter of the century, a group of linguists headed by Karl Brugmann formulated the theory that all sound change takes place in accordance with regular laws that have no exceptions. This so-called *Neo-Grammarian* group was attacked by various linguists who denied the functioning of these *Lautgesetze,* or "sound laws." The stand of the *Neo-Linguists,* as this group called itself, was that sound changes are sporadic and individualistic phenomena. The strength of the neo-grammarian approach was its insistence upon methodological rigor and its determination to deal only with the physical phenomena of language. This approach seemed to imply, however, that language had a sort of independent existence and that it was governed by forces beyond the power of human direction. Although the claims made by the Neo-Grammarians have been modified to some extent today, it was an important step forward for linguists to realize that language changes were not just optional tendencies but definite and clearly stateable laws.

THE ACCOMPLISHMENTS OF THE PHILOLOGISTS

A detailed description of the work of the nineteenth-century philologists is beyond the scope of this essay. We may, however, attempt to summarize here some of the most important results of this century of work.

The Discovery of Indo-European. By the beginning of the nineteenth century, theories propagating a Hebraic or Hellenic origin of all extant languages had been proven to be untenable. Instead, based upon correspondences too regular to be coincidental, the philologists saw that

Sanskrit, Greek, Latin, the Germanic, Celtic, and Slavonic languages had developed from an *Ursprache,* a common ancestor, no longer extant. To this language they gave the name *Indo-European,* subdividing it into nine groups, including the Greek branch. Indo-European is only one of many language families studied from a historical perspective in the nineteenth century as well as more recently.

Comparative Studies. Working from a variety of recorded sources, comparative philologists began to build up details of regular sound changes, and, to a lesser extent, changes in grammatical forms. From the detailed evidence of certain sound shifts, the philologists formulated conclusions about the regularity of such shifts. The most famous of such formulations, "Grimm's Law," demonstrates how certain consonants of the original Indo-European underwent a change in the Germanic languages, and how another shift took place in the division of German into High German and Low German. It is the most spectacular (and for our understanding of the relation between English and Greek, the most important) of hundreds of similar shifts that occurred when languages gradually broke off from their parent language.

The Classification of Languages. As the work of the philologists spread into other language families, there developed an attempt to classify all languages according to their basic structural features. Probably the best-known effort in this direction is the classification of languages into the categories of isolative, agglutinative, and inflectional. Some philologists advanced the theory that languages passed from one stage to the next in the order given above, the inflectional languages (like Greek and Latin) being the "most highly advanced." However, this hypothesis represented an oversimplified view of language, and today most linguists reject the notion of the superiority of inflected languages. Yet the view that Greek or Latin is the "best" language still occasionally crops up in studies of historical linguistics.

Advance in New Testament Greek Grammar. When the light of historical-comparative philology was turned upon the language of the New Testament, it revealed that New Testament Greek is nothing other than a natural development in the long history of the Greek language. It also revealed that Greek is not an isolated language but one that sustains vital relations with a great family of languages. These conclusions were first stated by the German philologist George Winer, who in 1822 inaugurated a new era in New Testament studies with the publication of his *Neutestamentliches Sprachidiom.* Winer's thesis that New Testament Greek was not a special "Holy Ghost" language but the ordinary tongue of the day was truly epoch-making.

Further progress was made by Alexander Buttmann (1859) and Friedrich Blass (1890), whose grammars were based on Winer's fundamental premise. In 1895, Adolph Deissmann published his *Bibelstudien,* and his *Neue Bibelstudien* followed in 1897. These "Bible Studies" condemned the isolation of biblical Greek from the so-called "profane Greek." Deissmann based his conclusions on the witness of Greek inscriptions and papyri to the language of the New Testament. In 1896, J. H. Moulton began the formal application of the new light from the papyri to the Greek New Testament in his *Introduction to the Study of New Testament Greek*. Moulton's subsequent *Grammar* (1906), as well as the mammoth work by A. T. Robertson, *A Grammar of the Greek New Testament in the Light of Historical Research* (1914), are works of greatest linguistic interest. Even though some of the conclusions drawn by these scholars are open to doubt, their demonstration that "Bible Greek" is vernacular Koine remains of permanent value. Nigel Turner's recent attempt in *Christian Words* (1980) to return to the pre-Deissmann era in the study of New Testament vocabulary is a demonstrable cul-de-sac.

The Twentieth Century: Descriptive and Generative Linguistics

While the nineteenth century was dominated by the historical-comparative and diachronic approach to linguistics, the twentieth century has been dominated by the descriptive and synchronic approach. Problems of language theory in general, as distinct from the study of individual languages, have also come to the fore, along with philosophical discussions on the nature of language very similar to those of the ancient Greeks. In America, linguistics began as an offshoot of anthropology, while in Europe structuralism was exerting a major influence in the field of linguistics.

AMERICAN DESCRIPTIVISM

While nineteenth-century Europe was engrossed in the comparative method of language study and the interest was largely in historical matters, in America a tradition was developing of studying languages whose history and relationships were unknown. As early as the seventeenth century, Roger Williams in Rhode Island was describing an Algonkian language under the rubric "the language of America." When the American Philosophical Society was founded by Benjamin Franklin, a number of its members, including Thomas Jefferson, showed a genuine interest in American Indian languages and their description. Around the beginning of the twentieth century, anthropologists began to record the culture of the fast-dying Indian tribes, and the American Indian languages were an aspect of this research. The work of those early scholars was for the most part haphazard and lacking cohesion, primarily because there were no firm guidelines for linguists to follow when they attempted to describe exotic languages.

This state of affairs changed with the emergence of the Yale linguists Edward Sapir (1884–1939) and Leonard Bloomfield (1887–1949). Sapir became the leading theoretical linguist in the field of American Indian languages, producing many important studies. Bloomfield began his career as a comparative linguist but soon began to take an interest in American Indian languages and in the whole American descriptivist approach. In 1914, he published a general work in linguistics which he later rewrote into a new work entitled simply *Language* (1933). Bloomfield's *Language* was quickly acknowledged as the best general introduction to linguistic science and the descriptive method. During the Bloomfieldian era large numbers of linguists, including many students of Sapir and Bloomfield, concentrated on writing descriptive grammars of both written and unwritten languages.

SAUSSURE AND STRUCTURALISM

As linguists in the United States became involved in the study of American Indian languages during the late nineteenth and early twentieth centuries, it became increasingly clear that the historical orientation of nineteenth-century European linguistics was no longer adequate. If any one person can be held responsible for this change in perception, it was the Swiss scholar Ferdinand de Saussure (1857–1913), whose *Cours de Linguistique General* was published after his death from notes compiled from his students. Saussure's crucial contribution was his explicit statement that all language items are essentially interlinked—an aspect of language that had not been stressed before. This approach to language is today called *structural* or *descriptive linguistics*. All linguistics since Saussure has been structural, as "structural" in the broad sense merely means the recognition that language is a system of interdependent elements rather than a collection of unconnected individual items.

STRUCTURALISM AND NEW TESTAMENT GREEK

With the publication of A. T. Robertson's *Grammar,* the American application of historical-comparative philology to New Testament Greek had reached its apex. Once the analytical methods for a philological approach to the language had been derived, however, scholars began shifting their attention to the new revolution in structural and descriptive linguistics. Although the achievements here have not been as unambiguous as in the area of historical-comparative linguistics, no less effort has been expended.

Characteristic of this new direction in New Testament studies is the three-volume *A Beginning-Intermediate Grammar of Hellenistic Greek* (1973) by Robert Funk, who earlier gave New Testament scholars an English edition of Blass (Debrunner). Funk's *Grammar* is a rigorous and scholarly attempt to organize all of New Testament Greek linguistics into a single body of theory and practice. A similar emphasis upon descriptive linguistics can be found in Eugene Van Ness Goetchius's *The Language of the New Testament* (1965), William Sanford LaSor's *Handbook of New Testament Greek* (1973), and Ward Powers's *Learn to Read the Greek New Testament* (1979). The morphemic analysis of New Testament words receives special attention in Bruce Metzger's *Lexical Aids for Students of New Testament Greek* (1969) and more recently in J. Harold Greenlee's *A*

New Testament Greek Morpheme Lexicon (1983). Each of these works is a serious attempt to update grammatical study, and LaSor's work in particular is an important advance over traditional grammars. Despite these promising beginnings, however, the descriptive approach to New Testament Greek grammar has not proved to be the dominant new tradition.

CHOMSKY AND GENERATIVE GRAMMAR

This history of the development of linguistics cannot be told without one more episode. In 1957, Noam Chomsky's *Syntactic Structures* presented a method of linguistic analysis that not only breaks sentences down into constituent morphemes but also reveals more of the inner structure of the language than any other method available at the time. It was Chomsky's theory that grammar should be more than a system for classifying the elements in sentences already produced but a system of generating sentences in the first place. By what process, he asked, is a sentence changed from active to passive voice, from simple to compound, from singular to plural, from present to future? Chomsky theorized that a great variety of sentences can be generated by transforming certain elements of the sentence—by interchanging, adding, or deleting linguistic forms; by reversing word order; or by combining two or more structures into one. In his words, a grammar will be "a device which generates all the grammatical sentences of a language and none of the ungrammatical ones." This theory is known as transformational-generative grammar or, more simply, TG.

The Chomskian revolution has pervaded all areas of linguistics, with its greatest impact on the study of syntax. In the spirit of this new approach, several works have attempted to apply TG to New Testament Greek, including Theodore Mueller's *New Testament Greek: A Case Grammar Approach* (1978), Reinhard Wonneberger's *Syntax und Exegese* (1979), Daryl Dean Schmidt's *Hellenistic Greek Grammar and Noam Chomsky: Nominalizing Transformations* (1981), and J. P. Louw's *Semantics of New Testament Greek* (1982). TG grammar has also been an important element in the theory of translation developed by Eugene Nida in *Toward a Science of Translating* (1964) and has been used extensively in the seminars and institutes on translation conducted by the United Bible Societies. However, studies such as these have tended to be specific applications of earlier results achieved in linguistics and as such have made a contribution to exegesis more than to the study of grammar.

Conclusion: Where Do We Go From Here?

Today the field of New Testament Greek philology has expanded beyond the wildest imaginings of previous generations. But this expansion of knowledge has ushered us into an age of new complexities, new patterns, and new challenges. In challenging the old assumptions, linguists have opened up a Pandora's box of fresh problems. After criticizing the traditional approach for being inconsistent, unscientific, and impractical, linguists have had difficulties standardizing their terminology, simplifying their discipline to a level realistic for classroom use, and demonstrating that the new grammar will aid exegesis and interpretation.

This last statement should be softened somewhat in that numerous linguists from the ranks of biblical scholarship have not been slack in bringing modern linguistics into the theological arena. Nonlinguistic views of theology and biblical language were initially criticized by James Barr, whose *Semantics of Biblical Language* (1961) mercilessly revealed that not all was apple pie in Exegesisland. Barr's writings have done much to reorder certain methods of biblical research along the lines of contemporary linguistic theory. Since Barr we have seen many innovations in the grammars of the biblical languages. But they have been innovations, for the most part, within the framework laid down centuries ago by a naive and simplistic society. This framework has confined the pursuit of knowledge in the universities to certain traditional areas of learning, with innovation limited to changes in emphasis from one area to another, or a change in instructional methods or materials.

To the extent that both traditional and linguistic grammars are descriptive disciplines, there is no reason each could not profit from the experience of the other. Adherence to the linguistic point of view entails a preference for a more revealing and exact description, and eventually explanation, of linguistic facts, but it need not entail a rejection of traditional values and emphases. Since it is a descriptive discipline, linguistics does not, because it cannot, prove or undermine any theological or philosophical position. But this rejection of "mentalism" in the study of language is the rejection of a grammatical method and not necessarily of a theological or philosophical commitment to the Bible as the Word of God. The most recent developments in biblical linguistics have, in fact, returned to the traditional goals of exegesis but with the rigor of the scientific methods developed by linguists over a period of years. Periodicals such as *The Bible Translator* (United Bible Societies), *Notes on Translation* (Summer Institute of Linguistics), *Neotestamentica* (South African Bible Society), *Linguistica Biblica* (Bonn), and *Filologia Neotestamentaria* (Córdoba), along with textbooks such as Moises Silva's *Biblical Words and Their Meaning* (1983), Peter Cotterell and Max Turner's *Linguistics and Biblical Interpretation* (1989), and the present writer's *Linguistics for Students of New Testament Greek* (rev. ed., 1995) demonstrate that interest in this interdisciplinary territory is alive and growing.

Nevertheless, important challenges remain. Significant scholarly discussion continues unabated, and of the numerous issues currently under investigation, the following seem to me to be among the most critical:

1. The problem of the reticence to break the traditional mold and strike out for newer and more productive territory. No longer can students of

Greek be considered knowledgeable if they still believe *the* grammar they were taught; it is now painfully obvious that there are *many* grammars—traditional, structural, transformational, etc.—and that each of these comes in a wide variety of sizes and shapes. And it seems a reasonable assumption that more will follow.

2. The problem of the atomization of methods currently employed in New Testament philology. To take just one example, in the United States, Chomskian linguistics once held the day, but today several other methods are being employed, such as Kenneth Pike's tagmemics, Charles Fillmore's case grammar, and Sydney Lamb's stratificational grammar. This diversity, including significant terminological confusion, remains a problem, and this situation is only exacerbated by the recent influx of methods currently in vogue in Europe.

3. The present crisis over the nature of "New Testament Greek." What is to be done about the strongly Semitic character of New Testament Greek, and can one speak of New Testament Greek as a linguistic subsystem when a comprehensive grammar of Hellenistic Greek has yet to be written?

4. The problem of defining the relationship between linguistics proper and New Testament "philology," which itself can refer both to *Literaturwissenschaft* (the study of the New Testament as a part of ancient Greek literature) and *Sprachwissenschaft* (the study of the Greek of the New Testament). This duel between diachronic and synchronic approaches must, it seems to me, be resolved if New Testament scholarship is to arrive at a synthesis capable of using the best of both approaches to language.

5. The riddle of the Greek verbal system: Can the tense structure of New Testament Greek continue to be described in terms of a rigid time structure when the latest research indicates that verbal aspect is the predominant category of tense (see especially the recent works by Buist Fanning and Stanley Porter)?

6. The challenge posed by "rhetorical criticism" in taking us beyond hermeneutics and structuralism. The recent revival of interest in rhetoric in New Testament studies bodes well for the future of our discipline, but neither James Muilenburg nor his school has produced a workable model of rhetorical criticism (though F. Siegert's 1984 dissertation is a positive step in the right direction).

7. The mention of structuralism raises the onerous hermeneutical question concerning surface and deeper linguistic meaning in the interpretation of New Testament texts, a question posed most radically by Erhardt Guttgemanns (1978) but certainly not by him alone.

8. The value of linguistics for NT Greek pedagogy. There are signs that a linguistic approach is becoming more acceptable to a new generation of Greek teachers. Phonology is seen as useful in that it helps students see that many seeming irregularities about Greek are perfectly normal and operate according to certain phonological "rules" in the language, while morphology

is especially helpful in acquiring and retaining vocabulary and in understanding the Greek verb system. The "slot and filler" approach to grammar used by the present writer in his *Learn to Read New Testament Greek* (exp. ed., 1994) helps students *understand* what they are learning (instead of just requiring them to memorize a phalanx of linguistic minutiae). Semantics reminds us that meaning is the ultimate goal of all linguistic analysis and that both syntagmatic and paradigmatic relations deserve careful study.

9. Finally, the place of discourse analysis (textlinguistics) requires further discussion. Traditional studies of New Testament Greek have tended to ignore the macrostructure of a given text (the "forest"), emphasizing instead the trees and the tiny saps. It is everywhere apparent that New Testament exegesis remains somewhat "word-bound," though more and more seminarians are being exposed to the dangers of a "wall motto" or "bumper sticker" mentality in doing exegesis. Discourse analysis is especially helpful in doing exegesis above the sentence level and promises to become a standard instrument in the pastor's toolbox.

These and other challenges will be around for some time to come and will offer plenteous grist for the scholar's mill. It may be hoped that these and other questions regarding New Testament Greek studies will inspire a new generation of Greek students to meet its destiny—aware of its opportunities, mindful of its responsibilities, eager to make fresh contributions. More than ever before, it now appears to be more than wishful thinking that the best of both traditional and linguistic approaches can be combined for a more exact and productive understanding of the biblical languages.

Bibliography

Arlotto, Anthony. *Introduction to Historical Linguistics.* Boston: Houghton & Mifflin, 1972.

Barr, James. *The Semantics of Biblical Language.* London: Oxford University Press, 1961.

Black, David Alan. *Learn to Read New Testament Greek.* Exp. ed. Nashville: Broadman and Holman, 1994.

————. *Linguistics for Students of New Testament Greek: A Survey of Basic Concepts and Applications.* Rev. ed. Grand Rapids: Baker, 1995.

————. *Using New Testament Greek in Ministry: A Practical Guide for Students and Pastors.* Grand Rapids: Baker, 1996.

Costas, Procope S. *An Outline of the History of the Greek Language.* Chicago: Ares, 1936.

Cotterell, Peter and Max Turner. *Linguistics and Biblical Interpretation.* Downers Grove, Ill.: InterVarsity, 1989.

Erickson, Richard J. "Linguistics and Biblical Language: A Wide-Open Field." *JETS* 26 (1983): 257–63.

Fanning, Buist M. *Verbal Aspect in New Testament Greek.* Oxford: University Press, 1990.

Funk, Robert W. *Language, Hermeneutic, and Word of God: The Problem of Language in the New Testament and Contemporary Theology.* New York: Harper, 1966.

Louw, J. P. *Semantics of New Testament Greek*. Philadelphia: Fortress, 1982.

Nida, Eugene A. "Implications of Contemporary Linguistics for Biblical Scholarship." *JBL* 91 (1972): 73–89.

Palmer, L. R. *The Greek Language*. Atlantic Highlands, N.J.: Humanities Press, 1980.

Porter, Stanley. *Verbal Aspect in the Greek of the New Testament, with Reference to Tense and Mood*. New York: Lang, 1989.

Schmidt, Daryl Dean. "The Study of Hellenistic Greek Grammar in the Light of Contemporary Linguistics." *PRS* 11 (1984): 27–38.

Siegert, F. *Argumentation bei Paulus gezeigt an Rom 9–11*. WUNT 34. Tübingen: Mohr Siebeck, 1985.

Silva, M. *Biblical Words and Their Meaning: An Introduction to Lexical Semantics*. Grand Rapids: Zondervan, 1983.

Sweet, H. *History of Language*. New York: Macmillan, 1900.

Notes

1. For a bibliography of works consulted in the preparation of this essay, see the list at the end of this article and the writer's *Linguistics for Students of New Testament Greek,* rev. ed. (Grand Rapids: Baker, 1995), 22, 141, 168–69. Chapter 6 of the latter work deals in greater detail with the subject of historical-comparative linguistics.

Chapter 12

Discourse Analysis

George H. Guthrie
Union University

One of my family's favorite stories is entitled *If You Give a Mouse a Cookie* (I have a six- and a three-year-old, but I confess this is one of my favorites, too). The discourse begins with the sentence, "If you give a mouse a cookie, he's going to ask for a glass of milk." The story continues by noting that if you give him a glass of milk, he will want a straw; then he will need a napkin. The possibility of a milk mustache prompts the lovable rodent to look in the mirror, which in turn reminds him that he needs a haircut. After the haircut the mouse sees he needs to clean up the cut hair in the sink, and on the story goes as the mouse thinks of task after task, each task inspiring the next. Finally, worn out by his endeavors the mouse is thirsty and wants a glass of milk. The author concludes, "And chances are if he asks for a glass of milk, he's going to want a cookie to go with it."[1]

If You Give a Mouse a Cookie has a number of features that make it an enjoyable read. The boy, the mouse, and the mouse's tasks cause the story to "hang together" nicely (linguists call this "cohesion"), and the author presents the tale in a singsong, rapidly progressing fashion that pulls the reader from page to page. Finally, we smile at the ending that has brought us back to the beginning, bringing a very pleasing closure to the narrative.

Now it just would not do to take the various parts of the story and scramble them. The progress inherent to *If You Give a Mouse a Cookie*, the cohesion borne of one task prompting another, with the cute rodent moving from one scene to another, would be destroyed. The story has parts that play specific roles by virtue of their positioning in the text, and we must allow them these roles if we are to participate in the act of communication initiated by the author. This particular discourse would decrease in its effectiveness if we started playing cut-and-paste with its organization of material. Its introduction introduces. Its body progresses according to the relationship between various tasks. Its conclusion wraps up the narrative.

The same could be said of this chapter. I have not begun with the conclusion or the second point of my "General Presuppositions" section. I move from this introduction, which hopefully is playing its role of gaining your attention, to definitions and general presuppositions, to a methodological approach, to an application of the method on a specific biblical text, and finally to a conclusion. These parts of the article are intended to progress logically as you follow the discourse point by point. The order of material is strategic and vital to this act of communication.

This is how communication works. Discourses, written or spoken, long or very short, communicate by organization of linguistic elements presented in relation to a given context or contexts. For example, even a simple "discourse" such as a stop sign has both organization and context that facilitate the intended message. The shape and color of the sign and the placing of the word *stop* in the middle of the sign are a form of organization of elements. If we saw *stop* written upside down, in small letters, along the top left edge of the sign, we would recognize immediately that something was amiss. We expect a stop sign to be organized a certain way. Yet the shape and color and letters might be different in different cultural and linguistic contexts. Also, we respond to a stop sign according to its intended function when it is placed appropriately at a crossroads, for example. If we are walking down the aisle of an antiques store and see an old stop sign hanging upside down from the ceiling, we do not respond according to the original intention of that "text." Why? It is out of an appropriate context for that message to be communicated.

In longer discourses as well, strategic organization of linguistic elements and context are vital for communication. Strategically organized words build phrases and clauses; phrases and clauses form sentences; sentences form paragraphs; and paragraphs are grouped to build articles, research papers, whole speeches, or chapters in a book. No discourse simply consists of a collection of words or sentences, so that if you added up the semantic content of all the individual words and all the individual sentences, you could make sense of the discourse. No, words and sentences only have meaning as they are grouped appropriately and given their places in context. Well-crafted texts are recognized as such in part because they are well organized. J. P. Louw notes:

> Whenever a person has something to say on a given subject, he is faced with the problem of how to say it, for it is by no means a matter of merely "throwing together" a number of randomly selected utterances. The material must be put in some order, and language normally offers a multiplicity of arrangements, all of which would serve differently to effect the purpose. . . . Selection becomes even more imperative in continuous discourse. Moreover, it may be said that the arrangement of the selected material becomes a vital factor as

soon as a number of utterances are linked together. These have to be ordered and articulated because any sensible string in communication is selective. This is especially true in the case of written material.[2]

Thus, Louw rightly notes, "the way or the manner, i.e. the structure, in which a notion is communicated, is the heart of its effectiveness."[3] To this we might hasten to add, "The way or the manner *as presented in a context* . . . is the heart of its effectiveness." Thus a key to understanding an act of communication—we could say *any* act of communication—is to understand the organization of material as related to a given context, and this is a major objective of a form of inquiry known as "discourse analysis."

The last half century has witnessed the rise of this very broad subcategory of general linguistics called "discourse analysis," or "text-linguistics." Some reserve the former designation for analysis of spoken discourse and the latter for written texts, and it is true that the dynamics involved in written and spoken language differ at points.[4] Yet these two labels often are used synonymously.[5] Discourse analysis has been used in an array of fields such as psychoanalysis, political science, literary studies, and the communication arts and, as a part of the broader discipline of linguistics, has become "one of the most important and most widely discussed and investigated areas of research."[6] In the past two decades especially, this form of investigation has made modest inroads to the world of biblical scholarship, being used much more broadly to date in Old Testament studies than in studies on the New Testament.[7] Although gaining attention and use in the field of New Testament[8] and boasting several vigorous schools of thought,[9] discourse analysis has yet to make much of an impact on exegetical methodologies as used by most New Testament scholars.

My purpose in this chapter is to present a clear introduction to discourse analysis for introductory-level biblical studies students and to make a case for its use as a part of the broader exegetical enterprise. I hope to demonstrate that, rather than being a superfluous, exotic criticism destined to pass as a scholarly fad, discourse analysis, when properly understood, provides a natural, logical extension of traditional exegetical means of study.

Definition

Broadly speaking, discourse analysis concerns a wide array of *linguistic dynamics* that interplay in language, various *forms* of discourse expressed within languages, and specific *contexts* in which those forms are expressed. Essentially, it concerns language as used as a tool of human communication.[10] In this chapter, however, we are interested specifically in that aspect of discourse analysis that addresses written texts, particularly the biblical literature. Thus, for our purposes at present, *discourse analysis* may be defined as "a process of investigation by which one examines the form and function of all the parts and levels of a written discourse, with the aim of better understanding both the parts and the whole of that discourse."

Now we must say from the start that any scholar addressing the biblical text in an attempt to understand the meaning of that text performs *aspects* of discourse analysis, whether the designation is claimed or not. Any time a scholar seeks to discern the syntax of a word in the Greek text (i.e., the relation of a word to other words in a sentence) or to outline a book of the New Testament, concerns of discourse analysis have been engaged. Yet discourse analysts suggest that an expansion of the analyses normally performed in New Testament studies is in order. Speaking to this expansion and the importance of discourse analysis being incorporated into the exegetical enterprise, Birger Olsson remarks:

> A text-linguistic analysis is a basic component of all exegesis. A main task, or the main task of all Biblical scholarship has always been to interpret individual texts or passages of the Bible. Among the many tools lexicon and grammar are the most important ones. To the *words* and to the *sentences* a textual exegesis now adds *texts*. The text is seen as the primary object of inquiry. To handle texts is as basic for our discipline as to handle words and sentences. Therefore, text-linguistic analyses belong to the fundamental part of Biblical scholarship.[11]

Note especially Olsson's assertion that the text must be seen as the *primary* object of inquiry. This means that if one does not have a degree of understanding of a whole discourse one cannot adequately appraise a unit under consideration. Thus, discourse analysis shifts the focus of biblical exegesis from individual words, and even passages, and places it on whole discourses. This does not mean that the individual words, sentences, and paragraphs are any less important than in traditional approaches to exegesis. Rather, discourse analysis moves the "text" or "discourse" from a place of ambiguity, and often obscurity, to a place of rigorous consideration and analysis. The presuppositions driving this shift in focus clarify discourse analysis as an approach to the text.

General Presuppositions

First, discourse analysts insist that *the primary locus of discourse meaning resides above the sentence level.* David Allen notes, "Modern linguistic theory is now recognizing that we may (and indeed must) talk about the structure of meaning beyond the sentence level, just as we can talk about the structure of clause and sentence."[12] Also, Talmy Givón, in an often-quoted remark states, "It has become obvious to a growing number of linguists that the study of the syntax of isolated sentences, extracted, without natural context from the purposeful constructions of speakers is a methodology that has outlived its usefulness."[13]

Traditionally, exegetical concerns have focused on the sentence level of the text. Intermediate Greek grammar classes zero in on syntax, that is the relationship between words, clauses, and phrases within New Testament sentences. Exercises often focus on sentences taken out of their textual contexts. Commentaries move section by section through a book, treating each section in a verse-by-verse, clause-by-clause, and sometimes word-by-word manner. Yet often there is little attempt to demonstrate how the words, clauses, and sentences in a paragraph work together to accomplish the author's goal for that paragraph in relation to the whole book or section of the book. Words and clauses, nevertheless, are given their specific meaning and functions by their surrounding "contexts."[14]

For example, in Philippians 3:2, Paul writes, "Beware of the dogs." Now if someone were to ask you, out of the blue, as you were walking down a street in your town, what the warning "Beware of the dogs" means, you probably would identify it as a caution related to canines! Yet, given both the cultural and literary context of Philippians 3, we understand that Paul is referring to evil, false teachers. The cultural and literary contexts make the words meaningful in a specific direction. Discourse analysts, however, vie for more than mere sensitivity to contexts, as vital as that is. An aim is to identify semantic and pragmatic functions of parts of the discourse above the sentence level, and this brings us to the second foundational presupposition of discourse analysis.

Discourse constituents, at various levels of the discourse, play roles that should be identified. In the passage just mentioned, the parts of Paul's warning concerning false teachers may be interpreted to play the following roles:

Warning:	Watch out for dogs;
Restatement/warning:	watch out for evil workers;
Restatement 2/warning:	watch out for the mutilators.
Basis of the warning:	For we are the circumcision,
description:	who worship God
Manner:	in the Spirit
	and
description 2:	boast about Christ Jesus
	and
contrast:	not about what we can accomplish
concession:	although I myself might have confidence
	in the flesh

Paul probably gives the triple warning for emphasis. He then follows with the basis of the warning: the readers should heed his warning because Paul and his associates provide the true paradigm of church leadership—they are the ones to whom the Philippians should be looking as exemplars of true Christianity, not the false workers. Notice that this statement of the warning's "basis" is expressed as a contrast. Paul then describes the religious posture of those who are the "circumcision." They worship God in a manner that is "in the Spirit" and boast about Christ, not human endeavors. Yet, even though he as a true Christian minister does not boast about human accomplishment, Paul points out that he could and would beat the false workers if playing the religion game by their standards.

"In the Spirit" might be identified as an instrumental dative of manner, but if we are going to grasp this phrase's immediate significance, it must be read as making a specific semantic contribution to the argument of these verses. Moreover, this brief passage fits in a broader section in which Paul holds himself up as an example of right leadership. The unit running from 3:2–16 could be entitled, "The Bad Workers and Paul." This unit in turn plays the role of supporting the center section of the book (1:27–4:9), which gives a series of examples that the Philippians should follow (Christ, Timothy and Epaphroditus, Paul).[15] So the fact that true Christian workers worship "in the Spirit" serves, by giving a characteristic of a true worker, as a small and significant counter to the false teachers who plague the church.

Brown and Yule comment on the roles played by various parts of a discourse:

> The analysis of discourses is, necessarily, the analysis of language in use. As such, it cannot be restricted to the description of linguistic forms independent of the purposes or functions which those forms are designed to serve in human affairs. While some linguists may concentrate on determining the formal properties of a language, the discourse analyst is committed to an investigation of what that language is used for.[16]

In terms of biblical studies, scholars focus the attention of Greek grammar almost entirely on the function of words at the sentence level. What the discourse analyst suggests is that this focus should be expanded to a consideration of roles at every level of the discourse, and identification of these roles should be systematized just as Greek syntax is presently.

A third general presupposition driving discourse analysis is that *various dynamics work together to give a discourse cohesion.* Cohesion is that quality of a text that gives it unity. Every text has a network of relationships between the words that make up the discourse. These relationships may be formal (i.e., a relatedness of form), semantic (related according to meaning), or pragmatic (related in function on the readers or hearers). For instance, when in Hebrews 1:1 the author uses alliteration (five words begin with π), the verse is given a higher level of cohesiveness by virtue of the form of words used. Yet these same words also are cohesive semantically, each playing a role in modifying the participle translated "having spoken." It could be said that the five words also are cohesive pragmatically in that they function to stimulate the hearers' thinking about God's act of speaking.

Similarly, but on a broader scale, Hebrews 11 has a very high level of cohesiveness due to formal, semantic, and pragmatic relationships. Formally, the author often presents his material in a pattern: the word *pistei* ("by faith"), followed by the name of the exemplar of faith, followed by the action or event by which faith was expressed, and then the positive outcome. Semantically the words are meaningful because of a historical backdrop that is understood—the names "fit together" because they form a tapestry of figures from the Old Testament era. For example, Abraham is not just any Abraham, and Moses is not just any Moses. The reader understands that these are heroes from the pages of biblical history. Pragmatically, the examples serve a unified purpose—to challenge the hearers to live by faith. Consequently, the cohesion provided by consistency of form, tight semantic frameworks, and pragmatic relationships provides the chapter with an overwhelming sense of "unity."

Maintaining a topic, using connection (e.g., conjunctions or words related logically), crafting pronouns with the same referents, repeating the same or related lexical items, and sustaining grammatical features such as subject, "actor," verb tense, person and number from sentence to sentence, all contribute to a text's semantic cohesiveness. The consistent use of a particular genre (e.g., parable or exhortation), or temporal and spatial indicators in a text, also can play significant roles in the semantic cohesion of a discourse.[17] An author may use all of these dynamics to make the text flow and hang together. Correspondingly, the author accomplishes a shift in the text to a new unit or section, marking the discourse with a shift in some of these tools of cohesion. He may change the subject, switch to the consistent use of another tense, or move the discourse to another time frame, for example. Such uses of language mark the movements in a text.

Method

Having presented three presuppositions most basic to discourse analysis, we must move to the question of methodology. Particularly we are interested in how discourse analysis relates to exegesis, and one of the primary questions the student or scholar must ask is how to address the interplay between the micro- (i.e., the sentence and paragraph levels) and macrolevel (i.e., the whole discourse) of the text. Discourse analysts adhere to a "bottom-up, top-down" approach.[18] This means that one moves from the smallest particulars of the text, such as morphemes, up through words, phrases, clauses, sentences, paragraphs (i.e. clusters of sentences), and sections until one reaches the level of the macro-discourse itself.

The semantic information from the parts contributes to an understanding of the whole. Then the process is reversed, moving from the highest level of the discourse back down through the discourse constituents. The individual parts of the discourse are read in light of one's understanding of the whole.

As we have seen, traditional exegesis focuses on the microlevel, treating questions of broader structure more informally. Discourse analysis, on the other hand, moves from the micro- to the macrolevel and back again, as many times as is necessary, attempting both to understand the dynamics within a unit and the role of that unit and its parts in the broader context of communication. An enhanced understanding of the broader scope of the discourse, then, enhances understanding of the unit and its parts.

Therefore, our method must incorporate both the aspects of "paragraph-level" exegesis and other analyses that address broader discourse concerns.

How then does a general approach to discourse analysis work with a process of exegesis? I propose that the two *already are* integrated when each is rightly conceived. This is why much of what we have already discussed simply sounds like good, contextually-sensitive exegesis. These are not two separate processes but, rather, one process executed on various levels. Discourse analysis incorporates all of what we normally consider exegesis, and thorough exegesis presupposes aspects of discourse analysis. For example, one cannot do discourse analysis without performing translation, word studies, analysis of syntax, evaluation of an author's uses of particular terms in the context of the whole work, or even analysis of broader biblical and theological contexts. On the other hand, when, in processes of exegesis, we consider "literary context," for example, we are presupposing that thorough work has already been done on the macro-discourse level.[19] Also, if we attempt to set a unit's boundaries or outline a passage under consideration, we have engaged aspects of discourse analysis. To perform a thorough discourse analysis, one must, in essence, move back and forth between the micro- and macrolevels of the discourse, engaging in exegesis both on and above the sentence and paragraph levels:

1. *(Microlevel):* Translate the text and begin a basic grammatical analysis.
2. *(Macrolevel):* Identify the unit boundaries[20] within the discourse by:
   a. identifying a change in genre.
   b. identifying transition devices in the text (e.g. statements of introduction or conclusion).
   c. identifying the uses of linguistic devices such as *inclusio*.[21]
   d. tracking shifts in cohesion dynamics such as time frame, topic, etc.
3. *(Microlevel):* Analyze the internal structure of each discourse unit, and perform a detailed study of the material in that unit.
4. *(Macrolevel):* Analyze the interrelationship between the various units of the discourse and identify the types of progression in the discourse.
5. *(Microlevel):* Consider further the interpretation of elements within each discourse unit.

The whole process must, of course, begin with translation and basic grammatical analysis (step 1). Ideally the exegete would start at the beginning of the whole discourse and translate through the whole text. This is the only way a thorough study can be carried out. However, aspects of discourse analysis can be used even if one begins by considering a subunit within a broader discourse. For example, if the student of Scripture asks a burning question about Romans 8, *aspects* of discourse analysis can be engaged in the study of that chapter. The semantic structure, for instance, can be studied. Yet questions are likely to arise, which will force consideration to broader reaches of the discourse. In the first verse one encounters the term *katakrima*, a word used in the New Testament only here and twice in

Romans 5. Thus, the question of the relationship between Romans 5 and Romans 8 has been raised. My point is that one need not have time to translate and analyze a whole discourse in order to use aspects of discourse analysis, but a deeper level of understanding will demand that the whole discourse be studied.

To a certain extent the first two points under "Identify unit boundaries within the discourse" (step 2) are somewhat intuitive. In Mark 4:3, Jesus begins the parable of the sower, which we recognize as belonging to a specific subgenre in the Gospels. This shift to a specific subgenre marks a new unit in 4:3–9. Just two verses earlier, however, Mark prepares us for the parable by placing it in a certain context. Mark 4:1 reads, "Once again he started to teach by the lake." The transitions in narrative are somewhat different from the transitions used in exposition and here correspond to "cohesion shifts" in "location" and "time frame" built into the narrative.[22] There is also a cohesion shift in "topic" as we move from the end of chapter 3 to the beginning of chapter 4, and Jesus' mother and brothers no longer are in the picture.[23]

How far does the unit initiated at 4:1 extend? In 4:1–2, Mark, having established the setting, states, "He began to teach them by using many parables." As one reads through the text, we come to a similar statement in 4:33, which reads, "He was speaking the word to them with many such parables." This statement, as a part of a summary statement in 4:33–34, constitutes the closing of an *inclusio* (i.e., the repeating of the same or a similar statement at the beginning and end of a section) that marks the unit as 4:1–34.

When we speak of analyzing the internal structure of a unit (step 3), we mean both the execution of syntax on the sentence level and semantic analysis on the paragraph level (see the example under "Application of the Method"). As syntactical analysis involves an evaluation of the relationship between words, phrases, and clauses on the sentence level, semantic analysis concerns similar relationships on the paragraph level. To do a good job of both, one must do good exegesis, studying word meanings, patterns of expression, and broader theological and biblical contexts.[24]

Once the unit boundaries are identified and the units themselves are studied thoroughly, the analyst must seek to ascertain how those units relate to one another and how they progress to move the discourse forward (step 4). For example, can large subsections of the discourse be discerned? How are these subsections subdivided? Further, does the discourse progress in a logical, step-by-step fashion, like the first eight chapters of Romans? Or is the structure more cyclical like the Book of Revelation? Or is the progression based on narrative dynamics as in Acts? These questions must be asked if the exegete is to ascertain the exact role of a given unit in the broader discourse. Finally, once a clearer understanding of the broader discourse is gained, there must be a return to the microdiscourse level to check our earlier interpretations of words, phrases, and clauses in light of insights from the discourse as a whole (step 5).

These five proposed steps in discourse analysis demand a thorough engagement in exegesis at every level of the discourse. The process is rigorous but pays great dividends in enhanced understanding of the text.

Application of the Method

We now consider a particular exegetical conundrum in order to demonstrate the potential of discourse analysis when understood as a vital aspect of the exegetical enterprise. In Hebrews 6:17, the author mentions "an oath" that relates in some way to "two unchangeable facts in which it is impossible for God to lie." He proclaims that these two facts (or things) give strong encouragement to believers. Much discussion has issued from commentators concerning the identification of these "two things." William L. Lane, in his Word Biblical Commentary, rightly notes that upon these two irrevocable facts "rests the assurance of receiving the blessings that are the content of Christian hope." Thus their identification is significant. Lane follows other commentators such as Otto Michel in identifying the unspecified items as God's promise and his oath.[25] Harold Attridge, F. F. Bruce, Donald Hagner, P. E. Hughes, and Victor Pfitzner, among others, also hold this position.[26] In a slight variation Attridge speculates that the author may be referring specifically to the word of Psalm 110:4, "which proclaims Christ as High Priest and the oath in the same context." F. Schröger expands this position to include the proclamations of both Psalm 2:7 and Psalm 110:4, passages juxtaposed in Hebrews 5:5–6.[27] B. Klappert adds an interesting dimension to the discussion by pointing out the parallels between Hebrews 6:13–20 and 7:19–21, linking the promise of chapter 6 with the quotation of Psalm 110:4 in chapter 7.[28]

It should be noted that most of the proposals above are mere speculation, drawing on weak appeals to the immediate context. Schröger and Klappert move the discussion to elements found at the level of the broader discourse, but their proposals have not convinced the majority of commentators. What might discourse analysis add to the discussion?

Consider the following semantic diagram of Hebrews 6:13–18:[29]

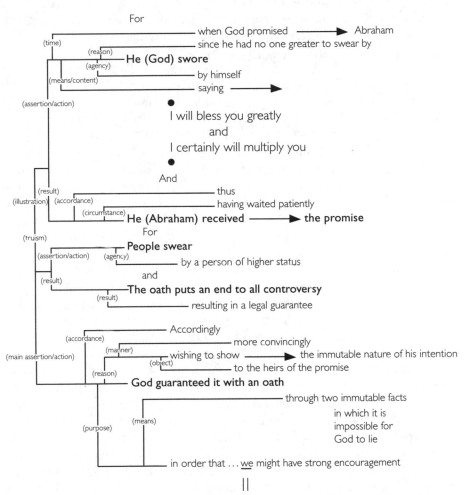

For

when God promised ⟶ Abraham

(time) since he had no one greater to swear by

(reason)

He (God) swore

(agency)

(means/content) by himself

saying ⟶

(assertion/action)

●

I will bless you greatly

and

I certainly will multiply you

●

And

(result) thus

(illustration) (accordance) having waited patiently

(circumstance) He (Abraham) received ⟶ the promise

For

(truism)

(assertion/action) (agency) People swear

by a person of higher status

and

(result) The oath puts an end to all controversy

(result) resulting in a legal guarantee

Accordingly

(accordance)

(manner) more convincingly

(main assertion/action) wishing to show ⟶ the immutable nature of his intention

(object) to the heirs of the promise

(reason) God guaranteed it with an oath

through two immutable facts

in which it is
impossible for
God to lie

(means)

(purpose)

in order that ... we might have strong encouragement

||

the ones fleeing to grab hold of the hope in front of us

I have presented the main clauses in bold typeface to highlight what might be called the "backbone" of the passage.[30] The main clauses are positioned on the left margin; modifying elements are indented three spaces on the words they modify; conjunctions are indented five spaces on the words or clauses they join; and objects are preceded by an arrow at the end of the clause to which they relate. As is plain in the diagram, the semantic function of each phrase or clause is marked on the line leading to that phrase or clause. If, for the moment, we strip away the bulk of the support material surrounding these main clauses, we have the following:

an illustration	*assertion/action:*	God swore
	result:	Abraham received
a truism	*assertion/action:*	People swear
	result:	a legal guarantee
main point	*assertion/action:*	God guaranteed with an oath
	intended result:	encouragement

So the author moves from a general illustration with which the audience would be familiar to a universal truth with which they certainly would agree, to the main point he wants to communicate. The illustration and the truism lay the foundation and build toward the author's main point. Notice the parallelism crafted in the passage. Moreover, the assertion that people swear (a universal truth) is preceded and followed by assertions that God swore.

Therefore, from the semantic structure of Hebrews 6:13–18 we can say the following about the enigmatic "two unchangeable facts" of verse 18. First, they are part of the climax of the passage (vv. 17–18) and as such are vital to the author's intention for the whole of the passage. Second, this climax follows the pattern established by the illustration of verses 13–15 and the truism of verse 16: an act of swearing and its result. This climax specifically has to do with God's making a guarantee with an oath in order to bring about encouragement to the heirs of the promise. Furthermore, the oath is intended to give encouragement *by means of* these two immutable facts. Third, notice that the *two* facts are the means by which encouragement is delivered through *one* oath. Fourth, notice that throughout the passage the concepts of "oath" and "promise" are somewhat synonymous. God's promise to Abraham, "I will bless you greatly, I certainly will multiply you," is the content of his oath. The oath and the promise are one and the same. Thus, the interpretation held by those many commentators who read the "two things" as God's "oath" and "promise" should be called into question. We are dealing with a *single* action by God when we speak of his oath and promise, not two. What we have, rather, is "two things" that are tied to a single oath (i.e., promise).

Thus far we have executed an aspect of discourse analysis on the paragraph level, and that analysis has accomplished two things. First, it has helped to clarify the logic of the whole passage and the specific role played by the reference to "two things" in verse 18. Second, the analysis has raised doubts about the widely published speculation that the "two things" of that verse are God's oath and his promise. Nevertheless, we still have not identified the "two things." For this task we must move to a higher level of the discourse.

In my book, *The Structure of Hebrews: A Text-Linguistic Analysis*, I identified unit boundaries by marking the author's uses of *inclusio* and tracking cohesion shifts in the discourse. Having marked the unit boundaries, I attempted to evaluate how the units interrelate. This was accomplished by paying close attention to lexical items in the text and identifying the author's uses of transitions. When I carried out this analysis, the section of Hebrews running from 5:1 through 7:28 was shown to have the following structure:[31]

A. The Appointment of the Son as a Superior High Priest
    1. Introduction: The Son Taken from among Men and Appointed according to the Order of Melchizedek (5:1–10)

The Present Problem with the Hearers (5:11–6:3)
Warning: The Danger of Falling Away from the Christian Faith (6:4–8)
Mitigation: The Author's Confidence in and Desire for the Hearers (6:9–12)
Intermediary Transition: God's Promise Our Basis of Hope (6:13–20)

    2. The Superiority of Melchizedek (7:1–10)
    3. The Superiority of Our Eternal, Melchizedekan High Priest (7:11–28)

Furthermore, the final passage in this section, Hebrews 7:11–28 may be subdivided into two movements. Hebrews 7:11–14 concerns Christ's appointment as high priest by a criterion other than tribal lineage. Whereas the Levitical priests were appointed by virtue of being Aaron's descendants, Jesus was appointed according to the order of Melchizedek. As the second subdivision, Hebrews 7:15–28 focuses on the eternality of Christ's priesthood.

Notice that the concept of "oath" as providing hope plays a prominent role in this latter unit. In 7:19b–22, the author proclaims:

> And a superior hope is brought in through which we draw near to God. And it was not apart from an oath. Other people became priests without an oath, but he (became a priest) with an oath, by the agency of the one saying to him, "The Lord has sworn and will not change his mind; you are a priest forever." According to this oath Jesus has become the guarantee of a superior covenant.

Here the oath (i.e., the content of Ps. 110:4) given to Jesus upon his appointment as high priest is said to be an item for great encouragement. Remember that in 6:17–19 the hope is also tied to the oath given by God. Also in 6:19–20, the hope is said to enter the "inner room behind the curtain" where Jesus functions in the role as high priest according to the order of Melchizedek. Thus, the concepts of "oath," "hope," and Jesus' "high priesthood" converge in Hebrews 6:13–20 and 7:11–28. In the latter passage, however, the oath is clearly presented as being the words of Psalm

110:4: "You are a priest forever, according to the order of Melchizedek" (7:17, 21). We can also point out that the two parts of this oath form the two movements of 7:11–28 and do so in inverse order as given in the psalm:[32]

| "You are a priest forever" | Hebrews 7:15–28 |
| "According to the order of Melchizedek" | Hebrews 7:11–14 |

It may be suggested that these two parts of Psalm 110:4, laid out crisply in Hebrews 7:11–28, are the mysterious "two unchangeable facts" of Hebrews 6:18. Why are they "unchangeable"? Because "The Lord has sworn and will not change his mind." It is impossible for God to lie (6:18). Why do these two facts give encouragement to those who have fled to take hold of hope (6:18–19)? Because Christ's priesthood is eternal and of a superior order—the order of Melchizedek. He, as a priest who will not die, is able to save forever those who, through his high priesthood, draw near to God (Heb. 7:24–25).

Having identified the "two unchangeable facts" is not enough, however. Discourse analysis demands that we ascertain why the author alludes to Psalm 110:4 at Hebrews 6:18. The following may be suggested and relates to the outline of Hebrews 5:1–7:28 offered above. The whole of Hebrews 5:1–7:28, with the exception of the strategic exhortation of 5:11–6:20, focuses attention on the appointment of Jesus as a superior high priest, and the text upon which the author bases his treatment of that appointment is Psalm 110:4. This verse is introduced as the centerpiece of the author's introduction to the topic found in Hebrews 5:1–10. Before developing an exposition of this text, however, the writer to the Hebrews interjects a strategic interlude meant to heighten their attention. In this interlude, Hebrews 5:11–6:12, he confronts the hearers with their spiritual problem (5:11–6:3), gives them a harsh warning (6:4–8), and then softens his warning by speaking confidently of their appropriate response to God (6:9–12).

In 7:1, the author rejoins his topic of Christ's Melchizedekan high priesthood in earnest. Hebrews 7:1–10 demonstrates that Melchizedek was a priest superior to the Levites. Then, as we have seen and on the basis of Psalm 110:4, the author argues for the superiority of Jesus' Melchizedekan high priesthood along the lines of the two proclamations of Psalm 110:4: "you are a priest forever" and, "according to the order of Melchizedek."

What then of the role played by Hebrews 6:13–20 in which our phrase, "two unchangeable facts," is found? This passage plays an important role as what might be called an "ingressive intermediary transition." This type of transition stands between two major sections of the discourse and thus is "intermediary." It is "ingressive" in that it picks back up on the topic from which the author departed at 5:11, "Christ's Appointment as a Melchizedekan High Priest," and leads back into a focused discussion of that topic (7:1–28). Since the author had left the topic and inserted a strategic interlude (5:11–6:12), he needed a means of transitioning back to his discussion of Psalm 110:4. The exact point at which the author begins moving back into his discussion of the Christ's Melchizedekan high priesthood is Hebrews 6:17–18, for here he alludes to Psalm 110:4 with its "oath" and "two unchangeable facts."

It may be pointed out that the identification of the "two unchangeable facts" of Hebrews 6:18 could not be ascertained in the immediate context of that verse. Moreover, the exploration of the function of units such as Hebrews 7:11–14 and 7:15–28 was necessary to that identification. Finally, the specific role played by the "two unchangeable facts" in Hebrews—an allusion playing part in a transition—could not be grasped apart from an examination of the roles played by *all* the units of discourse in 5:1–7:28. This is the work, the effectiveness, and the necessity of discourse analysis.

What Discourse Analysis Has to Offer Exegesis

In making our case for the use of discourse analysis as an aspect of exegesis, how might we summarize the benefits of going through the necessary learning curve? The above examination of Hebrews 6:13–20 shows that such methodology is not easy and demands both rigorous work and patient reflection. First, discourse analysis has to do with general linguistic dynamics. In this sense it is a methodology that can incorporate and use various valid "criticisms" of the New Testament. Rhetorical criticism, literary criticism, and sociological exegesis, for example, all have to do with discourse, and the insights they offer can be embraced within the framework of discourse analysis. Because it is a field of inquiry with tremendous breadth, it might serve to address the splintering of New Testament studies into a plethora of competing criticisms. Thus, discourse analysis may serve as a tool of integration.

Second, in a systematic way, discourse analysis provides a framework for analyzing meaning relationships above the sentence level. Traditional Greek grammar has provided extensive means for discussing the relationships between words in a sentence. Yet much work is needed to formalize the way we speak of meaning relationships on the paragraph and discourse levels. Terms like *promise, sequence, progression, basis, restatement, question/answer,* and *verification* need to become as much a part of the vocabulary of New Testament studies as *reference, apposition,* and *sphere.* Also, many of the terms we use now on the sentence level can be co-opted for higher levels of a discourse.

Third, as with the enigmatic "two unchangeable facts" of Hebrews 6:18, some exegetical questions cannot be addressed by immediate context alone. Thus, they are "whole discourse" questions and demand a discourse analysis for a systematic treatment of the questions. As a master's student in seminary, I asked the question, "What is the function of Psalm 110:1 in the Book of Hebrews?" This verse from Psalms, the most-cited Old Testament passage in the New Testament, is quoted in Hebrews 1:13 and alluded to in

1:3, 8:1, 10:12, and 12:2. I had asked a question that could not be answered by an appeal to sentence-level syntax or even immediate context. I had asked a "whole discourse" question. My search for a viable means of answering the question led me step-by-step down a path to an eclectic version of discourse analysis. Discourse analysis gave me a broad enough framework to deal with dynamics in the discourse as varied as rhetorical features, uses of inclusions, cohesive dynamics, and transitions. Discourse analysis provides a means for dealing with meaning relationships outside of immediate literary contexts.

Fourth, discourse analysis provides a means for dealing with discourse structure, including the identification of boundaries between units in a discourse. Currently, little consensus exists concerning how to determine a proper outline for a book or section of a book of the New Testament—perhaps that is why the outlines vary so widely from scholar to scholar. Discourse analysis offers means of discussing unit boundaries and the functions of units on the discourse level. It moves the discussion from merely thematic and even literary grounds to broader considerations such as transitions, cohesion, semantic patterns, and logical relationships between paragraphs or sections.

Therefore, it may be suggested that discourse analysis has much to offer exegesis. We must work well with the words and sentences of the text, but we must be just as rigorous in our considerations of the paragraph and discourse as a whole. Where are the scholars who will move New Testament studies to a systematic consideration of grammar above the sentence level?

Bibliography

Beekman, John, John C. Callow, and Michael Kopesec. *The Semantic Structure of Written Communication*. Dallas: Summer Institute of Linguistics, 1981.

Black, David Alan, ed. *Linguistics and New Testament Interpretation: Essays on Discourse Analysis*. Nashville: Broadman & Holman, 1992.

———. *Linguistics for Students of New Testament Greek: A Survey of Basic Concepts and Applications*. Grand Rapids: Baker, 1995.

Brown, G., and G. Yule. *Discourse Analysis*. Cambridge: Cambridge University Press, 2d ed., 1983.

Callow, Kathleen. *Discourse Considerations in Translating the Word of God*. Grand Rapids: Zondervan, 1974.

Cotterell, Peter, and Max Turner. *Linguistics and Biblical Interpretation*. Downers Grove: InterVarsity, 1989.

de Beaugrande, R. and W. Dressler. *Introduction to Text Linguistics*. London: Longman, 1981.

Guthrie, George H. *The Structure of Hebrews: A Text-Linguistic Analysis*. Sup. to Novum Testamentum, 73. Leiden: E. J. Brill, 1994; Grand Rapids: Baker, 1998.

Halliday, M. A. K., and R. Hasan, *Cohesion in English*. London: Longman, 1976.

———. *Language, Context, and Text: Aspects of Language in a Social-Semiotic Perspective*. Oxford: Oxford University Press, 1989.

Levinsohn, Stephen H. *Discourse Features of New Testament Greek: A Coursebook.* Dallas: Summer Institute of Linguistics, 1992.

Longacre, Robert E. *The Grammar of Discourse: Notional and Surface Structures.* New York: Plenum, 1983.

Louw, Johannes P. *The Semantics of New Testament Greek.* Atlanta: Scholars Press, 1982.

———. "Discourse Analysis and the Greek New Testament." *The Bible Translator* 24 (January 1973):101–19.

Nida, E. A., J. P. Louw, A. H. Snyman, and J. V. W. Cronje. *Style and Discourse.* Cape Town: Bible Society of South Africa, 1983.

Porter, Stanley E., and D. A. Carson, eds. *Discourse Analysis and Other Topics in Biblical Greek.* JSNT Sup., 72. Sheffield: Sheffield Academic Press, 1995.

Reed, Jeffrey T. *A Discourse Analysis of Philippians: Method and Rhetoric in the Debate over Literary Integrity.* JSNT Sup., 136. Sheffield: Sheffield Academic Press, 1997.

———. "Discourse Analysis." In Stanley E. Porter, ed., *Handbook to Exegesis of the New Testament.* Leiden: E. J. Brill, 1997.

van Dyke, T. A. *Text and Context: Explorations in the Semantics and Pragmatics of Discourse.* London: Longman, 1977.

Notes

1. Laura Joffe Numeroff, *If You Give a Mouse a Cookie* (HarperCollins Publishers, 1985).

2. Johannes P. Louw, "Discourse Analysis and the Greek New Testament," *The Bible Translator* 24 (January 1973): 101.

3. Ibid.

4. Gillian Brown and George Yule, *Discourse Analysis* (Cambridge: Cambridge University Press, 1983), 4–5. Brown and Yule, for example, use the term "text" technically to refer to the verbal record of an act of communication (p. 6). David Nunan uses "text analysis" to refer to linguistic analysis of a written record of a communicative event and "discourse analysis" to refer to an interpretation of a text. See the discussion in David Nunan, *Introducing Discourse Analysis* (New York: Penguin Books, 1993), 5–7.

5. See the discussion in Nunan, *Introducing Discourse Analysis,* 5–6.

6. Stanley E. Porter, "Discourse Analysis and New Testament Studies: An Introductory Survey," in *Discourse Analysis and Other Topics in Biblical Greek,* ed. Stanley E. Porter and D. A. Carson (Sheffield: Sheffield Academic Press, 1995), 17. For an extensive and categorized bibliography on discourse analysis, see Walter Bodine, ed., *Discourse Analysis of Biblical Literature,* Society of Biblical Literature Semeia Studies (Atlanta: Scholars Press, 1995), 213–53.

7. E.g., Walter R. Bodine, ed., *Discourse Analysis of Biblical Literature,* (Philadelphia: Scholars Press, 1995); Robert D. Bergen, *Biblical Hebrew and Discourse Linguistics: What It Is and What It Offers* (Dallas: Summer Institute of Linguistics; Winona Lake: Eisenbrauns, 1994). Work has been done to introduce New Testament scholars to discourse analysis and linguistics generally, such as the work associated with the Summer Institute of Linguistics; see J. P. Louw, *The Semantics of New Testament Greek* (Scholars Press, 1982); Louw and others, *Style and Discourse: With Special Reference to the Text of the Greek New Testament* (Cape Town: Bible Society, 1983); David Alan Black's two volumes, *Linguistics for Students of New Testament Greek*

(Grand Rapids, Mich.: Baker, 1995) and the more technical *Linguistics and New Testament Interpretation: Essays on Discourse Analysis* (Nashville: Broadman Press, 1992), and the helpful introduction by Peter Cotterell and Max Turner, *Linguistics and Biblical Interpretation* (Downers Grove, Ill.: InterVarsity Press, 1989).

For helpful, article-length introductions to discourse analysis, see Jeffrey T. Reed, "Discourse Analysis," in *Handbook to Exegesis of the New Testament*, ed. Stanley E. Porter (Leiden: E. J. Brill, 1997), 189–217; and Porter, "Discourse Analysis and New Testament Studies: An Introductory Survey," 14–35.

8. See, for example, Jeffrey T. Reed, *A Discourse Analysis of Philippians: Method and Rhetoric in the Debate over Literary Integrity*, JSNT Sup., 136 (Sheffield: Sheffield Academic Press, 1997; George H. Guthrie, *The Structure of Hebrews: A Text-Linguistic Analysis*, Novum Testamentum Sup., 73 (Leiden: Brill, 1994; reprint: Grand Rapids, Mich.: Baker, 1998); David L. Allen, "The Discourse Structure of Philemon: A Study in Textlinguistics," in David Alan Black, ed., *Scribes and Scripture: New Testament Essays in Honor of J. Harold Greenlee* (Winona Lake, Ind.: Eisenbrauns, 1992), 77–96.

9. On the various schools of discourse analysis see Porter, "Discourse Analysis and New Testament Studies," 24–34.

10. Reed, "Discourse Analysis," 189–217.

11. Birger Olsson, "A Decade of Text-Linguistic Analyses of Biblical Texts at Uppsala," *Studia Theologica* 39 (1985): 107.

12. Allen, "The Discourse Structure of Philemon," 77.

13. Talmy Givón, "Preface," in *Syntax and Semantics. XII. Discourse and Syntax* (New York: Academic Press, 1979), xiii.

14. Linguists make a distinction between *context*, which refers to the historical, social, and cultural situation of the text, and the *co-text*, which refers to the surrounding words, sentences, and paragraphs in the text. I have chosen to continue to use the term *context* (as in "literary context") because such language is so widely used in biblical studies circles.

15. George H. Guthrie, "Cohesion Shifts and Stitches in Philippians," in Porter and Carson, *Discourse Analysis and Other Topics*, 44–46, 58.

16. Brown and Yule, *Discourse Analysis*, 1.

17. Guthrie, *The Structure of Hebrews*, 49–54.

18. Porter and Reed, "Greek Grammar Since BDF," 158.

19. For a process of exegesis that incorporates aspects of discourse analysis, see George H. Guthrie and J. Scott Duvall, *Biblical Greek Exegesis: A Graded Approach to Learning Intermediate and Advanced Greek* (Grand Rapids, Mich.: Zondervan, 1998), 99–165. This method focuses on the treatment of individual passages in a New Testament book but presupposes that some work has already been done on the discourse as a whole.

20. On the identification of unit boundaries within New Testament texts, see Guthrie, *The Structure of Hebrews*, 49–55.

21. *Inclusio* was used by ancient authors to mark the beginning and ending of a unit by using distant lexical parallels. For more on this phenomenon, see Guthrie, *The Structure of Hebrews*, 14–15, 76–89.

22. For example, see the ten distinct transition devices used in Hebrews in Guthrie, *The Structure of Hebrews*, 94–111.

23. In this narrative what might be called cohesion continuity is provided by Jesus being the main "actor" and the crowds being his main audience.

24. For a detailed explanation of how to do semantic diagramming, see George H. Guthrie and J. Scott Duvall, *Biblical Greek Exegesis: A Graded Approach to Learning*

Intermediate and Advanced Greek (Grand Rapids: Zondervan, 1998), 27–53.

25. William L. Lane, *Hebrews 1–8*, Word Biblical Commentary (Dallas: Word, 1991), 152.

26. Harold Attridge, *The Epistle to the Hebrews*, Hermeneia (Philadelphia: Fortress, 1989), 181–82; F. F. Bruce, *The Epistle to the Hebrews*, The New International Commentary on the New Testament (Grand Rapids: Eerdmans, 1990), 154; Donald Hagner, *Hebrews*, New International Biblical Commentary (Peabody, Mass.: Hendrickson, 1990), 98; P. E. Hughes, *A Commentary on the Epistle to the Hebrews* (Grand Rapids: Eerdmans, 1977), 233; Victor C. Pfitzner, *Hebrews*, Abingdon New Testament Commentaries (Nashville: Abingdon Press, 1997), 102.

27. F. Schröger, *Der Verfasser des Hebräerbriefes als Schriftausleger* (Regensburg: Pustet, 1968), 128–29.

28. Bertold Klappert, *Die Eschatologie des Hebräerbriefs* (Munich: Kaiser, 1969), 27–32.

29. For an explanation on the method of grammatical and semantic diagramming, see Guthrie and Duvall, *Biblical Greek Exegesis*, 27–53. The diagram here is presented in English because of this book's target audience. However, semantic diagrams are most beneficial if presented in Greek because word patterns and parallels can be identified.

30. Guthrie, *The Structure of Hebrews*, 37.

31. Ibid., 144.

32. Inverting order is a stylistic device used by the author of Hebrews at a number of places.

Chapter 13

The Diversity of Literary Genres in the New Testament

Craig L. Blomberg
Denver Seminary

Casual readers of Scripture often treat the Bible itself as if it were all a book of proverbs. They quote, interpret, and apply their favorite verses with little awareness of the contexts in which those texts appear. More serious readers often know enough to interpret a verse in light of the paragraph in which it appears and in view of the overall structure and themes of the particular book in which it is found. But even people who have been studying the Bible for years often do not realize that one cannot treat a passage in Joshua the same way one deals with one of the Psalms, a portion of Romans, or a section of the Book of Revelation. Each of these four biblical books represents a different literary "genre," and each has distinctive principles that must guide legitimate interpretation. A genre may be defined as "a group of texts that exhibit a coherent and recurring configuration of literary features involving form (including structure and style), content, and function."[1]

In the New Testament four primary genres appear: gospels, a book of "acts," epistles, and an apocalypse. As obvious an observation as this is, it is remarkable that until recently a majority of New Testament surveys and introductions, commentaries, and guides to hermeneutics said little about the distinctives of these four genres. But times are changing. In the last three decades a spate of specialized studies has appeared, spawning a new discipline often known as "genre criticism." This article can only survey some of the high points of recent research, but its goal is to demonstrate how crucial it is for correct interpretation and application to be able to answer the questions: What is a gospel? What is an "acts"? What is an epistle? What is an apocalypse? The reader who desires more detail at a foundational level should consult the introductory handbooks by Gordon D. Fee and Douglas Stuart (*How to Read the Bible for All Its Worth*),[2] Robert H. Stein (*Playing by the Rules: A Basic Guide to Interpreting the Bible*),[3] or Leland Ryken (*Words of Life: A Literary Introduction to the New Testament*),[4] works designed especially with the layperson in mind. The most thorough survey of technical research, but still readable for the average theological student, is David Aune's *The New Testament in Its Literary Environment*.[5]

What Is a Gospel?

At first glance most readers would probably call the Gospels biographies of Jesus. On closer inspection, they would discover that none of the four Gospels looks like the modern biographies with which they are familiar. For example, Mark and John say nothing about Jesus' birth, childhood, or young adult years. Luke 1–2 and Matthew 1–2 include selected incidents related to his birth and one episode about his teaching in the temple at age twelve, but otherwise they too are silent. On the other hand, all four Gospels devote a disproportionately large amount of their space to the last few weeks and days of Christ's life. Almost half of John's Gospel (chaps. 12–21) deals with the period of time beginning with "Palm Sunday" (five days before his crucifixion). The main events of Jesus' life that are recorded appear in different orders in the different Gospels. Many of the details vary too. Only John reveals that Jesus' ministry occupied a three-year period or longer, and all four Gospel writers are only rarely concerned to tell us how much time elapsed between any two events.

As a result, many modern scholars have abandoned the identification of the Gospels with the genre "biography." Many also have given up believing that the Gospels may be viewed as historically reliable, except in certain places. Instead they conclude that Matthew, Mark, Luke, and John wrote to express their theological understandings of the person and work of Christ and to record instructions relevant for the Christian communities to whom they wrote. The four evangelists had relatively few historical or biographical intentions in mind. Contradictions of many kinds, scholars would allege, appear on virtually every page of a Gospel synopsis. But one may look beyond the disagreement and discover key themes on which all the writers agree and which reflect the heart of early Christian faith.

If the Gospels are for the most part neither historical nor biographical, what then do contemporary critics believe them to be? Several proposals have competed with one another. A few have identified the Gospels with well-known genres of Greco-Roman fiction. Some have called the Gospels "aretalogies"—accounts of episodes from the life of a "divine man," usually embellishing and exaggerating the feats of some famous hero or warrior of the past.[6] Some have viewed them as "parables," highlighting the pervasiveness of metaphor and mystery.[7] Still others have applied to them language of the playwrights, associating the Gospels with "comedies" (stories with a triumphant ending) or "tragedies" (stories in which the protagonist is defeated, despite having shown signs of ability and knowledge to do better).[8] Focusing on Jewish backgrounds, evangelical scholar Robert Gundry generated considerable controversy in the 1980s by proposing that Matthew was a "midrash"—a complex mixture of fact and fiction that embellished Mark, much as various ancient Jewish works rewrote portions of the Old Testament.[9] But more differences than similarities appear between the Gospels and these various genres so that none of these identifications is widely held today. Most would probably term them unique literary creations that defy classification. W. G. Kümmel's summary represents the views that a majority might endorse:

> Viewed as a literary form, the Gospels are a new creation. They are in no way lives after the manner of Hellenistic biographies, since they lack the sense of internal and external history (as in lives of heroes), of character formation, of temporal sequence, and of the contemporary setting. Neither do the Gospels belong to the genre, memoirs, in which the collected stories and sayings from the lives of great men are simply strung together. Nor do they belong to the genus, miracle stories, in which the great deeds of ancient wonder-workers are glorified in a more or less stylized manner.[10]

Nevertheless, there is a sizeable and growing minority of scholars that believes the Gospels should be equated with a known historical or biographical genre from the Hellenistic world of the first century.[11] Luke 1:1–4 provides the most important clues to these generic identifications. In these verses Luke describes his work in language paralleled in other Greco-Roman historical and biographical texts. Loveday Alexander has demonstrated that the closest of these parallels occur in Greco-Roman "technical prose," which she broadly describes as "scientific" literature—treatises on such topics as medicine, philosophy, mathematics, engineering, and rhetoric.[12] Casting his net even more widely, Richard Burridge has examined numerous pre- and post-Christian *bioi* ("lives") of eminent individuals and found a substantial cluster of parallels between the Gospels and Hellenistic biography.[13]

What led modern interpreters away from a historical or biographical genre was that the Gospels did not seem to match up to *modern* conventions for these types of works. But when they are set side by side with various *ancient* sources, the Gospels compare quite favorably. Ancient historical standards of precision in narration and in selection and arrangement of material were much less rigid than modern ones. Few, if any, ancient works were written merely for the sake of preserving the facts; almost all were trying to put forward and defend certain ideologies or morals. But propaganda need not distort the facts, though it sometimes does. Of course, any genre may be modified, and there are uniquely Christian features in the Gospels. Robert Guelich offers a compromise proposal which seems judicious:

Formally, a gospel is a narrative account concerning the public life and teaching of a significant person that is composed of discreet [*sic*] traditional units placed in the context of Scriptures. . . . *Materially*, the genre consists of the message that God was at work in Jesus' life, death, and resurrection effecting his promises found in the Scriptures.[14]

The Gospels thus exhibit formal parallels to other historical and biographical writings, while materially they remain unique. But not even all of those who support a partial equation of the Gospels with known historical or biographical genres are equally confident of how much of their narratives may be viewed as trustworthy. C. H. Talbert, for example, is still fairly skeptical of the level of historical reliability; for him, calling the Gospels biographies means that they have a mythical structure, an origin in the legends of the "cult" or ritual of a religious community devoted to the traditions of its founder, and an optimistic, "world-affirming" perspective reacting against the many pessimistic philosophies of the day.[15] On the other hand, Martin Hengel associates the Gospels with those kinds of biographies that supplied a "relatively trustworthy historical report,"[16] while Terrence Callan finds significant parallels to Luke's preface in the histories of Herodotus, Tacitus, Arrian, Dio Cassius, Sallust, and Josephus, all of whom are generally viewed by modern historians as more reliable than not in what they record.[17]

Unique problems emerge when we turn to the Fourth Gospel. The numerous differences between John and the Synoptics have suggested to many that, however historical or biographical Matthew, Mark, and Luke may be, John must be viewed differently. Several studies have likened John to a drama, especially to a Greek tragedy,[18] while A. S. Harvey plausibly analyzes the Fourth Gospel as a Hebrew trial (*ribh*), as in sections of Old Testament prophecy in which God brings a "lawsuit" against his people.[19] Granted the differences between John and the Synoptics, John is still much more like the "gospel" genre they created than any other ancient compositional form, and its recurring themes of "witness" and "truth" demonstrate that its author thought he was presenting factual information, even if via different generic conventions than we might use today.[20]

Perhaps the best term to use to define *gospel* is, then, "theological biography."[21] One may not excuse the seeming discrepancies among the Gospels by denying a historical intention on the part of the four evangelists. Apparent contradictions must be evaluated. In fact, when this is done, plausible resolutions of all of them may be discerned. One cannot always prove what the best solution is in any given case, but there are no "contradictions" or "errors" that necessarily impugn the integrity of any of the Gospel writers or that threaten the trustworthiness of what they have written.[22] At the same time, none of the evangelists was a mere chronicler of information. Virtually every teaching and episode from Jesus' life that they have preserved was included for a theological reason—to teach us something about who Jesus was and how people should live. It is increasingly common to identify a third perspective besides the historical and theological approaches from which to view the Gospels, namely a literary perspective. This is dealt with in an earlier chapter in this volume. In the broader world of literary criticism, genre criticism usually forms one subdiscipline.

Implications for interpreters are numerous. As one is studying any individual passage in the Gospels, one must try to understand it in light of that author's overarching purposes and not immediately obscure them by comparing it with parallel information in other accounts. The reason the Gospels differ as they do is because the four Evangelists were each trying to emphasize different aspects of the life of Christ. Reading Matthew's account of the resurrection should make one aware of his concern to answer Jewish charges that the disciples had stolen Christ's body (27:62–66; 28:11–15). Reading Mark's account should highlight the initial fear and silence of the women who came to Jesus' tomb (16:8). Luke stresses that the resurrection was a fulfillment of all of the Jewish Scriptures (24:25, 44, 46–47). John emphasizes Jesus' encounter with Thomas to prove that Jesus was God himself (20:24–28). Each of these four emphases fits in closely with a dominant theme of the Gospel in which it appears. Each emphasis is also fairly distinctive to the Gospel in which it is found. All four themes are usually missed when one deals with a composite "harmony" of the various resurrection accounts. Yet such a harmony is also valuable in demonstrating that none of the four accounts contradicts another.[23]

Recognizing the Gospels as theological biographies also affects the way one relates a particular passage to its larger context. The individual events in the Gospels do not always appear in chronological order. Many times the four Evangelists write topically. Much of Mark 1–8 falls into just such an outline. Mark 1:21–45 presents a series of Jesus' healings. Mark 2:1–3:6 gives a series of controversies with the Jewish leaders. Mark 4:1–34 links together several of Jesus' parables. Mark 4:35–6:6 tells of several of Jesus' more dramatic miracles over the forces of nature (and concludes by contrast with his inability to work them in Nazareth because of widespread disbelief there).

When one sees where several of these passages appear in the other Gospels, it is clear that all of them cannot be in chronological order. So it is safe to assume that no chronology is implied unless it is explicitly present in the text (and unfortunately, English translations often use the word *then* when the Greek need only be translated as "and"). For example, one dare not assume that Luke 9:51–18:14 represents one consecutive series of Jesus' teachings as he traveled from Galilee to Jerusalem (even though it is often called the Perean ministry, as if this were the case). For one thing, that would mean that he had already arrived at Jerusalem's outskirts (Bethany) in 10:38–42 (cf. John 11:1, which tells where Mary and Martha lived) but was somehow back north again on the border between Samaria and Galilee in 17:11. Rather, this nine-chapter section of Luke's Gospel, almost exclusively devoted to Jesus' sayings, is a topically arranged collection of Jesus' teaching "under the shadow of the cross" (9:51). The significance of the order of Luke 11:1–4, 5–8, and 9–13 is therefore that they are all teachings about prayer, not necessarily that they were all spoken in the same place or in that order or one right after the other.[24]

It is amazing how often students of Scripture miss either the historical or theological elements in the Gospels, or, worse still, pit one against the other. Both are present, and they do not conflict. In fact, it is often precisely when one understands an Evangelist's theological rationale for a given version of an episode from Christ's life that apparent contradictions with parallel accounts evaporate.[25] For example, Luke's account reverses the order of the second and third of Christ's temptations by Satan. Matthew ends with Jesus' seeing all the kingdoms of the world (Matt. 4:8–10); Luke, with Jesus being tempted to throw himself off the temple (Luke 4:9–12). But Luke never says the "third" temptation happened *after* the "second." Most likely he has arranged the temptations in the order he has to end with the climax of Jesus at the temple in Jerusalem, because Luke is the Gospel writer most interested in Jesus' relationship with the temple and with Jerusalem. There is no contradiction, but the change in sequence is not arbitrary. Luke wants to highlight Jesus as the one whose ministry zeroed in increasingly more narrowly on the Jewish people and finally in on Jerusalem, as well as to underscore Jerusalem as the center from which Christian proclamation subsequently went out to all the world (Acts 1:8).[26]

What Is the Acts of the Apostles?

As the second volume in Luke's two-part work, Acts raises expectations of closely resembling the Gospels in genre. If the Gospels are best described as theological biographies, then Acts is best described as a theological history.[27] Instead of focusing on one main character, Jesus, as in a biography, Acts broadens its scope to present key episodes from the first generation of Christian history involving dozens of characters.[28] The title, Acts of the Apostles, is actually misleading, because most of the apostles disappear quickly from view after the opening chapters. Most of Luke's narrative focuses on Peter and Paul, with subordinate characters, such as the deacons Stephen and Philip, garnering the next greatest amount of attention. The "Acts of the Holy Spirit" might be a more descriptive title, since Luke sees the coming of the Spirit at Pentecost and his subsequent filling of believers as accounting for the expansion and growth of the fledgling Christian community.

As with the Gospels, most interpreters have tended to create false dichotomies between theology and history. Throughout the past century, two clearly discernible "camps" have competed with each other in interpreting Acts. One group of commentators, primarily British, has compared Acts favorably with the more reliable ancient Greek historians, such as

Herodotus and Thucydides, and has argued for a substantial measure of historicity. The trailblazer for this group was the British archaeologist Sir William Ramsay, whose turn-of-the-century excavations in Asia Minor converted him from skeptic to one who was extremely confident of Luke's historical intentions and success in carrying them out.[29] More recently, Colin Hemer has laid out in painstaking detail all the correspondences between Acts and other ancient historical information from the Greco-Roman world.[30] Building on Hemer's work, a wide-ranging, five-volume series on *The Book of Acts in Its First-Century Setting* provides massive additional support for the historicity of Acts.[31] Essays devoted exclusively to genre point out significant parallels between Acts and the "short historical monograph," "ancient intellectual biography," and "biblical [i.e., Old Testament] history," while also recognizing that, as in the Gospels, the end product of Acts is a unique mixture of genres.[32]

These various scholars, however, have not always emphasized as strongly the key theological motives and elements of Acts. A second group of commentators, primarily German, has therefore swung the pendulum in an opposite direction. Giving Luke very poor marks as a historian, they have concentrated instead on his theological concerns. Even then, they have often found him largely inferior to the Epistles of Paul, both in his presentation of Christianity in general and in the credibility of his portrayal of Paul in particular. Ernst Haenchen's massive commentary on Acts has proved foundational for this group,[33] and much liberal scholarship internationally has followed in his footsteps.

A third, primarily American group has also recently emerged. Elaborated at greatest length by Richard Pervo, this approach classifies Acts as a historical novel.[34] In other words, Luke had more in common with other Greco-Roman writers of fiction than he did with authors of history or biography. Pervo believes his approach is a helpful advance on the stalemate of the history versus theology debate. He underlines the elements of adventure and excitement in Luke's narrative style and points out numerous features which Acts shares with other ancient novels. But all of these features appear in genuine histories as well. When one reads Pervo's work closely, it becomes apparent that, despite his disclaimers to the contrary, his case ultimately depends on a series of implausibilities which he identifies in the narratives of Acts. As with the so-called contradictions in the Gospels, all of these matters have been plausibly explained by more conservative commentators, though Pervo ignores most of these explanations. A better solution to the theology/history debate is to affirm an element of both at the same time, rather than to look for a third alternative.[35]

When one turns to implications for interpretation, one discovers that Acts is much more concerned to narrate events in chronological order than is any of the Gospels. Still there are occasions when Luke reverts to a topical sequence. Josephus (*Ant.* xx,ii.5; xix,viii.2), for example, makes it plain that the famine which Luke records in Acts 11:27–30 occurred about two to three years after the death of Herod Agrippa (Acts 12:1–24). Luke has told the story of the famine earlier most likely because Agabus predicted it in Antioch, and in Acts 11:19–26, Luke has just been relating information about the development of Christianity in Antioch. So readers dare not assume that the events at the beginning of Acts 12 somehow depend on those at the end of chapter 11, since the latter in fact occurred at a later date.

Sensitivity to Luke's theological concerns without denying his trustworthiness as a historian also helps contemporary readers to recognize Luke's main emphases within any given passage. In light of modern debates about water baptism, baptism in the Spirit, and eternal security, readers of Acts 8 usually raise such questions as: Why didn't the Spirit come immediately when the Samaritans believed Philip's preaching? Was Simon Magus ever really saved, and if so, did he lose his salvation? Is it significant that Philip baptizes the Ethiopian eunuch as soon as the chariot in which they are riding passes a sufficiently large body of water? Although all of these are legitimate questions, probably none was in Luke's mind as he penned this chapter of Acts. Once one realizes that the outline for his book (Acts 1:8) is concerned with the expansion of Christianity into successively less and less Jewish circles, the two most striking features of Acts 8 become the reception of the gospel by Samaritans and by a eunuch, both considered highly unclean by orthodox Jews. The main applications of Acts 8 for Christian living today should therefore not center on the pros and cons of the charismatic movement or debate the issue of believer's versus infant baptism; rather, they should call all Christians today to determine who are the Samaritans and eunuchs in modern society. Whoever today's "untouchables" or "outcasts" are, these are the ones on whom significant Christian ministry should center.

What Is an Epistle?

An epistle is obviously a letter. For a long time scholars said little else, except to note that most of the New Testament Epistles followed typical Hellenistic convention by beginning with a greeting and statement of the author and persons being addressed, by continuing with an appropriate prayer or thanksgiving, by often containing a section of instruction or exhortation toward the end and by concluding with further greetings and a farewell formula. In just the last two decades, however, interest in analyzing the body of an epistle has increased dramatically. Today several good introductions to a whole host of subgenres of Hellenistic letters are available,[36] while a significant number of helpful classifications of specific New Testament Epistles enhance the interpreter's ability to understand the biblical writers' original intentions.

For most of the past century, the work of Adolf Deissmann dominated scholarship on the Epistles. Based on his study of Egyptian papyri, Deissmann subdivided the letter genre into "real" and "nonreal" letters. Real letters, like the papyri, were private, nonliterary, informal, and artless, addressing specific circumstances. Nonreal letters, like more classical Greek treatises, were public, deliberately literary, and designed to address a general audience without regard to occasion. For Deissmann, Paul's letters were real, private, nonliterary, and artless.[37] But these distinctions proved to be too cut-and-dried. Deissmann's dichotomy was based exclusively on materials from one Egyptian province and did not take into account the literary nature of either other papyri or Paul's letters. At the same time, general letters often tended "to avoid or even suppress typically epistolary forms and styles for other types of discourse."[38]

Recent genre criticism of the Epistles has tended to head in two somewhat different directions. Some scholars have tried to classify the Epistles functionally according to specific sub-genres of letter-writing. Others have analyzed the rhetoric of the Epistles, associating various New Testament letters with one or more of the major species of Greco-Roman rhetoric used in a variety of different kinds of speaking and writing, including letter-writing.

Two functional categories of epistle that are represented in the New Testament are the parenetic letter and the letter of recommendation. First Thessalonians is a good example of a parenetic or exhortational letter.[39] This kind of epistle is designed primarily to persuade or dissuade an audience concerning a specific action or attitude. Many readers of 1 Thessalonians have been surprised at how much praise Paul lavishes on this particular church throughout chapters 1 to 3, even though he has some pointed moral instruction to give them in 4:1–12 and crucial theology to correct in 4:13–5:11. When 1 Thessalonians is seen as a parenetic letter, Paul's strategy makes excellent sense. One of the key features of this kind of letter is that the author establishes his friendship with his audience and emphasizes how well they are doing and how little they really need any further instruction. But, in fact, they do need some additional encouragement to correct beliefs and lifestyle. So the author has tactfully prepared his readers for the exhortation with which the letter concludes.

The Pastoral Epistles, especially 1 and 2 Timothy, are additional examples of parenetic letters. Here Paul relies heavily on personal reminders of his past behavior to encourage Timothy to imitate his example. Inasmuch as the church at Ephesus where Timothy is ministering is troubled by false teachers, this exhortation becomes all the more crucial. More specifically, Benjamin Fiore identifies 1 Timothy and Titus as "mandate" letters closely parallel to documents sent from imperial officials to their subordinates instructing them in their responsibilities.[40] This increases the likelihood of these letters being authentically Pauline, given that their "strange combination of elements may be due, not to the clumsy inefficiency of someone trying to imitate [Paul's] other letters, but to the conventions of epistolary form that Paul himself used as freely as he did others in the amazing range of letters found in the Pauline collection."[41] Other New Testament letters do not correspond as closely to the formal style of a parenetic letter but do contain substantial portions of exhortation. First Peter is perhaps the best example of this kind of writing.[42]

Philemon provides an excellent illustration of a letter of recommendation (also called a letter of introduction or intercessory letter). This kind of letter was common among the papyri, designed to introduce the bearer of the letter to its recipient and then requesting a certain favor. Often the writer of the letter was a close friend or relative of the recipient and was promising to return the favor in some way.[43] Thus Paul is asking Philemon to welcome his runaway slave, Onesimus, back home without punishing him. Paul promises to pay any damages Philemon has incurred and reminds him of the debts he owes Paul. The entire Epistle is a masterpiece of tact and persuasion, as Paul steers a delicate course between pleading and demanding. Since it was a well-established genre of writing, Philemon could have been expected to recognize the kind of letter Paul sent and to comply with his requests. Third John appears to be a second canonical letter of recommendation—on behalf of the traveling Christian missionaries whom John encourages Gaius to welcome.[44]

More common among the genre criticism of the Epistles has been rhetorical analysis. The three major species of rhetoric which Greco-Roman writers identified were judicial (forensic, apologetic), deliberative (symbouleutic, hortatory), and epideictic (demonstrative, laudatory). Judicial rhetoric sought to convince an audience of the rightness or wrongness of a past action. Deliberative rhetoric tried to persuade or dissuade an assembly concerning the expediency of a future action. Epideictic rhetoric used praise and blame in order to urge a group of people to affirm a point of view or set of values in the present. A full-blown rhetorical speech would contain all the following features, though often one or more sections might be missing:

> *Exordium (proemium)*—stated the cause and gained the hearers' attention and sympathy.
> *Narratio*—related the background and facts of the case.
> *Propositio (divisio, partitio)*—stated what was agreed upon and what was contested.
> *Probatio (confirmatio)*—contained the proofs, based on the credibility of the speaker, appeals to the hearers' feelings, and/or logical argument.
> *Refutatio (confutatio)*—refuted opponents' arguments.
> *Peroratio (conclusio)*—summarized argument and sought to arouse hearers' emotions.[45]

These sections can also be subdivided into further rhetorical categories and/or arranged in varying sequences. A spate of recent commentaries and technical studies of the Epistles attempts to create similar outlines to make sense of each New Testament letter writer's narrative flow.[46]

The most well-known example of an application of rhetorical analysis to the New Testament Epistles appears in Hans-Dieter Betz's major commentary on Galatians.[47] Betz believes that Galatians is an apologetic letter using judicial rhetoric to defend Paul's past actions in preaching independently of the Jerusalem apostles and to summon his audience to side with him and against the Judaizers who were infiltrating Galatia. This analysis implies that Paul's primary thrust was not so much an exposition of the doctrine of justification by faith as a polemic against legalism, in which he attempted to justify himself. Several studies, reacting to Betz, have agreed that rhetorical analysis greatly helps one's understanding of Galatians but prefer to analyze it in terms of deliberative rhetoric.[48] The exhortational material in 5:1–6:10 fits in more with the purpose of a speaker who is trying to convince his audience to act a certain way in the future than with one who is simply defending himself. And even 1:12–2:14, the most autobiographical section of Galatians, is more a defense of the divine origin of Paul's gospel than of Paul's personal behavior or motives.[49]

Second Thessalonians affords a second probable example of deliberative rhetoric.[50] Here Paul wishes to dissuade his readers from believing that the day of the Lord had already come (2:2) or was so imminent that they could stop working (3:6–15). In fact, many of the New Testament letters have elements of deliberative rhetoric in them, because one of the primary purposes of the Epistle writers was to tell people how to act or how not to act in the Christian life.

Epideictic rhetoric has proved helpful in an analysis of Romans. Commentators have long recognized various uniquenesses in this Epistle. It reads more like a theological treatise than a personal letter. Yet chapters 1 and 16 frame the Epistle with numerous personal and informal remarks. Romans also divides abruptly into theological (1:16–11:36) and ethical material (12:1–15:13). Epideictic rhetoric provides a structure which incorporates all of these disparate sections into a coherent whole. The features of a personal letter at beginning and end establish Paul's credibility and relationship with the Romans. In between appear the *propositio* (1:16–17) and *confirmatio* (1:18–15:13),[51] which can in turn be subdivided into numerous additional rhetorical elements.[52]

Robert Jewett has narrowed down the genre of Romans even more specifically—it is an ambassadorial letter. Paul is paving the way for a hoped-for visit to Rome by commending his understanding of the gospel to the church there and by explaining the purposes of his travels. One application of this genre identification is that it makes the long list of greetings in chapter 16 an integral part of the letter rather than a hypothetical fragment of some other letter (such as Ephesians), as has often been proposed.[53] Stanley Stowers has also identified the rhetoric of Romans more specifically, pointing out that most of chapters 1–11 form a diatribe. A diatribe was a conversational method of instruction among ancient philosophers and religious teachers in which hypothetical objectives from opponents were regularly considered and answered. So when Paul frequently discusses how someone might reply to his presentation of the gospel (e.g., Rom. 2:1, 9; 4:1; 6:1, 15; 7:7), one must not assume that such objectors were actually present in the Roman church. Rather, Paul was anticipating the type of response he could imagine his letter eliciting and answering those charges before they ever arose.[54]

Epistolary and rhetorical genre criticism also support the case for the unity of several Epistles which have often been viewed as collections of independent fragments of letters. Duane Watson, for example, has shown that the outline of Philippians closely corresponds to that of a deliberative letter, although he has to bracket 2:19–30 as an epideictic digression.[55] More specifically, Loveday Alexander outlines Philippians as a "family letter" with 3:1–4:1 and 4:2–20 reflecting Paul's two major expansions of this form of letter to deal with the major danger and the major expression of gratitude that have generated this Epistle.[56]

Linda Belleville has suggested that 2 Corinthians 1–7 follows the paradigm for an apologetic self-commendatory letter, with the body opening in 1:8 and the transition to the request section in 6:1.[57] I have elsewhere proposed that these same seven chapters may also be seen as a chiasmus (inverted parallelism), the climactic center of which is Paul's discussion of his ministry of reconciliation in 5:1–11.[58] Of course, it is always possible that a later editor has imposed one of these structures on the various fragments of letters which he inherited. But the main reason Philippians and 2 Corinthians are usually seen as composite letters is because there seems to be no overarching outline to unite the different sections of the Epistles as they currently stand. Once this objection is removed, there is really no good reason to continue to see them as composite collections of fragments.

The two kinds of epistolary criticisms surveyed here remain in a certain tension with each other. Rhetorical analysis requires the assumption that epistles are to be treated more as written speeches than as pure letters. The primary literature for justifying such a transfer postdates the New Testament, while older writers largely distinguish the two.[59] It does seem that the categories have been applied so broadly in much recent literature that elements of two or all three of the major species of rhetoric are perceived in a given epistle and that these letters at times bear only a vague resemblance to the classical outlines they are said to follow. Still, it is worth noting some of the more persuasive proposals, even if we cannot necessarily demonstrate corresponding authorial intent.[60]

Genre criticism of Hebrews, James, Jude, and the Epistles of Peter and John prove somewhat more daunting. Several of these letters lack the conventional openings or closings and may not be ordinary epistles at all.

Hebrews, for example, refers to itself as "a word of encouragement (or exhortation)" (Heb. 13:22). The only other place this phrase occurs in the New Testament is in Acts 13:15 where it refers to a sermon. Hebrews is therefore best understood as a sermon or homily. It may well have been written to be preached before it was given an epistolary closing and used as a letter.[61] If this is the case, then it goes without saying that Hebrews should be taken seriously as a text to be preached today. Among other things, this means it is unlikely that the numerous warnings against apostasy throughout the letter (esp. 2:1–4; 3:7–4:11; 6:4–12; 10:19–39; 12:14–29) are merely hypothetical. The writer of Hebrews seriously believed that at least some in his congregation were in danger of abandoning their profession of Christian faith. Whether such people were ever truly believers is not an issue that genre criticism can solve, but it at least suggests that the debate is not academic!

Perhaps the most significant study of the genre of James is Peter Davids's analysis of the letter as a complex chiasmus. Three themes dominate the Epistle: trials and temptations, wisdom and speech, and wealth and poverty. James 1 introduces each of these themes twice (1:2–4, 5–8, 9–11; 1:12–18, 19–26, 27), while 2:1–26, 3:1–4:12 and 4:13–5:18 unpack them in greater detail in inverse order.[62] This kind of outline refutes two widely held notions about the letter. First, James is not simply a collection of teachings loosely strung together, like the Book of Proverbs. Second, James's main concern is not faith versus works, though that has been the primary preoccupation of commentators ever since Martin Luther. Important as it is, James's discussion of a faith which produces no works as being dead (2:18–26) is actually a subordinate point under the larger and more crucial topic of the right use of one's material resources (see 2:14–17 and 1–13).

First John neither begins nor ends like a letter. Of several proposals which have been made, perhaps David Aune's is the best: it is a "deliberative homily."[63] Like Hebrews, it resembles a sermon more than a letter. Like other forms of deliberative rhetoric, it is designed to persuade the Ephesian church, to which it was probably addressed, to side with John and embrace true Christian doctrine and practice over against the false teachers who had promoted heresy and ungodliness and begun to split the church (2:19).

Richard Bauckham has broken fresh ground with his detailed analysis of 2 Peter. Taking his cue from 1:14–15, Bauckham identifies 2 Peter as a testament.[64] This was a well-known Jewish and Greco-Roman form of address depicting the final instructions of an aged teacher or leader to his sons or followers shortly before his death. Numerous other details of 2 Peter match features prominent in such books as the *Testaments of the Twelve Patriarchs* (an important collection of intertestamental Jewish writings). Now most ancient testaments were pseudonymous. That is to say, they were not actually written by the revered individuals to whom they were ascribed. But no deceit was intended in this attribution of authorship, and no one was misled by the literary convention, any more than modern audiences object to or are misled by ghostwriters. In fact, in many instances such pseudonymity was an ascription of honor to a teacher to whom one owed credit for his ideas. Bauckham thus believes that the early church would have recognized and accepted 2 Peter as a testament written by one of Peter's disciples in the generation following his death (usually assumed to be in the late 60s) to contemporize Peter's message for the church of a later date (probably near the end of the first century).[65]

Pseudonymity has traditionally been a difficult concept for evangelicals to accept. This is largely because arguments for pseudonymity have usually depended on interpretations of certain passages in a given biblical book which placed them in opposition to portions of other biblical writings believed to be authentic.[66] Sometimes scholars have flatly declared that certain portions of Scriptures were forgeries.[67] But these approaches to pseudonymity, though still widespread, are increasingly giving way to hypotheses like those of Bauckham in which the integrity of the unknown writers is in no way impugned and in which the unity and consistency of Scripture may still be maintained. It is doubtful if Bauckham's hypothesis may be considered to be proved, but it is at least an option which evangelicals should consider seriously and not dismiss out-of-hand as by definition incompatible with a high view of Scripture.[68] If an ancient writer could have written the name *Peter* and expected his readers to realize that it was not the apostle Peter writing (as, for example, if he were already dead) but that the thoughts of the letter were those the writer could have imagined Peter speaking if he were alive, then such practice is morally no more objectionable than when a modern author uses a pen name or when a public figure writes an "autobiography" which was really composed by a professional assistant to whom he told his life story. But the jury is still out on whether such practice was deemed acceptable in the earliest years of Christianity. From the mid-second century onward it often was not, because of the proliferation of heretical literature under the guise of apostolic authorship.[69]

What Is the Book of Revelation?

The great reformer, John Calvin, admitted that he wasn't sure what to do with the Book of Revelation and therefore did not write a commentary on it, even though he had completed volumes on almost all of the rest of the New Testament. Readers throughout the ages have shared Calvin's perplexity, and not a few commentators on the book might have done better to follow in his footsteps. Still, genre criticism can help the careful student sift the more likely from the less likely interpretations in a maze of opinions that compete for attention.

Formally, Revelation shares features with three distinct genres—prophecy, apocalyptic, and epistle.[70] As a letter, to be circulated among seven churches in Asia Minor, John addressed the contemporary circumstances which his audience was experiencing. Chapters 2–3, which most specifically address these seven congregations, contain various enigmas which are deciphered when one studies the historical background of each individual city.[71] When, for example, John calls the Laodicean church to be either hot or cold and not lukewarm (Rev. 3:15–16), he is not encouraging them to take a clear stand either for or against Christ. Both hot and cold water are positive metaphors. Laodicea did not have its own water supply and so depended on water piped in either from the cold mountain streams near Colossae or from the natural hot springs at Hierapolis. Unfortunately, by the time it arrived at Laodicea, the water was often lukewarm and insipid. The church was resembling its water supply, and John was commanding them to become either therapeutically warm or refreshingly cool.

As prophecy, one can also expect Revelation to refer to actual events which will occur at some time in the future. Old Testament prophecies which were fulfilled in New Testament times sometimes unfolded as the literal occurrence of events previously predicted (e.g., Mic. 5:2; cf. Matt. 2:6). Frequently, however, the New Testament writers found merely a typological correspondence between ancient prophecy and contemporary events (e.g., Hos. 11:1; cf. Matt. 2:15)—that is to say, patterns of history were repeating themselves in ways too "coincidental" not to be attributed to the hand of God.[72] So to say that Revelation depicts certain events which had not yet happened at the time of its writing does not enable one to determine how literally they were being described. There is an approach of interpreting Scripture which requires that all texts be taken literally unless there is clear evidence of the use of figures of speech, but however helpful this approach may be for other literary genres, it is almost certainly more misleading than helpful when one approaches prophecy. What John records represents what he actually saw in his visions, but to what extent those visions can be compared to photographs of what will happen in the end times or to what extent God used well-known imagery and symbolism which John and his readers would have understood (much like the political cartoons of today that picture the U.S. as an eagle or Russia as a bear) cannot be determined apart from meticulous study and research.

The most significant genre for interpreting Revelation is apocalyptic. Apocalyptic works were common in both Jewish and Greco-Roman circles in antiquity. A somewhat technical but nicely comprehensive definition of an apocalypse is that of John J. Collins.

> "Apocalypse" is a genre of revelatory literature with a narrative framework, in which a revelation is mediated by an otherworldly being to a human recipient, disclosing a transcendent reality which is both temporal, insofar as it envisages eschatological salvation, and spatial insofar as it involves another, supernatural world.[73]

Other good examples of apocalypses from ancient Jewish and Christian writers include 4 Ezra, 2 Baruch, the Apocalypse of John the Theologian, and the Apocalypse of Peter. Apocalypses regularly used highly unusual, even bizarre or grotesque imagery to communicate truths about the last days. They tended to believe that the world would end with a cataclysmic intervention by God, who would bring justice and create a perfect society. They often encouraged a beleaguered religious community to persevere during times of persecution. All of these features recur in the Book of Revelation.

On the other hand, Leon Morris nicely summarizes seven key features of Revelation absent from typical apocalypses: (1) regular references to the book as prophecy; (2) typically prophetic warnings and calls for repentance; (3) lack of pseudonymity; (4) an optimistic world-view; (5) no retracing of past history in the guise of prophecy; (6) realized eschatology (the end times have begun with the first coming of Christ); (7) little interpretation by angels; and (8) belief that the Messiah has already come and made atonement.[74]

When people misinterpret Revelation, therefore, it is usually because they focus too exclusively on either the prophetic or the apocalyptic element. Many liberal commentators do not adequately take into account the prophetic element. Adela Collins, for example, writes that "a hermeneutic which takes historical criticism seriously [by which she means understanding Revelation as apocalyptic] can no longer work with an interventionist notion of God."[75] In other words, modern readers cannot seriously expect the world to end with God's supernatural intervention by means of the various plagues and tribulation which Revelation describes and certainly not by the universally visible and bodily return of Jesus Christ from heaven. Yet it is precisely this much which an understanding of Revelation as prophecy must affirm, however much different schools of interpretation disagree concerning other details. It is an antisupernatural bias, not a correct use of historical (or genre) criticism, which leads Collins to her conclusions. On the other hand, many conservative commentators, especially popular writers like Hal Lindsey, do not adequately take into account the apocalyptic element when they try to find detailed counterparts in current events to each of the different images in Revelation. Ironically, such interpretation often eliminates the supernatural element just as much as more liberal views do. For example, Lindsey's famous interpretation of the locusts in Revelation 9 as armed helicopters[76] misses the point that these are not human creations but demonic, otherworldly creatures, coming up from the Abyss (9:1–3, 11), described in terms designed to horrify ancient readers accustomed to the ravages of locust plagues but wholly ignorant of the methods of twentieth-century warfare.

Fortunately, more and more scholars of both conservative and liberal persuasions are coming to recognize Revelation as a mixture of prophecy and apocalyptic.[77] Several international colloquia on apocalyptic writings have begun to rectify the previous, widespread lack of interest in Revelation on the part of most scholars.[78] Works like those of Robert Mounce, Gregory Beale, and G. R. Beasley-Murray offer students a good spectrum of plausible evangelical commentary.[79]

Numerous details still remain puzzling, and there is room for tolerating a fair amount of disagreement. But for an interpretation of a given passage in Revelation to be relatively convincing, several criteria must be satisfied. (1) When John interprets a particular symbol, that interpretation must be preferred to any other speculations (e.g., the lampstands of 1:12 are the seven churches to whom John writes [v. 20]). (2) When key Old Testament texts, or for that matter other Jewish texts well-known in the first century, use imagery in a consistent way which John seems to imitate, those meanings should be carried over into Revelation (e.g., the "son of man" in 1:13 almost certainly harks back to Daniel 7:13). (3) When other historical information accessible to first-century Asian readers sheds light on particular details, it should be used (e.g., the five months of 9:5 was the average life cycle for a locust and, therefore, not necessarily a literal reference to the length of demonic persecution during the tribulation but merely a length appropriate for symbolism involving locusts). (4) When imagery seems merely to support the central truth of a passage, no specific, allegorical interpretation should be given to it (e.g., all the jewels adorning the walls of the new Jerusalem simply reinforce the picture of its magnificence and do not each stand for some particular attribute [21:19–21]).

Above all, any interpretation which could not have been deduced by John's original readers must be rejected out of hand.[80] When details seem cryptic, it is more likely the modern reader who is missing something which would have been clearer to Revelation's original recipients. To be sure, when the prophet-apocalypticist Daniel described his visions, there were elements even he did not understand. And the angel told him to seal up the words of his scroll until the end when all would become clear (12:4, 8–10). But Revelation deliberately reverses this strategy, with the angel's caution to John "not to seal up the words of the prophecy of this book, because the time is near" (Rev. 22:10). John wrote to encourage persecuted Christians to persevere because God would soon avenge their ill treatment, and he used a combination of well-established genres (however strange they may seem to people today) to inform them in language they were meant to understand about what would happen at the end of history.[81]

Conclusion

Understanding the genre of a particular New Testament book scarcely solves all the interpretive issues arising from it. But it does help readers avoid some basic errors which come from a lack of appreciation of literary form. At the level of individual portions of a book, it is widely realized that one cannot interpret a parable the same way as, say, a miracle, or prose in the same fashion as poetry. At last, more and more students of Scripture are recognizing that the same is true when comparing a Gospel with an Epistle or the Book of Acts with the Book of Revelation. Genre criticism is still in its adolescence as a discipline, and further refinements are surely to be expected. It also runs the risk of overemphasizing the similarities between Scripture and noncanonical writings, just as traditional Christianity has often overemphasized the differences. But the study of genre is here to stay, and it should be welcomed by all serious Bible readers even as they examine each individual hypothesis with a healthy measure of skepticism.

Bibliography

Alexander, Loveday. *The Preface to Luke's Gospel.* Cambridge: CUP, 1993.

Aune, David E. *The New Testament in Its Literary Environment.* Philadelphia: Westminster, 1987.

Burridge, Richard A. *What Are the Gospels?* Cambridge: CUP, 1992.

Collins, John J., ed. *The Encyclopedia of Apocalypticism,* 3 vols. New York: Continuum, 1998.

Malherbe, Abraham J. *Ancient Epistolary Theorists.* Atlanta: Scholars, 1998.

Ryken, Leland. *Words of Life: A Literary Introduction to the New Testament.* Grand Rapids: Zondervan, 1987.

Stirewalt, M. Luther, Jr. *Studies in Ancient Greek Epistolography.* Atlanta: Scholars, 1993.

Stowers, Stanley K. *Letter-Writing in Greco-Roman Antiquity.* Philadelphia: Westminster, 1986.

Stuart, Douglas, and Gordon D. Fee. *How to Read the Bible for All Its Worth.* Grand Rapids: Zondervan, 1994.

White, John L. *Light from Ancient Letters.* Philadelphia: Fortress, 1986.

Winter, Bruce W., and Andrew D. Clarke, eds. *The Book of Acts in Its Ancient Literary Setting.* Grand Rapids: Eerdmans, 1993.

Notes

1. David E. Aune, *The New Testament in Its Literary Environment* (Philadelphia: Westminster, 1987), 13. The term *genre* is used in a variety of ways in biblical and literary criticism. A balanced review and assessment of its various uses appears in Grant R. Osborne, "Genre Criticism—Sensus Literalis," *TrinJ* 4 (1983): 1–27. Tom Thatcher ("The Gospel Genre: What Are We After?" *RestQ* 36 [1994]: 129–38) argues for focusing more on features of composition, social context, and ideology.

2. Grand Rapids: Zondervan, 1994.

3. Grand Rapids: Baker, 1994.

4. Grand Rapids: Zondervan, 1987.

5. See n. 1. An important collection of samples of Greco-Roman literary genres most relevant for interpreting the New Testament appears in David E. Aune, ed., *Greco-Roman Literature and the New Testament* (Atlanta: Scholars, 1988).

6. E.g., Morton Smith, "Prolegomena to a Discussion of Aretalogies, Divine Men, the Gospels and Jesus," *JBL* (1971): 174–99.

7. Werner Kelber, *The Oral and the Written Gospel* (Philadelphia: Fortress, 1983), 131.

8. E.g., respectively, Dan O. Via Jr., *Kerygma and Comedy in the New Testament* (Philadelphia: Fortress, 1975); Gilbert Bilezikian, *The Liberated Gospel: A Comparison of the Gospel of Mark and Greek Tragedy* (Grand Rapids: Baker, 1977).

9. Robert H. Gundry, *Matthew: A Commentary on His Literary and Theological Art* (Grand Rapids: Eerdmans, 1982). Gundry revised his work and responded to his critics in idem, *Matthew: A Commentary on His Handbook for a Mixed Church Under Persecution* (Grand Rapids: Eerdmans, 1994).

10. Werner G. Kümmel, *Introduction to the New Testament* (Nashville: Abingdon, 1975), 37. So also Larry W. Hurtado, "Gospel (Genre)," in *Dictionary of Jesus and the Gospels*, ed. Joel B. Green, Scot McKnight, and I. Howard Marshall (Downers Grove: IVP, 1992), 276–82.

11. Joel B. Green (*The Gospel of Luke* [Grand Rapids: Eerdmans, 1997], 2) goes so far as to speak of a "broad consensus" that places at least Luke-Acts "squarely within the literary tradition of ancient historiography." My survey of the literature does not yet disclose such a consensus for either Luke or Acts (and it is almost certainly not present for Mark and Matthew), but Green's comment definitely reflects the direction recent trends have been heading.

12. Loveday Alexander, *The Preface to Luke's Gospel* (Cambridge: CUP, 1993), 21.

13. Richard A. Burridge, *What Are the Gospels?* (Cambridge: CUP, 1992). For some of the limitations of Burridge's study, see Adela Y. Collins, "Genre and the Gospels," *JR* 75 (1995): 239–46.

14. Robert A. Guelich, "The Gospel Genre," in *Das Evangelium und die Evangelien*, ed. Peter Stuhlmacher (Grand Rapids: Eerdmans, 1991), 206.

15. C. H. Talbert, *What Is a Gospel?* (Philadelphia: Fortress, 1977). Philip L. Shuler (*A Genre for the Gospels: The Biographical Character of Matthew* [Philadelphia: Fortress, 1982]) classifies Matthew as encomium or laudatory biography but is not overly optimistic about the amount of accurate history it contains. John Fitzgerald ("The Ancient Lives of Aristotle and the Modern Debate about the Genre of the Gospels," *RestQ* 36 [1994]: 209–21) finds significant parallels between the Gospels and the lives of Aristotle in both historical and nonhistorical elements.

16. Martin Hengel, *Acts and the History of Earliest Christianity* (London: SCM, 1979), 16. Cf. Aune, *New Testament*, 64–65.

17. Terrence Callan, "The Preface of Luke-Acts and Historiography," *NTS* 31 (1985): 576–81.

18. E.g., Neal Flanagan, "The Gospel of John as Drama," *BibTod* 19 (1981): 264–70; W. R. Domeris, "The Johannine Drama," *JTSA* 21 (1983): 29–35.

19. A. E. Harvey, *Jesus on Trial: A Study in the Fourth Gospel* (Atlanta: Knox, 1977).

20. Cf. further Craig L. Blomberg, "To What Extent Is John Historically Reliable?" in *Perspectives on John: Method and Interpretation in the Fourth Gospel*, ed. Robert B. Sloan and Mikeal C. Parsons (Lewiston: Mellen, 1993), esp. 48–53.

21. Cf. I. Howard Marshall, "Luke and His Gospel," in *Das Evangelium und die Evangelien*, 289–308.

22. I have defended this claim at length in my book, *The Historical Reliability of the Gospels* (Leicester: IVP, 1987), which is heavily indebted to the six-volume series, *Gospel Perspectives*, ed. R. T. France, David Wenham, and Craig Blomberg (Sheffield: JSOT, 1980–86).

23. For all of the examples in this and the next paragraph and for a brief introduction to the theological distinctives and narrative structures of each Gospel, see my *Jesus*

and the Gospels: An Introduction and Survey (Nashville: Broadman and Holman, 1997, ad loc).

24. Cf. esp. my "Midrash, Chiasmus, and the Outline of Luke's Central Section," in *Gospel Perspectives*, vol. 3, 217–61.

25. Cf. esp. my "The Legitimacy and Limits of Harmonization," in *Hermeneutics, Authority, and Canon*, ed. D. A. Carson and John D. Woodbridge (Grand Rapids: Baker, 1995, repr.), 139–74.

26. Cf. esp. Kenneth R. Wolfe, "The Chiastic Structure of Luke-Acts and Some Implications for Worship," *SWJT* 22 (1980): 60–71.

27. Robert Maddox, *The Purpose of Luke-Acts* (Edinburgh: T & T Clark, 1982), 16. Cf. W. C. van Unnik, "Luke's Second Book and the Rules of Hellenistic Historiography" in *Les Actes des Apôtres: Traditions, rédaction, théologie*, ed. Jacob Kremer (Gembloux: Duculot, 1979), 37–60.

28. Because of the obvious unity of Luke-Acts, attempts have been made to label both volumes as biography or both as history. But the Gospel of Luke is clearly about Jesus, whereas the Acts of the Apostles depicts the ministries of numerous early Christian characters in the broader context of the expansion of the church in the Roman Empire.

29. William Ramsay, *St. Paul the Traveller and a Roman Citizen* (London: Hodder and Stoughton, 1895).

30. Colin J. Hemer, *The Book of Acts in the Setting of Hellenistic History* (Tübingen: Mohr, 1989).

31. Ed. Bruce W. Winter (Grand Rapids: Eerdmans, 1993–96).

32. See respectively, Darryl W. Palmer, "Acts and the Ancient Historical Monograph," in *The Book of Acts in Its Ancient Literary Setting*, ed. Bruce W. Winter and Andrew D. Clarke (Grand Rapids: Eerdmans, 1993), 1–29; L. C. A. Alexander, "Acts and Ancient Intellectual Biography," in ibid., 31–63; Brian S. Rosner, "Acts and Biblical History," in ibid., 65–82; and I. Howard Marshall, "Acts and the Former Treatise," in ibid., 163–82. Kota Yamada ("A Rhetorical History: The Literary Genre of the Acts of the Apostles," in *Rhetoric, Scripture and Theology*, ed. Stanley E. Porter and Thomas H. Olbricht [Sheffield: SAP, 1996]: 230–50) argues that Acts reflects "rhetorical" as opposed to "political" history.

33. Ernst Haenchen, *The Acts of the Apostles* (Oxford: Blackwell, 1971). Cf. also Eberhard Plümacher, *Lukas als hellenistischer Schriftsteller* (Göttingen: Vandenhoeck und Ruprecht, 1972).

34. Richard I. Pervo, *Profit with Delight: The Literary Genre of the Acts of the Apostles* (Philadelphia: Fortress, 1987).

35. For further critique of Pervo's position, particularly in light of Acts' abrupt ending that lacks key information about the ends of the lives of Peter and Paul, information that one would expect in a novel, see William F. Brosend II, "The Means of Absent Ends," in *History, Literature, and Society in the Book of the Acts*, ed. Ben Witherington III (Cambridge: CUP, 1996), 348–62. For another historical-theological analysis and a detailed comparison of Luke-Acts with pre-Christian, Hellenistic-Jewish "apologetic historiography," see Gregory E. Stirling, *Historiography and Self-Definition: Josephos, Luke-Acts and Apologetic Historiography* (Leiden: Brill, 1992). Stirling finds telling parallels in the common commitments of the works he surveys to commending the history of a religion or people to the broader Greek world.

36. John L. White, *Light from Ancient Letters* (Philadelphia: Fortress, 1986); Stanley K. Stowers, *Letter-Writing in Greco-Roman Antiquity* (Philadelphia: Westminster, 1986); Abraham J. Malherbe, *Ancient Epistolary Theorists* (Atlanta: Scholars, 1988); M. Luther Stirewalt Jr., *Studies in Ancient Greek Epistolography* (Atlanta: Scholars, 1993).

292   CRAIG L. BLOMBERG

37. Adolf Deissmann, *Light from the Ancient East* (London: Harper & Bros., 1922), 146–251.

38. Aune, *New Testament*, 218. Cf. Stowers, *Letter-Writing*, 18–19.

39. See esp. Abraham J. Malherbe, *Paul and the Thessalonians: The Philosophic Tradition of Pastoral Care* (Philadelphia: Fortress, 1987), 68–78; Steve Walton, "What Has Aristotle to Do with Paul? Rhetorical Criticism and 1 Thessalonians," *TynB* 46 (1995): 229–50. More specifically, Abraham Smith (*Comfort One Another: Reconstructing the Rhetoric and Audience of 1 Thessalonians* [Louisville: Westminster John Knox, 1995]) analyzes 1 Thessalonians as a "letter of consolation" with three main sections and objectives: laudation (1:6–2:16), positive examples (2:17–3:13), and precepts of consolation (4:1–5:22) (pp. 75–76). Juan Chapa ("Is First Thessalonians a Letter of Consolation?" *NTS* [1994]: 150–60) does not think the entire letter sufficiently parallels the structure and contents of a letter of consolation but agrees that it contains elements of this subgenre within its broader parenetic framework.

40. Benjamin Fiore, *The Function of Personal Example in the Socratic and Pastoral Epistles* (Rome: BIP, 1986) 79–84. Cf. Stowers, *Letter-Writing*, 97.

41. Luke T. Johnson, *Letters to Paul's Delegates: 1 Timothy, 2 Timothy, Titus* (Valley Forge: TPI, 1996), 107–08.

42. Aune, *New Testament*, 121–22.

43. Ibid., 211–12; Stowers, *Letter-Writing*, 155.

44. Ibid., 156. Cf. Duane F. Watson, "A Rhetorical Analysis of 3 John: A Study in Epistolary Rhetoric," *CBQ* 51 (1989): 479–501.

45. George A. Kennedy, *New Testament Interpretation Through Rhetorical Criticism* (Chapel Hill, N.C: University of North Carolina Press, 1984), 24.

46. Particularly significant is the series of "socio-rhetorical commentaries" by Ben Witherington III on 1 and 2 Corinthians (*Conflict and Community in Corinth* [Grand Rapids: Eerdmans, 1995]); Galatians (*Grace in Galatia* [Grand Rapids: Eerdmans, 1998]); and also on *The Acts of the Apostles* (Grand Rapids: Eerdmans, 1998).

47. Hans-Dieter Betz, *Galatians* (Philadelphia: Fortress, 1979). Most recently see also Troy Martin, "Apostasy to Paganism: The Rhetorical Stasis of the Galatian Controversy," *JBL* 114 (1995): 437–61.

48. Esp. Robert G. Hall, "The Rhetorical Outline for Galatians: A Reconsideration," *JBL* 106 (1987): 277–87; Joop Smit, "The Letter of Paul to the Galatians: A Deliberative Speech," *NTS* 35 (1989): 1–26.

49. Robert G. Hall ("Arguing like an Apocalypse: Galatians and an Ancient *Topos* Outside the Greco-Roman Rhetorical Tradition," *NTS* 42 [1996]: 434–53) elaborates on the juridical elements as owing to the Jewish apocalyptic influences on the letter, reminding us that we cannot explain New Testament epistolary rhetoric solely in Hellenistic categories.

50. Robert Jewett, *The Thessalonian Correspondence: Pauline Rhetoric and Millenarian Piety* (Philadelphia: Fortress, 1986), 63–87; G. S. Holland, *The Tradition That You Received from Us: 2 Thessalonians in the Pauline Tradition* (Tübingen: Mohr, 1988), 6.

51. Wilhelm Wuellner, "Paul's Rhetoric of Argumentation in Romans: An Alternative to the Donfried-Karris Debate over Romans," in *The Romans Debate*, ed. Karl P. Donfried (Minneapolis: Augsburg, 1977), 168. Cf. Kennedy, *Rhetorical Criticism*, 152–56. Challenging this emerging consensus, Anthony J. Guerra (*Romans and the Apologetic Tradition* [Cambridge: CUP, 1995]) argues for a "protreptic" genre and apologetic purpose that combines elements of all three species of rhetoric and seeks to commend Paul's ministry and gospel.

52. The most detailed *tour de force* in this respect is David Hellholm, "Amplificatio in the Macro-Structure of Romans," in *Rhetoric and the New Testament*, ed. Stanley E. Porter and Thomas H. Olbricht (Sheffield: JSOT, 1993), 123–51.

53. Robert Jewett, "Romans as an Ambassadorial Letter," *Int* 36 (1982): 5–20.

54. Stanley K. Stowers, *The Diatribe and Paul's Letter to the Romans* (Chico: Scholars, 1981).

55. Duane F. Watson, "A Rhetorical Analysis of Philippians and Its Implications for the Unity Question," *NovT* 30 (1988): 57–58. In "The Integration of Epistolary and Rhetorical Analysis of Philippians," in *The Rhetorical Analysis of Scripture*, ed. Stanley E. Porter and Thomas H. Olbricht (Sheffield: SAP, 1996), 398–426, Watson shows how these two kinds of genre criticism can be seen as converging on the same outline.

56. Loveday Alexander, "Hellenistic Letter Forms and the Structure of Philippians," *JSNT* 37 (1989): 87–101. This is endorsed by Gordon D. Fee (*Paul's Letter to the Philippians* [Grand Rapids: Eerdmans, 1995], 3–4) as part of his larger discussion of Philippians as a "hortatory letter of friendship" (pp. 2–14).

57. Linda L. Belleville, "A Letter of Apologetic Self-Commendation: 2 Cor. 1:8–7:16," *NovT* 31 (1989): 142–63.

58. Craig L. Blomberg, "The Structure of 2 Corinthians 1–7," *Criswell Theological Review* 4 (1989): 3–20. I am grateful to A. Boyd Luter and Michelle V. Lee ("Philippians as Chiasmus: Key to the Structure, Unity and Theme Questions," *NTS* 41 [1995]: 89–101) for their affirmation of my criteria for identifying chiasmus, though I am not as convinced as they are that their chiastic outline of Philippians satisfies these criteria. Stanley E. Porter and Jeffrey T. Reed ("Philippians as a Macro-Chiasm and Its Exegetical Significance," *NTS* 44 [1998]: 213–31) demonstrate the numerous problems with Luter's and Lee's outline but misrepresent and make false inferences from some of my criteria.

59. See Stanley E. Porter, "The Theoretical Justification for Application of Rhetorical Categories to Pauline Epistolary Literature," in *Rhetoric and the New Testament*, 100–22. Cf. also the articles by Classen and Reed in the same volume, as well as J. A. D. Weima, "What Does Aristotle Have to Do with Paul? An Evaluation of Rhetorical Criticism," *CTJ* 32 (1997): 458–68.

60. A reasonable compromise has been articulated by Janet Fairweather ("The Epistle to the Galatians and Classical Rhetoric," *TynB* 45 [1994]: 1–38, 213–43), who finds it telling that John Chrysostom already recognized numerous elements of classical rhetoric in Galatians, even though she doubts if Paul ever formally studied Greco-Roman rhetoric. Rather, the influences were more informal and less conscious. Somewhat similar but even more cautious are the conclusions of R. Dean Anderson Jr., *Ancient Rhetorical Theory and Paul* (Kampen: Kok, 1996).

61. William L. Lane, "Hebrews: A Sermon in Search of a Setting," *SWJT* 28 (1985): 13–18. Andrew H. Trotter Jr. (*Interpreting the Epistle to the Hebrews* [Grand Rapids: Baker, 1997], 159–80) analyzes the genre of Hebrews and concludes that it is "a complex literary form, basically a sermon but clearly reconstructed as an epistle" (p. 79).

62. My slight modification of Peter H. Davids, *The Epistle of James* (Grand Rapids: Eerdmans, 1982), who built on Fred O. Francis, "The Form and Function of the Opening and Closing Paragraphs of James and 1 John," *ZNW* 61 (1970): 118–21. Lauri Thurén ("Risky Rhetoric in James," *NovT* 37 [1995]: 262–84) shows how this overall structure could also fit the major sections of a speech with deliberative rhetoric.

63. Aune, *New Testament*, 218. Duane F. Watson ("Amplification Techniques in 1 John: The Interaction of Rhetorical Style and Invention," *JSNT* 51 [1993]: 99–123) analyzes the numerous devices of repetition and elaboration that seem to make this

Epistle, more so than all others in the New Testament, defy standard linear outlines, and he prefers to label the rhetoric as epideictic.

64. Richard J. Bauckham, *Jude, 2 Peter* (Waco: Word, 1983), 131–63. Duane F. Watson (*Invention, Arrangement and Style: Rhetorical Criticism of Jude and 2 Peter* [Atlanta: Scholars, 1988]) finds 2 Peter a combination of testamentary genre and deliberative rhetoric.

65. Cf. also Richard J. Bauckham, "Pseudo-Apostolic Letters," *JBL* 107 (1988): 469–94. A similar approach to 2 Timothy has been taken by Seán C. Martin, *Pauli Testamentum: 2 Timothy and the Last Words of Moses* (Rome: Gregorian University Press, 1997).

66. E.g., Mark Kiley, *Colossians as Pseudepigraphy* (Sheffield: JSOT, 1986). But see George E. Cannon (*The Use of Traditional Materials in Colossians* [Macon: Mercer, 1983], 136–66), who uses genre criticism to compare the rhetorical structure of Colossians with the undisputed Pauline letters, discovering parallels that would not easily be imitated by a different writer.

67. E.g., Lewis R. Donelson, *Pseudepigraphy and Ethical Argument in the Pastoral Epistles* (Tübingen: Mohr, 1986), who even argues that this trait characterized an entire pseudepigraphic genre.

68. The most detailed evangelical treatment of pseudepigraphy is David G. Meade, *Pseudonymity and Canon* (Grand Rapids: Eerdmans, 1987), who believes that before the mid-second century it was generally acceptable. More briefly, and arguing the contrary position, is Donald Guthrie, *New Testament Introduction* (Downers Grove: IVP, 1990), 1011–28. Cf. further the chapter in this volume by Terry Wilder.

69. For the genre criticism of New Testament Epistles not specifically mentioned in this chapter, see Linda L. Belleville, "Continuity or Discontinuity: A Fresh Look at 1 Corinthians in the Light of First-Century Epistolary Forms and Conventions," *EQ* 59 (1987): 15–37; Holland Hendrix, "On the Form and Ethos of Ephesians," *USQR* 42 (1988): 3–15; Duane F. Watson, "A Rhetorical Analysis of 2 John According to Greco-Roman Convention," *NTS* 35 (1989): 104–30; and Bauckham, *Jude, 2 Peter*, 3–6.

70. An excellent discussion of each of these categories as they apply to Revelation appears in David E. Aune, *Revelation 1–5* (Dallas: Word, 1997), lxx–xc. For a survey of recent literature, see Dave Mathewson, "Revelation in Recent Genre Criticism," *TrinJ* 13 (1992): 193–213.

71. See esp. Colin J. Hemer, *The Letters to the Seven Churches of Asia in Their Local Setting* (Sheffield: JSOT, 1986).

72. See esp. R. T. France, *The Gospel According to Matthew* (Grand Rapids: Eerdmans, 1985), 40.

73. John J. Collins, "Introduction: Morphology of a Genre," *Semeia* 14 (1979): 9.

74. Leon Morris, *The Book of Revelation* (Grand Rapids: Eerdmans, 1987), 25–27.

75. Adela Y. Collins, "Reading the Book of Revelation in the Twentieth Century," *Int* 40 (1986): 242.

76. Hal Lindsey, *There's a New World Coming* (Santa Ana: Vision House, 1973), 124.

77. The pioneering study was George E. Ladd, "Why Not Prophetic-Apocalyptic?" *JBL* 76 (1957): 192–200. Cf. Elisabeth S. Fiorenza, *The Book of Revelation: Justice and Judgment* (Philadelphia: Fortress, 1985), 133–56; J. Ramsey Michaels, *Interpreting the Book of Revelation* (Grand Rapids: Baker, 1992), 21–33.

78. Results are published in *Semeia* 14 (1979); 36 (1986); David Hellholm, ed., *Apocalypticism in the Mediterranean World and the Near East* (Tübingen: Mohr, 1983);

and John J. Collins, ed., *The Encyclopedia of Apocalypticism*, 3 vols. (New York: Continuum, 1998).

79. Robert H. Mounce, *The Book of Revelation* (Grand Rapids: Eerdmans, 1997); Gregory K. Beale, *The Book of Revelation* (Grand Rapids: Eerdmans, 1998); G. R. Beasley-Murray, *The Book of Revelation* (London: Oliphants, 1974).

80. Fee and Stuart, *How to Read the Bible*, 235.

81. For excellent, recent, evangelical summaries of the message and application of Revelation, see Donald Guthrie, *The Relevance of John's Apocalypse* (Grand Rapids: Eerdmans 1987); Graeme Goldsworthy, *The Gospel in Revelation* (Exeter: Paternoster, 1984); and Richard Bauckham, *The Theology in the Book of Revelation* (Cambridge: CUP, 1993).

Chapter 14

Pseudonymity and the New Testament

Terry L. Wilder
Midwestern Baptist Theological Seminary

In nineteenth-century America Samuel L. Clemens wrote popular novels like *Huckleberry Finn* and *The Adventures of Tom Sawyer*, though few of his readers were familiar with his real name. Rather, they associated such works with his pseudonym: Mark Twain. Clemens's use of the pseudonym was acceptable for two reasons. First, there had been no historical figure named "Mark Twain" with whom the public might have confused the actual author of these books. Second, Clemens did not use his pseudonym in an effort to secure recognition or authority for his work, as might the author of a work who had used the pseudonym of a historical figure. On the contrary, Clemens used an unremarkable literary convention of the day.

Many contemporary scholars believe that pseudonymous letters exist in the New Testament. Others, including me,[1] do not accept pseudonymity in the New Testament for historical, theological, ethical, and psychological reasons. Indeed, whether the practice of pseudonymity was ever embraced as a literary convention by the early church has been the topic of much debate.

What is pseudonymity? A text is pseudonymous when it is "not by the person whose name it bears in the sense that it was written after his death by another person or during his life by another person who was not in some way commissioned to do so."[2] On the basis of this definition, a Pauline letter written by means of an amanuensis, or one written by a colleague for the apostle's later approval would be authentic. A letter of this latter variety might even feature some indication of Pauline endorsement, such as a signature. For example, if Colossians was written by Timothy on behalf of

Paul, then Colossians 4:18 would be a sign of such approval. On the other hand, a letter written subsequent to Paul's death but incorporating Pauline material would be regarded as pseudonymous, unless the author was attempting to fulfill a Pauline request to prepare existing material for subsequent distribution.[3]

Strictly speaking, those New Testament works most often classified as pseudonymous by critical scholars are certain Pauline and Petrine letters and those of James and Jude[4]—namely, Ephesians, Colossians, 2 Thessalonians, the Pastoral Epistles, 1 and 2 Peter, James, and Jude. One might also note that several pseudoapostolic works exist outside of the New Testament canon—for example, *3 Corinthians*, the *Epistle to the Laodiceans*, and the *Gospel of Peter*.

When discussing pseudonymity, one should also consider anonymity. Several anonymous works exist within the New Testament. For example, the Gospels, Acts, and Hebrews do not make definite claims to authorship. That is to say, the authors of these works did not specifically identify themselves, though they may have been well-known to their recipients.

To understand further the topic of pseudonymity and the New Testament, this essay will (1) explore historical developments concerning the subject, (2) survey past and present scholarship on the problem, (3) propose some factors for understanding the issue, and (4) examine briefly the authorship of the Pastoral Epistles with a view to scrutinizing the proposal that these letters are pseudonymous.

Historical Developments in the Study of Pseudonymity

When studying the topic of pseudonymity, a helpful approach is first to examine the phenomenon's literary history in Greek, Jewish, and Christian circles. This study is necessary because many scholars feel that the authors of the disputed New Testament letters, if pseudonymous, had followed an analogous precedent. Second, the attitudes of persons in Greek, Jewish, and Christian antiquity toward pseudonymity need to be considered because scholars generally agree that the problem must be settled in accordance with the literary standards and judgments of the ancient world and not those of the modern day. One may find that people in antiquity were not as open or closed minded to the practice of pseudonymity as is sometimes thought. And third, a historical survey of biblical scholarship on this subject will be offered in order that it may be seen how ideas from the past have helped to shape modern opinion.

PSEUDONYMITY IN GRECO-ROMAN WRITINGS

From Greco-Roman sources, the pseudonymous didactic letters of the philosophical schools (for example, the Pythagorean, Cynic, and neo-Platonic writings) are often cited as analogous to alleged pseudonymous letters in the New Testament. Some of these Epistles do share some affinity with the New Testament works in question—for example, in their form and use of paraenesis.[5] Moreover, while the disputed New Testament letters are presented as having been written by an authoritative apostle to instruct, encourage, and admonish Christian believers in the churches, many of the epistles from the schools purport to be from philosophers who instruct and exhort their recipients to live the philosophic life.[6] However, the same similarities noted here may also be found in a comparison between authentic Greco-Roman epistles and the disputed New Testament letters mentioned earlier.

While some of the pseudepigraphal epistles from the philosophical schools share some affinity with the disputed New Testament letters, in several ways the latter writings differ from the former. For example, some of the Greco-Roman pseudepigraphal epistles were composed as literary exercises out of respect for philosophical masters, or for students to sharpen their letter-writing skills. Still others were written solely as propaganda. The disputed Pauline letters, however, were written neither for literary purposes nor for propaganda. Rather, they were written as actual correspondences addressing specific situations in the churches. Furthermore—and this fact should be stressed—while documentation exists for the presence of Greco-Roman schools in antiquity, evidence is lacking for the existence of, say, a Pauline school after the death of that apostle.

GRECO-ROMAN ATTITUDES CONCERNING PSEUDONYMITY

Many justify the presence of pseudonymity in the New Testament with an appeal to the acceptance of the practice in the Greco-Roman schools, namely, in the context of a master-disciple relationship. Good external evidence exists which indicates that some pseudonymity was accepted in such settings. For example, Iamblichus described the Pythagoreans and their writings in the following manner:

> It was a fine custom of theirs also to ascribe and assign everything to Pythagoras, and only very seldom to claim personal fame for their discoveries, for there are very few of them indeed to whom works are ascribed personally.[7]

> If it be agreed that some writings now circulated are by Pythagoras, but others were composed on the basis of his lectures, and on this account the authors did not give their own names, but attributed them to Pythagoras as his work.[8]

At least three things may be concluded from Iamblichus's remarks. First, pseudonymous works written in the name of Pythagoras were fairly widespread, accepted, and praiseworthy. Indeed, it was a "fine custom of theirs to ascribe and assign everything to Pythagoras." Second, to ascribe one's work to Pythagoras seems to have been motivated by humility. Iamblichus indicates that these pseudonymous authors desired no personal renown for their writings. Third, the Pythagoreans attributed many of their writings to Pythagoras because their works appear to be based on ideas which belonged to him. Perhaps they did not ascribe their writings with their own names because it would have been considered dishonest to attribute the thoughts in their works to anybody but their rightful owner, namely, Pythagoras. Although some modern scholars do not regard Iamblichus's remarks on pseudo-Pythagorean works as entirely trustworthy,[9] the text above still provides some indication that much of the pseudo-Pythagorean literature was written acceptably.

Porphyry the neo-Platonist identified 280 "authentic books" within the Pythagorean corpus.[10] Of these 280 "authentic books," however, he maintained, "Only 80 books are from Pythagoras himself, the other 200 stem from 'mature men who belong to the group of Pythagoras, to his party and to the heritage of his knowledge.'"[11] Porphyry seems to have considered the 200 Pythagorean books authored by "mature men" as acceptable pseudepigrapha. When he spoke of an "authentic book," Porphyry did not necessarily mean that a writing actually had to be authored by the person to whom it was attributed.

In like fashion Olympiodorus made the following remarks about Pythagoras, his disciples, and their writings:

> Pythagoras did not leave behind any personal writings, saying that one should not leave behind lifeless writings, since they were not able to speak in their defense; but that indeed he *was* leaving spirited writings behind, i.e. disciples who were able to defend both themselves and their teachers. His disciples then, having created writings through goodwill, inscribed (them with) the name of Pythagoras. And for this reason all of the writings handed down in the name of Pythagoras are spurious.[12]

Olympiodorus noted that Pythagoras had not left behind any writings of his own for subsequent generations to read. However, he went on to say that the renowned philosopher had left behind "spirited writings," namely, his disciples who wrote works in his name out of goodwill. Thus, some of the Pythagorean literature may have constituted a case of widely recognized pseudepigraphy which was not impaired by its known pseudepigraphal character, at least for many readers.

Not all school productions, however, were created acceptably in the context of a master-disciple relationship. To be sure, sometimes deceptive pseudepigrapha were expressly written to defend philosophical teaching. According to W. Speyer, "In the battle between philosophical schools of thought one sought especially since Hellenistic times to disparage the enemy through literary forgeries."[13] In this context, one could use pseudonymity to support his interpretation of a philosophical master against an opponent's view.[14] For example, as N. Gulley maintains, the author of pseudo-Plato's *Epistle VII* writes against those who have been criticizing the political theory of Plato.[15] In such a setting one might also compose documents under the name of another school's master in order to denounce him.[16] For example, Diogenes Laertius 10.3 informs us that the Stoic Diotimus maliciously wrote fifty letters under the name of Epicurus in order to reproach him.[17]

At least one other opinion from Greco-Roman antiquity concerning pseudonymity ought to be considered. David, the neo-Platonist, commented on a practice of unknown writers in his day: "Whenever someone was slight and unrespected, but wanted to insure that his writing would be read, he wrote under the name of an ancient and respected man so that through this appearance his work was well received."[18] David's remarks indicate that authors of no reputation would write using the pseudonym of an older, reputable figure in order to secure a hearing for their own works. Evidently, these writers wanted their documents to carry authority which they themselves did not have.

PSEUDONYMITY IN JEWISH WRITINGS

Jewish literature is not particularly helpful to a study of pseudepigraphy in early Christianity. Pseudonymity among the Jews occurred mostly in apocalyptic writings rather than in epistles.[19] Only two pseudonymous letters seem to have come down to us from Jewish sources: the *Letter of Aristeas* and the *Epistle of Jeremiah*.[20] The former work, strictly speaking, is not a letter because it does not occur in epistolary form.[21] It is an apologetic narrative which gives an account of the Hebrew Old Testament being translated into Greek. The latter writing, a sermon which warns the Jews against pagan idolatry, calls itself a letter and identifies its senders and addressees but does not begin like New Testament letters: "A *copy* of a letter which Jeremiah sent to those who were to be taken to Babylon as captives . . . to give them the message which God has commanded him."[22]

Other pseudonymous Jewish letters exist—for example, *1 Baruch, 2 Baruch 78–87, 1 Enoch 92–105,* and some letters contained in *1* and *2 Maccabees*—but such writings occur within composite, apocalyptic, or narrative frameworks. Thus, such Jewish letters seem to have had a different form and function from the disputed New Testament Epistles[23] and are not quite relevant to the latter.[24] That is to say, they are "embedded" or "reported" letters written within larger contexts and not "stand-alone" letters like those, for example, of Paul.

JEWISH ATTITUDES CONCERNING PSEUDONYMITY

Not much documentation exists on how the Jews felt about pseudonymity. Nonetheless, some evidence is extant. Arguably, the practice of pseudonymity in Jewish apocalyptic writings is due to a general belief among the Jews that prophetic inspiration had ceased after 200 B.C. Josephus, the Jewish historian, reflected this commonly held belief when he discussed the twenty-two books limited to the Hebrew canon: "From Artaxerxes to our own time the complete history has been written, but has not been deemed worthy of equal credit with the earlier records, because of the failure of the exact succession of the prophets."[25] Similarly, the *Babylonian Talmud, Sanhedrin* 11a mentions the cessation of inspired prophecy: "Since the death of the last prophets, Haggai, Zechariah and Malachi, the Holy Spirit (of prophetic inspiration) departed from Israel."[26] This external evidence from Jewish antiquity makes plausible the theory that by 200 B.C. apocalyptic writers had to write under a name that reverted back to an earlier time in order to gain both authority and a hearing for their works.[27] Like many Greco-Roman writers of little or no reputation, evidently some Jewish authors also wanted their pseudonymous writings to carry "punch."

PSEUDONYMITY IN CHRISTIAN WRITINGS

Some pseudonymous letters can be found in Christian circles, but, as is well-known, they are few and unimpressive—for example, the *Letters of Christ and Abgarus*, the *Letter of Lentulus*, the *Correspondence of Paul and Seneca*, the *Epistle of Titus*, the *Epistle to the Laodiceans*, the *Epistle of the Apostles*, *3 Corinthians*, and the pseudo-Ignatian letters. These pseudepigraphal writings do not closely resemble the disputed New Testament Epistles, were written fairly late, and are not all marked with the name of an apostle as a pseudonymous letter would have been if present in the New Testament.

The evidence shows that many pseudepigraphal epistles were composed in Greco-Roman antiquity,[28] but relatively few pseudonymous letters[29] exist in the religious literature of the Jews and Christians. And one is indeed hard pressed to find any pseudonymous epistles from antiquity to which the disputed New Testament letters are entirely comparable. D. Guthrie wisely cautioned, "The absence of any close contemporary epistolary parallels must put the investigator on his guard against a too facile admittance of the practice in New Testament criticism."[30] In other words, scholars should not be so quick to consider the presence of pseudonymity in the New Testament because no contemporary pseudonymous writings exist which are just like the disputed New Testament letters.

And yet evidence has been seen above which indicates that some people in certain quarters of antiquity accepted the use of pseudonymity. However, just because some persons in the ancient world accepted pseudepigraphy does not mean that the early Christians would have had the same viewpoint toward the practice. Such an assumption portrays the early church with a "monkey-see, monkey-do" mentality. On the contrary, early Christians often ran counter to the practices of their culture. Since Christians were committed to truth as a moral ideal, then it follows that they would not have written pseudonymous letters purporting to be works of the apostles. To evaluate the attitudes of early Christians on pseudonymity, both the New Testament evidence concerning the practice and the known responses of early Christian leaders toward the phenomenon will be examined.

NEW TESTAMENT EVIDENCE CONCERNING PSEUDONYMITY

The New Testament itself does not contain much evidence on the subject of pseudonymity. However, some biblical passages that have tremendous bearing on the question ought to be considered.

In 2 Thessalonians 2:2, Paul warned the church against accepting the false teaching of a "spirit, word, or letter as through us." In other words Paul cautioned the Thessalonians that, no matter through what agency the heresy came to them, though attributed to him and his associates, they had nothing to do with it. He does not seem to have had a specific pseudonymous letter in mind. Nonetheless, it can be said from 2 Thessalonians 2:2 that Paul would have objected to a pseudonymous letter being attributed to him which contained falsehood, wrong teaching, or inauthentic material that he did not write. If one couples this general categorical disclaimer in 2:2 with the Pauline signature in 2 Thessalonians 3:17, then Paul clearly puts a moratorium on pseudonymity in his name.

The Pauline signatures in the New Testament provide us with more internal evidence related to the practice of pseudonymity. Three of Paul's letters which are normally undisputed bear his signature: 1 Corinthians 16:21, Galatians 6:11, and Philemon 19. Two of the disputed Pauline letters in the New Testament also bear the apostle's mark: Colossians 4:18 and 2 Thessalonians 3:17. These greetings in Paul's own handwriting, which indicated the use of a secretary, provided a sign of his letters' authority and authenticity.[31] They should be interpreted in the following way: "This letter is an authoritative utterance composed by me, Paul, and I have attested it as such by my signature, and therefore you must pay heed to it." In the light of this interpretation, surely Paul would have frowned on someone's using a facsimile of his signature in a pseudonymous letter which purported to be his.

Though not specifically about the practice of pseudonymity, Revelation 22:18–19 should be also considered in a study of the New Testament evidence. Writers of ancient Near Eastern texts frequently invoked a warning or curse upon anyone who defaced or altered a document's words.[32] Similarly, in these verses John warned that no one was to tamper with what he had written in the Revelation by rewriting it in any way. (If someone did alter the text of Revelation, the subsequent impression would be given that the added or subtracted words belonged to the actual author.) No one was to violate John's inspired written work. One can extrapolate from this interpretation of these verses to somebody writing another book and falsely attributing it to him by means of pseudonymity. John would have objected to a pseudonymous letter being attributed to him which contained falsehood, wrong teaching, or inauthentic material that he did not write. For to write a pseudonymous work and attribute it to somebody is a sort of extension of tampering with an existing document. Thus, to enlarge pseudonymously an existing body of literature—for example, the Pauline corpus—by adding a few inauthentic works is to tamper with Paul's actual writings.

The New Testament also contains several appeals for truth that are difficult to reconcile with the thinking of an author who had used pseudonymity deceptively. Interestingly, many such entreaties occur in the disputed New Testament letters themselves. For example, in 1 Timothy 4:1–2 Paul warned his readers against embracing the doctrine of "deceitful spirits" and "hypocritical liars"; in Ephesians 4:15, he instructed his readers to "speak the truth in love"; in Ephesians 4:25, he exhorted the church to "put off falsehood and speak truthfully"; and in Colossians 3:9, he admonished his readers: "Do not lie to one another."

Furthermore, the Holy Spirit, who indwells each believer (1 Cor. 6:19; 12:13) and is described as the "Spirit of Truth" (John 14:17; 16:3), created an ethos in the Christian community in which deceptive pseudonymity would have been frowned upon and thus could not have flourished. Guthrie appropriately cautioned that "pseudepigraphic hypotheses must assume that the author's notion of the truth contained nothing inconsistent with a literary method which he must have known would deceive many if not all his readers."[33]

Despite such appeals for truth, some scholars[34] have sought to justify the use of deceptive pseudonymity in the New Testament on the basis of a Greek idea known as the "noble falsehood," which says that deception is permissible when used for good purposes.[35] However, a careful study of the terms for "deception" (cf. *apataō* and the entire *pseud*-word group) makes it difficult to show a concept of legitimate deception for the New Testament.[36]

THE ATTITUDES OF EARLY CHURCH LEADERS TOWARD PSEUDONYMITY

Many scholars neglect or discount prematurely the judgments of the early church fathers concerning pseudonymity. However, the latter evidence is the only extant documentation of known early Christian responses to pseudepigraphy. Thus, this evidence, coupled with the evidence earlier viewed from Scripture, arguably must be the point of departure in any study of pseudonymity and the New Testament. This documentation should likewise favor any conclusion which one might reach concerning the authenticity of the disputed New Testament letters. The study in this section will be limited primarily to the attitudes of the Ante-Nicene Fathers toward pseudonymity because their responses are nearest to the apostolic era.

Eusebius's comments on the *Shepherd of Hermas*[37] shed light on the attitudes of early church leaders toward pseudonymous documents. This book, which some apparently thought had been written by the Hermas mentioned by Paul in Romans 16:14,[38] was probably written in the early second century. While discussing the *Shepherd of Hermas*, Eusebius remarked that this work was "rejected by some, and for their sake should not be placed among accepted books."[39] Despite the latter remark by Eusebius, some read this work publicly in the churches anyway because they believed that it contained valuable teaching.[40]

However, the judgment of the Muratorian Canon on the *Shepherd of Hermas* is clear about the book's status: "Hermas wrote the *Shepherd.* . . . And therefore it ought indeed to be read; but it cannot be read publicly to the people in church either among the prophets, whose number is complete, or among the apostles, for it is after [their] time."[41] When the Muratorian Canon does not accept the canonicity of the *Shepherd of Hermas*, it does so because the writing did not come from the time period of the apostles and thus cannot be admitted to the canon. On the basis of this evidence, one can infer that, if a pseudoapostolic work had been written later than apostolic times, then it would have been excluded from the list of acceptable books and prohibited from being read in church.

Eusebius also recorded the response of Serapion, bishop of Antioch (c. A.D. 190), to the use of the apocryphal *Gospel of Peter* in the church at Rhossus. Serapion initially had allowed the church to read the book, seemingly because he thought it was authentic. However, when the bishop further examined the work, he discovered that it contained heresy and forbade its use. Serapion declared, "For our part, brethren, we receive both Peter and the other apostles as Christ, but the writings which falsely bear their names we reject, as men of experience, knowing that such were not handed down to us."[42] At least three points may be concluded from Serapion's remarks. First, he clearly would not have accepted pseudoapostolic works—whether orthodox or heretical in content. The bishop drew a sharp distinction between genuine apostolic writings ("as Christ") and pseudoapostolic works ("pseudepigrapha"). Second, though Serapion had the heresy[43] of the *Gospel of Peter* in mind when he rejected the writing, he also clearly considered the pseudonymous authorship of the work. The latter conclusion is reached because, in the bishop's statement, the phrase "in their names" is used to describe the pseudepigrapha he rejected. Third, Serapion pointed out that the church did not knowingly hand down pseudoapostolic writings. Both the heresy contained in the *Gospel of Peter* and its claim to authorship by an apostle were factors in the book's rejection by Serapion.

Tertullian wrote a work entitled *On Prescription Against Heretics* in which he emphasized that orthodox Christian doctrine should originate only from the apostles.[44] He stated, "It remains, then, that we demonstrate whether this doctrine of ours, of which we have now given the rule, has its origin in the tradition of the apostles, and whether all other *doctrines* do not ipso facto proceed from falsehood."[45] Tertullian clearly was concerned about both the authorship and the content of a work. Neither was to be excluded when considering writings for acceptance by the church.

Tertullian[46] also recorded that Asian church elders ousted a colleague from his post for writing out of "love for Paul" the apocryphal *Acts of Paul*, which included the pseudoapostolic letter of *3 Corinthians*. Despite the presbyter's profession that he had meant well when he wrote the work, his action warranted removal from office. The elders condemned the man either for writing a work that fictitiously bore Paul's name or for composing a fiction about the apostle, and not because, in the apocryphal story, he had allowed a woman to baptize. The latter conclusion is reached because, in Tertullian's account, the elders condemned the presbyter immediately after he had confessed that he was the author of the *Acts of Paul*. Only later did Tertullian complain about the book's teaching on baptism. The early church clearly regarded the fictive use of an apostle's name with disdain.

Defenders of pseudonymity in the New Testament have sometimes used a remark of Tertullian to help support the idea that an established convention of pseudonymity existed among the early Christians.[47] Tertullian indicated that "it may well seem that the works which disciples publish belong to their masters."[48] Some scholars have used the latter remark to bolster their view that the letter of Ephesians was written pseudonymously by a later disciple of Paul.[49] Perhaps some justification exists, on a cursory reading of Tertullian's statement, to suppose he taught that the reading public would generally credit the works of disciples to their masters. However, if one digs deeper, he will discover that Tertullian made this particular statement to help confirm the canonicity of the Gospels of Mark and Luke. Since neither Gospel was authored by an apostle, Tertullian helped establish their dependency upon the authority of the apostles Peter and Paul.[50] Thus, as Lea has well expressed, "This statement of Tertullian's must not be used as a broad sweeping defense of the practice of pseudonymity. We should limit its usage to a confirmation of the authority of Mark and Luke."[51] When Tertullian's comment is considered within its appropriate context, one cannot maintain from his remarks that an established convention of pseudonymity existed among orthodox Christians.

While discussing the corporeality of God, Origen mentioned the *Doctrine of Peter*, which he rejected because it was "not included among the books of the Church and . . . not a writing of Peter nor of any one else inspired by the Spirit of God."[52] Origen rejected the *Doctrine of Peter* because of its inauthenticity. He does not sound like someone who would have approved of pseudonymity.

Though he did not specifically discuss pseudonymity, the comments of Dionysius of Alexandria on the Book of Revelation are helpful to this study. Dionysius acknowledged that a "holy and inspired person"[53] named John authored the Revelation, but he questioned whether John the apostle wrote the book:

> But I could not so easily admit that this was the apostle, the son of Zebedee, the brother of James, and the same person with him who wrote the Gospel which bears the title *according to John*, and the catholic epistle. But from the character of both, and the forms of expression, and the whole disposition and execution of the book, I draw the conclusion that the authorship is not his.[54]

Though the fuller context of Dionysius' remarks shows that he was not concerned with authorship for its own sake,[55] his assessment of Revelation's authorship is nonetheless relevant. His appraisal clearly shows that early Christian writers were capable of critically evaluating documents. Thus, it becomes difficult to charge early Christians with being entirely naïve or having a precritical mind-set.[56] Dionysius was not sure who the author of Revelation might have been, but he felt certain that the book had been written by a Christian man named John.[57] If Dionysius had concluded that a pseudonymous author had written the Book of Revelation, he might have easily accounted for the differences he pointed out between Revelation, the Gospel of John, and the Epistle, and further show, for his purposes, that the apostle John did not write the book. However, when presented with that opportunity, he did not do so.

The work entitled the *Constitutions of the Holy Apostles* has sometimes been assigned to the apostolic age and also attributed to Clement, the bishop of Rome.[58] However, the book is most likely a third-century document, which has had later additions.[59] This document consists of moral laws and instructions, guidelines for church leaders, and exhortations for those facing martyrdom.[60] One passage in this work censures pseudepigraphal writings:[61]

> For you are not to attend to the names of the apostles, but to the nature of the things, and their settled opinions. For we know that Simon and Cleobius, and their followers, have compiled poisonous books under the name of Christ and of his disciples, and do carry them about in order to deceive you who love Christ, and us His servants.[62]

Some point out that this writer's words plainly indicate that the early church fathers were concerned about the content of writings and not their authorship.[63] However, this generalization does not hold true if the statement above is interpreted in the following way: "These particular works are not from the apostles; we know that these writings are not by the apostles because they are heretical. Therefore, do not pay attention to the names attached to these documents as though they were authored by the apostles." Clearly, the passage above reflects some early Christian writer's opinion towards pseudonymity which has originated from heretical sources. For him, like the early church, both the orthodox content of a work and its authorship were factors when scrutinizing a document.

Other writings exist which indicate that the early church was quite concerned with the authorship of works and not just content. The latter statement is reflected in the fact that certain apostolic pseudepigrapha, though orthodox in their content and raising no doctrinal objections, were nonetheless excluded from the church's canon.[64] Some works of this nature are the *Preaching of Peter*, the *Apocalypse of Peter*, the *Epistle of the Apostles*, the *Correspondence of Paul and Seneca*, and the extant *Epistle to the Laodiceans*.

Some of the language which early church leaders used to describe pseudonymous writings should also be considered briefly. These terms were certainly not complimentary and indicate that pseudoapostolic works were viewed by them as fraudulent and deceptive writings—for example, "falsely written"[65] (*perperam scripta*), "forged"[66] (*finctae*), and "pseudepigrapha"[67] (*pseudepigrapha*). Surely the early church did not embrace pseudonymous writings that it described in such a pejorative manner.

The exclusion of pseudepigrapha by the early church favors the following positions. First, both the authorship of writings and their content were criteria used by the early church when determining which books were to be recognized or rejected as having normative status. These criteria fit together hand in hand. The content of a document was often used as a barometer to gauge its authenticity. If a writing was heretical, it was considered inauthentic, and if inauthentic, then the work was not used publicly in the churches. Only where a work appeared to meet both of these criteria was it ever recognized as normative and accepted for public reading in the churches. In other words, the early church would not have knowingly accepted or allowed either pseudoapostolic or heretical works to be read publicly in the churches along with the apostolic writings. Second, evidence is lacking for a convention of pseudonymity which existed among orthodox Christians. Third, early Christians did not regard the fictive use of an apostle's name with indifference.

Despite the latter conclusion, some scholars object that the evidence of later, Gentile Christian attitudes toward pseudepigrapha is anachronistic and should not be used to judge the first-century, Jewish Christian phenomenon of pseudonymity. However, the clear, undeniable fact is that second-century orthodox Christianity strongly disapproved of pseudonymity, and it is improbable that first-century Christians had a different opinion on the matter.[68]

Some scholars also object that all of the evidence above comes from a period when a great deal of heretical literature attributed to the apostles was circulating. Thus, this fact possibly affected the way that pseudepigraphy per se was viewed by orthodox bishops and others who were concerned about heresy. In other words, this phenomenon possibly colored the way that orthodox churchmen looked at all pseudonymity. However, though the evidence may be colored by a period in which heresy flourished, the early church could conceivably have responded differently—for example, by only screening the content of documents and not their authorship. Notably, the early Christians did no such thing; instead they used both standards. Also, if there had been no heresy, there would have been no need to establish criteria for the inclusion or exclusion of certain writings.

PSEUDONYMITY AND THE NEW TESTAMENT APOCRYPHA

The New Testament apocrypha are "writings which originated in the first centuries of Church history, and which through title, *Gattung* or content stand in a definite connection with the NT writings."[69] These works were not received into the canon of Scripture.

Many of the apocrypha are pseudonymous. A variety of motives, some of which overlap, led to the use of pseudonymity in these writings. Sometimes authors wrote apocryphal works to supplement the canonical texts.[70] Along these lines, the *Infancy Gospel of Thomas* and the *Protevangelium of James* attempted to fill in the gaps in the canonical Gospel record by providing fictional stories about Jesus' birth and childhood.[71] Other apocrypha were composed with specific interest in New Testament persons.[72] For example, the *Acts of Paul* glorified the apostle Paul and provided fictional accounts of his life. Some apocryphal documents were created for purposes of entertainment or propaganda.[73] Various other Acts of the apostles may have arisen from this motive. Still other apocryphal writings advanced variant traditions of Jesus which were dependent upon and inferior to the canonical Gospels.[74] Though fiercely debated, the *Gospel of Thomas*, a collection of sayings emanating from Gnostic circles, should be placed into this latter category.

Edgar Hennecke's helpful two-volume *New Testament Apocrypha*, recently revised by Wilhelm Schneemelcher, presents many apocryphal fragments and documents which provide information concerning a literary milieu near the New Testament period. These apocryphal works were rejected by the early church as spurious and did not achieve normative status. Though scholars debate the exact criteria used by the early church to determine the authenticity of writings, Schneemelcher notes, "What was fundamental and apostolic was given precedence, but what was apostolic was determined by what was fundamental, i.e. by the confession and faith of the Church."[75] Failure in either regard—pseudonymous authorship or false teaching—merited disqualification for a document.

Two catalogues of the books included in the New Testament by the early church provide help in appraising the criteria that early Christians used to ascertain the authenticity of documents. The first of these lists is the Muratorian Canon, which bears the name of L. A. Muratori who discovered the work and published it in 1740.[76] This document provides insight into the status of the New Testament canon in the second century.[77] The compiler of the Muratorian Canon listed those documents which were permitted for use and were refused by the early church in the West.[78]

In his list the author of the Muratorian Canon mentions two works that had been falsely attributed to the apostle Paul: "There is current also (an epistle) to the Laodiceans, another to the Alexandrians, forged in Paul's name for the sect of Marcion, and several others, which cannot be received in the catholic Church; for it will not do to mix gall with honey."[79] Both an epistle to the Laodiceans and one written to the Alexandrians are viewed as "forged in Paul's name." These letters were not admitted into the canon recognized by the church. Strangely enough, though purportedly belonging to the ancient past and in no sense a New Testament apocryphon, the author of the Muratorian Canon recognized the *Wisdom of Solomon*, "written by friends of Solomon in his honour."[80] However, the *Wisdom of Solomon* should not be considered strictly pseudonymous because it does not have Solomon's name specifically ascribed in it as the author. Rather, the writer of the latter work simply takes on the role of Solomon in his writing. The compiler of the Muratorian Canon went on to voice reluctance about the *Apocalypse of Peter*, which some people did not want to be read in the church. In the light of the evidence above, one may say that the author of the Muratorian Canon clearly did not admit forgeries into the canon. Surely he would not have knowingly accepted documents having a pseudonymous authorship.

Another early list of writings included in the New Testament is provided by Eusebius, bishop of Caesarea, in his *Ecclesiastical History*. Eusebius divided books into three different categories: "recognized," "disputed," and "spurious."[81] Among the "recognized" books he included the four Gospels, Acts, the Pauline Epistles (not specifically named), 1 John, and 1 Peter. The "disputed" writings mentioned by Eusebius are James, Jude, 2 Peter, and 2 and 3 John. He related that some (including himself) counted Revelation among the recognized writings but that some rejected the book. Eusebius also did not mention Hebrews, but this is probably because he considered it as one of the Pauline Epistles.[82] Among the "spurious" books Eusebius included the *Acts of Paul*, the *Shepherd*, the *Apocalypse of Peter*, the *Epistle of Barnabas*, and the *Teachings of the Apostles*. He explained that the "spurious" writings were those in which "the type of phraseology differs from apostolic style, and the opinion and tendency of their contents is widely dissonant from true orthodoxy and clearly shows that they are the forgeries of heretics."[83] The word "forgery" *(anaplasma)* denoted that which was fabricated or fictional.[84] Eusebius' remarks show that he rejected works which had a known pseudonymous authorship and writings which contained heresy. For him, documents of this nature did not meet the necessary standards.

The church today is indebted to Eusebius for his skill as a historian. His remarks indicate that early Christian leaders used the twin criteria of apostolic authorship and orthodox content to distinguish genuine canonical writings from those which were not.

PAST SCHOLARSHIP ON PSEUDONYMITY (UP TO 1960)

Earlier, the views of persons towards pseudonymity in Greco-Roman, Jewish, and Christian antiquity were highlighted. In this section some opinions on the subject from the time of the Reformation up to the year 1960 will be reviewed.

The Reformation brought a renewed focus on the Scriptures, which in turn led to many questions about the Bible, some of which concerned the authenticity of certain writings in the New Testament canon. For example, Martin Luther relegated the Epistle of James to a lesser status in his New Testament canon. He did so, not on account of pseudonymous authorship, but because he felt that the letter did not "promote Christ": "That which does not teach Christ is still not apostolic, even if it were the teaching of Peter or Paul. On the other hand, that which preaches Christ, that would be apostolic even if Judas, Annas, Pilate or Herod did it."[85] Presumably, Luther might have accepted a pseudonymous letter which met his criterion of primary canonicity, regardless of who wrote the work.

John Calvin, another Reformation-era scholar, commented upon the canonicity and authorship of 2 Peter:

> If it is received as canonical, we must admit that Peter is the author, not only because it bears his name, but also because he testifies that he lived with Christ. It would have been a fiction unworthy of a minister of Christ to pretend to another personality. Therefore I conclude that if the epistle is trustworthy it has come from Peter; not that he wrote it himself, but that one of his disciples composed by his command what the necessity of the times demanded.[86]

Unlike most contemporary critical scholars, Calvin did not believe that 2 Peter was pseudonymous. Instead he concluded that the letter had been written by a secretary under Peter's direction.

Edward Evanson, an Englishman, apparently first made the claim that pseudonymity was present in the New Testament.[87] However, it was F. C. Baur, the leading scholar of the Tübingen school, who most successfully promoted this view. Baur held the principle that one pseudepigraphon present in the New Testament leads to the probability of several others.[88] With this kind of reasoning, he came to believe that all of the New Testament letters bearing Paul's name were inauthentic, except Romans, 1 and 2 Corinthians, and Galatians. While discussing the authorship of the Pauline Epistles that he viewed as pseudonymous, he remarked, "What gives these Epistles their claim to the name of the apostle is simply the circumstances that they profess to be Pauline and make the apostle speak as their author."[89]

On the question of the moral culpability of such works, Baur assumed that the writing of pseudo-Pauline letters "must not be judged according to the modern standard of literary honesty."[90] In such cases he refused to call pseudonymity "deception or wilful forgery."[91] Nonetheless, Baur appeared to be comfortable with a certain degree of ambiguity regarding the practice, for he also referred to it as the "forging of such epistles."[92] Baur's work has clearly influenced much subsequent scholarship.

Adolph Jülicher agreed with Baur's principle approach concerning pseudonymity and tried to substantiate its presence in the New Testament with more data than most scholars at the time. He avoided using the word *forgery* to describe pseudonymous writings and claimed that "the ethical notion of literary property" was "a plant of modern growth."[93] Jülicher justified the presence of pseudonymity in the New Testament with an appeal to the "boundless credulity of ecclesiastical circles."[94] He also defended the idea with the claim that "believers frequently borrowed from the books of other believers, or of unbelievers" without thinking they did anything wrong.[95]

Moreover, he asserted that early Christian writers put words into the apostles' mouths without considering themselves deceptive;[96] for Jülicher, they "were quite indifferent as to the form in which it was clothed."[97] To support his claim that the early Christians had a strong yet naïve tendency toward using "literary disguises," Jülicher cited examples of pseudepigrapha from both the Greek and Jewish cultures.[98] Though he did not entirely follow Baur's lead and rejected all but four of Paul's Epistles, some of Jülicher's arguments on pseudonymity are still used today to defend the practice in the New Testament.

Martin Dibelius, well known for his form-critical study of the Gospels, also claimed that pseudonymity existed in the New Testament. When considering the authorship of 2 Peter, he confidently asserted, "Obviously in this case we have the beginning of pseudonymity in the literary sense."[99] After studying the language of the Pastoral Epistles, Dibelius decided, "The Paulinist makes use here of conceptions which are foreign to the Pauline letters which have come down to us."[100] Consequently, he concluded that the Pastorals were not authentic. Dibelius saw nothing wrong with pseudonymity because he viewed the practice as a literary convention of that day.

James Moffatt justified the presence of pseudonymity in the New Testament with an appeal to what he claimed were Greek and Jewish literary antecedents. For him, early Christians simply had adopted a widespread custom that many people in antiquity had practiced. Moffatt felt that modesty was a chief motive in the production of pseudonymous writings by which a disciple was prompted "to reproduce in his own language the ideas, or what he conceived to be the ideas, of his master, and yet forbade him . . . to present these under his own name."[101] Moffatt's grasp of pseudonymity illumined for him the practice as he thought it varied in some New Testament books:

> This throws light upon the ethos of NT writings like Ephesians and the
> Pastorals. While 2 Peter represents in the NT Canon a pseudonymous epistle,

pure and simple, the Pastoral epistles, on the other hand, were composed by a Paulinist who must have had access to certain notes or papers of the great apostle, which he incorporated in his own writings.[102]

Moffatt further explained pseudonymity by calling attention to the practices of Greek and Roman authors. He pointed out that ancient historians often composed pseudonymous letters which were "true to the general spirit of the situation and the supposed writer," but "undoubtedly due to the creative imagination of the author himself."[103] According to Moffatt, the latter practice led to the production of speeches in the New Testament which consisted of "(a) compositions made up from previous materials, usually genuine in the main; and (b) more or less free compositions, which, without being purely rhetorical exercises, represent what the writer's historical sense judged appropriate to the situation."[104] With these methods the supposed author was made to express what the actual writer felt he would have said had he been present.

Similarly, P. N. Harrison claimed that a pseudonymous author had some genuine fragments of Pauline material set before him and that he incorporated these fragments into the Pastoral Epistles as he wrote them.[105] Harrison came to believe this mainly by comparing the language of the Pastorals with the Epistles of Paul. He claimed that the pseudonymous author of these letters did not consciously misrepresent or deceive anybody and that those to whom he had written surely knew what he had done. Accordingly, Harrison viewed pseudonymity as an acceptable, transparent, literary device.

Edgar Goodspeed expressed some concerns about how pseudepigrapha were examined. He cautioned against studying pseudonymous works in isolation from other like writings: "It is evident that this whole literature must be studied together from the point of view of its pseudonymous character, if we are to escape the fatal fault of atomism in our treatment of these documents."[106] Apparently, Goodspeed believed, like Baur earlier, that the presence of several pseudonymous writings made it likely that there would be others. He initially assumed that Jude and 2 Peter were pseudonymous and gradually added Ephesians, 1 Peter, James, and the Pastoral Epistles to his list. To defend pseudonymity, Goodspeed echoed what Moffatt had earlier expressed, "For a disciple to put forth his interpretation or restatement of his master's teaching under that master's name was a practice not unknown in antiquity."[107]

F. W. Beare believed that a pseudonymous author wrote 1 Peter. He defended pseudonymity as "an accepted and harmless literary device, employed by a teacher who is more concerned for the Christian content of his message than for the assertion of his own claims to authority."[108] According to Beare, the author of 1 Peter sought in his work to "re-create the personality of the one whose name he has chosen, and to make him speak in his personality and accents."[109]

J. C. Fenton surveyed three factors which he thought led to pseudonymity in the New Testament.[110] First, he claimed that pseudonymous writings were produced when disciples wished to attribute their works to their teachers. Second, Fenton surmised that authors wrote pseudonymously when they encountered heresy in order to "recall the faithful to apostolic teaching."[111] Third, he asserted that pseudonymity was a literary genre acceptably and widely used by all in antiquity, including heretical and orthodox Christians.

With little or no supporting documentation, the scholars highlighted in the foregoing discussion defended the view that the early church readily accepted the practice of pseudonymity. However, the evidence that has been seen thus far indicates that such an assumption is far from certain. As shall be seen, not all biblical scholars recognized pseudonymity as a literary convention which is present in the New Testament. The following discussion will rehearse the views of three individuals who rejected the practice.

J. S. Candlish investigated the early church's response to pseudonymous works and rejected the practice on ethical grounds. He concluded that in early Christianity pseudonymous works were considered morally culpable and determined that no external evidence exists to support the view of pseudonymity as a recognized literary convention which did not intend to deceive.[112] Though Candlish suggested that inspired works could use any form of composition accepted in that day,[113] he did not include pseudonymous documents in the latter category because he believed that they were deliberately written to deceive. According to him, such writings were inconsistent with divine inspiration.[114]

R. D. Shaw likewise rejected pseudonymity on the basis of its ethical inconsistency. He found it difficult to believe that the New Testament age could produce "so consummate a literary artist" who could write a pseudonymous Pauline letter that would be universally accepted as authentic.[115] Nonetheless, Shaw said, "If there were no conscious transgression of any moral principle, it would be impossible to refuse inspiration to a pseudonymous writing on the mere ground of its pseudonymity."[116] However, he believed that the authors of pseudonymous works did intend to deceive; thus, their writings could neither be inspired nor considered canonical.[117]

When discussing views of pseudonymity and the Pastoral Epistles, J. I. Packer argued that the advocates of such theories fail to grasp two concepts.[118] First, they do not understand the authority and importance of the apostolate. Apostolicity guarantees that the Pastorals are part of the Christ-inspired, authoritative, apostolic teaching which has been given to the churches. Second, defenders of pseudonymity in the Pastorals do not comprehend the biblical notion of Scripture. This concept demands that claims to authorship in these letters "should be received as truth from God."[119] Packer theologically concluded, "Pseudonymity and canonicity are mutually exclusive."[120]

The conclusion of this survey will rehearse the views of two scholars who, in the 1930s, specifically discussed the psychology and ethics of pseudonymity among early Christians. Interestingly, the men reached opposite conclusions. On the one hand, Arnold Meyer proposed, in an extensive survey of pseudepigrapha, that the ethical dilemma posed by an author using a pseudonym was not a sufficient argument against the practice. He claimed that if a prophet could speak in the name of God, "then it is no great step from there for one to believe himself justified also to be able to write in the name of a patriarch or an apostle."[121] Meyer felt that pseudonymous works were present in the New Testament because the acceptance or rejection of them was "according to the measure of ecclesiastical truth, not literary authenticity."[122] He claimed that since pseudonymity was so widespread and accepted in antiquity, Christians also would have used it. For Meyer the practice was a literary device which had no intention to deceive.

On the other hand, F. Torm argued that the practice of pseudonymity by Christians was problematic in the light of certain ethical and psychological impediments to its use.[123] He believed that the custom posed greater problems for religious writers than it did for pagan authors. Torm held that the use of pseudonymity by Greek and Roman writers was consistent with their way of thinking. However, he found it troublesome that a sincere Christian could write a pseudonymous letter given that such an act would have been one of deception.

The historical survey in this section highlighted the views of scholars on the subject of pseudonymity from the time of the Reformation up to the year 1960. Opinions extended across a broad spectrum. At one end, John Calvin believed that 2 Peter had been written by a secretary under the direction of the apostle Peter. At the other end, F. C. Baur radically rejected the authenticity of every Pauline letter except Romans, 1 and 2 Corinthians, and Galatians. On the one hand, defenders of pseudonymity in the New Testament often justified it with an appeal to the influence and widespread acceptance of pseudepigrapha written by Jews and Greeks. Advocates of pseudonymity neither viewed these writings as forgeries nor saw the authors of these works as being dishonest. On the other hand, those who objected to the idea of pseudepigrapha in the New Testament saw definite theological problems in trying to mix pseudonymity with canonicity. They also expressed certain ethical incongruities and psychological impediments to its use by the early Christians. Defenders of authenticity maintained that the practice is deceitful and found difficulty reconciling it with a religious people who were committed to truth and morality. The latter problem is still the center of discussion in many studies of pseudonymity and the New Testament.[124]

Other earlier scholars whose views might be considered in a study of pseudonymity and the New Testament include: B. S. Easton (1948), C. L. Mitton (1951), and J. A. Sint (1960).

Contemporary Scholarship on Pseudonymity

In this section the views of some more recent scholars on the subject of pseudonymity and the New Testament will be highlighted. This survey will also illustrate the variety of expression on the topic.

Kurt Aland posited a pneumatic theory to explain the problem of pseudonymity. He investigates both anonymity and pseudonymity, and argues that the two phenomena are linked.[125] Aland limits his study to the first two centuries. During this period many anonymous writings were produced—for example, the Gospels, *2 Clement*, the *Epistle of Barnabas*, etc. Regarding the *Epistle of Barnabas*, Aland suggests that the author was a channel through which spiritual knowledge flowed to his readers. He cites the *Didache* as an example of pseudonymity, which he views as "the shift of the message from the spoken to the written word."[126] According to Aland, a charismatic wrote the *Didache*, read it in the course of worship to his own congregation, and claimed that it was the Lord's message through the apostles. The message's content confirmed this claim; the church acknowledged it; and thus "the *Didache* achieved recognition in the Church of those days."[127]

According to Aland, anonymous writings and pseudonymous works in the apostles' names were quite normal then. For him, pseudonymity did not intend to deceive because the writer was simply the tool of the Holy Spirit who was seen as the actual author of the work. However, Aland assumes there is no distinction in how canonical and noncanonical writers were inspired.[128] Moreover, his hypothesis makes the apostle Paul, who wrote using his own name, appear to be less spiritual than anonymous and pseudonymous authors who did not.[129] Furthermore, Aland cares little about the ethics and psychology of pseudonymity and neglects the fact that documentation from the early church shows that Christians did not accept pseudonymity.

Bruce Metzger has written a helpful article in which he concisely explains a range of motives behind the production and circulation of pseudonymous writings in antiquity.[130] He also discusses problems regarding canonical pseudepigrapha and maintains that patristic writers rejected pseudonymous works for literary and doctrinal reasons.[131] Metzger considers different views of pseudepigrapha in antiquity and decides that "the prevalence of differing degrees of sensitivity to the morality of such productions, should warn us against attempting to find a single formula that will solve all questions."[132] After asserting that pseudonymity does not need to be viewed as deceptive, Metzger concludes that "it cannot be argued that the character of inspiration excludes the possibility of pseudepigraphy among the canonical writings."[133] Unfortunately, Metzger does not provide a discussion that demonstrates why inspiration cannot rule out pseudonymity in the New Testament.

Norbert Brox claims that no single solution is sufficient to solve the problem of New Testament pseudonymity. He posits three main features to explain the phenomenon. First, he argues that the early church fathers were more concerned with the content of writings than their authorship.[134] Second, Brox says that Christians used pseudonymity to take part in the "superior past."[135] That is to say, like others in antiquity, they admired whatever was old and believed that whatever was old was true. Thus, by using the pseudonym, writers could attribute their works to an earlier date and command such respect. Third, Brox contends that, because the idea of the "noble falsehood" pervaded antiquity, deception could be used to promote one's aims.[136]

In this manner he believes that pseudonymity was used deliberately to support the religious content of works. However, Brox too quickly discounts the documentary evidence which shows that the early church was concerned with both the content and the authorship of documents. Moreover, one struggles to see how love for antiquity could have motivated pseudepigraphers composing works written shortly after the deaths of the apostles.[137] Furthermore, Brox imposes the Greek idea of the noble falsehood upon writings of a primarily Jewish origin.[138] His support of a legitimate concept of deception for the New Testament is indeed difficult to prove.

In encyclopedic fashion, Wolfgang Speyer has gathered and analyzed numerous ancient pseudepigrapha and literary forgeries.[139] In his study of religious pseudepigrapha, Speyer classifies these works into three distinct categories.[140] First, he discusses "genuine religious pseudepigrapha." These works were spread mainly in the Near East by the Jews but were also known in Greece and Rome. For Speyer, such writings are not deceptive because they stem from a mythical-religious experience. In other words, the writers believed that they were possessed and inspired by a spirit (whether that of a god, spirit, or a godly wise man of the past) with the result that they did not pen their own words but those of the one controlling them. Speyer does not place Christian pseudepigrapha into this category.

Second, he explains "falsified religious pseudepigrapha." The authors of these works imitated genuine religious pseudepigrapha, used the name of one who carried authority within a religious tradition, and wrote to deceive their readers. Speyer locates most Christian pseudepigrapha within this category.

Third, he evaluates "fictive religious pseudepigrapha." These works are artistic literary creations which belong to the realm of poetry and art and are not viewed as deceptive. Speyer finds none of these works in Christian literature. Speyer claims that the early Christians used forgeries "to explain, defend and spread the faith authoritatively."[141] He says that even orthodox Christians did not reject the use of the "necessary lie."[142] For example, Speyer views *3 Corinthians* as one of many counterforgeries written to defend the church's teaching against heretics,[143] and he views the Pastoral Epistles and 2 Peter as forgeries composed out of high moral motives serving "the development of the faith and church discipline."[144]

Despite Speyer's extensive research, evidence is lacking that a pseudonymous author ever thought that he was possessed by a spirit in such a way; moreover, had these authors really undergone such mystical-religious experiences, it is difficult to imagine why they did not write in their own names.[145] Furthermore, Speyer's belief that the early church winked at forgery and used it for their own purposes is inconsistent with a people who were presumably committed to truth and moral ideals.

Especially significant among "later disciple" theories of pseudonymity is the monograph written by David Meade entitled *Pseudonymity and Canon*.[146] According to Meade, the use of the pseudonym does not indicate the literary origins of a document but rather the authoritative tradition within which it is written. Consequently, he views the authors of the Pastoral Epistles, Ephesians, and 1 and 2 Peter as later writers who were convinced of the continuity and truth of their assertions with those of their pseudonyms and who simply "reactualized" the apostles' teaching for a new generation.[147] Meade reaches this conclusion because he claims to have found such a tradition of pseudonymity in Jewish and Christian literature.

For Meade, deception only enters the scene in such works when one asks how such documents were circulated, and then it must be radically qualified. He explains that deception can run on two levels: first, the literary origins of a book (who really wrote it?), and second, the truth or content of a work (are the ideas within those of the purported author or someone else's?).[148] Meade contends that in modern practice these two levels cannot be separated and that it is their combination which causes scholars to equate deception with forgery. However, he insists that in his study of Jewish and Christian literature the two can be separated; thus, the pseudonym acceptably serves to sanction the more important level of authoritative content. That is to say, authors used pseudonyms to deceive their readers, but the practice was not culpable because it acceptably promoted the content of a work.

Meade gives the analogy of slavery as evidence to support his viewpoint. He says that today slavery is viewed as incompatible with the gospel, but in New Testament times this was not the case. Similarly, though the modern world does not accept authorial deception, Meade claims the matter was different in the first century; he argues that Christians used deceit in the fashion described by him. However, his appeal to changing moral sensitivities as justification for his views concerning deception is weak. Moreover, Meade's strong dichotomy between literary origins and the content of works is extremely difficult to prove from the evidence. Furthermore, Meade assumes throughout his work that the New Testament contains pseudonymity and then attempts to rationalize it.[149]

Lewis Donelson argues that the author of the Pastorals combines pseudepigraphy and Greco-Roman ethics in these letters to make an ethical and theological argument to his church.[150] He believes that pseudepigraphy should be considered primarily Greco-Roman and not Jewish and makes three generalizations about it in the Pastoral Epistles: first, the letters were written in response to heresy; second, the author used the "pedagogical lie" (i.e., he used the pseudonym to get his readers to accept the truth contained in these letters); and third, the letters appealed to the apostle and his authority to make the writer's arguments forceful and credible. Donelson clearly sees the author of the Pastorals as having intended to deceive his readers. He views pseudonymity as a dishonorable practice and maintains that if pseudonymous writings were discovered they were rejected and their authors condemned. Yet Donelson contends that Christians often used pseudonymity because the need for the "good lie" was so great. However, like others, Donelson unabashedly attributes deliberate deception to a people who surely would have been concerned about truth and morals.

In an article on pseudoapostolic letters, Richard Bauckham provides fresh criteria for distinguishing pseudepigraphal from authentic letters in the New Testament.[151] First, he explains the special features of the pseudepigraphal letter "by setting it within the context of a comprehensive classification of types of letters in antiquity."[152] Second, he finds, in a fairly comprehensive analysis, that ancient Jewish pseudepigraphal letters and pseudoapostolic letters among the New Testament apocrypha conform to these types. On the basis of his study, Bauckham concludes that 2 Peter[153] and the Pastoral Epistles are probably pseudonymous, while Ephesians, James, and 2 Thessalonians are only possibly pseudepigraphal. He also finds Colossians, 1 Peter, and Jude to be authentic and suggests that Timothy wrote the Pastoral Epistles. Furthermore, Bauckham observes that "the readers of a pseudepigraphal letter cannot read it as though they were being directly addressed either by the supposed author or by the real author; they must read it as a letter written to *other* people, in the past."[154] In other words, pseudonymous letters required a distinction between the supposed addressee(s) and the real readers of a pseudepigraphal letter. Consequently, this gap had to be bridged somehow. Bauckham maintains that the author of a pseudonymous letter could bridge the gap for his readers in one of three ways. First, he could address the forebears of the real readers in a situation which has not changed up to the present. Second, he could depict the historical situation of the supposed addressees as a kind of type for the similar present situation of the actual recipients. Third, he could address the immediate hearers and future generations by means of a testament or farewell speech. However, Bauckham's work encounters a problem because it is not certain whether pseudonymous letters ever had any actual recipients who read such works in this manner.

In his recent commentary, I. H. Marshall argues that the early church might easily have received the Pastoral Epistles as authoritative knowing full well that they were not written by Paul.[155] He suggests that these letters therefore be termed "allonymous" rather than pseudonymous, so that no censure attaches to their production. Marshall's case relies heavily on a comparison between the writing of the Pastoral Epistles, as he understands it, and what he sees as three plainly innocent forms of literary composition.[156] First, he notes that an author may write letters in his lifetime using a secretary to whom he delegates power to write on his behalf. Second, he points out that one may acceptably edit an authentic work after an author's death to circulate it for future generations. Third, he writes, "it is not too great a step to a situation in which somebody close to a dead person continued to write as (they thought that) he would have done."[157] Thus, for him the Pastorals lie on a continuum with these non-deceptive practices, rather than being akin to plain forgery.

Marshall argues that the Pastoral Epistles applied "fresh formulations of Pauline teaching" to deal with growing opposition in Ephesus and Crete.[158] The same author (or group that possibly included Timothy and Titus) wrote all three letters just after Paul's death, incorporating genuine Pauline material into them. Second Timothy was based on an authentic last letter of Paul to Timothy. That letter generally began to confront the opposition. Second Timothy provided the spur for the subsequent writing of 1 Timothy and Titus to deal more fully and specifically with the hostility and heresy in the two places. The Epistles provided Pauline backing for Timothy, Titus, and other church leaders to help protect their congregations from false teaching. According to Marshall, they were not deceptive in any way, as this convention was familiar to both sides. The letters say only what Paul would have said in reaction to the circumstances had he been alive.

In the end, though Marshall's proposal is welcome, it seems vulnerable to some of the same criticisms as the "fragment theory" view of the Pastorals' authorship—the idea that a pseudonymous author incorporated some genuine Pauline fragments into his letters as he wrote them. The theory invites some searching questions. For example, how does one accurately determine which parts of the Pastorals rely on authentic Pauline materials and which do not? By what standard can such a judgment be made?

Any theory of pseudonymity or unauthorized allonymity in the New Testament must assume that the early Christians tolerated the practice. However, as the reader has seen, the available documentary evidence shows that the early church soundly rejected pseudo-apostolic works upon their discovery. Thus, the view that pseudepigraphic or allepigraphic writings in the names of the apostles were gladly accepted by the early church is not secure.

Modern scholarship also has its defenders of the authenticity of the New Testament writings. The following discussion highlights some scholars who oppose the idea that pseudonymous works exist in the New Testament canon.

Michael Green acknowledges a weighty case against the apostolic authorship of 2 Peter but rejects the idea that the letter is pseudonymous on textual, historical, and ethical grounds. He says, however, if the evidence were to indicate that 2 Peter was an orthodox pseudepigraphon, then "I, for one, believe that we should have to accept the fact that God did employ the literary genre of pseudepigraphy for the communication of his revelation."[159]

F. F. Bruce resists the idea that the New Testament canon contains pseudonymous writings and believes that the standard of apostolicity is still fitting where the authorship of the New Testament writings is concerned. However, he applies the criterion in a different way. For him, the acceptance of Luke's Gospel does not hinge on its validation by direct apostolic authority. Rather, he thinks Luke's record is based on "authentic apostolic preaching" received from eyewitnesses and others.[160] Similarly, the Book of Hebrews "needs no apostle's name to certify its credentials" as a first-century writing which presents the significance of Christ's work as sacrifice and high priest for his people.[161]

Donald Guthrie devoted his doctoral thesis to the subject of pseudonymity[162] and in a related essay examined the disputed New Testament letters against the background of Jewish and noncanonical examples of pseudepigrapha.[163] Guthrie believed that one should recognize the practice of pseudepigraphy in Judaism, while being careful not to assume uncritically that a Christian writer would adopt the practice due to the absence of relevant epistolary parallels. According to Guthrie, what available evidence exists in the Christian period points to the practice of pseudepigraphy as being questionable, both ethically and psychologically. For him such deception was difficult to reconcile with the ethos of the New Testament. In yet another article Guthrie discussed the development of the idea of canonical pseudepigrapha and concluded: "There is no evidence in Christian literature for the idea of a conventional literary device, by which an author as a matter of literary custom and with the full approbation of his circle of readers publishes his own productions in another's name. There was always an ulterior motive."[164]

In his discussion of Paul as a letter writer, Michael Prior observes three factors which have bearing on the authorship of the Pastoral Epistles.[165] First, he points out that Paul wrote several letters in coauthorship with other persons. Only Romans, Ephesians, and the Pastoral Epistles list Paul's name alone as the author; all the other Pauline letters mention someone else's name with Paul's.[166] Thus, Prior maintains that "the person named together with Paul had a real share in the authorship of the letters."[167] Second, he proposes that, while several of Paul's letters to churches were written with secretarial help, the Pastorals were not. Third, Prior notes that the Pastoral Epistles were written to individuals rather than to church communities. For him these qualities account for the differences often pointed out between the Pastoral Epistles and the other Paulines. In the light of these characteristics, Prior sees no need to resort to a pseudonymous authorship in the Pastorals to resolve these variances.

In an essay which primarily addresses the issue of whether pseudoapostolic documents should be retained in the canon of Scripture, E. E. Ellis claims that such writings were a tainted enterprise from the very start and could not avoid the odor of forgery throughout the history of the early church.[168] He assumes that the disputed New Testament letters are pseudonymous and finds what he believes is sufficient evidence for a deceptive intention in them based on three factors: first, the evidence for literary fraud in Greco-Roman antiquity; second, the role of the New Testament apostle in the early church; and third, certain features of the disputed New Testament letters themselves. Ellis concludes that these writings cannot be identified as pseudonymous and simultaneously considered to be innocent documents with the right to a place in the canon of Scripture.

The survey in this section reveals a broad range of opinion on the subject of pseudonymity and the New Testament. Scholars who believe that pseudonymity exists in the New Testament canon find no ethical dilemma in this idea. They get around the ethical difficulty simply by saying that the authors of pseudonymous works were not dishonest or deceitful. Or if they do acknowledge that such writings were deceptive, then they claim, by means of the "noble lie," that this practice of deceit was not morally culpable. Accordingly, psychological objections to the presence of pseudonymity in the New Testament hold no validity for defenders of the practice. They usually are also not convinced by the known responses of the early church to pseudonymity, which do not support the practice as acceptable. Most argue that the early Christians were more concerned about the content and doctrine of writings rather than their authorship. Leading the way today as a representative of the latter belief is David Meade, who believes that the pseudonym was an attribution of authoritative tradition, not literary origins.[169]

Contrary to the group above, those who object to the concept of pseudonymity in the New Testament do so for a variety of reasons. Many oppose the prospect of pseudonymous works in the New Testament on the basis of theological arguments. For them inherent in the practice of pseudonymity is falsehood and present in the concept of canon is truth; the two simply do not mix. Most scholars who reject pseudonymity in the New Testament do so because of the ethical difficulties the idea presents. For them the deception involved in the production of pseudonymous works simply cannot be reconciled with the New Testament writings which teach truth and morality. They also argue that tremendous psychological obstacles impede the idea of a moral Christian writer who composed a pseudonymous work under a false name. Finally, these scholars also argue that the early Christian leaders who scrutinized documents would not have knowingly admitted a pseudonymous writing into the New Testament. The known attitudes of the early church toward pseudonymity clearly favor the latter position.

Other recent scholars whose views on pseudonymity might be considered in a study on the subject include: J. N. D. Kelly (1963), A. T. Hanson (1966, 1982), C. Spicq (1969), H. Balz (1969), M. Hengel (1972), M. Smith (1972), M. Rist (1972), W. Trilling (1972, 1980), W. Stenger (1974), J. Jeremias (1975), A. Lindemann (1977), P. Trummer (1974, 1978), J. Zmijewski (1979), D. N. Penny (1980), T. D. Lea (1984, 1991), M. Kiley (1986), E. Schnabel (1989), M. Wolter (1988), A. T. Lincoln (1990), C. Gempf (1992), B. Steimer (1992), D. W. MacDougall (1993), R. I. Pervo (1994), C. K. Horn (1996), T. L. Wilder (1998), and J. Duff (1998).

Conclusion

Scholars should take into account several factors when studying the subject of pseudonymity and before making a decision about the authorship of a New Testament document. First, they should consider the internal evidence of the New Testament writings and the external evidence of how the early church received those writings. Reputable scholars have examined the identical evidence and yet have reached opposite conclusions concerning the apostolic authorship of New Testament books. For example, M. Dibelius, H. Conzelmann, A. T. Hanson, C. K. Barrett, and Norbert Brox all believe that Paul did not write the Pastoral Epistles; but Ceslaus Spicq, Joachim Jeremias, Donald Guthrie, J. N. D. Kelly, and Gordon Fee all conclude that Paul did author those letters. The latter fact might lead one to think that such decisions are reached subjectively.[170] They should not be. Scholars must genuinely look at the available internal and external evidence when they evaluate the practice of pseudonymity. The extant evidence on the subject clearly indicates that the early church did not accept pseudonymous writings; when discovered, such works were rejected.

Second, scholars should recognize the ethical dilemma that is created when one accepts the presence of pseudonymity in the New Testament. The problem here is the belief that the early church was committed to truth as a moral ideal, encouraged its members to practice it, and yet approved of deliberate deception in the production of pseudonymous writings. Lea correctly observes, "It appears inconsistent for the writer of Ephesians to urge his readers to 'put off falsehood' (Eph. 4:25) if he were not Paul."[171]

Third, students must realize that psychological obstacles accompany the idea that pseudonymity exists in the New Testament. Is it psychologically probable that an early Christian writer would resort to a literary practice which he knew was dishonest and would be rejected by church leaders? Such troublesome questions must be answered by those who advocate pseudonymity in the New Testament.

Fourth, the important crux of apostolic authorship must not be neglected. One of the criteria used by the early church to recognize whether a writing was inspired of God and thus canonical was apostolicity—that is, whether a book had been written by an apostle or by someone under his supervision or with his approval, such as a protégé or amanuensis. Sometimes this criterion is difficult to explain and apply to canonical works such as the anonymous Book of Hebrews, but it is even more difficult to do so with the idea of a canonical writing which has been authored pseudonymously.[172] On the one hand, defenders of the authenticity of the New Testament writings often argue that using the apostles' names in pseudonymous letters usurped their unique status and high authority for one's own unscrupulous purposes. On the other hand, supporters of pseudonymity in the New Testament frequently contend that the apostles' names had to be used pseudonymously to invest letters with needed authority in order to pass on apostolic tradition to a future generation or to fight heresy with apostolic teaching. However, the existing evidence shows that such a practice was not acceptable to the early church. Also, many neglect the fact that the high authority of the apostles did not prevent others from writing in their own names or in works that are now anonymous (for example, Hebrews, *1* and *2 Clement*, *Epistle of Barnabas*, Ignatius, Polycarp). Moreover, the early church often fought heresy in letters without using apostolic pseudonyms, and, for that matter, even without using the apostles' names (for example, Jude and possibly the Book of Hebrews were written against false teaching). Included among the many works written by the early church fathers in their own names against heresy are Irenaeus, *Against Heresy*; Origen, *Against Celsus*; Tertullian, *On Prescription Against Heretics*, and *Against Marcion*. Furthermore, the early Christians often transmitted the teachings of an authority figure without using pseudonymity. For example, Paul himself, when passing on the authoritative tradition of the Old Testament, used introductory formulae such as "It is written."

Rather than writing a pseudonymous letter in an apostle's name, might not an author have written, "The apostle has said," and achieved the same result? Other examples of the transmission of authoritative teaching by the early church without using pseudonymity include: an anonymous author who began his work as "The Teaching of the Twelve Apostles" (the *Didache*); Mark, who introduces his Gospel as "the beginning of the gospel about Jesus Christ"; and Luke's Acts, which gives a largely third-person narration of the teaching of the apostles.[173] Evidently, it was unnecessary to write using the apostles' names pseudonymously.

Finally, students should understand that some New Testament books were written anonymously and not pseudonymously. The Book of Hebrews, as mentioned earlier, is a classic example of anonymity in the New Testament. The writing contains no authorial attribution; the author did not ascribe his name. Pseudonymity occurs when an author purposely conceals his identity behind the name of another person. Though Hebrews did come to be treated as Paul's by the Eastern Church, this designation was not the recognition of a pseudonymous work.[174] Rather, the authorship of the writing was misattributed to Paul. The early church likely recognized Hebrews as canonical under the misconception that Paul wrote it. The latter identification was mistaken. However, the decision by the church to recognize the book as normative and admit it into the New Testament was not mistaken because the book is clearly in accord with apostolic teaching.

Pseudonymity and the Pastoral Epistles

Scholars cast more doubt on the authenticity of the Pastoral Epistles than on any of the other Pauline letters. Some argue that the Pastorals were written after Paul's death by a writer who used the apostle's name to strengthen the authority of these letters. Others suggest that these writings were composed by a later admirer of Paul who included some genuine notes from Paul in his work. Those who argue against the Pauline authorship of the Pastorals do so on the basis of the following criteria.

First, they stress that the vocabulary and style of these letters differ from the other Pauline Epistles. Many words found in the Pastorals do not occur in the other Pauline writings[175]—for example, the term "godliness" (*eusebeia*, 1 Tim. 6:11). Moreover, 175 different *hapax legomena* appear in the Pastoral Epistles which are found nowhere else in the New Testament[176]—for example, the terms "slave dealers" (*andrapodistēs*, 1 Tim. 1:10), "perjurers" (*epiorkos*, 1 Tim. 1:10), and "integrity" (*aphthoria*, Titus 2:7). Stylistic differences also exist between the Pastorals and the rest of the Pauline corpus—for example, several particles are absent from the Pastoral Epistles but present in the other Paulines.[177] Such contrasts lead many to believe that Paul did not write the Pastoral Epistles. However, this argument does not consider that the variations in subject matter, occasion, purpose, and addressees may account for many of these differences.[178] The use of a secretary by Paul may also explain the presence of many words in the Pastorals. Stylistic arguments tend to be subjective and unimpressive.

Differences exist within the other Pauline letters which are just as extensive as those between the Pastorals and the rest of the Pauline corpus.[179] Furthermore, the Pastoral Epistles are simply too brief to determine with accuracy the writing habits of a particular author.[180]

Second, defenders of pseudonymity in the Pastorals contend that the church structure in these letters is too advanced for Paul's time.[181] That is to say, the Pastorals are said to correspond to a later period when church government was more organized and controlled.[182] Moreover, opponents of authenticity often argue that the Pastoral Epistles reflect a church government of monarchial bishops. However, the fact that Paul appointed elders at the start of his missionary work strongly shows his concern for orderly church government (cf. Acts 14:23).[183] Other biblical passages also indicate that church structure played a key part in Paul's ministry (cf. Acts 20:17–28; Phil. 1:1; etc.). Furthermore, the instructions regarding bishops in 1 Timothy and Titus simply do not reflect the monarchial church government which began to develop in the second century.[184] For example, in Titus 1:5–7 the word *bishop* is used interchangeably with *elder*, and since elders are to be appointed in every town, there is no indication of monarchial government.

Third, those who argue against the Pauline authorship of the Pastorals date the heresy opposed in these letters later than Paul's lifetime. In the second century Gnostic heretics came on the scene denying the resurrection of Christ and practicing both a moral license and rigid asceticism.[185] Advocates of pseudonymity in the Pastorals argue that the words *myths* and *genealogies* in 1 Timothy 1:4 pertain to a developed Gnosticism of the second century.[186] They also contend that the Greek term for "opposing arguments" (*antitheseis,* another hapax) in 1 Timothy 6:20 referred to the title of a second-century work written by the heretic Marcion. However, those who defend the Pauline authorship of the Pastorals point out that Gnosticism in its incipient form stretched back into the first century and likely operated in Paul's time.[187] Moreover, they note that the false teaching in these letters contained many Jewish elements (1 Tim. 1:7; Titus 1:10, 14; 3:9) as well as Gnostic characteristics.[188] Consequently, the heresy combated in the Pastoral Epistles is not a developed Gnosticism that requires a date later than Paul's lifetime.

Fourth, supporters of pseudonymity contend that the Pastorals do not emphasize characteristic Pauline doctrines like the Fatherhood of God, the believer's union with Christ, the work of the Holy Spirit, and the cross.[189] Many also suggest that too much of a concern for the transmission of "sound teaching," i.e. tradition (1 Tim. 2:4), and the use of creeds (cf. 1 Tim. 3:16, 2 Tim. 1:13–14; 2 Tim. 2:2; Titus 2:11–14, etc.) in the Pastorals reflect Christianity at the end of the first century.[190] However, standards of this nature are not accurate criteria for determining authenticity. The so-called absence of typical Pauline themes is overstated. For example, the lack of references to the Holy Spirit in the Pastoral Epistles (found only in 1 Tim. 4:1; 2 Tim. 1:14; Titus 3:5) is not as big a problem as it first may seem. Colossians and 2 Thessalonians mention the Holy Spirit only once; Philippians also refers to the Spirit very few times. Moreover, the emphasis on Christian doctrine in the Pastorals does not require a later date. During his ministry Paul stressed holding firmly to tradition (cf. 1 Cor. 11:2), and often cited creedal sayings and hymns in his letters (cf. 1 Cor. 15:3–5; Phil. 2:6–8; Col. 1:15–17, etc.).[191]

Finally, opponents of the Pauline authorship of the Pastoral Epistles argue that these letters contain historical allusions to Paul's life that cannot be placed within the Book of Acts. For example, Paul has been with Timothy and left him in Ephesus to combat false teachers while he went to Macedonia (1 Tim. 1:3); similarly, he has left Titus in Crete (Titus 1:5); Paul also referred to Onesiphorus, who had been seeking for him in Rome (2 Tim. 1:16–17); and he is now a prisoner (2 Tim. 1:8, 16; cf. 4:16). This objection suggests that only what is recorded in the Book of Acts may be considered authentic. Traditionally, defenders of the authenticity of the Pastorals respond to this argument with the theory that Paul was released from his imprisonment in Acts 28, traveled back to the East, and was later arrested and imprisoned in Rome again.[192] Under this view the references to Paul in the Pastorals cannot be placed within the data of Acts because they happened at a later date. Those who hold to the Pauline authorship of the Pastorals also point out that the Book of Acts does not record many details of Paul's life (cf. 2 Cor. 11).[193] Thus, the fact that Acts does not record a second Pauline imprisonment in Rome is not unusual. If Paul had been martyred at the end of his imprisonment recorded in Acts 28, it is difficult to imagine that the author would have completed his work without mentioning this event.[194] Moreover, the fact that Paul expected to be released from prison in Philippians (1:19, 25; 2:24), while he did not in the Pastorals (2 Tim. 4:6–8), also suggests a subsequent Roman imprisonment. Furthermore, a social-historical study of Paul in Roman custody in Acts 28 indicates that Paul was likely released.[195]

External evidence from the early church also attests to the Pauline authorship of the Pastoral Epistles. Several early church leaders accepted these letters as canonical and Pauline—for example, Ignatius, Polycarp, Clement of Alexandria, Tertullian, and Irenaeus. Eusebius, the early church historian, said, "The epistles of Paul are fourteen, all well known and beyond doubt."[196] These "fourteen epistles" included the Pastorals. Furthermore, the Pastoral Epistles are included among the Pauline letters in the Muratorian Canon. The Pauline authorship of the Pastorals was not seriously questioned until the nineteenth century.[197]

In the light of the cumulative evidence, there is no need to resort to a pseudonymous authorship for the Pastoral Epistles. They, like the rest of the New Testament writings, may be relied upon as authentic and trustworthy.

Those who say that pseudonymity exists in the New Testament really need to take a closer look at the evidence for the burden of proof weighs heavily upon them.

Bibliography

Aland, Kurt. "The Problem of Anonymity and Pseudonymity in Christian Literature of the First Two Centuries." *The Authority and Integrity of the New Testament*, 1–13. London: SPCK, 1965.

Bauckham, Richard. "Pseudoapostolic Letters." *JBL* 107 (September 1988): 469–94.

Brox, Norbert. *Falsche Verfasserangaben zur Erklärung der frühchristlichen Pseudepigraphie*. Stuttgart: KBW, 1975.

———. (ed.) *Pseudepigraphie in der heidnischen und jüdischen-christlichen Antike*. Darmstadt: Wissenschaftliche Buchgesellschaft, 1977.

Bruce, F. F. *The Canon of Scripture*. Downers Grove, Ill.: IVP, 1988.

Carson, D. A. "Pseudonymity and Pseudepigraphy," in *Dictionary of New Testament Background*. Ed. Craig A. Evans and Stanley E. Porter, 857–64. Downer's Grove, Ill.: IVP, 2000.

Ellis, Earle E. "Pseudonymity and Canonicity of New Testament Documents." *Worship, Theology and Ministry in the Early Church: Essays in Honour of Ralph P. Martin*. Ed., J. Wilkins and T. Paige, 212–24. Sheffield: Sheffield Academic Press, 1993.

Guthrie, Donald. "Acts and Epistles in Apocryphal Writings." *Apostolic History and the Gospel*. Ed. W. Ward Gasque and Ralph P. Martin, 328–45. Grand Rapids: Eerdmans, 1970.

———. "The Development of the Idea of Canonical Pseudepigrapha in New Testament Criticism." *The Authority and Integrity of the New Testament*, 14–39. London: SPCK, 1965.

———. "Epistolary Pseudepigraphy." Appendix in *New Testament Introduction*, 4th ed., 1011–28. Downers Grove, Ill.: IVP, 1990.

Lea, Thomas D. "The Early Christian View of Pseudepigraphic Writings." *JETS* 27 (March 1984): 65–75.

———. "Pseudonymity and the New Testament." *New Testament Criticism and Interpretation*. Eds. David Alan Black and David S. Dockery, 535–59. Grand Rapids: Zondervan, 1991.

Meade, David. *Pseudonymity and Canon*. Grand Rapids: Eerdmans, 1986.

Metzger, Bruce M. "Literary Forgeries and Canonical Pseudepigrapha." *JBL* 91 (1972): 3–24.

———. *The Canon of the New Testament*. Oxford: Clarendon Press, 1987.

Speyer, Wolfgang. *Die literarische Fälschung im heidnischen und christlichen Altertum*. Munich: Beck, 1971.

Notes

1. This chapter is a revision of the work by Thomas D. Lea, "Pseudonymity and the New Testament," in *New Testament Criticism and Interpretation*, eds. D. A. Black and D. S. Dockery (Grand Rapids: Zondervan, 1991). I have followed the same basic outline and format of Dr. Lea's previous article. In some places I have followed Lea closely; in others I did not. However, any shortcomings in this article should not be attributed to Dr. Lea.

2. I. Howard Marshall, "The Problem of Non-Apostolic Authorship of the Pastoral Epistles" (unpublished paper, 1985), 1.

3. Ibid., 2. Marshall also allows for a letter subsequent to Paul's death and incorporating Pauline material in which the degree of redactional intrusion is minimal.

4. E. E. Ellis ("Pseudonymity and Canonicity of New Testament Documents," *Worship, Theology and Ministry in the Early Church: Essays in Honor of Ralph P. Martin*, ed. M. Wilkins [Sheffield: Sheffield Academic Press, 1993], 212–224; 220) notes that *only* the Pauline and Petrine Epistles can be classified as pseudepigrapha. He says that the letters of James and Jude cannot be classified as such because the names of the authors ("Jude . . . brother of James" [Jude 1] and "James . . . servant of the Lord Jesus Christ" [James 1:1]) "are less precise and could refer to a number of individuals." However, nearly all critics think that the names *James* and *Jude* refer to famous individuals of this name, and many scholars think they are used pseudonymously.

5. For a comparison between Greco-Roman pseudepigraphal epistles and the disputed NT letters, see R. J. Bauckham, "Pseudoapostolic Letters," *JBL* 107 (September 1988): 469–94. Cf. also L. R. Donelson, *Pseudepigraphy and Ethical Argument in the Pastoral Epistles* (Tübingen: Mohr, 1986), 7–66.

6. Though such philosophers do not have precisely the same kind of authority as an apostle, they are nonetheless authority figures of sorts.

7. Iamblichus, *De Vita Pythagorica* § 198.

8. Ibid., § 158.

9. For example, J. Dillon and J. Hershbell (*Iamblichus: On the Pythagorean Way of Life*, SBLTT, eds., H. D. Betz and E. N. O'Neill, no. 29 [Atlanta: Scholars Press, 1991], 203, n. 12) comment on *De Vita Pythagorica* § 198: "This statement might have validity in Aristoxenus' time, but hardly makes much sense subsequent to the publication of the pseudo-Pythagorean writings (forty-three authors other than Pythagoras are represented in Thesleff's collection)."

10. N. Brox, *Falsche Verfasserangaben zur Erklärung der frühchristlichen Pseudepigraphie*, SBS 79 (Stuttgart: KBW, 1975), 73.

11. Ibid.

12. Translation from the Greek text of Busse, *Olympiodori*, 13, 14 (cited from M. Kiley, *Colossians as Pseudepigraphy* [Sheffield: JSOT], 22f.).

13. W. Speyer, *Die literarische Fälschung im heidnischen und christlichen Altertum* (Munchen: Beck, 1971), 139 [translation mine].

14. D. Penny, *The Pseudo-Pauline Letters of the First Two Centuries* (unpublished Ph.D. thesis, Emory University, 1980), 41.

15. N. Gulley, "The Authenticity of the Platonic Epistles," in K. von Fritz, ed., *Pseudepigrapha I* (Genève: O. Reverdin, 1972), 105–30, 128.

16. Penny, *Pseudo-Pauline Letters*, 41.

17. Speyer, *Fälschung*, 139.

18. Cited in Speyer, *Fälschung*, 132 [translation mine].

19. T. D. Lea, "Pseudonymity and the New Testament," *New Testament Criticism and Interpretation* (Grand Rapids: Zondervan, 1991), 535–59. Also Guthrie, "Epistolary Pseudepigraphy," in *New Testament Introduction*, 4th ed. (Downer's Grove, Ill.: IVP, 1990), 1011–28, 1012.

20. Guthrie, "Epistolary Pseudepigraphy," 1012; M. Prior, *Paul the Letter-Writer and the Second Letter to Timothy*, JSNTSup 23 (Sheffield: JSOT, 1989), 20.

21. Concerning the *Letter of Aristeas*, P. S. Alexander ("Epistolary Literature," *Jewish Writings of the Second Temple Period*, CRINT 2.2 , ed. M. E. Stone [Assen: Van

Gorcum/Philadelphia: Fortress Press, 1984], 579–596; 580) says that despite its title, the work "is not a letter: it is not in epistolary form, nor was it recognized as a letter by the earliest writers who refer to it."

22. *Epistle of Jeremiah* v. 1 [italics mine].

23. As Donelson (*Pseudepigraphy and Ethical Argument*, 15, ftn. 37) has correctly noted.

24. For example, R. J. Bauckham (*Jude, 2 Peter*, WBC 50 [Waco: Word, 1983], 133) views *2 Apoc Bar 78–86* as a "testamentary letter" that is analogous to 2 Peter. However, he also acknowledges that "this letter within the framework of a fictional history is not entirely comparable with 2 Peter." Nonetheless, Bauckham goes on to argue that 2 Peter is pseudonymous.

25. Josephus, *Against Apion*, 1.41. Reference cited from Flavius Josephus, *The Works of Josephus*, Loeb Classical Library, trans. H. St. J. Thackeray and R. Marcus, 9 vols. (London: Heinemann, 1926–65).

26. *BT Sanhedrin* 11a. Reference cited from I. Epstein, ed., *The Babylonian Talmud: Seder Nezekin*, 8 vols. (London: Sorcino, 1935).

27. R. H. Charles, ed., *The Apocrypha and Pseudepigrapha of the Old Testament in English*, vol. 2 (n.p.: 1913; reprint, Oxford: Clarendon Press, 1963), ix.

28. These works cannot be surveyed comprehensively in this study. For more thorough surveys, see Bauckham, "Pseudoapostolic Letters," 469–494, and D. Guthrie, *Early Christian Pseudepigraphy and Its Antecedents* (unpublished Ph.D. thesis, London University, 1961).

29. Guthrie, "Epistolary Pseudepigraphy," 1012. Guthrie correctly notes that though the epistolary genre should not be regarded entirely in isolation from other forms of pseudepigraphic literature, it is clearly more important than other types because those works in the NT alleged to be pseudonymous are letters (1011).

30. Ibid., 1017.

31. On the Pauline signatures, see E. R. Richards, *The Secretary in the Letters of Paul*, WUNT 2.42 (Tübingen: Mohr [Siebeck], 1991), 172.

32. M. Fishbane, "Varia Deuteronomica," ZAW 84 (1972): 349–52, 350.

33. Guthrie, "Epistolary Pseudonymity," 1021.

34. For example, Brox, *Falsche Verfasserangaben*.

35. For example, see Plato's *Republic* 3.389b.

36. As E. Schnabel ("History, theology and the biblical canon: an introduction to basic issues," *Themelios* 20/2 (January 1995): 16–24; esp. 19; idem, "Der biblische Kanon und das Phänomen der Pseudonymität," *Jahrbuch für Evangelikale Theologie* 3 Jahrgang" (1989): 59–96; 92–95) has correctly pointed out.

37. Speyer (*Fälschung*, 37f.) correctly sees this book as a case of homonymity, and not pseudonymity.

38. Eusebius, *Eccl Hist*, 3.3, 6: "But since the same Apostle in the salutations at the end of Romans has mentioned among others Hermas, whose, they say, is the Book of the Shepherd." All references from Eusebius are cited from Eusebius, *Ecclesiastical History*, Loeb Classical Library, trans. J. E. L. Oulton, 2 vols. (London: Heinemann/New York: Putnam's, 1932).

39. Ibid., cf. 3.25.

40. Ibid.

41. Translation of Muratorian Canon by B. M. Metzger, *The Canon of the New Testament* (Oxford: Clarendon Press, 1987), 307. Future references to the Muratorian Canon taken from Edgar Hennecke, *New Testament Apocrypha*, rev. ed., ed. Wilhelm

Schneemelcher, trans. R. McL. Wilson, 2 vols. (Louisville: Westminster/John Knox Press, 1991), 1:34–36.

42. Eusebius, *Eccl. Hist.* 6.12, 2ff.

43. But see J. W. McCant ("The Gospel of Peter, Docetism Reconsidered," *NTS* 30 [1984]: 258–73) who argues that the *Gospel of Peter* does not contain heretical teaching. If so, this further supports the theory that Serapion rejected the work because of its pseudoapostolicity.

44. Lea, "Pseudonymity," 539.

45. Tertullian, *On Prescription Against Heretics* 21. Cf. *Against Marcion* 4.3 where Tertullian suggests that a true version of the gospel is not that of Marcion but that which is from the apostles. All references from the Ante-Nicene Fathers are cited from Alexander Roberts and James Donaldson, eds., *The Ante-Nicene Fathers: The Writings of the Fathers down to* A.D.. *325*, 10 vols. (Edinburgh: T&T Clark, 1986–90).

46. Tertullian, *On Baptism*, 17.

47. Lea, "Pseudonymity," 539.

48. Tertullian, *Against Marcion* 4.5.

49. For example, A. T. Lincoln, *Ephesians*, WBC 42 (Dallas: Word, 1990), lxxii.

50. Lea, "Pseudonymity," 539. So also F. F. Bruce, *The Canon of Scripture* (Downers Grove, Ill.: IVP, 1988), 257; and D. Meade, *Pseudonymity and Canon* (Grand Rapids: Eerdmans, 1986), 10.

51. Lea, "Pseudonymity," 539. So also D. Guthrie, "Tertullian and Pseudonymity," *ExpTim* 67 (1956): 341f.

52. Origen, *On Principles*, Preface 8.

53. Eusebius, *Eccl. Hist.* 7.25, 7.

54. Dionysius, *Extant Fragments* 1.4; see also Eusebius, *Eccl. Hist.* 7.25, 17–18.

55. Many agree (e.g., W. G. Kümmel, *Introduction to the NT* [Nashville: Abingdon, 1975], 471) that Dionysius is writing in connection against the apocalyptic doctrine of chiliasm, and thus says that Revelation was written by a John other than the apostle John; Dionysius wants to establish the dissimilarities between Revelation on the one hand, and the Gospel and Epistle of John on the other (cf. Eusebius, *Eccl. Hist.* 7.25, 27).

56. Lea, "Pseudonymity," 540; idem, "Early Christian View," 70.

57. Ibid.

58. As noted by A. Roberts and J. Donaldson, *Ante-Nicene Fathers*, vol. 7: 387–90, 389.

59. Ibid., 388.

60. As correctly noted by Lea, "Pseudonymity," 540; idem, "Early Christian View," 70.

61. This is notable because the following words occur in a document that itself might arguably be called pseudonymous.

62. *Constitutions of the Holy Apostles* 6.16.

63. For example, Meade, *Pseudonymity and Canon*, 12.

64. Ellis, "Pseudonymity," 218.

65. Description of the *Acts of Paul* in Tertullian, *On Baptism* 17.

66. Description in the Muratorian Canon of the *Epistles to the Laodiceans* and the *Alexandrians*.

67. Description by Serapion of pseudoapostolic works recorded in Eusebius, *Eccl. Hist.* 6.12, 2ff.

68. As noted by I. Howard Marshall, "Prospects for the Pastoral Epistles," in *Doing Theology for the People of God: Studies in Honor of J. I. Packer*, eds. Donald Lewis and Alister McGrath (Downers Grove, Ill.: IVP, 1996), 137–55; 146f. David Meade (*Pseudonymity and Canon*, 206) denies that there was a continuity of attitudes between the first and later centuries, but his arguments are unconvincing; see the thesis of T. L. Wilder, *New Testament Pseudonymity and Deception* (unpublished Ph.D. thesis, University of Aberdeen, 1998).

69. Edgar Hennecke, *New Testament Apocrypha*, rev. ed., ed. Wilhelm Schneemelcher, trans. R. McL. Wilson, 2 vols. (Louisville: Westminster/John Knox Press, 1991), 1: 61.

70. Ibid., 55.

71. C. L. Blomberg, "Gospels (Historical Reliability)," in *Dictionary of Jesus and the Gospels*, eds. Joel B. Green, Scot McKnight, I. Howard Marshall (Downers Grove, Ill./Leicester, England: IVP, 1992), 291–97.

72. Hennecke, *NT Apocrypha*, 55.

73. Ibid., 56.

74. Blomberg, "Gospels," 293.

75. Hennecke, *NT Apocrypha* (1965), 1: 36. Interestingly, the present writer could not find the same remark in the revised edition of the same work.

76. Hennecke, *NT Apocrypha* (1991), 1: 34.

77. As Metzger (*Canon of the NT*, 194), Bruce (*Canon of Scripture*, 158), *et al.*, maintain. But most recently see G. M. Hahneman (*The Muratorian Fragment and the Development of the Canon* [Oxford: Clarendon, 1992], 215), who argues that the fragment "is an Eastern list of New Testament works originating from the fourth century."

78. Hennecke, *NT Apocrypha*, 1:27.

79. Translation of Muratorian Canon from Hennecke and Schneemelcher, *NT Apocrypha*, 1:36.

80. Quotation of Muratorian Canon from Hennecke and Schneemelcher, *NT Apocrypha*, 1:36. Some even believe that the author was referring to the biblical Book of Proverbs and not the *Wisdom of Solomon*.

81. Eusebius, *Ecclesiastical History*, 3.25.

82. Ibid., cf. 3.3: "And the fourteen letters of Paul are obvious and plain, yet it is not right to ignore that some dispute the Epistle to the Hebrews, saying that it was rejected by the church of Rome as not being by Paul."

83. Ibid., 3.25.

84. G. W. H. Lampe, ed., *A Patristic Greek Lexicon* (Oxford: Clarendon Press, [1961] 1987), 116f.

85. Martin Luther's "Preface to James," quoted from F. F. Bruce, *Canon of Scripture* (Downer's Grove, Ill.: IVP, 1988), 244.

86. John Calvin, *The Epistle of Paul the Apostle to the Hebrews and the First and Second Epistles of St. Peter*, eds. D. W. Torrance and T. F. Torrance, trans. W. B. Johnston, *Calvin's Commentaries* (Edinburgh: St. Andrew Press, 1963), 325.

87. E. Evanson, *The Dissonance of the Four Generally Received Evangelists* (Ipswich: G. Jermyn, 1792), 255–89. See D. Guthrie, "The Development of the Idea of Canonical Pseudepigrapha in New Testament Criticism," in *The Authority and Integrity of the New Testament* (London: SPCK, 1965), 14–39, 16.

88. Guthrie, "Canonical Pseudepigrapha," 18.

89. F. C. Baur, *Paul, His Life and Works*, trans. A. Menzies, 2 vols. (London: Williams and Norgate, 1875), II:109.

90. Ibid., II:110.

91. Ibid., II:110f.

92. Ibid., II:110.

93. A. Jülicher, *An Introduction to the New Testament,* trans. J. P. Ward (London: Smith, 1904), 52.

94. Ibid.

95. Ibid.

96. Ibid.

97. Ibid., 53.

98. Ibid. For example, the Pythagorean literature and Jewish apocalyptic.

99. M. Dibelius, *A Fresh Approach to the New Testament and Early Christian Literature* (New York: Scribner's, 1936), 207.

100. Ibid., 232.

101. James Moffatt, *Introduction to the Literature of the New Testament,* 3d. ed. (Edinburgh: T&T Clark, 1918), 41.

102. Ibid.

103. Ibid., 42.

104. Ibid., 43.

105. P. N. Harrison, *The Problem of the Pastoral Epistles* (London: Oxford, 1921).

106. Edgar J. Goodspeed, *New Chapters in New Testament Study* (New York: Macmillan, 1937), 172.

107. Ibid., 173.

108. F. W. Beare, *The First Epistle of Peter* (Oxford: Blackwell, 1961 [1947]), 29.

109. Ibid., 30.

110. J. C. Fenton, "Pseudonymity in the New Testament," *Theology* 58 (February 1955): 51–56.

111. Ibid., 54.

112. J. S. Candlish, "On the Moral Character of Pseudonymous Books," *The Expositor* 4, series 4 (London: Hodder, 1891), 103, 262.

113. Ibid., 273f.

114. Ibid., 276.

115. R. D. Shaw, *The Pauline Epistles: Introductory and Expository Studies,* 4th ed. (Edinburgh: T&T Clark, 1913), 481.

116. Ibid., 482.

117. Ibid.

118. J. I. Packer, *Fundamentalism and the Word of God* (London: InterVarsity Fellowship, 1958), 184.

119. Ibid.

120. Ibid.

121. A. Meyer, "Religiöse Pseudepigraphie als ethische-psychologisches Problem," in N. Brox, ed., *Pseudepigraphie in der heidnischen und jüdischen-christlichen Antike* (Darmstadt: Wissenschaftliche Buchgesellschaft, 1977), 90–110, 107 [translation mine].

122. Ibid., 109 [translation mine].

123. F. Torm, "Die Psychologie der Pseudonymität im Hinblick auf die Literatur des Urchristentums," in N. Brox, ed., *Pseudepigraphie,* 111–147.

124. As Lea ("Pseudonymity," 547) and others have noted.

125. K. Aland, "The Problem of Anonymity and Pseudonymity in Christian Literature of the First Two Centuries," in *The Authorship and Integrity of the New Testament* (London: SPCK, 1965), 1–13.

126. Ibid., 8.

127. Ibid., 7.

128. Lea, "Pseudonymity," 548.

129. As Meade (*Pseudonymity and Canon*, 13f.) and others have noted.

130. B. M. Metzger, "Literary Forgeries and Canonical Pseudepigrapha," *JBL* (1972): 3–24.

131. Ibid., 15.

132. Ibid., 19.

133. Ibid., 22.

134. Brox, *Falsche Verfasserangaben*, 26–36.

135. Ibid., 52f., 105–106.

136. Ibid., 82ff.

137. Criticism noted by Meade, *Pseudonymity and Canon*, 12.

138. Ibid.

139. W. Speyer, *Fälschung*. See also idem, "Religiöse Pseudepigraphie und Literarische Fälschung im Altertum," in Brox, ed., *Pseudepigraphie*, 195–263; and idem, "Fälschung, pseudepigraphische freie Erfindung und 'echte religiöse Pseudepigraphie,'" in K. von Fritz, ed., *Pseudepigrapha I* (Genève: O. Reverdin, 1972), 333–66 with discussion 367–72. Similar to Speyer's monograph, though not as detailed, is the earlier work of J. A. Sint, *Pseudonymität im Altertum, ihre Formen und ihre Gründe* (Innsbruck: Universitätsverlag, 1960).

140. See Speyer's summary in "Religiöse Pseudepigraphie und Literarische Fälschung," 262.

141. Speyer, *Fälschung*, 219.

142. Ibid., 94f., 97.

143. Ibid., 278f.

144. Ibid., 285f.

145. As Meade (*Pseudonymity and Canon*, 8–9) *et al.* have noted.

146. Meade, *Pseudonymity and Canon* (Grand Rapids: Eerdmans, 1986).

147. Ibid., see esp. 103–93.

148. Ibid., 197.

149. As many scholars have commented.

150. Donelson, *Pseudepigraphy and Ethical Argument in the Pastoral Epistles*. See especially chapter 1 of his monograph.

151. Bauckham, "Pseudoapostolic Letters," 469–94.

152. Ibid., 469.

153. R. Bauckham (*Jude, 2 Peter*, WBC 50 [Waco: Word, 1983]) believes that the pseudonym in 2 Peter is a device used by the writer to mediate faithfully the apostolic message.

154. Bauckham, "Pseudoapostolic Letters," 475.

155. I. Howard Marshall, in collaboration with Philip H. Towner, *A Critical and Exegetical Commentary on the Pastoral Epistles*. ICC (Edinburgh: T&T Clark, 1999), 59-108.

156. Ibid., 83-84.

157. Ibid., 84. Marshall believes that writings in which students attributed their works to their philosophical teachers may be categorized here.

158. Ibid., 92. For the summary presented in this paragraph, see Marshall's conclusion on p. 92.

159. Michael Green, *2 Peter and Jude*, Tyndale New Testament Commentaries, rev. ed. (Grand Rapids: Eerdmans, 1987), 38.

160. Bruce, *Canon of Scripture*, 276f.

161. Ibid., 277.

162. Guthrie, *Early Christian Pseudepigraphy and Its Antecedents*.

163. Guthrie, "Epistolary Pseudepigraphy," 1011–28.

164. Guthrie, "Canonical Pseudepigrapha," 14–39; 38.

165. M. Prior, *Paul the Letter-Writer and the Second Letter to Timothy*, JSNTSup 23 (Sheffield: JSOT, 1989), 37–57.

166. Ibid., 38.

167. Ibid., 39.

168. Ellis, "Pseudonymity and Canonicity," 212–24.

169. As Lea ("Pseudonymity," 551) has correctly noted.

170. As noted by Lea, "Pseudonymity," 552.

171. Lea, "Pseudonymity," 552.

172. Ibid., 552f.

173. Ellis, "Pseudonymity," 220.

174. As Lea ("Pseudonymity," 553) and others have emphasized. Because of some comments made by Origen on Hebrews, some argue that the early church would have viewed a pseudonymous letter which imparted Pauline teaching as acceptable. Origen said, "I should say that the thoughts are the apostle's, but that the style and composition belong to one who called to mind the apostle's teachings and . . . made short notes of what his master said" (cp. Eusebius, *Eccl. Hist.* II: 6.25, 13). However, the position that the early church would have accepted pseudonymity cannot be maintained on the basis of these remarks because Hebrews clearly is anonymous. Origen went on to say, "But who wrote [Hebrews], in truth God knows" (*Eccl. Hist.* II: 6.25, 14).

175. D. Guthrie, *New Testament Introduction* (Downers Grove, Ill.: IVP, 1990), 619.

176. Ibid.

177. Ibid.

178. Ibid., 633.

179. For examples, see Guthrie, *Introduction*, 635.

180. Lea, "Pseudonymity," 553.

181. Guthrie, *Introduction*, 615.

182. Ibid., 616.

183. Ibid., 625.

184. Ibid., 627.

185. Lea, "Pseudonymity," 554; Guthrie, *Introduction*, 617.

186. Lea, "Pseudonymity," 554.

187. Guthrie, *Introduction*, 617.

188. Lea, "Pseudonymity," 554; Guthrie, *Introduction*, 628.

189. Ibid., 618.

190. Ibid., 619.

191. Ibid., 632.

192. As Lea ("Pseudonymity," 555) has succinctly summarized.

193. Guthrie, *Introduction*, 622.

194. Ibid., 624.

195. Brian Rapske, *Paul in Roman Custody: The Book of Acts in Its First Century Setting*, vol. 3, ed. Bruce W. Winter (Grand Rapids: Eerdmans/Carlisle: Paternoster, 1994), 191. He states, "The custody in Rome as Luke reports it and the probable material basis

of the deliberations leading to that custody . . . constitute a significant and highly placed Roman estimate of the trial's probable outcome; i.e., that Paul will be released."

196. Eusebius, *Ecclesiastical History* 3.3.

197. As Lea ("Pseudonymity," 555) and many others have noted.

Chapter 15

Interpreting the Synoptic Gospels

Robert H. Stein
The Southern Baptist Theological Seminary

Upon reading the four canonical Gospels, one becomes immediately aware that they can be divided into two groups. One group consists of the Gospels of Matthew, Mark, and Luke, and the other contains the Gospel of John.[1] The reasons for grouping Matthew, Mark, and Luke together are: (1) they contain a great deal of common material; (2) this material is arranged in a similar order; and (3) the wording of this material is close and at times identical. In contrast, John contains a great deal of material not found in Matthew, Mark, and Luke, and the order and wording are different. The accounts found in John also tend to be considerably longer than those found in the first three Gospels. As a result, Matthew, Mark, and Luke have been referred to as the "Synoptic Gospels," because they are to be "viewed (*opsesthai*) together (*sun*)."[2]

The similarity of the Synoptic Gospels raises for the serious reader several important issues. One involves the question of why Matthew, Mark, and Luke look so much alike. How does one explain their look-alike character? This is the essence of what is called the "Synoptic Problem." Another issue that arises in the study of the Synoptic Gospels involves the question of what the traditions and sayings found in these Gospels were like before they were written down and how they were "delivered"[3] during the period before their incorporation into our present Gospels. This area of investigation involves the discipline of "Form Criticism." Whereas the look-alike character of the Synoptic Gospels raises these kinds of questions, the differences in these Gospels raise another set of questions. One involves the theological emphases found in these differences. This area of investigation involves the discipline of "Redaction Criticism." Another area of investigation raised by these differences involves historical questions. How does one deal with the differences in order and wording of various events and sayings in these Gospels?

Few areas of the New Testament have been so extensively investigated and debated as this one. Explanations for the similarity of Matthew, Mark, and Luke have involved historical, theological, oral, and literary solutions. Some have suggested that their look-alike character is due to their being accurate representations of what Jesus said and did. Yet how does one then explain their differences and the significant differences between the Synoptic Gospels and John? Others have explained their similarity as being due to their being inspired by the Holy Spirit, but what then of John? Few people who argue for the inspiration of Matthew, Mark, and Luke deny the inspiration of John. Thus historical and theological solutions of the Synoptic Problem have never been very convincing. More convincing is the view that each of the Evangelists used a common oral tradition of the events and sayings of Jesus. As a result of using this common oral tradition, they look alike.

THE IDEA OF A COMMON ORAL TRADITION

The suggestion that underlying the look-alike character of the Synoptic Gospels is the use of a common tradition is probably correct, but was this common element "oral" in nature? There are a number of reasons a common oral tradition is an inadequate solution for the Synoptic Problem. First, a common oral tradition is insufficient to explain the degree of similarity in wording between the Synoptic Gospels. To illustrate this one need only compare in a synopsis such passages as Mark 10:13–16; 12:18–27; 13:5–8 and their parallels in Matthew and Luke. A common oral source is a less likely explanation for these similarities than a common written source. More convincing still is the common order of the material. If one compares Mark 3:31–6:6a and 8:27–10:52 with the parallels in Matthew and Luke, one is impressed by their great similarity. It is difficult to explain the similar order of all this material as being due to a common oral tradition. This is because during the oral period of gospel tradition the material found in Mark 3:31–6:6a and 8:27–10:52 was memorized and passed down primarily as small units or pericopes.[4]

Another argument against a common oral source explaining the Synoptic Problem involves the presence of similar parenthetical material within these Gospels. In Mark 13:14 and Matthew 24:15, we find the exact editorial comment, "Let the *reader* [note!] understand" (NIV here and elsewhere). It is difficult to believe that this was found in the *oral* tradition of Jesus' saying. Oral explanations that seek to account for these common editorial comments are far less convincing than those that see them as being due to a comment found in a written source. In a similar manner the parenthetical comments found in Matthew 9:6/Mark 2:10/Luke 5:24 ("He said to the paralytic") and Mark 5:8 and Luke 8:29 ("For Jesus was saying to him") are more easily explained by the use of a common written source than an oral one.

A third argument against the oral source explanation involves the similarity we find in various biblical quotations contained in the Synoptic Gospels. Such a similarity would not be significant if the quotations were identical to that found in the Hebrew (the masoretic text) or Greek Old Testament (the Septuagint). However, there are times when we find verbal agreement in these Gospels of an Old Testament quotation that follows neither the masoretic nor Septuagintal text. In Matthew 3:3/Mark 1:2/Luke 3:4 and Matthew 15:9/Mark 7:7, we find agreements in the Old Testament quotations that disagree with both the Hebrew and Greek Old Testament. This is more convincingly explained by the use of a common written source than a common oral one, for in the oral retelling of a tradition, the Old Testament quotation would tend to be "corrected" to the known Hebrew or Greek form with which the community was familiar.

Finally, it should be noted that in Luke 1:1–4, whereas the Evangelist does refer to the passing on of oral traditions (1:2, "as they were handed down to us"), he speaks of others who "had undertaken to draw up an account of the things which have been fulfilled among us" (1:1). He furthermore speaks of his having investigated all these things carefully "from the beginning" (1:3). The similarity of Luke to Matthew and Mark is most easily explained in his having investigated and used a common written source (or sources). For the above reasons the vast majority of scholars argue that the similarity of Matthew, Mark, and Luke is due to their having used a common written source (or sources).

THE IDEA OF A COMMON WRITTEN SOURCE (OR SOURCES)

Once scholars became convinced that a common written source(s) was the reason Matthew, Mark, and Luke look alike, the question arose as to the nature of this source. Did it look more like Matthew, Mark, or Luke? For reasons that we shall soon discuss, the majority of scholars became convinced that the common source underlying the Synoptic Gospels looked more like Mark. As a result this source began to be referred to as "proto-Mark." As time went on, however, "proto-Mark" began to look so much like Mark that the question arose as to why it could not simply have been the canonical Mark. Today the great majority of scholars who investigate this question are convinced that the look-alike character of Matthew, Mark, and Luke is due to the fact that Matthew and Luke in writing their Gospels used Mark as their basic source.

The Priority of Mark

While it must be remembered that the "priority of Mark" is a hypothesis and not a "proof," the evidence in support of the view that Matthew and Luke used Mark is quite convincing. Several arguments have led scholars to this conclusion:[5]

1. The fact that Matthew and Luke are considerably larger than Mark is more easily explained by Matthew and Luke's adding material to their

Gospels than Mark's having eliminated that material. For example, it is much easier to conceptualize Matthew and Luke adding to their Markan source their birth accounts, the Sermon on the Mount/Plain, resurrection accounts, etc., than to conceive of Mark's omitting this material from his Matthean or Lukan source. Some scholars have attempted to explain the brevity of Mark as being due to his seeking to write an "abridged" Gospel. This explanation, however, is refuted by the fact that those stories common to these Gospels are almost always longer in Mark.[6] It is hard to understand why Mark would seek to abridge Matthew and/or Luke by eliminating various accounts and sayings and at the same time lengthening those accounts that he included.

2. Mark generally possesses a literary style inferior to Matthew and Luke. The issue here is not whether Mark wrote acceptable Greek but why his Greek is less polished than that of Matthew and Luke. The improvement of Mark's literary style by Matthew and Luke is more readily understood than the reverse.[7]

3. In Mark we come across several passages containing theological problems that we do not find in the parallel accounts in Matthew and/or Luke. Again it is easier to understand Matthew and Luke's seeking to ameliorate the problems that the reading in Mark creates than Mark changing Matthew and/or Luke in a way that would create such problems. In comparing Mark 10:18 and Matthew 19:17, it is much easier to think of Matthew's having used Mark and seeking to alleviate the difficulty that Mark's wording creates than to think that Mark used Matthew here and made his account more difficult for his readers.[8]

4. If one underlines the parallel accounts in the Synoptic Gospels, it becomes clear that whereas on numerous occasions Matthew and Mark agree against Luke, and Mark and Luke agree against Matthew, there are few agreements of Matthew and Luke against Mark in the triple tradition, i.e., in the accounts found in all three Gospels. This is true both with respect to the wording of the accounts in the triple tradition and the order of these accounts in their respective Gospels. Without denying that Matthew-Luke agreements (in wording but not in order) against Mark do exist in the triple tradition, it should be pointed out that they are considerably fewer than the Matthew-Mark and Mark-Luke agreements. This is best explained on the basis of Matthew and Luke's not "knowing one another," that is, not having used the other. The Griesbach Hypothesis (Matthew was first, Luke used Matthew, and Mark used both Matthew and Luke) can explain how such agreements might have arisen, but it encounters insurmountable objections.[9] There simply is no ancient precedent for such an alleged, complicated use of sources by Mark.[10]

5. There are several instances in the Synoptic Gospels where the literary agreement can best be explained by Matthew's and/or Luke's use of Mark. An example of this is found in Mark 1:10 and Matthew 3:16. The "and

immediately" found in Mark fits well his use of this expression to connect various accounts. In the Matthean parallel, however, the "and immediately" is confusing to say the least. In Mark, after Jesus was baptized, while coming out of the water he "immediately" saw the heavens opening. In Matthew, however, after Jesus was baptized, he "immediately" came up out of the water. It appears that Matthew in this instance followed Mark's order but did not realize the consequence of his having changed Mark's verb, "baptized," to a participle and Mark's participle, "coming out," to a finite verb. As a result the "immediately" in Mark, which describes the heavens opening, now describes Jesus immediately coming out of the water.[11]

6. The final argument in favor of Markan priority that will be mentioned is the argument from redaction criticism. The use of Mark by Matthew and Luke explains well their editorial work and theological emphases. When one looks at the Christological title "Son of David" in Matthew, we find that it appears eleven times compared to only four times in Mark and Luke. It is much easier to understand this emphasis of Matthew (cf.1:1) in 2:23; 15:22; and 21:9 and 15 as being added by Matthew to his Markan source than being deleted by Mark (and Luke) from a Matthean source. It is also easier to see Matthew as having added his emphasis "this was to fulfill" in 5:17–18 (cf. Luke 16:16–17) and in 8:17; 12:17; 13:14; 21:4; and 26:54 (cf. the parallels in Mark and Luke) than to think of the other Evangelists' having for some reason omitted this expression. This is especially true with regard to Luke, who strongly emphasizes the fulfillment of Scripture.[12] Similarly, when one compares the Lukan emphasis on the importance of prayer in 3:21; 4:1, 14; 5:17; 11:13 (cf. 4:16–21) with the parallels in Mark and Matthew, it is clear that he has added this to his Markan (or Q) source.

Whereas the above arguments in favor of Markan priority, when considered individually, may not seem absolutely convincing, when considered together they become quite compelling. As a result, the great majority of scholars involved in the investigation of the Synoptic Problem believe that the best explanation for their look-alike character is that Matthew and Luke used Mark.

The Existence of Q

Common material exists in Matthew and Luke that is not found in Mark. Some of this material is, at times, almost identical.[13] The easiest explanation of this common material, which consists of about 235 verses, is that either Matthew used Luke as a source or that Luke used Matthew. Such an explanation is simple and straightforward and does not require the positing of an unknown, hypothetical source. There are convincing reasons, however, for concluding that Matthew and Luke did not know each other, i.e., that one of these Gospel writers did not use the Gospel of the other.

1. Luke never uses any of the Matthean additions to the Markan narrative (and vice versa). Some clear examples of this can be found in Matthew

8:17; 12:5–6, 11; 13:14–15; 18:3–4. Why would Luke never have included in his Gospel something that Matthew has in his account but is not found in Mark? If Luke did not use Matthew, this is understandable, but if he used the Gospel of Matthew and copied so carefully some of this Q material, it is difficult to understand why he never included Matthean additions to the Markan narrative in his Gospel.[14]

2. Luke never leaves the Q material in the same context that we find it in Matthew. In Matthew the Q material is arranged artistically into five sections (chapters 5–7; 10; 13; 18; 23–25), and all of these sections end similarly with something like "When Jesus had finished saying these things" (7:28; 11:1; 13:53; 19:1; and 26:1 [NOTE: "When Jesus had finished saying *all* these things"]). In Luke this material is arranged in two uneven sections: 6:20–8:3 and 9:51–18:14. If Luke knew Matthew, that is, if he obtained his Q material from Matthew, it is difficult to understand why he rearranged them in such a totally different and inferior (at least "artistically") way. The independent use of a common source Q explains more easily why the two Evangelists arranged the material of Q in radically different ways.

3. At times the Q material appears to be more primitive, that is, less developed theologically, in Luke and at times in Matthew. If Luke obtained his material from Matthew, one would expect that almost always his version of the Q material would be more developed. What we find, however, is that, whereas many times the material in Luke is more primitive (Luke 6:20, 21, 31; 11:2, 20; 14:26–27), at times it is the material in Matthew that is more primitive (Matt. 5:44; 6:8, 12; 7:11; 8:22; 10:34). This phenomenon is most easily explained on the basis of Matthew and Luke not knowing each other and independently using a common source, which scholars call Q.

4. Luke never agrees with Matthew against Mark in the order of the material. Again it is difficult to explain, if Luke at times so carefully copied Matthew in order to obtain the Q material, why he would never side with Matthew in his ordering of the material over against Mark. This is quite easily explained if Matthew and Luke did not know each other. (The same argument is applicable if one argues that Matthew supposedly knew Luke.)[15]

"M" and "L"

Matthew and Luke obviously contain material not found in either Mark or Q. This material is referred to as *M* material (material found only in Matthew) and *L* material (material found only in Luke). It is not only possible but also probable that some of this material came from Q. If, for example, Matthew followed Q at a certain point but Luke for some reason decided to exclude this material, it would appear in Matthew as *M* material. Similarly, if Luke followed Q at a certain point but Matthew decided to exclude this material, it would appear in Luke as *L* material. It is speculative to speak of an *M* or *L* source as specific written sources. It is best to view *M* and *L* as representing the material unique to Matthew and Luke respectively. This unique material might come from *Q*, one of several other written sources, as well as from the oral traditions with which they were both familiar.

The Gospel Traditions during the Oral Period

After scholars believed that they had explained why Matthew, Mark, and Luke looked so much alike and delineated the literary relationships that caused this look-alike character, a new question arose. What were these gospel traditions in the Synoptic Gospels like before they were written down? This question concerning oral sources, which was already under discussion in OT studies, came to the forefront of gospel studies after World War I. The discussion was initiated by a trio of German scholars.[16] The new discipline called *Formgeschichte* or "Form Criticism" was based on a number of presuppositions. Some of these have been generally acknowledged, whereas others are hotly disputed.

The presuppositions generally conceded by most scholars included:[17]

1. "Before the Gospels were written the gospel traditions circulated in oral form within the Christian community." There is little disagreement over this. Unless the Gospels were written before the ascension of Jesus into heaven, Christians must have shared the Jesus traditions orally with others. No one dates the writing down of the Jesus traditions so early as to preclude such an oral period. Luke 1:2 furthermore expressly refers to the oral passing on of the traditions recorded in his Gospel.

2. "During this period the gospel traditions tended to be passed on as individual and isolated units with the exception of the passion tradition." Except for the general context of the life and teachings of Jesus possessed by the Christian community, individual traditions appear to have circulated as isolated units. A good analogy of this can be seen in the knowledge Christians today possess of such traditions as the Lord's Prayer, the healing of the paralytic, the conversion of Zacchaeus, individual sayings of Jesus, the parable of the prodigal son, etc. Whereas the knowledge of these individual traditions may be quite good, the only context most people have for them is their general knowledge of the life and teachings of Jesus. There is seldom any knowledge of what immediately precedes or follows these individual traditions, and such knowledge is unnecessary. One can know and understand the Lord's Prayer, the parable of the prodigal son, and the healing of the paralytic, etc. without knowing what immediately precedes or follows them. Interpreted within the general context of Jesus' life and teachings, these isolated units make perfectly good sense. On the other hand, it is difficult to speak of the passion of Jesus without telling the entire story. Such elements as the arrest of Jesus, his trial before the Sanhedrin, his trial before Pontius Pilate do not possess satisfactory breaking points, because from the arrest on, one is prone to ask, "And then what happened?"[18]

3. "The gospel traditions can be classified according to various forms." This presupposition must be qualified. Some of the traditions can be classified nicely according to their form. Miracle stories of healing and pronouncement stories by their very nature follow a specific format. In a healing miracle you have: a description of the problem (diagnosis); usually, but not always, a reference to faith; the healing proper (prescription); and the result (cure). These are necessary elements in any account of a healing miracle. In a pronouncement story the story always end with the pronouncement for which the story exists. Other forms attributed to the gospel traditions, such as stories about Jesus, parables, and various sayings of Jesus, however, are classified more by their subject matter than by their literary form.

4. "The gospel traditions were preserved and passed on because of their religious value to the Christian community." It is self-evident that not everything Jesus said or did is recorded in the Gospels (John 21:25). What we have is a selection (John 20:30–31), and this selection was governed primarily by the religious interests and needs of the Christian community. We do not have accounts in our Gospels of Jesus' eating meals in which nothing significant occurred, even though there must have been many such occasions. Most gospel traditions were preserved and passed on because they met various Christian apologetical, polemical, catechetical, and liturgical needs. It would be misleading, however, to assume that such needs existed prior to and brought about the creation of such traditions. At one time early Christian prophets were posited as creating much of the gospel tradition, but there seems to be little justification for such an assertion.[19] It was the community's reverence and commitment to the Jesus traditions that created its needs and interests. These in turn caused the community to preserve the source of these needs and interests. The latter were created and determined, however, by the traditions and not vice versa.

Some of the other presuppositions associated with form criticism that are much more disputed include:

5. "The gospel tradition lacks any interest in temporal, geographical, or biographical concerns." This presupposition has taken a valuable insight and unfortunately absolutized it. The existence of most of the Jesus traditions as isolated units during the oral period shows that by nature they require no immediate temporal or geographical ties with the other traditions. The general context of Jesus' life and teachings sufficed. Of course, certain traditions have clear temporal associations with the beginning (the appearance of John the Baptist, Jesus' baptism, the temptation, the call of the disciples) or the end of Jesus' ministry (the betrayal, arrest, trial, crucifixion, and resurrection). The other traditions, however, were simply understood as occurring between these main events. Apart from an occasional temporal tie ("And after six days," Mark 9:2), most traditions and sayings in the gospel tradition lack any necessary chronological tie with another

event. Similarly, although some traditions possess geographical ties to certain cities (Capernaum—Mark 1:21, 29; 2:1; 9:33; Nazareth—Mark 6:1; Tyre—Mark 7:24; Dalmanutha—Mark 8:10; Bathsaida—Mark 8:22; Caesarea Philippi—Mark 8:27; Jerusalem—Mark 11:1ff.; etc.) or regions (Sea of Galilee—Mark 2:13; 3:7; 4:1, 35; 5:1; etc.; across the Jordan—Mark 10:1; etc.), most are not tied to any particular geographical designation.

As for the assertion that the gospel traditions display little biographical interest, the issue depends on how one defines *biographical*. The traditions clearly are interested in Jesus' life and teachings and seek to help their hearers understand "Who then is this, that even wind and sea obey him?" (Mark 4:41). Yet when compared to the concerns of modern-day biographers, they have little in common. They have essentially no interest in the first thirty years of Jesus' life. The only incident recorded outside of the events surrounding Jesus' birth involves the visit of the boy Jesus at the age of twelve to the temple in Jerusalem (Luke 2:41–51). No modern biography would pay so little attention to the "formative years" of Jesus' childhood. For the gospel tradition, however, Jesus was, is, and always will be the Son of God. No psychological development of this awareness is hinted at in the tradition. Yet to say that the gospels portray no interest in temporal, geographical, or biographical concerns is grossly exaggerated.

6. "The laws governing the Jesus tradition during the oral period can and should be learned in order to work backwards to the more primitive tradition." At one time there was great confidence that oral traditions were passed on via certain unalterable principles. These principles were ascertained from observing the development of various traditions in the Synoptic and apocryphal gospels, rabbinic literature, and German folklore.

The work of E. P. Sanders, however, raised serious questions concerning the legitimacy of such "laws." When he compared five possible tendencies or laws (the increasing of length and detail, diminishing of Semitisms, the increasing use of direct discourse, and the conflation of various accounts), he discovered that there were no hard and fast rules of development.[20]

At times traditions in the Gospel accounts tend to become more specific (the high priest's servant's ear—Mark 14:47; the high priest's servant's *right* ear—Luke 22:50; the high priest's servant's, named *Malchus*, right ear—John 18:10), but at times they become less specific (*green* grass—Mark 6:39; grass—Matt. 14:19). How useful for arriving at the more primitive form of a tradition is a "law" that states that at times traditions become more specific and at times they become less specific? Even more important, however, is the criticism that has been raised that the alleged laws for the passing on of oral traditions have come out of the observing of how *written* traditions were passed on. On what basis are we to assume that oral tradition were passed on and developed according to the same rules as written traditions? It has even been suggested by some that the development of oral traditions follow quite different rules.[21]

7. "The eyewitnesses played no significant role in the passing on of the gospel traditions." This presupposition is seldom stated, but it is both assumed and necessary for those who believe that the present form of the traditions in our Gospels has experienced radical corruption.[22] This denial is built on several additional presuppositions. One involves the nature of the early church. In the minds of some scholars the early church was a free, democratic, and charismatic organization that was "unhindered" by any rigid form of leadership. Such a view, of course, finds little support in the New Testament where issues are brought to the "apostles and elders (Acts 15:2)" for resolution (cf., Gal. 2:1–10).

An even more important presupposition, however, that comes into play in this area involves a narrow understanding of the historical-critical method by many form critics. In their understanding of this method, miracles are arbitrarily determined as being impossible. As a result, by definition the life of Jesus must have been free of the supernatural.[23] If the Gospels (the third *Sitz im Leben*) portray a supernatural Jesus (and of course they do), and if Jesus' life (the first *Sitz im Leben*) was by definition free of the supernatural, then a great deal of distortion and corruption of the gospel tradition must have taken place during the oral period (the second *Sitz im Leben*). Radical form critics assume the gospel traditions were radically transformed and corrupted during the oral period. They also assume, however, that the eyewitnesses and disciples were not deceitful. Since the eyewitnesses and disciples knew from their experience only a non-supernatural Jesus, they therefore could not have had any serious connection and control of the Jesus traditions during this period of great corruption.

The problem with such a presupposition is that the earliest evidence available for understanding how the gospel traditions were transmitted during the oral period places the eyewitnesses and disciples at the heart of the transmission process. Luke writes that the events recorded in his Gospel were originally "handed on to us by those who from the beginning were eyewitnesses and servants of the word" (1:2). These words clearly stand in stark contrast and opposition to this presupposition of the radical form critics. In this regard it should be noted that Luke lived some nineteen hundred years closer to this period in history than these critics. In fact, he lived during this very period and even claims to have investigated all of these traditions firsthand. It is evident that, if one begins with the presupposition that Jesus' life and ministry were non-supernatural, one is then forced to eliminate the eyewitnesses from any significant role in the passing on, preserving, and controlling of the gospel traditions. If one is open to the supernatural in the life of Jesus, however, then one is able to take seriously the words of Luke 1:2. Luke furthermore argues that his own account is in agreement with these traditions, because he believed his Gospel would help Theophilus "know the certainty of the things [he had been] taught" through the oral tradition (1:4).

There also existed in the time of Jesus a precedent within the culture of Jesus and the early disciples for the passing on of oral traditions. This came from the rabbinic practice of passing on oral tradition over the centuries. Here, rather than a carefree and charismatic attitude of passing on traditions, we find instead the practice of careful memorization using mnemonic devices and constant repetition. There is much debate as to how legitimate it is to read the practice of second- and third-century rabbinic Judaism into the first-century. Nevertheless, it is more likely that the passing on of the gospel traditions by the eyewitnesses and ministers of the word has more in common with such rabbinic practice than the view of the radical form critics that the apostles and eyewitnesses played no significant role in this process.[24]

THE RELIABILITY OF THE GOSPEL TRADITION

The faithful transmission of the Jesus tradition during the oral period is witnessed to by several considerations. One of these is the lack of any material within the Jesus tradition that deals with some of the early church's major conflicts. The single most pressing issue the early Christian community faced involved what to do with non-Jews who wanted to become part of the community. The importance of this issue is seen in both the amount of space Luke (Acts 10–11, 15) and Paul (Gal. 3–5; Rom. 4) devote to it and the importance of the issue in their thinking. Did Gentiles have to be circumcised in order to become Christians? In other words, did becoming a Christian for a Gentile also involve becoming a Jew? No Jesus tradition deals with this issue. In fact, if anything, the only tradition discussing this issue seems to support the need for circumcision (John 7:22).

The debate of the early church on this issue (Acts 11; 15; Gal. 2) never focused on a saying of Jesus! On the contrary, the issue was decided by the fact that God had unconditionally accepted Gentiles without their being circumcised. This was confirmed by his giving them the gift of the Spirit. What must be noted in all the church's discussion of this is that no one in the church created a Jesus tradition to resolve this issue. Their reverence for the Jesus tradition did not permit such an approach. In the same manner Paul, in dealing with the issue of divorce, made a clear distinction between what the Jesus tradition said on this issue ("To the married I give this command [not I, but the Lord]," 1 Cor. 7:10) and his own teaching ("To the rest I say [I not the Lord]" 1 Cor. 7:12). Paul did not think he could simply place his teachings, even though they were authoritative and came from the Lord, on the lips of the historical Jesus. Paul even believed it was not so much that the church was given the gospel traditions and commanded to preserve them as that the church itself was handed over to these traditions and they preserved the church (Rom. 6:17)!

The reliability of the Jesus tradition is also witnessed to by the presence of difficult dominical sayings within the tradition. One need only look up such passages as Mark 9:1; 10:18; 13:32; Matthew 10:15; etc., and it becomes clear that these sayings were not created by the early church community. On the contrary they must go back to the historical Jesus. In a similar manner, when one compares the favorite Christological titles found in Acts to Revelation and Matthew to John, the difference is quite striking. In Acts to Revelation the favorite titles of the Christian community for Jesus are "Lord" and "Christ." These are found, however, sparingly in the Gospels. In the Gospels the favorite title and self-designation of Jesus is "Son of Man." Yet in Acts to Revelation this title appears only four times, and only once (Acts 7:56) is it used in the same sense that it is occurs in the Gospels. How is this to be explained? The simplest explanation is that, although Jesus described himself by the designation "Son of Man," the early church preferred to describe him as "Lord" and "Christ." In so doing, however, they refused to read their favorite title back into the Jesus traditions. Instead they continued faithfully to transmit the gospel traditions even though these traditions described Jesus as the "Son of Man." They did not change these traditions to reflect their preferred Christological titles.

The Evangelists as Theologians

In the 1950s a new stage in the study of the Synoptic Gospels arose in Germany.[25] Up to this time form-critical research thought in sociological terms and focused their attention on the "anonymous early church" and the oral period of gospel transmission. In so doing they viewed the Evangelists simply as "scissors and paste men" with little theological interest or concern. Various scholars, however, began to react against this anti-individualistic view and to recognize the theological contributions of the individual Evangelists. The two most important scholars who influenced the new movement were Hans Conzelmann and Willi Marxsen.[26] Earlier writers had emphasized the theological contribution of the Evangelists,[27] but Conzelmann in his attempt to demonstrate a uniquely Lukan theological emphasis and Marxsen in his defining of the now-accepted three *Sitze im Leben* truly founded *Redaktionsgeschichte* or redaction criticism. Today it is assumed in Gospel studies that the Evangelists were theologians who interpreted and shaped the gospel tradition according to their own particular theological understandings. They were not only "recorders" of the gospel traditions but "interpreters" of that tradition as well.

In the past those practicing redaction criticism have sought to make this discipline do more than it was intended to do. Markan redaction criticism is not interested in ascertaining the entire theology of Mark. Its goal is much more limited. It seeks rather to discover the unique views of the Evangelist, the unique emphasis he placed on the traditions he inherited, his theological purpose (or purposes) in writing his Gospel, and the situation in life out of which he wrote.[28]

PRACTICING REDACTION CRITICISM IN LUKE

In attempting to understand how the individual Evangelists interpreted the gospel tradition, the importance of solving the Synoptic Problem becomes apparent. If Mark were in fact the first Gospel written and Matthew and Luke used Mark in writing their Gospels, then one can ascertain their emphases by comparing in a synopsis how they used Mark. If, on the other hand, Matthew was first and Mark and Luke used it, then we would have to compare in the same synopsis how they used Matthew! The results would be quite different. The comparison of how Matthew and Luke used Mark has resulted in clear and understandable Matthean and Lukan theological emphases that lend support to the hypothesis of Markan priority. Matthew's and Luke's use of Mark with their resulting theological emphases can be easily visualized, whereas these emphases cannot be envisioned nearly as well on the basis of the Matthean priority.

The practice of redaction criticism is best accomplished with the use of a synopsis. An example of how one discovers the theological emphases of Luke can be found in observing how he adds his own theological emphasis to his Markan source. In the following examples notice how he has added to his Markan source the material in italics: "the Holy Spirit descended upon him *in bodily form* as a dove" (3:22); "And Jesus, *full of the Holy Spirit*, returned from the Jordan, and was led by the Spirit for forty days in the wilderness" (4:1); "And Jesus returned *in the power of the Spirit* into Galilee" (4:14); "*And the power of the Lord was with him to heal*" (5:17: cf. the connection of "*power*" and the Spirit in 1:35 and Acts 1:8). Note also how Luke has added to the Q tradition the following italicized material: "In that same hour *he rejoiced in the Holy Spirit* and said" (10:21), and "how much more will the heavenly Father give *the Holy Spirit* to those who ask him" (11:13). To this can be added the references to the Spirit found in the material unique to Luke (the *L* material): 1:15, 17, 35, 41, 67; 2:25–27; 4:18; 24:49.

Another unique Lukan emphasis involves the centrality of prayer in the life of Jesus and the early church. In his Gospel we find him adding to his Markan source the following italicized material: "when Jesus also had been baptized *and was praying*" (3:21); "But he withdrew to the wilderness *and prayed*" (5:16); "In these days he went out to the mountain *to pray; and all night he continued in prayer*" (6:12); "Now it happened *that as he was praying alone* the disciples were with him" (9:18); "and went up on the mountain *to pray. And as he was praying*" (9:28–29); "*He was praying* in a certain place" (11:1); "*And as he arose from prayer*" (24:45). To these can be added all the references in Acts where key decisions and events are preceded by prayer.[29]

PRACTICING REDACTION CRITICISM IN MATTHEW

In a similar way we are able to discover Matthew's particular emphasis on the fulfillment of Scripture most clearly in the places where his Markan source lacks such an emphasis. Note for example the following additions of Matthew to Mark that are in italics: *"This was to fulfil what was spoken by the prophet Isaiah"* (8:17f.); *"This was to fulfil what was spoken by the prophet Isaiah"* (12:17f.); *"With them indeed is fulfilled the prophecy of Isaiah which says"* (13:14f.); *"This was to fulfil what was spoken by the prophet"* (13:35f.); *"This took place to fulfil what was spoken by the prophet, saying"* (21:4f.); *"But then how should the scriptures be fulfilled, that it must be so?"* (26:54). To this can also be added the fulfillment quotations found in Matthew's unique material, namely, the M material: 1:22f.; 2:15, 17f., 23; 4:14f.; 27:9f., the various instances in which Matthew has added an Old Testament quotation to his Markan source (9:13; 12:7; 21:16) or to Q (12:40), and where he has added "it is written" to Q (4:6 and 7). It is clear from these additions to his sources that, although this theme is not unique to Matthew, the Evangelist certainly gives his own unique emphasis to this issue.[30] As in the emphases of Luke shown above, so here also it is much easier to understand on the basis of Markan priority how and why Matthew added these to his Markan (and Q) source. On the other hand, it is much more difficult on the basis of Matthean priority to perceive of why Mark and Luke would have wanted to remove these references from their accounts.

PRACTICING REDACTION CRITICISM IN MARK

The practice of redaction criticism in Mark is much more difficult than in Matthew and Luke. The reason for this is evident. We have the major source of Matthew and Luke—Mark! Thus we can compare how they used Mark. We can also, when comparing Matthew and Luke, frequently ascertain the likely form of the Q source they used. The investigation of their editorial hand in the M and L material, however, is much more difficult, because we have nothing with which to compare this material. Similarly, in investigating the Gospel of Mark, we have no clear source or sources with which to compare it. We have no copy of the source(s) he used. Nevertheless the situation is not entirely hopeless. If our discussion concerning the transmission of the gospel traditions during the oral period is correct, we are able to observe the hand of the Evangelist in a number of areas.[31] These involve the investigation of:

1. The Markan Seams. If the gospel traditions tended to circulate before Mark as individual units, then we can expect to find the creative hand of the Evangelist in the places where he joins together, that is, sews together as seams, these individual units. Compare, for example, the Markan emphasis on Jesus' teaching found in 1:21–22.

2. The Markan Insertions. On occasion we can see the clear hand of the Evangelist in his insertion of material into the tradition. Note for example his explanation clauses in 1:34b (cf. 3:11; 5:7) and 7:3–4.

3. The Markan Summaries. Summaries of the individual traditions most probably would not have circulated during the oral period. When these traditions were brought together, such summaries became necessary. Several clear Markan theological emphases are found in such summaries as 1:32–34; 3:7–12; 8:31; 9:30–31; 10:32–34. There is little doubt that the Evangelist in such instances used traditional material, but the shaping of this material into summaries was his own doing and thus reveals his theological emphases.

4. The Markan Arrangement of the Material. If we believe that the traditions before Mark circulated primarily as isolated units, then the arrangement of much of this material must be due to the hand of Mark. Numerous scholars have seen the threefold repetition of passion saying—disciple error—discipleship teaching in 8:27–10:52 as due to the hand of Mark. Similarly the "Markan sandwich" in which one account is sandwiched between another (cf. Mark 3:22–30 into 3:19b–21 and 31–35; 5:25–34 into 5:21–24 and 35–43; 6:14–29 into 6:6b–13 and 30f.; 11:15–19 into 11:12–14 and 20–25; 14:3–9 into 14:1–2 and 10–11) is almost certainly due to the hand of the Evangelist.

5. The Markan Introduction. Since Mark had to create the introductory words of his work, the opening verse of his Gospel should reveal something about his purpose and emphasis. In 1:1, Mark reveals that he wants the rest of the Gospel to be read "Christologically," for his work is about Jesus Christ, the Son of God.[32]

6. The Markan Vocabulary. In reading Mark certain terms come up with great frequency. These include: teacher, teaching, to teach; to preach; gospel, authority, power, to amaze, cause to wonder; to follow; etc. These are furthermore found with great frequency in the seams, insertions, and summaries of Mark. The investigation of this vocabulary provides insight into the theological emphases of the Evangelist.

7. The Markan Christological Titles. The particular titles Mark used to describe Jesus no doubt also reveal something of his theological emphasis. Granted that Mark found such titles in the tradition he inherited, his overall use of Christological titles reveals something of his understanding of who Jesus of Nazareth is.

We may look to find the hand of Mark in a number of other areas, but to each of them a number of objections can be raised.

8. The Markan Modification of the Materials. The subjective nature of this is self-evident. It is far from clear how one can know exactly where and how Mark modified the tradition.

9. The Markan Selection and/or Omission of Material. The problem with this criterion is that we are unaware of what materials Mark had

before him. If Mark possessed ten times the number of exorcism stories and chose to include only what we find in his Gospel but if he included every one of the healing miracles he knew, this would suggest that he perhaps sought to underplay Jesus as an exorcist. We simply do not know, however, how many accounts of exorcisms and how many healing miracles he possessed. In a similar way we do not know how much of the teachings of Jesus Mark possessed when he wrote. As a result we can only speculate why so little of the teaching material is found in his Gospel.

10. The Markan Conclusion. The problem here lies in the debate over exactly how the Gospel of Mark ended. Although a majority of scholars today believe that Mark ended at 16:8, there is good reason to believe that the original ending of Mark has been lost. We have in 14:28 and 16:7 (which are possible Markan insertions) sayings that lead the reader to anticipate a meeting between Jesus and the disciples in Galilee. Yet, if the Gospel originally ended in 16:8, we read of no such meeting. It would appear therefore unwise to build a case for a particular Markan theological emphasis too heavily on the assumption that Mark originally ended his Gospel at 16:8.

Insights into the Interpretation of the Synoptic Gospels

Research in the Synoptic Gospels has resulted in a number of insights that enable us to understand these books better. Three of these insights include the nature of the order of events found within them, the Evangelists' role as theologians, and the religious purpose of the Gospel accounts.

THE ORDER OF EVENTS

Already in the early part of the second century, Papias commented concerning the Gospel of Mark, "Mark became Peter's interpreter and wrote accurately all that he remembered, not, indeed, in order, of the things said or done by the Lord."[33] Over the centuries this insight of Papias has been neglected. Those who constructed various "harmonies" of the Gospels were well aware of the fact that at times the order of events in the Gospels seem to "conflict." Often elaborate and unconvincing harmonies were constructed to explain the different order of events found in the Gospels. The most famous of such attempts was that of Osiander.[34] It was Griesbach who first produced a "synopsis" in which harmonistic concerns for placing similar events into a common chronological order were laid aside.[35] Here the guiding principle was no longer the desire to create a harmonious chronology of the events in Jesus' life but rather to place side by side the similar sayings and events found in the Gospels in order to be able to compare them.

The observations of form criticism that during the oral period the gospel traditions tended to be passed on as isolated units and that many of the traditions lacked chronological and geographical concerns lend support to Papias' insight. Redaction criticism also supported the insight of Papias. The

Gospels were no longer understood as straightforward "chronologies of Jesus' life." Mark, for example, arranged his Gospel, in part at least, along geographical lines. In the first nine chapters he speaks of the events in Jesus' ministry that occurred in Galilee and its environs. Chapter 10 serves as a transition in which Jesus moves from Galilee to Jerusalem. Then in chapters 11 through 16, Mark recounts various events that occurred in or around Jerusalem. Matthew and Luke in their use of Mark followed a similar format. Yet if, as John indicates, Jesus traveled between Galilee and Jerusalem on several occasions, then events that occurred early in Jesus' ministry in Jerusalem would have to be placed late in the ministry, that is, when Matthew, Mark, and Luke focus on Jesus' ministry in and around Jerusalem. Similarly, events that occurred late in Jesus' ministry but that occurred in Galilee would have to be placed early in Matthew, Mark, and Luke because they focus on Jesus' ministry in Galilee early in their Gospels. It is thus evident that chronological considerations do not form the main organizing principle of the Synoptic Gospels.

In similar fashion Matthew, who arranged his Gospel artistically by alternating stories about Jesus (chapter 1–4, 8–9, 11–12, 14–17, 19–22, 26–28) and the teachings of Jesus (chapters 5–7, 10, 13, 18, 23–25), also reveals that he did not construct his Gospel along chronological lines. To be sure certain events had to be placed at the beginning (birth, baptism, temptation) and the end (Last Supper, Gethsemane, trial, crucifixion, resurrection), but other events and various teachings he placed as he did for reasons other than chronology.

Understanding that the order of events in the Synoptic Gospels are not chronological in nature or purpose is helpful in several ways. For one, it allows us to focus our attention on what the author is seeking to teach by his arrangement of the gospel traditions, i.e., what he saw as important for faith and practice. Second, it relieves us from the task of creating unconvincing harmonizations of these events that the Evangelists never saw a need to harmonize. Why should we seek to harmonize accounts to fit a specific chronology when the Gospel writers never meant these events to be understood as occurring in chronological order? A classic example of what this can lead to was the famous attempt by Osiander to harmonize the accounts of the raising of Jairus' daughter from the dead. In Mark this event (5:21–43) takes place immediately after Jesus crosses the Sea of Galilee and arrives at Capernaum (5:21). In Matthew, however, Jesus, after crossing the Sea of Galilee (9:1), heals a paralytic (9:2–8), calls Matthew to follow him (9:9–13), and teaches about fasting (9:14–17). Only then does he raise Jairus' daughter from the dead (9:18–26). Osiander's chronological harmonization was that these events took place consecutively and that Jairus' daughter was raised from the dead twice![36] Such harmonizations are misguided attempts to defend the chronological order of events that the Gospel writers did not place in chronological order. A correct understanding of the purposes of the Evangelists enables us to concentrate on the intention of the biblical authors and not to impose a chronological order upon them which they never intended. Calvin, himself, pointed out that

> the Evangelists did not definitely set down a fixed and distinct time sequence in their records. They neglected the order of days, and were content to put together the chief events in Christ's career as they saw them. They certainly took note of the years. . . . But they freely confuse [i.e., intermix] the miracles which occurred at much the same period, and this we shall see clearly from a number of cases.[37]

THE EVANGELISTS AS THEOLOGIANS

With the coming of redaction criticism as a discipline, the focus of attention switched from concentrating on the first *Sitz im Leben* (studies in the life and teachings of Jesus) and the second *Sitz im Leben* (studies of the early church in relation to the Jesus tradition) to the third *Sitz im Leben*. This is not to imply that the individual interests of the Evangelists were unknown up to this time. Wrede's discussion of the messianic secret in Mark preceded redaction criticism by half a century. Similarly, Matthew's interest in the fulfillment of Scripture was well-known long before redaction criticism became the focus of Gospel studies. Nevertheless, just as one is more likely to find a four-leaf clover when one is looking for one, so in similar fashion scholars discovered more of the theological emphases of the Evangelists than they had before simply because they were now looking for them. We have already given examples of some of these theological emphases.

The recognition of the Evangelists as theologians has been a major contribution to the study of the Synoptic Gospels. Whereas some critical scholars see the contribution of the Evangelists to the gospel traditions as unfortunate and even as corruptions of the original teachings of Jesus, evangelical scholarship sees itself doubly blessed. We possess both the teachings and the acts of the Son of God and the inspired interpretation of these teachings and acts by the Evangelists. At times we can discover what Jesus himself said and meant and then read how an Evangelist, led by the Spirit (John 14:26) contextualized this for his own situation. An example of this can be found in the parable of the lost sheep. We find in Luke 15:1–3 the context and purpose of Jesus in originally telling the parable of the lost sheep (Luke 15:4–7). In Matthew 18:12–14, however, we discover how the Evangelist applied this teaching to his own church situation (cf. Matt. 18:2–5, 6–10). Thus the reader receives the double benefit of being able to understand both the meaning of the original parable of Jesus (Luke 15:4–7) and the Evangelist's interpretation of this parable to his own situation (Matt. 18:12–14). On other occasions an Evangelist by his interpretation of a saying of Jesus reveals how this saying should be understood. One need only compare how a "word for word" interpretation of Jesus' teaching in Luke

14:26–27 is explained in the "thought for thought" interpretation found in Matthew 10:37–38.

THE RELIGIOUS PURPOSE OF THE GOSPEL ACCOUNTS

One final contribution of modern Gospel studies should be mentioned. Form criticism has pointed out that the reason most gospel traditions were preserved and passed on was due to their value in ministering to the practical needs of the early church. John states, "Jesus did many other things as well [that are not recorded in this gospel]. If every one of them were written down, I suppose that even the whole world would not have room for the books that would be written" (John 21:25).

After making allowance for the hyperbolic nature of John's statement, the fact remains that one of the primary purposes, if not the primary one, for the preservation of the gospel traditions was the fact that they met various religious needs in the Christian community. This encourages us to read the Gospel accounts for a similar purpose. To investigate the Gospels for information about Jesus and the early church is clearly legitimate and worthwhile. The Gospels certainly can be studied with this in mind. Yet we need to keep foremost in our minds the religious value of the Gospels and their traditions. How much richer our experience will be if, as we read the gospel traditions, we ask ourselves, "Why was this story/teaching of Jesus preserved whereas many others were not? What religious need(s) of the early church did this story/teaching minister to?" We may be wonderfully surprised to discover that the same needs they met for the early church they continue to meet today.

Bibliography

Bellinzoni, Jr., A. J. *The Two-Source Hypothesis: A Critical Appraisal*. Macon: Mercer, 1985.

Black, C. C. *The Disciples According to Mark: Markan Redaction in Current Debate*. Sheffield: JSOT, 1989.

Catchpole, D. R. *The Quest for Q*. Edinburgh: T & T Clark, 1993.

Farmer, W. R. *The Synoptic Problem: A Critical Analysis*. New York: Macmillan, 1964.

Farrer, A. M. "On Dispensing with Q." *Studies in the Gospels*. Oxford: Blackwell, 1955, pp. 55–88.

Fitzmyer, J. A. "The Priority of Mark and the 'Q' Source in Luke." *Jesus and Man's Hope*. Pittsburgh: Pittsburgh Theological Seminary, 1970, pp. 131–70.

Gerhardsson, B. *Memory and Manuscript*. Lund: Gleerup, 1961.

Hawkins, J. C. *Horae Synopticae*. Oxford: Clarendon, 1909.

Hultgren, A. J. *Jesus and His Adversaries*. Minneapolis: Augsburg, 1979.

Kloppenborg, J. S. *The Formation of Q: Trajectores in Ancient Wisdom Collections*. Philadelphia: Fortress, 1987.

Marxsen, W. *Mark the Evangelist: Studies on the Redaction History of the Gospel*. New York: Abingdon, 1969.

Neirynck, F. *The Minor Agreements of Matthew and Luke Against Mark with a Cumulative List*. Leuven: University Press, 1991.

————. "The Griesbach Hypothesis: The Phenomenon of Order," *EphTheolLov 58* (1982): 111–22.

Osborne, G. R. "Redaction Criticism." *Dictionary of Jesus and the Gospels.* Downers Grove, Ill.: InterVarsity, 1992, pp. 662–69.

Reicke, B. *The Roots of the Synoptic Gospels.* Philadelphia: Fortress, 1986.

Sanders, E. P. *The Tendencies of the Synoptic Tradition.* Cambridge: University Press, 1969.

Stein, R. H. "Synoptic Problem." *Dictionary of Jesus and the Gospels.* Downers Grove, Ill.: InterVarsity, 1992, pp. 784–92.

————. "The Matthew-Luke Agreements Against Mark: Insight from John." *CBQ 54* (1992): 482–502.

————. *The Synoptic Problem: An Introduction.* Grand Rapids: Baker, 1987.

Streeter, B. H. *The Four Gospels.* London: Macmillan, 1924.

Tuckett, C. M. "The Argument from Order and the Synoptic Problem," *TZ 36* (1980): 338–54.

————. *The Revival of the Griesbach Hypothesis: An Analysis and Appraisal.* Cambridge: University Press, 1983.

Wansbrough, H., ed. *Jesus and the Oral Gospel Tradition.* JSNT Sup. 64. Sheffield: JSOT Press, 1991.

Notes

1. See for example, Augustine, *De Consensu Evangelistarum,* I.2 (4).

2. It was apparently J. J. Griesbach who in 1776 first used the term *Synopsis* with respect to Matthew, Mark, and Luke.

3. Cf. Luke 1:2; Heb. 2:3; cf. also 1 Cor. 11:23ff.; 15:3ff.; etc.

4. A discussion of "The Gospel Traditions during the Oral Period" follows later in this chapter.

5. For a more detailed discussion of the literary sources involved in the composition of the Synoptic Gospels, see the article by Scot McKnight, "Source Criticism."

6. See Robert H. Stein, *The Synoptic Problem: An Introduction* (Grand Rapids: Baker, 1987), 48–52.

7. Ibid., 52–62.

8. Ibid., 62–67.

9. See McKnight, "Source Criticism."

10. See F. Gerald Downing, "Compositional Conventions and the Synoptic Problem," *JBL* 107 (1988): 69–85.

11. See Stein, *The Synoptic Problem,* 70–76, for additional examples.

12. See Robert H. Stein, *Luke,* NAC (Nashville: Broadman Press, 1992), 37–38.

13. Cf. for example Matthew 6:24; 7:7–11; 11:25–27; 23:37–39; etc. with the Lukan parallels.

14. Some examples of Lukan additions to the Markan narrative not found in the parallel accounts in Matthew are Luke 5:39; 9:31–33, 48d; 18:34; 21:24.

15. For further discussion see McKnight, "Source Criticism," and Stein, *The Synoptic Problem,* 91–103.

16. This issue was raised in three works that appeared almost simultaneously: Karl Ludwig Schmidt, *Der Rahmen der Geschichte Jesu* (1919); Martin Dibelius, *Die Formgeschichte des Evangeliums* (1919); and Rudolf Bultmann, *Die Geschichte der Synoptischen Tradition* (1921).

17. For a more detailed discussion of these presuppositions, see Stein, *The Synoptic Problem*, 162–85.

18. For the opposing view, see Werner H. Kelber, *The Passion in Mark* (Philadelphia: Fortress Press, 1976), esp. 153–59.

19. In support of such a view, see David Hill, "On the Evidence for the Creative Role of Christian Prophets," *NTS* 20 (1979): 262–74. For the opposing view see David E. Aune, *Prophecy in Early Christianity and the Ancient Mediterranean World* (Grand Rapids: Eerdmans, 1983).

20. E. P. Sanders, *The Tendencies of the Synoptic Tradition* (Cambridge: Cambridge University Press, 1969).

21. See M. D. Hooker, "On Using the Wrong Tool," *Theology* 75 (1972): 572; Werner H. Kelber, *The Oral and the Written Gospel* (Philadelphia: Fortress, 1983), 14–32.

22. See D. E. Nineham, "Eye-Witness Testimony and the Gospel Tradition," *JTS* 9 (1958): 13–25; 243–52; and 11 (1960): 253–64.

23. For a more detailed discussion, see Robert H. Stein, "Where You Start Determines Where You Finish: The Role of Presuppositions in Studying the Life of Jesus," in *Jesus the Messiah* (Downers Grove, Ill.: InterVarsity Press, 1996), 17–24.

24. For a more detailed discussion, see Stein, *The Synoptic Problem*, 197–203.

25. For a more detailed discussion, see Grant R. Osborne, "Redaction Criticism" in this volume, and Stein, *The Synoptic Problem*, 231–72.

26. See Hans Conzelmann, *The Theology of St. Luke*, trans. Geoffrey Buswell (New York: Harper & Row Publishers, 1961; from the German, *Die Mitte Der Zeit*, 1953) and Willi Marxsen, *Mark the Evangelist* (Nashville: Abingdon Press, 1969; from the German, *Der Evangelist Markus*, 1956).

27. William Wrede, Ernst Lohmeyer, Karl Kundsin, Adolf Schlatter, Robert Henry Lightfoot, and James M. Robinson are but a few.

28. See Robert H. Stein, "What Is Redaktionsgeschichte?" *JBL* 88 (1969): 53–54.

29. Cf. Acts 1:14, 24–26; 2:42; 3:1; 6:6; 8:15; 9:11, 40; 10:4, 9, 30–31; 11:5; 12:12; 13:3; 14:23; 16:25; 21:5; 28:8.

30. We can also trace this theme in the following passages found in his sources (Mark, Q, and M): 2:6; 3:3; 4:10; 10:35–36; 11:10; 15:4, 8–9; 18:16; 19:4, 5, 18–19; 21:9, 13, 42; 22:24, 32, 37, 38, 44; 23:39; 26:26, 56, 64; 27:35.

31. What follows is essentially a summary of Robert H. Stein, "The Proper Methodology for Ascertaining a Markan Redaction History," *NT* 13 (1971): 181–98.

32. There is a textual problem involving "Son of God." Does the fact that Mark in his redactional work emphasized that Jesus of Nazareth is the "Son of God" lend internal support to accepting these words as Markan?

33. Eusebius, *Ecclesiastical History*, 3.39.15–16 (Loeb).

34. Andreas Osiander, *Harmoniae Evangelicae* (Basel, 1537).

35. Johann Jacob Griesbach, *Synopsis Evangeliorum Matthaei, Marci et Lucae* (Halle, 1776).

36. Osiander also believed that there were four separate healings of blind men at Jericho, two healings of the Gerasene maniac, that Jesus was crowned with thorns two times at his trial, etc. Both Calvin (*A Harmony of the Gospels Matthew, Mark, and Luke* on Matthew 20:29–34 and parallels) and Luther (Jaroslav Pelikan [ed.], *Luther's Works* [St. Louis: Concordia Publishing, 1957], 22:218–19) rejected the approach of Osiander to such matters.

37. John Calvin, *A Harmony of the Gospels Matthew, Mark, and Luke*, ed. David W. Torrance and Thomas F. Torrance (Grand Rapids: Eerdmans, 1972), on Matthew 4:18.

Chapter 16

Interpreting the Gospel of John

Gary M. Burge
Wheaton College

The Fourth Gospel not only introduces us to "the beloved disciple" but is itself the "beloved Gospel" of the Christian church. From the earliest centuries, the Gospel of John has been set apart as offering a unique story that probes a spiritual depth unsurpassed anywhere else. Already by the second century Clement of Alexandria had labeled John "the spiritual Gospel," and this reputation has remained to this day. The lofty heights gained by the prologue (1:1–18) and the grace and power found in John's portrait of Jesus provided reason enough for ancient copyists to symbolize the Gospel with an eagle. In fact, medieval Christians so venerated John's prologue that its verses were read over baptized children and the seriously ill. Copies were placed in amulets and worn around the neck to ward off evil. Even the major ecumenical councils of the fourth and fifth centuries found John's Gospel playing a major role shaping doctrines that would have a permanent place in Christian theology.

But the Gospel of John has also inspired tremendous scholarly interest and debate. Each year hundreds of journal articles and books sift its words and offer hypotheses for its origins and meaning. Evangelical interpreters need to be conversant with these developments and have a well-reasoned understanding of the Gospel's structure and message. This chapter provides a survey of interpretative developments in John and outlines some of the key issues for interpretation.

A Brief History of Interpretation[1]

My first exposure to Johannine criticism came in the autumn of 1972 at the American University of Beirut in Lebanon, where I was taking a course on the Gospels with a French Jesuit scholar. At one point he remarked that the New Testament nowhere gives evidence that Jesus went to Samaria. I eagerly offered some reference to John 4 (the story of Jesus and the Samaritan woman), whereupon he remarked, "Ah yes, but that account appears in the Fourth Gospel, and as everyone knows, *John is not histori-cally trustworthy!*" Defeated by what seemed to be an important scholarly argument, I retreated.

Today when scholars reconstruct the life of Jesus, they constantly meas-ure the quality of their sources. The trustworthiness of John is a case in point. Is the Fourth Gospel a reliable source for the life of Jesus? We could answer this as a statement of faith ("It is in the Scriptures, isn't it?"), but this will mean little to those who do not share our convictions. On the other hand, we could benefit from knowing what has been said about this Gospel—the history of its interpretation—and thereby equip ourselves to address some of these academic challenges head-on. If I had done this in 1972, I would have learned that my college professor was completely out of step with current Johannine scholarship.

In the New Testament a considerable body of literature is traditionally attributed to John: a Gospel, three letters, and the Book of Revelation. In addition is a host of extrabiblical writings that make some claim on his name: the legendary *Acts of John* was written almost two hundred years later and provides a fictional biography of the apostle. The Syriac *History of John* shows the apostle to be a magic-working evangelist. Gnostic sources such as the *Gospel of Philip* show fragments of Johannine-style sayings, while others provide accounts of his contact with Jesus, his mission and martyrdom. But while this apocryphal literature may be set aside with ease, still the significance of the biblical Johannine material has aroused consid-erable academic debate.

THE EARLY PERIOD

In the early church the Fourth Gospel was given the highest place of honor. Since it was thought to originate with the apostle (the Beloved Disciple) who was one of the closest to Jesus, it was esteemed as the most valuable Gospel. John offered a depth of insight that was unparalleled in the synoptics. But unfortunately even the heretics loved it. A second-century Gnostic writer in Egypt penned the *Gospel of Truth,* and it shows surpris-ing Johannine parallels. Even the earliest commentaries on John were Gnostic (Heracleon, a disciple of Valentinus). Themes in the Gospel were so popular, one charismatic leader (Montanus) claimed that he was the coming Paraclete or Comforter described in John 14–16! Because of this Gnostic interest, many orthodox leaders were so reluctant to promote the Gospel that many of them were openly opposed to it. But on the whole, where it was accepted, John was deeply revered.[2]

Early Christian leaders such as Irenaeus (c. 175) also learned that John's incarnational theology was an important resource against the sort of heresies being spawned in Christian-gnostic circles. Later in the fourth century when the Arians were depicting Jesus as fully subordinate to the Father—a creature along with us—Athanasius and the leaders of Nicea looked to the Fourth Gospel's incarnational theology and doctrine of Christ as an uncompromising affirmation of Jesus' divinity.[3]

Medieval Christendom gave the Gospel this same respect. From Augustine to Aquinas, John provided the portrait of a Jesus who directly revealed the Father. Mysticism and sacramentalism likewise found in John the language and symbolic images they enjoyed. Therefore commentaries from this period abound.

All of this came to an abrupt end during the Enlightenment of the eighteenth and nineteenth centuries. In this period the Gospels came under careful scrutiny, while a skepticism about supernatural religion won the day at European universities. For example, in 1778 the lecture notes of Hermann Samuel Reimarus were published, which denied Jesus' claim to messiahship, argued that the Gospels were later fabrications, and urged the implausibility of the resurrection. A quest was launched to find the real Jesus of history, that is, a history dictated by rationalistic, Enlightenment standards.

The following questions were continually at issue for more than 150 years since Reimarus was studied. First, was the supernatural admissible as genuine history? Second, what were the relative merits of the Gospels? And third, what was the essence of Jesus' message? This third question brought special nuances. Did Jesus preach about an ultimate crisis or catastrophe for Judaism and the world with himself at the center (eschatology)? Indeed, did Jesus even claim to be the Son of God or the Messiah?

John's Gospel was enjoying an interesting history. Because it contained fewer miracles and described Jesus' giving lengthy Socratic discourses, it was favored among many. Karl Hase (1800–1890) argued that the Johannine miracle stories seemed more authentic and less prone to embellishment. The famous Friedrich Schleiermacher (1768–1834) embraced John fully in lectures he gave in 1832 (published in 1864). John is an eyewitness, Schleiermacher argued, who gives us a Jesus of depth and substance. No doubt John offered something that resonated in the liberal nineteenth-century soul.

But critical objections were soon to follow. In 1835, David Strauss (1808–1874) published his influential volume, *The Life of Christ*, and forced the Johannine question. Strauss believed that each of the Gospel writers was promoting some preconceived theological portrait of Jesus, thus rendering the Gospel presentations unhistorical. This was especially true of John. This Gospel was inferior because it served a literary and theological schema and was influenced by second-century dogmas. Strauss simply pointed to John's baptismal narrative, the calling of the first disciples (1:29–51), and especially the absence of Jesus' "Gethsemane struggle" to show that the Fourth Gospel was the conscious result of "devotional, but unhistorical embellishment."[4]

He even showed how the language of Jesus in the Fourth Gospel was John's own language by comparing it with the Johannine Epistles. Strauss forced New Testament scholarship to make a choice between John and the Synoptics. Their differences were utterly irreconcilable.

Strauss had been a pupil in Germany's Tübingen University studying with Ferdinand Christian Baur (1792–1860).[5] It was Baur who propelled Strauss into biblical criticism, and now it was left to the instructor to seal the fate of John's Gospel. Baur and the later-known "Tübingen School" were deeply influenced by the philosophy of Hegel, who asserted that all history was an outworking of the dialectic of thesis, antithesis, and synthesis. For example, major historical movements (thesis) are often met with opposition (antithesis) and this results in a synthesis over the course of time. Baur applied this sweeping framework to early Christianity: Judaism and Hellenism had intermingled to produce Christianity. Baur further emphasized to the point of exaggeration how Jewish elements in the church (Peter) opposed Greek interests (Paul), resulting in a consensus or early Catholicism. He even clarified New Testament documents as fitting this schema: Romans, 1 and 2 Corinthians, and Galatians were Paul's Gentile-Christian salvos; Matthew and the Apocalypse were the Jewish-Christian response; and Acts and the Pastoral Epistles were the documents of reconciliation and consensus.

What about the Fourth Gospel? Baur believed that John stemmed from a Greek community (thus its Hellenistic accent) that had been permeated by Jewish interests. It thus came from a later era—possibly 150–170—in which early Christianity was reconciling itself with its diversity. It did not originate with the apostolic circle nor did it reflect the early Palestinian Judaism of Jesus' day.

For the balance of the nineteenth century, criticism of the Fourth Gospel along the lines of Strauss and Baur continued unabated. Refinements to the thesis surfaced, to be sure, but the broad contours remained unchanged. Many objected, especially outside of Germany. For example, at Trinity College in Cambridge University, J. B. Lightfoot (1828–1889) dismantled Baur's reconstruction of early Christian history through an exhaustive study of the Patristic Fathers. His colleague, B. F. Westcott (1825–1901), published a commentary on John in 1880 defending the Gospel's apostolic origins. In Germany Adolf Schlatter (1852–1938) dissented against Baur in his volumes *Die Sprache und Heimat des 4. Evangelisten (The Language and Province of the Fourth Gospel)* (1902) and *Der Evangelist Johannes, wie er spricht, denkt, und glaubt (The Fourth Evangelist: His Speech, Thought, and Belief)* (1930). Nevertheless the die had been cast, and for many the Fourth Gospel never survived the nineteenth century as a trustworthy source for reconstructing the life of Christ.[6]

Throughout this period two important conclusions resulted that still have influence today. First, the synoptic Gospels, not John, are viewed as the primary evidence for the life of Jesus. John is interested in theology instead of history. The Fourth Gospel presents an "idea" of Jesus (a myth, Strauss said) and cannot be seen as a historical account. Second, the cultural setting of John is Hellenistic rather than Jewish since it was penned by a second-century Christian community far removed from the Jesus of Palestine. It is, quite simply, an attempt to express the gospel in the terms of Greek philosophy.

In 1910, William Sanday of Oxford University chronicled this severe trend in biblical studies in his volume, *The Criticism of the Fourth Gospel*. Sanday uncovered the serious prejudice against John and summed up the period as "an uncompromising rejection" of the Fourth Gospel. Sanday reported how many scholars were urging that John was an intermediate step between Paul and Gnosticism, a purer expression of Paul's gospel now freed from any link to Judaism and the historical events in the life and death of Jesus.

THE JEWISH CHARACTER OF JOHN'S GOSPEL

Sometimes an academic thesis persists only to be broadsided from an utterly unexpected source. Stephen Neill remarks how, in 1924, Israel Abrahams, a rabbinics scholar at Cambridge and an orthodox Jew, addressed the theological society of the university with the words, "To us Jews, the Fourth Gospel is the most Jewish of the four!"[7]

A cursory reading of John might well lead to the same sort of question. Does not the Gospel contain numerous allusions to the Old Testament? Do not semitic hints abound? And if this is so, what happens to Baur and the Tübingen thesis? Is it right to view John as the product of the Greek Christian church of the second century?

Already J. B. Lightfoot and Adolf Schlatter had been suggesting that rabbinic literature and the Old Testament were the best tools for interpreting John.[8] Now at the turn of the century, evidence seemed to be accumulating. John uses numerous references to the Old Testament, but many are dissimilar to, say, Matthew's citations. John alludes to Old Testament texts and seems to assume that his readers know the reference intimately (compare John 10 with Ezek. 34; John 3:14 with Num. 21:9).[9] Similarly the discourses of Jesus presuppose some knowledge of the theological symbolism behind the Jewish festivals (Passover, John 6; Tabernacles, John 7; Dedication, John 10). They even employ rabbinic arguments, such as the way Jesus debates his opponents in chapter 5. John 6 is a midrash (or Jewish commentary) on "bread from heaven" (Exod. 16:4), while 10:34 is a midrash on Psalm 82:6. This is hardly the sort of literature one would expect from a Greek community. On the other hand, it could be argued that John uses language dissimilar to that of Judaism. His dualism (light/darkness, above/below) and abstract expressions (truth, faith, spirit) are unlike most Jewish literature. But in the 1940s archaeologists uncovered the Dead

Sea Scrolls at Qumran and there learned of a Jewish sectarian community using language similar to that found in John.[10]

In 1922, C. F. Burney of Oxford advanced the thesis that not only was John influenced by Semitic concepts but the Gospel itself had originally been written in Aramaic.[11] The language of the text, argued Burney, betrays an Aramaic original which is now translated into Greek. This in turn explains the Gospel's simple, often wooden, Greek. Similarly, in 1967, Matthew Black of St. Andrews, Scotland, suggested that the Fourth Gospel's language is evidence of an author's writing in Greek whose native tongue is Aramaic.[12]

John also seems to know a surprising amount about the customs, culture, and land of first-century Palestine. Note how in John 4 he casually describes Samaria and its outlook. In John 5, he describes the five-porch pool of Bethesda in Jerusalem (which was only recently uncovered near St. Anne's Church).[13] The geography of Palestine is accurate as are Jesus' appearances at the Jewish festivals. He likewise gives us an enormous amount of local detail.[14] John even describes the temple using incidental detail (see 8:20) when this structure was destroyed by the Romans in A.D. 70.

Finally, this century Greek papyrus fragments have come to light providing us with early portions of the New Testament. In fact, we possess more papyrus fragments of John (17 in all) than any other New Testament book. For example, P^{52} is an Egyptian scrap with about five verses from John 18 (about 3.5 by 2.3 inches). Discovered in 1920 and published in 1935, it is the oldest New Testament fragment we possess and is usually dated at A.D. 125.[15] If we allow time for it to circulate throughout the church as far as Egypt, this pushes the date of John right into the first century and provides us with the latest possible date for the Gospel (perhaps A.D. 80 or 95).

However, we must be clear that a consensus had *not* been reached. Others were pursuing different avenues of investigation still convinced that John was a by-product of pagan mysticism and Hellenistic Gnosticism. In 1921, Alfred Loisy published a commentary along these lines. At Tübingen an effort had been launched to discover the "history of religions" and see how one faith evolved into newer forms. Many scholars such as Richard Reitzenstein (1861–1931) were emphasizing now-popular Hellenistic mystery religions and the newly discovered writings of the Mandeans.[16] A myth of a "descending redeemer" had been popular in the Near East, and John had applied Jesus to its drama. It was left for Rudolf Bultmann (1884–1972) of Marburg University to publish his magisterial commentary on John in 1941 (ET: 1971) that made full and compelling use of these sources. To a certain extent Bultmann's influence in Johannine studies is still significant.[17] In 1980 (ET: 1984), E. Haenchen published his two-volume commentary on John, using Bultmann's outlook fully.

The question of John's Jewish roots still remains unsolved for many. But it is an essential subject as we seek to determine the Gospel's date and origin. A Jewish background suggests that the origins of the Fourth Gospel must not be found in Hellenistic religious systems but must be sought in the world of first-century Judaism. Indeed, as Peder Borgen has recently suggested, the ideas in John that appear linked to Hellenism must be seen as coming through a Jewish context shaped by Christian thinking.[18] And if John is principally Jewish, the way is open to view it as a by-product of the world of Jesus and his apostles.

HISTORICAL TRADITIONS IN JOHN'S GOSPEL

We have seen that John's cultural setting has been a major issue that has vexed scholars throughout the century. A second possibly more important question was soon to join it. Did John's account of the life of Jesus contain any historical data? If so, what was its relation to the Synoptic Gospels?

Already scholars had determined that Matthew, Mark, and Luke were dependent on one another in their Gospels. This resulted in a complex literary puzzle that even today enjoys considerable attention. At the turn of the century, most assumed that since John was the latest Gospel written its author knew and used the Synoptics.[19] Implicit in this hypothesis was an assessment of John's historicity: when a story in John paralleled, say, Mark, the account was deemed trustworthy. When the Fourth Gospel diverged from the Synoptics, its historical value plummeted.

We need to look closely at this subject to gain some perspective on its importance. B. F. Westcott estimated that 93 percent of Mark could be found hidden in Matthew and Luke. But John was different. Only 8 percent was paralleled in the Synoptics, and fully 92 percent was unique for the Johannine story.[20] For instance, the cleansing of the temple story can be found in John 2:14–22, Matthew 21:12–13, Mark 11:15–17, and Luke 19:45–46. Likewise, the feeding of the five thousand (John 6:1–14) appears in all four Gospels. But other major accounts such as the dialogue with Nicodemus (John 3), the Samaritan Woman's story (John 4), the raising of Lazarus (John 11), and Jesus' upper room discourses (John 13–16) are absent from the Synoptics. Does this mean that John invented them? And when we look closely at the parallel material such as the cleansing of the temple, discrepancies appear: John records this event at the beginning of Jesus' ministry, while the Synoptics put it at the end. Even the great feeding miracle is concluded in John with a lengthy monologue about Jesus as the "bread of life" (6:15–59). Does this evidence prove that when John used the Synoptics he freely embellished their narratives? If this was his tendency, then his independent stories such as Jesus' private discussion with Pilate, 18:18–19:16, must fall by the wayside.

The thesis deserves restating: if John knew and used the Synoptics, then his divergences make him suspect. Such was the view of John until 1938 when P. Gardner-Smith wrote a critique of the evidence that John even knew the Synoptics in the first place (*St. John and the Synoptics*). Gardner-Smith demonstrated how fragile were the arguments for dependency, and it is doubtful whether his criticisms have ever been refuted. Nevertheless he sounded a call that began to be echoed elsewhere. Scholars began to ask whether John's accounts stem from independent traditional sources that *antedated* the Synoptics. In 1953, C. H. Dodd concluded *The Interpretation of the Fourth Gospel* with an appendix rejecting the "symbolic" use of place names in John. He concluded that the Gospel may contain original traditional narratives associated with southern Palestine. Place names (like Bethesda) are indeed geographical locations. He wrote: "The *prima facie* impression is that John is, in large measure at any rate, working independently of other written gospels."[21]

In 1963, Dodd offered his full-fledged study boldly entitling it *Historical Tradition in the Fourth Gospel*. This volume was a watershed in Johannine studies in which Dodd concluded, "The above argument has led to the conclusion that behind the Fourth Gospel lies an ancient tradition independent of the other gospels, and meriting serious consideration as a contribution to our knowledge of the historical facts concerning Jesus Christ."[22] Dodd began with a thorough study of the passion narrative and concluded that, rather than a reshuffling of the Synoptics, John's story was ancient, Jewish, possibly dated before A.D. 70, and even "better informed than the tradition behind the Synoptics!"[23]

It goes without saying that scholarly unanimity has not been reached on this subject either. In 1978, C. K. Barrett published the second edition of his 1955 commentary still defending—even defensively—his view that John was familiar with Mark (and possibly even Luke) and had minimal historical value.[24] R. H. Lightfoot's commentary of 1956 claimed that John knew all three Synoptic Gospels. But these views are not winning the day. An important shift has occurred. Writers are now more than ever inclined to say that John records ancient traditions that stem from the same wellspring as that of the Synoptics. Occasionally he shares these primitive traditions with the Synoptics, but he does not employ the Synoptics themselves.[25]

The importance of this shift cannot be missed. As Gardner-Smith wrote in 1938, "If in the Fourth Gospel we have a survival of the type of first century Christianity which owed nothing to synoptic developments, and which originated in quite a different intellectual atmosphere, its historical value may be very great indeed."[26] Indeed, impressive new light has been shed on the Fourth Gospel making it an *independent, authoritative* witness to the traditions about Jesus on a par with any historical claims found in the Synoptics.

THE NEW LOOK ON THE GOSPEL OF JOHN

Many writers have chronicled these developments, but none so famous as J. A. T. Robinson of Trinity College, Cambridge. In 1957, Robinson announced a "new look" on the Fourth Gospel in a paper read at Oxford.[27] In it he distinguished an "old look" on John that was under siege and that consisted of five major propositions: (1) that the fourth Evangelist is dependent on sources and in particular on the Synoptics; (2) that his background is different than that of his subjects—that the author is Greek writing with significant Gnostic influence; (3) that John is not a serious witness to the Jesus of history; (4) that he is evidence of the latest stage of first-century theological development; (5) and that the author of the Fourth Gospel is not the apostle John or an eyewitness.

Robinson went on to outline the demise of these views and to illustrate how they are all interlocked. Above all, the "new look," while not just over-turning these propositions, affirms a genuine connection between the fourth Evangelist and historical traditions about Jesus. And if the "new look" is embraced, questions about the date, cultural background, and authorship must all be decided in the locale of early first-century Jewish Christianity. In sum, the "new look" has earnestly sought to affirm the value of the "Johannine tradition." The presumption no longer holds that John fails to merit the historical trustworthiness of his synoptic peers.

The new look's insistence on John's independence from the Synoptics and John's Jewish orientation has been well received. But the third advance—that John offers genuine history—has resulted from a more real-istic appraisal of all four Gospels. Each Evangelist presents theology along with history and "interprets" Jesus for his reader. Thus Luke has given shape to the portrait of Jesus in ways once reserved strictly for John. But this is in no way to disparage historical value within the Gospel.

In the 1970s Robinson's interest in John led him to reread Dodd's *Historical Tradition in the Fourth Gospel*. He was forced to rethink not only the date of John but also the entire New Testament, publishing his results in 1976 (*Redating the New Testament*). He even suggested that John could have stemmed from the sixties of the first century. Why? John is conspicu-ously silent about the doom of Jerusalem, which the Romans razed in A.D. 70, and he presupposes a pre-70 outlook (see 2:19–20; 11:47–52). John even employs details of the city as if it were still standing (see 5:2). Added to this is the widespread evidence defended also by Dodd that John is aware of the "psychological divisions of Palestine before the war"—which "would be barely intelligible outside a purely Jewish context in the earliest period."[28] Robinson ended his life pouring his energies into Johannine scholarship. In the final volume of his career, *The Priority of John* (1985), Robinson offered a massive summing up of his conservative, unconventional views. It is an exhaustive defense of John's antiquity, authority, and Jewish orientation. *The Priority of John* argues what its title suggests. It is the climax of the "new look" that Robinson had signaled thirty years earlier.[29]

However, we must be quick to add that not all scholars have agreed with these results. In fact, *The Priority of John* has been given scant attention in some academic circles that are still convinced that John is a significantly late Gospel whose heritage is Hellenistic.[30]

THE SIGNIFICANCE OF THE NEW LOOK

These issues that we have been discussing are important because they will directly affect the way we value and interpret the Gospel of John. We are forced to make decisions. If we conclude that the cultural background of the Gospel is Hellenistic (as do Bultmann, Haenchen, and to a degree, Barrett), it will influence our interpretation. For example, the miracle at Cana where Jesus turns water into wine may reflect a Christianizing of the Greek Dionysus myth if the Gospel is Hellenistic. On the other hand, if it is a Jewish story from early Palestinian Judaism, we shall need to look to Old Testament and Jewish antecedents (as do the commentaries of Marsh, Brown, Morris, Carson, and Beasley-Murray).

The same is true for the value of the Johannine traditions. It is not enough to accept merely those accounts that parallel the Synoptics. As Stephen Smalley urges, "We can now reckon seriously with the possibility that the Fourth Gospel, including John's special material, is grounded in historical tradition when it *departs* from the synoptics *as well as* when it overlaps them."[31] Hence exclusively Johannine stories such as Nicodemus, the Samaritan woman, and Lazarus must no longer be viewed as fictional. They bear important historical worth.

CURRENT TRENDS

The question of John's historicity (and thereby the Gospel's authenticity) is certainly an important issue. But for some, especially those outside the evangelical camp, these questions are no longer pressing. New trends in Johannine research are following other movements in biblical studies and in literary criticism and these need to be noted.

1. Source Criticism

A compelling interest among many Johannine scholars today is the quest to unravel the literary structure of the Fourth Gospel. The Gospel has left us some evidence showing traces of its own history. For instance, 2:11 and 4:54 record that the signs of Jesus were being numbered, but the system of numbering is not consistent. There also seems to be a pattern relating the discourses to these signs throughout the first half of the Gospel. There is even evidence that John's Gospel is irregularly "stitched" together and the flow of the narrative uneven: consider the way the geography of Jesus' movements make him bounce between Galilee and Judea in chapters 3–7.

No doubt Robert Fortna has established himself as a most ambitious writer who is uncovering the "literary seams" in the Gospel and separating John's sources.[32] But Fortna has undoubtedly set the agenda for much future research, and as he does so, it will be important to ask critical questions about his chief presuppositions. Source criticism is another approach to locate behind the Gospel trustworthy, historical data; and, in this case, the narrative "signs" source is deemed to be the most ancient. One problem with this comes when we see how intricately the sign source and the discourse source are connected—and how uniform is their language.

Raymond Brown has done similar work in this area. He believes that we can detect multiple "layers" of tradition in the Gospel and these each give us a period of the history of the book's composition.[33] While not many have rushed to endorse these reconstructions, still a near consensus seems at hand: that a community of Christians did indeed collaborate in the development and preservation of these Johannine traditions. And the evidence of their work is still present in the Gospel. Debate continues, however, about the degree to which this community preserved, shaped, and even reinvented traditional materials.

Once again, questions will have to be raised with regard to the presuppositions of such a hypothesis. It is the tacit understanding of Brown, Fortna, and others that the narrative of the Fourth Gospel is in fact telling us more about the history of the Johannine community (its "lives, loves, and hates," as Brown puts it in his subtitle) than about Jesus.

2. Sociology and Theology

This interest in the Gospels as windows into the life and times of a particular New Testament community has been taken up by scholars with a keen interest in sociology. This trend has been with us for some time and reflects the interests of the late twentieth century as we study the diversity and the complexity of our own social organizations. For instance, Bruce Malina is a biblical scholar who examines life and values in the New Testament world, employing the categories of cultural anthropology.[34] One problem with studying the New Testament communities in this manner is that there is little evidence—direct evidence—that tells us about the character of early Christian life. The only access possible is to view writings such as the Gospels as windows that do not clarify the life of Jesus but do tell us about the community that produced it.

Johannine sociological analysis is simply the attempt to reconstruct the value system, community characteristics, and worldview of the Christians who produced the Fourth Gospel. David Rensberger's book, *Johannine Faith and Liberating Community*, attempts this in a consistent and thoroughgoing fashion.[35] Thus John 3 and 9 are "communal symbols" showing the inner tensions of the community and the severe choices each member had to make. The trial sequence in the Gospel (along with John 5) tells us about the Johannine worldview of hostility and suspicion.

Perhaps the most troubling problem of such reconstructions is that the interpreter can almost find in the fourth gospel whatever he or she is seeking. That is, *the sociological grid may be made to fit even when the ancient evidence is not appropriate to the study at hand.* For example, in chapter 6, Rensberger employs the liberation theology categories of Jose Miranda to prove that the Johannine church was an "oppressed community" seeking liberation from powerful authorities. In fact, this is the meaning of the Johannine christology: Jesus' conflict with the Jews is simply the church's conflict with the world. Even the Nicodemus narrative is put to use: Nicodemus, we are told, is challenged "to be born into a people"—to undertake "deliberate downward mobility" and to take a stand with the "oppressed community."[36] "Good works," according to John, really translates into "the eschatological transformation of the world and its social systems on the basis of love and justice."[37]

While this is a fascinating suggestion, we are right to wonder if the interpreter is bringing categories to the text that may not be there. In this case, the author neglects the major themes of inwardness, individual piety, and mysticism that are so central to John. How do we know when we are bringing our own social framework to the text?

3. Rhetorical Criticism

If there is a "cutting edge" to Johannine study, many writers would like to find it here.[38] Scholars in this field "do not ask, at least primarily, questions about the history of the text, the state of the Johannine community, the degree of John's historical trustworthiness, what sources can be detected, or the like. Rather they ask how to make sense of the text as it stands."[39] Above all, the "sense of the text" is determined by the reader as he/she interacts with the story.

It is important to understand the key used by these interpreters to unlock the Gospel's message. In this case theories of communication provide universal structures that can then be found in virtually any composition. Thus John is viewed as a writing to which we react, which forces us to make a response as the story of Jesus unfolds.

One of the most comprehensive treatments of John from this vantage belongs to Alan Culpepper in his book, *The Anatomy of the Fourth Gospel. A Study in Literary Design.*[40] Culpepper sets out to make the first thorough rhetorical examination of the Fourth Gospel, using the interdisciplinary tools of today's literary critics. For instance, he studies the plot, the relation between the narrator and the assumed reader, narrative time, the characters (and their relation to the narrator), and the real author (who stands behind the narration itself). For instance, we as readers are carried along through the story that unfolds as the narrator gives us hints of what is really happening. Thus in 2:11, the narrator explains about the signs and glory of

Jesus. He has inside information so that we can see what the characters are thinking and feeling. And then (21:24) we suddenly are told that indeed this narrator is the Beloved Disciple who all along has been evidencing an intimacy with Jesus in the story.

What we have here is a shift at work in the notion of truth and its relation to the historical narrative. Biblical studies for centuries have understood the "truth" as a value that is tied to the "historical facts" given in the text. That is why heated debates have always raged around the historicity and Jewishness of the biblical narratives. But here we are learning that "truth" comes in other ways as well. The novel, for instance, conveys truth about the realities of life, and it may be an entirely fictional setting. *Thus truth does not have to be necessarily tied to historicity.*[41] Truth-claims can still be made through a narrative that provides poor history or no history at all. In fact, it is the drama itself, the literary world that the author creates, which ushers new truth to the reader.

In the work of Culpepper and others, serious questions will always have to be asked of this method.[42] Chief among these are questions concerning the appropriateness of using categories from the modern novel to interpret first-century gospels. But evangelicals will have a more serious complaint. Carson argues rightly when Culpepper says that the Gospel should not be a window into the life of Jesus but a mirror in which we see ourselves reacting, learning, and discovering what the narrative gives us. But here, in the words of Carson, "We have sacrificed the Gospel's claims to certain historical specificity, to eyewitness credibility, to the *truth claims* of this Gospel, and set sail on the shoreless sea of existential subjectivity."[43]

Today many scholars have given up any interest in rebuilding the Johannine world or pursuing the historicity of John's story, urging that such reconstructions are impossible; and when they are attempted, they simply become a platform for the scholar to introduce his or her worldview into the story. Frozen at a hermeneutical impasse in which few objective facts can be discovered, these writers now offer "readings" of John as open admissions of their own hermeneutical bias. Therefore, creative analyses of John from a personal perspective have become the order of the day.[44]

CONCLUSION

Each of the trends we have discussed offer both promise and challenge to the interpreter today. But any novice who looks at current literature—commentaries, monographs, or journal articles—must be aware of these trends and be able to critically evaluate them. For instance, a new commentary was mailed to me recently to review for a journal. At a glance it was evident that the author still held to a completely Hellenistic interpretation of John but, finding that unsatisfying for the modern audience, looked to themes in modern liberation theology for the message of the Gospel. My sincere hope is that students who find this commentary in the library will see it as a volume that is in conversation with decades of Johannine research. And since so many of its theses are still being debated, the book will be used with care and critical insight.

Important Introductory Questions

WHO WROTE JOHN'S GOSPEL?

The authorship of the Gospel of John has been notoriously difficult, and a handful of positions represents the present terrain. (1) The Gospel was written by John the son of Zebedee (or some other major New Testament figure). (2) The Gospel was written by a pious disciple in the second century who read many of his own experiences back into the life of Jesus. (3) The Gospel was a community production which rewrote the story of Jesus making it relevant to their own (Hellenistic) context. (4) The Gospel represents ancient traditions of the apostle John who bequeathed them to the community he founded. These were then written up by his followers after John's death.

At the center of this question are the very issues that informed the debate about the "new look" on John that I mentioned earlier. Robinson saw clearly that the logical result of the New Look was reopening the question about authorship. If John's date belongs in the first century, if the Gospel's cultural milieu is Jewish, and if it is a valuable witness to the Jesus of history, it is not implausible to argue for apostolic authorship. In doing so, however, we are not compelled to exclude the possibility of other editorial hands. Stephen Smalley puts it this way: "John the Apostle, also known as the Beloved Disciple, handed on to some of his own followers his eyewitness account of the Jesus story, and in turn they were responsible for the publication of the Fourth Gospel in its finished form. Thus the work is apostolic, but not in fact *written* by the apostle."[45]

The earliest complete Greek manuscripts of John employ the heading "Kata Iōannēn" (according to John). Which John is meant? John the Baptist is the only "John" named in the Gospel, and he is doubtless not the author.[46] Of course we think of John, the brother of James, son of Zebedee, who features prominently in the Synoptics (Mark 1:19f). But nowhere is this person mentioned. In 21:2, the "sons of Zebedee" are listed (showing that James and John were known), but the name "John" is never provided. The absence of any reference to this apostle is curious—it increases the mystery of the puzzle before us.

The best evidence comes from an anonymous figure described as "the Beloved Disciple" (13:23; 19:26; 20:2; 21:7, 20). This must have been intelligible to someone, and we can safely assume that John's readers know this disciple's name already. Perhaps it is a title of respect or veneration. The same is true of the mother of Jesus. Nowhere is she named "Mary"—and if the Fourth Gospel were our only source for her, she would never have been known by name. Something similar is evidenced in the Dead Sea Scrolls of

Qumran. That community's leader was "The Teacher of Righteousness," but nowhere in the Qumran literature is he named.

The Beloved Disciple is first introduced in the upper room before Jesus' arrest (13:21–30). The Synoptics make clear that this meal was reserved for the Twelve (Mark 14:17), and so we may be able to deduce that the Beloved Disciple must have been an apostle. He also reclined next to Jesus and was able to lean back easily against Jesus to ask the name of the traitor in their company. The text shows intimacy and suggests that the Beloved Disciple knew Jesus well and could make inquiries for the other eleven.

John 19:26 shows him standing at the foot of the cross with Jesus' mother. Jesus indicates to this disciple that he is now to care for Jesus' mother. If 20:25–26 is compared with the same account found in Matthew 27:56, it appears that Jesus' "mother's sister" (Mary's sister or Jesus' aunt) may be the same as the "mother of the sons of Zebedee." This would make John the maternal cousin of Jesus and explain why the apostle is assigned to care for Mary.[47]

On Easter morning Peter and the Beloved Disciple race to the empty tomb (20:2–10). The account shows the disciple having great virtue: he outruns Peter, sees the evidence of the Resurrection, and even though Peter enters the tomb first, the Beloved Disciple is first to "see and believe." Obviously the readers of this Gospel are to view the Beloved Disciple as a model of virtue and faith.

The comparison of the Beloved Disciple to Peter comes up again in chapter 21. He alone identifies the resurrected Jesus on the shore (21:4–7); and though Peter sprints to Jesus' side, the Beloved Disciple stays with the miraculous catch. This leads to Jesus' inquiries about Peter's love (21:15–17) and an oblique description of Peter's martyrdom (21:18–19).

Perhaps the most important reference is found in 21:20–24. The fate of the Beloved Disciple becomes a natural subject following the discussion in 21:18–19 about Peter's death. But it appears that a well-known saying of Jesus was subject to considerable misunderstanding ("If it is my will that he remain till I come, what is that to you?" 21:22). Apparently the popular view was that the Beloved Disciple would not die but witness Christ's second coming personally. Now in light of the Beloved Disciple's apparent death, 21:23 must make the correction explicit.

This brings us to verse 24 which, according to many (Westcott, Nunn), is the earliest evidence of authorship. "This is the disciple [the Beloved Disciple] who is bearing witness to these things—and who has written these things." Despite his death the Beloved Disciple nevertheless continued to nurture his followers by providing the Gospel itself as a written testimony to the life of Jesus. Now his disciples pen a final credit to him complete with words of respect—"and we know that his testimony is true." These verses apply not just to the previous verses in chapter 21, but to the entire Gospel. The Beloved Disciple is the eyewitness source to the Fourth Gospel's testimony.

Note the language of the text carefully: the Beloved Disciple is the source of testimony as an *eyewitness,* and he authored something as a record. Nevertheless, other participants or editors have contributed substantially to the Gospel's story.

There may be other indirect references to this disciple in other texts as well. John 19:34–37 corroborates the role of the Beloved Disciple in 21:24. Here an unnamed disciple is witness to the events of the cross. In 19:35 his eyewitness role is explicit, "He who saw it has born witness—his testimony is true and he knows that he tells the truth." Of course, we cannot be certain whether this is also the Beloved Disciple in 19:35, and there is no suggestion of authorship. But still, the text is saying that the story we are reading originated from an eyewitness tradition—someone who was there and who later gave a report. This verification holds striking similarities to that in 21:24 and urges that they point to the same person.

More evidence of a prominent unnamed disciple occurs in two other places. In 18:15–16, it is "the other disciple" who gains Peter access to the high priest's courtyard. Is the reader meant to understand that this is the Beloved Disciple? On the one hand it would seem unlikely that one of the Twelve would be a personal acquaintance of the high priest.[48] Then again, the close connection with Peter here reminds us of the two narratives we have already seen in which the Beloved Disciple and Peter play a complimentary role (20:1–10; 21:4–8). From a literary standpoint at least, we cannot exclude this as a possible reference to the Beloved Disciple.

A similar occasion appears in 1:35–42. Who is the unnamed disciple with Andrew? Presumably he, too, has a brother since on one reading of verse 41, Andrew was the first to find his brother (and then the other disciple found his brother, too). Evidence connecting this passage to the other texts is slim, however.

Who is this enigmatic "Beloved Disciple"? Bultmann suggested that he was no historical person at all but a literary figure—an ideal disciple offered as a model to the reader. Certainly the Beloved Disciple is held aloft as an exemplary Christian, but he does play another role. He is also the foundational witness to the Gospel's historical tradition. One way or another, he must be a genuine person.

Nominees for the Beloved Disciple have been legion. Among them, Lazarus deserves special mention. If we use only the Gospel itself as a source, he is the one person whom Jesus specifically "loved" (11:3, 11, 36). The Beloved Disciple passages also occur *after* the Lazarus episode (ch. 11). But why would the text mention him by name in chapter 11 and then disguise it thereafter? Further, chapter 13 says that the Beloved Disciple was at Jesus' Passover meal; and since Lazarus was not one of the Twelve, it is uncertain that he was present.[49] On the other hand, this proposal has intriguing literary support from within the Gospel. In chapter 21, there is some confusion about why the Beloved Disciple might die. If this were

Lazarus, it might refer to chapter 11—Lazarus had already experienced a "resurrection" and would he not be impervious to death? Jesus had said in Bethany, "I am the resurrection and the life, he who believes in me, *though he die*, yet shall he live, and whoever lives and believes in me *shall never die*" (11:25f NKJV). Furthermore, since the Lazarus episode is at the literary center of the gospel and is a clear parallel to the story of Jesus' death and resurrection in chapter 19 and 20, it should not surprise us to learn that its hero is the source of the Fourth Gospel.

John Mark is another well-known candidate (Acts 12:12; Philem. 24). He lived in Jerusalem and would know southern Judah well as the Gospel certainly does. Mark is also associated with Peter (Acts 12:12; 1 Pet. 5:13), and this may explain the Gospel's rivalry between Peter and the Beloved Disciple. He even had priestly connections since Barnabas *the Levite* was his cousin (Col. 4:10). But John Mark was also not a member of the Twelve, and tradition has always associated him with the writing of the Second Gospel.

The most recent—and most thorough—survey of the question of authorship has come from James Charlesworth in *The Beloved Disciple*.[50] After examining the evidence for suggested authors for more than one hundred pages, he disqualifies all comers and argues that the Beloved Disciple is actually Thomas, "the Twin." For instance, only the Beloved Disciple sees Jesus' lance wound on the cross (19:32–35)—and it is this evidence that Thomas wants to see later at the resurrection (20:24–25). Charlesworth provides about a dozen arguments to support his case and concludes that a "School of Thomas" flourished in antiquity, rivaled the western church at Rome, and led to a devotion and respect for Thomas, resulting in the later Coptic Gospel of Thomas and Gnostic writings found at Nag Hammadi.

For many scholars, it is still completely defensible to argue that John the son of Zebedee is the most promising candidate. Some important evidence includes: (1) He was one of the Twelve, and in the Synoptics he along with Peter and James formed an "inner circle" around Jesus. This would explain the intimacy of John's picture of Jesus. (2) In the Synoptics John appears most often with Peter—and this continues in the Book of Acts. They arrange the details of the Last Supper (Luke 22:8). Later they are together in Jerusalem (Acts 3:1, 11) and are placed in custody together (Acts 4) boldly speaking to the Sanhedrin (4:13). They reappear in Samaria as envoys from Jerusalem (8:14). In Galatians 2:9, Paul even refers to Peter and John (along with James) as the "pillars of the church." Thus the comparison with Peter in the Fourth Gospel is not out of character. (3) The Gospel individualizes the names of many disciples (Thomas, Nathanael, Andrew, Peter, etc.), and it is surprising that John is not listed among them. This unusual silence is satisfied if the Beloved Disciple is concealing John's role. (4) The logic of chapter 21 points directly to John. The context of the fishing scene shows that the disciples present are Peter, Thomas, Nathanael, and the two sons of Zebedee. Peter is obviously not the Beloved Disciple, and there is little evidence or tradition that Thomas (*contra* Charlesworth) or Nathanael ever knew Jesus intimately or produced any gospel. Of the sons of Zebedee, James was martyred early, according to Acts 12:2. This leaves John as the remaining possibility.

Is it possible to develop a profile of the author using indirect evidence within the Gospel? As early as 1881, the famous New Testament scholar B. F. Westcott did just this and amassed impressive data to defend the following arguments that build on one another: (1) the author was a Jew; (2) the author was a Jew of Palestine; (3) the author was an eyewitness of what he describes; (4) the author was an apostle; (5) the author was the apostle John. Many would agree with these steps but hesitate only with the last two. But for Westcott, the link between the beloved disciple and the son of Zebedee seemed irrefutable. Westcott's colleague, J. B. Lightfoot, exhaustively asserted the same in an article in 1890 (published with lecture notes in 1893), and it is doubtful whether the arguments presented there have ever been overturned.

We must remember that the question of authorship—especially when it comes to internal evidence—no longer turns on the discovery of *new* evidence. There is no new evidence, only re-sifting of what has been known for years. And as Lightfoot urged, no argument has ever been advanced to show the *impossibility* of the author's being John the apostle.[51]

A major objection has always been that if John penned this Gospel would he refer to *himself* as "the disciple whom Jesus loved"? But it loses its force when we recognize the possibility of *stages of authorship*. It is likely that the apostle John originated the historical traditions of the Gospel and that these may even have been written. These texts were treasured by his disciples, and when he died, they took it upon themselves to organize and even edit them. This explains the Gospel's final verses (21:20–24). By this account "the Beloved Disciple" became *a title of veneration* employed by John's disciples to revere their deceased leader.

The suggestion that the apostle John was the author of the Fourth Gospel is (not surprisingly) echoed by a strong postapostolic tradition. Not only do early second-century writers betray knowledge of the Gospel, but by the late second century writers like Irenaeus and Polycarp can provide a full explanation for the origins of the Gospel.[52] A great deal could be said about these sources (we could refer to the Muratorian Fragment or the Anti-Marcionite Prologue), but this would take us far beyond the scope of the present study.[53] But it is at least important to note that our instincts concerning the internal evidence resonates with what we find coming from the postapostolic era.

HOW THE GOSPEL OF JOHN WAS WRITTEN

In a recent issue of *The Expository Times*, Stephen Smalley reported that the literary origins and structure of John were some of the most pressing concerns in Johannine scholarship.[54] This puzzle of literary structure was the first critical issue recognized in the Gospel. As early as the second century, Tatian's Diatessaron rearranged major portions of John to fit the Synoptics. But the process of textual dislocation must have been widespread. The Sinaitic Syriac version found in 1892 at St. Catherine's monastery in the Sinai desert of Egypt rearranged John 18 (the order of the Caiaphas/Annas interrogation) in order to "improve" the narrative.

What we seem to have are internal clues—perhaps we might label them literary seams—that betray a history of composition in this Gospel. Unfortunately the solution to this problem is unlike that in the Synoptics where multiple traditions can be compared. For instance, if Matthew and Luke used Mark, their patterns of dependence and divergence might be analyzed. On the contrary, John's sources have left only subtle traces of their history.

Since John's sources are not "given away," scholars have developed techniques to unravel the Gospel's mysteries.[55] First we might look for *stylistic evidences* where additional editorial hands are suspected. In John, for example, we could note how *logos* (or word) is employed in chapter 1 and then drops away. But the best studies have rejected this tool. The careful linguistic work of Edward Schweitzer and Eugene Ruckstuhl have fatally weakened source theories based on style and convinced us that the same hand was at work from chapters 1–21.[56]

Second, we might look for *ideological tendencies* in which rival points of view are in the text. John has witnessed a good deal of attention here, too. When any author adopts a source, he may exhibit disagreements with it even if on an unconscious level. Where these disagreements are discernable, the source and the editor may be distinguished. No doubt Bultmann was the expert at this sort of detective work. He cataloged numerous tendencies such as interest in the Beloved Disciple, works versus signs, and eschatology. Note how in 3:26 and in 4:1 very traditional narratives tell us that Jesus was providing water baptism. And then much to our surprise, in 4:2 the story is corrected to say that Jesus really did not baptize—only his followers did. Bultmann would urge that this is evidence of disagreement between an author and his source.

But critics have been equally harsh with this approach too. D. Moody Smith and Robert Fortna question our ability to discern ideological strata.[57] The themes in John are too subtle, too nuanced—and besides, any author may write employing a number of inner tensions. To assign one view to a more primitive level and another view to a redactor or editor simply lacks an objective basis.

A third tool is more promising: *contextual evidence*. This evidence in John is surprisingly the best and the least exploited evidence of all. It is by far the distinguishing feature of John's literary puzzle. Contextual evidence is that which shows some irregularity in the text, some narrative rift, and it comes in a variety of forms: First, there is *textual evidence* where ancient manuscripts show discrepancies in the tradition. One Greek manuscript may record a paragraph or sentence one way while another offers a different version. The pericope of the adulteress (7:53–8:11) comes quickly to mind, but seldom do textual discrepancies bear a major significance for the interpretation of the Fourth Gospel (cf. 1:13, 18, 41; 3:34; 6:69; 14:3).[58]

A second contextual tool is to locate and study the *parenthetical remarks* of the narrator/editor. These are comments that interrupt the story in order to assist the reader, and they imply that the author is using materials, sources, or traditions that his readers may not understand. These are frequent in John. For instance, in John 1:42, we are taught that the Aramaic name "Cephas" means Peter. In 19:31, we are told that the Jewish Sabbath is a "high day." In 4:9, Jewish/Samaritan tensions are footnoted ("for Jews have no dealings with Samaritans"). Occasionally John explains some awkwardness in the logic of the text. For example, in 2:9 the steward of the wedding party may not have known the origin of the wine, but the narrator reminds us that the servants were genuine witnesses to the miracle. The same "reader helps" can be found in 4:2, where we are reminded that Jesus did not baptize anyone. But usually the narrator just assists the story as in 6:1, when he says that the Sea of Galilee and the Sea of Tiberias are one and the same. This is where the source critic sits up. If John's reader understood "Sea of Tiberias" and if John wrote the entire narrative without sources, why didn't John use this phrase in the first place? Other passages with such comments can be found in 2:22 and 3:11.

The third contextual tool is where we identify what I label *literary seams* in the text. These are instances where the chronological, topical, or dramatic flow of the narrative appears disjointed. John's Gospel abounds with these in a way that is completely different from the Synoptics.

These phenomena are so common that they have even received a technical name. In 1907, Edward Schwartz coined the term *aporia* for these "difficulties."[59] Today this term has been taken up by Robert Fortna and Howard Teeple.[60] In English the earliest work on this problem followed Schwartz by three years and can be found in Warburton Lewis, *Disarrangements in the Fourth Gospel*.[61]

What are these "aporias" in John, and how do they evidence "seams" in the Gospel's narrative? While dozens can be found, a mere sampling will establish their significance.

1. First take note of the Johannine Prologue (1:1–18) with its distinctive idiom and poetic style. Without it the Gospel would begin at 1:19 with John the Baptist and parallel the traditional synoptic starting point. What is the origin of this poem? Who wrote it? What is its relation to the body of the Gospel?

2. Note how John uses the term *sign* for Jesus' miracles. In 2:11 and 4:54, these are numbered (the first and second "signs"); but the numbering

system is not maintained; and besides, many have asked, how can 4:54 be the second sign when 2:23 says that Jesus had done multiple signs earlier in Jerusalem?

3. In 3:22, the text says that Jesus "came into the land of Judea." The problem is that he has been in Judea all along since he had attended a Passover Feast in Jerusalem from 2:23–3:21.

4. Many point to the sequence of John 5 and 6. The present order makes Jesus move abruptly from Samaria to Galilee to Jerusalem back to Galilee again and back once more to Jerusalem without transitions. In chapter 5, Jesus is engaged in a debate in Jerusalem. Now look at 6:1, "After this Jesus went to the other side of the Sea of Galilee." It is like reading a letter from a friend who has just described his vacation in Scotland salmon fishing. Then when you turn the page, he says, "And after this, we crossed to the other side of Chicago." Surely, you say, something was left out. As a solution many scholars would like to rearrange the chapters completely (John 3, 4, 6, 5, 7).

5. A fifth *aporia* comes in 7:3–5. Jesus is urged to reveal his signs in Judea as if he had not yet been there; but in 2:23 and in chapter 5 he has already done so.

6. A seventh *aporia* could be noted at John 11:2. Here Mary of Bethany is introduced as the woman who "anointed the Lord with ointment and wiped his feet with her hair." The only problem is that this anointing does not take place until the next chapter (chapter 12).

7. In 14:31, it appears that Jesus has completed his upper room discourse. He implies that his arrest is at hand by saying, "I will no longer talk much with you for the ruler of this world is coming" (14:30). Then he says, "Rise, let us go hence." The striking thing is that Jesus *does* have much to say—86 verses or so!—before the coming of Judas. Should 14:31 be followed by 18:1? If you read the story in this sequence, you will be surprised by the ease with which the narrative flows.

8. Another *aporia* is found at 16:5, "None of you ask me 'Where are you going?'" On the contrary, just the opposite is the case since in 13:36 Peter has asked the identical question and in 14:5 Thomas has done the same. This has inspired a host of rearrangement theories that try to place 16:5 before 13:36.

If we are going to wrestle seriously with the text of John as we have it, we must at least come to terms with these contextual seams. A few of the current explanations are as follows: (1) Some have said that the author never finished the Gospel (W. F. Howard; W. Grundmann). (2) Others have argued that the author produced two editions of his Gospel and these have been artificially joined (P. Parker[62]). (3) One popular solution is to say that John wrote with disjointed stories (R. Schnackenburg, E. Käsemann). Wilhem Wrede thought that John was simply confused. Eduard Meyer suggested that he was clumsy. Walter Bauer thought that John just could not write. This at least is more charitable than Ernest Renan, who in 1867 chalked it up to John's increasing senility! (4) The least likely possibility is that, subsequent to its completion, completed folio leaves were switched around. This theory assumes the unlikely prospect that John even had a folio format.

Most recent critics posit a series of later redactors or editors who compiled various diverse sources. For example, C. K. Barrett feels that these were written from traditions found in Mark. Others such as C. H. Dodd believe that John's sources were oral, older than the Synoptics, and thus bearing a high degree of historicity. Sometimes as in the case of Raymond Brown or Oscar Cullmann, this reworking of the Gospel is attributed to a "Johannine School" or a community of disciples of John who complied, organized, and edited their master's teachings.

Let's try to sum up the usefulness of this data for exegesis. What importance may we attribute to these literary seams?

First, most scholars think that a consensus is nearing in Johannine scholarship that the Fourth Gospel is made up of sources. These *aporias* then are literary seams that betray the diverse historical traditions combined to make up the fabric of John. These seams are *positive objective data* and bear vital clues for us. Of course, this result is nothing new. Scholars from Bultmann to Moody Smith have been weighing the evidence for signs, narrative sources, and discourse sources all along.

Conservative exegetes may find that these results work to some advantage. Johannine source criticism may lead us in the same direction as the Synoptic Problem: rather than being the literary inventions of three prolific Christians, the Synoptics are well-crafted collections of ancient historical units preserved by the earliest Christians. Now similar claims are possible for the Fourth Gospel. If John is using early traditions, his Gospel is hardly a late first-century invention. On the contrary, it possesses an antiquity and authenticity, that is striking. To my mind, sources point to antiquity and antiquity points to authenticity.

The danger here is to say that uncovering earlier strata will get us back to an earlier, more pristine message from John. This is, by the way, how Johannine form critics have eliminated things such as futurist eschatology and sacramental interest from John. Similarly Bruce Woll and Fernando Segovia have recently argued that the original core of the Farewell Discourse is found in 13:31–14:31 and all else is secondary.[63] But this neglects the overall literary and theological unity of John. Most recently Robert Fortna has published his attempt to locate the earliest stratum, the narrative source, which was subsequently edited by a redactor. And his premise is clear: the Fourth Gospel is like an old Victorian house whose grandeur and heritage will be seen only when the later efforts of painters and carpenters have been removed.[64]

Second, the recognition of *aporias* suggests that the process of writing, compiling, and editing the Fourth Gospel was more complex than we ever realized. Raymond Brown, for example, supports multiple stages of editing. Tied to this is the likelihood that the Gospel is the product of a community, and at various times various hands made their contribution. All of this began, in my judgment, with John, the Beloved Disciple. The numerous reflexes to eyewitness testimony (19:35) must at least mean this. But it may be true that his community, his intimate followers, collated his teachings, organized them, and edited them. John 21:20–23 may even suggest that John had died.

Does 21:24 reveal the identity of a Johannine disciple? Again, what does verse 24 mean when the writer says, "*We* know that *his* testimony is true?" Clearly other parties are buttressing the Beloved Disciple's report. And if this is true, we may have ready evidence that editors have substantially reshaped the text.

While complete rearrangement theories have not won the day, the Johannine *aporias* have clearly affected our understanding of source criticism, authorship, and literary format. Even today authors still argue for reversing chapters 5 and 6. Nevertheless, despite these difficulties and tensions, it seems that a very early hand completed the final edition of the Gospel. Far too many themes unite John theologically, giving this Gospel a power and conviction that is uncanny. Overarching literary unity can be seen in the delicate construction of plot/narrative (Alan Culpepper[65]), dramatic suspense (S. Smalley[66]), irony (P. D. Duke[67]), or even forensic motifs (A. A. Trites, A. E. Harvey[68]). It is John's complexity, his mixing of these elements that troubles us. In 1953, C. H. Dodd cleverly described the Fourth Gospel as a musical fugue: "A theme is introduced and developed up to a point; then a second theme is introduced and the two are interwoven; then a third and so on. A theme may be dropped and later resumed and differently combined, in all manner of harmonious variations."[69]

If the seams in John suggest to us a patchwork quilt, a combining of sources by some editor, then it should not surprise us to find that scholars have sought to look beneath the surface of the Gospel. Rudolf Bultmann was the first to work out a thorough explanation of this Johannine collage.[70] He suggested that the Fourth Gospel originated with a "Signs Source," a narrative of miracle stories and conflicts that may have included the passion narrative at the end. Then at a later date an editor revised these stories and supplied the lengthy speeches or discourses of Jesus.

In 1988, Robert Fortna published what is to date the most comprehensive study of this mystery.[71] In 314 pages of detective work, Fortna tries to separate this ancient narrative source, to sift out editorial comments, and to reweave the theology of the original document. He even dates this source in the 40s or 50s. And he claims to be able to discern when the editor disagreed with the source.[72]

These efforts are common today among Johannine scholars, but understandably evangelicals have been reluctant to join in. Two reservations may be appropriately lodged. First, much of this spadework is entirely speculative. Even Fortna himself hopes that a mere 50 percent of it will find acceptance. Sometimes it is virtually impossible to reconstruct the literary history of a given chapter. And the chief problem is that, unlike the Synoptics, we have no other documents with which to compare John. We might be able to study the editorial efforts of Matthew by looking at Mark (a text Matthew may have known by some accounts). But the Fourth Gospel gives us nothing similar.

Second, Johannine scholarship is fascinated with the *development* of communities and faith. While this has academic interest, how is it assisting the exegete to open up and understand the biblical text before us? In many of these studies the aim is to reconstruct the communities of Christians who stand behind the text and show how their faith changed and developed as new voices hidden in the Gospel struggled to be heard.[73] There is certainly value in understanding that early Christianity was dynamic. For instance the Epistle of James is no doubt a *response* to a theological development that Jewish-Christians found troubling. And First John likely is a response to the misuse of the Fourth Gospel's christology and pneumatology.[74] But it may be dubious to locate development within a single text such as this.

And so we have a puzzle. The Fourth Gospel is a text with a history—seismic seams, literary lacunae, editorial traces are abundantly evident. It is a phenomenon that cannot be lightly dismissed. And the interpreters must be aware of them as they move through the text. It may help explain rough passages (such as 14:31 and 16:5) and enlighten us when the text shows the tensions of development.

But the exegete's task is best served when we study the text as we have it. A long tradition of commentaries represented by Bultmann, MacGregor, and recently Koester (among many others) viewed exegesis as a dismantling and rebuilding exercise. But a new, infinitely more beneficial commentary today seeks the theological message within the canonical form of the text. Scholars such as Brown, Barrett, Morris, Carson, and Beasley-Murray (among others) know the older tradition but choose for theological reasons to make sense of the Gospel as we have it: to explore its own coherence (instead of its hidden strata) and to examine its final message (instead of trace the process of its development).

THE LITERARY FORM OF THE GOSPEL

This brings us to an important next step. If it is true that the interpretation of John must take into account the larger theological drama presented in the Gospel, we need to understand the literary structure of the Gospel as we have it today. Does the present canonical text show an organization that might be useful for exegesis?

If we scan the entire Gospel, we at once can see some natural divisions. All along, however, we must keep in mind that the chapter divisions in the Gospel are artificial. We want to locate any natural literary divisions. It seems that Jesus is at work in public in chapters 1–12, showing signs and teaching to diverse public audiences. Then in chapters 13–17, he is in private speaking to his followers, almost saying "farewell" to them. Finally, the story ends with a detailed passion/resurrection account. We might illustrate the text thus:

Literary Divisions in the Fourth Gospel

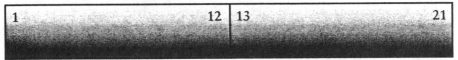

If we look at the transitions between these chapters carefully, chapter 12 seems to be a clear climax to the public ministry: it ends with a "summing up" of Jesus' efforts, a cry of despair concerning disbelief, and a final reaffirmation of the divine origins of Jesus' words. John 13:1 switches the scene to Passover, remarks that Jesus is now departing from the world, and narrows the stage to those who have followed him.

Chapter 17 ends a lengthy prayer, and another geographical shift (the Kidron Valley) moves us to yet another scene: Jesus' arrest, trial, and death. *Lengthy discourses give way to dramatic narrative.* Scholars have been quick to note these divisions and label them. Chapters 1–12 is called the "Book of Signs" since it records Jesus' numerous revelatory miracles. Chapters 13–21 (uniting the upper room and Passion sections) is termed the "Book of Glory," since on the cross Jesus is glorified (13:31).

THE BOOK OF SIGNS (JOHN 1–12)

In this first "book" note how the hymn at the beginning is almost an overture, a curtain-raiser to the drama that really begins at verse 19. This is followed by a unit centered on John the Baptist and his disciples (and their earliest contacts with Jesus). Then the story moves quickly from scene to scene: a miracle at Cana, cleansing the temple, and Nicodemus.

If we sort these units by theme, major narrative shifts become evident. At once it is clear that these sections are *topically arranged.* In chapters 2–4, Jesus is working miracles on institutions in Judaism; in chapters 5–10, he is making appearances at a series of Jewish festivals (note how each festival is actually named in each section). In each of these—institutions and festivals—he is replacing some Jewish symbol with abundance, messianic abundance (water > living water; manna > living bread, for example).

Each literary unit is also marked by an internal indicator for the division. Note how many of the literary units are shown by internal indicators of each division. Episodes in Cana (miracles each of which are numbered) frame the section on Jewish institutions. The festival section clearly refers to each respective festival, exploits a major symbol in the festival (Sabbath/work, Passover/bread, Tabernacles/water and light, Rededication/Jesus' consecration), and generally offers a discourse expanding the meaning of the symbols (see 6:15–35 as a comment on Passover). The final reference to John the Baptist (10:40–42) refers back to the beginning of the entire sequence of signs (1:19ff), making another closing frame and reiterating the value of Jesus' signs. Finally, the closing two chapters serve as a sobering warning of what is to come.

What conclusions can we draw from this? Suddenly it appears that the Fourth Gospel may be topically arranged (at least in chapters 1–12), even though the units or stories themselves have a clear historical and chronological character. John is telling us more about Jesus' messianic impact on Judaism than he is about the sequence of events in Jesus' ministry. And the episodes are arranged by no accident. The final edition of John that we possess has a careful, intentional organization.

THE BOOK OF GLORY (JOHN 13–21)

Much the same can be argued for the Book of Glory (chapters 13–21). In this major section Jesus now turns in private to his disciples during his final Passover. Remarkably, all nine chapters center on just a few days of Jesus' life. Chapter 18 opens the story of the trial and death of Jesus. As an extended narrative, it reads much like the Synoptics, moving quickly from scene to scene without the characteristic Johannine discourses. The cross is followed by a detailed Resurrection account in which Jesus anoints his followers with the Spirit. Finally, chapter 21 is likely an addition which adds Resurrection stories in Galilee and Jesus' lengthy discussion with Peter.

The Book of Glory is dominated by the events of the upper room and the Passion account. In chapters 13–17, Jesus is center stage preparing his disciples for his death. He teaches them privately about servanthood, washes their feet, explains the coming Holy Spirit in terms of personal revelation and persecution, and prays at length for his followers and their disciples. If each "sign" in the Gospel is accompanied by a discourse, this may be the "great discourse" explaining the "great sign" of the cross. Chapter 18, on the other hand, is a different sort of story. It seems that the account of Jesus' trial and death was firmly established in early Christianity, perhaps by oral tradition. John 18–19 has more parallels with the Synoptic Gospels than any other section. This is why C. H. Dodd began with the passion narrative of John when he probed the Fourth Gospel's historical worth.[75] He concluded, though, that while the Gospel echoes the Synoptics, its divergences were such that it probably recorded an ancient and authentic strain of the oral tradition about Jesus' death.

But what at first sight appears to be a smooth narrative shows up on closer inspection to be a story assembled in much the same way as the Book of Signs. Jesus' farewell (13:31–17:26), for instance, reads like a patchwork of teachings. We have already noted how 16:5 and the question of "going" follows 13:36 with difficulty. Commentators often point out the many parallels between chapters 14 and 16, suggesting that we may have two renditions of similar materials. Nevertheless the final edition of the Gospel combined these sources of tradition, organized them here, and worked to give a coherent presentation of Jesus' final days.

A helpful diagram might serve to underscore the layout of the literary units in the Gospel as they develop John's overall themes.

Conclusion

It is time to sum up what we have said and draw some conclusions. It is clear that the text of John is made up of sources that have been pieced together to form a unified narrative. If we look carefully, we can discern the seams where these sources have been stitched together. Some of them are rough, rugged signs of an awkward assembly. But that is fine. It shows us that John—no less than the Synoptics—is made up of sources, ancient sources, that predate the author's own efforts.

But this raises important questions. If John has been edited, should we give a different worth, say, to the miracle stories than to the discourses? If the editor was free to shape these narratives, how much did he influence their final form? It is interesting to remember that the language of the First Epistle of John is exactly like that of Jesus in the Fourth Gospel. How much freedom did such editors have?

When we work with a passage in the Fourth Gospel, it is crucial that we realize where in the longer text our passage comes from. John's layout is not haphazard. If, say, we are discussing Jesus' claim to be living bread (6:35), we *must* see the larger context in the Book of Signs. Each theme is knit into the larger fabric, and when we pause to stand back, the book we call the Fourth Gospel takes on a striking and wonderful quality.

To study John's Gospel in detail for the first time is like becoming heir to an ancient, beautiful tapestry. Its artistry astounds. And the closer we examine it, the more we are awed by mysteries hidden from the casual observer. To understand the part we must stand back and comprehend the whole. And when we investigate its background and its history, its value and uniqueness—even its message—acquire an entirely new depth.

The Structure of John's Gospel

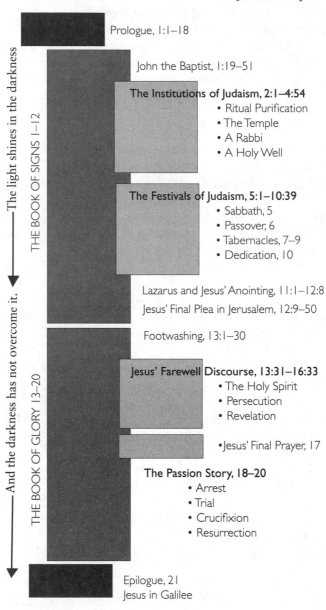

The light shines in the darkness ⟶

And the darkness has not overcome it. ⟶

Prologue, 1:1–18

John the Baptist, 1:19–51

The Institutions of Judaism, 2:1–4:54
- Ritual Purification
- The Temple
- A Rabbi
- A Holy Well

The Festivals of Judaism, 5:1–10:39
- Sabbath, 5
- Passover, 6
- Tabernacles, 7–9
- Dedication, 10

Lazarus and Jesus' Anointing, 11:1–12:8

Jesus' Final Plea in Jerusalem, 12:9–50

Footwashing, 13:1–30

Jesus' Farewell Discourse, 13:31–16:33
- The Holy Spirit
- Persecution
- Revelation

•Jesus' Final Prayer, 17

The Passion Story, 18–20
- Arrest
- Trial
- Crucifixion
- Resurrection

THE BOOK OF SIGNS 1–12

THE BOOK OF GLORY 13–20

Epilogue, 21
Jesus in Galilee

Bibliography
Anderson, C. C. *Critical Quests for Jesus.* Grand Rapids: Eerdmans, 1959.

Ashton, J. *Understanding the Fourth Gospel.* Oxford: Clarendon Press, 1991.

Briggs, R. C. *Interpreting the New Testament Today.* Nashville: Abingdon, 1973.

Brown, C. *Jesus in European Protestant Thought 1778–1860.* Grand Rapids: Baker, 1985.

Brown, R. "The Relation Between the Fourth Gospel and the Synoptic Gospels." *New Testament Essays.* London: Chapman, 1965. 143–216.

Brown, R. E. *The Community of the Beloved Disciple.* New York: Paulist, 1979.

Bruns, J. E. "The Confusion Between John and John Mark in Antiquity," *Scripture* 17 (1965), 23–26.

Carson, D. A. "Recent Literature on the Fourth Gospel: Some Reflections" *Themelios* 9.1 (September 1983): 8–18.

———. "Selected Recent Studies of the Fourth Gospel." *Themelios* 14.2 (January 1989), 57–64.

———. "Current Source Criticism of the Fourth Gospel. Some Methodological Questions." *JBL* 97 (1978): 411–29.

Charlesworth, J. *The Beloved Disciple. Whose Witness Validates the Gospel of John?* Valley Forge, Pa.: Trinity Press, 1995.

Cullmann, O. *The Johannine Circle.* Philadelphia: Westminster, 1976.

Culpepper, A. *The Anatomy of the Fourth Gospel. A Study in Literary Design.* Philadelphia: Fortress, 1983.

Culpepper, R. A., and C. C. Black. *Exploring the Gospel of John.* Louisville: Westminster/John Knox, 1996.

deJonge, M. "The Beloved Disciple and the Date of John." E. Best and R. McL. Wilson, eds. *Text and Interpretation: Studies in the New Testament for Matthew Black.* Cambridge: University Press, 1979, 99–114.

Dodd, C. H. *Historical Tradition in the Fourth Gospel.* Cambridge: University Press, 1963.

———. *The Interpretation of the Fourth Gospel.* Cambridge: University Press, 1953.

Ellis, P. *The Genius of John. A Composition-Critical Commentary on the Fourth Gospel.* Collegeville, Minn.: Liturgical Press, 1984.

Filson, F. "Who Was the Beloved Disciple?" *JBL* 68 (1949): 83–88.

Fortna, R. *The Fourth Gospel and Its Predecessor. From Narrative Source to Present Gospel.* Philadelphia: Fortress, 1988.

———. *The Gospel of Signs. A Reconstruction of the Narrative Source Underlying the Fourth Gospel.* Cambridge: University Press, 1970.

Freed, E. D. *Old Testament Quotations in the Gospel of John.* Leiden: Brill, 1965.

Gardner-Smith, P. *St. John & The Synoptic Gospels.* Cambridge: University Press, 1938.

Guthrie, D. *New Testament Introduction.* Downers Grove, Ill.: IVP, 1970, 241–71.

Henry, P. *New Directions in New Testament Study.* Philadelphia: Westminster, 1979.

Higgins, A. J. B. *The Historicity of the Fourth Gospel.* London: Lutterworth, 1960.

Hoskyns, E. C. and F. N. Davey. *The Fourth Gospel.* London: Faber & Faber, 1947, 58–135.

Howard, W. F. Revised by C. K. Barrett. *The Fourth Gospel in Recent Criticism & Interpretation.* London: Epworth, 1955.

Hunter, A. M. *According to John. The New Look at the Fourth Gospel.* Philadelphia: Westminster, 1968.

Kümmel, W. G. *Introduction to the New Testament.* ET: Nashville: Abingdon, 1975. 196–99.

———. *The New Testament: The History of the Investigation of Its Problems.* ET: Nashville: Abingdon, 1972.

Kysar, R. *The Fourth Evangelist and His Gospel. An Examination of Contemporary Scholarship.* Minneapolis: Augsburg, 1975.

———. *John: The Maverick Gospel.* Atlanta: John Knox, 1976.

Lightfoot, J. B. "Internal Evidence for the Authenticity and Genuineness of St. John's Gospel," "External Evidence for the Authenticity and Genuineness of St. John's Gospel." *Biblical Essays.* London: MacMillan, 1893, 1–198.

Lindars, B. "Some Recent Trends in the Study of John." *Way* 30 (1990): 329–38.

Malatesta, E. *St. John's Gospel 1920–1965.* Rome: Pontifical Biblical Institute, 1967.

Moody-Smith, D., *The Composition and Order of the Fourth Gospel. Bultmann's Literary Theory.* New Haven: Yale University Press, 1970.

Neill, S. *The Interpretation of the New Testament 1861–1986,* 2nd ed. New York: Oxford University Press, 1988.

Nunn, H. P. V. *The Authorship of the Fourth Gospel.* Oxford: Blackwell, 1952.

Painter, J., *The Quest for the Messiah. The History, Literature, and Theology of the Johannine Community.* Edinburgh/Nashville: T&T Clark/Abingdon, 1993.

Parker, P. "John and John Mark." *JBL* 79 (1960): 97–110.

———. "John the Son of Zebedee and the Fourth Gospel." *JBL* 81 (1962): 35–43.

Robinson, J. A. T. *Redating the New Testament.* Philadelphia: Westminster, 1976.

———. *The Priority of John.* London: SCM, 1985.

Sanday, W. *The Criticism of the Fourth Gospel.* Oxford: Clarendon Press, 1910.

Sanders, J. N. "St. John of Patmos." *NTS* 9 (1962/63): 75–85.

———. "Who Was the Disciple Whom Jesus Loved?" F. L. Cross, ed., *Studies in the Fourth Gospel.* London: Mowbray, 1957, 72–82.

Schnackenburg, R. *The Gospel According to John,* 3 vols. ET: New York: Seabury, 1968.

Scott, E. F. *The Fourth Gospel, Its Purpose & Its Theology.* Edinburgh: T & T Clark, 1906.

Sloyan, G., *What Are They Saying about John?* New York: Paulist, 1991.

Smalley, S. *John, Evangelist & Interpreter.* Exeter: Paternoster, 1978; Downer's Grove, Ill.: IVP, 1999.

Smith, D. M. *Johannine Christianity. Essays on Its Setting, Sources, and Theology.* Columbia: University of South Carolina Press, 1984.

Snape, H. C. "The Fourth Gospel, Ephesus and Alexandria." *HTR* 47 (1954): 1–4.

Sparks, H. F. D. *The Johannine Synopsis of the Gospels.* New York: Harper & Row, 1974.

Teeple, H. *The Literary Origin of the Gospel of John.* Evanston, Ill.: Religion and Ethics Institute, 1974.

Wiles, M. F. *The Spiritual Gospel. The Interpretation of the Fourth Gospel in the Early Church.* Cambridge: University Press, 1960.

Notes

1. Much of this material has been adapted and revised from G. M. Burge, *Interpreting the Gospel of John* (Grand Rapids: Baker, 1992, rev. 1998).

2. See M. Hengel, *The Johannine Question* (London: SCM, 1989), 1–23.

3. M. Wiles, *The Spiritual Gospel: The Interpretation of the Fourth Gospel in the Early Church* (Cambridge: University Press, 1960); R. Schnackenburg, *John*, 1:193–210;

J. N. D. Kelly, *Early Christian Doctrines* (London: A&C Black, 1977), 52–79, 223–51; see the thorough though now-dated bibliography of E. Malatesta, *St. John's Gospel, 1920–1965* (Rome: Pontifical Institute, 1967), 157–71, "John in the History of Exegesis." For an appreciation of John's incarnational theology, see E. Harrison, "A Study of John 1:14," in R. Guelich, ed., *Unity and Diversity in New Testament Theology* (Grand Rapids: Eerdmans, 1978), 23–36; and M. Meye-Thompson, *The Humanity of Jesus in the Fourth Gospel* (Philadelphia: Fortress, 1988).

4. D. F. Strauss, as cited in W. G. Kümmel, *The New Testament: The History of the Investigation of Its Problems* (Nashville: Abingdon: 1972), 126; cf. A. Schweitzer, *The Quest for the Historical Jesus* (London: A&C Black, 1954), 85–88

5. S. Neill, *The Interpretation of the New Testament 1861–1986* (Oxford: University Press, 1988), 20–29.

6. J. Ashton, *Understanding the Fourth Gospel* (Oxford: Clarendon Press, 1991), 9–43.

7. S. Neill, *The Interpretation of the New Testament 1861–1986*, 338f.

8. In 1925, M. J. Lagrange, the founder of the Ecole Biblique in Jerusalem, published a widely influential commentary along these lines. See J. Murphy-O'Connor, *The Ecole Biblique and the New Testament* (Freiburg, 1990), 22–25.

9. See C. K. Barrett, "The Old Testament in the Fourth Gospel," *JTS* 481 (1947): 155–69; D. A. Carson, "John and the Johannine Epistles," in *It is Written. Scripture Citing Scripture. Essays in Honor of Barnabas Lindars*, D. A. Carson, H. G. M. Williamson, eds. (Cambridge: University Press, 1988), 245–64.

10. See J. H. Charlesworth's collection of essays, *John and Qumran* (London: G. Chapman, 1972).

11. C. F. Burney, *The Aramaic Origin of the Fourth Gospel* (Oxford: University Press, 1922).

12. M. Black, *An Aramaic Approach to the Gospels and Acts* (Oxford: University Press, 1967).

13. Earlier writers, commenting on these details in John 5, interpreted them symbolically, suggesting that the five porticoes (or porches) were the five books of Moses.

14. See J. A. T. Robinson, *The Priority of John* (London: SCM, 1985), 48–67.

15. For a detailed study see J. Finegan, *Encountering New Testament Manuscripts* (Grand Rapids: Eerdmans, 1974), 85–90; also V. Salmon, *The Fourth Gospel. The History of the Text* (Collegeville, Minn.: Liturgical Press, 1976).

16. The Mandeans, who live in rural Iraq and Iran, claim that John the Baptist was messiah and are highly critical of orthodox Christianity.

17. Bultmann's commentary is still in print and widely influential (Philadelphia: Westminster, 1971). The influence of Bultmann, who pointed to these Hellenistic sources in the interpretation of John, can be seen recently in H. Koester, *Introduction to the New Testament*, 2 vols. (Philadelphia: Fortress, 1982), 2:178–98.

18. P. Borgen, "The Gospel of John and Hellenism. Some Observations," in R. A. Culpepper, and C. C. Black, *Exploring the Gospel of John* (Louisville: Westminster/John Knox, 1996), 98–123.

19. B. H. Streeter, *The Four Gospels* (Oxford: University Press, 1924); more recently, see C. Blomberg, *The Historical Reliability of the Gospels* (Downers Grove, Ill.: IVP, 1987), 153–89.

20. Most synopses compare only the Synoptics. However, attempts to study the Johannine material are available. See especially H. F. D. Sparks, *The Johannine Synopsis of the Gospels* (New York: Harper & Row, 1976), and K. Aland, *Synopsis of the Four Gospels* (Stuttgart: United Bible Society, 1971 [Eng. Text], 1975 [Gk. Text]).

21. C. H. Dodd, *The Interpretation of the Fourth Gospel*, 449.

22. *Historical Tradition in the Fourth Gospel*, 423. For a critique of Dodd, see D. A. Carson, "Historical Tradition in the Fourth Gospel. After Dodd, What?" in R. T. France and D. Wenham, *Gospel Perspectives* (Sheffield: JSOT Press, 1981), 83–145.

23. *Historical Tradition in the Fourth Gospel*, 120; so too, T. W. Manson, "Materials for the Life of Jesus in the Fourth Gospel," *Studies in the Gospels and Epistles* (Philadelphia: Westminister, 1962), 105–122.

24. See also C. K. Barrett, "John and the Synoptic Gospels," *ExpTim* 85 (1973/74): 228–33; John's assumption that his reader knows Mark has recently been defended by R. Bauckham, "John for Readers of Mark," in R. Bauckham, ed., *The Gospels for All Christians. Rethinking the Gospel Audiences* (Grand Rapids: Eerdmans, 1998), 147–72.

25. See the recent remarks of S. Smalley, "Keeping Up with Recent Studies. XII. St. John's Gospel," *ExpTim* 96 (1986/87): 103; cf. D. M. Smith, *Johannine Christianity* (Columbia: University Press, 1984), 95–172

26. *St. John and the Synoptic Gospels*, 96, as cited in R. H. Lightfoot, *John*, 29.

27. Published in *Studia Evangelica TU* (73: 1959): 338–50; also in J. A. T. Robinson, *Twelve New Testament Studies* (London: SCM, 1962), 94–106.

28. C. H. Dodd, *Redating the New Testament* (Philadelphia: Westminster, 1976), 264.

29. J. A. T. Robison, *The Priority of John* (London: SCM, 1985); typical of this trend, see the recent C. F. Coakley, "The Anointing at Bethany and the Priority of John," *JBL* 102 (1988): 241–56.

30. See, for example, G. Sloyan, *What Are They Saying about John?* (New York: Paulist, 1991).

31. S. Smalley, *John, Evangelist and Interpreter* (Exeter: Paternoster, 1978), 29; now reissued in the U.S. by Intervarsity Press: *John, Evangelist and Interpreter*, "Gospel Profiles 4" (Downer's Grove, Ill.: IVP, 1998).

32. R. Fortna, *The Gospel of Signs. A Reconstruction of the Narrative Source Underlying the Fourth Gospel* (Cambridge: University Press, 1970); idem, R. Fortna, *The Fourth Gospel and Its Predecessor. From Narrative Source to Present Gospel* (Philadelphia: Fortress, 1988).

33. R. E. Brown, *The Community of the Beloved Disciple* (New York: Paulist, 1979).

34. B. J. Malina, *The New Testament World. Insights from Cultural Anthropology* (Atlanta: John Knox, 1981). Also, Howard C. Kee, *Knowing the Truth. A Sociological Approach to New Testament Interpretation* (Minneapolis: Fortress, 1989).

35. David Rensberger, *Johannine Faith and Liberating Community* (Philadelphia: Westminster, 1988). Rensberger offers an introductory chapter (pp. 15–36) in which he charts the development of this approach so far.

36. Ibid., 114.

37. Ibid., 127.

38. D. A. Carson, *The Gospel According to John* (Grand Rapids: Eerdmans, 1991), 38.

39. Ibid., 38.

40. Alan Culpepper, *The Anatomy of the Fourth Gospel. A Study in Literary Design* (Philadelphia: Fortress, 1983).

41. See further H. Frei, *The Eclipse of the Biblical Narrative* (New Haven: Yale University Press, 1974), and M. Sternberg, *The Poetics of Biblical Narrative* (Indiana University Press, 1985).

42. See D. A. Carson's review of Culpepper, *Trinity Journal* 4 (1983): 122–26.

43. D. A. Carson, *The Gospel According to John* (Grand Rapids: Eerdmans, 1991), 65.

44. See F. Segovia, ed., "What Is John?" *Volume 1: Readers and Readings of the Fourth Gospel* (Atlanta: Scholar's Press, 1996); also, *idem, "What Is John?" Volume 2: Literary and Social Readings of the Fourth Gospel* (Atlanta: Scholar's Press, 1999).

45. S. Smalley, "Keeping Up with Recent Studies. XII St. John's Gospel," *Expository Times* 96 (1986): 102–08.

46. The earliest full preface to the Gospel belongs to the "Muratorian Canon" (about A.D. 180–200). This lengthy addition gives a fantastic (and fictional) rendition of the Gospel's origin from John the son of Zebedee.

47. This alignment is very well-known but far from certain. See Bernard, *John*, 1:xxxv; and Brown, *John*, 1:xcvii and 2:905f.

48. However, we know that Mary was related to Elizabeth, wife of Zechariah the priest (Luke 1:36, a *suggenes*, a female relative, not necessarily a cousin), giving the family a priestly connection (cf. Luke 1:5). If John's aunt is Mary (see above), then he, too, may have had a similar connection. At least the possibility of a priestly link to John is not implausible. See the confidence of Dodd in this regard, *The Historical Tradition in the Fourth Gospel*, 86–88.

49. The current defense of the Lazarus theory can be found in V. Eller, *The Beloved Disciple: His Name, His Story, and His Thought* (Grand Rapids: Eerdmans, 1987).

50. James Charlesworth, *The Beloved Disciple* (Valley Forge, Penn.: Trinity Press, 1995).

51. As does Barrett, *John*, 119–23.

52. Primary sources for this "external evidence" can be found in G. Burge, *Interpreting the Gospel of John* (Grand Rapids: Baker, 1992), 45–52.

53. Every major New Testament introduction will cover this in considerable detail.

54. S. Smalley, "Keeping Up with Recent Studies: St. John," *The Expository Times* 96 (1986): 102–08.

55. See R. Fortna, *The Gospel of Signs. A Reconstruction of the Narrative Source Underlying the Fourth Gospel* (Cambridge: University Press, 1970), 1–22. More recently, R. Fortna, *The Fourth Gospel and Its Predecessors. From Narrative Source to Present Gospel* (Philadelphia: Fortress, 1988).

56. E. Schweizer, *Ego Emi. Die religionsgeschichtliche Herkunft und theologische Bedeutung der johanneischen Bildreden, Zugleich ein Beitrag zur Quellenfragan des vierten Evangeliums* (Göttingen: Vandenhoeck, 1938, 1965); E. Ruckstuhl, *Die literarische Einheit des Johannesevangeliums: Der gegenwärtige Stand der einschlägigen Forschungen* (Friburg: St. Paul, 1951).

57. D. Moody Smith, *The Composition and Order of the Fourth Gospel: Bultmann's Literary Theory* (New Haven: Yale University Press, 1965); R. Fortna, *The Gospel of Signs* (1970) and *The Fourth Gospel and Its Predecessor* (1988).

58. For a study of the text of John, see V. Salmon, *The Fourth Gospel. A History of the Text* (Collegeville: The Liturgical Press, 1976)); commentaries on the Greek text of John (esp. that of C. K. Barrett, 1978) generally point out specific text problems.

59. From the Greek *aporia* (a difficult passing; cf. *aporē*, "to be at a loss") which described either an impassable maritime strait (*aporos*) or, in debate, a difficulty in logic. See E. Schwartz, "Aporien im vierten Evangelium," in *Nachrichten von der Königlichen Gesellschaft der Wissenschaften zu Göttingen* (1907): 342–72; (1908): 115–88, 497–50.

60. R. Fortna, *The Gospel of Signs*; H. Teeple, *The Literary Origin of the Gospel of John* (Evanston: Religion and Ethics Institute, 1974).

61. Warburton Lewis, *Disarrangements in the Fourth Gospel* (Cambridge: University Press, 1910).

62. P. Parker, "Two Editions of John," *JBL* 75 (1956): 303–14.

63. D. B. Woll, "The Departure of the Way: The First Farewell Discourse in the Gospel of John," *JBL* 99 (1980): 225–39; F. F. Segovia, "The Structure, *Tendenz*, and *Sitz im Leben* of John 13:31–14:31," *JBL* 104 (1985): 471–93.

64. R. Fortna, *The Fourth Gospel and Its Predecessor* (Philadelphia: Fortress, 1988).

65. A. Culpepper, *The Anatomy of the Fourth Gospel* (Philadelphia: Fortress, 1983).

66. S. Smalley, *John: Evangelist and Interpreter* (New York: Nelson, 1978).

67. P. Duke, *Irony in the Fourth Gospel* (Atlanta: John Knox, 1985).

68. A. A. Trites, *The New Testament Concept of Witness* (Cambridge: University Press, 1977); A. E. Harvey, *Jesus on Trial. A Study in the Fourth Gospel* (London: SPCK, 1976).

69. C. H. Dodd, *The Interpretation of the Fourth Gospel* (Cambridge: University Press, 1953), 383.

70. See Rudolf Bultmann's commentary, *The Gospel of John* (1966; ET: Philadelphia: Westminster, 1971); cf. D. M. Smith, *The Composition and Order of the Fourth Gospel. Bultmann's Literary Theory* (New Haven: Yale University Press, 1965).

71. Robert Fortna, *The Fourth Gospel and Its Predecessors. From Narrative Source to Present Gospel* (Philadelphia: Fortress, 1988).

72. For example, the source promotes the signs of Jesus as if they had merit for faith. Thus 2:11 says after the Cana miracle, "This, the first of his signs, Jesus did at Cana of Galilee, and he manifested his glory; *and his disciples believed in him*." Now compare the critique of "signs faith" in 4:48, 6:26, and elsewhere. Apparently on later reflection the Johannine editor concluded that faith that possessed no "sign" had greater merit. Thus the affirmation is given to Thomas in 20:29, "Blessed are those who have not seen and yet believe."

73. Important examples of this can be found in R. E. Brown's *Community of the Beloved Disciple* (NY: Paulist, 1979) and J. L. Martyn, *History and Theology in the Fourth Gospel*, 2d ed. (Nashville: Abingdon, 1979).

74. See the study of the dynamic and diverse New Testament community given by James D.G. Dunn, *Unity and Diversity in New Testament Theology* (Philadelphia: Westminster, 1977).

75. C. H. Dodd, *Historical Tradition in the Fourth Gospel* (1963), 21–151; F. F. Bruce, "The Trial of Jesus in the Fourth Gospel," *Gospel Perspectives I. Studies of History and Tradition in the Four Gospels,* ed. R. T. France and D. Wenham (Sheffield: JSOT Press, 1980), 1:7–20; D. Carson, "Historical Tradition in the Fourth Gospel. After Dodd, What?" *Gospel Perspectives II. Studies of History and Tradition in the Four Gospels,* ed. R. T. France and D. Wenham (Sheffield: JSOT Press, 1981), 2:83–145.

Chapter 17

Interpreting the Book of Acts

John B. Polhill
The Southern Baptist Theological Seminary

The Acts of the Apostles is unique among the writings of the New Testament. It alone deals with the history of the Jerusalem church from Pentecost to the persecution by Agrippa (chapters 1–12). Only Acts provides the outline of Paul's missionary activity, from his conversion to his Roman imprisonment (chapters 13–28). As will be evident in the discussion that follows, much of the scholarly attention on Acts has focused on the issue of its historical reliability. The issue is crucial: apart from Acts we have no other canonical source for the history of the church during this period.[1]

The Genre of Acts

What kind of writing is Acts? It is clearly the second volume of a two-volume work. The introductions to the Gospel of Luke (1:1–4) and Acts (1:1) link the two together. Both books are dedicated to a person named Theophilus. Acts 1:1 refers back to the "former book," which dealt with "all that Jesus began to do and to teach." If one examines the issue further, numerous links will be observed between the conclusion of Luke (24:44–53) and the beginning of Acts (1:1–12), including Jesus' teaching on his death and resurrection, the mission of the disciples, and Christ's ascension. We categorize Luke as a Gospel, which is a genre debate all its own. But what shall we call Acts?

The book originally had no title. The term *Acts* was applied to it later. It is first found in the Muratorian Canon, where it is called "The Acts of All the Apostles." That is an obvious misnomer. The book does not cover the acts of "all" the apostles, only of Peter and Paul. The term *Acts* stuck, however, and by the third century became the dominant usage. Most contemporary interpreters describe Acts in terms of Hellenistic historiography, using terms like "historical monograph,"[2] or "institutional history,"[3] or "political history."[4]

C. H. Talbert has suggested that Luke and Acts be described in terms of a single genre, that of a Hellenistic "succession narrative." This consists of a biography of a founder of a philosophical school, followed by a biography of his successors. Talbert points to the numerous parallels between Jesus in Luke and the apostles in Acts as evidence for this succession pattern.[5] The category of biography is questionable for both Gospel and Acts. It is also debatable whether the Gospel and Acts should be placed in the same genre. Without detracting from the obvious links between Luke's two works, it does not necessarily follow that they are works of the same literary genre.[6]

Richard Pervo has suggested that Acts be placed in the category of the Hellenistic romance, a fictional writing that used entertaining stories for purposes of edification.[7] Pervo's judgment on the historical basis of the Acts narrative is extreme, though he has made his point convincingly that Luke wrote with considerable attention to bringing "delight" to his readers.

The question of genre is obviously connected with one's view of Acts' historical reliability. The more highly one views the historical accuracy of Acts, the more likely one is to place the writing in the category of ancient historiography.

Author and Date

Traditionally, Acts has been attributed to Luke, the physician and traveling companion of Paul. This view is clearly set forth in the latter half of the second century in the Muratorian Canon and in Irenaeus. Irenaeus based his conclusions on the passages where the writer of Acts wrote in the first person (the "we" passages). Irenaeus enumerated these (16:10–17, 20:5–21:18, 27:1–28:16) and pointed out that they showed the writer to be present with Paul on these occasions. He identified the writer as the Luke whom Paul mentioned in Colossians 4:14 and 2 Timothy 4:11 (*Against Heresies* 3.14.1).

Little is known of Luke. Paul called him a physician in Colossians 4:14. Attempts to bolster the tradition of Lukan authorship on the basis of supposed medical language in Luke and Acts have failed.[8] Luke did not use technical medical language. He wrote in the language of the cultured laity; he wanted to be understood. The church fathers identified him as an educated Gentile who wrote in the best Greek of the four Gospel writers. He was often described as coming from Antioch, although this tradition cannot be traced before Eusebius in the early fourth century (*Hist. eccl.* 3.4.6). Most modern interpreters see Luke as a converted Gentile. A dissenting voice is Jervell, who sees Luke as being a Jewish Christian who, if not a Jew himself, was at least a converted God-fearer.[9]

A number of scholars reject the tradition of Lukan authorship. They usually base this on the argument that the Paul of Acts is too different from the

Paul of the epistles for Acts to have been written by a traveling companion of Paul. They maintain that the theology of Acts differs too widely from the theology of the Epistles and that the eloquent, miracle-working Paul of Acts is radically different from the Paul who spoke of his unimpressive speaking presence (2 Cor. 10:10).[10] Space does not permit a full rebuttal. Suffice it to say that these interpreters overdraw the theological differences between Paul and Acts. The Paul of the Areopagus speech sounds much like the Paul of Romans 1. The Paul of the Miletus address is much like the Paul of the Pastorals. True, Paul did not boast of his miracle-working. Converts like the Corinthians were too likely to overemphasize that sort of thing, anyway. Paul was more concerned that they learn Christian humility. But Luke wrote about Paul from a different perspective and for a different purpose. Naturally his portrait of Paul differs.

Acts is dated variously. In general, there are two early datings and two late datings. Those who follow traditional Lukan authorship date the book during Luke's lifetime. One group dates Acts between A.D. 62 and 64. This view is generally based on the abrupt ending of Acts, which does not relate the outcome of Paul's trial. The book is therefore dated before the trial and before the outbreak of the Neronic persecution (A.D. 64).[11] This early dating creates real difficulties if Luke used Mark as a source for his Gospel, which seems to have been the case. Tradition places Mark after the death of Peter, *after* the Neronic persecution had begun. Most of those who advocate Lukan authorship thus see the Gospel of Luke as written after A.D. 70 and Acts still later. The dominant view is A.D. 75–90. Among those who deny Lukan authorship, two dates are advocated. Those who see Acts as dependent on Josephus date it between A.D. 95 and 105. Those who see Acts as an irenic and those who emphasize its affinity to the later Christian apologists date it as late as A.D. 120–150.

The Text of Acts

Acts presents a special text-critical problem: there are two widely divergent texts. Actually, there are three major groups of witnesses. One is the Alexandrian, represented by the early uncial (capital letter) manuscripts Sinaiticus and Vaticanus. A second is the Byzantine text, represented by the majority of the minuscule (small letter) manuscripts. The majority of text critics favor the Alexandrian text, arguing that the Byzantine (or koine) text is a later, harmonizing text. A vocal minority argue that the Byzantine text, the basis for the textus receptus, is the original, more reliable text. There are significant individual variants in Acts between these two texts. For instance, Acts 8:37 is found in the Byzantine tradition but is not present in the Alexandrian witnesses. The differences, however, are limited and mostly insignificant. The same cannot be said for the Western tradition, which differs radically from the other two. It is nearly 10 percent longer than they.

The Western text of Acts is represented primarily by a bilingual manuscript, Codex Bezae, which has Greek and Latin texts of the New Testament in parallel columns. It is also found in a couple of early papyri (P38 and P48), several early versions, such as the Old Syriac and the Old Latin, as well as a number of individual readings in the church fathers. Bezae is not a complete manuscript, and for some readings (especially after chapter 22) the main witnesses are the versions, particularly the marginal notes of the Harclean Syriac.[12] Most of the differences between the Western text and the others are insignificant. The Western text tends to be more wordy. Sometimes it "clarifies" a passage, such as the note in 16:30 that the Philippian jailer secured the other prisoners before exiting with Paul and Silas. The Western text sometimes betrays a bias when compared to the non-Western texts. For instance, it seems to be more prejudiced against both Jews and women.[13]

Recently two French scholars have revived a theory first suggested by F. Blass. They see Luke as having himself produced both major textual traditions, with the Western text representing his original draft and the other two representing his later, edited text.[14] Most scholars tend still to opt for the non-Western witnesses. No English translation is based on the Western text. The KJV follows the Byzantine tradition of the textus receptus. Most newer versions follow a text based more on the Alexandrian witnesses. A number of text critics, however, argue that the Western text should not be dismissed out of hand. Following an "eclectic" method, scholars should consider each textual variant separately on its own merit.[15]

The Sources of Acts

CLASSICAL SOURCE CRITICISM

A major area of Acts research has been the quest for its sources. Unlike the Synoptic Gospels, Acts has no parallel writings, no points of comparison. Any source theory has to be based solely on internal criteria. This was the procedure followed during the heyday of source criticism of Acts (mid-nineteenth to early twentieth century). Adolf Harnack may serve as an example.[16] His source theory was perhaps the most influential of them all. Since he accepted traditional Lukan authorship, he assumed that Luke needed no sources for chapters 16–28, where he would have relied on his personal reminiscences as Paul's missionary companion. What would he have depended on for chapters 1–15? Harnack proposed an elaborate source theory based on the criteria of places, persons, and doublets. The recurrence of certain characters, such as Stephen and Philip, would indicate a source that recounted their ministries. The prominence of places, such as Jerusalem and Antioch, would indicate a source originating in those churches. Thus, Harnack spoke of a Stephen source (6:1–8:4), which he coupled with an Antioch source (11:19–30; 12:25; 13:1–15:35). He placed the Philip tradition (8:5–40), Peter's ministry to Dorcas and Cornelius (9:29–11:18), and Peter's escape from prison (12:1–23) in a "Jerusalem Caesarean" source. He saw the Pauline conversion narrative (9:1–28) as being based on a separate written source.

Harnack attributed chapters 1–5 to a "Jerusalem" source. This is where he appealed to the criterion of doublets. He argued that Luke had two sources for his Jerusalem traditions, as indicated by these doublets. One source was historically reliable, Jerusalem source A. The other he saw as unreliable, Jerusalem source B. Examples of his doublets are the two accounts of an outpouring of the Spirit in chapters 2 and in 4:23–31. Harnack claimed that the account of chapter 4, which contains no miraculous phenomena, came from the reliable source A. The account of chapter 2, with its tongues of fire and speaking in foreign languages, belonged, said Harnack, to the inferior source B. It is hard to see how anyone would ever see 4:23–31 as a doublet of Pentecost. In his delineation of the two sources, however, it is not at all hard to see Harnack's rationalistic bias.

The kind of source criticism performed by Harnack is no longer in vogue. It is a basically subjective, futile task. After a long investigation of the various source proposals, Jacques Dupont concluded that he could not find any that met with anything like a scholarly consensus.[17]

SEMITIC SOURCES

A second kind of source investigation maintains that Semitic sources can be detected behind the early chapters of Acts. This was first suggested by C. C. Torrey, who noted the extensive Semitisms in Acts 1–15.[18] He argued that an Aramaic original lay behind these sections. Today, these Semitic expressions are generally viewed as being due to the influence of the Septuagint on Luke's style, or perhaps as being reflective of a "synagogue" koine employed by Luke to give verisimilitude to the narrative.[19]

THE "WE SOURCE"

A third type of source criticism, still very much alive, is the question of the "we passages." There are four main approaches to this material. The first is that of Irenaeus: to see Luke as the author of Luke-Acts and the "we passages" as evidence of his presence on Paul's mission. A second approach speaks of a "we source" and sees the author of Luke-Acts as a different person from the one responsible for the "we" narrative. In this view the writer of these passages was a traveling companion of Paul. He may or may not have been Luke. The writer of Acts used his writing as a source for his narrative. A third view is a modification of the second. Instead of speaking of a "we source," one talks of a "diary" or "itinerary" that was kept by Paul's traveling companion and later used by the author of Acts.

With the rise of literary-critical study of Acts, a fourth approach has been advocated. It argues that the "we" is a literary device that is characteristic of ancient sea narratives.[20] This approach is rarely advocated today.

It has been shown that third-person narration is actually more common than first-person in ancient sea narratives. It also might be observed that Luke himself often used the third and not the first person when narrating Paul's voyages.[21]

ORAL SOURCES AND LOCAL TRADITIONS

A fourth kind of source criticism is perhaps the least demonstrable of all. It argues for individual local traditions and/or reports being behind Luke's narrative. This kind of source delineation can be either conservative or skeptical. In the latter category would be Haenchen, who throughout his commentary postulated that isolated, often legendary traditions, lie behind much of Luke's material.[22] In contrast is Hemer's view that much of Luke's material may have been gathered from the various Christian communities in the form of eyewitness reports (Luke 1:2). He suggested that since Luke eventually accompanied Paul on his voyage from Palestine to Rome he may have been present in Palestine during the two years of Paul's Caesarean imprisonment. During that time he could have visited the various congregations like Antioch and Jerusalem, gathering reports.[23]

Luke as Historian

Of all the New Testament writers, Luke shows the most interest in linking the Christian movement to world history. This is evident in the Gospel in those places where he dates Christian events by mentioning the various local and world leaders (Luke 1:5, 2:1–2, 3:1–2). In Acts, Luke mentioned the emperor Claudius, the Roman procurators and governors (Gallio, Felix, Festus), and the two Jewish kings Herod Agrippa I and II. It was his way of saying that Christianity was a movement of world-historical significance, a sentiment perhaps best summed up in the phrase "not done in a corner" (Acts 26:26).

Despite his personal concern with history, Luke has not always fared well with the critics as a historian. One of the first to radically question Luke's reliability was F. C. Baur. Writing in the last half of the nineteenth century, Baur applied the philosophy of Hegel to early Christianity. Hegel argued that history moves through a process whereby two opposing ideologies (a thesis and its antithesis) engage in a struggle that subsequently produces a resolution of the conflict (a synthesis) that embodies elements of both. Baur argued that early Christianity was marked by a severe conflict between Jewish Christianity, represented by Peter, and Gentile Christianity, represented by Paul. The conflict was resolved in the early second century by a synthesis of the two into what Baur called the "early catholic (universal) church." Acts does not reflect this conflict. In fact, Peter is presented as the advocate of Paul's Gentile mission in Acts 15. Baur thus claimed that Acts was a second-century writing, deriving from the early-Catholic synthesis. He called it an "irenic," a deliberate attempt on Luke's part to smooth over the clash between Pauline and Petrine Christianity. He judged Luke's reconstruction to be totally unhistorical, a deliberate distortion of the actual events.

Baur's theory was ultimately discredited. J. B. Lightfoot pointed out that Baur's historical sources for the Pauline-Petrine conflict were all much later than the first century. William Ramsay took on Baur's evaluation of Acts. Through many years of personal on-site investigation, Ramsay showed that down to the smallest detail the archaeological evidence proves Luke to have been meticulously accurate in his account.[24] Ramsay's heritage has been continued in recent years, particularly in the work of C. J. Hemer and in the major series entitled *The Book of Acts in Its First Century Setting*.[25]

Though few today would espouse Baur's full theory, his skepticism about the historical veracity of Acts is still shared by many scholars. For instance, Barrett's treatment of Acts 15 sees the account as a primarily Lukan contribution in much the same terms as Baur's irenic approach.[26] Acts comes under particular fire from many Pauline scholars. It is viewed by them as a tendentious, secondary, and inaccurate account of Paul's ministry. Particularly is attention drawn to the places where Acts seems to conflict with Paul's Epistles—on such matters as the number of times Paul visited Jerusalem or the nature of the Jerusalem Conference in Acts as compared with Galatians. What is *not* observed are the many places where Paul's Epistles are in agreement with Acts, instances that far outnumber the differences.

A number of scholars insist on basing any treatment of Paul on his Epistles rather than on Acts. Attempts to do so have proved to be thin indeed. The fact is that we would know little about Paul if we had only his letters. We depend on Acts for details about his background, his conversion, and his mission. It is one thing to acknowledge that the Epistles are the primary source for Paul. It is quite another to see the account in Acts as unreliable. Discrepancies between the Epistles and Acts should be carefully considered, but their frequency has been greatly exaggerated in much contemporary scholarship.[27]

A special category of historical investigation in Acts are recent studies that employ the methodology of social history. A pioneering work in this area is Ronald Hock's study of Paul's tent-making.[28] Other studies have focused on such diverse subjects as apartment dwellings in Greek cities, the social makeup of the Christian congregations, and the features of travel in the Graeco-Roman world.[29] A number of studies have combined literary study with sociological investigation, such as P. F Esler's study on the community of Luke-Acts,[30] and John Lentz's study of Paul's social status in Acts.[31] Various aspects of social theory have been applied to Acts research, such as the concepts of symbolic universes and of honor and shame in Mediterranean society.[32] The sociological investigation of Acts is just beginning and offers great promise, especially in the area of social history, which is at bottom a contemporary form of background studies.

Luke as Writer

Henry Joel Cadbury pointed out long ago that Luke was a self-conscious writer.[33] He was a "man of letters," who wrote for a public. This can be seen in his producing a well-designed, two-volume work, each with its own literary preface. Each preface contains the literary convention of a dedication, which in Luke-Acts is to a certain Theophilus. Cadbury suggested that Theophilus may have been Luke's patron, who underwrote the expenses of his writing projects. *Theophilus* means "lover of God," and it may well be that he was a recent convert, perhaps a former "God fearer" like Cornelius, whom Luke wished to inform more fully about the "certainties" of the faith (Luke 1:4).

In any event, Luke was a skilled writer. He wrote in a fluent Hellenistic Greek with a vocabulary that rivals that of the Greek historians. He knew how to adapt his language. In Acts, Jews speak in "synagogue" Greek, the Athenian philosophers emulate the Attic of the Golden Age, and the tribune Lysias writes in the formal style of an official Graeco-Roman letter. Luke's skill as a writer involved more than his good grammar. He was an excellent storyteller. For an example, take Acts 12, where Luke showed how the Christians' archenemy Herod in the end received his just deserts. Is it by accident that the Good Samaritan and the Prodigal Son are found only in Luke's Gospel? He recognized and included the best. Or which infancy narrative do we generally prefer to read at Christmas, Matthew's or Luke's?

In recent years Acts has been investigated extensively with literary methodologies.[34] Since Acts consists primarily of narrative, it lends itself well to narrative-critical investigation. Often this kind of study is done in conjunction with the Gospel of Luke. Many themes are carried through in both the Gospel and Acts, such as the role of the Jews and Jerusalem in salvation history, the salvation brought by Christ, and the inclusion of the Gentiles.[35] Narrative critics have been quick to note the many parallels between Jesus in the Gospel of Luke and the apostles in Acts and between Peter and Paul in Acts. They work the same sorts of miracles; they experience the same kinds of opposition and rejection. These parallels serve to unify the narrative of the two volumes and to highlight Luke's main themes.

One contribution of narrative criticism is the concept of the "implied author," that is, the author who can be distinguished from within the text itself. As we have seen, tradition gives us little reliable information about Luke other than his being Paul's traveling companion. The text itself, however, tells us a great deal more about Luke, about his interests, his knowledge, his culture, his faith. Text-based studies have helped us to learn more about the Luke who is implicit in his writings.[36]

Acts lends itself to narrative criticism in a number of other ways. It is filled with any number of interesting characters, many of whom are rather complex, having a considerable degree of "roundness." A number of recent studies have been devoted to characterization in Acts.[37] A special sort of study is that of Luke's "narrative asides," places where he intrudes into the text and provides a note of information that he feels the reader needs to know.[38] These asides are helpful in determining the "implied reader," the type of person Luke seems to have had in mind as his reader. Narrative analysis offers many other possibilities for understanding Acts. Repetition, for instance, tells a great deal about the author's emphases. It is not by accident that Peter's vision of God's accepting the Gentiles is repeated no fewer than three times in Acts 10 and 11. Another signal indicative of emphasis is narrative time. When the time line slows down, it indicates the importance of the events being narrated. For example, the Acts narrative often covers months, even years in a few verses. Chapter 19 covers a period of three years. The narrative between Acts 21:27 and 24:11, in comparison, involves only "twelve days," indicating that the events covered during this period are of unusual importance for understanding the message of Acts.

A specialized type of study is that of an author's literary devices. For example, Luke is famous for being a master of *litotes*, a figure of speech that emphasizes through understatement. Luke preferred to speak of "no small commotion" rather than "a great big commotion." He also occasionally used irony. John Darr has pointed out how Luke may well have used irony in Gamaliel's speech.[39]

Though studies which have attempted rhetorical analyses of the New Testament sometimes seem a bit forced, this is not true for Acts. Ancient rhetoric was primarily an oral skill, related to speech-making. Acts is full of speeches. The speeches in Acts lend themselves quite naturally to rhetorical analysis, especially the forensic speeches of Paul's trials.[40]

Since Acts is a masterpiece of ancient literature, it is not surprising that it has received so much attention from a literary perspective. It would perhaps now be helpful to look at some of the main kinds of building blocks which Luke employed in constructing his narrative.

Luke's Main Materials

THE EPISODES

Acts has rightly been characterized as having an "episodic" style. It is in no sense a continuous, sequential narrative written in the manner of a modern history. Luke was highly selective in what he included. Despite the Muratorian canon, he did not write about all the apostles, only two of them. He didn't give a history of the early Christian mission, only primarily of Paul's. Christianity was strong in Alexandria by the early second century. How did it get there? Luke doesn't tell us. It wasn't on his agenda. Neither does he tell us how Christianity reached Rome. It was already there when Paul reached the outskirts of the city (Acts 28:14–15). Luke doesn't even give a full picture of Paul's missionary activity. We know from Paul's

Epistles that he established a church at Colosse, but Luke does not relate its founding. We know from 2 Corinthians that Paul made at least one more trip to Corinth than the two that Acts mentions. In Romans 15:19, Paul spoke of preaching the gospel as far as Illyricum (on the Adriatic coast north of Macedonia). Acts is silent about Paul's work in that area.

Luke simply did not set out to write a full history of early Christianity, no matter how much we might have liked him to. What he did provide us with was an edifying story of how Christianity moved from its Jewish roots in Jerusalem to the heart of the Gentile world, Rome. He tells how this took place through a series of stories. These stories are not intended as mere history. They instruct and inspire the reader in the essentials of Christian outreach.

Take Acts 19, for example. It covers the three years during which Paul ministered in Ephesus. We are not told of the number of Ephesian converts or the number of house churches established or how the gospel was taken to the surrounding villages. We are only told in the broadest summary that the word of the Lord reached all the province of Asia (19:10). What is included in Acts 19 is a series of episodes that illustrate the kind of ministry Paul accomplished in Ephesus. First, there were the disciples of John the Baptist whom Paul introduced to Christ (vv. 1–7). The story reminded Luke's readers that there were others like these disciples of John, those who had an incomplete knowledge of the faith and were ready for a total witness. Next Luke related how Paul had to switch from synagogue to lecture hall, following a familiar pattern when he was unable to continue his witness to the Jews (vv. 8–12). These verses are the least "episodic," the most like a historical summary of anything in the chapter.

The next episode involves the sons of Sceva, seven would-be exorcists, who attempted to manipulate the name of Jesus to their own advantage (vv. 13–16). It relates a common theme of Acts, a reminder that the name and Spirit of Jesus are a powerful blessing for the faithful but are not subject to abuse by those who seek to use them for selfish ends. Verses 17–20 tell of the burning of expensive magical books that was prompted by Paul's preaching, a reminder that genuine Christian faith has nothing to do with magic and superstition. Verses 21–22 are a break in the episodes, a "directional signal" for the entire narrative of Acts. The passage tells of a vision Paul had in Ephesus informing him of his final destiny in Rome. The "centerpiece" of the entire chapter is the story of Paul's encounter with the Ephesian silversmiths (vv. 23–41). It reminds the reader of how proclaiming the truth sometimes encounters strong opposition, especially when it crosses powerful social and economic forces.

When one looks back at chapter 19, it is obvious that it gives us few "raw data" about Paul's Ephesian mission. On the other hand, the "episodes" tell us a great deal about the kind of ministry Paul conducted, the opposition he encountered, and the power of the Spirit that undergirded his work. Not only does it tell us about Paul's mission, but it also challenges us for our own.

Acts has many different kinds of stories. Some are similar to those in the Gospels, especially the miracles worked through Peter and Paul, which are much like those of Jesus. Acts has a unique form of miracle, the punitive miracle, where a person is punished for resistance to the work of God. An example is the temporary blindness that struck the magician Elymas for his opposition to Paul's witness (13:9–12). Another characteristic form in Acts is the "escape" narrative, when the apostles are miraculously delivered from prison. Usually they do not run away but continue in the vicinity to bear their testimony. Acts is filled with visions in which God leads the Christian witnesses to a new field of ministry. A unique sort of visionary experience is when two visions occur to different people at the same time and serve to confirm one another, such as those of Ananias and Paul in chapter 9 and Cornelius and Peter in chapter 10. A number of other types of narratives occur in Acts. These will serve to illustrate something of their diversity.

THE SPEECHES

One of the most characteristic types of material in Acts is the speech.[41] Depending on how one counts, there are 24 or 28. Together they comprise approximately 30 percent of the total text of Acts. In contrast, the Gospel of Luke has only one discourse that could be compared to the Acts speeches, the address of Jesus in the Nazareth synagogue (Luke 4:16–30). Acts has ten major speeches. Three are Peter's (2:14–40, 3:12–26, 10:34–43). Three are Paul's missionary speeches (13:16–41; 17:22–31; 20:18–35). Three are Paul's defense speeches (22:1–21; 24:10–21; 26:1–29). The tenth is the address of Stephen before the Sanhedrin, the longest of them all (7:2–53). Paul's three missionary speeches are of particular note. One occurs on each of his three missionary journeys, and each is to a different type of audience. The Pisidian Antioch sermon (13:16–41) is on the first journey and is to Jews. The Areopagus speech (17:22–31) on the second journey is to Gentiles. The Miletus address (20:18–35) on the third journey is to Christians.

The extent to which Luke is responsible for the speeches is a matter of considerable debate among scholars. Some would see them as based on written notes by eyewitnesses. Others see Luke as having composed the speeches himself. A third group sees the final form of the Acts' speeches as being due to Luke's own writing but based on reliable reports. They see Luke as having preserved the essence of what was said. Something like that process seems best to account for the facts. The speeches of Acts are in a uniform style, both when compared with one another and with the entire narrative of Acts. They are obviously condensations of what were probably originally rather long speeches. None of the speeches of Peter and Paul takes more than several minutes to read out loud. There are affinities between the speeches of like kind. Peter and Paul's speeches to Jews in chapters 2 and 13 use some of the same Old Testament texts. Paul's speeches to pagans at Lystra and Athens use similar arguments. Paul's defense speeches resemble one another. On the other hand, there is considerable diversity within the speeches, particularly when different types of audiences are involved. The speeches fit their historical contexts, which is strong evidence for their reliability.

For purposes of interpretation, one should note how Luke used the speeches to advance the narrative. The speeches are a vivid means of interpreting the significance of the events. In many ways, the theological meat of Acts is found in the speeches. The episodes are more entertaining, and it is easy to major on them and neglect the speeches. To do so is to miss much of the message of Acts.

THE SUMMARIES

One of the characteristic forms in Acts is the summary statement. Summaries are not unique to Acts. They are found in the Gospels, where they furnish broad summaries of the ministry of Jesus, often focusing on his teaching or his working of miracles (e.g. Mark. 4:33, 6:56). Two types of summaries occur in Acts. The major summaries are found in the first five chapters and are three in number.[42] Acts 2:42–47 describes the life of the church after Pentecost. Acts 4:32–35 summarizes the sharing of the Christian community. Acts 5:12–16 depicts the apostles' reputation for miracles. There are also seven minor (short) summaries: 1:14; 6:7; 9:31; 12:24; 16:5; 19:20; 28:30–31. The minor summaries all deal with the growth of the church, describing how peace came to it and how it was able to continue its witness and flourish. The single exception is 1:14, which summarizes the prayer life of the early community as they awaited the coming of the Spirit. In this respect, 1:14 probably belongs with the major summaries. Together they depict the ideal life of the earliest Christians—their prayer life, their fellowship, their teaching and witnessing, their worship, their sharing, their experience of the Spirit's power. The summaries present a pattern that the church of every age would do well to turn back to again and again as it seeks renewal.

THE ITINERARIES

One of the most common and yet perplexing of the kinds of material in Acts is the type of long itinerary that one finds in passages like 20:13–15 and 21:1–3. Why these long lists of places that Paul's group sailed past, especially ones where they didn't even stop? It was their detail that led Dibelius to believe that Luke must have kept a diary. But, even if he did, why did he include this material in his narrative in a day when writing materials were quite expensive? Why take up the space? Luke may have been seeking to be complete in his account or to lend the appearance of verisimilitude. On the other hand, he may have intended these to serve a missionary purpose.[43] The detailed travel notes give the impression that the gospel is on the move. Though no stops are made, one feels as if all these ports are within the scope of the Christian message. Most of the places were well-known in Luke's day. Some were the homes of celebrated persons and were famous for that. It may be that this was Luke's way of saying that on another occasion, perhaps even through another missionary, these too were places ripe for Christian witness.

The Themes of Acts

A major question in contemporary research involves Luke's purpose in writing his two-volume work.[44] Luke stated his purpose clearly in the preface to his Gospel: "to write an orderly account . . . so that you may know the certainty of the things you have been taught" (Luke 1:3–4). Whoever Theophilus was, he seems to have already been well acquainted with the Christian faith. He was most likely already a believer. Luke wrote to give him a deepened understanding of and certainty in his faith. Beyond Luke's express statement, it is probably impossible to probe into his mind and further determine his "purposes." To speak of the themes of Luke-Acts is another matter; they are a property of the objective text and not of the author's subjective mind.

In the nineteenth century a great deal of attention was devoted to the question of Luke's purposes. The investigation is known as "tendency criticism." The tendency critics assumed that Luke wrote his history with a decided slant or "tendency." Baur was the first of them. He saw Luke writing with an *irenic* slant on early Christian history. Others followed him, suggesting other tendencies: that Luke sought to explain the rise of the Gentile mission, that he wrote to present an apology to the Roman world, and the like.

In the middle of the twentieth century, redaction criticism came into vogue. In many ways the redaction critics were the heirs of the tendency critics, as they sought out the major emphases of the author. Classic redaction criticism is based on a comparison of parallel accounts and is best suited to Synoptic studies. A pioneering redaction critic was Hans Conzelmann, who applied the method to both Luke and Acts.[45] In actual fact he derived his understanding of Luke's theological themes primarily from a synoptic study of the Gospel and then proceeded to trace the same themes in Acts. Conzelmann saw Luke's main theology as that of salvation history. He argued that Luke wrote to legitimize the Christian movement in light of the "delayed parousia." He personally viewed Luke's perspective negatively, as a loss of the original eschatological passion of early Christianity. He presented Luke as a theologian and not a reliable historian. Conzelmann provoked an intense debate over whether Luke should be viewed as a theologian or as a historian. Most evangelical scholars view this as a false dichotomy. Luke wrote as a conscious historian, but he selected his material in such a way as to highlight certain themes or theological emphases.[46]

In many ways redaction criticism and recent narrative studies are related. Both are literary-critical methodologies; both are concerned with the themes of the works they investigate.[47] Below are listed some of the main themes which have been uncovered by the two methods.[48]

WORLD MISSION

The missionary purpose of Acts is obvious. In many ways Acts 1:8 sets the theme of the entire book. The disciples are called to be witnesses to Christ. They are sent forth on a mission and promised the Spirit to empower their mission. The verse provides a rough geographical outline of the whole of Acts. The mission begins with the Jews in Jerusalem (chapters 1–5). With Stephen and his fellow Hellenists it begins to spread beyond the environs of Jerusalem and the confines of the Jewish people into all Judea and Samaria (chapters 6–12). With Paul it spreads in an ever-widening circle toward the ends of the inhabited earth (chapters 13–28).[49]

Luke's two-volume work is concerned above all with the salvation that is in Jesus Christ. The angel's words to the shepherds set the theme: Christ is to be the Savior "for all the people" (Luke 2:10). The progress of the narrative in Luke-Acts makes it clear that "all the people" includes both Jews and Gentiles. Acts is preoccupied with evangelism, mission, conversion. There are at least ten conversion narratives in Acts and a great number of additional passages which make reference to conversions.[50] Acts is about sharing the good news of salvation in Christ. In a real sense, every theme in Acts could be subsumed under its primary missionary purpose.[51]

PROVIDENCE OF GOD

Recent narrative-critical studies have shown that God is probably to be viewed as the main character in Acts.[52] The presence of God is seen in many different ways: in the visions that direct the paths of the Christians, through the intervention of angels, through the activity of the Spirit. The direction of God, Christ, and the Spirit are often virtually indistinguishable in Acts. For example, when Paul is led to Troas and the Macedonian vision, the divine leading is attributed to all three persons of the Trinity: the Holy Spirit (16:6), the Spirit of Jesus (16:7), and God (16:10). Perhaps the strongest indication of God's providence in Acts is the many places where "divine necessity" is expressed in terms of Scripture having to be fulfilled. God willed it. He has revealed it in Scripture. Therefore, it must be fulfilled (e.g. Acts 1:16). A similar emphasis on God's sovereignty is expressed by the frequent emphasis in Acts on God's having chosen people for salvation and God's adding people to the Christian community (e.g. 2:47).

THE POWER OF THE SPIRIT

The Spirit is so prominent in Acts that many would rename the book "The Acts of the Holy Spirit." The Spirit is explicitly mentioned in 17 of the 28 chapters, and even when not, the Spirit's presence is evident through references to the Spirit's activity, such as the inspiration and bold witness of the Christians. Pentecost empowers and enables the Christian mission, and the Spirit is present in every major breakthrough which the Christians experience. When a new group is reached for the Lord, Acts shows the Spirit descending upon them in order to "legitimize" the work. This is true of the Samaritans (8:17–25), the Gentiles (10:44–48), the disciples of John the Baptist (19:6–7).[53]

RESTORED ISRAEL

Luke-Acts is obviously concerned with the place of the Jews in the Christian movement. In his infancy narrative (Luke 1–2) Luke shows how Jesus was the Jewish Messiah, born of pious Jewish parents who observed the law down to its smallest detail. Jesus' sermon at Nazareth, however, strikes an ominous note. Jesus pointed out how in the past God had sent his prophets to deliver people outside Israel (Luke 4:24–27). The rest of Luke-Acts unfolds the story of how the same occurred with Jesus' ministry. Jerusalem rejected Him, just as it had rejected the prophets.[54] In Acts, the Jewish leaders of Jerusalem and the synagogues of the Dispersion reject the Christian mission as well. Finally, at the end of the story, in the last chapter of Acts, one finds Paul witnessing mainly to Gentiles in the heart of Gentile territory, the capital city of Rome.

The motif of Jewish rejection is especially prominent in the recurring pattern of Paul's being rejected by the synagogues and turning to the Gentiles. It first occurs in Pisidian Antioch (Acts 13:46). In the very next town he visits, however, Paul again begins in the synagogue (14:1) until forced to leave. This pattern of synagogue expulsion, turning to the Gentiles, and returning to the synagogue happens over and over again. The final occurrence is in the last chapter, where Paul once again turns from the Jews to the Gentiles (28:28). Was this last time definitive?[55] Did Luke intend for us to see Paul turning his back altogether on a witness to the Jews? Some scholars think so.[56] Others believe that Luke wrote altogether from a Jewish perspective, that even the Gentile mission should be seen as a Jewish Christian endeavor to include them in the only people of God, the Jewish people.[57] However one views the Jewish question, one thing is clear: a major concern of Luke was to show the inclusion of *all* persons in the people of God.

INCLUSIVE GOSPEL

The Gentile mission is obviously a major theme of Acts.[58] It is actually an aspect of an even larger emphasis, that of the inclusive Christian gospel that knows no racial, economic, political, or physical barriers. Frank Stagg pointed out quite convincingly how Acts depicts a gospel unhindered by the barriers of human discrimination.[59] In Acts the gospel reaches out to everyone, whether it be a black eunuch or a Gentile centurion, a God-fearing businesswoman or a Roman governor. The greatest division of all was between Jew and Gentile. Even for the Christians, the Torah-free Gentiles and the Torah-strict Jewish Christians were radically different. Luke was at pains to show how they overcame their differences and found their unity in Christ. This is the theme of chapter 15. Not by accident, it occurs at the very center of the book.

RELATIONSHIP TO THE WORLD

One of the main themes emphasized by the tendency critics was the apologetic motif. Some saw Acts as being written *primarily* to offer an apologetic for Christianity to the Graeco-Roman world. The apology was seen to have two aspects. First, it presented Christians as law-abiding citizens whom the Roman authorities recognized as such. Second, Christians were to be seen as a form of Judaism, a sect or "Way" within Judaism. Judaism was recognized as a legal religion (*religio licita*) by the Roman authorities and enjoyed various rights and exemptions granted by the emperors. According to this theory, Luke wanted to associate Christians with the Jews so that they would enjoy these Jewish rights and protections.

It is doubtful that Luke wrote to offer an apologetic to the Roman world. Theophilus seems to have been a Christian. Luke wrote not to outsiders but to insiders, to those who already professed the Christian faith. Christians are indeed presented as law-abiding citizens, and Roman officials as those worthy of the gospel. There is certainly a strong apologetic element in Acts, but it is for *Christians*. Luke presents Peter and Paul as models of how to handle oneself before one's critics. They embody sound principles by which one can offer an effective defense of the gospel.[60]

TRIUMPHANT GOSPEL

Without doubt, Acts depicts the gospel as triumphant. It overcame obstacles from within and without. From outside came imprisonments, expulsions, natural disasters, angry mobs. From inside came the distrust sown by those like Ananias and Sapphira and the sincere theological differences between groups within the church. Despite its differences, the church succeeded in finding its unity. Despite its opponents, it grew, even flourished, until there was a witness established all along the way from Jerusalem to Rome.

Because of this triumphant note, Acts has sometimes been accused of promoting a false theology of glory as opposed to a theology of the cross. In actuality, both emphases are present in Acts. The theme of the faithful witnesses must be placed alongside that of the triumphant gospel. The gospel triumphed because witnesses were willing to suffer for it. For instance, the apostles were brutally scourged for their testimony, but they praised God for the privilege of suffering in Jesus' name (5:41). Peter was imprisoned for Christ on more than one occasion. Stephen became the ultimate witness: he gave his life for his testimony to Christ. Paul was stoned, shipwrecked, and jailed for five or more years. At the end of Acts, one finds him still in jail but able to preach the gospel quite openly (28:30–31). Perhaps that is why the book ends so abruptly, without telling what happened to Paul. Luke wanted to focus on the gospel, not on Paul. The hero of Acts is the gospel, not the apostles. The gospel triumphed precisely because faithful witnesses were willing to suffer for it. In Rome the triumphant gospel was proclaimed quite openly and unchained because the faithful witness, Paul, was willing to render his testimony even in chains.

Bibliography

Barrett, C. K. *A Critical and Exegetical Commentary on the Acts of the Apostles.* International Critical Commentary. 2 vols. Edinburgh: Clark, 1994, 1998.

Bauckham, Richard, ed. *The Book of Acts in Its Palestinian Setting.* Vol. 4 of *The Book of Acts in Its First Century Setting.* Grand Rapids: Eerdmans, 1995.

Bruce, F. F. *The Acts of the Apostles, Greek Text with Introduction and Commentary.* Third revised and enlarged edition. Grand Rapids: Eerdmans, 1990.

Fernando, Ajith. *Acts.* NIV Application Commentary. Grand Rapids: Zondervan, 1998.

Fitzmyer, Joseph A. *The Acts of the Apostles.* Anchor Bible. New York: Doubleday, 1998.

Gill, David and Conrad Gempf, eds. *The Book of Acts in Its Graeco-Roman Setting.* Vol. 2 of *The Book of Acts in Its First Century Setting.* Grand Rapids: Eerdmans, 1994.

Longenecker, Richard N. *The Acts of the Apostles.* The Expositor's Bible, vol. 9: *John-Acts,* 207–573. Grand Rapids: Zondervan, 1981.

Marshall, I. Howard. *Acts, An Introduction and Commentary.* Tyndale New Testament Commentaries. Liecester, England: InterVarsity, 1980.

Polhill, John. *Acts.* New American Commentary. Nashville: Broadman, 1992.

Stagg, Frank. *The Book of Acts, the Early Struggle for an Unhindered Gospel.* Nashville: Broadman, 1955.

Talbert, Charles H. *Reading Acts, A Literary and Theological Commentary on the Acts of the Apostles.* New York: Crossroad, 1997.

Tannehill, Robert C. *The Narrative Unity of Luke-Acts: A Literary Interpretation.* Vol. 2: *The Acts of the Apostles.* Minneapolis: Fortress, 1990.

Thompson, Richard P. and Thomas E. Phillips. *Literary Studies in Luke-Acts, Essays in Honor of Joseph B. Tyson.* Macon, Ga.: Mercer University Press, 1998.

Winter, Bruce and Andrew Clarke. *The Book of Acts in Its Ancient Literary Setting.* Vol. 1 of *The Book of Acts in Its First Century Setting.* Grand Rapids: Eerdmans, 1993.

Witherington, Ben III. *The Acts of the Apostles, A Socio-Rhetorical Commentary.* Grand Rapids: Eerdmans, 1998.

Notes

1. Some scraps of information can be gleaned from Paul's Epistles, but they are scant. The later "apocryphal" Acts cover this period, but they are secondary to the canonical Acts at best and pure legend at their worst.

2. D. W. Palmer, "Acts and the Ancient Historical Monograph," *The Book of Acts in Its Ancient Literary Setting*, vol. 1 of *The Book of Acts in Its First Century Setting*, ed. Winter and Clarke (Grand Rapids: Eerdmans, 1993), 1–29. B. Witherington advises that Acts has more in common with Greek than Roman historiography (*The Acts of the Apostles, A Socio-Rhetorical Commentary* [Grand Rapids: Eerdmans, 1998], 2–39).

3. H. Canick, "The History of Culture, Religion and Institutions in Ancient Historiography: Philological Observations Concerning Luke's History," *JBL* 116 (1997): 673–95.

4. E. Plümacher, "Die Missionsreden der Apostelgeschichte und Dionys von Halikarnass," *NTS* 39 (1993): 161–77.

5. C. H. Talbert, *Reading Acts, a Literary and Theological Commentary on the Acts of the Apostles* (New York: Crossroad, 1997), 3–17.

6. M. C. Parsons and R. I. Pervo, *Rethinking the Unity of Luke and Acts* (Minneapolis: Fortress, 1993).

7. R. I. Pervo, *Profit with Delight: The Literary Genre of the Acts of the Apostles* (Philadelphia: Fortress, 1987). L. Alexander points out that in Hellenistic historiography, the line between fact and fiction is often indistinguishable: "Fact, Fiction and the Genre of Acts," *NTS* 44 (1998): 380–99.

8. For a full discussion of the "medical theory," see J. B. Polhill, *Acts*, NAC (Nashville: Broadman, 1992), 24–27.

9. J. Jervell, *Die Apostelgeschichte*, 17e. Auflage, Kritisch-exegetischer Kommentar über das Neue Testament (Göttingen: Vandenhoeck & Ruprecht, 1998), 79–86.

10. A classic presentation of this view is that of P. Vielhauer, "On the 'Paulinism' of Acts," *Studies in Luke-Acts*, ed. L. Keck and J. L. Martyn (Nashville: Abingdon, 1966), 33–50.

11. The pre-64 dating is advocated by W. J. Larkin Jr., *Acts*, IVP New Testament Commentary (Downers Grove, Ill.: InterVarsity, 1995), 18–19.

12. The fullest treatment of the Western text is by J. H. Ropes in vol. 3 of *The Beginnings of Christianity*, all of which is devoted to the text of Acts (Foakes-Jackson and Lake, eds., *The Beginnings of Christianity*, Part I: *The Acts of the Apostles* [5 vols.; London: Macmillan, 1920–33]). A thorough listing of the individual witnesses to Acts is provided by C. K. Barrett, *A Critical and Exegetical Commentary on the Acts of the Apostles*, Vol. I: *Preliminary Introduction and Commentary on Acts I–XIV*, ICC (Edinburgh: T. & T. Clark, 1994), 2–29. See also, Vol II: *Introduction and Commentary on Acts XV–XXVIII* (Edinburgh: T. T. Clark, 1998), xxi–xxii.

13. E. J. Epp, *The Theological Tendency of Codex Bezae Cantabrigiensis in Acts*, SNTSMS 3 (Cambridge: University Press, 1966); B. Witherington, "The Anti-Feminist Tendencies of the 'Western' Text in Acts," *JBL* 103 (1984): 82–84.

14. M.–E. Boismard and A. Lamouille, *Le Texte occidental des Actes des Apôtres: Reconstruction et rehabilitation* (2 vols.; Paris: Editions Recherche sur les Civilisations, 1984). On different grounds (his theory that the longer text is the original) A. C. Clark also argued that the Western text was the earlier. He saw the shorter text as non-Lukan and due to later editorial changes: *The Primitive Text of the Gospel and Acts* (Oxford: Clarendon, 1914).

15. G. D. Kilpatrick, "Western Text and Original Text in the Gospels and Acts," *JTS* 44 (1943): 24–36; A. F. J. Klijn, "In Search of the Original Text of Acts," *Studies in Luke-Acts*, 103–10.

16. A. Harnack, *The Acts of the Apostles*, trans. J. R. Wilkinson (London: Williams and Norgate, 1909), 162–202.

17. J. Dupont, *The Sources of Acts: The Present Position*, trans. K. Pond (London: Darton, Longman and Todd, 1964), 166.

18. C. C. Torrey, *The Composition and Date of Acts* (Cambridge: Harvard University Press, 1916). Recent attempts by Wilson and others to revive the Aramaic source theory are flatly rejected by J. Fitzmyer, *The Acts of the Apostles,* The Anchor Bible (New York: Doubleday, 1998), 81–82.

19. J. M. Watt calls this "code-switching," a bilingual speaker adapting his language to different social situations: *Code-Switching in Luke and Acts*, Berkeley Insights in Linguistics and Semiotics 31 (New York: Peter Lang, 1997).

20. V. K. Robbins, "The We-Passages in Acts and Ancient Sea Voyages," *BR* 20 (1975): 5–18.

21. S. M. Praeder, "Acts 27:1–28:16: Sea Voyages in Ancient Literature and the Theology of Luke-Acts," *CBQ* 46 (1984): 683–706.

22. E. Haenchen, *The Acts of the Apostles: A Commentary*, trans. B. Noble and G. Shinn (Philadelphia: Westminster, 1971). For a similar list of local traditions, but with a more conservative estimate of their trustworthiness, see Fitzmyer, *The Acts of the Apostles*, 85–88.

23. C. J. Hemer, *The Book of Acts in the Setting of Hellenistic History*, ed. C. H. Gempf (Tübingen: Mohr/Siebeck, 1989), 335–64.

24. For a fuller discussion and references, see Polhill, *Acts*, 50–52.

25. A six-volume set, published by Eerdmans between 1993 and 1996. Four of the volumes involve "background" studies on such topics as the social and political history of Diaspora and Palestinian Judaism, the Graeco-Roman setting of Acts, and the Roman legal system. All serve not only to cast further light on the Acts narrative but to bear out the accuracy of Luke's account.

26. Barrett, *Critical and Exegetical Commentary on Acts*, II:xxxiii–xli.

27. Luke was an *ancient* historian, and his conventions are those of his own day, not ours. For a balanced treatment, see J. D. G. Dunn, *The Acts of the Apostles, Epworth Commentaries* (London: Epworth, 1996), xv–xix.

28. R. F. Hock, *The Social Context of Paul's Ministry: Tentmaking and Apostleship* (Philadelphia: Fortress, 1980).

29. Many of the articles in vol. 2 of *The Book of Acts in Its First Century Setting* fall into this category: *The Book of Acts in Its Graeco-Roman Setting* (Grand Rapids: Eerdmans, 1994).

30. P. F. Esler, *Community and Gospel in Luke-Acts*, SNTSMS 57 (Cambridge University Press, 1987).

31. J. C. Lentz Jr., *Luke's Portrait of Paul*, SNTSMS 77 (Cambridge: University Press, 1993).

32. For the former, see S. J. Joubert, "The Jerusalem Community as a Role-model for a Cosmopolitan Christian Group. A Socio-Literary Analysis of Luke's Symbolic Universe," *Neot* 29 (1995): 49–59. For the latter, see R. A. Bondi, "Become Such as I Am: St. Paul in the Acts of the Apostles," *BTB* 27 (1997): 164–76.

33. H. J. Cadbury, *The Making of Luke-Acts* (New York: Macmillan, 1927).

34. For a summary of research, see F. S. Spencer, "Acts and Modern Literary Approaches," *The Book of Acts in Its Ancient Literary Setting*, vol. 1 of *The Book of Acts in Its First Century Setting* (Grand Rapids: Eerdmans, 1993), 381–414.

35. See especially R. C. Tannehill, *The Narrative Unity of Luke-Acts: A Literary Interpretation* (2 vols.; Philadelphia: Fortress, 1986, 1990).

36. For a study of the implied author of Luke-Acts, see J. B. Tyson, *Images of Judaism in Luke-Acts* (Columbia, S.C.: University of South Carolina, 1992).

37. For example, see the influential study of the Pharisees in Luke-Acts by D. B. Gowler, *Host, Guest, Enemy and Friend: Portraits of the Pharisees in Luke and Acts*, Emory Studies in Early Christianity 2 (New York: Peter Lang, 1991).

38. S. M. Sheeley, *Narrative Asides in Luke-Acts*, JSNTSS 72 (Sheffield: University Press, 1992).

39. J. A. Darr, "Irenic or Ironic? Another Look at Gamaliel Before the Sanhedrin (Acts 5:33–42)," in *Literary Studies in Luke-Acts, Essays in Honor of Joseph B. Tyson* (Macon, Ga.: Mercer University Press, 1998), 121–39.

40. See B. W. Winter, "Official Proceedings and the Forensic Speeches in Acts 24–26." *The Book of Acts in Its Ancient Literary Setting*, 305–36.

41. The most comprehensive treatment of the speeches is that of M. L. Soards, *The Speeches in Acts, Their Content, Context, and Concerns (Louisville: Westminster/Knox, 1994).*

42. For a recent treatment which sees the summaries as primarily apologetic in purpose, see G. E. Sterling, "'Athletes of Virtue': An Analysis of the Summaries in Acts (2:41–47; 4:32–35; 5:12–16)," *JBL* 113 (1994): 679–96.

43. See D. Marguerat, "Voyages et voyageurs dans le livre des Actes et la culture gréco-romaine," *RHPR* 78 (1998): 33–59.

44. See R. Maddox, *The Purpose of Luke-Acts* (Edinburgh: T. T. Clark, 1982).

45. H. Conzelmann, *The Theology of St. Luke*, trans. G. Buswell (New York: Harper and Row, 1960).

46. For a balanced perspective, see I. H. Marshall, *Luke: Historian and Theologian* (Grand Rapids: Zondervan, 1971).

47. B. R. Gaventa argues persuasively for narrative-critical methods being superior to redaction criticism for determining the main theological themes of Acts: "Toward a Theology of Acts: Reading and Rereading," *Int* 42 (1988): 148–149.

48. For a full treatment of these themes, see Polhill, *Acts*, 57–72.

49. Whether "ends of the earth" refers to Rome, Spain, Ethiopia, or the limits of human habitation is often debated. See T. S. Moore, "'To the Ends of the Earth': The Geographical and Ethnic Universalism of Acts 1:8 in Light of Isaianic Influence on Luke," *JETS* 40 (1997): 389–99.

50. C. H. Talbert, "Conversion in the Acts of the Apostles: Ancient Auditors' Perceptions," *Literary Studies in Luke-Acts*, 141–53. See also D. L. Matson, *Household Conversion Narratives in Acts*, JSNTSS 123 (Sheffield Academic Press, 1996).

51. For a recent treatment of missionary strategy in Acts, see H. Dollar, *St. Luke's Missiology, A Cross-Cultural Challenge* (Pasadena, Calif.: William Carey Library, 1996).

52. R. L. Brawley, *Centering on God: Method and Message in Luke-Acts*, Literary Currents in Biblical Interpretation (Louisville: Westminster/Knox, 1990).

53. For a characterization of the Spirit in Acts, see W. H. Shepherd Jr., *The Narrative Function of the Holy Spirit as a Character in Luke-Acts*, SBLDS 147 (Atlanta: Scholars, 1994).

54. See M. C. Parsons, "The Place of Jerusalem on the Lukan Landscape: An Exercise in Symbolic Cartography," *Literary Studies in Luke-Acts*, 155–71.

55. That the motif of the Jews' "blindness" (28:26–27) leaves the door open for repentance is argued by V. Fusco, "Luke-Acts and the Future of Israel," *NovT* 38 (1996):1–17.

56. See the debate in *Literary Studies in Luke-Acts*. The chapters by Tannehill and Sanders argue that the rejection of the Jews is final. Those by Brawley and Thompson see the door still being open for a Jewish witness.

57. J. Jervell, *The Theology of the Acts of the Apostles*, New Testament Theology (Cambridge: University Press, 1996).

58. It is a theme already strongly present in the Gospel of Luke. See T. J. Lane, *Luke and the Gentile Mission, Gospel Anticipates Acts,* European University Studies, series 23, vol. 571 (Frankfurt: Peter Lang, 1996).

59. F. Stagg, *The Book of Acts: The Early Struggle for an Unhindered Gospel* (Nashville: Broadman, 1955).

60. J. T. Squires argues that Luke wrote with an apologetic purpose of equipping Christians to defend their faith in the Hellenistic world: *The Plan of God in Luke-Acts*, SNTSMS 76 (Cambridge: University Press, 1993). For an application of Luke's apologetic to the contemporary scene, see A. E. McGrath, "Apologetics to the Romans," *BSac* 155 (1988): 387–93.

Chapter 18

Interpreting the Pauline Epistles

Thomas R. Schreiner
The Southern Baptist Theological Seminary

Introduction

The Pauline letters have played a decisive role in the formation of Christian theology over the centuries. Paul's influence was primary in the theologies of Augustine, Aquinas, Luther, Calvin, and Barth. The theological impact of Paul may blind us to the most striking feature of his writings. He never wrote a systematic theology in which all the elements of his thought are related together and presented in a coherent and logical fashion. Instead he wrote letters to churches (or individuals), and these letters were addressed to the particular circumstances faced by the churches. The Pauline letters are not theological treatises in which a full-fledged theological system is elaborated. They are addressed to specific situations and problems in various churches. If Paul's goal were simply to compose a systematic theology, responses to individual churches would be superfluous. Paul could have simply sent the same *magnum opus* to all the churches once it was completed. No need would exist to write one letter to the Galatians and a different letter to the Colossians. The Pauline letters, as J. C. Beker reminds us, are *contingent*, written to particular locales and addressing specific circumstances.[1]

Emphasizing the occasional nature of the Pauline letters does not cancel out their theological contribution. Borrowing from Beker again, the letters may be directed to particular situations, but they also flow from a *coherent* Pauline gospel.[2] The contingency of the letters does not cancel out a theological worldview. We must mine Paul's theology from the letters addressed to the various churches. When interpreting the Pauline letters, we must grasp both the contingency and the coherence of the Pauline gospel. If the contingency of the letters is ignored, Paul's letters become timeless treatises,

412

severed from the historical circumstances in which they were birthed. If the coherence of Paul's gospel is forgotten, the letters become isolated snippets of Paul's thought, divorced from a larger worldview.

The Occasional Nature of the Letters

If what I have said above is correct, Paul's letters are not systematic treatises but pastoral responses to problems and situations in his churches. Galatians is not a measured and calm disquistion on the topic of justification. Paul counterattacks adversaries who insisted that the Galatians must submit to circumcision in order to be right with God. The entire letter is a rejoinder to opponents who advocated a return to the Mosaic Law. Similarly, Philippians is not merely a delightful little manual upon joy. Substantial grounds exist for thinking that the Philippian church was rent by disunity (Phil. 1:27–2:4; 4:2–3).[3] Paul wrote the letter to unify the church, so that they would live ardently for the cause of the gospel. Virtually everything in the letter is designed to attain this specific goal. In Colossians certain adversaries trumpeted ascetic practices, the observance of the sabbath, festival days, and "the worship of angels" (Col. 2:18). Scholars debate whether the Colossian philosophy hails from mystical Judaism, a pagan-Jewish syncretism, or even a form of Gnosticism. The profile of the Colossian philosophy should not detain us now. We must see, however, that the letter addresses a deviant teaching, which threatens the Colossian community.

The occasional character of the letters is evident in 1 Thessalonians, where Paul responds joyfully to recent news that the Thessalonians have persisted in the faith despite trials and persecutions. The letter closes with various exhortations so that the believers will be strengthened for the rest of their earthly sojourn. The focus on eschatology (1 Thess. 4:13–5:11) indicates that confusion existed over this matter for these new Christians. Apprehension continued over eschatological matters in Thessalonica, and so Paul needed to address such issues again in 2 Thessalonians. Often scholars have identified the Pastoral Letters (1–2 Timothy, Titus) as manuals for church organization. Describing the letters in such a way, however, is fundamentally misleading, for they are not miniature monographs on church structure. Paul wrote all three letters because false teaching menaced the churches.[4] I am not denying that all three letters have much to teach us about church structure today. Any contemporary application, however, must first grapple with the first-century context in which the letters were written to ensure that the historical particularity of the letters is not erased. Moreover, we must also beware of lumping together the three pastoral letters indiscriminately. Titus is addressed to a church that was recently established, and there are indications that the church is more rough-hewn than the church in Ephesus (addressed in 1 Timothy) that had existed for a number of years.[5] The situation in 2 Timothy is different yet again. The call to suffer for the gospel takes center stage. All of the examples cited teach the same lesson: When we read the Pauline letters, the occasional nature of the letters must be etched into our consciousness.

In the history of interpretation Romans has been classified as a theological treatise.[6] Describing Romans as a full exposition of Paul's entire gospel is understandable, for it is certainly the most comprehensive of all Paul's letters. Topics like faith, hope, sin, justification, the law, the death of Christ, the Christian life, the role of Israel, and ethics are all examined extensively. And yet a number of themes are missing in Romans, or at least lack any detailed treatment. The reflective christological statements of Philippians 2:5–11 and Colossians 1:15–20 really have no parallel in Romans. The return of Christ is assumed in Romans, but it is only referred to in a glancing way in contrast to 1 and 2 Thessalonians where Christ's return is prominent. The theology of the church, which is beautifully portrayed and explained in Ephesians, does not have the same focus in Romans. Nor is there any mention of the Lord's Supper in Romans. Other lacunae could be mentioned, but the point is obvious. Even though Romans is deeply theological, not all of Paul's theology is contained in the letter. Indeed, more and more scholars believe—rightly in my view—that Romans was addressed to a specific situation in Rome.[7]

Both Romans 9–11 and 14–15 imply that tensions existed between Jews and Gentiles in Rome. I would suggest that Romans was written to unify Jews and Gentiles, so that they would support Paul's mission to Spain. If Roman Christians disagreed with Paul's gospel, they could scarcely endorse its extension to Spain. Therefore, Paul had to tackle the issues that were crucial for bringing Jewish and Gentile Christians together. It is not surprising, then, that the law and justification, the place of Israel, and the matter of eating clean foods arise in the letter.

Paul does not merely examine these issues as "topics" needing responses. He explains them in the light of his gospel, so that the Romans will have deep comprehension of the issues involved. The only other letter that could qualify as a theological treatise is Ephesians. Certainly the letter does not contain a comprehensive exposition of the Pauline gospel since some themes from other Pauline letters are omitted. Some have suggested that even here Paul responds to false teaching, though this seems doubtful since clear references to opponents are lacking. Perhaps the letter is an encyclical, sent to a number of churches in Asia Minor, and this might account for its more expansive feel. Richard Longenecker's designation "tractate letter" seems to be fitting in the case of Ephesians.[8]

Letters or Epistles?

How should we understand the Pauline compositions? Adolf Deissmann early in the century argued that they should be designated as letters rather than epistles.[9] Epistles were artistic works, designed for a larger audience and intended to last forever as literary compositions. Letters, on the other hand, were addressed to specific situations, dashed off to meet the immediate needs of readers. Paul, Deissmann insisted, did not write careful literary compositions that were intended for posterity, which were intended to function authoritatively in the life of the church over the years. He wrote in the ordinary language of his day in response to situations as they arose.

Deissmann, despite the validity of some his insights, overstated his case. All would agree that Paul wrote occasional letters, addressed to particular circumstances in the churches. It is also true that the ordinary language of Paul's day was used, an insight that was clear to Deissmann when he compared the language of the Pauline letters to the papyri. Nonetheless, most scholars no longer see Deissmann's sharp cleavage between letters and epistles as credible. First, even though Paul's letters responded to specific situations in the churches, they show every indication of being carefully constructed. The distinction between Paul's letters and most letters from the papyri collections is evident at this very point, for Paul's letters have a literary quality lacking in the papyri. Indeed, some contemporary scholars believe that Paul's letters are patterned after Greek rhetoric (see below). Even if this latter theory is incorrect, the proposal itself calls into question Deissmann's thesis, for the theory would not even be seriously considered if the letters were not carefully structured.

The second feature of the Pauline letters, which was overlooked by Deissmann, is their authoritative character. The letters were not merely private missives. Paul wrote them as an apostle of Jesus Christ, and he expected them to be read in the churches and obeyed (1 Cor. 14:37; 1 Thess. 5:27; 2 Thess. 3:14). The authority of the Pauline letters is communicated by the admonition to public reading. In the synagogue the OT Scriptures were read aloud, and Paul expects *his letters* to be read and his admonitions to be heeded. It is instructive as well that the Colossians are enjoined to pass his letter on to the Laodiceans (Col. 4:16). Even though Colossians is addressed to specific circumstances in that church, Paul believes it will be useful to the Laodiceans as well, demonstrating that his instructions had a significance that transcended local circumstances. This is not surprising because Paul believed his instructions in the letters were authoritative (Gal. 1:8; 1 Cor. 14:37). His letters were not merely good advice but were part of the gospel (cf. 1 Thess. 2:13). Thus, Deissmann underestimates the authoritative status of the Pauline letters and the extent to which letters addressed to one church could also apply to another.

Mirror Reading in the Letters

Thus far we have seen that Paul's letters are occasional in nature, and yet they are also authoritative. The majority of the letters address specific situations in the churches, and Paul often counters false teaching. Our ability to reconstruct the teaching of opponents will help us gain a sharper profile of

Paul's own instructions, for we shall understand more clearly the circumstances he faced. A disadvantage arises immediately, for we learn about the opponents only from Paul's perspective. Morna Hooker remarks that we are placed in the position of hearing only one end of a telephone conversation.[10] The historical particularity of the letters surfaces here, for a detailed description of the situation of the letters was unnecessary for the readers since the letters were written to them, and they knew their own circumstances. The Galatians, for instance, scarcely needed from Paul a full portrait of those proclaiming the other gospel. And yet for readers in the twenty-first century a summary of their activities and beliefs would be enormously helpful. We are reminded that the letters were not written to us but to people who lived nearly two thousand years ago.

A particularly vivid example of the historical distance between the first readers and us emerges in 2 Thessalonians 2:5–7. Paul informs the Thessalonians that he is merely reminding them of his oral instructions since they already know what is restraining the mystery of lawlessness from erupting. They know who the restrainer is because Paul already communicated such orally. He does not bother to tell them again since they are already well instructed on this point. Modern readers, on the other hand, are frustrated by Paul's indirect reference to the restrainer, and we cannot identify the restrainer with certainty. The perplexity of scholars is evident by canvassing some of the options presented for identifying the restrainer. Commentators have said the restrainer is the Holy Spirit, Satan, the government, Paul as a missionary, and others. The disparity of interpretations reveals our historical distance from the first readers. The Thessalonians knew who the restrainer was since Paul told them, whereas certitude eludes us.

Three other situations in the Thessalonian letters are of the same nature. The Thessalonians were apparently convinced that fellow believers who had died since coming to faith were at a disadvantage when the Lord returned (1 Thess. 4:13–18). What precisely were the Thessalonians thinking? Why did they think that believers who had died were at some disadvantage? Many theories have been suggested, but we must admit that certainty eludes us. We know that they thought Christians who had died were impaired in some way, but we do not know why they believed such.

A similar problem emerges in 2 Thessalonians 2:1–12. Apparently the Thessalonians were convinced that the day of the Lord had arrived or was impending. Paul clarifies that this cannot be correct since the apostasy had not yet occurred and the man of lawlessness had not been revealed.

We are interested in knowing what led them to think that the day of the Lord had arrived, but Paul does not fill us in on their thinking process since both he and they knew the answer to that question! Once again we learn *what* they were thinking, but we are frustrated if we try to discern *why*.

In this latter instance I have my own suspicion. I suspect that the Thessalonians thought the end had arrived because of the intensity of persecution

(2 Thess. 1:3–10). Such a judgment can function only as a guess, for the text does not specify the reason. I am not suggesting, incidentally, that such guesses are historically worthless. Any attempt to make sense of historical documents involves some reading between the lines, and most would agree that some readings are more viable than others. I am only pointing out that our need to guess was not shared by the first readers.

The last example hails from 2 Thessalonians 3:6–11. We learn from this text that some in the church were idle and lazy. Why were they acting that way? Many scholars suggest that they were idle because they believed that the end of history was coming soon. I am of the opinion that this view is probably correct. But once again we must note that Paul does not tell us *why* the Thessalonians were indolent and slothful. In reading the Pauline letters we often know *what* is happening and are much less certain as to *why.*

When we attempt to reconstruct the situations Paul addresses in the churches, our knowledge is partial. For example, a comprehensive understanding of the Colossian philosophy (Col. 2:8), which threatened the Colossian church, is not available to us. We could possibly conclude that attempting to delineate the features of the Colossian philosophy is pointless since the validity of our reconstruction is uncertain. It is imperative at this juncture to make some necessary distinctions and to avoid extremes.

First, we can understand the basic message of every Pauline letter without a comprehensive understanding of the situation. Even the original recipients of the letter to the Colossians did not have a complete grasp of what was at stake since total understanding is impossible for human beings. On the other hand, they knew the situation much better than we. And yet we can understand the letter to the Colossians even if we grasp imperfectly the Colossian philosophy. Our inability to pin down every feature of the Colossian philosophy does not produce despair about the meaning of the letter as a whole.

The letter itself provides enough information so that we can understand its basic message. We can apply this principle to the Pastoral Epistles. Identifying the adversaries in these letters is extraordinarily difficult, for the opponents are vilified, but their views are not expounded in any detail. I would suggest that we can still grasp the message of these letters even though we lack much information about the opposition.

The second point is related to the first. If we believe in divine providence, we are confident that God has given us enough information *within the confines of the individual letters* to understand them. No extrabiblical information provides the key by which they will be unlocked for future generations.

Third, we should not conclude from this that study of the situation informing the letters is unnecessary, for our understanding of the letters can be sharpened, confirmed, or even called into question through such research. Extrabiblical research may provoke us to reexamine the text afresh so as to discern if we were reading our views *into the text*. For example, whether

Colossians 2:16 refers to the Jewish sabbath or to pagan observance of the same is significant when we interpret the text of Colossians. Other primary sources from the ancient world, both Jewish and Hellenistic, can help us to resolve this issue.

Fourth, the principal means by which we discern the circumstances addressed in the Pauline letters is from the letters themselves. We must beware of imposing an outside situation upon the letters. For instance, in previous generations some scholars read Gnosticism from the second and third centuries A.D. into the New Testament letters, so that the opponents in almost every Pauline letter were identified as Gnostics. Virtually no one advocates the Gnostic hypothesis today, for it is illegitimate to read later church history into first-century documents. The Gnostic detour could have been avoided if scholars had read the Pauline letters themselves more carefully, for evidence for full-fledged Gnosticism cannot be read out of his letters. Scholars are prone to engage in "parallelomania" where information from the Dead Sea Scrolls or Nag Hammadi or the Church Fathers is imposed upon the New Testament documents.[11]

The method used to identify the opponents in the Pauline letters is crucial.[12] I would suggest the following principles, which overlap in some respects. The internal evidence from the letter itself must be primary in delineating the opponents. This principle has already been mentioned, but it must be stated again since it is often overlooked *in practice*, even when it is subscribed to theoretically. Scholars desire to provide a sharp profile of the Pauline adversaries, and thus they are tempted to fill out the local situation from evidence outside the letter. In my opinion, Clint Arnold commits this error in his fine work on the opponents in Colossians.[13]

Arnold rightly documents the pervasiveness of magic in Asia Minor during the period when Colossians was written. What is lacking, however, is any firm evidence that magic was actually the problem in the letter to the Colossians. There is no reference *in Colossians itself* to magic, spells, invocations, conjurations, sorcery, etc. Many religious movements vied for the attention of the populace in the first century. We need primary evidence from the letter itself to establish a particular religious influence in the letter under consideration. Sharon Hodgin Gritz falls prey to the same error in her analysis of 1 Timothy when she posits the influence of the mother goddess, Artemis cult.[14]

Certainly such a cult functioned in Ephesus, but Hodgin Gritz fails to show that the cult lies behind the situation in 1 Timothy. To see a connection with the Artemis cult on the basis of sexual impurity (1 Tim. 5:11–14) and greed (1 Tim. 6:3–5) is unpersuasive, for these sins, as we all know, may emerge in almost any religious movement.[15] Hodgin Gritz does not explain adequately how myths and genealogies (1 Tim. 1:3–4), devotion to the Mosaic Law (1 Tim. 1:8–11), asceticism (1 Tim. 4:1–3), and knowledge

(1 Tim. 6:20–21) relate to the Artemis cult. The features of the Artemis cult appear to be superimposed upon the contents of 1 Timothy.

The internal evidence of the letters may also be ignored in the attempt to provide a *global* view of the Pauline opponents. F. C. Baur, in his magnificent attempt to write a history of early Christianity, went astray at this point.[16] Baur assumed that the opponents in *all* the Pauline letters were Judaizers. Therefore, he could raid all the Pauline letters (i.e., those he considered to be authentic) to garner information about the Judaizers. Baur does not practice a sound historical method here, for he needs to establish the opponents inductively from each letter instead of simply assuming that the adversaries are the same in each letter.

A careful comparison of Galatians and 1 Corinthians is instructive. The opponents in Galatians are likely Judaizers as Baur himself suggested, but to read the same out of 1 Corinthians is highly questionable since the features present in Galatians (e.g., an insistence upon circumcision for salvation) are lacking in 1 Corinthians.

Walter Schmithals follows the same path as Baur in suggesting a single front opposition in all of Paul's letters.[17] Schmithals departs from Baur in identifying these opponents as Gnostics. The same tendency to come up with a totalizing scheme in which all the letters become grist for one mill is evident. To sustain his hypothesis Schmithals is forced to argue that Galatians 3–4 contains traditional material unrelated to the situation at Galatia.[18] Some of the evidence in the letter itself, according to Willi Marxsen, may actually mislead one about the identity of the opponents.[19] In this latter instance, the hypothesis trumps the inductive material present in the letter. Instead of wresting the material of each letter in support of some global scheme, we must derive the opponents from an inductive analysis of the letters themselves.

The next principle to be considered was also mentioned above. Documents from a later date must not be read into the Pauline letters. Once again Baur and Schmithals function as bad examples. Baur posited a distinction between Pauline and Petrine Christianity, and one of his bases was the Psuedo-Clementine Homilies of the second century A.D. A document from the next century, however, is not a secure foundation for discerning the circumstances when Paul's letters were written, for too much time has elapsed to assume that the situation is similar. Schmithals committed the same error by reading the Gnosticism of later church history into the Pauline letters. For example, Schmithals identified the opponents in Galatia as Gnostics. This is illegitimate, for we cannot assume that circumstances in the second or third century A.D. existed in the first century. The full-fledged Gnosticism of the later church history did not exist in the first century A.D.[20]

An incipient form of Gnosticism was present, but Schmithals makes the error of reading later Gnosticism into the first-century documents. Richard and Catherine Kroeger follow in Schmithals's footsteps in positing the background to 1 Timothy.[21] They call the heresy "proto-Gnostic," but in fact they often appeal to later sources to define the false teaching.[22] External evidence can only be admitted if it can be shown that the religious or philosophical movement was contemporary with the New Testament.

Internal evidence from the letter is primary in delineating the opponents. How do we discern the situation of the letter using internal evidence? Explicit statements about opponents are the most important in reconstructing the teaching of adversaries. We can discern from Galatians 1:6–7 (cf. 5:10), for instance, that some were proclaiming a different gospel in Galatia. We also know from Galatians 6:12–13 that they were advocating circumcision, and some Galatians were contemplating circumcision (Gal. 5:2–4) and the observance of the OT calendar (Gal. 4:10).

In Colossians Paul explicitly refers to a philosophy that was threatening the faith of his readers (Col. 2:8). We are also informed that the errorists prohibited certain foods and drinks, observed various days and festivals, and worshiped angels (Col. 2:16–23). In 2 Corinthians Paul says the adversaries are peddlers of God's word (2 Cor. 2:17), commend themselves to the Corinthians (2 Cor. 3:1; 10:12–18), boast about their credentials (2 Cor. 5:12; 11:18), claim to be super-apostles (2 Cor. 11:5–6; 12:11), and demand payment as apostolic messengers (2 Cor. 11:12–15), criticize Paul as fleshly (2 Cor. 10:2) and hypocritical (2 Cor. 10:10–11), act tyrannically (2 Cor. 11:21), appeal to their Jewish heritage (2 Cor. 11:21–23), and demand proof of Christ's speaking through Paul (2 Cor. 13:2–3). On the other hand, it is much more difficult to discern whether opponents actually exist in 1 Thessalonians. Paul nowhere refers to them expressly. Yet some scholars believe that adversaries are in view when Paul defends his apostleship in 1 Thessalonians 2:1–12. It is also possible, however, that Paul rehearses his ministry so that the Thessalonians will imitate his behavior.

I conclude that explicit statements clearly demonstrate the presence of opponents and perhaps some of the elements of their teaching, and yet the lack of express statements does not prove opponents did not exist. In the latter instance, it is much more difficult to reach a definite conclusion.

Explicit statements are fundamental in discerning opponents in Pauline letters, and yet other passages in letters may yield information about the situation if they cohere with or shed light on explicit statements. We have already seen from explicit statements in Galatians that opponents exist and are demanding circumcision. Nowhere in Paul's discussion of the law in Galatians 3–4 does he mention circumcision, and yet we rightly infer that Paul's words on faith, the law, the Spirit, and righteousness are in response to the Judaizing threat. Similarly, the segment on Paul's apostleship in Galatians 1–2 most likely rebuts an attack on the same by the Judaizers. No unambiguous statement demonstrates that Paul defends himself against criticism, though such an idea is implied by both Galatians 5:11 and 6:17. Moreover, Paul's defense of his apostleship in the first verse signals a counterattack against the agitators since this defensive tone is distinctive in his greetings. It is also sensible to think that opponents of Paul would criticize him as a messenger in order to substantiate their own gospel.

The validity of appealing to sections of the letters that are not explicitly polemical can also be defended from Colossians. We know from Colossians 2:18 that the philosophy promoted "the worship of angels." This information is extremely useful in interpreting the rest of the letter, for in the Colossian hymn Christ's superiority to and creation of "thrones, dominions, rulers, and authorities" is featured (Col. 1:16). Almost all scholars agree that these are angelic powers, and Christ's preeminence over them is proclaimed because the opponents were overestimating the importance of angels.

Similarly, God has disarmed, exposed, and triumphed over angels through Christ (Col. 2:15). No explicit statement about the opponents exists in this verse, but it is hard to believe that they are not countered here. Similarly, the word *fullness* in Colossians does not appear where Paul sketches in the teaching of the philosophy. And yet the word appears both in the Colossian hymn and in Paul's response to the philosophy (Col. 1:19; 2:9–10). We cannot be certain, but it is probable that the opponents claimed that fullness was attained by following ascetic practices, observing days, and through devotion to angels.

The same method can be employed in 2 Corinthians. We have seen above that a fair bit of information about the opponents can be derived from explicit statements. Other parts of the letter, then, may yield information about the situation. For instance, it is probable that the opponents called into question Paul's reliability in 2 Corinthians 1:12–2:2. Indeed, Paul's apology for his ministry (see esp. 2 Cor. 2:14–7:4) is likely a response to his adversaries.

I am scarcely suggesting a fail-safe method for detecting the historical situation of Paul's letters. The fragmentary nature of the evidence precludes such confidence. And yet radical agnosticism should be eschewed as well. We often have enough information to gain quite a clear, though not a perfect, outline of the opponents. What is fundamental in tracing the outline of the adversaries or in delineating the historical situation that precipitated one of the Pauline letters is the text of the letter itself. Scholars have gotten off track by reading data from later church history into the letters, by coming up with some global picture of the opponents that suppresses the evidence from individual letters, or even by imposing some contemporary parallel religious movement upon the letters. We must decipher the teaching or views of the adversaries from the letters themselves, acknowledging carefully what we do know and what is only conjecture. At the same time information from extrabiblical sources may be useful in confirming or refuting some hypothesis about the identity of the opponents. The evidence from the letters themselves is fundamental, but it does not follow from this that other evidence should be overlooked.

Rhetorical Criticism

In recent years Paul's letters have been investigated from the standpoint of rhetorical criticism.[23] Did Paul use the patterns of argumentation and structure recommended in the Greco-Roman handbooks, especially in the works of Quintilian and Cicero? Many scholars now answer such a question in the affirmative, and a growing body of literature reflects the attempt to comprehend Paul's letters as rhetorical compositions. Rhetoric can be classified into three types: (1) judicial, (2) deliberative, and (3) epideictic. Judicial rhetoric is the language of the law court where language of defense and accusation predominate, and guilt and innocence are under consideration. Deliberative rhetoric summons human beings to consider the future, seeking to persuade or dissuade them from a certain course of action.

When speakers use epideictic rhetoric, they are celebrating common values or aspirations, or indicting something that is blameworthy. Most rhetorical speeches have four elements: (1) the *exordium* which introduces the speech and attempts to create empathy for what will follow; (2) the *narratio* which contains the main proposition and background information relevant to the argument; (3) the *probatio* in which the arguments for the proposition are set forth; and (4) the *peroratio* in which the whole argument is summarized and brought to a ringing conclusion so that the hearers will be persuaded.

The work which seems to have launched rhetorical criticism in Paul is Hans Dieter Betz's commentary on Galatians.[24] He divides Galatians as follows, identifying it as a judicial apologetic letter:

> Prescript 1:1–5
> Body 1:6–6:10
> *Exordium* 1:6–11
> *Narratio* 1:12–2:14
> *Propositio* 2:15–21
> *Probatio* 3:1–4:31
> *Paraenesis* 5:1–6:10
> Postscript (containing *Peroratio*) 6:11–18

Betz's work is enormously interesting, and we can immediately see the plausibility of the structure proposed. Indeed, one of the benefits of rhetorical criticism is that it reminds us that the Pauline letters are carefully structured and written. Nonetheless, there are serious questions that finally render Betz's proposal doubtful.[25] First, the *exordium* in Galatians hardly creates goodwill with the audience. Instead of thanking God for his work in their lives Paul expresses astonishment at their departure from the gospel (Gal. 1:6–11). No attempt to establish rapport with the readers is evident here! Second, much of Galatians is comprised of parenesis (Gal. 5:1–6:10), but parenesis has no place in the rhetorical handbooks. Third, Betz does not provide any literary examples of an apologetic letter which would function as a comparison with Galatians. Fourth, Paul's Jewish background is completely ignored in the composition of the letter.

Some scholars have responded to Betz by suggesting that Galatians should be classified as deliberative rather than judicial rhetoric.[26] Seeing Galatians as fundamentally persuasive in intent seems correct, and yet it is still questionable whether it conforms so precisely to the pattern of Greek rhetoric. Rhetorical schemas have been suggested now for virtually every Pauline letter. The detailed suggestions seem to suffer from the problem of imposing a form on the Pauline letters that does not fit them precisely. The unique features of his letters can easily be extinguished by some prefabricated pattern that squelches what the letter actually says.

This is not to say that the new rhetorical approaches are without value. They remind us that the letters are carefully structured and crafted, for the new proposals would not be worthy of serious consideration if Paul's letters were organized poorly. Moreover, Paul was probably familiar with such rhetoric to some extent, for he was an educated person, and the impact of Hellenism was evident even in Palestine.[27] Even if he was unaware entirely of Greek rhetoric (which is unlikely), it still follows that we could detect some rhetorical features in his letters since the rhetorical handbooks identify elements of effective communication that are used even by those who know nothing of Greek rhetoric. Nevertheless, we must seriously question whether he actually structured entire letters in accordance with the rhetorical handbooks.[28]

The rules of rhetoric in these handbooks were designed for *speeches,* not for written discourse. Rhetorical handbooks rarely refer to *letters,* and they do not contain prescriptions in terms of the type of argument employed (judicial, deliberative, or epideictic), nor do they recommend the following of a certain outline (*exordium, narratio, probatio, peroratio*).

Stanley Porter concludes his study of the impact of the rhetorical handbooks upon letters by saying, "There is, therefore, little if any theoretical justification in the ancient handbooks for application of the formal categories of the species and organization of rhetoric to analysis of the Pauline epistles."[29]

It is also instructive that early church fathers did not identify the Pauline letters as conforming to Greek rhetoric.[30] A number of the fathers were familiar with or trained in rhetoric, and yet they do not give any indication that they understood Paul's letters to be patterned after such rhetoric. If anything, they sometimes seemed embarrassed by the rudeness of his style. The most serious problem with classifying the Pauline letters as rhetoric has already been mentioned. The detailed schemes appear to be imposed upon Paul's writings.

Epistolary Features of the Letters

Examining the epistolary features of Paul's letters is more promising than rhetorical criticism. All of Paul's letters consist of the opening, the body, and the closing. The opening of letters usually has four elements: (1) the sender (e.g., Paul); (2) the recipients (e.g., the Philippians); (3) the salutation (e.g., grace and peace to you); and (4) prayer (usually a thanksgiving). Interpretive significance can be discerned from Paul's variation from the pattern and from what he emphasizes in the opening. For example, the defensive tone of Galatians 1:1 is unparalleled in the Pauline letters, suggesting that the opponents call into question the legitimacy of his apostleship.

Paul not only lists himself as the sender in Galatians 1:2 but also mentions "all the brothers with me." With these words he communicates the truth that the gospel he preaches is not merely his private opinion. All the believers with Paul acknowledge it as well, and so the Galatians are not renouncing Paul alone if they repudiate his gospel.

Usually Paul announces himself as an apostle, but in Philippians 1:1, he designates both Timothy and himself as "slaves." Why does he avoid the term *apostle*? Probably because the Philippian church suffered from some division, and thus Paul represents Timothy and himself as models for the Philippians. Dissension is overcome through living like a servant, not by claiming authority over others.

The surprising reference to "overseers and deacons" (Phil. 1:1) may also signal that they play a central role in the problems surfacing in the Philippian church. Since Paul typically begins with a thanksgiving, the lack of the same in Galatians 1 is significant.[31] Paul is not thankful but astonished with the defection in the church. Usually the opening of the letter is brief, two or three verses. Again Galatians stands out since the opening consists of five verses. The longest opening of all is found in Romans, for here Paul writes to a church that was not established by him, and so he emphasizes his unique apostolic role and the gospel he proclaims, to establish a common bond and understanding from the inception of the letter.

The substance of Pauline letters is found in the body. Here the Pauline letters display remarkable creativity, and no consistent pattern is readily observable. The task of the interpreter is to trace Paul's argument carefully, letting the text itself dictate the structure.[32] The body of the letters highlights the distinctive nature of the Pauline letters. Despite some overlap with other letters in the Greco-Roman world, they also have unique features, features that demand thorough and careful interpretation.

The closing of letters is also interpretively significant, though the pattern varies, and discerning where the closing begins may be difficult.[33] The following elements are often present, and I will cite only two examples for each, though more could be given: (1) travel plans or personal situation (Rom. 15:22–29; 1 Cor. 16:5–9); (2) prayer (Rom. 15:33; 1 Thess. 5:23); (3) commendation of coworkers (Rom. 16:1–2; 1 Cor. 16:10–12); (4) prayer requests (Rom. 15:30–32; Col. 4:2–4); (5) greetings (Rom. 16:3–16; 1 Cor. 16:19–21); (6) final instructions and exhortations (Rom. 16:17–20a; 1 Cor. 16:13–18); (7) holy kiss (1 Cor. 16:20; 2 Cor. 13:12); (8) autographed greeting

(1 Cor. 16:21; Gal. 6:11); and (9) a grace benediction (Rom. 16:20; 1 Cor. 16:23–24).

The closing of Romans is particularly significant, and this is evident from its length alone (either Rom. 15:14–16:17 or 15:22–16:27). The contribution of the closing in interpreting letters is aptly illustrated from Galatians 6:11–18, though it must be observed that the importance of the closing varies from letter to letter.[34] The autograph formula (v. 11) signals the weight of the closing, for Paul writes with large letters to emphasize the significance of what follows. Most striking are the contrasts between the opponents and Paul. They boast in the circumcision of the Galatians (vv. 12–13), but Paul boasts in the cross of Christ only (v. 14). The agitators "avoid persecution for the cross" (v. 12), but Paul "accepts persecution . . . for the cross" (v. 17), and bears the marks of that persecution upon his body.[35] The adversaries are attempting to force circumcision on the Galatians (vv. 12–13), but Paul views both circumcision and uncircumcision as *adiaphora* (v. 15). The opponents live under the power of this world (v. 14), but Paul has been inducted into the age to come, "the new creation" inaugurated by Christ (v. 15).

A careful reading of the closing discloses that the fundamental issue in Galatians is the cross of Christ. Paul summarizes the major issue in the letter by reminding his readers of the significance of the cross (see also Gal. 1:4; 2:19–21; 3:1, 13; 4:4–5; 5:1, 11, 24). Since the closing reprises central themes of the letter, we are also given help in defining "the Israel of God" (Gal. 6:16). Paul labors throughout the letter to emphasize that all those who belong to Christ are children of Abraham and share the blessing of Abraham. It is quite likely, then, that he uses the term *Israel of God* to designate both Jewish and Gentile believers in Christ, summarizing one of the major themes of the letter at its conclusion. Reading the closing of a letter may cast significant light on the rest of the letter, especially when the closing is more extended as in Galatians and Romans.

Doing Pauline Theology

It is impossible in a brief essay to tackle adequately the task of doing Pauline theology. In some ways Paul's theology is more difficult than that of any other writer in the New Testament because all thirteen letters must be assessed in order to determine his theology. Some might even think such a theology is impossible since the letters were written to specific situations. We should remind ourselves again of Beker's distinction. Paul's letters were directed to *contingent* situations, but his advice for particular communities stemmed from a *coherent* gospel. Paul did not respond spontaneously and uncritically to every circumstance that arose. He responded to each new situation in the light of the gospel of Jesus Christ he proclaimed. At the end of the day, however, seeing coherence in the Pauline gospel is a *theological* judgment.

New Testament scholars must not think that they are merely objective historians, free from any dogmatic biases. The history of New Testament theology reveals the naivete of many of its practitioners, since they claimed to be doing "objective" historical research without any presuppositions. Such a claim was naïve, for they actually operated from an Enlightenment worldview that excluded the possibility of the miraculous.

Adolf Schlatter rightly noted that the historical work of some is fundamentally atheistic.[36] At the same time we can learn much about Pauline theology, even from those who have a naturalistic worldview. Such scholars may have detected themes in Paul's writings that were squelched by the theological commitments of other scholars. Conservatives may be so committed to their respective theological systems that they obscure segments of Paul's theology. Scholars who are free from such systems may perform a service for us in helping us see what is really there, even if they deny the fundamental truth of the Pauline gospel.

The task of Pauline theology is not an easy one, for dangers exist on every side. No one approaches Paul neutrally, and thus we must examine afresh the legitimacy of our presuppositions. And even after we have done this, we may not see what Paul says because of our own cultural or psychological limitations. Opening up ourselves to other scholarly work on Paul may remove some blinders that hindered us from seeing what is truly there.

When we do Pauline theology, we must be careful to interpret each letter on its own terms. In other words, we must beware of reading Romans into Galatians or Romans into the Pastoral Epistles. Each document must be interpreted in light of its own unique context. Otherwise the distinctive contribution of, say, 2 Thessalonians may be suppressed. Similarly, we may become so entranced with a particular theme that we fail to see or may even squeeze out another theme in Paul. For instance, Paul's famous teaching on justification by faith (e.g., Rom. 3:21–4:25) may prevent us from seeing that he also teaches that believers must do good works in order to inherit eternal life (e.g., Rom. 2:5–11; Gal. 5:21; 6:8–9; 1 Cor. 6:9–11).[37]

Conversely, we must beware of going to the other extreme and insisting that we can learn nothing about Galatians from Romans. If Paul was a coherent thinker, then we would expect that he would return to some major themes often and that his teaching on these themes would be consistent. Thus, if a verse or a paragraph is somewhat obscure or difficult to comprehend in Galatians, we may gain insight into Paul's meaning if the same subject is discussed in Romans. Naturally the danger of reading Romans into Galatians must be avoided. On the other hand, if the letters are segregated from one another in a rigid way, insight into the coherence and unity of the Pauline gospel will be overlooked. Obviously much more can and should be said about Pauline theology than is possible in this brief essay on interpreting Paul's Epistles. To have said nothing at all would be even worse, for the impression would be given that Paul's letters could be understood apart from any theological framework, for a grasp of the whole of Paul's theology provides wisdom in interpreting his individual letters, just as intensive exegesis in the letters sheds light on the whole of his theology.

Applying Paul to Today

Paul's writings have endured two thousand years because most readers have believed that they are part of the canon of Scripture and that they speak authoritatively to our lives. Knowing how to apply Paul's letters to present circumstances, therefore, is a crucial issue.[38] Given space constraints I will limit myself briefly to some observations on the cultural particularity of Paul's letters. The contingency of the letters creates a distance between Paul and us, which makes their applicability uncertain. What message is there for us when Paul asks Timothy to bring him a cloak and parchments (2 Tim. 4:13)? We certainly cannot do what Timothy presumably attempted. Nor have I ever met a Christian who thought that fellow believers who had already died were at some disadvantage at the resurrection (cf. 1 Thess. 4:13–18). Apparently the Thessalonians believed that those whom they loved and who had died were at such a disadvantage for reasons that are now lost to us. Paul goes to some lengths to say that the believing dead will precede the living at the resurrection and that the believing dead will not be left out at the resurrection, and yet most modern believers have never thought that their deceased beloved will suffer some detriment because of their early demise.

The cultural particularity of Paul's letters is evident in a number of texts. Should we prescribe wine for stomach problems (1 Tim. 5:23) or greet one another with a holy kiss (1 Cor. 16:20; 2 Cor. 13:12; 1 Thess. 5:26)? Should women wear shawls (1 Cor. 11:2–16) or be prohibited from speaking in church (1 Cor. 14:33b–36)? Should we pattern our worship services after Paul's instructions in 1 Corinthians 14:26–33? Do Paul's words on slavery constitute an endorsement of the practice (Eph. 6:5–9; Col. 3:22–4:1; 1 Tim. 6:1–2; Titus 2:9–10)? Should wives submit to their husbands (Eph. 5:22–24; Col. 3:18), and are they confined to working at home (Titus 2:3–5)?

Two errors must be avoided at the outset. First, we could dismiss Paul's teaching altogether, arguing that we cannot apply it to today since circumstances have been altered dramatically. Such a verdict confines Paul to his day and is a frank acknowledgment that his teaching does not constitute a word from God for us. Second, it would be an error to apply Paul woodenly to our culture. Some might think that if Paul prescribed wine for stomachaches, then wine must be the best remedy for stomach problems even today. Or some might think that we must literally practice the holy kiss since Paul instructed believers to greet one another that way. Others might insist that women wear shawls or veils or their hair tied up onto their heads in a bun (scholars disagree on what the custom was). We know that some

Christians previous to and during the American Civil War defended slavery on the basis of biblical instructions. Transporting Pauline admonitions to our day *carte blanche* is unsatisfactory, for the occasional nature and historical particularity of the letters are ignored on such a scheme. Before applying the text, the specific situation addressed must be explored, and we must also recognize that our culture at the beginning of the twenty-first century is remarkably different from the culture of the Greco-Roman world.

What positively can we say about applying Paul's letters to contemporary society? First, the whole of Paul's theology must be taken into consideration. Our application may be distorted if all of Paul's words on a particular theme are not consulted. For example, Paul's words on women being silent in the church are not the only text about women in Paul. All of his teaching must be consulted before suggesting an application, and in 1 Corinthians 11:2–16, Paul defends the legitimacy of women praying and prophesying in the assembly. Another danger, on the other end of the spectrum, also exists. We may suppress the relevance of a particular text in order to sustain a "general" teaching that is more congenial to our way of thinking. For instance, the text on women being silent in the church may be excluded altogether, so that it does not play any role when we formulate Paul's teaching on women. The whole of Paul's teaching must be included when we consider how it relates to us today. Engaging in such a task can be extraordinarily difficult, for it involves careful exegesis of all the texts and the formation of a theory as to how they all relate. Both induction and deduction play a role in the process.

Second, in every text a principle or norm must be deduced. Once again the difficulty of the task must be acknowledged. The principle we formulate may veer away from or even distort Paul's instructions. Interpreters disagree over what is culturally limited and what is a norm for all time.[39] Norms that transcend situations are rooted in God's nature or the created order. It follows from this that admonitions to live in love, or truthfully, or righteously still apply today because they correspond to God's nature.

Other commands are relevant because we are God's creatures. Therefore, we should be humble and not proud. Other admonitions apply because they are rooted in God's created order. Polygamy and divorce are excluded by God's intention in creation, for he made one man and one woman (Gen. 2:18–25). Similarly, homosexuality, though it is fiercely debated today, is prohibited since it violates God's creation order (Rom. 1:26–27). Giving a holy kiss, however, is not clearly related to either God's nature, our role as creatures, or God's created order. It seems to be a particular cultural practice of churches in the Greco-Roman world. Demanding it today would be awkward to the extreme in some cultures. It does not follow from this that no norm exists in such a command. The principle underlying the admonition is that fellow believers should greet one another warmly, but the specific way we greet one another may vary from culture to culture. Similarly, to insist that we all take wine for stomachaches is a wooden application of the text. Paul was recommending the medicinal means available in that day. Today we might recommend an antacid for those with frequent stomach ailments. The principle of the text is not hard to grasp. Those suffering from disease should use the requisite medicine. We also learn from this that Paul did not expect every one to be healed and actually encouraged the use of medicine for illnesses.

How should we assess the injunction for women to wear shawls? The interpretive issues are particularly vexing in this case. Paul appeals to the relationship between the Father and the Son as the ground for his admonition (1 Cor. 11:3). He also grounds the admonition on the relationship between men and women established during creation (1 Cor. 11:8–9). On the other hand, it is hard to see how wearing something on one's head represents a universal norm. The injunction seems similar to the holy kiss in this regard. Probably the best solution is to see a norm or principle that lasts for all time, namely, women are to prophesy in the assembly with a demeanor or manner that does not subvert male headship. At the same time, the specific practice is culturally limited, for very few people today conclude that women are rebellious if they fail to wear shawls.

Could the same principle apply to 1 Timothy 2:11–12 where Paul prohibits women from teaching or exercising authority over men? We should be open to an affirmative answer. Some scholars suggest that the principle is that women who are uneducated should desist from teaching or exercising authority. Others maintain that women who have fallen prey to false teachers should refrain from teaching. In my estimation both of these suggestions fail, for they cannot be sustained from a careful exegesis of the text.[40] So in this case the principle and the wording of the text coalesce. Once again the comments here are too brief to handle the issue of application satisfactorily, but it is hoped that they will stimulate further thinking, for ultimately we study Paul's letters to do what they say.

Conclusion

Interpreting the Pauline Epistles is no easy task, though it is a joyful one. Readers must recognize the historical distance between Paul's letters and our own day. The letters are not systematic treatises but occasional documents sent to churches struggling with specific problems. Understanding the circumstances of the letter or the Pauline opponents in the letter is of immense help in interpretation. Readers must also try to discern the structure of the Epistle which is being studied.

The openings and closings of letters are of special importance since Paul may foreshadow or summarize main themes at the beginning and end of his letters. Typical epistolary features should be identified. Departures from the usual pattern signal a distinctive emphasis. Analyzing the body of a letter is more difficult since each one is distinctive. Here readers must be sensitive to the structure of the argument, allowing each letter to make its own contribution.

The task of Pauline theology is also complicated since we have thirteen letters but no coherent treatise that weaves all into a logical system. But we also believe that Paul was an inspired writer who was a coherent theologian. Satisfying presentations of his thought can be and have been produced, even if a comprehensive and definitive Pauline theology is impossible. Finally, Paul's letters are the Word of God, and they speak to today. We should not succumb to the hermeneutical nihilism that despairs of understanding or applying Paul's letters. Hard work is certainly involved, but the Spirit of God enables us to apply the historical and authoritative word of Paul to our world.

Bibliography

Beker, J. C. *Paul the Apostle: The Triumph of God in Life and Thought.* Philadelphia: Fortress, 1980.

Dunn, James D. G. *The Theology of Paul the Apostle.* Grand Rapids: Eerdmans, 1998.

Kim, Seyoon. *The Origion of Paul's Gospel.* Grand Rapids: Eerdmans, 1982.

Sanders, E. P. *Paul, the Law, and the Jewish People.* Philadelphia: Fortress, 1983.

Ridderbos, Herman. *An Outline of Paul's Theology.* Grand Rapids: Eerdmans, 1975.

Seifrid, Mark A. *Christ, Our Righteousness: The Justification of the Ungodly as the Theology of Paul.* Forthcoming from Eerdmans.

Schreiner, Thomas R. *The Law and Its Fulfillment: A Pauline Theology of Law.* Grand Rapids: Baker, 1993.

———. *Paul, Apostle of God's Glory in Christ: A Pauline Theology.* Forthcoming from InterVarsity Press.

Thielman, Frank. *Paul and the Law: A Contextual Approach.* Downers Grove, Ill.: InterVarsity Press, 1994.

Westerholm, Stephen. *Israel's Law and the Church's Faith: Paul and His Recent Interpreters.* Grand Rapids: Eerdmans, 1988.

Notes

1. J. C. Beker, *Paul the Apostle: The Triumph of God in Life and Thought* (Philadelphia: Fortress, 1980), 11–16.

2. Ibid.

3. Supporting the idea that Philippians was written to unify the church is Davorin Peterlin, *Paul's Letter to the Philippians in Light of Disunity in the Church* (SupNovT 79; Leiden: Brill, 1995). Unfortunately, in making his case Peterlin overstates his thesis.

4. For a fine exposition of this view, see G. D. Fee's fine commentary *1 and 2 Timothy and Titus* (Peabody: Hendrickson, 1988).

5. Cf. L. T. Johnson, *Letter's to Paul's Delegates: 1 Timothy, 2 Timothy, Titus* (Valley Forge, Penn.: Trinity Press International, 1996), 212–13.

6. This view has a long history. For a modern proponent of the view, see A. Nygren, *Commentary on Romans* (Philadelphia: Fortress, 1949), 4.

7. For a defense of this view of *Romans,* see T. R. Schreiner, *Romans* (BECNT; Grand Rapids: Baker, 1998), 10–23.

8. R. N. Longenecker, "On the Form, Function, and Authority of the New Testament Letters," in *Scripture and Truth,* ed. D. A. Carson and J. D. Woodbridge (Grand Rapids: Zondervan, 1983), 104–05.

9. A. Deissmann, *Light from the Ancient East: The New Testament Illustrated by Recently Discovered Texts in the Graeco-Roman World* (London: Hodder & Stoughton, 1927), 228–41; idem, *Bible Studies: Contributions Chiefly from Papyri and Inscriptions to the History of the Language, the Literature, and the Religion of Hellenistic Judaism and Primitive Christianity* (Peabody: Hendrickson, 1988), 3–59.

10. M. D. Hooker, "Were There False Teachers in Colossae?" in *Christ and Spirit in the New Testament,* ed. B. Lindars and S. S. Smalley (Cambridge: Cambridge University Press, 1973), 315.

11. For the danger of parallelomania, see the famous article by S. Sandmel, "Parallelomania," *JBL* 81 (1962): 2–13.

12. See especially J. M. G. Barclay, "Mirror Reading a Polemical Letter: Galatians as a Test Case," *JSNT* 31 (1987): 73–93; J. L. Sumney, *Identifying Paul's Opponents: The Question of Method in 2 Corinthians,* JSNTSS 40 (Sheffield: JSOT Press, 1990).

13. C. E. Arnold, *The Colossian Syncretism: The Interface between Christianity and Folk Belief at Colossae* (Grand Rapids: Baker, 1996).

14. S. Hodgin Gritz, *Paul, Women Teachers, and the Mother Goddess at Ephesus* (Lanham: University Press of America, 1991).

15. Ibid., 114–16.

16. See F. C. Baur, *Paul the Apostle of Jesus Christ, His Life and Work, His Epistles and His Doctrine,* 2 vols. (London: Williams & Norgate, 1876).

17. W. Schmithals, *Gnosticism in Corinth* (Nashville: Abingdon, 1971) and *Paul and the Gnostics* (Nashville: Abingdon, 1972).

18. For Schmithals's view of the Galatian opponents, see pp. 13–64 in *Paul and the Gnostics* and his more recent article, "Judaisten in Galatien?" *ZNW* 74 (1983): 27–58.

19. Willi Marxsen, *Introduction to the New Testament: An Approach to Its Problems* (Oxford: Blackwell, 1968), 53–58.

20. So E. Yamauchi, *Pre-Christian Gnosticism,* 2d ed. (Grand Rapids: Baker, 1983).

21. R. C. Kroeger and C. C. Kroeger, *I Suffer Not a Woman: Rethinking 1 Timothy 2:11–15 in Light of Ancient Evidence* (Grand Rapids: Baker, 1992). For devastating criticisms of the Kroegers's method, see S. M. Baugh, "The Apostle among the Amazons," *WTJ* 56 (1994): 153–71; A. Wolters, "Review: *I Suffer Not a Woman,*" *CTJ* 28 (1993): 208–13; R. W. Yarbrough, "I Suffer Not a Woman: A Review Essay," *Presbyterion* 18 (1992): 25–33.

22. Arnold (*Colossian Syncretism*) appeals to magical papryi that are also post-New Testament (2nd and 3rd century A.D). He makes a good case, however, for the stability of invocations and curses over the centuries. Thus, the principle of dating must not be applied rigidly. On the other hand, I am less convinced when he appeals to mystery religions and Mithraism to inform the Colossian situation. The late date of the sources renders any influence improbable.

23. For a useful introduction to Greek rhetoric, see G. A. Kennedy, *New Testament Interpretation through Rhetorical Criticism* (Chapel Hill: University of North Carolina, 1984); cf. also B. L. Mack, *Rhetoric and the New Testament* (Minneapolis: Fortress, 1990); D. F. Watson and A. J. Hauser, *Rhetorical Criticism of the Bible: A Comprehensive Bibliography with Notes on History and Method* (Leiden: Brill, 1994).

24. H. D. Betz, *A Commentary on Paul's Letter to the Churches in Galatia* (Philadelphia: Fortress, 1979).

25. For an evaluation of Betz, see W. D. Davies, P. W. Meyer, and D. E. Aune, "Review: *Galatians: A Commentary on Paul's Letter to the Churches in Galatia* by Hans Dieter Betz," *Religious Studies Review* 7 (1981): 310–28.

26. See e.g. R. G. Hall, "The Rhetorical Outline for Galatians: A Reconsideration," *JBL* 106 (1987): 277–87; J. Smit, "The Letter of Paul to the Galatians: A Deliberative Speech," *NTS* 35 (1989): 1–26. The improbability of Smit's thesis is attested by his theory that Galatians 5:13–6:10 was inserted into the letter later by Paul.

27. This point is disputed. For an entrée into the discussion, see J. A. D. Weima, "What Does Aristotle Have to Do with Paul? An Evaluation of Rhetorical Criticism," *CTJ* 32 (1997): 464–65.

28. See especially the article by Weima, "What Does Aristotle," though I am less certain that Paul was uninstructed in Greek rhetoric. In contrast to Weima, I also think it is possible that Paul's negative comments about rhetoric in 1 Corinthians 2:1–5 should be restricted to his preaching, so that they do not rule out the use of rhetoric in his writings. I think Weima is correct, however, when he says that evidence is lacking to substantiate the use of such rhetoric in Paul.

29. S. E. Porter, "The Theoretical Justification for Application of Rhetorical Categories to Pauline Epistolary Literature," in *Rhetoric and the New Testament: Essays from the 1992 Heidelberg Conference*, ed. S. E. Porter and T. H. Olbricht (Sheffield: JSOT Press, 1993), 115–16.

30. For this point, see Weima, "What Does Aristotle," 467.

31. The prayer section often foreshadows important themes in the letter. See P. Schubert, *Form and Function of Pauline Thanksgivings* (Berlin: Töpelmann, 1939); P. T. O'Brien, *Introductory Thanksgivings in the Letters of Paul* (Leiden: Brill, 1977); G. P. Wiles, *Paul's Intercessory Prayers: Prayer Passages in the Letters of St. Paul* (London: Cambridge University Press, 1974).

32. For a method of tracing the argument in Paul, see T. R. Schreiner, *Interpreting the Pauline Epistles* (Grand Rapids: Baker, 1990), 97–126.

33. See J. A. D. Weima, *Neglected Endings: The Significance of Pauline Letter Closings,* JSNTSup 101 (Sheffield: Sheffield Academic Press, 1994).

34. My work here depends especially on the essay by J. A. D. Weima, "Gal. 6:11–18: A Hermeneutical Key to the Galatian Letter," *CTJ* 28 (1993): 90–107.

35. Ibid., 94.

36. For A. Schlatter's programmatic essay on doing biblical theology, see his "The Theology of the New Testament and Dogmatics," in *The Nature of New Testament Theology*, ed. and trans. R. Morgan (Naperville, Ill.: Allenson, 1973).

37. See e.g. T. R. Schreiner, "Did Paul Believe in Justification by Works? Another Look at Romans 2," *Bulletin for Biblical Research* 3 (1993): 131–58.

38. For a fuller discussion on how to apply the text to today's world, see W. J. Larkin, *Culture and Biblical Hermeneutics: Interpreting and Applying the Authoritative Word in a Relativistic Age* (Grand Rapids: Baker, 1988), esp. 325–60.

39. T. Theissen helpfully explores some principles for applying Paul to today in "Towards a Hermeneutic for Discerning Universal Moral Absolutes," *JETS* 36 (1993): 189–207.

40. For my understanding of the text, see T. R. Schreiner, "An Interpretation of 1 Timothy 2:9–15: A Dialogue with Scholarship," in *Women in the Church: A Fresh Analysis of 1 Timothy 2:9–15*, ed. A. J. Köstenberger, T. R. Schreiner, and H. S. Baldwin (Grand Rapids: Baker, 1995), 105–54.

Chapter 19

Interpreting the General Epistles

J. Daryl Charles
Taylor University

In considering the relationship most Christians—whether theologians or laypersons—have to the General Epistles (GEs), one is reminded of the proverbial story of "Lucky Jack." Jack, through no effort of his own, had stumbled upon a lump of gold. In time, however, this lump proved to be too impractical and burdensome to carry around; thus, he exchanged it for something more amenable to his perceived needs. First, he exchanged the gold for a horse, then the horse for a cow, then the cow for a pig, the pig for a goose, and finally the goose for a whetstone—which he eventually threw into the pond without any appreciable loss. What he now gained, so he thought, was complete freedom.

How long this state of delusion lasted and how excruciating the moment of awakening from that delusion are left to the imagination. Is it possible that the Christian community in effect has done the same thing in its handling of Scripture, by neglecting—or failing to appreciate—the contributions and wealth of insights afforded by the GEs? Have we not perhaps, like Jack, moved from exchange to exchange, from interpretation to interpretation, and consequently been disenfranchised of substantial riches—riches that the Christian community originally possessed? And have we not thereby lost—in our theology, studying and preaching—a treasure of inestimable value? Can the riches of the GEs, once again valued and newly appropriated, help equip the church, both in its pastoral and academic theology, as it navigates its way into the third millennium? Are there particular benefits that the church stands to accrue by retrieving the GEs from the periphery of the NT canon? And how might the social locations mirrored in these letters illuminate and speak to our own cultural situation?

At the close of the twentieth century, the GEs have the dubious distinction of being the Rodney Dangerfield of the NT corpus, rarely if ever afforded the respect or attention that they deserve. One anticipated objection by religious conservatives to such a claim might be that James is indeed used for preaching and teaching—and arguably, 1 Peter as well. But even if this concession is granted, few would deny that 2 Peter, Jude, and 1, 2 and 3 John are relatively—if not wholly—neglected. This state of affairs is readily confirmed when the GEs are placed beside the Synoptic Gospels, the Fourth Gospel, or the Pauline epistles. In the end, both among academic theologians and pastor-teachers, the GEs have suffered relative neglect and beckon the Christian community to "recover" them. Indeed, the neglect of which D. J. Rowston spoke twenty-five years ago remains and can be applied to the corpus of the GEs as a whole.[1] Those who dare to venture into the study of 2 Peter, Jude, or the Johannine epistles are seemingly few.[2]

Although the thesis of "recovery" can be applied at two levels—in pastoral use and in academic theology—the two domains are not unrelated. It is only natural that neglect in teaching and preaching follows the neglect of scholarship, since the guild serves as a resource for the pastor-teacher and the layperson. Stated negatively, recovering the GEs suggests overcoming misconceptions and particular biases about this valuable part of the NT canon. Stated positively, recovery means freshly discovering and appropriating the message, themes, and theology of these writings. It is to that specific task that this essay is largely devoted.

Obstacles to Interpretation

Why have the GEs been afforded low priority in the church's life and study? Initial exploration of this phenomenon necessitates that we revisit formative influences on our reading of the NT. James D. G. Dunn, through his commentary on the "early Catholic" thesis, reveals basic assumptions that have guided NT scholarship for much of the present century:

> We must observe first the historical fact that no Christian church or group has in the event treated the New Testament writing as uniformly canonical.
> Perhaps most arresting of all, we must remind ourselves that . . . orthodoxy itself is based on a canon within a canon. . . . Certainly, if the New Testament serves any continuing usefulness for Christians today, nothing less than that canon within the canon will do. . . . Nor would I want to say . . . that the New Testament writings are canonical because they were more inspired than other later Christian writings. Almost every Christian who wrote in an authoritative way during the first two centuries of Christianity claimed the same sort of inspiration for their writing as Paul. . . . And I would want to insist that in not a few compositions Martin Luther and John Wesley, for example, were as, if not more[,] inspired . . . than the author of II Peter.[3]

By this view it is understood that there is little or no difference in the writings of the first two centuries with respect to claims to apostolic authority and right to canonicity. Any authority the NT writings might possess inheres in a "canon within a canon." A perusal of most standard introductions to the NT quickly confirms this and cognate assumptions about the NT documents. Willi Marxsen, in his *Introduction to the New Testament*, resolutely states what is a sine qua non for critical scholarship:

> If it is possible to allot the separate writings [of the NT] their place in the various lines of tradition and to understand them in their historical context, then a problem which has often been hotly disputed becomes considerably less important—that of pseudonymity. So long as we assume the traditional idea of canonicity and accept as permanently normative only what derives from the apostles or the disciples of the apostles, "not genuine" is a serious charge to make. . . . But if we admit its pseudonymity we are far more likely to place the letter in its particular historical context and to be able to understand it. . . . Whether we draw the line at the beginning of the second century or earlier is simply a matter of choice. . . . We could perhaps exchange 2 Peter for the Didache and Jude for 1 Clement, but this is of no significance as far as basic principles are concerned, and we should therefore not make it a problem.[4]

In 1958, Marxsen published his influential *Der 'Frühkatholizismus' im Neuen Testament*—roughly concurrent with the period in which German NT scholar Ernst Käsemann was making inroads in biblical scholarship with the "early Catholic" thesis.[5] That it is impossible to explore the GEs—Jude and the Petrine epistles in particular—without passing the tollbooth of "early Catholicism" is evidenced by several factors, notably the relative neglect of the GEs as well as the highly derivative nature of commentary associated with these writings. Few, it would seem, have questioned the need even to pay the toll in the first place. While an "early Catholic" reading of the NT is by no means confined to the GEs, it is here that it is applied in its most concentrated form. To use the term *Catholic* in connection with a NT document is to suggest that for biblical scholars a writing is viewed as a postapostolic development in the life of the church—a period several generations removed from the apostles and eyewitnesses of the Lord. In his massive *Die Mitte der Zeit*, Siegfried Schulz categorically asserts:

> The early Catholicism of the New Testament cuts off the foregoing temporary period of . . . early Christianity, with its characteristic apocalyptic approach to the Parousia. . . . Strictly speaking, early Catholicism no more belongs to the early church, which conceived of itself in apocalyptic terms.[6]

Likewise, for Käsemann, perhaps the most influential proponent of "early Catholicism," it becomes "apparent that nascent catholicism was the historically necessary outcome of an original Christianity whose apocalyptic expectation had not been fulfilled."[7]

"Early Catholicism," by definition, purports to reflect the institutionalization of the postapostolic church, wherein the reader encounters the codification of beliefs into creedal confessions (the *fides qua creditur*) and the notion of a canon for the purposes of defending the faith against gnostic heresy. Evidences of the need for a teaching office—which replaces the charismatic work of the Spirit—and the church's growing institutionalization—evidenced by a growing dichotomy of clergy and laity—are features of the postapostolic mentality. Also characterizing this transition from earliest Christianity to the so-called ancient church is the disappearance of the imminent expectation of Christ's Second Coming and the emergence of a legalistic "endurance ethic."

A poignant example of how the "early Catholic" interpretive grid has colored NT commentary on the GEs is traditional commentary on 2 Peter. Addressing the Berliner Gemeinschaft für Evangelische[8] Theologie[9] in 1952, Käsemann concluded that "the Second Epistle of Peter is from beginning to end a document expressing an early Catholic viewpoint and is perhaps the most dubious writing in the canon."[10] An even less enthusiastic assessment of 2 Peter comes from Gunter Klein, in an essay titled "Der zweite Petrusbrief und der neutestamentliche Kanon":

> The author does a miserable job of presenting his case. . . . He wants to restore the fragile doctrine of last things to a new credibility, but he is only able to destroy it yet further. In spite of how vigorously he asserts himself, he is basically helpless. . . . The dubious manner with which he treats his subject is a clear reflection of the writer's own lack of self-assurance.[11]

While 2 Peter alone is not the focus of our study, scholarly attitudes toward this epistle—attitudes that are not confined to a minority of NT scholars—graphically demonstrate the "identity problem" of the GEs. Klein concludes:

> It is precisely such a New Testament writer with this sort of mentality—the only person [in the New Testament] defending the newly emergent canonical awareness—who fits our idea of a unified canon the least. . . . This writer could not have possibly dreamt that his own letter would join—and in fact follow—in the same canonical collection the letters of Paul, whose writings he held to be suspect. . . . For this reason, the clearly inescapable question puts our assurance of faith to the test, namely, whether we can ultimately consider the epistle of 2 Peter, with its conceptualization of canon, to be canonical.[12]

The rather uncomplementary view of the GEs, finding its most vivid expression in commentary on 2 Peter[13] (with Jude not far behind), leaves one with a settled impression. Among biblical scholars the supposed presence of "early Catholicism" in the NT[14] is the theological equivalent of eating spinach or kissing one's sister. While by no means the real thing, these documents—for better or worse—are part of canonical realities nonetheless, and therefore, must be tolerated. Thus R. H. Fuller:

> Not all aspects of early Catholicism are salutary, e.g., its conventional bourgeois morality, its propositional understanding of faith, its relegation of the eschatological hope to the last chapter of dogmatics, the total suppression of the charismata. But these writings are balanced by the presence of earlier apostolic writings in the New Testament, viz., the gospel tradition, the kerygmatic traditions in Acts and the genuine Pauline letters.[15]

The GEs, then, would appear to have earned the "Rodney Dangerfield" moniker. This lack of respect is owing initially to the assumptions of critical scholarship—assumptions that have relegated the GEs to less than authoritative status in the NT canon. Given this "half embrace" by critical scholars, it is no wonder that the GEs labor under a heavy load. Not only do they constitute a generally neglected part of the canon, but by virtue of their reputed subapostolic origin[16] they have consistently been thought to lack authority and theological value.[17] This devaluation has meant a considerable pastoral and theological loss. In practical terms this loss has blunted the church in terms of ethics, doctrinal definition, the ability to confront heresy and heterodox teaching, and the character of pastoral ministry—all of which are pressing issues in the contemporary church.

In addition to this flawed theological perspective, a further cause for neglect of the GEs is the tendency of historical-critical scholarship to overlook their literary and paraenetic character. In these letters literary-rhetorical conventions are borrowed and artfully crafted in such a way as to mirror implicitly the social location of the readership in ways that might escape the merely theological eye.[18]

If, by way of example, James' allusion to Abraham, Rahab, Lot, and Job reflects contemporary Jewish usage of tradition material more than mere allusion to OT narratives, our appreciation of the particular hermeneutic on display may lead our interpretation of James in a slightly different direction.[19] Similarly, if Jude's near-verbatim citation of 1 Enoch (dating ca. mid-second century B.C.) is understood less as his personal veneration of Enochic literature (presupposed uniformly by critical scholarship) and more as a possible literary device based on the readers' familiarity with Enochic literature, it may therefore be seen as part of an overall strategy that has as its focus first-century Palestinian Jewish-Christians who need a hortatory reminder from paradigms of the past. And if we view the strikingly pagan and seemingly "unchristian" metaphysical and ethical language in 2 Peter as a borrowing of contemporary—specifically Stoic—categories with which to admonish believers in a pagan cultural environment (e.g., Asia Minor), the writer's literary strategy, and hence, the readers' social location, becomes more recognizable.

Contrary to what mainstream critical scholarship has promoted, the GEs represent a maturing, not a degenerating, phase of Christian theological development.[20] Thomas Oden has put the matter succinctly:

> The crucial question before the churches then was: How, in a period of cross-cultural pluralism, syncretism, political alienation, and vast historical mutation, is it possible to pass the tradition learned from the earliest Christians on to succeeding generations? How can we teach it accurately without distortions, and how can we defend it against interpretations that would profoundly diminish it?[21]

The GEs raise—and address—questions of a critical nature that reverberate today. How, amidst cultural and ideological pluralism, can classic Christian faith be affirmed in a cultural climate of lawlessness, moral skepticism, apostasy, and Gnostic religion? What theological and pastoral insights are to be gleaned from a fresh and enthusiastic reading of the GEs?

Before such questions can be addressed, however, basic interpretive issues present themselves. How do the GEs function within the corpus of the NT? What is their literary character? What important themes emerge? What social situations and pastoral needs are being mirrored, and what sorts of strategies are employed by the writers to address these particular needs? It is to the matter of interpretive strategy that we now turn.

Interpretive Issues in the General Epistles

USE OF THE OLD TESTAMENT IN THE GENERAL EPISTLES

The GEs reflect a conspicuous debt to the OT[22] and to contemporary Jewish exegesis of the OT. They are rich in their appropriation of characters, events, and imagery associated with Israel's history. In the main it is the literary tendency of the GEs to display their relationship to the OT technically through indirect allusions rather than direct citations. This is frequently found in the context of moral and hortatory instruction on the part of the writers.

Unlike the Pauline epistles, many of which contain an explicitly theological formulation of doctrinal matters, the GEs mirror the practical dimensions of moral tensions arising from the church's contact with surrounding culture. And unlike the Gospel narratives, whose apologetic aim is to demonstrate that Jesus Christ is the fulfillment of the law, the prophets, and the writings, the GEs typically are paraenetic in character, alluding to the OT for the sake of ethical illustration. Where a markedly Palestinian Jewish-Christian substratum is evident, such as in James and Jude, a stronger indebtedness to OT and Jewish tradition is exhibited. By comparison, where a more Gentile social environment is suggested, as in 2 Peter, the literary strategy of the writer calls for more numerous touch-points with pagan culture.[23]

More recent scholarship, stimulated in no small way by interest in Christian origins, Jewish apocalyptic, and the Dead Sea Scrolls, has devoted itself largely to the question of the NT writers' exegetical technique. The result has meant a fruitful yield for the student of the NT. Creative and penetrating interpretations arise from the awareness that the writers of the NT are in conversation with Jewish contemporaries, evidence of which suggests familiarity with and borrowing of contemporary exegetical methods. A fresh appreciation for the literary-rhetorical strategies being applied in the GEs is helpful in refining the interpreter's perspective. Elucidating the extent to which the language and thought-world of both the OT and contemporary Judaism pervade the GEs is the aim of the discussion that follows.

An investigation of NT dependence on the OT is no cut-and-dried matter. Intertextual relationships are complex and often defy neat categorization.

Alone determining whether we are dealing with a quotation or an allusion is at times problematic. Moreover, the citation or allusion, as for example in the case of James 4:5, may be unidentified. Thus, proof of literary borrowing can be elusive. As already noted, the main lines of recent research have followed the question of exegetical method. This has been particularly the case in tracing current Jewish exegetical practice in Pauline literature, Acts, and the Gospels—for example, in the use of formula quotations, collections of OT texts (testimonia), and the role of the LXX in citation.[24] More recent attempts have been made to uncover the underlying midrashic structure of passages in the GEs.[25] The social location of "midrashic" or paraphrastic use of the OT is typically found in current events, with a scriptural allusion serving as a means of illustration or reapplication. Certain phenomena in the GEs are best understood in light of contemporary midrashic techniques and not merely the actual OT passage from which the tradition derives. A comparison of extrabiblical Jewish writings that are roughly contemporary to the NT documents offers impressive material parallels.[26]

In addition to paraphrastic or midrashic use, the NT makes typological use of the OT. In the GEs this usage is less for explicitly theological than for ethical reasons. A typological exegetical approach grows out of the conviction that contained within Israel's history—history that is inscripturated—are all the principal forms of divine activity that point to the ultimate purposes of God.[27] The theological "center" of this, of course, is the life, death, and resurrection of Jesus Christ. Beyond christological or theological typology, however, lies moral typology. Types or foreshadows find various correspondences to antitypes by way of illustration or comparison. That is, OT characters and events project themselves in ways that allow them to serve as paradigms in the Christian paraenetic tradition. It is the abundance of this category—use of the moral paradigm—that makes the corpus of the GEs such a rich and distinct contribution to the NT canon.

Much of the illustrative material in James, for example, consists of moral exhortation to endure as the people of God. With no direct or discernible OT passages in support, Abraham and Rahab, the prophets, Job, and Elijah are cited as exemplars.[28] (Extrabiblical Jewish traditions frequently "fill in the gap" in explaining the context of those particular references.) In 1 Peter, Sarah is the model wife, submissive to her husband's authority, while Noah is a paradigm of patience amidst persecution.[29] In Jude and 2 Peter, the fallen angels, Sodom and Gomorrah, and Balaam function in the context of evocative warnings to the readers.[30] Noah and Lot illustrate in 2 Peter the need for perseverance amidst pagan surroundings, while unbelieving Israel, Cain, Korah, and Michael the archangel are added to the catalog of paradigms in Jude.[31] And in 1 John, Cain is a type of anyone who does not love his brother.[32]

As it turns out, the moral fiber of the community surfaces as a primary theme in virtually all of the GEs. Admonitions to good works (James), patient endurance (1 Peter), faithfulness (Jude), virtuous living (2 Peter), and undivided commitments (1 John) are the didactic trajectory of these letters.

USE OF NONCANONICAL TRADITION MATERIAL IN THE GENERAL EPISTLES

Of the GEs, James, 1 Peter, and Jude in particular reflect a conspicuous debt to Jewish exegetical tradition. In their use of both the Hebrew Scriptures and noncanonical tradition material, they mirror a Jewish religio-cultural matrix to which their message as well as mode of literary expression are owing.[33] While evincing continuity with contemporary exegetical practice, these epistles also exhibit considerable variation in exegetical tendencies.

For example, the arguments set forth in James, 1 Peter, and Jude betray the hand of a skilled haggadist, exercised in the application of Jewish midrash for didactic purposes, not unlike what one finds in rabbinic literature. Jude and 2 Peter contain instances of prophetic typology that are brought to bear on the Christian community for the purpose of condemning the apostate and exhorting the faithful. James unfolds as a collection of loosely knit paraenetic sayings cast in the form of a diatribe for a highly rhetorical effect. Both Jude and 2 Peter offer a targumic assessment of OT characters, while simultaneously making use of pagan proverbs or legends (in addition to a Stoic catalog of virtues in the latter) that underscore the reality of divine truth. Jude and 1 Peter contain christologized allusions—explicit in the former and faint in the latter—to apocalyptic writings of sectarian Judaism. And 1 John at times shows conceptual resemblance to the literature of Qumran in its theological dualism.

Within the great exegetical diversity on display in the GEs, one feature stands out. Indirect allusions to characters or events in the OT, rather than explicit citations, are the general rule. These nondirect allusions are representative of contemporary Jewish exegetical procedure. An awareness of this "indirect" approach to exegesis has been shown to be indispensable for the student of the NT. Thereby we acquire insight into the intimate relationship between Jewish and Christian hermeneutics and the Jewish matrix out of which the early church emerged.

The relevance of noncanonical tradition material in the NT is important not just for NT studies as a whole but especially the GEs, where pastoral arguments are creatively marshalled for the Christian community as it moves from a Palestinian to an increasingly Gentile cultural milieu.[34]

The history of the interpretation of the GEs, when not neglect, has not infrequently been one of misunderstanding. Most readers of the NT, puzzled by cryptic references to Enoch, Noah, Balaam, Cain, Michael the archangel, the devil, the rebellious angels, and a slate of OT characters, only naturally gravitate toward other parts of the NT, which require less contextualizing on the part of the reader.

Although this obstacle, coupled with the sheer diversity of Jewish tradition material found in the GEs, tends to intimidate students of the NT, the significance of noncanonical sources for biblical exegesis can scarcely be overstated. Their value lies in their ability to clarify theological concepts, inform us of Jewish religious history, elucidate Jewish attitudes toward the Scriptures, and most importantly, illuminate the first-century Jewish-Christian context of which the GEs are a part. In the GEs, theological truth is clothed in literary arguments of the day. Literary sources, all part of a well-calculated literary strategy, are marshalled with a view of addressing urgent pastoral needs. Lessons from the past bear forcefully on the present, with enormous implications for the future. It is with an appreciation for this literary strategy on the part of the writer that the following discussion proceeds.

Because any discussion of NT use of noncanonical tradition material refracts in some way on the question of canon and inspiration, guiding presuppositions about the biblical text are to be detected. What Jewish religious works were regarded as divinely inspired, and thus, normative for faith and practice? By what criteria were these revered works judged sacred, and in what sense did the sacred books—the "canonical" writings—possess divine authority? Such questions raised by the NT use of Jewish tradition material constitute part of our critical examination that requires some reflection.

The GEs present the reader with a remarkably clear window through which to observe the considerable influence and rich variety of first-century Jewish hermeneutics. The use of Jewish midrash as a didactic tool (whether the pesharim of Qumran that contemporize the prophetic corpus or the rabbinic model of moralizing through historical paradigms), paraenetic sayings, typology, and apocalyptic all surface in the GEs. These exegetical approaches reflect both language and themes of the Hebrew Scriptures, however contemporized and modified, so as to make them relevant for the Christian community.

Renewed interest in Christian origins, modern study of Jewish pseudepigrapha, and insights from Qumran literature—already noted—reveal a notably sophisticated Judaism concurrent with the early Christian church. This sophistication was adapted into the NT writings by the early Christian disciples, the acknowledgement of which overturns particular literary assumptions that governed NT scholarship earlier this century.[35] In truth, the writings of the NT (the GEs in particular), as well as intertestamental Jewish literature, indicate a highly cultured status of Palestinian Jews and Christians, as James Charlesworth[36] has ably shown. And given the fact that the GEs traditionally have been associated with the acknowledged "pillars" of the Jerusalem church—Peter, James, and John (Gal. 2:9)—in addition to a brother of James (Jude 1), it is justified to assume that the writings attributed to them mirror the Jewish mind both in Palestine and the diaspora. Thus it is that some scholars view the GEs as "Jewish-Christian tractates."

It is less with a movement than with a Jewish mind-set that this facet of NT interpretation is concerned.

All told, one encounters in the GEs a pluriform assortment of OT citations, OT allusions, secular proverbs, and extracanonical tradition material. Because indirect allusions to OT characters and events rather than explicit quotations tend to color the fabric of these writings, the logical question of exegetical method comes into focus. To observe method is to gain understanding into the religio-cultural milieu from whence it derives. While biblical scholarship in the main has categorized first-century Jewish hermeneutical practice according to three broad types—a literalistic interpretation (found in rabbinic literature), allegorizing (as practiced by Philo), and the use of midrash (as practiced both by mainstream and sectarian Judaism)—it is the last, haggadic midrash, that is of primary interest.

The four dense volumes comprising Strack and Billerbeck's *Kommentar zum Neuen Testament aus Talmud und Midrasch*[37] have long been the primary source for parallels between rabbinic literature and the NT. Rabbinic interpretation of the OT Scriptures traditionally have been designated "midrash" (from the Hebrew verb *derash*, "to search out," "to seek"). Midrashic interpretations of the Bible have as their goal the contemporary application of the Scriptures, an "actualization" of a text, for later generations. Jewish midrash can either be halakhic, that is, legalistic, or haggadic, that is, moral and historical, in its teaching emphasis. It is the latter category that occurs with relative frequency in the GEs.

Haggadic midrash employs historical anecdotes and legendary material set within a didactic context. So it is that paradigms or types (*hypodeigma*, James 5:10, 2 Pet. 2:6; *hypogrammos*, 1 Pet. 2:21; *deigma*, Jude 7) abound in the GEs—for example, Rahab, Abraham, Job, the prophets, and Elijah in James; Noah in 1 and 2 Peter; the fallen angels, Sodom and Gomorrah, and Balaam in 2 Peter and Jude; Cain in Jude and 1 John; and Michael the archangel, Cain, Balaam and Korah in Jude. The reader comes to recognize that the significance of midrashic material for the GEs is indeed immense.

Moving away from mainstream Judaism roughly contemporary to the early church, we encounter another literary convention that leaves its imprint on the GEs. Apocryphal apocalyptic writings of the second century B.C. to the second century A.D. such as 1 Enoch, Jubilees, the Testaments of the Twelve Patriarchs, 4 Ezra, and 2 Baruch indulge in apocalyptic "revelations" ascribed to heroes from Israel's past—Enoch, Moses, Isaiah, Ezra, and the like. While the significance of Jewish apocalyptic for the study of the NT is undeniable, a proper balance of perspective is necessary for their assessment. In general terms, the presence of apocalyptic elements, concepts, and imagery can be said to derive more from literary conventions associated with Jewish culture than from the purely theological orientation of Jewish writers themselves, many of whom were wrestling with the seeming lack of fulfillment of the divine promise as Persian, Greek, and Roman empires marched by with agonizing slowness. First and 2 Peter and Jude incorporate imagery and motifs that are part and parcel of Jewish apocalyptic.[38] In all three writings the cryptic world of the fallen angels is alluded to for the sake of illustration and yet remains tantalizingly unqualified. In 1 Peter, Christ's proclamation of conquest to the "imprisoned spirits" is depicted in much the same way that 1 Enoch portrays the vindication of the righteous and judgment of the wicked.[39] This is done parenthetically and in veiled fashion, whereas in Jude and 2 Peter the reference is explicit.[40]

Although the importance of Jewish apocalyptic for understanding the NT cannot be denied, neither should it be exaggerated. Whereas apocalyptic language and concepts are to be found in the NT, the reverse is not the case, due to eminently theological reasons. Thus, we are concerned foremost with the use of literary style and convention rather than evidence for the NT writer's wholesale embracing of a Jewish apocalyptic worldview and theological orientation.

Apart from authenticity, the focal point of most commentary on Jude and 2 Peter is the obvious literary relation between the two letters. The general theme of apostasy runs throughout both writings. In Jude it would appear less advanced than in 2 Peter, where "false teachers" are compared to "false prophets" of ancient Israel. However, Jude accents the irrevocability of judgment, whereas in 2 Peter both judgment's certainty and deliverance of a righteous remnant are stressed. Both letters counter a movement toward apostasy with a literary strategy of midrashic typology that borrows heavily from Jewish tradition material. They differ in that Jude reflects a distinctly Palestinian provenance, whereas the language of 2 Peter appears to address a more Hellenized audience.

Literary dependence, whether one argues for the priority of Jude, 2 Peter, or a common third source, should not obscure the difference in literary strategy between the two writings. The Jewish flavor of Jude's style and illustrations suggests a markedly Jewish-Christian matrix to which his readers belong; hence, the appropriate paradigms—namely, Israel's deliverance from Egypt, fallen angels, Sodom and Gomorrah, and the cities of the plain, Moses, Michael the archangel, and the devil, Cain, Balaam and Korah, and "Enoch, the seventh from Adam." Second Peter, on the other hand, while incorporating some of the same, reflects a conspicuously pagan social environment; hence the use of a Stoic catalog of virtues, a reference to "Tartarus," Lot's depiction as a "righteous" sufferer amidst pagan debauchery, Balaam as a spiritual prostitute, the use of two common secular proverbs, and flood-fire typology couched in Stoic terms that is directed against moral relativists—all of which elements form the backbone of the writer's apologetic.[41]

Jude clothes his argument, by which the orthodox and the apostate are contradistinguished, in conspicuously Jewish-Christian apocalyptic garb. To this end two sets of triplets are employed. A hardened Israel, the angels of

God who deserted their glory, and Sodom and Gomorrah share one thing in common: they each departed and consequently were disenfranchised. The notion of fallen angels as "imprisoned spirits" is well developed in Jewish apocalyptic literature. Lists of historical paradigms depicting hardheartedness are commonplace in intertestamental literature. Among the most frequently cited in these lists are apostate Israel, Sodomites, the fallen angels, Assyria, the giants, Korah, and the Canaanites. These examples are employed as a teaching device in the Apocrypha, the pseudepigrapha, and in rabbinic literature as well—for example, 1 Enoch 1–36, T. Naph. 2:8–4:3; Jub. 20:2–7; 3 Macc. 3:7; Sir. 16:5–15; CD 2:14–3:12; and m.Sanh. 10:3.

As an elaboration of the apostates' irrationality, Jude casts them as polar opposites of Michael the archangel, who though possessing incomparable authority exhibited striking humility and subordination. The tradition upon which the conflict between Michael and the devil reputedly is based, the Assumption of Moses, is apocryphal in origin, perhaps circulating in oral form during the first century and having numerous parallels in Qumran literature. The Assumption, which admits no apparent connection to Deuteronomy 34 but incorporates imagery from Zechariah 3, is known to us through several subapostolic sources, initially through Origen (De prin. 3.2.1)

Jude's description of the judgment of the ungodly includes a near-verbatim citation of 1 Enoch 1:9, a pseudepigraphal expansion of theophany statements that occur with frequency throughout the OT—most notably, the Sinai-theophany tradition of Deuteronomy 33. In Jude as in 1 Enoch, theophany and judgment merge in response to the apostate. The fate of the wicked is certain. Further borrowing of Jewish apocalyptic imagery surfaces in the same contextual flow, Jude 12–13 (cf. 1 Enoch 67:5–7; 80:2–8), where the apostate are cast as "wandering stars."[42]

Absent the distinctly Palestinian flavor that is manifest in Jude, 2 Peter relies on extrabiblical tradition material with a pagan social context in view. The christianized version of a Hellenistic catalog of virtues in 1:5–7 is representative of this strategy.[43] To the list of characteristic Stoic virtues such as moral excellence, knowledge, self-control, and piety are added the Christian virtues of faith, endurance, brotherly love, and agape. The present situation, in which the writer counters a "faith" devoid of ethical fiber, calls for a rhetorical response that is immediately apparent. The Petrine catalog mirrors a discussion of virtues commonplace among Hellenistic philosophers, with the addition of the Christian ethical distinctive—faith and love—that the secular ethic wholly misses. Furthermore, it is plausible to argue, as does Jerome Neyrey,[44] that the general structure of 2 Peter suggests itself as drawing inspiration from a contemporary anti-Epicurean polemic which builds upon four apologetic arguments—ordered cosmology, restricted human autonomy, predestination, and moral accountability.

In 2 Peter, the profile of apostasy (chapter 2) shows the greatest degree of literary relationship to Jude. Whereas the historical paradigms in the latter underscore irrevocable judgment; in the former they highlight both certain judgment and deliverance of a righteous remnant.[45] That the situation behind 2 Peter calls for a unique response is shown by the presence of Noah and Lot as midrashic types of God's merciful deliverance. That Lot is a "model" of righteous suffering is rooted not in the OT narrative alone (cf. Genesis 19), rather in extrabiblical Jewish tradition, where he appears alongside Noah, Abraham, Jacob, and Joseph as a "virtuous" man (see, e.g., Wis. 10:4–10). In 2 Peter, Lot is "righteous" not so much by example as by comparison. The syntax of 2 Peter 2:4–10 clarifies the proper sense in which Lot is *dikaios*: "If God . . . rescued Lot . . . , who was vexed . . . , then he knows how to rescue" (vv. 4–9).

Taken together, the ungodly in 2 Peter are reminiscent of one noted OT character—Balaam, "who loved the wages of evil" (2:15). Balaam is notorious in Jewish tradition material; he reflects a Jewish mind-set that is fascinated—and repulsed—by the prophet who led Israel into idolatry (Philo, Vit. Mos. 1.295–99; Jos., Ant. 4.6.6; cf. Num. 31:16) and thus had no place in the life to come (m.Sanh. 10:2). In rabbinic literature Balaam is the antithesis of Abraham (e.g., m.'Abot 5:19). Absent from 2 Peter are Cain and Korah as paradigms (cf. Jude 11), the former serving as "type and teacher" of ungodliness in Jewish tradition (Philo, *De post. Caini* 38), the latter being arguably the most arresting case of insubordination in the OT due to his opposition to Moses, the man who walked with God. With Balaam as their spiritual mentor, the apostate are vividly depicted by means of a double metaphor—a dog returning to its vomit and a pig returning to the mud. While the dog metaphor finds a parallel in the Book of Proverbs 26:11), the pig metaphor finds its analogue in the Egyptian Story of Ahiqar: "My son, you were to me like a pig which had been in a hot bath . . . , and when it was out and saw a filthy pool went down and wallowed in it."[46]

It is not infrequently claimed that the language and thought-world of the Qumran community resemble that of the Fourth Gospel. Less frequent, however, is the link to 1 John established. According to an earlier generation of scholars, 1 John was to be dated late, and therefore, was "Gnostic" in its conceptualization. The discovery of the Dead Sea Scrolls, however, changed this complexion. The form of expression in 1 John is strikingly similar to the Qumran outlook. Principal among these parallels is a theological dualism that expresses itself in several ways—namely, sons/children of light and truth versus sons/children of darkness, deceit and the devil; spirits of truth and light vs. spirits of deceit and darkness; angels of truth versus angels of darkness (1 John 3:10,13,24–25; 4:5–6,17; 3:18–21,24; 5:10; cf. 1 QS 1:9–10; 2:2,5).

Several thematic links are also to be detected—that is, angels, spirits, and the devil (1 John 3:8–10; 4:1–6; cf. 1 QS 3:13–14,20–22; 5:20–21,24; 9:14);

love, community, and koinonia (1 John 1:3–7; 2:9–11; 3:10; 4:7–12; cf. 1 QS 1:1,12,16; 2:22; 3:12; 5:1; 8:1,5; knowledge (in 1 John, *oida* is used eleven times and *ginosko* fourteen times; cf. 1 QS 4:26; 1 QH 12:11; 13:18–19; 14:12–13,25; 16:2–7); confession of sin and cleansing from lies (1 John 1:6–10; 2:13; cf. 1 QS 1:23–26; 4:20–22; 11:9–10; 1 QH 1:21–26; 3:23–25; 17:18–19); and hatred of the world (1 John 3:13; cf. 1 QH 2:12–17,23–25; 3:6–8; 4:7–27; 5:1–32).

From this comparison it should be emphasized that 1 John is not to be regarded as a theological development of Qumran theology, despite the many similarities. Rather, the parallels help to elucidate the first-century Palestinian and Jewish mind-set. We are once more thereby reminded that the writers of the NT did not give expression to their ideas in a cultural vacuum but were very much an extension of a particular religious-cultural milieu.

It has been the lot of the GEs to be regarded largely as pseudonymous writings.[47] Critical scholarship has traditionally accepted the presence of pseudonymity in the NT on the basis of its purported widespread use by heterodox groups both before and after the Christian advent. In this regard the distinction between form and content, between literary convention and theological orientation, deserves recognition. In general terms, pseudonymity normally took on the form of apocalypses rather than epistles, though samples of both genres are extant. Moreover, that pseudepigrapha flourished in some sectarian Jewish circles is no sure indication that the NT writers would have sanctioned their usage.[48] Indeed, Paul would seem to indicate the opposite. In his Thessalonian correspondence he admonishes the Christian community "not to become . . . alarmed by some prophecy, report or letter supposed to have come from us, saying that the day of the Lord has already come. Don't let anyone deceive you in any way" (2 Thess. 2:2–3). Concluding 2 Thessalonians, the apostle asserts: "I, Paul, write this greeting in my own hand, which is the distinguishing mark in all my letters. This is how I write" (3:17–18). The implication is clear: a letter falsely ascribed to him could only be designed to deceive. As Donald Guthrie notes, one's literary method must be consonant with the message itself; pseudepigraphy as a literary convention would have been constructed to deceive some if not all of its readers[49] and poses an ethical dilemma.[50]

Patristic evidence, too readily dismissed by the modern critic, would also weigh against the legitimacy of a pseudonymity hypothesis.[51] Material judged to be heretical as well as authorship judged to be inauthentic would have disqualified a work from canonical consideration.[52] There is no example of a known pseudepigraphal work being granted canonical status in the NT.[53] The fact that Jude and 2 Peter engendered some doubts in the early church was due in part to the fact that spurious works had circulated in the first and second centuries. Attestation of both orthodoxy and apostolicity[54] plays a pivotal role in the adjudication of writings vying for NT canonical status.[55]

Jude is the only instance of which extracanonical tradition material is cited verbatim and authoritatively in the NT. Rather than conform our notion of inspiration and canonicity to the presence of one known extra-canonical citation (Jude 14–15 = 1 Enoch 1:9), it is preferable to assess this one citation in light of the author's broader literary strategy and the twin criteria of orthodoxy and apostolicity that historically and consensually have guided the church in matters of interpretation. It is entirely plausible that Jude makes "inspired" use of extracanonical tradition material based on the background and needs of his audience.[56]

Recovering What Has Been Lost

Interpretive and exegetical issues are not free-floating; rather, they illuminate authorial intent and literary-rhetorical strategy, and they inform us of the readers' social location and pastoral need. In the GEs, ethics receives a higher profile than doctrine.[57] The hortatory character of the writings reflects the struggle between faith and culture, thereby underscoring the abiding value of these writings for the Christian community.[58]

In perhaps no area of Western Christendom is the failure to take account of itself more apparent than in the area of self-discipline and moral formation. Stated bluntly, pastoral obligations of the Christian community as they relate to surrounding therapeutic culture and religious anomie have been largely abandoned. Miming common culture, the church would rather make people feel good about themselves than have them conform to ethical and communal norms. The GEs very much counter this tendency.

Attention has already been directed to the examples of moral typology in James, 1 and 2 Peter, and Jude as well as divided commitments in the Johannine epistles. Together these serve as a warning to the Christian community that, inter alia, (1) deeds must accompany and validate true faith; (2) an abiding ethical standard exists by which the community must be measured; (3) lawlessness and a cheapening of divine grace are not tolerable; and (4) divine wrath awaits those who persist in disobedience. Paraenetic language is employed again and again in the GEs to remind the community of its ethical obligations.

Contrary to the assumption of mainstream historical-critical scholarship, the church in the GEs is not mirroring the formation and hardening of ecclesiastical offices; rather, the members of the community themselves are admonished—in the strongest terms—to administer discipline.[59] Correlatively, the Holy Spirit has not been relegated to an office; rather, it is presumed that the members of the community are to respond to the Spirit's leading themselves.[60] It is a scandal when the Christian community divorces morality from the message of divine grace. The result is an absurd contradiction, a denial of the faith that is being purported. Such "maligning of the truth" must be dealt with in the strongest terms pastorally, for it undermines the community's witness.[61]

The same unwillingness within the contemporary church to embrace controversy in moral matters applies to the sphere of doctrine as well. Orthopraxy and orthodoxy go hand in hand. Tragically, Western Christendom, desperately striving for accommodation, demonstrates a reticence to engage in theological reflection and theological recovery. Religion degenerates to the point at which it becomes indistinguishable from broader culture. Unquestionably, one of the most fundamental of issues confronting the North American church—conservative or liberal—is what it means to be a confessional church in a pluralistic world.

> Christianity is by nature confessional. The Church—at least the Church Militant—never exists apart from a cultural context. The longstanding alliance between Protestantism and American democracy makes the Church particularly vulnerable to a confusion of creed and context, of confessional status and pluralistic environment. Our quandary over the confession by which we live and the pluralistic culture in which we live is sometimes like trying to play football on a field without sidelines and end zones.[62]

Thomas Oden has quipped that "the leading candidate for 'most ugly issue in theology today' is without question heresy; hence, we avoid it like the plague."[63] And why? Because, in Oden's words, "We are programmed to affable religious permissiveness and the rhetoric of compliance. . . . Our least favored interaction pattern as Christian teachers is the role of a harsh judge."[64] And yet to affirm and confess belief is to negate what it opposes. And what does the NT oppose? The GEs afford us a glimpse—and a frequently graphic one at that. What one professes matters enormously.[65]

The legend of "Lucky Jack" is by no means the last word on the GEs. The church poised on the advent of the Third Millennium has much to gain from a recovery of documents that for too long have languished on the periphery of NT canon. It is high time that the church appropriate the riches that await her as a result of fresh examination of the GEs. Surely it is no exaggeration to suggest that there have been periods during the church's history when these writings were the most relevant books in all the NT.

Bibliography

Bauckham, R. J. "James, 1 and 2 Peter, Jude," in D. A. Carson and H. G. M. Williamson, eds., *It Is Written: Scripture Citing Scripture. Essay in Honour of B. Lindars.* Cambridge: Cambridge University, 1988. Pages 303–17.

Beckwith, R. *The Old Testament Canon of the New Testament Church and Its Background in Early Judaism.* Grand Rapids: Eerdmans, 1985.

Charles, J. D. *Literary Strategy in the Epistle of Jude.* Scranton/London/Toronto: University of Scranton/Associated University Presses, 1993.

———. "Noncanonical Writings, Citations in the General Epistles." R. P. Martin and P. H. Davids, eds. *Dictionary of the Later New Testament.* Downers Grove/Leicester: InterVarsity, 1997. Pages 814–20.

————. "The Old Testament in the General Epistles." R. P. Martin and P. H. Davids, eds. *Dictionary of the Later New Testament*. Downers Grove/Leicester: InterVarsity, 1997. Pages 834–41.

————. "The Use of Tradition Material in the Epistle of Jude." *BBR* 4 (1994): 1–14.

————. *Virtue amidst Vice*. JSNTSS 150; Sheffield: Sheffield Academic Press, 1997.

Charlesworth, J. H. *The Old Testament Pseudepigrapha and the New Testament. Prolegomena for the Study of Christian Origins*. Cambridge: Cambridge University, 1985.

Chester, A. and R. P. Martin. *The Theology of the Letters of James, Peter, and Jude*. Cambridge: Cambridge University Press, 1994.

Davids, P. "Tradition and Citation in the Epistle of James." W. W. Gasque and W. S. LaSor, eds. *Scripture, Tradition, and Interpretation*. Grand Rapids: Eerdmans, 1978. Pages 113–26.

Davies, W. D. "Reflections about the Use of the Old Testament in the New and Its Historical Context." *JQR* 74 (1983). Pages 105–36.

Ellis, E. E. *Prophecy and Hermeneutic in Early Christianity*. WUNT 18. Tübingen: Mohr, 1978.

————. "Pseudonymity and Canonicity of New Testament Documents." M. J. Wilkins and T. Paige, eds. *Worship, Theology and Ministry in the Early Church: Essays in Honor of R. P. Martin*. JSNTSS 87. Sheffield: Sheffield Academic Press, 1992. Pages 212–24.

Evans, C. A. *Noncanonical Writings and New Testament Interpretation*. Peabody: Hendrickson, 1992.

Fitzmyer, J. A. "The Use of Explicit Old Testament Quotations in Qumran Literature and in the New Testament." *NTS* 7 (1960/61): 297–333.

Forestell, J. T. *Targumic Traditions and the New Testament: An Annotated Bibliography with a New Testament Index*. SBLAS 4. Chico: Scholars, 1979.

Fornberg, T. *An Early Church in a Pluralistic Society: A Study of 2 Peter*. ConBNT 9. Lund: C.W.K. Gleerup, 1977.

Gertner, M. "Midrashim in the New Testament," *JSS* 7 (1962): 267–92.

Goppelt, L. *Typos. The Typological Interpretation of the Old Testament in the New*. Tr. D. H. Madvig. Grand Rapids: Eerdmans, 1982.

Guthrie, D. "The Development of the Idea of Canonical Pseudepigrapha in New Testament Criticism." R. P. Martin, ed. *Vox Evangelica I*. London: Tyndale, 1962. Pages 43–59. (= idem, in K. Aland, ed. *The Authority and Integrity of the New Testament*. London: SPCK, 1965. 14–39.)

A. T. Hanson, *The Living Utterances of God. The New Testament Exegesis of the Old*. London: Darton, Longman & Todd, 1983.

Hoffman, T. A. "1 John and the Qumran Scrolls" *BTB* 8 (1978): 117–25.

Lampe, G. W. H. and K. J. Woollcombe, *Essays on Typology*. Naperville: Allenson, 1957.

Lea, T. D. "The Early Christian View of Pseudepigraphic Writings." *JETS* 27 (1984): 65–75.

————. "Pseudonymity and the New Testament." D. A. Black and D. S. Dockery, eds. *New Testament Criticism and Interpretation*. Grand Rapids: Zondervan, 1991. Pages 535–59.

Longenecker, R. N. *Biblical Exegesis in the Apostolic Period*. Grand Rapids: Eerdmans, 1975.

McNamara, M. *Targum and Testament. Aramaic Paraphrases of the Hebrew Bible: A Light on the New Testament*. Grand Rapids: Eerdmans, 1982.

Miller, M. P. "Targum, Midrash, and the Use of the Old Testament in the New Testament." *JSJ* 2 (1970): 29–82.

Neyrey, J. H. "The Form and Background of the Polemic in 2 Peter." *JBL* 99 (1980): 407–31.

Schutter, W. L. *Hermeneutic and Composition in 1 Peter.* Tübingen: Mohr, 1989.

Smith, D. M. "The Use of the Old Testament in the New." J. M. Efird, ed. *The Use of the Old Testament in the New and Other Essays.* Durham: Duke University Press, 1972. Pages 3–65.

Snodgrass, K. R. "The Use of the Old Testament in the New." D. A. Black and D. S. Dockery, eds. *New Testament Criticism and Interpretation* Grand Rapids: Zondervan, 1991. Pages 409–34.

Strack, H. L. and P. Billerbeck. *Kommentar zum Neuen Testament aus Talmud und Midrasch.* 4 vols. Munich: Beck, 1922–28.

Wall, R. W. "James as Apocalyptic Paraenesis," *RestQ* 32 (1990): 11–22.

Notes

1. D. J. Rowston, "The Most Neglected Book in the New Testament," *NTS* 21 (1974/75): 554–63.

2. Commentaries aside, with only several exceptions, one is hard-pressed to identify scholarly monographs written since 1900 that are wholly devoted to exegetical and theological issues raised by 2 Peter, Jude, or the Johannine epistles. Even the number of journal articles is meager.

3. J. D. G. Dunn, *Unity and Diversity in the New Testament: An Inquiry into the Character of Earliest Christianity* (Philadelphia: Westminster Press, 1977) 374, 386 (emphasis his).

4. W. Marxsen, *Introduction to the New Testament: An Approach to Its Problem,* tr. G. Buswell (Philadelphia: Fortress Press, 1970), 12–13.

5. Käsemann's investigation of the "early Catholic" phenomenon, by his account, began in the early 1940s as he encountered the "problem of contradictory concepts of Spirit, Church, office and tradition . . . within the New Testament" that were "at first extremely disturbing" to him. This problem, according to Käsemann, was "immediately radicalized and complicated because it was very soon apparent that it could not be confined to the two strands of Paulinism and the theology of Luke together with the Pastorals" ("Paul and Early Catholicism," in *New Testament Questions of Today* [Philadelphia: Fortress Press, 1969], 236).

6. S. Schulz, *Die Mitte der Zeit: Frühkatholizismus im Neuen Testament als Herausforderung an den Protestantismus* (Stuttgart/Berlin: Kreuz Verlag, 1976), 77 (my translation). Similarly, F. Hahn writes: "Even though the implications might not yet be clearly seen, there is a practical awareness that the apostolic era is surely closed and that the immediate postapostolic period is soon ending. Hence, now the present tradition material must be preserved in its basic meaning and form" ("Randbemerkungen zum Judasbrief," *TZ* 37 [1981] 209–10 [my translation]).

7. Käsemann, "Paul," 242.

8. The German "Evangelische" denotes the theology of mainline German Lutherans, i.e., *Staatskirche*, and not that of Protestant evangelicals as would be typically understood in North America.

9. See F. Mussner, "Frühkatholizismus," *TTZ* 68 (1959): 237–45; idem, "Spätapostolische Briefe als frühkatholisches Zeugnis," in J. Blinzer et al., eds., *Neutestamentliche Aufsätze für J. Schmid* (Regensburg: F. Pustet, 1963), 225–32; idem,

"Die Ablösung des Apostolischen durch das nachapostolische Zeitalter und ihre Konsequenzen," in *Wort Gottes in der Zeit* (Festschrift K. H. Schelkle; Düsseldorf: Patmos, 1972), 166–77; H. Küng, "Frühkatholizismus im Neuen Testament als kontroverstheologisches Problem," *ThQ* 142 (1962): 385–424; K. H. Schelkle, "Spätapostolische Briefe und Frühkatholizismus," in *Wort und Schrift. Beiträge zur Auslegung und Auslegungsgeschichte des Neuen Testaments* (Düsseldorf: Patmos, 1966), 117–25; J. H. Elliott, "A Catholic Gospel: Reflections on 'Early Catholicism' in the New Testament," *CBQ* 31 (1969): 213–23; A. Vögtle, "Kirche und Schriftprinzip nach dem Neuen Testament," *BuL* 12 (1971): 153–62,260–81; K. H. Neufeld, "Frühkatholizismus—Idee und Begriff," *ZKT* 94 (1972): 1–28; and U. Luz, "Erwägungen zur Entstehung des 'Frühkatholizismus,'" *ZNW* 65 (1974): 88–111.

10. For an English translation of this address, see "An Apologia for Primitive Christian Eschatology," in *Essays on New Testament Themes* (London: SCM, 1964), 135–57.

11. G. Klein, "Der zweite Petrusbrief und der neutestamentliche Kanon," in *Ärgernisse. Konfrontationen mit dem Neuen Testament* (Munich: Kaiser, 1970), 111–23 (my translation).

12. Ibid., 112.

13. To further illustrate this bias, Wolfgang Schrage, author of a highly acclaimed primer on NT ethics (*The Ethics of the New Testament* [tr. D. E. Green; Philadelphia: Fortress Press, 1988]) in which a total of seven lines are devoted to 2 Peter and Jude, writes of 2 Peter in his commentary on the GEs: "Even when the epistle is lacking in theological depth and spiritual energy . . . it is not simply worthless. Above all, it mediates historical insights into the church's crisis resulting from second-century heresy" (H. Balz and W. Schrage, *Die katholischen Briefe: Die Briefe des Jakobus, Petrus, Johannes und Judas* [NTD 10; Göttingen: Vandenhoeck & Ruprecht, 1973], 123). For scholars like Siegfried Schulz, not only is the debate over 2 Peter's place in the canon "inappropriate" (*unsachgemäss*) apart from subordination to the early Catholic scheme it is in fact "boring" (*langweilig*), and therefore, pointless (*Mitte der Zeit*, 294).

14. In his commentary on 2 Peter, R. J. Bauckham has correctly called for a "reexamination" of the "early Catholic" thesis (*Jude, 2 Peter* [WBC 50 (Waco: Word, 1983): 8]).

15. R. H. Fuller, *A Critical Introduction to the New Testament* (London: Gerald Duckworth, 1966), 167.

16. It must be emphasized that the problem with the "early Catholic" thesis is not in its observation of second-century ecclesiastical phenomena. That these phenomena emerge in the subapostolic era is indisputable. Nor can it be denied that the NT contains foreshadows of "early Catholic" theological tendencies that come to full bloom in the second century. Rather, the problem of the thesis lies with its starting point. "Early Catholicism" begins with the assumption that apostolic authorship presents an "obstacle" to NT exegesis. Being presupposed is that (1) the writer is far removed from the beginnings of the church; (2) pseudonymity allows us to grasp the full meaning of the letter; and (3) writings such as the *Didache* or *1 Clement* or *Barnabas*, with no theological consequence, can be substituted in the canon for writings such as Jude or 2 Peter.

17. For a more thorough assessment of the "early Catholic" rubric, see J. D. Charles, *Virtue Amidst Vice* (JSNTSS 150; Sheffield: Sheffield Academic Press, 1997), 11–43.

18. The *logos parainetikos* typically incorporates the use of paradigms, rules of conduct, ethical proscriptions, ethical justifications, warnings, and catalogs of vice and/or virtue. On the paraenetic tradition in general, see K. Berger, "Hellenistiche Gattungen im Neuen Testament," in W. Haase, ed., *Aufstieg und Niedergang der römischen Welt*.

Geschichte und Kultur Roms im Spiegel der neueren Forschung (Berlin: de Gruyter, 1984), II.25.2, 1075–77.

19. See, e.g., M. Gertner, "Midrashim in the New Testament," *JSS* 7 (1962): 267–92.

20. Thus T. C. Oden, *After Modernity . . . What? Agenda for Theology* (Grand Rapids: Zondervan, 1990), 146.

21. Ibid., 146–47.

22. See J. D. Charles, "The Old Testament in the General Epistles," in R. P. Martin and P. H. Davids, eds., *Dictionary of the Later New Testament* (Downers Grove/Leicester: InterVarsity, 1997), 834–41.

23. See in this regard T. Fornberg, *An Early Church in a Pluralistic Society: A Study of 2 Peter* (ConBNT 9; Lund: C. W. K. Gleerup, 1977), and related commentary on 2 Peter in E. Waltner and J. D. Charles, *1 Peter, 2 Peter and Jude* (Scottdale: Herald Press, forthcoming).

24. See, e.g., J. A. Fitzmyer, "The Use of Explicit Old Testament Quotations in Qumran Literature and in the New Testament," *NTS* 7 (1960/61): 297–333; M. P. Miller, "Targum, Midrash, and the Use of the Old Testament in the New Testament," *JSJ* 2 (1970): 29–82; R. N. Longenecker, *Biblical Exegesis in the Apostolic Period* (Grand Rapids: Eerdmans, 1975); D. M. Smith, "The Use of the Old Testament in the New," in J. M. Efird, ed., *The Use of the Old Testament in the New and Other Essays* (Durham: Duke University Press, 1972), 3–65; W. D. Davies, "Reflections about the Use of the Old Testament in the New in Its Historical Context," *JQR* 74 (1983): 105–36; A. T. Hanson, *The Living Utterances of God. The New Testament Exegesis of the Old* (London: Darton, Longman & Todd, 1983); and K. R. Snodgrass, "The Use of the Old Testament in the New," in D. A. Black and D. S. Dockery, eds., *New Testament Criticism and Interpretation* (Grand Rapids: Zondervan, 1991), 409–34.

25. E.g., E. E. Ellis, "Prophecy and Hermeneutic in Jude," in *Prophecy and Hermeneutic in Early Christianity* (Tübingen: Mohr, 1978), 221–36, and R. J. Bauckham, "James, 1 and 2 Peter, Jude," in D. A. Carson and H. G. M. Williamson, eds., *It Is Written: Scripture Citing Scripture. Essays in Honour of B. Lindars* (Cambridge: Cambridge University Press, 1988), 303–17.

26. Two important resources in this regard are J. T. Forestell, *Targumic Traditions and the New Testament: An Annotated Bibliography with a New Testament Index*, SBLAS 4 (Chico: Scholars, 1979), and C. A. Evans, *Noncanonical Writings and New Testament Interpretation* (Peabody: Hendrickson, 1992).

27. See G. W. H. Lampe and K. J. Woollcombe, *Essays on Typology* (Naperville: Allenson, 1957), and L. Goppelt, *Typos: The Typological Interpretation of the Old Testament in the New*, tr. D. H. Madvig (Grand Rapids: Eerdmans, 1982).

28. James 2:14–26; 5:7–11,17–18. See P. H. Davids, "Tradition and Citation in the Epistle of James," in W. W. Gasque and W. S. LaSor, eds., *Scripture, Tradition, and Interpretation* (Grand Rapids: Eerdmans, 1978), 113–26.

29. 1 Peter 3:1–6,13–22. See G. L. Green, "The Use of the Old Testament for Christian Ethics in 1 Peter," *TynB* 41/42 (1990): 277–89.

30. 2 Peter 2:4–10a,15–16; Jude 5–7.

31. 2 Peter 2:4–10a; Jude 9,11. See J. D. Charles, *Literary Strategy in the Epistle of Jude* (Scranton/London/Toronto: University of Scranton Press/Associated University Presses, 1993), and idem, *Virtue Amidst Vice*, JSNTSS 150 (Sheffield: Sheffield Academic Press, 1997).

32. 1 John 3:12. While it is generally conceded that direct influence of the OT, with the exception of 1 John 3:12, is absent from the Johannine epistles, it should be noted that the substructure underlying the writer's polemic in 1 John reveals more about his

opponents' confession than their social location. Parallels between Johannine and Essene literature suggest that 1 John initially circulated in a Jewish-Christian orbit, and thus, is firmly rooted in a Jewish-Christian milieu. Most if not all of the moral paradigms in the GEs are meaningful as they find reinterpretation and reapplication in extrabiblical Jewish literature. Not infrequently, the use of these paradigms in the GEs has more in common with contemporary exegetical practice than any OT passages to which they might be traced.

33. See J. D. Charles, "Noncanonical Writings, Citations in the General Epistles," in R. P. Martin and P. H. Davids, eds., *Dictionary of the Later New Testament* (Downers Grove/Leicester: InterVarsity, 1997), 814–20.

34. That this particular corpus since the early patristic era has been denominated "catholic epistles" is somewhat misleading, to the extent that to the term *katholikos* has been attached the understanding that these epistles have "universal" application. A close reading of 1 and 2 Peter, James, and Jude, however, coupled with a mere cursory reading of 2 and 3 John, yields the awareness of a markedly local—and deeply pastoral—character of their teaching and instruction. Even Jude and 2 Peter, the origin and destination of which allude any certainty, contain evidences of a concrete local situation in which grave pastoral needs are present.

35. The notion of the disciples as "illiterate peasant- or fisherman-types" (cf. Acts 4:13) had achieved fairly wide currency among modern critical scholars and is expressed in the commentary of P. Feine, J. Behm, and W. G. Kümmel in their *Introduction to the New Testament* (Nashville/New York: Abingdon, 1965), 299–305.

36. *The Old Testament Pseudepigrapha* (2 vols.; Garden City: Doubleday, 1983, 1985); and *The Old Testament Pseudepigraph and the New Testament Prolegomena for the Study of Christian Origins* SNTSMS 54 (Cambridge: Cambridge University Press, 1985).

37. Strack, and Billerbeck, *Kommentar zum Neuen Testament aus Talmud und midrasch* (Munich: Beck, 1922–1928).

38. 1 Peter 3:18–20; 4:6 (cf. 3:22); 2 Peter 2:4–17; 3:7,12–13; Jude 4–16. While Jewish apocalyptic concepts appear in 2 Peter, J. H. Neyrey ("The Form and Background of the Polemic in 2 Peter," *JBL* 99/3 [1980]: 407–31); C. P. Thiede ("A Pagan Reader of 2 Peter: Cosmic Conflagration in 2 Peter 3 and the OCTAVIUS of Minucius Felix," *JSNT* 26 [1986]: 79–96); and R. Riesner ("Der zweite Petrus-Brief und die Eschatologie," in G. Maier, ed., *Zukünftserwartung in biblischer Sicht. Beiträge zur Eschatologie* [Wuppertal: Brockhaus, 1984], 124–43) have presented convincing arguments that Stoic cosmology is being denounced. E. Loevestam ("Eschatologie und Tradition im 2. Petrusbrief," in W. C. Weinrich, ed., *The New Testament Age: Essays in Honor of B. Reicke* [2 vols.; Macon: Mercer University Press, 1984], 2.287–300) also examines the eschatological question in 2 Peter, observing the writer's use of Jewish flood-typology in chapter 3 as a response to the moral skeptics and citing parallels from intertestamental literature in support thereof. What is missing from Loevestam's otherwise helpful treatment of eschatology and ethics in the epistle is a discussion of literary, social-cultural, and theological distinctives that might set 2 Peter apart from Jude. On the Epicurean denial of providence, which is the thrust of Neyrey's essay noted above, see also more recently J. H. Neyrey, *2 Peter, Jude: A New Translation with Introduction and Commentary*, AB 37c (New York: Doubleday, 1993), 230–31,239.

39. 1 Peter 3:15–4:6.

40. Jude 6; 2 Peter 2:4.

41. Contra B. Reicke (*The Epistles of James, Peter, and Jude*, AB 37 [New York: Doubleday, 1964], 112) and others, the literary strategy in 2 Peter calls not for a polemic

against Gnosticism but a reminder of the foundations of moral reasoning, consistent with the Hellenistic moral and Christian parenetic tradition.

42. Because Jude's Enoch citation is direct and because he states that Enoch "prophesied," commentators assume that Jude regarded Enochic literature as "inspired" and on the level of the Hebrew Scriptures. If, however, Jude's literary strategy called for exploiting a work that was highly esteemed not so much by himself as by his *audience*, a plausible interpretive option suggests itself. Enoch can be said to "prophesy" in much the same way as a Cretan poet is said to be a "prophet" by the Apostle Paul (Titus 1:12) for illustrative purposes. Seen thusly, Jude's citation of 1 Enoch might derive less from his *personal elevation* of Enochic literature than from that of his readers.

43. See J. D. Charles, "The Language and Logic of Virtue in 2 Peter 1:5–7," *BBR* 8 (1998): 1–20.

44. Jerome Neyrey, "Form and Background," 407–31.

45. On the contrast between 2 Peter and Jude, see related commentary in Waltner and Charles, *1 Peter, 2 Peter and Jude*.

46. R. H. Charles, *The Apocrypha and Pseudepigrapha of the Old Testament* (Oxford: Clarendon, 1913), 2.772.

47. The volume of literature on pseudonymity is massive. Representative pseudonymity theory, which takes a variety of approaches and responses to questions raised by pseudonymity theory, includes: F. Törm, *Die Psychologie der Pseudonymität im Hinblick auf die Literatur des Urchristentums* (Gütersloh: Bertelsmann, 1932); A. Meyer, "Religiöse Pseudepigraphie als ethisch-psychologisches Problem," *ZNW* 35 (1936): 262–79; J. A. Sint, *Pseudonymität im Altertum. Ihre Formen und ihre Gründe* (Innsbruck: Universitätsverlag, 1960); D. Guthrie, "The Development of the Idea of Canonical Pseudepigrapha in New Testament Criticism," in R. P. Martin, ed., *Vox Evangelica I* (London: Tyndale, 1962), 43–59; and idem. *New Testament Introduction* (Leicester/Downers Grove: InterVarsity, 4th ed., 1990), 824–27; W. Speyer, "Religiese Pseudonymität und literarische Fälschung im Altertum," *JAC* 8/9 (1965/66): 88–125; idem; *Die literarische Fälschung im heidnischen und christlichen Altertum: Ein Versuch ihrer Deutung*, HAW 1/2 München: Beck, 1971); B. M. Metzger, "Literary Forgeries and Canonical Pseudepigrapha," *JBL* 91 (1972): 3–23; M. Rist, "Pseudepigraphy and the Early Christians," in D. E. Aune, ed., *Studies in New Testament and Early Christian Literature: Essays in Honor of A. P. Wikgren*, NovTSup 33 (Leiden: Brill, 1972), 75–91; M. Smith, "Pseudepigraphy in Israelite Literary Tradition," in K. von Fritz, ed., *Pseudepigrapha I* (Geneve: Revedin, 1972), 191–215; O. Knoch, *Die 'Testamente' des Petrus und Paulus. Die Sicherung der apostolischen Überlieferung in der spätapostolischen Zeit*, SBB 62 (Stuttgart: Katholisches Bibelwerk, 1973); N. Brox, *Falsche Verfasserangaben. Zur Erklärung der frühchristlichen Pseudepigraphie* (Stuttgart: KBW, 1975); idem., ed., *Pseudepigraphie in der heidnischen und judisch-christlichen Antike* (Darmstadt: WBG, 1977); K. M. Fischer, "Anmerkungen zur Pseudepigraphie im Neuen Testament," *NTS* 23 (1976): 76–81; T. D. Lea, "The Early Christian View of Pseudepigraphic Writings," *JETS* 27 (1984): 65–75; idem, "Pseudepigraphy and the New Testament," in D. A. Black and D. S. Dockery, eds., *New Testament Criticism and Interpretation* (Grand Rapids: Zondervan, 1991), 535–59; D. G. Meade, *Pseudonymity and Canon. An Investigation into the Relationship of Authorship and Authority in Jewish and Earliest Christian Tradition*, WUNT 39 (Tübingen: Mohr, 1986); and E. E. Ellis, "Pseudonymity and Canonicity of New Testament Documents," in J. Wilkins and T. Paige, eds., *Worship, Theology and Ministry in the Early Church: Essays in Honor of R. P. Martin*, JSNTSS 87 (Sheffield: Sheffield Academic Press, 1992), 212–24.

48. Given the problem of Petrine authorship among critical scholars, it is the view of O. Knoch (*Die 'Testamente,'* 28) and R. J. Bauckham (*Jude, 2 Peter*, WBC 50 [Waco:

Word, 1983], 132–34) that in 2 Peter the pseudonymous testamental genre, or farewell speech, mediates and "preserves" the apostolic tradition. Because the testamental function of the farewell speech in no way proceeds from the apostolic witness and guarantor of apostolic tradition himself, the testament is understood to reveal an attempt by a later generation to "guarantee" the apostolic tradition faithfully. For an evaluation of Bauckham's argument that 2 Peter is a last will or testament, see Charles, *Virtue*, 49–75. On the farewell speech elsewhere in the writings of the NT, see W. S. Kurz, *Farewell Addresses in the New Testament* (Collegeville: Liturgical Press, 1990).

49. D. Guthrie, "The Development of the Idea of Canonical Pseudepigrapha in New Testament Criticism," in R. P. Martin, ed., *Vox Evangelica I* (London: Tyndale, 1962), 43–59; and idem., *New Testament Introduction* (Leicester/Downers Grove: InterVarsity, 4th ed., 1990), 824–27.

50. The ethical question has been addressed by B. M. Metzger, "Literary Forgeries and Canonical Pseudepigrapha," *JBL* 91 (1972): 3–23; T. D. Lea, "The Early Christian View," 65–75; idem, "Pseudepigraphy," 535–59; and M. Green, *2 Peter and Jude*, TNTC 18 (Leicester/Grand Rapids: InterVarsity/Eerdmans, 3rd ed., 1989), 34–35.

51. See, in this regard, K. K. Hulley, "Principles of Textual Criticism Known to St. Jerome," *HSCP* 55 (1944): 104–09; D. Guthrie, "Tertullian and Pseudonymity," *ExpTim* 67 (1956): 341–42; idem, *Early Christian Pseudepigraphy and Its Antecedents* (Dissertation: University of London, 1961); and R. E. Picirell, "Allusions to 2 Peter in the Apostolic Fathers," *JSNT* 33 (1988): 57–83.

52. Historically the church has not judged any of the writings of the NT canon to be pseudepigraphal, nor has it deemed them "fictional" representations (contra Bauckham *[Jude, 2 Peter*, 134], who argues that Petrine authorship of 2 Peter "was intended to be an entirely *transparent* fiction" [emphasis his], and others).

53. That the documents of the NT resist our attempts to be classified with nonapostolic pseudepigrapha is by no means an arbitrary ecclesiastical verdict. From the beginning the Christian community recognized that the NT documents are bound up with revelation that is imparted "apostolically" and within history. Writes R. B. Gaffin Jr.: "Apostolic witness . . . is infallibly authoritative, legally binding deposition . . . Accordingly, that witness embodies a canonical principle . . . , the emergence of a new body of revelation to stand alongside the covenantal revelation of the Old Testament" ("The New Testament as Canon," in H. M. Conn, ed., *Inerrancy and Hermeneutic: A Tradition, A Challenge, A Debate* [Grand Rapids: Baker, 1988], 176).

54. It is significant that in his essay "Der zweite Petrus-Brief und die Eschatologie" (see n. 37), R. Riesner, a German, suggests the possibility of a dating for 2 Peter that might fall within the apostle's lifetime.

55. This has been ably argued by T. D. Lea, "The Early Christian View," 65–75; idem., "Pseudepigraphy," 535–59; R.B. Gaffin, Jr., "The New Testament as Canon," 165–83; and E. E. Ellis, "Pseudonymity and Canonicity of New Testament Documents," in W. J. Wilkins and T. Paige, eds., *Worship, Theology and Ministry in the Early Church*, JSNTSup 87 (Sheffield: JSOT Press, 1992), 212–24. Even Richard Bauckham's masterful commentary—which maintains 2 Peter to be a last will or testament (131–35, 158–62) and thus builds on the insights of J. Munck ("Discours d'adieu dans le Nouveau Testament et dans la litterature biblique," in *Aux sources de la tradition chretienne*, Festschrift M. Goguel [Paris: Neuchatel, 1950], 164ff) and O. Knoch (*Die 'Testamente'* [see n. 47])—falls short of offering a satisfactory explanation for pseudonymity. For Bauckham, 2 Peter is "fictionally represented as written shortly before Peter's death." Michael Green (*2 Peter and Jude*, 34–35) summarizes the problems left unanswered by Bauckham, who

believes that the literary genre to which 2 Peter belongs made it perfectly evident to the first readers that it was a pseudegraph. Accordingly, no possible question of morality arises. 2 Peter is both a letter and also an example of the type of work we meet in the Testaments of the Twelve Patriarchs. That is to say, it sets out the supposed message of the deceased Peter to meet the exigencies of a late-first-century situation where antinomianism was present, heresy was rife and the parousia was mocked. The author's aim was to defend apostolic Christianity in a subapostolic situation, and this he does, not by having recourse to his own authority, but by faithfully mirroring apostolic teaching which he adapts and interprets for his own day. "Peter's testament" formed the ideal literary vehicle for his plans. Not only did the Testament genre have a long and honoured history in Judaism both within and outside the Old Testament; not only do the main contents of 2 Peter (ethical admonitions and revelations of the future) precisely correspond to those found in most Testaments; but everyone knew these were pseudepigraphs. It went without saying that the same held good of 2 Peter. Nobody ever imagined it came from Peter himself. The literary convention of the Testament was too well known. Such is the theory.

On the character of the NT writings, F. F. Bruce ("Tradition and the Canon of Scripture," in D. K. McKim, ed., *The Authoritative Word: Essays on the Nature of Scripture* [Grand Rapids: Eerdmans, 1983], 74) has written:

The principal criterion of New Testament canonicity imposed in the early church was not prophetic inspiration but apostolic authorship—or, if not authorship, then authority. In an environment where apostolic tradition counted for so much, the source and norm of that tradition were naturally found in the writings of apostles or of men closely associated with apostles.

56. In a recent monograph D. G. Meade (*Pseudonmity and Canon* [see n. 47]) surveys the landscape of various pseudonymity theories. Meade's concern is to address the "fundamental lack in the history of the investigation of New Testament pseudonymity" (15); the project proceeds by an examination of diverse positions on the theological spectrum. Meade concludes that pseudonymity and canonicity are not mutually exclusive; rather, pseudonymity could be a "legitimate part of the early Christian's . . . moral conscience" (pp. 3–4). For a critical evaluation of Meade's position and a dissenting view, see Ellis, "Pseudonymity and Canonicity," 212–24; Charles, *Literary Strategy*, 81–90, and more recently, Charles, *Virtue and Vice*, 49–75.

57. This is not to contend that the GEs have no theological perspective. It is rather to acknowledge the strong paraenetic character of these writings, which allows them an important function in the canon of the New Testament.

58. A reading of the entire NT, which takes into account both ethical and doctrinal emphases at differing times in different documents, prevents, in the words of R. W. Wall, both the formation of faith without validating works as well as a legalism that is void of grace ("James as Apocalyptic Paraenesis," *RestQ* 32 [1990]: 22).

59. E.g., James 4:7–10; 5:13–19; 1 Peter 5:1–9; 2 Peter 1:10; 3:1–2,14,17–18; Jude 3,20–23; 1 John 4:1,6,21; 2 John 10.

60. Cf Jude 19–21.

61. Cf. James 4:7–10; 2 Peter 2:1–2; Jude 4; 1 John 2:1,19,22; 3:4,6,10,18; 4:3,16–17.

62. J. R. Edwards, "A Confessional Church in a Pluralistic World," *Touchstone* 6/1 (1993): 16.

63. Oden, *After Modernity*, 156.

64. Ibid.

65. Cf. 2 Peter 2:1–2; Jude 3–4,17; 1 John 2:22; 4:1–3; 5:6–12; 2 John 7–11.

Chapter 20

Interpreting the Book of Revelation

Boyd Luter
The Criswell College

Much of the recent tidal wave of interest in the Book of Revelation among evangelicals, mostly related to eschatology, will likely recede significantly now that the Y2K/year 2000 hysteria has passed. That is most unfortunate. After all, Revelation is the only biblical book that pronounces a blessing on those who hear and heed it: "Blessed is the one who reads the words of this prophecy, and blessed are those who hear it and take to heart what is written in it, because the time is near" (1:3). In other words, beyond focusing on "the blessed hope—the glorious appearing of our great God and Savior, Jesus Christ" (Titus 2:13), there is considerably more "blessing" available to the reader/responder in the Apocalypse.

To lay out only two additional timely practical examples: (1) In a culture obsessed with winning, the most developed New Testament teaching on victory is the "overcomer" (Gk. *nikē/nikaō*) material in Revelation (2:7, etc.; 12:11; 21:7); (2) many evangelical churches, as well as evangelistic, discipleship, and missions organizations, made the year 2000 a strategic target date in regard to the fulfillment of the Great Commission.[1] Such emphases should, of course, continue unabated "to the very end of the age" (Matt. 28:20; see also 24:14). Since much of Revelation apparently deals with the climactic events of the age, it would seem likely to have real significance in regard to the culmination of Christ's Commission.[2]

The following is an overview of the ongoing and emerging areas and issues related to proper interpretation of the Apocalypse. Due to space limitations, it is strongly suggested that the reader follow up by consulting resources in the bibliography and notes that deal with areas of further interest or questions.

The Book's Unity and the Status of Critical Study

Before attempting to analyze the Book of Revelation, it should be understood that, for much of the earlier part of this century, the bulk of broader scholarship took the perspective that it was not a unified document.[3] Aune goes so far as to say, "More source-critical analyses of the Apocalypse of John have been proposed than for any other NT composition."[4]

One of the most "imaginative"[5] of such multisource schemes was propounded by Josephine Massyngbaerde Ford.[6] Significantly, though, in the process of fresh study leading to the revision of her *Anchor Bible* commentary volume, Ford recently concluded that Revelation is a compositional unity.[7] This change of perspective is a striking example of the contemporary scholarly backdrop in which there is, in Aune's words, "a widespread tendency to regard Revelation as a composition that exhibits internal unity and coherence."[8]

This scholarly consensus must not be taken to mean, however, that the unity of the Book of Revelation is finally secured against assault. A liberal scholar like Yarbro Collins still asserts cautiously that earlier source-critical studies "definitively established that the author of Revelation did use sources."[9] Moreover, even a broader evangelical like Aune has recently suggested an elaborate source-critical approach,[10] though this approach must be considered quite tenuous, given the suspect evidence Aune has marshaled to make his case.[11]

On the other hand, the fact that Beale's recent massive commentary, which treats in some depth almost every other substantial issue, does not even directly discuss the issue[12] strongly implies that there is a basic "ruling consensus" in favor of unity. At the least, it can be said that wider scholarship has largely turned to literary studies of Revelation that virtually assume its unity.[13]

Genre Considerations

In the past, spirited disagreement has existed on the literary genre of the Book of Revelation. Not a few have viewed the initial phrase of the book, "the Revelation (Gk. *apokalupsis*) of Jesus Christ" (1:1) as both a title and a genre identification of the book as apocalyptic literature. Others have correctly noted the prominent references to prophecy (e.g., 1:3; 19:10; 22:7, 18–19) and have championed the prophecy genre. Still others have contended that, since Revelation begins (1:4) and ends (22:21) like a letter and includes seven shorter letters to churches in the same geographical vicinity (chs. 2–3), the genre epistle could not be left out of the discussions.

Perhaps the most widespread view today is that Revelation is "a prophecy cast in an apocalyptic mold and written down in a letter form."[14] In a general sense, this is undoubtedly correct. Yet this does not help as much as it might initially seem in attempting to interpret the book. How do you shift gears between the principles of interpretation for each particular genre when you are not sure which one (or more) you are dealing with in a certain passage? In this regard, Michaels' suggestion of "mixed genres"[15] is significant, as is the conclusion of Carson, Moo, and Morris that "'epistle' may be the single best categorization."[16]

The concept of blended genres perhaps can greatly enhance the interpretation of Revelation. It allows the narrowing or specifying of how to determine the "big picture" issue of overall interpretative approach as well as how to deal with the strong presence of symbolism (see below) in the book. In other words, a mixed genre makes for useful comparisons with other NT documents that have previously not seemed useful parallels.

For example, drawing upon the above understanding that "epistle" provides the wider genre framework, it is worth noting that Ephesians contains both symbolic imagery ("the foundation of the apostles," 2:20; compare Rev. 21:14) and a discussion of timeless spiritual warfare (6:10ff.; compare Rev. 2:9–10, etc.; 12:7ff.) that are very similar to those in Revelation. Likewise, aspects of 1 and 2 Thessalonians and Jude are heavily prophetic or apocalyptic within the epistolary framework.

Heretofore, insightful biblical genre parallels have been sought in venues like the Olivet Discourse and Daniel (which are clearly very helpful). Now, however, although familiarity with all three genre types is certainly still required,[17] seemingly less "exotic" material in the Epistles can be extremely valuable in interpreting Revelation.

This is a very telling point since, as Osborne correctly emphasizes, "Meaning is genre-dependent."[18] Among other things, this means that while the symbolism in the Apocalypse is *quantitatively* much more common than in the Epistles, it is not necessarily *qualitatively* totally different, as it has been treated for the most part. As will be seen, this may have sizable ramifications for interpreting Revelation. If nothing else, it clearly limits the tendency simply to assume that the meaning of symbolism leans toward the spiritualizing (even allegorizing) side of the aisle, a common practice (even today) in interpreting apocalyptic.

Major Historical Interpretive Approaches

In the long history of interpretation of Revelation, four major schemes have emerged.[19] These four approaches are the: (1) preterist (contemporary historical) view, which focuses on the historical setting contemporary with the original writer and his original readers; (2) historicist (continuous historical) view, which sees Revelation as a preview of the entire sweep of church history; (3) idealist (timeless symbolic) view, which understands the book as a symbolic depiction of principle related to the ongoing clash between God and Satan, good and evil; and (4) futurist (eschatological) view, which takes the vast bulk of the Apocalypse as referring to events surrounding the Second Coming of Christ and subsequent events.

Three of these schools of thought have obvious strengths and almost as many obvious weaknesses. The preterist view rightly emphasizes the original setting (in the spirit of historical-grammatical exegesis) but tends to undervalue the end-times aspect of Revelation. The idealist view correctly emphasizes the spiritual warfare angle and seeks relevant timeless principles in every context but is not historically rooted. The futurist view correctly spotlights the climactic events of the end of the age but is weak in demonstrating the present-tense relevance to the original audience (or even readers today).

The historicist view, as attractive as it seems at first glance, given nineteen centuries of church history between the writing of the Apocalypse and today, turns out to be an interpretive "tower of Babel." No two historicist commentators who are not of the same generation, or directly dependent on each other, have ever reflected widespread consensus on what particular passages in Revelation are referring to church history. This utter confusion shows that the historicist view is hardly to be considered on par with the other three views and cannot be viewed as a viable option.

Given the general recognition of the above analysis, blended combinations of the above standard views began to emerge. In fact, such eclectic views have become so common that it has become rare in recent years for a serious commentator to argue for any of these views in pure form.[20] It is quite common for those taking such an eclectic approach to attempt to proceed as if all the contributing views have equal validity.[21] Yet others choose to give the upper hand to one or two of the views in the blend. Beale, for example, terms his eclectic approach "modified idealism."[22] By contrast, Mounce seems to opt for a preterist-futurist bottom line understanding.[23]

The Interpretation-Application Process and the Apocalypse

With continued refinements in the understanding of valid application of Scripture, it appears that additional related factors may need to be considered before deciding on an overall interpretive scheme for Revelation. Chief among these factors is the nature of application and its relationship to interpretation.[24]

Zuck refers to the bridge between proper interpretation and application as "principlizing."[25] Interpretation seeks to understand what the biblical text *meant* specifically in its original historical setting. Before we can legitimately deal with what it *means* specifically (or applicationally) for modern readers, however, a generalizing step must take place. You must carefully determine the "timeless truth" that applies equally well in both the original and the modern setting before specifying the exact applications for today.

It is significant that this widely accepted applicational procedure in effect renders the idealist view redundant. The ongoing appeal of the idealist approach is predominately its focus on relevant "timeless principles" in Revelation. But, since the generalizing of such principles is part and parcel of the rightly expected[26] movement from interpretation to application, it is premature to consider them center stage in the interpretation of the Apocalypse. In other words, to include the idealist perspective at the point of interpretation is to confuse later applicational procedure with interpretation, to get the cart before the horse.

In the end, the best overall interpretive approach to Revelation is a preterist-futurist view,[27] rooted firmly in both the original first-century context and the future setting of eschatological fulfillment. As stated above, the historicist perspective is of marginal value, at best. The idealist understanding, however, inevitably comes back into play in generalizing timeless principles in the succeeding applicational process.

The focus of this chapter is not to deal directly with applicational issues,[28] which are frequently acknowledged to be the single most difficult aspect of expounding the Apocalypse. With that challenge in mind, it is important to note here at least one new major evangelical work on the Book of Revelation that places a premium on application without de-emphasizing proper prior interpretation. Kendell Easley's excellent volume in the Holman New Testament Commentary series will prove very suggestive for those who struggle not just with interpretation but also with the intimidating task of the practical application of Revelation.[29]

Text, Grammar, and Style

In regard to the text of Revelation, three factors distinguish it from the rest of the New Testament.[30] First, there are considerably fewer Greek manuscripts than for any of the other NT books, perhaps due to early canon-related concerns in the Eastern churches. Second, apparently at least partly due to the smaller number of textual witnesses, the available text types are distinctive. Third, there are proportionately more variants between the so-called "Critical Text"[31] and "Majority Text"[32] schools of textual criticism, and thus their related translations,[33] than with any other NT book, though none of the variants have major theological consequences.

Grammatically, the Greek of the Book of Revelation is "odd,"[34] to say the least.[35] Yet this somewhat irregular, and even frequently awkward, Greek is not necessarily "bad" Greek at all and turns out to be not even notably difficult (in either style or vocabulary) to read.[36]

Over the years, it has been concluded that most of the examples of unusual style in Revelation are reflective of either Hebrew style (thus termed "Hebraisms") or of the style of the Septuagint, the Greek translation of the OT (called "Septuagintalisms"). Though related issues are far from fully resolved, Beale's explanation for this phenomenon is well considered: These stylistic peculiarities indicate the presence of an allusion to the Old Testament (see below) and are likely intended to "create a 'biblical' effect in the hearer and, hence, to show the solidarity of the writing with that of the OT."[37] If this understanding is essentially correct, it would not be unlike the contrasting effect of reading passages from the King James Version at various points in an informal contemporary worship service.

Author and Date

Among those who hold a high view of Scripture, two positions on who wrote the Apocalypse, and two on when it was written, have persevered as credible.[38] From time to time, other possibilities come and go,[39] getting their hearing, but none has proved to have staying power.

On the authorship question, the writer calls himself "John" (Rev. 1:1, 4, 9; 22:8). The bulk of commentators through church history have understood that to mean John the Apostle, partly because the book reflects the Son of Zebedee's Jewish-Christian background and partly because a number of the earlier church fathers clearly back that identification.

However, often because of the apparent differences in theology and style between Revelation and the Fourth Gospel, there have been a number of dissenters going back to the third century A.D. Generally, the alternate view has been John "the Elder," often supposed to be a different writer of at least 2 and 3 John (see 2 John 1; 3 John 1). But the theological differences are not as great as often trumpeted (especially given the different literary genres of the books), and the theological similarities are fairly significant. Thus, while there can be no more certainty here than with most other biblical authorship questions, there is no compelling reason to conclude other than that John the Apostle wrote Revelation.

The dating issue revolves mostly around the identification of the suffering of John (1:9) and at least some of his immediate readers (e.g., 2:9–10). Among evangelicals, the "persecutions" under the Roman Emperors Nero (mid- to later 60s) and Domitian (mid-90s) are the likely candidates.[40] The Neronian view looks for support to internal material in Revelation 13 and 17 that seems to echo Nero's reign or rumors surrounding his death in A.D. 68. The Domitianic view understands the same evidence differently but also relies on the ancient tradition that Revelation originated from John's exile to Patmos near the end of Domitian's reign (A.D. 95–96).

Little, if anything, that would dislodge either conclusion has been forthcoming in recent times, other than perhaps the wider reasoning of John A. T. Robinson in regard to dating all NT documents. Robinson asserted that, if an event as traumatic as the destruction of Jerusalem and the temple in A.D. 70 had already taken place, it would be recorded in the NT[41] (which it is not, directly). His conclusion, then, was that it had not yet taken place; thus the entire NT, including Revelation, predates A.D. 70.

Preterists and others who follow Robinson's reasoning are usually very comfortable with the later 60s dating. The majority position, however, is still the mid-90s view. And, with the exception of chapters 13 and 17, the view chosen does not significantly alter the interpretation of the book.

The Use of the Old Testament and Other Writings

One of the underdeveloped areas in the interpretation of the Book of Revelation, until recently,[42] has been the extensive use of the Old Testament in Revelation. Estimates of the number of allusions to, or echoes of, the OT in the Apocalypse vary astoundingly, from a low total of about 275 to a mind-boggling ceiling of 1,000.[43]

Considerable disagreement may continue to exist on how many OT uses there are in Revelation. However, Beale's categories regarding such allusions are helpful in attempting to determine which are valid. The book includes no strict scriptural citations (though the echoes of Dan. 7:13 and Zech. 12:10 in Rev. 1:7, among several other possibilities, are close). The remaining phenomena can be broken down as: (1) Clear allusions: The wording is almost identical to the OT source, shares somewhat the core meaning, and could not likely have come from somewhere else. (2) Probable allusions: Though the wording is not as close, it still contains an idea or wording that is uniquely traceable to the OT text or exhibits a structure of ideas uniquely traceable to the OT passage. (3) Possible Allusions: The language is only generally similar to the purported source, echoing either its wording or concepts.[44] Such distinctions can, at least, prevent basing too much on a long-shot allusion at a key interpretive juncture.

Given this range from the clear and specific to the vague and general, it must also be asked: How *conscious* was John of the presence of these allusions? If his mind was saturated with the OT, could it not be that what is seen in much of Revelation is simply familiar images in which he unconsciously chooses to express his visions? That is how many understand it. Others, however, hold that John was completely aware of how he was echoing the OT, perhaps using the allusions for their "evocative and emotive power."[45] Still others conclude that there is a mixture of unconscious and conscious usage and that it is often virtually impossible to tell where one stops and the other starts, especially in passages that exhibit clusters of several allusions.

Where do the allusions come from in the OT? All the way from the earliest chapters of Genesis (echoed extensively in Rev. 21–22) and Exodus (many of the plagues and the "Song of Moses" [Rev. 15:3ff; cf. Exod. 15:1–18]) to Zechariah (e.g., the four horses [Rev. 6:1–8; cf. Zech. 1:8, etc.]) and Malachi (the Elijah prophecy [Rev. 11:6a; Mal. 4:5]). It is commonly understood that over half of the OT books are well represented. The most heavily used books appear to be Psalms (e.g., Ps. 2:1a, in Rev. 11:18a), Isaiah (e.g., the "new heavens and earth" passages in Isa. 65–66, in Rev. 21–22), Ezekiel (e.g., eating the scroll in Ezek. 3:1–3, in Rev. 10:9–10), and Daniel.

Given Daniel's dramatically shorter length than Psalms, Isaiah, or Ezekiel, it is not without significance that there are proportionately more allusions from Daniel. Within Daniel, the most come from chapter 7,[46] though chapter 2 is also "heard" at key junctures (see the following discussions of "Symbolism" and "Structure"). The Danielic flavor of Revelation is also sprinkled with notable echoes from Daniel 1, 4, 10 and 12, with the possible role of chapter 9 debated (see below).

Knotty relevant questions have to do with why and how the OT passages are used. One of the reasons for this has to do with creating a "biblical feel," as discussed earlier. Additionally, repeated uses of certain passages and books call attention to the OT context[47] and some type of linkage with the passage in Revelation. The kinds of linkage answers the "why" questions. It may be fulfillment of OT prophecy, typological usage, or some other type of comparison for theological and/or applicational reasons. It is even possible that an OT book, in this case most likely Daniel,[48] serves as a "literary prototype" that provides a specific structure for the Book of Revelation (see below under "Structure").

It is also necessary to ask whether the OT setting shapes the use in Revelation or vice versa. Historically and logically, the simplest answers are that either: (1) the OT setting "controls" the meaning of the allusion in Revelation (or "transfer of images"); or (2) the context in the Apocalypse "nails down" the use of the OT (or "transformation of images"[49]).

The problem, however, is that, in the stretching process of interpreting Revelation, it is not at all clear that it is one way or the other. It seems usually to be more "transfer" when the wording or imagery in Revelation is close to that in the OT context but more "transformation" when the passage in Revelation makes notable changes or additions. In speaking of this kind of "reciprocal interpretative interplay," Beale aptly concludes: "The place of the OT in the formation of thought in the Apocalypse is that of both a servant and a guide."[50]

This conclusion seems justified in light of another important aspect of the use of the OT in Revelation: the general hermeneutical principle usually known as "progressive revelation." As Osborne states, "Later passages do not replace the earlier; rather, they clarify the earlier passages."[51] Admittedly, the use of the OT in Revelation is a complex instance of the progress of revelation. Nevertheless, the concept of "progressive clarification" through the course of biblical revelation adds a helpful element to the discussion.

The remaining issue here has to do not with the use of the OT but with the possibility of echoes from even beyond, in extrabiblical literature. Certainly, with a clear example like the citation of 1 Enoch 1:9 in the apocalyptic setting of Jude 14–15,[52] the presence of apocryphal allusions is quite possible. Having said that, though, it is worth asking how far such possible wider echoes *should* be pursued.

Both Aune's and Beale's commentaries go considerably further in such pursuits than other contemporary commentators.[53] But beyond a lingering first glance, the similarity ends. In comparison with Beale's almost always carefully balanced secondary use of extrabiblical materials, many of Aune's lengthy discussions of extrabiblical material (interspersed with biblical discussions, with basically no differentiation) verge on "parallelomania" (i.e., seeing relationship, even dependence, of thought in similar words or ideas where none exists). Elwell and Yarbrough wisely remind us that, even if a sizable number of such examples prove suggestive, we must avoid the "impression that the primary literary background of the New Testament is pagan or sectarian writings, or even writings like the Old Testament apocrypha, which the New Testament writers seldom or ever cite, much less base doctrines on."[54]

The Use of Symbolism and Numbers

One of the first things most newer readers of the Apocalypse are struck by is the cover-to-cover presence of strange symbolism, little of which is interpreted (e.g., 1:20). From the images in the initial "Son of Man" vision in chapter 1 to the descriptions of the eternal state near the end of the book, the symbolic imagery is as thick as rush-hour traffic and equally challenging.

With sensitivity to genre and other factors, approaches to the interpretation of the symbolism in Revelation have more and more left behind simplistic hermeneutical summaries. "Interpret normally (literally) unless it is abnormal to do so" and the purported "dual hermeneutic" (i.e., interpret prophecy in a different [figurative-spiritual] way from other biblical literature) may be hermeneutical opposites, but they are equally oversimplified and shortsighted.

Beale is essentially correct in his twofold understanding of the great significance of the words usually rendered "made known" (Gk. *sēmainō*) in Revelation 1:1. First, it echoes wording in Daniel 2:28–30, 45, which has major ramifications for the literary structure of the Apocalypse (see below). Second, and to the point here, its interpreted force is to "make known *by signs or symbols*."[55]

Given the conclusion on mixed literary genre above (i.e., apocalyptic-prophecy-epistle), though, it seems to be going too far to say that the symbolism in Revelation is so "predominant" as to require an almost universally figurative interpretive approach.[56] That would mean in practice that, for the bulk of the book, there would have to be a compelling reason *not* to interpret an apparent symbol (or number) figuratively. Instead, it is wiser not to stereotype in advance the book's rich symbolic component but rather to interpret each symbol on its own terms. This recognizes that, much as John uses the OT in a fresh variety of ways, there can also be different degrees of figurative intent, with some being quite minimal.

Though potential for "spiritualizing" abuse exists, there is still much to be said for Beale's four "levels of communication in most segments of Revelation, especially from chapter 4 and onward." These levels are: (1) linguistic: the biblical text that is read or heard; (2) visionary: John's experience of the visions; (3) referential: historical identification of the objects in the visions; and (4) symbolic: what the visionary symbols connote about their historical referents (i.e., Level 3).[57]

As long as the symbolic component is not universalized (see above), or the impact of "commonplace" imagery (see below) from elsewhere is not overplayed, these four levels provide a helpful means of working with the symbolic imagery of the Apocalypse. Realistically, though, if the interpretive "back door" is left open, spiritualizing, if not allegorizing, can get out of hand, as it so often has in church history.

What is the bottom-line, practical function of the widespread symbolism in Revelation? One of Beale's most piercing insights is that "the symbols have a parabolic function and are intended to encourage and exhort." That means "hardening" in the case of unbelievers while "jolting" believers, and those who will believe, to proper response.[58]

It must be clearly understood here that "parabolic" function does not imply allegorical interpretation. That would only be true if all parables are taken to be fully allegorical, the very historical hermeneutical "quicksand pit" into which the interpretation of parables tends to sink.[59]

In addition to general symbolism, quite a few numbers are also used repetitively in Revelation. Many of these symbols and numbers follow on the heels of well-trafficked (or "commonplace") uses in earlier Scripture (and, possibly, significant extrabiblical literature). Thus, in attempting to derive their meaning in Revelation, it is necessary to consider carefully the previous usage.

For example, in Revelation the number seven (used for at least seven blessings, the group of churches receiving the book; seals on the scroll; trumpet and bowl judgments) is understood to signify "completeness," as does twelve (which may also include the nuance of "unity within diversity" [e.g., 12 tribes of Israel or 12 apostles]). The number four also seems to speak of completeness, at least in the sense of "universal" (e.g., "the four winds of the earth").[60] On this there is almost total interpretive consensus. Things change, however: (1) when other, particularly "multiplied," numbers are worked with; and (2) when the presumed meaning of well-known numerical usage elsewhere is brought into play to interpret that number in the Apocalypse.

As an example of the first case, are the "144,000" (Rev. 7:1–8; 14:1–5) or the various measurements of the New Jerusalem (21:16–17), all of which are multiples of twelve, to be "nailed down" in meaning by that multiple? Those with a "predominant" figurative understanding of the book usually say, "Yes." Many who consider each numerical usage on its own merits will say, "Not necessarily."

As an example of the second case, the use and meaning of various, well-known numerical time references in the Book of Daniel are usually taken as determinative for their meaning in Revelation. What often happens is that the Danielic wording (e.g., "time, times, and half a time" [Dan 7:25; Rev. 12:14]) is assumed to be a commonplace figure for "the period of tribulation," but otherwise generally undefined lengthwise.[61] On the other hand, no less a revered Semitics scholar than Gleason Archer concludes that such numerical time references in Daniel mean exactly what they say time-wise.[62] Thus, the number should almost surely be taken the same way in the Apocalypse, unless there is some clear reason for doing otherwise. In the end, Osborne is correct in saying that, in interpreting such symbolism, "The final arbiter is still the immediate context."[63] That leads to our discussion of the structure of Revelation, the "big picture" aspect of context.

"Reading" and "Hearing" the Literary Structure

Before seeking to interpret the structure of Revelation, we do well to consider how the original readers would have "heard" it. Aune makes clear that "the one who reads the words of this prophecy" (1:3) is reading *aloud*, the normal practice of the day.[64] Thomas explains further:

> Because writing materials were expensive and scarce, so were copies of the books that were part of the biblical canon. As a rule, one copy per Christian assembly was the best that could be hoped for. Public reading was the only means that rank-and-file Christians had for becoming familiar with the contents of these books.[65]

Alan Johnson offers the very real possibility that "the entire book was designed to be heard as a single unit in the public worship service."[66] This seems particularly plausible, considering that this seems to be exactly what was to be done in the churches in Thessalonica (1 Thess. 5:27) and Colossae (Col. 4:16). Hence, it appears a fairly safe assumption that, from the beginning, understanding of the Apocalypse was to proceed from *repeated whole readings* of the book.

As such reading and *re*reading takes place, more and more *internal* structural clues and imbedded *external* "echoes" (see "Use of the OT" above) begin to stack up and clarify. With increasing familiarity, this evidence starts to come together into possible skeletal outline form, though perhaps in more ways than one.

The more obvious internal clues[67] are: (1) the possibility that 1:19 may be a sort of preview outlining device;[68] (2) the arrangements of seven: churches (chs. 2–3), seals (6:1–8:1), trumpets (8:6–11:19), and bowls (ch. 16); (3) the opening of the scroll (5:1–8:1; see below for possible theological ramifications); (4) the so-called "interludes" (i.e., slowing and orienting literary devices in chapter 7, 10:1–11:14, chapters 12–14 and 17:1–19:5);

(5) the literary fade-out of the blameworthy "earth-dwellers" (3:10; 6:10; 8:13; 11:10; 13:8; 17:2, 8) in favor of Babylon the Great (14:8; 16:19; 17:5; 18:2, 10, 21); (6) the varied three-and-a-half year wording in chapters 11–13 (see under "Theology"); (7) the interplay of "holy city" (11:2; 21:2) and "great city" (11:8; 14:8, etc.); and (8) the "face-off" comparison between Babylon the harlot and consort of the Beast (esp. chs. 17–18) and the pure Bride of Christ (chs. 19, 21).

At the same time, wording and imagery recalling the OT is accumulating, notably from the Book of Daniel. As the density of its usage, especially in chapters. 1, 4–5, 12–13, 14, 17, 20 and 22[69] becomes compelling, the possibility that Daniel may prove to be the "literary prototype" for Revelation (see above) begins to come into focus. However, if that is true, it does not answer what type of framework Daniel might provide for Revelation: merely thematic or in some sense chronological (e.g., Revelation deals with the yet unfulfilled part of Daniel's prophecies at the end of the age).

Some outlines that emerge from this type of study will emphasize either the internal or external evidence. It is, however, possible to fuse *both* together in an overview outline like the following, which proceeds on internal clues within the framing wording of the echoes of Daniel 2:28–30, 45 in Revelation 1:1, 19; 4:1; and 22:6:[70]

I. Introduction and Son of Man vision (echoing Daniel) (1:1–20)
II. Letters to the seven churches in Asia (chs. 2–3)
III. Visions of the end of the age and new heaven and earth (4:1–22:5)
    A. The heavenly throneroom, the sealed scroll, and the Lamb (chs. 4–5)
    B. Removing the seven seals, opening the scroll (6:1–8:1)
    C. Sounding the seven trumpets, announcing judgment (8:2–11:19)
    D. Introducing signs and characters before the final wrath (chs. 12–14)
    E. Pouring out the seven bowls of the climactic wrath of God (15:1–19:5)
    F. The return, reign, and final judgment of the King of kings (19:6–20:15)
    G. The new heaven and earth and New Jerusalem (21:1–22:5)
IV. Conclusion (using earlier wording/imagery) (22:6–21)[71]

While such an outline accurately reflects the basic literary movement of the book, it does not address two key interpretive questions: (1) Is the forward movement of Revelation a spiraling "recapitulation" or a chronological progression? (2) How do you best account for the "breaks" in the movement (i.e., "interludes")?

Beale is an example of those who conclude that the recapitulation view is correct. Regarding internal evidence, he sees the seals, trumpets, and bowls sequences as speaking of the same period from different angles. Externally, he believes the movement of the Apocalypse is derived from five parallel (i.e., dealing with roughly the same subject and temporal focus) prophecies in Daniel (chs. 2, 7–12).[72]

On the other hand, it is also quite possible to argue for chronological progression from the seals to the trumpets to the bowls. Internally, the obvious surface similarities are outweighed by greater differences and escalating intensity in the three sequences. Externally, the five focal Daniel prophecies are seen as suggestive for the structure of Revelation but not truly parallel (thus not "previewing" some kind of recapitulated structuring of Rev.). Daniel 7 builds on and clarifies chapter 2, while chapter 8 was fulfilled by Antiochus IV Epiphanes. Daniel 9 gives a temporal framework not provided by the others, and chapters 11–12 "telescope" from the Greek Empire (up to 11:36) to the eschatological "tribulation" and resurrection (12:1–2).

Attempts to explain the structural "rough points" have varied, including dramatic effect or emphasis, or, at the extreme end of the scale, even source-critical explanations. As a classic example, Aune has recently claimed: "The most striking literary characteristic in Revelation is the presence of approximately twelve relatively independent textual units that have little to do with their immediate contexts or indeed with the macronarrative of Revelation."[73] According to Aune, these "stick out like a sore thumb" passages are chapters 7, 10; 11:1–13, chapters 12–14; chapters 17–18, 19:11–16; 20:1–10, 20:15; 21:9–22:5.[74]

What Aune has apparently not considered is the possibility that these seemingly awkward passages may actually point to yet another outline. In other words, not only do these passages serve a purpose in the structure tracked above (i.e., as interludes and expansions), they also fit beautifully into a complementary structure (see, e.g., below).

The plausibility of multiple outlines has recently been surveyed briefly by Michelle Lee, who suggests the insightful grand chiastic (inverted parallel) structuring included below, which is the most compelling this writer has seen.[75] Beale also considers a number of other chiastic proposals, concluding that there is viability in some,[76] though he apparently does not draw notably upon such in his commentary.

Lee has marshaled impressive evidence for her chiastic "pairings" and has explained that it meets rigorous criteria for chiastic presence.[77] In so doing, she has, in effect, demonstrated that every one of Aune's "troubling" passages fits beautifully opposite its clearly parallel section, seriously calling into question much of Aune's entire approach to Revelation.

Though much about this outline is significant, the major remaining questions in regard to Lee's proposal have to do with its central pairing: Is its midpoint both *specific* enough and *significant* enough to warrant its "spot-lighted" location in the book-encompassing inverted structure?[78] The answer on both counts is "yes." The middle layer J, J' (see below) showcases two crucial points of decision. Some will decide to follow and worship the Beast, who persecutes the saints (ch. 13); others will follow the Lamb, who will judge the beast-worshipers (ch. 14). Both decisions have eternal consequences.

Michelle Lee's Proposed Chiastic Structure of Revelation

A   (ch. 1) Prologue
   B   (chs. 2–3) Present Situation: Letters to the seven churches
      C   (chs. 4–5) Fundamental Paradigm: Worship of God, worthiness of the Lamb
         D   (ch. 6) Judgment of God's enemies (note rider on white horse)
            E   (ch. 7) Faithful believers (note "great multitude")
               F   (chs. 8–10) Judgment of God's enemies (II; note first two "woes")
                  G   (ch. 11) False power of the Beast: Defeat through the two witnesses' resurrection
                     H   (12:1–6) Woman brings salvation
                       I   (12:7–18) Judgment of God's enemies (III): Dragon
                         J   (ch. 13) *Moment of Decision: Worship the Beast!*
                         J'   (ch.14) *Moment of Decision: Follow the Lamb!*
                     I'   (chs. 15–16) Judgment of God's enemies (III): Climactically on Babylon
                  H'   (17:1–6) Woman killing saints
                G'   (17:7–18) False power of the Beast: Defeat by the King of kings
              F'   (ch. 18) Judgment of God's enemies (II; note repeated "woe, woe" over Babylon)
            E'   (19:1–10) Faithful believers ("great multitude")
         D'   (19:11–21) Judgment of God's enemies (rider on white horse)
      C'   (20:1–10) Fundamental Paradigm: Damnation of Satan, worthiness of the saints
   B'   (20:11–22:5) Future Situation: The new heaven and earth and New Jerusalem
A'   (22:6–21) Epilogue[79]

In the center sections of this structure, Lee has also astutely noted a "twin peaks" effect related to two almost identical challenges to faithful endurance (13:10 and 14:12). These statements are, in effect, the *central (applicational) point* of the wider centerpoint sections of the book.[80]

Additionally, though, it is worth noting that 14:12 leads into the second of the seven makarisms (i.e., "blessing" statements) of the book (14:13). While this could be coincidence, it could also be an indicator (i.e., a literary "hook") of yet another level of structuring. Talbert, for example, long ago noted the presence of such a triple structure in some important ancient works.[81] So a third literary "side-by-side" structure in Revelation is not altogether unlikely.

What could the nature of such a structure be? One real possibility is a "spread chiasma" (i.e., of smaller textually separated ideas) of the seven beatitudes of the Apocalypse. The obvious questions here are: Is anything like this purported spread chiasma effect seen in regard to Revelation and is such an effect present in other biblical books?

The answer to both questions is positive. First, Bauckham has indeed noted a chiasma related to the well-known "Alpha and Omega," "first and last," "beginning and end" terminology in 1:8 (A); 1:17 (B); 21:6 (B'); and

22:13 (B').[82] Second, a chiasma of spread blessing statements has been detected in Genesis: 12:3 (A; note: "all the *families* of the earth"); 22:18 (B; "all the *nations*"); 26:4 (B'; "all the *nations*"); and 28:14 (A'; "all the *families* of the earth").[83]

Beyond that, David Johnson discerns a wider framing effect between the first and sixth blessings (1:3 and 22:7) and concludes that all seven beatitudes should be read together for total effect.[84] Also, within the inclusio relationship of 1:3 and 22:7 there is even a minichiastic effect: a (1:3a) heed; b (1:3b) "The time is near"; b' (22:7a) "I am coming quickly"; a' (22:7b) heed.

Given these factors, the following outline is suggested as an understanding of the structure of the seven blessing statements of Revelation:

A (1:3) (See above)
   B (14:13) Death and blessing beyond
      C (16:15) Alertness (echoes Matt. 24:42–44; 25:1–13)
      C' (19:9) Invitation to marriage supper (echoing Matt. 25:1–13)
   B' (20:6) Resurrection beyond death
A' (22:7) (See above)
D (22:14) Concluding offer of "blessing" to the converted

Though this structure may not seem initially plausible, it is exactly parallel to the structure of the Book of Ruth.[85] And, if it seems not to hold much significance, it should be considered that the important logical "blessings-curses" contrast (e.g., Lev. 26; Deut. 28) may be in view here. If so, the centered effect (i.e., between C [16:15] and C' [19:9]) proves to frame the divine "curse" rained down on Babylon the Great (16:17–19:5).

We have considered but three of a number of possible overall structurings of the Book of Revelation that emerge from repeated readings and close study of the book: A consecutive outline, a chiastic outline, and a "blessings and curses" outline. The first two could be "the" single outline of the book. However, it is not at all unlikely that two of the three, or all three, could coexist as interactive interpretive frameworks, as suggested above. If that is the case, such a double or triple structure could prove invaluable in the huge interpretative task facing the reader of Revelation by further specifying contextual meaning, thus subtracting some of the "guesswork" in regard to symbolism.

Biblical Theology on the "Bridge" Toward Application

There are two crucial balancing points that have to do with the theology of the Apocalypse: (1) though there is much related to eschatology[86] in Revelation, there is also *much more* theologically significant material in Revelation than just eschatology, as will be developed briefly below;[87] and (2) theological principles are not at all an end in themselves, since they comprise the contextualizing (or principlizing)[88] "bridge" to valid application (see above).

The wording "thousand years" (Rev 20:2–6) has become the debated basis of three major *millennial* (taken from the Latin for "thousand") views. Wider interpretive decisions made in this area are usually bound up with how "literally" the related symbolism and numbers (see above) are handled, as well as how persuasive the recapitulation interpretation of the book's structure is viewed to be versus the straightforward movement of the text (see above).

The *premillennial* (meaning "before the millennium") view holds that Christ will return to earth (Rev 19:11ff.) to set up his kingdom for a period of one thousand years (20:4–6), following the straightforward movement of the text. Among general premillennialists, there is also a narrower view, based on one reading of 20:4, that the focus of the earthly "kingdom" is the martyrs.[89]

The *amillennial* (meaning "no [earthly] millennium") takes the expression "thousand years" figuratively, as referring to a lengthy period of time of unknown duration. It holds that Revelation 20 recapitulates the period before the Second Coming (Rev. 19) in some sense.

The *postmillennial* (meaning "after the millennium") approach asserts that Christ will come back after the world has become progressively "christianized" by the spread of the gospel and biblical values. When that process is complete, there will be a "millennium," which some hold to be an actual thousand years, while others view the time factor figuratively. Recapitulation of Revelation 19, 20 is at the heart of this view, though it is somewhat less figurative than the amillennial understanding.

Premillennialists who understand certain numerical expressions of time in Revelation, notably the varied expressions for three and a half years (11:2–3; 12:6, 14; 13:5), in a less "symbolic commonplace" manner disagree on exactly when prior to the Second Coming that Christ will come for the church (see "Numbers" and "Structure" above). This is at the heart of the so-called "tribulation" issue.

Two related preliminary interpretive issues need to be answered, *not just assumed.* (1) When in Revelation does the "tribulation period" begin? Many assume that it is at the start of the body of the book (ch. 4) or at the initiation of the "seals" sequence (ch. 6). It is quite possible, though, that it does not start until the scroll of chapter 5 is completely open (i.e., after the last seal is lifted [8:1], at the beginning of the "trumpets" [8:6ff.]).[90] (2) How long does the tribulation period last? It is more common to take it as seven years long, either by adding the length of the two witnesses' ministry (11:3) to the length of the Beast's reign (13:5) or by importing the presumed remaining unfulfilled seven-year period from Daniel 9:27.[91] If all five of the key variously worded references in chapters 11–13 are seen as equivalent, the tribulation could be only three and a half years long.

Only after these interpretive questions, as well as the meaning of "kept from the hour of trial" (Rev. 3:10), are answered is the reader in a knowledgeable position to attempt to determine a position on the so-called Rapture question. There are three major definable positions, with variations of each.

The *pretribulational* (prior to) view places the Rapture either: (1) between chapters 3 and 4; (2) when John hears the wording "Come up here" in 4:1; or (3) if the scroll is not open until after the unsealing sequence, with the "great multitude" taken to heaven in 7:9ff. The *midtribulational* (in the midst of) understanding position typically places the Rapture with the "come up here" wording to the two witnesses in 11:12. The recent *Prewrath Rapture*[92] view is a variant kind of midtribulational view, which begins the tribulation at the earlier point and sees the Rapture in 7:9ff, which is roughly three-fourths of the way through the seven-year period. The *posttribulational* (at the end of) position usually sees the Rapture as the first stage of the Second Coming of Christ (19:11ff.). Recently Easley has laid out his theory that the Rapture may be at the point of the "harvest" in 14:14ff.,[93] which occurs quite close to the Second Coming (i.e., the end of the tribulation).

Even in the midst of this ongoing disagreement, though, it must never be forgotten that there is a crucial central aspect—the *most important* aspect—on which all agree: Christ's future return, whatever the surrounding details, is a "blessed hope" for those that are his own. All believers can wholeheartedly agree with John's concluding prayer: "Come, Lord Jesus" (22:20).[94]

This vital lingering christological coloring of the eschatology of Revelation leads into the book's other great theological emphasis. The book's apparent title, "The Revelation of Jesus Christ" (1:1), among other things, previews the extensive christology of the Apocalypse. Within this one amazing book, Christ is variously portrayed as the glorified Son of Man (1:12–16), the Lion of Judah, the worthy Lamb (5:8ff.), the Son who is universal ruler (12:5), the Bridegroom (19:7–9), the victorious Warrior/Word of God (19:11ff.), as well as the model witness/martyr (1:5; 12:11),[95] among others. In one of the most enigmatic statements of this difficult book, it is even said: "The testimony of Jesus is the spirit of prophecy" (19:10).

Revelation's extensive use of the OT (see above), frequently in fulfillment of prophecy, as well as the strongly worded warnings against altering Scripture (22:18–19), are striking contributions to bibliology. The book's climactic victory is a classic biblical example of the sovereignty of God. Relatedly, the "Lord God Almighty"[96] is the constant focus of both the heavenly throneroom (4:8) and the eternal state (21:22). Even the relatively scanty material about the Holy Spirit in Revelation shows up at key junctures: in the concluding appeals for the churches to "hear" (2:7, etc.) and in connection with the second beatitude (14:13).

The book's well-known references to "overcoming" fit within the scope of sanctification. But some of the references to "repentance" deal with unbelievers (e.g., 9:20–21; 16:9, 11) as a virtual equivalent to eternally damning unbelief, the settled sinful state of the "earth-dwellers" (3:10; 6:10; 8:13, etc.). The sole mention of "gospel" (14:6) seems to define proper response as fearing God and glorifying him (14:7). The redemptive "heart" of the gospel message is spelled out (1:5; 5:9), and a concluding evangelistic offer is even made in the beautiful imagery of the final beatitude (22:14).[97]

The only uses of "church" (Gk. *ekklēsia*) are in chapters 1–3 and at the conclusion of the book (22:16). Still the presence of terms like *saints*, widely used for Christians elsewhere, and the "blood" connection between John and the seven churches (1:4–6) with all who are redeemed by Christ (5:9–10), the martyrs (6:10; 12:11; 18:24), and the "great multitude" (7:14; 19:1ff.) implies some close relationship. There is even a future for believing Israel, if either the 144,000 or the rest who "fear God and give glory to him" (11:13; see above) are Jewish, or if the meaning attached to the twelve gates of the New Jerusalem is ethnic (21:12).

These theological realities are played out, as it were, in front of curtains often open into the unseen realm, providing a remarkable view of what has come to be called "spiritual warfare" (see also Eph. 6:10ff.). Some of the most extensive angelology in the entire Bible is in Revelation, including much on Satan (his presentation as "the Serpent of Old" is interpreted in 12:7–9 and 20:1–3) and the demons (portrayed in ch. 9 under the imagery of both horrific locusts and horses). The Apocalypse provides a great word of encouragement that, even though the devil and his hordes will not go down without a cosmic fight, their doom is indeed sure![98]

Conclusion

Many have noted that Calvin conspicuously did not write a commentary on Revelation, given his well-respected contributions on all the other NT books. Similarly, in an earlier teaching assignment, I ended up offering Revelation, essentially because no one else wanted to deal with it (and that initially included me!), given its history as a virtual hermeneutical minefield.

In the same vein, W. A. Criswell tells the story of the great New Testament scholar, A. T. Robertson, who was handling Revelation in one of his courses. In a class period dealing with interpreting the Apocalypse, Robertson walked into the classroom with a double armful of books, dropped them on the table with a thud and announced, "Here are the various approaches to interpreting Revelation. Take your pick."

Certainly, it gives pause to note immensely capable scholars and pastors who opt to avoid the Book of Revelation or go with the "it will all pan out in the end" cop-out. Yet, along with the caution such examples engender, there is still a note of loss, even tragedy. To fail to engage the Apocalypse makes no more sense than reading through the entirety of a fascinating book, only to refuse to face the final chapter (which, by the way, does conclude with an *eternally* "happy ending"!).

Admittedly, a treatment of this length can do little more than skim the surface of the complex web of issues related to interpreting the Book of Revelation. And no less an authority on the interpretation of the book throughout church history than Gerhard Maier referred to the Apocalypse as "the exercise field of hermeneutics par excellence."[99] Even such an introductory treatment may leave the intellectual and spiritual muscles a little sore. However, continued exercise in interpreting Revelation will quickly work through to enhanced skill and understanding.

Michaels has well said: "There is no denying that Revelation is a difficult book, but students can take heart from the fact that it was never intended to be a closed book (see 22:10: Do not seal up the words of the prophecy of this book, for the time is near.)"[100] The Lord intended this open book to be a continual blessing to all who "read and heed" its inspired content.

Certainly, in many senses, John's Apocalypse is a profound challenge to the interpreter, worthy of a lifetime of study. Just as true, though, is the realization that "at the heart of the Book of Revelation is a story, the same gospel story that echoes throughout the entire New Testament, about a slain Lamb victorious over death and evil and a God who makes everything new."[101]*

Bibliography

Aune, David E. *Revelation 1–5*. Word Biblical Commentary 52A. Dallas: Word Books, 1997.

———. *Revelation 6–16*. WBC 52B. Nashville: Thomas Nelson, 1998.

———. *Revelation 17–22*. WBC 52C. Nashville: Thomas Nelson, 1998.

Bauckham, Richard. *The Theology of the Book of Revelation*. New Testament Theology. Cambridge: Cambridge University Press, 1993.

Beale, G. K. *The Book of Revelation*. New International Greek Testament Commentary. Grand Rapids: Eerdmans, 1999.

Easley, Kendell H. *Revelation*. Holman New Testament Commentary. Nashville: Broadman & Holman, 1998.

Johnson, Alan F. "Revelation," in the *Expositor's Bible Commentary*. Gen. ed. Frank E. Gaebelein. Grand Rapids: Zondervan, 1981. 12:399–603.

Lee, Michelle V. "A Call to Martyrdom: Function as Method and Message in Revelation." *NovT* 40 (1998): 164–94.

Michaels, J. Ramsey. *Interpreting the Book of Revelation*. Guides to New Testament Exegesis. Grand Rapids: Baker, 1992.

Mounce, Robert H. *The Book of Revelation*. Rev. Ed. New International Commentary on the New Testament. Grand Rapids: Eerdmans, 1998.

Osborne, Grant R. *Revelation*. Baker Exegetical Commentary. Grand Rapids: Baker, forthcoming.

Patterson, L. Paige. *Revelation*. Two Vols. New American Commentary. Nashville: Broadman & Holman, forthcoming.

Thomas, Robert L. *Revelation 1–7.* Chicago: Moody Press, 1992.

———. *Revelation 8–22.* Chicago: Moody Press, 1995.

Yarbro Collins, Adela. "Revelation" in the *Anchor Bible Dictionary.* Gen. ed. David Noel Freedman. New York: Doubleday, 1992. V, 994–1708.

Notes

1. For a succinct discussion of this important theme, see A. Boyd Luter, "Great Commission," *ABD,* II, 1090–91.

2. This point has been made in more detail in "Concluding the Great Commission and Recovery," chapter 15 of Boyd Luter and Kathy McReynolds, *Disciplined Living: What the New Testament Teaches about Recovery and Discipleship* (Grand Rapids: Baker, 1996), esp. p. 179.

3. See the helpful summary in D. A. Carson, Douglas J. Moo, and Leon Morris, *An Introduction to the New Testament* (Grand Rapids: Zondervan, 1992), 477.

4. David E. Aune, *Revelation 1–5* WBC 52A (Dallas: Word Books, 1997), cvi.

5. The wording is that of Carson, Moo, and Morris, *Introduction to the New Testament,* 477.

6. J. M. Ford, *Revelation* AB (Garden City, N.Y.: Doubleday, 1965).

7. Aune, *Revelation 1–5,* cxi.

8. Ibid., cvii.

9. Adela Yarbro Collins, "Revelation," *ABD,* V, 697.

10. See Aune's extensive discussion and apologetic, cv–cxxxiv.

11. See the section in this chapter on Structure, as well as my reviews of all three of Aune's volumes, forthcoming in the *Journal of the Evangelical Theological Society.*

12. G. K. Beale, *The Book of Revelation,* NIGTC (Grand Rapids: Wm. B. Eerdmans, 1999), 3.

13. Carson, Moo, and Morris, *Introduction to the New Testament,* 481.

14. Ibid., 479, echoed by Beale, *The Book of Revelation,* 39.

15. J. Ramsey Michaels, *Interpreting the Book of Revelation,* Guides to NT Exegesis (Grand Rapids: Baker, 1992), 30–32, echoed by Beale, *The Book of Revelation,* 39.

16. Carson, Moo and Morris, *Introduction to the New Testament,* 479.

17. Besides relevant material in this volume, one of the best sources combining insightfulness and readability is Grant R. Osborne, *The Hermeneutical Spiral: A Comprehensive Introduction to Biblical Interpretation* (Downers Grove: IVP, 1991). In addition, it is expected that Osborne's forthcoming treatment of Revelation in the Baker Exegetical Commentary series will make a useful wider contribution.

18. Ibid., 8.

19. Useful accessible discussions of the historical roots of these views can be found in Alan F. Johnson, "Revelation," *EBC,* 12:408–11; and Robert H. Mounce, *The Book of Revelation.* rev. ed. NICNT (Grand Rapids: Eerdmans, 1998), 24–30.

20. Robert L. Thomas, *Revelation 1–7* (Chicago: Moody, 1992), who rousingly champions the (pure) futurist perspective, is a decided exception to that rule.

21. E.g., Walter A. Elwell, "Revelation," in the *Evangelical Commentary on the Bible,* ed. W. A. Elwell (Grand Rapids: Baker, 1989), 1201–02.

22. Beale, *The Book of Revelation,* 48–49.

23. Mounce, *The Book of Revelation,* 30.

24. Though I do not share his final conclusion, I believe Thomas is absolutely right to bring up the interpretation-application process as a key issue in his discussion of what is the correct overall interpretive approach to Revelation, *Revelation 1–7* (pp. 31–32).

25. Roy B. Zuck, "Application in Biblical Hermeneutics and Exposition," in *Walvoord: A Tribute*, ed. Donald K. Campbell (Chicago: Moody, 1982), 27–28. Zuck's concept was later helpfully developed in his chapter, "Applying God's Word Today," in R. B. Zuck, *Basic Bible Interpretation* (Wheaton: Victor Books, 1991), 279–92.

26. Professor Howard Hendricks is the first I heard speak to this effect: "Interpretation without application is an abortion (of God's purpose in Scripture)." In considering the entire sequence of historical-grammatical interpretation and application, it is helpful to summarize thusly: "God gave the Bible into historical time, that we might draw timeless principles for timely application."

27. This conclusion may be also strengthened by the insightful inference drawn by David L. Turner, "The Structure and Sequence of Matthew 24:1–41: Interaction with Evangelical Treatments," *Grace Theological Journal* 10.1 (1989): 3–27. After concluding that the Matthean Olivet Discourse must be preterist-futurist in orientation, if Jesus answered both questions by the disciples about: (1) the destruction of the Temple, and (2) signs related to the Second Coming/end of the age, (Matt. 24:3), Turner notes the strong similarity between Matthew 24 and Revelation 6 (p. 27), suggesting that Revelation may well also best be understood from a preterist-futurist perspective.

28. See, however, the overview treatment of applicational issues related to preaching the NT in Richard Wells' chapter in this volume.

29. Kendell H. Easley, *Revelation*, HNTC (Nashville: Broadman & Holman, 1998). It is also quite possible that a similar contribution will be made by Craig Keener in his forthcoming work on Revelation in the NIV Application Commentary series, though, given the nature of the series design, the interpretive underpinnings may not be quite as strong proportionately.

30. A brief but helpful specialized discussion in this area is Carson, Moo, and Morris, *Introduction to the New Testament*, 479–80. The most extensive recent wider evangelical discussion is Aune, *Revelation 1–5*, cxxxiv–cxlviii. For a wider discussion related to text critical issues in the NT, see Michael Holmes' earlier chapter on "Textual Criticism."

31. Of which the most current major versions are *Novum Testamentum Graece*, 27th ed., eds. K. Aland, M. Black, C. Martini, B. Metzger, and A. Wikgren (Stuttgart: Deutsche Bibelgesellschaft, 1993)—better known as the Nestle-Aland text; and the United Bible Societies' *Greek New Testament*, 4th ed., eds. B. Aland, K. Aland, J. Karavidopoulos, C. Martini, and B. Metzger (Stuttgart: Deutsche Bibelgesellschaft, 1994)—usually referred to as the UBS text, between which there is minimal difference.

32. Currently reflected chiefly by Zane C. Hodges and Arthur L. Farstad, *The Greek New Testament according to the Majority Text* (Nashville: Thomas Nelson, 1982) or its revision.

33. E.g., modern translations like NIV, NASB, and NRSV used textual bases closely related to the existing Nestle-Aland texts, while NKJV worked with a Majority Text basis much like Hodges-Farstad. A wise and readable introductory source for sorting out NT text critical issues is David Alan Black, *New Testament Textual Criticism: A Concise Guide* (Grand Rapids: Baker, 1994).

34. Michaels, *Interpreting the Book of Revelation*, 89.

35. Aune, *Revelation 1–5*, clxii, goes so far as to assert, "The Greek of Revelation is the most peculiar Greek in the NT."

36. In comparison to, say, the complex Greek of Luke-Acts.

37. Beale, *The Book of Revelation*, 103; See also the helpful, but somewhat different, view of Stanley E. Porter, "The Language of the Apocalypse in Recent Discussion," *NTS* 35 (1989): 582–603.

38. An excellent succinct discussion of these issues is found in Carson, Moo, and Morris, *Introduction to the New Testament*, 468–76.

39. Among such was the inventive view of J. M. Ford, *Revelation*, 3–37, who suggested that John the Baptist may have written a good portion of Revelation (an understanding she has now abandoned).

40. There is, frankly, no consensus on whether the focused persecution in either of these time frames was widespread (throughout the Empire) or more localized and sporadic.

41. J. A. T. Robinson, *Redating the New Testament* (Philadelphia: Westminster, 1976), 221–53.

42. Both Aune's and Beale's commentaries are incredibly detailed in this area. In addition, significant among Beale's other relevant works are his published Cambridge dissertation, *The Use of Daniel in Jewish Apocalyptic Literature and in the Revelation of St. John* (Lanham: University Press of America, 1984); "The Use of the Old Testament in Revelation," in *It is Written: Scripture Citing Scripture*, eds. D. A. Carson and H. G. M. Williamson (Cambridge: Cambridge University Press, 1988), 318–36; and *John's Use of the Old Testament in Revelation*, JSNT Supplements Series (Sheffield: Sheffield Academic Press, 1998).

43. Beale, *The Book of Revelation*, 77, catalogs a number of widely varying listings. Though this extremely wide range indicates that there is little agreement on what constitutes a "use of the OT," it does at least underline the strong proportion of the OT backdrop. The remaining question is only: "Is there merely *a lot* of OT usage, or *even more* OT usage?"

44. Ibid., 78.

45. G. B. Caird, *A Commentary on the Revelation of St. John the Divine*, Harper's New Testament Commentaries (New York: Harper and Row, 1966), 25.

46. Beale, *The Book of Revelation*, 77.

47. Ibid., 81–86, is correct in noting that the OT context in question may be literary, historical, or thematic (or some combination).

48. This is the view of Beale, Ibid., e.g., 86–87, which I share (with some important variations). Cases have been attempted to make Ezekiel, Exodus, and even Zechariah such a literary prototype for the Apocalypse, but these are far less convincing.

49. See esp. Austin M. Farrer, *A Rebirth of Images: The Making of St. John's Apocalypse* (Boston: Beacon, 1949).

50. In an important respect, this view is not dramatically different from that briefly articulated by Darrell Bock in connection with wider use/fulfillment of the OT in the NT issues, in "Why I am a dispensationalist with a Small 'd,'" *JETS* 41 (1998): 390.

51. Osborne, *The Hermeneutical Spiral*, 11.

52. See the helpful treatment of Carroll D. Osburn, "The Christological Use of I Enoch 1.9 in Jude 14, 15," *NTS* 23 (1977): 334–41.

53. The background and command of the original sources, as well as the specific preparation of both for writing their respective commentaries, borders on awe-inspiring.

54. Walter A. Elwell and Robert W. Yarbrough, eds. *Readings from the First-Century World*, Encountering Biblical Studies (Grand Rapids: Baker, 1999), 11.

55. Beale, *The Book of Revelation*, 50–52. Thomas, 56, while admitting this force, counters with this warning: "It in no way gives license for a departure from the normal grammatical-historical system of hermeneutics."

56. Ibid., 52.

57. Ibid., 52–54. This material is adapted from Vern S. Poythress, "Genre and Hermeneutics in Rev. 20:1–6," *JETS* 36 (1993): 41–54.

58. Ibid., 69.

59. See the discussion in Osborne, *The Hermeneutical Spiral*, 235–51, who claims, with very good reason, that parables and apocalyptic have been among the most "hermeneutically abused portions of Scripture" (235).

60. Beale, *The Book of Revelation*, 58ff.

61. E.g., Ibid., 669, who understands this phraseology as "applied to the entire time of the church's existence," as he does the other expressions for three and a half years in Revelation 11–13.

62. G. L. Archer Jr., "Daniel" in *EBC*, 7:94. Whether it is "ten days" (p. 36; Dan. 1:11ff.) or "2,300 evenings and mornings" (p. 103; Dan. 8:14), Archer makes a highly plausible case for understanding the time references in Daniel in a straightforward manner that can be credibly followed in interpreting Revelation.

63. Osborne, *The Hemeneutical Spiral*, 231.

64. Aune, *Revelation 1–5*, 20–21.

65. Thomas, *Revelation 1–7*, 60.

66. A. F. Johnson, "Revelation," 418. See also David L. Barr, "The Apocalypse of John as Oral Enactment," *Interpretation* 40 (1986): 243–56.

67. Though I am not in complete agreement with the analysis and conclusions of either, the two best accessible discussions of internal structural factors are Michaels, *Interpreting the Book of Revelation*, 51–71; and Beale, *The Book of Revelation*, 108–51.

68. There remains sharp disagreement on the grammatical structure of 1:19 and its ramifications. See, e.g., Thomas, *Revelation 1–7*, 43, 113–16 versus Beale, *The Book of Revelation*, 152–70.

69. To my knowledge, Beale was the first scholar to explore carefully these allusions in his published dissertation, *The Use of Daniel*, and it has been something of a programmatic interest ever since.

70. The understanding here is that the vision in Daniel 2 (or, for some, a remaining unfulfilled aspect) gives initial orientation to the focus of the Book of Revelation.

71. Adapted from A. Boyd Luter, "Revelation" notes in the *Nelson Study Bible*, gen. ed. Earl D. Radmacher (Nashville: Thomas Nelson, 1997), 2162–63.

72. Beale, *The Book of Revelation*, 121ff. The odd thing about it is that, while Beale lays out how this supposed parallelism might play out specifically in Revelation in a helpful diagram on p. 136, this understanding is not reflected in the commentary outline from which he works (seen at a glance on pp. x–xvi).

73. Aune, *Revelation 1–5*, cxix.

74. Ibid.

75. M. V. Lee, "A Call to Martyrdom: Function as Method and Message in Revelation," *NovT* 40, 2 (1998): 174, 193–94.

76. Beale, *The Book of Revelation*, 130ff.

77. Lee. "A Call to Martyrdom," 174–90, drawing upon the clearly stated and detailed criteria of Craig Blomberg, "The Structure of 2 Corinthians 1–7," *Criswell Theological Review* 4 (1989): 4–8.

78. Though "main points" related to sophisticated chiastic structures are often found in the outer layer (see below), the centerpoint is almost always disproportionately important.

79. Adapted from Lee, "A Call to Martyrdom," 174.

80. Ibid., 191.

81. Charles H. Talbert, "Artistry and Theology: An Analysis of the Architecture of John 1, 19–5, 47," *CBQ* 32 (1970): 363.

82. Richard Bauckham, *The Theology of the Book of Revelation,* NTT (Cambridge: Cambridge University Press, 1993), 57.

83. A. Boyd Luter, "The Relationship between Israel and the Nations in God's Redemptive Plan," in *Israel: The Land and the People,* ed. H. Wayne House (Grand Rapids: Kregel, 1998).

84. D. H. Johnson, "Blessing," *Dictionary of the Later New Testament and Its Developments,* eds. Ralph P. Martin and Peter H. Davids (Downers Grove, Ill.: IVP, 1997), 131.

85. A. Boyd Luter and Richard O. Rigsby, "An Adjusted Symmetrical Structuring of Ruth," *JETS* 39/1 (1996): 15–28.

86. It is not thought necessary to face directly the reemerging questions of universalism and annihilationism here, especially since the relevant final judgment (Rev. 20:11–15) and New Heavens and Earth (chs. 21–22) passages are not hotly debated and also because these views have been little (and poorly) argued from Revelation.

87. Though this compact discussion does not follow his categories, the best "readable at a sitting" treatment of the theology of the Apocalypse is that of Bauckham, *The Theology of the Book of Revelation.*

88. Osborne, *The Hermeneutical Spiral,* 336–37, 345–47, citing Zuck, "Application in Biblical Hermeneutics," 27–28.

89. E.g., Mounce, *The Book of Revelation,* 365–70.

90. This is the well-considered position on the scroll and seals by Easley, *Revelation,* 90–91. Though it is not Easley's view, this understanding would mean that it is possible to place the Rapture as late as Revelation 7 and still be pretribulational (though the usual "imminency" is blunted somewhat).

91. Archer, "Daniel," 113, employs the latter kind of reasoning in his discussion of Daniel 9:24–27.

92. Beginning with the publication of ex-pretrib. Marvin Rosenthal's *The Pre-wrath Rapture of the Church* (Nashville: Thomas Nelson, 1990).

93. Easley, *Revelation,* 252–55.

94. Because of the self-conscious theological focus of the New American Commentary series, it is anticipated that Paige Patterson's forthcoming Revelation volumes will pointedly expound the theological dimensions of the Apocalypse, notably eschatology.

95. A. Boyd Luter, "Martyrdom," *DLNTID,* 719–20.

96. This is Eugene Boring's candidate for the focal point of the theology of Revelation ("The Theology of Revelation: The Lord Our God the Almighty Reigns," *Interpretation* 40, 3 [1986]: 257–69).

97. D. H. Johnson, "Blessings," 131, sees both this point and even wider theological/canonical significance to the beatitude in 22:14.

98. Much of the above discussion is an adapted expansion of the "Interpreting Revelation" and "Theology" segments in my "Revelation" notes in the *Nelson Study Bible,* 2162, 2195.

99. G. Maier, *Die Johannesoffenbarung und die Kirche* (Tübingen: J.C.B. Mohr, 1981), 622.

100. Michaels, *Interpreting the Book of Revelation,* 18.

101. Ibid., 147.

*I must express my deep appreciation to my assistant, Caroline Creel, for her proofreading skill and to Katherine Squires, Th.M. , for her insightful suggestions and editorial help with this chapter.

Chapter 21

The Foundations of
New Testament Theology

Brad Green
Union University

The New Testament is theologically driven and theologically centered. The New Testament documents are ultimately theological documents, and any attempt to understand them in a nontheological sense will fail to do justice to the character of the documents themselves. Thus, it is appropriate in a volume such as this to pay attention to the nature of the New Testament documents as theological literature and to outline the key issues involved in viewing the New Testament theologically.

George B. Caird suggests "that there is no such thing as New Testament theology" (and this at the very beginning of his own tremendous five-hundred-page *New Testament Theology*!).[1] But even if this statement is hyperbolic, it does point us to the fact that the discipline of "New Testament Theology" is not easily definable, nor do all agree on its nature.

In one sense, every time a Christian reads the New Testament, he or she is engaged in "New Testament theology," for every Bible reader generally tries to understand and make sense of what they read—they "theologize." There is the conviction—even if it has not been thought through and even if it would be difficult to articulate—that there is a theological unity and coherency to the Bible that allows the Bible reader to attempt to synthesize different texts and attempt to make theological sense of the Bible as a whole. Werner G. Kümmel has written that "most Christian Bible readers, . . . if he has not already been influenced by the insights of modern theology, probably will just as naturally assume that the Old Testament and New Testament are unitary, each in itself, and that therefore one can with full justification ask about the teachings of *the* Old and *the* New Testaments, and that he can unequivocally answer these questions."[2] In this sense "New Testament

481

theology" is simply the everyday experience of Bible readers to understand and make sense of what they read in the Bible.[3]

At another level New Testament theology *precedes* the New Testament documents and gives rise to the documents themselves. In this sense New Testament theology is the theology believed and preached and taught by Jesus, the disciples, Paul, and the early Christians who lived immediately before and during the development of the New Testament documents them-selves—what Robert Sloan has called "apostolic theology."[4] Thus, New Testament theology here is that theology which *resulted in* the New Testament documents, rather than that theology which is *derived from* the New Testament documents.[5]

At still another level, and closely related to the preceding paragraph, New Testament theology is that theology which is derived from the New Testament documents. That is, the interpreter seeks to articulate what kind of theological truths flow from the documents. Ultimately, this sort of New Testament theology must be harmonious with that New Testament theology which resulted *in* the New Testament documents. One might say that this type of New Testament theology is concerned with stating what kind of the-ological truths the documents lead to or necessitate rather than what type of apostolic theology existed that led to the New Testament documents.

My goal in this chapter is to outline the central foundations of New Testament theology. I am doing this from the perspective of the evangelical tradition, in that I am working from the perspective of a high view of Scripture, the centrality of the gospel in all theological endeavors, and the essential theological unity of the canon.[6] While there is not space here to jus-tify in detail these theological commitments, it is hoped that the essay as a whole will illustrate the importance and need of such commitments. After a brief survey of the main contours of the history of New Testament theology, I will attempt to show the creedal and confessional nature of the New Testament. Finally, I will outline key foundations for the practice and endeavor of New Testament theology.

A Brief History of New Testament Theology[7]

When one attempts to outline the central "foundations" of New Testament theology, it is worth asking a basic question: would the church of ages past have recognized nomenclature such as "New Testament theol-ogy"? That is, in the premodern age, would there have ever been an article devoted to the topic of New Testament theology? I have my doubts. When one reads the central theologians of ages past, it is intriguing how unaware they are of the divisions and classifications that pervade the contemporary academy of biblical and theological studies. For example, when one reads Calvin's *Institutes*, one encounters a grand task by the preacher of Geneva to outline the main contours of the *principia theologiae*. There is no sense that Calvin is moving *between* Old Testament theology, New Testament theology, historical theology, and systematic theology. Rather, Calvin and older theologians saw themselves as expounding theological truths, working primarily from Holy Scripture. Indeed, before the modern age, virtually *every* orthodox theologian saw himself as one who expounds Scripture, while at the same time working within a context which put a high premium on those councils, creeds, and confessions that preceded him.[8]

New Testament theology as a discipline (or perhaps, at earlier stages, simply "biblical theology")[9] can at least be traced back to 1607, with the appearance of W. J. Christmann's *Teutsche biblische Theologie*, a collection of proof texts compiled in order to buttress Protestant orthodoxy.[10] Philip Jacob Spener, the "Father" of Pietism, in his *Pia Desideria* (1675), distinguished between *theologia biblica* (Spener's own theology) and *theologia scholastica* (Protestant orthodoxy).[11] G. T. Zachariae, in his *Biblische Theologie oder Untersuchung des biblischen Grundes der vornehmsten theologischen Lehren* (1771–86), subtitled, "An Investigation for the Biblical Basis for the Most Important Theological Doctrines," sought to isolate and identify theological truths in the biblical texts that could be used to support an orthodox theological position.[12]

With the development and backdrop of the Enlightenment, there develops what might be called a historicist impulse. A tendency emerges in which the Bible is viewed less as inspired literature but rather more as a common literary document. Johann Salomo Semler (1725–1791), in his *Treatise on the Free Investigation of the Canon* (1771–1775), distinguished between the words of Scripture and the Word of God that is revealed in Scripture, as well as between religion and theology. Thus, the Bible is ultimately treated as a common historical document that is to be interpreted and treated like other literature. These types of distinctions allowed a more critical investigation of the Bible and allowed "theology" to be studied with less of an emphasis on one's "religious" commitments. The "historicist impulse" here and elsewhere lies in an implicit and/or explicit diminishing of the revelatory nature of the biblical documents.[13]

However, the most significant early figure in the development of biblical theology is Johann Philipp Gabler. Gabler gave an address on March 30, 1787, titled, *De justo discrimine theologiae biblicae et dogmaticae regundisque recte utriusque finibus* [An Oration on the Proper Distinction Between Biblical and Dogmatic Theology and the Specific Objectives of Each].[14] It is clear from the title alone that *biblical* and *dogmatic* theology are being distinguished, but one must read closely to discern the exact nature of this distinction, and one must consider if Gabler's position and particular distinction was followed or affirmed by his successors. Gabler argued that biblical and dogmatic theology should be distinguished, but he did not want to argue that there was a radical dichotomy or hostility between the two disciplines.

Rather, if biblical theology is going to be true to itself, it must go about its task unencumbered by the expectation that it must prove the current dogmatic theological tradition. Thus, Gabler argued for a limited autonomy for biblical theology. However, once biblical theology had truly done its work, the dogmatician would be in a good position to use the findings of biblical theology in the forging and articulation of dogmatic theology. He ultimately made three key distinctions: (1) "true biblical theology"—this is biblical religion as it is seen in history; (2) "pure biblical theology"—this is where the eternal theological truths found in history are set out; (3) "dogmatics"—the church's dogmatic formulations, which are rooted in both "true" and "pure" biblical theology. One of Gabler's colleagues at Altdorf, Georg Lorenz Bauer (1755–1806), attempted a "purely historical" biblical theology and is the first person to publish a "New Testament theology" (1800–1802).[15] It is difficult for this "historical" emphasis to keep from slipping into "historicism," and Bauer's work gives evidence of a historicist and rationalistic tendency.

Although not necessarily intended by Gabler himself, one can trace to Gabler's work the modern tendency to distinguish between the *descriptive* and the *normative*. That is, do we find in biblical theology *descriptive* materials (i.e., what, say, *John* believed about the incarnation), or do we find in biblical theology *normative* materials (i.e., what *we* should believe about the incarnation), or should we fuse the descriptive and normative? Additionally, by emphasizing history and the importance of the *descriptive* task in biblical theology, one can see a foreshadowing of the history of religions school which will develop in the following century.

A line should be drawn from Gabler and Bauer to Ferdinand Christian Baur (1792–1860). Baur's New Testament theology was published posthumously in 1864. With the emphasis on history and historical development that preceded him, Baur affirmed that in the New Testament documents there was a struggle between Jewish and Gentile Christianity, a struggle that led to the later early Catholic synthesis. Jewish Christianity (seen in 1 and 2 Peter, Matthew, Revelation) was in antithesis to Gentile Christianity (seen in Galatians, 1 and 2 Corinthians, Romans, Luke). This struggle results in a later synthesis dubbed "early Catholicism" (seen in Mark, John, Acts). The shift here from premodern construals of theology should be noted. Whereas most premodern theologians were quite happy to affirm a thoroughgoing theological unity of Scripture, Baur has contradictory theological differences within the New Testament itself (leaving aside the issue of, say, the relation between the Testaments).

The historicist impulse is seen in the 1800s with the most significant figure in the "history of religions school," Wilhelm Wrede. Wrede, in his 1897 work *Über Aufgabe und Methode der sogenannten neutestamenliche Theologie* [*Concerning the Task and Method of So-Called New Testament Theology*], argued that the goal of the student of the New Testament is not to discover or construct a coherent and unified theology from the New Testament but to discover the historical setting and backdrop of the early Christian movement. "Religion" is a developing, historical phenomena, and the student's task is *descriptive*, rather than *normative*, in that the student of the New Testament for the most part is simply to describe the phenomena of this first-century religious movement.

There were a number of conservative responses to the historicist impulse, and the chief among these was Adolf Schlatter (1852–1938). Schlatter was a German scholar who spent much of his time at Tübingen (as a student and then as a professor).[16] Schlatter was a key voice that offered an alternative to the historicism of Baur and Wrede. Schlatter contended that the New Testament must be interpreted on its own terms, and he lamented the tendency of many of his peers to interpret the New Testament through the grid of modern sensibilities. This did not mean that Schlatter denied the importance of history. Indeed, Schlatter held that the interpreter must pay careful attentions to the history—to the *past*. The interpreter must engage in both "historical" work and "dogmatic" work. Schlatter wished to distinguish these two emphases without posing a dichotomy between them.

The historical work is more descriptive, in that we try to look at the data without regard to how such data impinges upon our own belief system: "We separate off our own connection to them from the investigation."[17] The historical task is more descriptive of the past, with less attention being paid (at least at first) to how our study speaks to our own faith commitments. As Schlatter writes, "Our work has a historical purpose when it is not concerned with the interests that emerge from the course of our own life, but directs its attention quite deliberately away from ourselves and our own contemporary interests, back to the past."[18]

Dogmatic work takes a further step, giving emphasis to how the subject matter impinges on us. This dogmatic task "grants an absolute position to the idea of truth," and the interpreter ascertains "what is true for us ourselves and how for us, and so for everyone, that truth becomes God's revelation by which we attain relationship with him."[19] This dogmatic task "goes on to ask questions about the truth of what is said in the unlimited sense of how it determines our own thinking and willing."[20] In short, the dogmatic work asks more normative questions and allows the past to impinge on the present.

While Schlatter does wish to emphasize the distinction between these two tasks, he is quick to note that these two tasks are not radically separated. Indeed, "in the unity of human existence there is always a two-way connection between them both [between the historical and dogmatic task]."[21] The background (at least in part) to Schlatter's concern is the "atheistic method" in theology, which according to Schlatter produced works that were hostile to Christianity because the "observer" (the interpreter) did not allow the historical material to speak for itself but imposed a modern atheistic grid onto the historical material.[22]

As one moves into the twentieth century, the work of Rudolf Bultmann must be noted. Bultmann was one of the twentieth century's most significant New Testament scholars. Bultmann's two-volume *Theology of the New Testament* was originally published in 1951 and 1955.[23] The first sentence of these volumes gives a hint of what is to come: "*The message of Jesus* is a presupposition for the theology of the New Testament rather than a part of that theology itself." Indeed, "theological thinking—the theology of the New Testament—begins with the *kerygma* of the earliest church and not before."[24] That is, New Testament theology cannot be said to have begun with Jesus, but only with the church *after* Jesus. Bultmann's significance is hard to overestimate. Stephen Neill and Tom Wright note that by "the time of his death he had become one of the great father figures of Western theology."[25]

At the risk of reductionism, we offer the following brief summary of the key elements of Bultmann's thought, particularly as they relate to New Testament theology. (1) In accord with Bultmann's existentialism, the self is primary in Bultmann's theological construals. Critics of Bultmann have contended that for Bultmann theology becomes anthropology, and there is truth in this charge. Bultmann can write that "theological thoughts are the explication of man's understanding of himself as mind (reason)."[26] (2) Bultmann is working with a commitment to naturalistic and "closed" worldview, in which the supernatural is effectively severed from the "natural" order.[27] (3) The New Testament is permeated by a first-century mythical worldview, and it is the task of the New Testament student to "demythologize" the New Testament in order to recover what is of true and eternal value. (4) The first-century historical Jesus is virtually unknowable, and this Jesus plays no significant role in Bultmann's theological work. (5) Bultmann sees the Hellenistic world as more central than Jewish thought as the background to understanding the New Testament.[28] (6) Although Bultmann is in part forging his thought in contradistinction to the history-of-religions school, he does not fully escape that world of thought.

Since the time of Bultmann, there has been a veritable explosion of works on New Testament theology, whether large, synthesizing treatises or treatments of a specific theme or themes. However, no one school or figure currently dominates the field. One can see the legacy of Bultmann in the work of Hans Conzelmann,[29] and one can see naturalistic and/or historicist tendencies in phenomena like *The Five Gospels*.[30] Many writings have been committed neither to historicism nor to Bultmann's paradigm: the salvation-historical approach of Oscar Cullmann,[31] Joachim Jeremias' *New Testament Theology*,[32] the work of Peter Stuhlmacher,[33] the work of George Eldon Ladd,[34] George B. Caird,[35] and the recent work of N. T. Wright.[36]

The Confessional and Creedal Nature of the New Testament

Before outlining key foundations of New Testament theology, it is important simply to point to the reality of the theological nature of the documents themselves. That is, in thinking theologically about the New Testament, it is important to see the confessional and creedal nature of the New Testament itself. By this I am contending that it is not the case that "doctrine" is a later, postscriptural development of the Christian community.[37] Rather, the New Testament documents already contain confessional and creedal formulas that give evidence of theological conviction, a theological conviction that would have *preceded* the existence of the documents.[38]

As J. N. D. Kelly has written, content of the "rule of faith," an early creedal formula that confesses the lordship of Christ, "was . . . in all essentials, foreshadowed by the 'pattern of teaching' accepted in the apostolic Church." Indeed, "its characteristic lineaments and outline found their prototypes in the confessions and creedal summaries contained in the New Testament documents."[39] Kelly is not arguing that the early Christian Church had an established written creed before the formation of the New Testament documents. Rather, Kelly's point is that "creeds of a looser sort, lacking the fixity and the official character of the later formularies [e.g. the Apostles' Creed] but nonetheless foreshadowing them, were in use comparatively early."[40]

The New Testament puts a high premium on transmitting authoritative doctrine, and the evidence points to authoritative teaching and doctrine at virtually every strata of the New Testament, from the earlier documents to the later.[41] The concept of "tradition(s)," "pattern," "gospel," "faith," and "the word" permeates the Pauline corpus. Although Paul can claim that he received his gospel "by a revelation of Jesus Christ" (Gal. 1:12 NASB), he also insists that the gospel is something both he and the Corinthians "received" (1 Cor. 15:1, 3): "Now I make known to you, brethren, the gospel which I preached to you, which also you received, in which also you stand," and Paul continues, "I delivered to you as of first importance what I also received, that Christ died . . . according to the Scriptures."[42] Paul can refer to "the gospel" (*to euaggelion*) in such a way as to give the impression that the readers/hearers knew this gospel quite well with no further elaboration (Gal. 2:2; Rom. 2:16; Rom. 16:25). Paul can refer to the "traditions" (2 Thess. 2:15; *tas paradoseis*—related to the Greek verb *paradidōmi*—"to pass on," "entrust," "deliver") which were "taught by us," and which must be "held" or "kept." Paul claims that his teaching on the Lord's Supper was "received" from the Lord (1 Cor. 11:23).

Paul refers to "teaching"/"forms of teaching," "preaching," the "word" that is preached, etc. Heart obedience to a "form of teaching" is commended, Christians are established by "the preaching of Jesus Christ" (an objective genitive—"the preaching *about* Jesus Christ"), and the "message preached" is the means by which God saves sinners (1 Cor. 1:21). The "word" was "received" (1 Thess. 1:6); this "word of the Lord" has already "sounded forth" from the Thessalonians; Paul requests prayer that this "word of the Lord" may continue to spread; this "word of the Lord" has come forth from the Corinthians (1 Cor. 14:36); Paul can give a command to "the one who is taught the word" (Gal. 6:6); and many brethren speak "the word of God" with more courage due to Paul's imprisonment (Phil. 1:14). Paul can speak of being "rooted" and "built up" in "the faith" (*tē pistei*) (Col. 2:7), of preaching "the faith" (*tēn pistin*) (Gal. 1:23), of "one faith" (*mia pistis*) (Eph. 4:5).

Later parts of the New Testament such as Jude, the Pastoral Epistles, and Hebrews are also marked by a creedal and confessional pattern. Jude can speak of the "the faith which was once for all delivered to the saints" (v. 3), while Paul can speak of "keeping faith" (1 Tim. 1:19), and of simply "the faith" (Titus 1:13; *tē pistei*). Paul can also speak of "the standard of sound words" (2 Tim. 1:13), of "sound doctrine" (2 Tim. 4:3; 1 Tim. 4:6), of "the faithful word" (Titus 1:9), of the "deposit" ("what was entrusted") to Timothy (1 Tim. 6:20), of "the good deposit" (2 Tim. 1:14 NASB: "the treasure which has been entrusted to you"), while the author of Hebrews can speak of "our confession" or "the confession" (*homologia*) (3:1; 4:14; 10:23).

The Book of Acts also evidences a confessional/creedal theology.[43] Acts 6:4 can speak of the ministry of "the word" (*tou logou*), and Acts 2:42 can speak of the devotion to "the apostle's teaching" (*tē didachē tōn apostolōn*). The centrality of Jesus as Messiah (*Christos*) is repeated throughout Acts and was one of the first themes of Paul's preaching after his conversion (9:22; cf. 5:42; 18:5, 28). The lordship of Christ is often stressed, as is seen in 10:36, where Peter speaks of "Jesus Christ" (*Christos* here being used as a proper name rather than simply a title), who is "Lord of all," and in 11:20, where some men are "preaching the Lord Jesus." The title "Son of God" is rare in Acts, but it is significant that in Paul's first recorded "sermon" Luke reports that Paul proclaimed Jesus, "saying, 'He is the Son of God.'"[44] Of particular importance, the basic gospel message of the death and resurrection of Jesus is often summarized in brief formulas in Acts. In Peter's preaching at Pentecost, he can preach of the death and resurrection of Jesus: "'You nailed [Jesus] to a cross by the hands of godless men and put him to death. And God raised him up again'" (2:23–24). Again, in addressing the Jews Peter can preach that "[You] put to death the Prince of life, the one whom God raised from the dead" (3:15).

From such texts it becomes evident that the New Testament documents are theological at their core and that the documents themselves contain numerous "confessions" or primitive "creedal" statements. This confessional and creedal nature of the New Testament reveals that thinking theologically about the New Testament, and the attempt to understand the theological nature of the New Testament, is not foreign to the New Testament documents because the documents *themselves* are *already* intrinsically theological. To approach the New Testament seeking to understand the theological message is not "imposing" something on the documents, since the documents are already theological at their core.

Key Components and Principles of New Testament Theology

Where does one start today in the task of New Testament theology? While there is no agreed-upon method for New Testament theology, it is possible to suggest some key components and principles of the task of New Testament theology. We offer the following themes as being at the heart of the task.

THE CENTRALITY OF JESUS CHRIST AND THE GOSPEL

At the heart of New Testament theology stands Jesus Christ and the gospel. Not only is Jesus Christ the *focus* of New Testament theology, but it can and should be argued that he stands at the center of the *origin* of New Testament theology.[45] That is, not only does New Testament theology concern itself *with* Jesus, but New Testament theology also *originates* with Jesus. An older theological liberalism denied this. For example, for Adolf von Harnack, the "essence" of Christianity was the fatherhood of God, the brotherhood of man, and the ethical teachings of Jesus. Indeed, Harnack could say that Christianity was ultimately not concerned with the *Son* at all but only with the Father.[46] Likewise, an older theological liberalism argued that Paul, not Jesus, was the founder of Christianity and that complex beliefs about Jesus (i.e., doctrinal affirmations) were an imposition onto Scripture of later theological development (often attributed to "Greek" philosophical influence and categories) and could not be legitimately traced to or rooted in Jesus and the earliest Christian witnesses to him.[47]

However, even theologians of a more traditional cast are not always quick to see Jesus Christ and/or the gospel as the "center" of New Testament theology. D. A. Carson has written, "One might say that the center of NT theology is Jesus Christ, but although at one level that is saying everything at another level it is saying almost nothing."[48] Perhaps this is the case, but I suspect the affirmation of the centrality of Jesus Christ and the gospel does indeed serve as a helpful center to New Testament theology.

Peter Stuhlmacher has argued that the preaching of Jesus Christ is both the origin and center of New Testament theology.[49] Indeed, Stuhlmacher contends that the center of the Christian canon (i.e., Old and New Testaments) "*is the witness to God's act of salvation for Jews and Gentiles in and through Christ.*"[50] The reality of Jesus, including both his person and his actions pervade the New Testament. While the Old Testament revelation was genuine and true, a fuller revelation has come in Christ (Heb. 1:1–2). He is the one through whom the world was created (John 1:3; Heb. 1:2; Col. 1:15ff.) and through whom the created order is sustained (Col. 1:17; Heb. 1:3). Christ is not only the agent of creation; he is also the head of a new creation, and this new creation is "in him," or "in Christ" (2 Cor. 5:17; Gal. 6:15).[51]

Jesus' earliest recorded teaching in his ministry entailed "preaching the gospel of God" (Mark 1:14). One can even argue, with Graeme Goldsworthy, that the center of the *Old* Testament is indeed Christ and the gospel. This conclusion can be justified by the following phenomena: Jesus' own teaching in Luke 24:25–27, 44–45 that Moses and the prophets wrote concerning himself, the fact that Paul's gospel—the death, burial, and resurrection—happened "according to the Scriptures" (1 Cor. 15:3–4; i.e. the Old Testament),[52] the New Testament's willingness to see Christ present in the Old Testament (e.g., Christ was the "rock" that provided spiritual drink in Israel's desert wanderings—1 Cor. 10:4), and the New Testament's vision of Christ as the fulfillment of Old Testament hopes and promises (Acts 13:32; 1 Cor. 5:7—Christ as the Passover lamb; Gal. 3:13—Christ as one who removes the curse of the law; Gal. 3:29—belonging to Christ means being Abraham's seed; Rom. 10:4—Christ as the end of the law). New Testament theology is properly focused on Christ, and Christ himself serves as the originating impulse behind New Testament theology.

The Legitimacy of Theology and the Theological Unity of Scripture

Ultimately, however, we must go further than simply to affirm the centrality of Jesus Christ in the task of New Testament theology. New Testament theology also requires a fundamental commitment to the legitimacy of *theology* and to the theological unity of the New Testament. That is, the interpreter of the New Testament, if he or she hopes to state the theological meaning of a text or book, must affirm that theology itself is a legitimate task. Has God truly spoken? Has God truly revealed himself? Is it possible to speak about God? Can language speak truly, if not exhaustively, about God and his purposes? While these sorts of questions would have been answered thoroughly in the affirmative by premodern theologians (with the possible exception of the apophatic tradition in relation to the possibility of speaking about God), as believers living in the modern world, theologians and biblical scholars must be able and willing to affirm that theology is a legitimate task and that theology is neither "religion" nor simply the study of past events.

In genuine theology, the conviction that we speak about God only because he has truly spoken to us must remain paramount. Although many voices—past and present—might urge otherwise, theology must affirm a supernaturalistic worldview in which God has truly spoken. Closely related to the question of the legitimacy of theology is the importance of the theological unity of Holy Scripture. It has been argued that while certainly theology is possible, the New Testament simply gives us contradictory and polyvalent theolog*ies*, not theological unity. While the different emphases, personalities, and concerns of the different writers must and should be affirmed, the task of New Testament theology becomes a dead end if it is approached without a commitment to the theological unity of the documents themselves. This unity is ultimately centered in Jesus Christ and his gospel. The four Gospels record the origin, life/teachings, death, and resurrection of Christ; Acts pictures the church in its growth as following her resurrected Lord; the Epistles focus on life in Christ (and all that entails); and the Apocalypse focuses on continued life in Christ and the ultimate culmination of history.

One might object by arguing that the New Testament consists of largely occasional literature, and therefore it is illegitimate to try to construct a consistent, coherent theology from these documents or, stated slightly differently, to try to discover the theological convictions underlying the documents. But there is a *non sequitur* here. The occasional nature of the New Testament documents does *not* mean that there is not a coherent, consistent theology that can be derived from the documents or that underlies the documents. A coherent and consistent theology could inform diverse responses to multiple situations without necessitating the conclusion that no coherent and consistent theology exists.[53]

Although a full *defense* of the theological unity of the New Testament is not offered here, a good place to start is simply the *existence* of the New Testament canon itself. Where did these books come from, and what were the motivating forces behind their collection? As Robert Sloan has argued, there is good reason to believe that an "apostolic theology" existed *before* the emergence of the New Testament documents and that this theology gave rise to and unifies the New Testament documents. If this is the case, there would be good reason to grant at least provisionally the theological unity of the documents. Indeed, if there were an "apostolic theology" generally shared by the early Christians and if this theology was considered authoritative (e.g., 1 Thess. 2:13), it would follow that the New Testament is ultimately the inscripturated form of this oral theology.[54]

The question of the theological unity of the Bible is ultimately a "meta" question that takes us into the realm of presuppositions and ultimate convictions. An affirmation of the theological unity of Scripture is usually tied to a conviction about who God is—a God whose character can be trusted and who tells the truth. While Schlatter is probably right that the interpreter of Scripture should (at least partially) put one's own interests aside in an honest attempt to understand the meaning of the ancient text, such a method does not deny the importance of presuppositions. Rather, such an interpretive method in the end has its *own* presuppositional commitment to certain convictions: that there is an ancient text, its message is worth retrieving, interpretation is a real possibility, the human mind in a real sense understands things the way they generally are, the text I am holding in my hand is not simply an illusion. It is best simply to admit such presuppositions and insist that *every* interpreter comes to the text with certain presuppositions that would be extremely difficult to "prove" at the bar of "neutral" reason.

The evangelical interpreter approaches the text knowing that this is God's world and that all things are to be done for God's glory (1 Cor. 10:31). The Christian comes to the text with a commitment to certain theological truths, and it is simply naive to contend that *all* or even most convictions are up for grabs when one interprets a text. The reality of the gospel, the deity of Christ, and the trustworthiness of God are convictions that would be hard for most evangelicals to reject, and these convictions will ultimately shape one's effort at interpretation. Methodological skepticism or neutrality should be called what it is: an illusion. It is not the case that the evangelical comes to the text with presuppositions, while the nonevangelical does not. Rather, *every* interpreter comes to the text with a whole network of presuppositions. Both interpreters think their presuppositions are true, and it is not necessary, in affirming the existence of such presuppositions, to conclude that both sets of presuppositions are equally valid or that both are simply human constructs. Rather, the evangelical believes his or her presuppositions really are true and that these presuppositions will result in fruitful interpretation, sound conclusions, and genuine scholarship.

HISTORY AND IMPORTANCE OF THE PAST

A legitimate and fruitful New Testament theology will affirm the centrality of history and the importance of the past. In describing his own efforts at New Testament theology as a *historical* discipline, Adolf Schlatter writes, "Our work has a historical purpose when it is not concerned with the interests that emerge from the course of our own life, but directs its attention quite deliberately away from ourselves and our own contemporary interests, back to the past."[55] Along with Paul (who "received" his gospel—1 Cor. 15:3), the student of the New Testament must put a higher premium on "receiving" than "construction." As Schlatter writes, in the task of New Testament theology, "receiving takes precedence over construction."[56] We must pay attention to what is "given." Schlatter again writes, "We cannot create anything without reference to what is given," for "the question of truth . . . is always related to what is *given*."[57]

Ultimately, New Testament theology is concerned with *history*, but must not succumb to *historicism*.[58] New Testament theology concerns itself with certain *historical* events—particularly the death, burial, and resurrection of Jesus, but a *historicist* interpretive grid distorts the New Testament's own theological interpretation of these events: this gospel—the death, burial, and resurrection of Jesus—is the story of the incarnate Son of God and of what God has done *in history* for the redemption of sinners. While we cannot deal in depth with the whole question of the "historical Jesus" and the various concomitant "quests," there is little doubt that the best New Testament theology must see itself as centered on a first-century, flesh-and-blood Jesus of Nazareth. With Werner Georg Kümmel, we must confess that "the Christian who inquires after the message of the New Testament *must* also inquire after the Jesus who justifies his faith. Hence there can be no doubt that the question of the historical Jesus belongs at the beginning of the concern with the theology of the New Testament."[59]

The past reveals its own importance when we stop and take note of the trend of literary criticism, as well as the more destructive strands of postmodernism.[60] A high premium on the past reminds one of the importance of history for the Christian faith. Whatever the strengths of contemporary literary criticism, a weakness of some literary criticism is a devaluation of the authorial intent and historical background of the New Testament documents in favor of an emphasis on the text itself (apart from historical reference) and/or the reader's engagement with the text.[61] N. T. Wright has advocated an approach to the New Testament that would emphasize three main components that constitute a legitimate understanding of the New Testament: literature, history, and theology.[62] By holding all three together, and by seeing the New Testament as literature, history, and theology, the interpreter is less likely to forget the past (indeed, to forget history) in favor of some contemporary trend in "literary" studies. Indeed, to treat the New Testament as "literature" without paying attention to its historical and theological nature is to misunderstand the nature of this literature.[63] Geerhardus Vos has remarked that the Christian faith is ultimately a faith that is vulnerable at its central point—the incarnation.[64] By being a *historical* faith, it is open to verification at its core, the person and work of Jesus Christ. Whereas other faiths, particularly radically transcendental religions, may make truth claims about meaning, value, and the "gods," historic Christianity has always affirmed the centrality of first-century historical events to its nature and mission. Christianity is ultimately an *incarnational* faith, and the Jesus whom Christians worship and seek to follow was truly here *with us*, and as such was a part of this world of history.

THE IMPORTANCE OF THE OLD TESTAMENT AND GOD'S REDEMPTIVE PLAN

New Testament theology must always see itself in fundamental continuity with the Old Testament and with God's relations with his covenant people. That is, New Testament theology is not autonomous. The New Testament reveals ultimately a *continued* work of God that is in organic connection to the Old Testament. If this is the case, we in turn would want to argue that New Testament theology is ultimately the culmination of biblical theology. Indeed, we might argue that New Testament theology—done correctly—*is* biblical theology. Biblical theology in the full sense of a theology of the whole Bible is an area in which much work could be done. Much work has been done on New Testament theology and Old Testament theology, but unfortunately less has been done on a unified biblical theology, if for no other reason than such a task is indeed daunting. However, the work of Brevard S. Childs, Graeme Goldsworthy, William Dumbrell, and in a more limited way, Francis Watson, are notable exceptions.[65]

The theological exegete must always keep in mind that on the Bible's *own* terms what is happening in the New Testament is inextricably linked to God's work in the past: creation, covenants, promises, blessings, and curses. Both Matthew (1:1–17) and Luke (3:23–38) recount the genealogy of Jesus, tracing Jesus' lineage back to Abraham (Matt. 1:1) and Adam (Luke 3:38). This Jesus of Nazareth is indeed Immanuel, as foretold by Isaiah (Isa. 7:14; Matt. 1:23). The New Testament applies Old Testament texts to the coming of Christ, even applying Old Testament Yahweh texts to Jesus (for Isa. 40:3 see Matt. 3:3; Mark 1:3; Luke 1:76; John 1:23; for Mal. 3:1 see Matt. 11:10; Mark 1:2; Luke 1:17; Luke 7:27; Rev. 22:16). Jesus is the "prophet like Moses" promised in Deuteronomy 18:15, 18 (cf. John 1:45; 5:46; 6:14; 7:40; Acts 3:22–26; 7:37). Jesus can teach that he came to fulfill the Law, not to abolish it (Matt. 5:17ff.). Jesus' work is compared to the Mosaic covenant, to which it is superior (Heb. 3). Jesus' priestly work is superior to the Old Covenant priestly administration, but Jesus' work is nonetheless in continuity with and the fulfillment of that prior administration (Lev. 1–7; Heb. 4:14–10:18). Jesus is the fulfillment of the Davidic covenant (2 Sam. 7:11–14; cf. Ps. 2:7; Matt. 1:11; Mark 1:11; John 1:49; 2 Cor. 6:18; Acts 2:25–36; Heb. 1:5). Jesus' death is portrayed in covenantal terms as the "new covenant," denoting both continuity and discontinuity with and fulfillment of God's redemptive covenantal workings in the Old Testament (Matt. 26:27–29; Mark 14:22–25; Luke 22:20–22; 1 Cor. 11:23–25). Jesus' death is clearly portrayed as a passover death, being the fulfillment and antitype of God's redemptive work of rescuing the Israelites from bondage in Egypt (Ex. 12; cf. Matt. 26:17–30; Mark 14:12–26; Luke 22:7–23; 1 Cor. 5:7). Paul recounts God's redemptive purposes from the choosing of the patriarchs (Acts 13:17) to the resurrection and concludes that the resurrection fulfills what "God has promised to our children [i.e. the Israelites]" (Acts 13:33). In describing conversion Paul explicitly uses creation language from Genesis 1:3 (2 Cor. 4:6).[66] Likewise, if someone is "in Christ"—if they are a Christian—they are a "new creature" (2 Cor. 5:17). If someone belongs to Christ, they are Abraham's "seed," and "heirs according to the [Abrahamic] promise" (Gal. 3:29). Particularly striking is Paul's extended teaching on the salvation of Jews and Gentiles found in Romans 9–11. While the gospel is for *both* Jews and Gentiles, salvation is *first* for the Jew (Rom. 1:16–17). The stubbornness of the Jews has led to their rejection (at least in part, and temporarily), and the inclusion of the Gentiles in God's salvific plan is "proven" from the use of Old Testament texts, which speak of people who are "not my people" [i.e. the Gentiles] becoming the people of God (Rom. 9:25–26). Indeed, the salvation of the Gentiles is motivated, at least in part, by God's desire to make the Jews envious, thus inciting the Jews to seek the Lord (Rom. 10:19; 11:11, 14, 25). Gentiles have been grafted into God's redemptive line, or "tree." But the tree is fundamentally a Jewish phenomenon, into which Gentiles have been graciously grafted (Rom. 11:11–24).

This cursory summary of some of the pan-biblical themes that run throughout both the Testaments reveals that in the end New Testament theology is ultimately biblical theology, since the themes that are being worked out in the New Testament documents are ultimately overarching biblical themes. In a truly New Testament theology, it must be confessed that the New Testament ultimately supplies us with the true picture of God's gracious dealings with mankind. Further, it must be confessed that the New Testament, on its own terms, claims that God's redemptive purposes accomplished in Christ provide *the* true culmination to God's activity of creation and redemption recorded in the Old Testament. Simply put, the Christian message is *the* true conclusion to the Old Testament message. A genuine New Testament theology will carry on its work with the conviction that God's activity in Christ is the only legitimate culmination of God's activity with Israel.

Conclusion

We have attempted in this chapter to summarize the key figures in the history of New Testament theology, demonstrate the confessional and creedal nature of the New Testament, and outline some key foundations for New Testament theology. In the task of New Testament theology, we suggest that one must recognize and confess the centrality of Jesus Christ and the gospel. Such a confession affirms that all endeavors are informed by certain presuppositions and faith commitments (whether Christian or otherwise), and neither surrenders objectivity to others (for all persons engage in their tasks informed by presuppositions and faith commitments) nor capitulates to a postmodern relativism (for the Christian confesses that his or her presuppositions and faith commitment are really *true*).

The whole of Scripture ultimately finds its center and culmination in the reality of God's activity in Christ. New Testament theology affirms the legitimacy of *theology*—in that it affirms that God truly has spoken and that we can truly speak faithfully of God and his purposes—and affirms the theological unity of Holy Scripture, a unity that is derived from the reality of the Triune God, whose Word can be trusted. New Testament theology, like the biblical writers themselves, places a high premium on the past and affirms that God's activity in history is crucial and that attention is to be given to *history*, while avoiding the errors of *historicism*. Finally, New Testament theology recognizes its organic relationship to all of God's activity in history, including the activity of God and his people recorded in the Old Testament. New Testament theology recognizes that God's activity in Christ is the culmination and fulfillment of all of God's creative and redemptive activity. Hence, the task of New Testament theology is ultimately the task of understanding God and his purposes, a task to be entered into humbly, engaged with passionately, and pursued joyously.[67]

Bibliography

Caird, G. B. *New Testament Theology*. Completed and Edited by L. D. Hurst. Oxford: Clarendon Press, 1994.

Carson, D. A. "Current Issues in Biblical Theology: A New Testament Perspective." *Bulletin for Biblical Research* 5 (1995): 17–41.

———. "New Testament Theology." In *Dictionary of Later New Testament and Its Developments*, ed. Ralph P. Martin and Peter H. Davids. Downers Grove, Ill.: InterVarsity Press, 1997, 796–814.

Childs, Brevard S. *Biblical Theology of the Old and New Testaments: Theological Reflection on the Christian Bible*. Minneapolis: Fortress, 1992.

Dumbrell, William J. *The Search for Order: Biblical Eschatology in Focus* (Grand Rapids: Baker, 1999).

Ellis, E. Earle. "Jesus' Use of the Old Testament and the Genesis of New Testament Theology." *Bulletin for Biblical Research* 3 (1993): 59–75.

Goldsworthy, Graeme. *Gospel and Kingdom: A Christian Approach to the Old Testament*. Carlisle, U.K.: Paternoster, 1981.

Goppelt, Leonhard. *Theology of the New Testament*. 2 vols. Translated by John Alsup. Philadelphia: Westminster, 1977.

Kümmel, Werner Georg. *The Theology of the New Testament According to Its Major Witnesses, Jesus—Paul—John*. Nashville: Abingdon, 1973.

Ladd, George Eldon. *A Theology of the New Testament*. Revised edition. Edited by Donald A. Hagner. Grand Rapids: Eerdmans, 1993.

Neuer, Werner. *Adolf Schlatter: A Biography of Germany's Premier Biblical Theologian*. Trans. Robert W. Yarbrough. Grand Rapids: Baker, 1995. Contains two important essays by Schlatter: "Adolf Schlatter on Method in New Testament Theology" and "Adolf Schlatter on Atheistic Methods in Theology."

Sloan, Robert B. "Unity in Diversity: A Clue to the Emergence of the New Testament as Sacred Literature." *New Testament Criticism and Interpretation*. Ed. David Alan Black and David S. Dockery. Grand Rapids: Zondervan, 1991. Pages 435–68.

Stuhlmacher, Peter. *How to Do Biblical Theology*. Princeton Theological Monograph Series 38. Allison Park, Pa: Pickwick Publications, 1995.

Wright, N. T. *The New Testament and the People of God*. Vol. 1, *Christian Origins and the Question of God*. Minneapolis: Fortress, 1992.

Notes

1. George B. Caird, *New Testament Theology*, completed and edited by L. D. Hurst (Oxford: Clarendon Press, 1994), 4.

2. Werner Georg Kümmel, *The Theology of the New Testament According to Its Major Witnesses, Jesus—Paul—John* (Nashville: Abingdon, 1973), 13.

3. It is imperative, for at least two reasons, that the theological student and the academic not mock such Bible reading and theologizing by the layperson: (1) in one sense, the goal (besides larger, ultimate goals such as the glory of God) of theological and biblical scholarship is to help the church in its understanding of God's Word, to help all of God's people be "Bereans," examining and studying the Scriptures every day to see if what the scholar is saying is true (Acts 17:11); (2) the "theologizing" of the laypersons in their Bible reading is a beautiful testimony to the perspicuity of Scripture, to the theological unity and harmony of God's Word, and to the fact that God has created man in such a way that theological understanding is truly possible.

4. See Robert B. Sloan, "Unity in Diversity: A Clue to the Emergence of the New Testament as Sacred Literature," in *New Testament Criticism and Interpretation*, ed. David Alan Black and David S. Dockery (Grand Rapids: Zondervan, 1991), 437–68. C. H. Dodd pointed toward the apostolic preaching, which he believed could be outlined, at least in broad strokes. Cf. Dodd's *The Apostolic Preaching and its Development*, 2nd ed. (London: Hodder, 1963). Alan Richardson, *An Introduction to the Theology of the New Testament* (New York: Harper and Brothers, Publishers, 1958), argued that there was indeed a common apostolic theology that underlies the New Testament documents. The question Richardson asks is, "Is it right to assume that the apostolic Church possessed a common theology and that it can be reconstructed from the New Testament literature?" (p. 9). Richardson attempts to answer this question in the affirmative by the following method: he starts with the hypothesis that there *is* such a common theology, and then he works through the documents themselves to see if such a hypothesis is justified.

5. Of course, from our position, our knowledge of this early apostolic theology *is* "derived from" the New Testament, for our only bridge to the theology that gave rise to the New Testament is the New Testament itself. But it is important to see that the documents arose out of theological conviction, and we do not somehow "impose" theology on the documents after the fact. Cf. C. F. D. Moule, *The Birth of the New Testament*, 3rd ed. (San Francisco: Harper & Row Publishers, 1982), 184–85, who speaks of a "foundation and superstructure" preached by early Christians (throughout which numerous appeals to Scripture are included): (1) Initial proclamation: "Jesus, approved by miracles and deeds of goodness, was handed over by the Jews to Pilate and killed; but God raised him from among the dead and made him Lord and Messiah. All this was according to the scriptures." (2) Initial appeal: "Therefore repent, be baptized, and you will receive the Holy Spirit." (A) Initial proclamation: Death, burial, resurrection of Jesus, the Lord and Messiah, according to the Scriptures. (B) Initial appeal: Call to repentance, baptism, reception of Holy Spirit.

6. To the extent that much of modern theology has forfeited the essential theological unity of Scripture, theology becomes more and more impossible. Gerald Bray is generally right: "Classical orthodoxy is synthetic and integrative in its approach to the New Testament, whereas modern criticism is analytic and divisive." See Gerald Bray, *Creeds, Councils and Christ: Did the Early Christians Misrepresent Jesus?* 2nd ed. (Ross-Shire, Great Britain: Mentor, 1997), 56. The previous volume of *New Testament Criticism and Interpretation* (Grand Rapids: Zondervan, 1991) featured two essays at least partially devoted to these issues: Mikael C. Parsons, "Canonical Criticism" (255–94), and Robert B. Sloan, "Unity and Diversity: A Clue to the Emergence of the New Testament as Sacred Literature" (437–68). On the authority of Scripture see Peter H. Davids' essay earlier in the current volume. Sloan's previous essay likewise saw the gospel, or what Sloan summarizes as the "crucified, risen, and exalted Lord," as "the originating influence and the reflective object of the theology that eventually gave rise to the New Testament literature

itself" (p. 463). The work of Graeme Goldsworthy has been particularly beneficial in helping me to attempt to understand Scripture from the vantage point of the Gospel. See his *According to Plan: The Unfolding Revelation of God in the Bible* (Leicester: InterVarsity Press, 1991); idem, *Gospel and Kingdom: A Christian Interpretation of the Old Testament* (Carlisle, U.K.: Paternoster Press, 1996); idem, *Gospel and Revelation: The Book of Revelation in Light of the Gospel* (Carlisle, U.K.: Paternoster Press, 1994).

7. The history of New Testament theology and issues of prolegomena related to New Testament theology have been treated in a number of places: Gerhard Hasel, *New Testament Theology: Basic Issues in the Current Debate* (Grand Rapids: Eerdmans, 1978); James Barr, "Biblical Theology," *IDB Supplement*, (Nashville: Abingdon, 1976), 104–11; Otto Betz, "History of Biblical Theology," *IBD* 1: 432–37; George B. Caird, *New Testament Theology*, completed and edited by L. D. Hurst (Oxford: Clarendon Press, 1994), 1–26; Brevard S. Childs, *Biblical Theology of the Old and New Testaments: Theological Reflection on the Christian Bible* (Minneapolis: Fortress, 1992), 3–29; Reginald Fuller, "New Testament Theology," in *The New Testament and Its Modern Interpreters*, ed. Eldon Jay Epp and George W. MacRae, S.J. (Philadelphia: Fortress; Atlanta: Scholars Press, 1989), 565–84; Leonhard Goppelt, *The Theology of the New Testament*, vol. 1, trans. John E. Alsup, ed. Juürgen Roloff (Grand Rapids: Eerdmans, 1981), 251–81; A. Vogtle, "New Testament Theology," *Sacramentum Mundi* 4:216–20; Hendrikus Boers, *What Is New Testament Theology? The Rise of Criticism and the Problem of a Theology of the New Testament*. Guides to Biblical Scholarship, New Testament Series (Philadelphia: Fortress, 1979); Donald A. Carson, "Current Issues in Biblical Theology: A New Testament Perspective," *Bulletin for Biblical Research 5* (1995): 17–41; idem, "New Testament Theology," in *Dictionary of the Later New Testament and Its Developments*, ed. Ralph P. Martin and Peter H. Davids (Downers Grove, Ill.: InterVarsity Press, 1997), 796–814. Though treating biblical theology in the broader sense, the two-part article by Charles H. H. Scobie is very helpful: "The Challenge of Biblical Theology" and "The Structure of Biblical Theology," *Tyndale Bulletin* 42, no. 1 (1991): 31–61, 163–94.

8. That is, theologians saw themselves as under the authority of Scripture, but the councils, creeds, and confessions served as helpful summaries of the key teachings of Scripture. Cf. Gerald Bray, *Creeds, Councils and Christ*; idem, *Biblical Interpretation: Past and Present* (Downers Grove, Ill.: InterVarsity Press, 1996). One whole volume of *Evangelical Review of Theology* (19.2, April 1995) is devoted to the question of "Scripture and Tradition," to which exponents of various traditions contributed (Eastern Orthodoxy, Roman Catholicism, Reformation Thought, Enlightenment Thought, World Council of Churches, Evangelical).

9. Ultimately, *biblical theology* is the preferable term as well as the preferable enterprise. New Testament theology, in the best sense, is biblical theology in that biblical theologians should be about the task of articulating and expounding the theological truths that pervade and flow out of the entire Christian canon. The Old and New Testaments are simply inseparable and must be treated together. As Francis Watson has noted regarding the Old and New Testaments, "Neither collection is self-sufficient; both of them are what they are only in relation to the other." See his *Text and Truth: Redefining Biblical Theology* (Grand Rapids: Eerdmans, 1997), 180. Indeed, Peter Stuhlmacher (*How to Do Biblical Theology*. Princeton Theological Monograph Series 38 [Allison Park, Pa.: Pickwick Publications, 1995]) has recently argued that the canonization process of the Old and New Testaments was actually "*one complex continuous process*," a process that includes the Septuagint as part of the canon. Stuhlmacher writes (p. 5, italicizing his), "*The New Testament books are not placed opposite an Old Testament*

which had long been fixed as to its contents; rather, they refer to a collection of 'Holy Scriptures' written in Hebrew and Greek which are still canonically unclosed, and they testify to a continuity of God's activity in and through Christ, a continuity of salvation history." See D. A. Carson, "Current Issues in Biblical Theology," as well as Charles H. H. Scobie's two-part article, "The Challenge of Biblical Theology" and "The Structure of Biblical Theology."

10. Cf. Carson, "New Testament Theology," 796.

11. Philip Jacob Spener, *Pia Desideria* (Philadelphia: Fortress, 1964). It should be noted that Spener was *not* rejecting the importance of orthodox theology and correct doctrine, as is sometimes suggested or implied. Rather, Spener argues for a genuine theological and moral renewal, not for a "heart" renewal at the expense of a "mind" renewal. For example, Spener writes, "Not only should we know what is true in order to follow it, but we should also know what is false in order to oppose it" (p. 49). And piety is central to the study of theology. Spener, referring approvingly to David Chytraeus, writes, "The study of theology should be carried on not by the strife of disputations but rather by the practice of piety" (p. 50).

12. Cf. Hendrikus Boers, *What Is New Testament Theology? The Rise of Criticism and the Problem of a Theology of the New Testament* (Philadelphia: Fortress, 1979), 23–24.

13. Cf. Hasel, *New Testament Theology*, 20–21. Careful distinctions are always important with key terms and concepts. I am using "historicism" here to denote that view which tends to emphasize secondary causes to the implicit or explicit rejection of first causes or that view which holds that in any given event what one observes is ultimately "all there is." In short, in this context, historicism is akin to a naturalistic and empirical view of historical events. This is not to deny the importance of history, as I have argued above. Indeed, on the one hand, what is wrong with treating Scripture as a historical document? Well, nothing, of course. The New Testament documents *are* historical documents and should be treated as such. At the same time, the best of Christian thinkers have always assumed that history is a realm in which God's purposes are being advanced, and any attempt to understand history that gives short shrift to the sovereign and redemptive purposes of God ultimately misreads history. Thus, when a subtle naturalism or empiricism lies behind one's view of "history," the New Testament documents will be treated in a way that is untrue to the documents and their own truth claims. As Carl F. H. Henry has noted, "For the New Testament as for the Old, faith in the living God cannot be divorced from historical actualities," for Scripture repeatedly affirms "the ongoing significance of the redemptive acts of God and their revealed meaning for man in all ages." Cf. Henry's *God, Revelation and Authority*, vol. II, *God Who Speaks and Shows* (Waco: Word, 1976), 256.

14. Gabler's address was originally written in Latin, and the most accessible English version is to be found in John Sandys-Wunsch and Laurence Eldredge, "J. P. Gabler and the Distinction Between Biblical and Dogmatic Theology: Translation, Commentary, and Discussion of His Originality," *Scottish Journal of Theology* 33 (1980): 133–58.

15. *Biblical Theologie des Neuen Testaments*, 2 volumes (Leipzig, 1800–02). Bauer had also published an Old Testament theology in 1796.

16. There has been somewhat of a revival of interest in Schlatter recently, and several volumes by and about Schlatter have been published in English. See Werner Neuer, *Adolf Schlatter: A Biography of Germany's Premier Biblical Theologian*, trans. Robert W. Yarbrough (Grand Rapids: Baker, 1995). Schlatter's key thoughts on theological method are found in two appendices in the Neuer volume: "Adolf Schlatter on Method in New Testament Theology" (169–210) and "Adolf Schlatter on Atheistic Methods in

Theology" (211–25). "Adolf Schlatter on Method in New Testament Theology" also appears as "The Theology of the New Testament and Dogmatics" in Robert Morgan, *The Nature of New Testament Theology*. Studies in Biblical Theology, second series 25 (London: SCM, 1973), 117–66. Andreas Köstenberger has recently translated Schlatter's two-volume New Testament theology into English: *The History of the Christ: The Foundation for New Testament Theology* (Grand Rapids: Baker, 1997); idem, *The Theology of the Apostles: The Development of New Testament Theology* (Grand Rapids: Baker, 1999). Robert Yarbrough has also provided a translation and commentary of Schlatter's "The Significance of Method for Theological Work" in *The Southern Baptist Journal of Theology* 1, no. 2 (Summer 1997): 64–77.

17. Schlatter, "The Significance of Method for Theological Work," 67.

18. Schlatter, "Adolf Schlatter on Method in New Testament Theology," 170.

19. Ibid.

20. Ibid.

21. Ibid., 177.

22. Schlatter, "The Significance of Method for Theological Work," 68.

23. Rudolf Bultmann, *Theology of the New Testament*, 2 vols., trans. Kendrick Grobel (New York: Scribner's, 1951, 1955). At the end of volume 2 (pp. 237–51), Bultmann includes an epilogue, "The Task and History of New Testament Theology," which outlines his view of New Testament theology. A helpful summary of Bultmann's thought and significance can be found in Stephen Neill and Tom Wright, *The Interpretation of the New Testament 1861–1986*, new ed. (Oxford: Oxford University Press, 1988), 237–51.

24. Bultmann, *Theology of the New Testament*, vol. 1, 3.

25. Neill and Wright, *Interpretation*, 237.

26. Bultmann, *Theology*, vol. 2, 249.

27. Probably the most accessible place to learn about Bultmann's program of demythologization is in Rudolf Bultmann et al., *Kerygma and Myth* (New York and Evanston: Harper and Row, Publishers, 1961). The volume consists of an opening essay by Bultmann, in which he summarizes his position in about forty-five pages, responses by Ernst Lohmeyer, Julius Schniewind, Helmut Thielicke, and Austin Farrer, and a final response by Bultmann. Bultmann's writing here is understandable, and the theological student might be surprised at Bultmann's forthright and aggressive rejection of a supernatural worldview. Bultmann's oft-quoted remark is still helpful: "It is impossible to use electric light and the wireless and to avail ourselves of modern medical and surgical discoveries, and at the same time to believe in the New Testament world of spirits and miracles." (p. 5). Bultmann, speaking of the atonement, writes, "What a primitive mythology it is, that a divine Being should become incarnate, and atone for the sins of men through his own blood!" (p. 7). Bultmann can also write about redemption, "For the redemption of which we have spoken is not a miraculous supernatural event, but an historical event wrought out in time and space" (p. 43).

28. Bultmann, *Theology*, vol. 2, 250.

29. *An Outline of the Theology of the New Testament* (London: SCM, 1969).

30. R. W. Funk, R. W. Hoover, and the Jesus Seminar, *The Five Gospels* (New York, 1993).

31. Oscar Cullmann, *Salvation in History* (New York: Harper & Row, 1967).

32. Joachim Jeremias, *New Testament Theology*, vol. 1, *The Proclamation of Jesus*, trans. John Bowden (New York: Scribner's, 1971).

33. The first volume of Stuhlmacher's New Testament theology has been published in German: *Biblische Theologie des Neuen Testaments*, vol. 1, *Grundlegung: Von Jesus*

zu Paulus (Göttingen: Vandenhoeck & Ruprecht, 1999). For the English reader, the most accessible introduction to Stuhlmacher is probably his *How to Do Biblical Theology*, which includes a helpful introductory essay by Scott Hafemann, "The 'Righteousness of God': An Introduction to the Theological and Historical Foundation of Peter Stuhlmacher's Biblical Theology of the New Testament" (pp. xv–xli).

34. George Eldon Ladd, *A Theology of the New Testament*, rev. Donald A. Hagner (Grand Rapids: Eerdmans, 1998).

35. George B. Caird, *New Testament Theology*, completed and edited by L. D. Hurst (Oxford: Clarendon Press, 1994).

36. Wright is currently writing a projected five-volume New Testament theology. To date two volumes are published: *The New Testament and the People of God*, vol. 1, *Christian Origins and the Question of God* (Minneapolis: Fortress Press, 1992); idem, *Jesus and the Victory of God*, vol. 2, *Christian Origins and the Question of God* (Minneapolis: Fortress, 1994).

37. Cf. J. N. D. Kelly, *Early Christian Creeds*, 3d ed. (New York: Longman, 1972), 5.

38. As Kelly, *Early Christian Creeds*, 6, notes, it has often been argued that concepts such as "doctrines" and "creeds" are later philosophical (often "Greek") impositions onto the New Testament documents. As Kelly notes, the argument runs something like the following: "A sharp antithesis was often drawn between the Spirit-guided, spontaneous New Testament phase and the second-century epoch on incipient formalism and institutionalism."

39. Ibid., 29. It is not our intent here to engage Kelly's discussion of whether *a* creed existed that is evidenced in the New Testament documents. We are simply contending that there were creedal and confessional elements within the New Testament documents themselves.

40. Ibid., 7.

41. Kelly deals with these texts in some detail in ibid., 8ff.

42. Paul's statements that he (1) received his gospel through a revelation of Jesus Christ but also (2) received his gospel (apparently from others) need not be seen as contradictory, but can be seen as complementary. Cf. Knox Chamblin, "Revelation and Tradition in the Pauline *Euangelion*," *Westminster Theological Journal* 48 (1986): 1–16; Ronald Y. K. Fung, "Revelation and Tradition: The Origin of Paul's Gospel," *Evangelical Quarterly* LVII, no. 1 (1985): 23–41; George Eldon Ladd, "Revelation and Tradition in Paul," in *Apostolic History and the Gospel: Biblical and Historical Essays presented to F. F. Bruce on his 60th Birthday*, ed. W. Ward Gasque and Ralph P. Martin (Grand Rapids: Eerdmans, 1970), 223–30; Seyoon Kim, *The Origin of Paul's Gospel* (Tübingen: J. C. B. Mohr, 1981).

43. Cf. David F. Wright, "Creeds, Confessional Forms," in *Dictionary of the Later New Testament and Its Developments*, ed. Ralph P. Martin and Peter H. Davids (Downers Grove: InterVarsity Press, 1997), 256.

44. "Son of God" appears elsewhere in Acts. In the story of the Ethiopian eunuch, who is inquiring as to why he cannot be baptized, some Greek manuscripts, at the end of Acts 8:36, read: "And Philip said, 'If you believe with all your heart, you may.' And he replied, 'I believe that Jesus Christ is the Son of God.'"

45. On Jesus as the *origin* of New Testament theology, see E. Earle Ellis, "Jesus' Use of the Old Testament and the Genesis of New Testament Theology," *Bulletin for Biblical Research* 3 (1993): 59–75.

46. Adolf von Harnack, *What Is Christianity? Lectures Delivered in the University of Berlin during the Winter Term 1899–1900*, trans. Thomas Bailey Saunders (New York: G. P. Putnam's Sons, 1903), 56–80, 154, 156.

47. See Stephen Neill and Tom Wright, *The Interpretation of the New Testament 1861–1986*, new ed. (Oxford: Oxford University Press, 1988), 230.

48. Carson, "New Testament Theology," 810.

49. Stuhlmacher, *How to Do Biblical Theology*, 15ff. Cf. Ellis, "Jesus' Use of the Old Testament."

50. Ibid., 81.

51. Gregory K. Beale contends that "new creation" is the most plausible center of New Testament theology. See his "The Eschatological Conception of New Testament Theology," in *'The Reader Must Understand': Eschatology in Bible and Theology*, ed. K. E. Brower and M. W. Elliott (Leicester, U.K.: APOLLOS, 1997), 11–52. This volume has recently been published in the U.S. by InterVarsity Press, titled *Eschatology in Bible and Theology* (1999).

52. See the following works by Goldsworthy: *Gospel and Kingdom*, *According to Plan*, and "Is Biblical Theology Viable?"

53. As Robert Sloan, "Unity in Diversity," 443, has written, "When we say that the New Testament writers did not write a systematic theology, we do not mean that they are not systematic *thinkers*." Sloan's contention is that there "was a core of theological belief that when confronted with specific problems and needs, was able to adapt itself in response."

54. Ibid., 446–63. Incidentally, the recognition of such an "apostolic theology" and that this theology relates to emergence of the New Testament documents is perhaps vital to an honest Protestant response to Roman Catholic objections to *sola scriptura*. Roman Catholics rightly point to such texts as 1 Thess. 2:13, where Paul points to the authority of his *preached* word as the word of God. Protestants are unwise to try to gloss over such texts. Rather, a proper Protestant response is to accept gladly such an authoritative preached word (i.e., "apostolic theology") but to contend that this apostolic theology in effect *became* Scripture over time. That is, the oral, authoritative teaching of the early Christians was eventually inscripturated, and *our* only infallible access to this teaching is through Holy Scripture.

55. Adolf Schlatter, "Adolf Schlatter on Method in New Testament Theology," in *Adolf Schlatter: A Biography of Germany's Premier Biblical Theologian*, ed. Werner Neuer, trans. Robert W. Yarbrough (Grand Rapids: Baker, 1995), 168. This essay can also be found as "The Theology of the New Testament and Dogmatics," in *The Nature of New Testament Theology*, Studies in Biblical Theology, 2nd series, no. 25, ed. Robert Morgan (London: SCM Press, 1973), 117–66.

56. Schlatter, "Method in New Testament Theology," 173.

57. Ibid. The themes of "givenness" and of paying attention to the past are repeated numerous times in this essay. For example, Schlatter writes, "What has happened in the past demands of us, by the very fact that it *has* happened, that we grasp it in its *givenness*." He also contends that the goal of New Testament theology is to "have an intellectual discipline whose only concern is to know and to understand what is *there* in the New Testament" (p. 178).

58. The reality of both the eternal (or nonmaterial) and temporal (or material) is a perennial issue in Christian thought with which the Christian church has continuously struggled. When the church was wrestling with trinitarian and christological issues in the first five centuries of its existence, the question of "being" found in Hellenistic thought provided the backdrop for much of the church's deliberations. In the modern era there is often another general tendency—the tendency to dismiss the supernatural and to emphasize the temporal or material realm. Robert Letham succinctly notes: "If the historical was neglected in the Hellenistic world it is absolutized in the modern era."

Cf. Letham's *The Work of Christ,* Contours of Christian Theology (Downers Grove: InterVarsity Press, 1993), 27.

59. Kümmel, *The Theology of the New Testament,* 25. For a helpful summary of the "quests" for the "historical Jesus" and the philosophical presuppositions involved therein, see E. Earle Ellis, "The Historical Jesus and the Gospels," in *Evangelium— Schriftauslegung—Kirche. Festschift für Peter Stuhlmacher,* ed. O. Hofius (Tübingen, 1997). A central tenet of Ellis' critique is that it is simply mistaken to believe that one can write history apart from interpretation. As Ellis notes, "Written history *is* interpretation" (p. 4). Thus, it is not the case that the Gospels are "biased" or in "error" because they are written as theological interpretations of the life and sayings of Jesus, while, say, the "secular" historian's summary of the War of 1812 is "unbiased" and "neutral" because the historian simply has "recorded the facts." Rather, *all* history is interpretation. Lest Ellis at this point be considered an advocate of a type of relativistic postmodernism, it should be added that he affirms that the theological interpretation of Jesus recorded in the Gospels is ultimately a true and trustworthy theological interpretation rooted in God himself, the One who inspires Scripture. For a helpful discussion of philosophical issues and presuppositions in the writing of history—although in a different sphere, that of the history of Israel—see Iain W. Provan, *Ideologies, Literary and Critical: Reflections on Recent Writing on the History of Israel* (Vancouver: Regent College Publishing, 1997) [originally published in *Journal of Biblical Literature* 114, no. 4 (1995): 585–606]. Criticizing those scholars who would see themselves as writing from a position above presuppositions, or above a confessional stance, Provan writes: "Confessionalism of a religious sort is attacked in the name of critical enquiry and objectivity; but the noisy ejection of religious commitment through the *front* door of the scholarly house is only a cover for the quieter smuggling in (whether conscious or unconscious) of a quite different form of commitment through the rear" (p. 34).

60. See the essay by J. Weima on literary criticism elsewhere in this volume, and Aida B. Spencer's contribution to the previous edition of this volume ("Literary Criticism," pp. 225–51). Scot McKnight offers a brief exposition and critique of literary criticism in his *Interpreting the Synoptic Gospels,* Guides to New Testament Exegesis (Grand Rapids: Baker, 1988), 121–37. Cf. Edgar V. McKnight, *The Bible and the Reader: An Introduction to Literary Criticism* (Philadelphia: Fortress, 1985); Leland Ryken, ed. *The New Testament in Literary Criticism* (New York: Frederick Ungar, 1984). The literature on postmodernism is continuously growing, although as a phenomenon it may be fading. When I speak of destructive strands of postmodernism, I have in mind the following general tendencies: the diminishing of the importance of reason; the rejection of objective truth; thoroughgoing skepticism regarding our ability to know truth (if it is there); a radical pluralism; a type of radical nominalism; an emphasis on the reader, not the author's determining the meaning of a text. On postmodernity see Richard Lints, *The Fabric of Theology: A Prolegomenon to Evangelical Theology* (Grand Rapids: Eerdmans, 1993), 191–256; Steven Connor, *Postmodernist Culture: An Introduction to Theories of the Contemporary* (Oxford: Blackwell, 1989). David Harvey, *The Condition of Postmodernity* (Cambridge: Blackwell, 1989); Richard Rorty, *Objectivity, Relativism, and Truth* (New York: Cambridge, 1991). For a brief response to contemporary trends, see the appendix to A. J. Conyers, *The Eclipse of Heaven: Rediscovering the Hope of a World Beyond* (Downers Grove: InterVarsity Press, 1992), where Conyers contends that nominalism is one of the key features of modernity. In this he follows Richard Weaver, *Ideas Have Consequences* (Chicago: University of Chicago Press, 1947). For an intriguing defense of "some unfashionable concepts" such as literal sense, authorial intention, and objective interpretation, see chapter 3 of Francis Watson's *Text and Truth,* "Literal

Sense, Authorial Intention, Objective Interpretation: In Defence of Some Unfashionable Concepts" (pp. 95–126). Watson contends that the rejection of such unfashionable concepts must itself be rejected: "The current hermeneutical dogmas [which deny literal sense, authorial intention, and objective interpretation]" are to be rejected *because they conflict with the dogmas held to be foundational to orthodox Christian faith and because, in the light of that conflict, certain inherent problems and implausibilities rapidly come to light* (p. 97).

61. N. T. Wright seeks to offer a nuanced affirmation of the importance of history and to avoid the errors of historicism, which he generally associates with modernity. Cf. his *The New Testament and the People of God*, 81–144. Wright is self-consciously attracted to narrative theology but writes that unlike "most 'narrative theology,' however, I shall attempt to integrate this approach with a historical focus" (p. 132).

62. Ibid., 3–144.

63. Wright (ibid., 81) notes the following: "In a good deal of modern literary criticism, as we have seen, there is so much emphasis on the text apart from the author, and indeed on the reader apart from the text, that any idea that one might be reading a text which referred to something beyond itself looks so wildly ambitious that it is left out of consideration entirely—at least in theory, and at least when convenient."

64. I believe this remark was in a conversation with J. Gresham Machen when both were at Princeton. The point is an important one and a point with which Paul would surely wholeheartedly agree (1 Cor. 15:12ff.).

65. Cf. Brevard S. Childs, *Biblical Theology of the Old and New Testaments: Theological Reflection on the Christian Bible* (Minneapolis: Fortress, 1993); Graeme Goldsworthy, *Gospel and Kingdom*; idem, *According to Plan*. A helpful summary of Goldsworthy's position can be found in his essay "Is Biblical Theology Viable?" in *Interpreting God's Plan*, ed. R. Gibson (Carlisle, U.K.: Paternoster, 1998), 18–46. Cf. William Dumbrell, *Covenant and Creation: A Theology of the Old Testament Covenants* (Carlisle, U.K.: Paternoster, 1984); idem, *The Search for Order: Biblical Eschatology in Focus* (Grand Rapids: Baker, 1994); Francis Watson, *Text and Truth: Redefining Biblical Theology* (Grand Rapids: Eerdmans, 1997). Also helpful is Scobie, "The Challenge of Biblical Theology" and "The Structure of Biblical Theology"; idem, "New Directions in Biblical Theology," *Themelios* 17, no. 2 (1992): 4–8. On the relationship between biblical theology and systematic theology, see Kevin Vanhoozer, "From Canon to Concept: 'Same' and 'Other' in the Relation Between Biblical and Systematic Theology," *Scottish Bulletin of Evangelical Theology* 12, no. 2 (Autumn 1994): 96–124; D. A. Carson, "Unity and Diversity in the New Testament: The Possibility of Systematic Theology," in *Scripture and Truth*, ed. D. A. Carson and John D. Woodbridge (Grand Rapids: Baker, 1992). For help tracking the maze of contemporary biblical theology, the following might be helpful: Carson, "Current Issues in Biblical Theology"; Brevard S. Childs, "Some Reflections on the Search for a Biblical Theology," *Horizons in Biblical Theology* 4 (1982): 1–12; Gerhard F. Hasel, "Biblical Theology: Then, Now, and Tomorrow," *Horizons in Biblical Theology* 4 (1982): 61–93; Walther Zimmerli, "Biblical Theology," *Horizons in Biblical Theology* 4 (1982): 95–130; Paul D. Hanson, "The Future of Biblical Theology," *Horizons in Biblical Theology* (1983): 13–24; A. K. M. Adam, "Biblical Theology and the Problem of Modernity *Von Wredestrasse zu Sackgasse*," *Horizons in Biblical Theology* 12 (1990): 1–18; Henning Graf Reventlow, *Problems of Biblical Theology in the Twentieth Century* (Minneapolis: Fortress, 1986).

66. Some contend that Paul is here alluding to Isaiah 9:1 (LXX), rather than Gen. 1:3. If he is alluding to the Isaiah passage, our point still stands: Paul expounds the reality of salvation in light of themes and terms from the Old Testament. For a brief discussion see

David E. Garland, *2 Corinthians,* The New American Commentary (Nashville: Broadman & Holman, 1999), 216–18.

67. I would like to thank two student assistants, Crystal Wilson and Josh Lefler, who helped in the research of this essay. I would also like to thank my wife, Diane Green, who helped in the editing of this essay.

Chapter 22

New Testament Interpretation and Preaching

C. Richard Wells
The Criswell College

There is an (apocryphal) old story about an uncut beginning seminarian who could not understand why he needed to study *exegesis*: "After all," he protested, "I just want to *preach Jesus*!" Then there is a more recent (true) story. A seminary professor recalled how an elderly woman approached him after his ordination service with her own charge to the candidate: "Just preach Jesus." "What a benediction that was," he remembered, "she had no degree in homiletics, but her advice was as profound as I have ever gotten or given in a seminary preaching class."[1]

Each of these stories in its own way reminds us that biblical preaching is often at odds with biblical scholarship. On the one hand, "just preach Jesus" is a biblical mandate.[2] On the other hand, biblical preaching depends on critical study. Preachers ought to "preach Jesus" without leaving "exegesis" undone!

Alas, that may be easier said than done—not for lack of resources, however, but because a veritable gulf separates the biblical scholar from the preacher.[3] The truth is, today's preacher has unparalleled access to resources for biblical interpretation—refined historical-critical scholarship, available through relatively inexpensive books and computer software, plus college and seminary training. Yet preaching is in crisis. After a full century of the most exhaustive biblical scholarship ever known, more accessible than ever before: "Preachers drift out of seminaries trained in historical-critical method, practiced in homiletical techniques, yet at a loss to preach 'biblically.'"[4]

One explanation for this rift is that "the cure is the disease." Leander Keck states flatly that "the most important factor in the present malaise of preaching *is the preacher's own ambivalence toward the Bible and toward*

506

biblical criticism."[5] The "cure" (biblical criticism) has become the "disease" (ambivalence and malaise)! On this view biblical scholarship has become a *problem* for preaching rather than a *tool*.

Of course, other factors exacerbate the problem. One is simply *lack of time*. David Buttrick invites us to the study of a typical pastor. On the desk you might see "a stack of books—counseling, management, perhaps biblical theology. But on the same desk there are apt to be back issues of a 'homily service,' and on the shelves there may be commentaries gathering dust."[6] Even with user-friendly tools, critical study is labor intensive. A preacher ruled by a Day-Timer will not likely venture far into the dark continent of the critics: "Sunday's coming, a word study will have to pass for exegesis!"

Another factor is *lack of expertise*. Lloyd-Jones said that to preach is "to deliver the message of God, a message from God to . . . people."[7] But today's seminary student is much more likely to "expend energy on learning analytical techniques of research" than to "concentrate on what the Bible says."[8] And yet, while most seminary graduates are familiar with "textual," "redaction," and the other "criticisms," they are often ill prepared to use them in preaching. In truth, says James Smart, the "average scholar does not appreciate how devastating his critical analysis can be to the preacher."[9] Overwhelmed by critical minutiae, the effect of critical study on the preacher is more like a drink of water from a fire hydrant than a "message from God."

A third factor is the *perceived irrelevance* of critical study for biblical preaching. Karl Barth once said that "theology . . . ought . . . to be nothing other than sermon preparation."[10] Not surprisingly, therefore, Barth questioned the relevance of critical studies, for in his view, modern historical criticism often fails as sermon preparation because it focuses almost entirely "on the historical and earthly form of the Bible" rather than on "the revelation of God."[11] Barth would agree with Arthur Wainwright that "as ingenious theories pile on top of each other, the inventiveness of experts can make the Bible more difficult to understand than it was before."[12]

Mere "irrelevance" may not be the worst of it. In truth, biblical criticism tends to undermine biblical authority by de-emphasizing both the supernatural character and historical factuality of Scripture. Thus Harold Lindsell's trenchant remark: "The historical-critical method is the Bible's greatest enemy."[13] Thus also Donald Guthrie's caution: "It is *not impossible*," he says, "to sustain full biblical authority at the same time as using critical faculties to determine the historical background of the biblical texts."[14] But critical assumptions are often questionable, so scholars must beware the "dubious results of human propositions."[15] As John Stott reminds us, the scholar's "dubious results" become the preacher's loss of nerve. The "age of doubt"[16] is death to preaching.

Yet another factor is the *dulling effect* of critical study. How many enthusiastic young preachers have wilted under the prediction that "seminary will ruin you"? Or consider the stereotypical professor in the pulpit—hopelessly arcane, stratospherically irrelevant, and (worst of all) painfully boring. We cannot dismiss the unease out of hand. Critical study involves a degree of objective detachment from the text of Scripture, what D. A. Carson calls "dislocation" and "distanciation." Necessary though it may be, this detachment is "costly," "difficult," and "disturbing."[17] Paradoxically, critical study tends to make matters worse (1) by focusing attention on the history "behind the text," (2) by proliferating complicated theories of explanation, and (3) by insisting that critical study is essential to full understanding—in short, transmogrifying the Bible into an "ancient document under the control of specialists."[18]

What Is "Criticism," and What Does It Have to Do with Preaching?

Such problems notwithstanding, in reality "we cannot escape historical-critical study of the Bible."[19] Any preacher who takes Scripture seriously has already become a critic of sorts, just because the Bible is historical. Listen to George Ladd: "The Word of God has been given to men through historical events and historical personages; and this very fact demands historical criticism, unless the true nature of the Bible is to be ignored."[20]

What Is "Criticism"?

Following Ladd, we may define *historical criticism* first as an *approach* to biblical study, rather than a particular research *tool*; that is, a *methodology* (a philosophy of study) rather than a *method* (a technique for applying the philosophy). Further, there are two different versions of historical-critical *methodology*, as shown by the following descriptions of "criticism." First, George Ladd:

> Criticism means making intelligent judgments about historical, literary, textual, and philosophical questions which one must face in dealing with the Bible, in the light of all available evidence, when one recognizes that the Word of God has come to men through the words of men in historical situations.[21]

Now quite a different account from Roy Harrisville and Walter Sundberg:

> Historical-critical study of the Bible is a necessary component of responsible theology. To employ historical-critical method is to subject the putatively factual material and literary structure of the Bible to independent investigation in order to test their truthfulness and to discern their original historical meaning. This independent investigation assumes that the outcome of research will not be predetermined by a guarantee of the Bible's infallibility. The student of scripture, using historical-critical method, is placed under the imperative of the historian who must seek the facts no matter where they lead.[22]

Harrisville and Sundberg and Ladd would all agree that "historical-critical" study is "a necessary component of responsible theology." They differ as to the credibility of the texts. On Ladd's reading, a biblical text embodies "the Word of God," so scholars use historical criticism to *discern* the truthfulness of Scripture more fully. By contrast, Harrisville and Sundberg regard the texts as "putatively factual material," so critics use historical criticism to *test* their truthfulness. Translated to preaching, Ladd's version is expansive and enriching, the latter version is restrictive and crippling.

In *The Modern Preacher and the Ancient Text*, Sidney Greidanus elaborates on the difference between these two versions of historical criticism for preaching. According to Greidanus, traditional historical criticism (Harrisville and Sundberg) rests on three assumptions, all traceable to Ernst Troeltsch:[23] (1) The historicity of events can be established only in terms of probabilities (Principle of Criticism). (2) The key to criticism is the analogy of present events with past events (Principle of Analogy). (3) Any event must be understood in terms of cause and effect (Principle of Correlation). As an alternative, Greidanus proposes a "Holistic Historical-Critical Method."[24]

The "Holistic" Method (actually, *methodology*) adapts (or rather expands on) assumptions of traditional historical criticism. So Greidanus affirms the Principle of Correlation as a "valid principle *only* as long as it is open to *all possible causes* in history."[25] In short, look for "cause and effect" relationships, but remember that God is among the causes! Likewise, Greidanus affirms the Principle of Analogy with the proviso that "past events" are both "mediate" (where God works "unobtrusively through 'natural' causation") and "immediate" (where God acts uniquely.)[26] Greidanus reformulates the Principle of Criticism in the same way. The weight of "probability" lies on the side of biblical reliability.[27] Rather than doubt the historicity of the text, therefore, the preacher is freed to elucidate the meaning of the text more fully.

WHAT DOES "CRITICISM" HAVE TO DO WITH PREACHING?

The Bible then is the Word of God in human words, revelation and history at the same time. So biblical preaching necessitates historical critical study. But what kind, and how? What parameters are there to guide the preacher through critical study? What has biblical criticism to do with the "message of God"?

As a step toward an answer, think of the sermonic process in terms of three overlapping *phases:* (1) interpretation—original meaning; (2) theology—universal truth; and (3) homiletics—contemporary significance (see fig. 1). Each phase involves a *set of rules* which governs a *practice*, or (to borrow Bernard Ramm's happy metaphor) a "rule-book" which governs a "game."[28] In phase one, hermeneutics is the "rule-book," the "theory that guides exegesis," while exegesis is "the *practice* of and the set of *procedures* for discovering the author's intended meaning."[29]

In phase two, systematic theology provides the framework ("rule-book") for determining the (biblical) theology of the text ("game"). Recognize that preaching is the proclamation of biblical theology (the theological message of a particular text) "in the light of the whole system of revealed truth [systematic theology]."[30]

The final phase involves "exegeting the audience"[31] so as to proclaim this "universal truth [biblical theology] in a *hortatory* mode."[32] Preaching is hortatory, that is, persuasive. But persuasive communication has its own set of rules, classically known as *rhetoric* (the "rule-book"), for which *homiletics* proper is the "game" (thus older writers called homiletics "sacred rhetoric").

Figure 1

Homiletical Phases

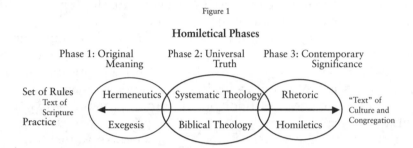

Biblical criticism clearly belongs to the first (interpretive) phase of homiletics, the aim of which is to elucidate "*what the text originally meant* by discovering the historical message intended by the author."[33] In practice, however, interpretation involves different "aims,"[34] in the pursuit of which different critical methods come into play.

According to Grant Osborne, "the 'message' of a written utterance has three foci: the author, the text and the reader."[35] Traditional historical-critical methods typically focus on either the "author" or the "text." "Author-oriented" (*diachronic*) methods focus on the historical context of the text. "Text-oriented" (*synchronic*) methods[36] focus on the text as such, not the (supposed) historical antecedents of the text.

All things being equal, however, critical methods, whether *diachronic* or *synchronic,* that work with the "text-as-is" have the greatest potential usefulness for preaching. Methods that attempt to "go beyond" or "get behind" the text are necessarily more speculative and the results more tenuous.[37]

Some *diachronic* methods, redaction[38] and textual criticism, for example, operate on the text in its present form. Other *diachronic* methods, however, such as source criticism, hypothesize some precanonical form(s) of the text. Form criticism operates still farther from the text-as-is—at a putatively oral stage of biblical tradition.[39]

In general, *synchronic* methods (such as literary and canonical criticism) operate "within the text,"[40] and can be especially useful in clarifying the theological emphasis of a text. Some *synchronic* methods of recent vintage, however, abandon the text altogether, and even history, as the primary locus of a text's significance. The primary interpretive datum for these newer approaches is either the psychological "set"[41] or political agenda of either the writer or (more typically) the reader. Often highly subjective and politically biased, methods such as structuralism, narrative criticism, and reader-response theory have little practical value for biblical preaching, except perhaps to caution us that our "own interpretations should remain the object of suspicion and critical evaluation."[42]

CASE STUDY: 2 CORINTHIANS 10–13

A good test case for assessing the value of critical methods is 2 Corinthians 10–13. Literary criticism (*synchronic*) has shown that the section takes the form of a self-defense, an *apologia pro vita sua*,[43] in stark contrast to Paul's tone in chapters 1–9. The comparison raises (*diachronic*) questions about the occasion for such a "mood alteration,"[44] and about the integrity of 2 Corinthians.

One solution, based on source criticism, is to identify 2 Corinthians 10–13 with the (otherwise unknown) letter referred to in 2 Corinthians 2:4—written "with many tears." Should the hypothesis prove true, we would have a much clearer picture of the background of 2 Corinthians 1–9. Barring a new discovery, however, the hypothesis will remain just that, in which case source-criticism contributes little other than (perhaps) some clues to the character of Paul's opposition in Corinth. Literary criticism will prove much more useful because in this case literary genre—specifically Paul's *apologia*—plays an important theological role. Paul defends himself (only) because his life and ministry are "inextricably bound up with the message entrusted to him as an ambassador."[45] To reject Paul is to do violence to the gospel itself. This theological emphasis has rich homiletical possibilities.

The Value of New Testament Criticism for Biblical Preaching

Back to our original question: Can critical study of the New Testament contribute to biblical preaching? And, if so, how? Clearly, the answer is yes, but "New Testament criticism" is not a set of "transcendent interpretive rules."[46] As noted earlier, New Testament criticism is both a (1) *methodology* (an approach to the study of the text), and (2) a (rather polymorphous) set of *methods* (techniques designed to apply critical methodology). As it turns out, these two aspects of "criticism" (*methodology* and *methods*) serve as convenient rubrics for assessing the value of New Testament criticism for preaching.

MACRO HOMILETICS: THE VALUE OF CRITICAL METHODOLOGY AS A "PRACTICE"

Quite apart from the value of any particular critical method, critical study, as a *practice*,[47] has value for preaching. By the "practice" of New

Testament criticism, we mean consistent work with critical resources so as continually (1) to achieve broader and deeper knowledge of the New Testament, and (2) to develop greater skills for exegesis. The "practice" of criticism has value for *macro homiletics*, developing the preacher as an exegete and equipping the preacher with a homiletical repertoire.

How so? At the most elementary level, the practice of critical study enables the preacher to *make use of the literature in New Testament studies.* Training in historical criticism is a kind of "initiation." Without it, observes R. B. Crotty, a good deal of material—including almost any recent commentary, study aid, or background work—will be "quite inaccessible."[48] The results can be tragic, if not dangerous. Like a miner without a lamp, the preacher may pass over jewels there for the taking. Or the preacher may mistake a worthless stone (or a scorpion!) for a gem.

Engaging in critical study also equips the preacher to *think more analytically about Scripture.* Critical methodology poses questions about the text—about its literary genre, historical and biblical context, its use of words, and more.[49] By practicing critical study, the preacher learns to pose such questions as "second nature." The preacher learns to look at a text from different angles so as to clarify the original meaning of the text.

To this end, almost any of the critical methods can help. Some knowledge of form criticism, for example, can lead to better understanding of the *pericope* as the basic unit of Synoptic material.[50] Likewise, a preacher can benefit from knowing that material found only in Matthew and Luke—the hypothetical *Q* of source criticism—tends to be more autobiographical and poetical, treats frequently of nature and common life, and consists mainly of the Lord's teaching.[51] In short, critical study enables the preacher to ask the right questions and frame the answers more usefully.

Third, the practice of criticism prepares the preacher to *preach more authoritatively.* Earlier we observed that critical study can work against preaching by casting doubt on Scripture. The flip side is that critical study can create a healthy awareness of real interpretative difficulties. Ignorance may be bliss, but preaching out of ignorance tends to be arrogant and authoritarian—not *authoritative.*

To illustrate, consider the following minidebate on the use of the Bible in evangelistic preaching. On one side, A. J. M. Wedderburn of St. Andrews complained that too many evangelicals merely string texts together, invoking "the Bible says" as authority, ignoring textual and historical difficulties.[52] T. E. Brinnington countered that evangelism is not the place to deal with critical questions,[53] not least because "evangelism presupposes certain conservative positions." Even so, he said, preachers should arrive at those positions in light of *"all the evidence."*[54] So, despite their differences, Wedderburn and Brinnington agree on one essential point: Dealing honestly and fully with the text makes preaching more, not less, authoritative.

Fourth, the practice of critical study *develops the preacher's scholarship*. Earlier we noted that, despite the accessibility of critical studies resources, time pressure keeps many preachers from using them consistently. Solving the time problem will not come easily—"this kind goeth not out" without self-discipline. But the payoff is huge. Homiletical scholarship develops depth in a preacher—more acute powers of critical reasoning,[55] more comprehensive and holistic knowledge of the Bible (not to mention history, sociology, psychology, theology, literature, and philosophy); and more effective use of imagination, owing to a deeper appreciation of historical context and of the character of Scripture both as Scripture[56] and as literature.[57]

Finally, preachers should not overlook the results, as such, of modern New Testament criticism, which can *enlarge the preacher's repertoire of biblical knowledge*. Gerald Bray has summarized the "main achievements"[58] of New Testament criticism over the last century. Some of the more important for preaching are as follows:

> (1) A text of the Greek New Testament has been reconstructed which is as close to the original as it is possible to get; (2) We now know that the New Testament is written in the vernacular [Greek], but with a particular flavour all its own; (3) The entire New Testament must now be dated in the first century, and possibly before AD 70. This considerably reduces the time available for oral tradition to have developed, and is a pointer to the greater historical accuracy of the text; (4) Mark's gospel was probably the earliest to have been written, in spite of the arguments put forward in favour of Matthaean priority. However, it is now clear that the synoptic problem cannot be resolved in any schematic or artificial way, and it seems most likely that the three gospels grew up alongside each other to some extent; (5) At the heart of Jesus' message was his proclamation of the 'kingdom of God.'

Micro Homiletics: The Value of Critical Methods as "Tools"

Now we shift gears—from *macro homiletics* to *micro homiletics*, from the repertoire of knowledge and skill which informs the homiletical task to the use of critical tools (methods) in preparing "next Sunday's sermon." What can New Testament criticism contribute in the study as a "tool" (or, better, a set of tools)?

A good place to begin is with *redaction criticism*, a relatively straightforward critical method, applied mostly to the Gospels, which preachers at different levels of competence can use profitably. Redaction criticism operates on the "text-as-is," and assumes that the author was also an editor (redactor), who (1) arranged materials others had written and (2) composed some material himself,[59] so as to produce a (self-conscious) work of "theology."[60] Since (as noted earlier) preaching is the proclamation of biblical *theology*, redaction criticism would seem to hold real promise for the preacher.

Like all the historical-critical methods, redaction criticism has some serious limitations,[61] not least that the earliest redaction critics (students of

Rudolf Bultmann) tended to discount biblical historicity.[62] But redaction criticism as such is simply an analytical tool to "aid the scholar [or preacher] in determining the special [theological] emphases of the evangelists."[63]

What of redaction-criticism as a homiletical tool? Grant Osborne mentions two possibilities: (1) detailed "composition analysis"—for the scholar or (presumably) the technically skilled preacher, to look "for the ways the writer used his sources;"[64] and (2) comparisons of parallel accounts—as an alternative for "non-specialists"—to identify "seams" (that "introduce sections and provide transitions") and "threads" ("recurring patterns and characteristic expressions" that are clues to the writer's emphasis).[65]

In doing rhetorical analysis, one useful exercise is to construct a theological outline of a book (or section of a book).[66] A theological outline differs from a grammatical diagram or a syntactical display[67] in that it highlights the flow of *ideas* in a book, rather than syntax, grammar, and vocabulary. Besides helping the preacher clarify theological themes in the text, the exercise helps isolate blocks of supporting material which can become preaching units.

For *micro homiletics*, redaction criticism may well be the most immediately useful of all the historical-critical methods. Still, it is only one method. In principle, preachers might use other methods with profit at times, even in preparing "next Sunday's message." To do so, however, preachers should keep in mind (1) that a critical method is merely a tool for engaging the text, not a substitute for engagement, and (2) that the value of a critical method is limited to (some) one aspect of the whole exegetical process. Using redaction criticism to look for "seams" and "threads" does not, for example, eliminate the need for analyzing syntax, grammar, or historical background.

Case Study: "The Syro-Phoenician Woman"

With these qualifications in mind, consider the notoriously difficult account(s) of the Syro-Phoenician woman (Matt.15:21–28 = Mark 7:24–30). In Matthew, this passage forms part of a section (13:1–16:20) that highlights "a growing polarization of response to [Jesus'] ministry."[68] The parables of the kingdom (13:1–52) explain the "polarization," while Jesus' use of parables differentiates between those who want to hear and those who do not (13:10–17). Jesus is then misunderstood (and rejected) at Nazareth (13:53–58), while Herod misinterprets reports about Jesus' ministry, identifying him with John the Baptist (14:1–12). Then follow three miracles—feeding the five thousand (14:13–21), walking on water (14:22–33), and healings in Gennesaret (14:34)—by which Jesus reveals himself to the Jews. At chapter 15, the tone changes slightly, but significantly, as the following *theological outline* suggests:

15:1–20   *The true worship of God is an obedient heart, not mere human forms and rituals.* ("Some Pharisees and teachers of the law" question Jesus about kosher regulations).

15:29–39   *The proper response to Jesus' ministry is to praise "the God of Israel" (15:31).* (Jesus performs miracles and feeds a multitude among Gentiles as he had previously done among Jews).

16:1–4   *It is wicked to seek a special sign when clear revelation is being clearly fulfilled.* (Back in Jewish territory, Jesus is accosted with a demand for "a sign from heaven").

16:5–12   *Beware of the corrupting influence of Pharisees' and Sadduccees' teaching.* (Jesus' private warning to his disciples privately about the teaching of the Pharisees).

Turning to rhetorical analysis, the accounts in Matthew and Mark (despite obvious similarities) differ in several ways. Matthew adds Jesus' saying that he was sent "only to the lost sheep of Israel." He also adds that the woman "came and knelt before him" and that the disciples urged Jesus to "send her away." Mark adds that "[Jesus] entered a house and did not want anyone to know it; yet, he could not keep his presence a secret." Matthew refers only to "a Canaanite woman." Mark calls special attention to her: "The woman was a Greek, born in Syrian Phoenicia." In Matthew the woman calls Jesus "Lord, Son of David," in Mark just "Lord."

In both cases the woman's faith—and only her faith—brings her the blessings of God. What differs in each account is the *significance* of that (theological) fact. Matthew clearly contrasts the Gentile woman's faith with *Jewish unbelief.* The Canaanite woman *believes* (and finds acceptance with God), while many Jews do not. Mark also emphasizes the woman's faith, though not in contrast to Jewish unbelief, rather in relation to her ethnicity and status. Writing to Gentiles, Mark stresses the universality of the gospel—"she believed, so can you." Matthew calls attention to the culpability of Jews, who should have known better—"*she* believed, how could *you* of all people, fail to believe?" A sermon from Mark's pericope, therefore, might stress the *universality* of the gospel message of Christ. One from Matthew might stress the greater *responsibility* of those who enjoy spiritual advantages.

Excursus: Criticism and Series Preaching

Paraphrasing Gordon Fee, the "obvious starting place [for exegesis] is with the choice of a text,"[69] the agony of which every preacher knows. Critical study cannot relieve the agony entirely, but it can help in developing a preaching strategy and in isolating a preaching text. The preacher's greatest ally here is series preaching,[70] whole books, character studies, thematic or historical sections of Scripture, lectionary texts, and more. And critical study can aid the development of series for preaching. Here are two examples—one from Philippians, the other from 1 Thessalonians.

A cursory reading of Philippians might suggest a sermon series on "joy in the midst of trials," since the word *joy* appears in various forms some sixteen times,[71] while "trouble" forms the backdrop of the letter.[72]

Historical-critical analysis of the *Sitz im Leben*, however, reveals that the "trouble" in Philippi ("contrary to first impressions," says Ralph Martin) arises from four versions of false teaching:[73] (1) itinerant Christian teachers of a sort "familiar in the Graeco-Roman world,"[74] who preach "out of self-ish ambition;"[75] (2) Pagan Greeks (1:27–30); (3) "Judaizing" and "gnosticizing" Christian propagandists;[76] and (4) Christian leaders who for material or sensual lust have defected from the gospel (3:17–19). The common denominator in the four groups is "an abandonment of the cross-side of the kerygma . . . a proud assertion of moral and religious superiority."[77]

Paul's "joy in Christ" (A. T. Robertson), therefore, is not merely a "positive mental attitude" amidst trials, but the supernatural by-product of embracing the cross. This theme could unfold naturally into a series using either Paul's many references to his own "joy in the cross," or "abandonment of the cross-side of the keryma" by the different opposition groups.

Abraham Malherbe's critical work on 1 Thessalonians[78] suggests another preaching series. According to Malherbe, Paul uses "family" both to describe and to exhort the new Christian community in Thessalonica. Tracing Paul's imagery to Jewish and Hellenistic sources, Malherbe shows that the apostle used "family" language to establish rapport with those who had "turned to God from idols" (1:9), and to give pagan converts a theological model for ordering their lives together. Here is rich material for a series on the "family" in the (theological) context of the "church as the family of God."

These examples suggest that some "reconnaissance" time spent in New Testament critical study can pay rich dividends for the preacher. Regular reading in theology, for example, is gold mining for sermon series.[79] Critical commentaries, theological dictionaries, and background studies, among other works, can all likewise help stimulate the preacher's thinking and lead to series.

Dealing Homiletically with Critical Problems

To restate: Any preacher who takes Scripture seriously must be a critic of sorts, because the Bible is historical. Now we must extend that point a bit further: *By its very nature, biblical criticism creates "critical problems," with which biblical preachers must contend.* For example, today's preacher faces "critical problems" just because parishioners use *modern translations*, which differ at many points with the Authorized Version, and with one another! A biblical preacher must come to grips "with the problem of (critical) problems"—handling critical questions in the sermon.

Types of Critical Problems

Of course, not all "critical problems" are created equal. Some problems (commonly called "textual problems") concern "the original wording of the New Testament"[80]—in short, the *text*. Others (commonly called "historical [or higher] critical" problems) concern authorship, date, occasion, background, and the like—in short, *history*. Each of the "types" presents different challenges for preaching.

Textual problems arise because the five thousand or so Greek manuscripts containing all or part of the New Testament[81] also contain some two thousand "variant"[82] readings. Most variants are inconsequential, either because they clearly lack substance or because the differences are insignificant; and no variant affects any fundamental doctrine. But *translations* differ because of these variants, and since preachers and congregations use different translations, variants pose a homiletical problem.

A striking case is 1 John 5:7–8. Verse 7 of the KJV is eliminated altogether in most modern translations, as are the words "in earth" in verse 8.[83] Many less dramatic cases might still require some explaining. For example, Colossians 1:14 (KJV) reads "redemption through [Christ's] blood," while most modern translations have only "redemption," since "through His blood" does not appear in many of the oldest Greek manuscripts. Likewise, Matthew 5:22 (KJV) reads, "angry with his brother without a cause." Most modern translations delete the phrase "without a cause."

With two thousand variants, we need not multiply examples. At a minimum preachers should be aware of textual problems as they prepare sermons, especially in view of differences in the translations. Indeed, the preacher's best guide here may be the translations themselves. Harold Scanlin points out that modern translation is actually a means of communicating New Testament textual criticism to the public.[84] Accordingly, most translations footnote significant deviations from the KJV in the margin; and these marginal notes provide the preacher a good "rule of thumb" for dealing with variants. The NIV footnotes the fewest number of these differences (129). The NASB has 209; others have more.[85] Some study Bibles also note significant variants affecting translation, and together with marginal notes help the preacher decide which textual problems to address, while also providing a reference point for the congregation when such problems are addressed.

Historical-critical problems present quite different, and frankly greater, challenges. To what extent should questions of authorship, date, the use of sources, occasion, and the like, be raised in preaching? And if they are raised, how should they be handled in the pulpit?

WHAT PROBLEMS TO RAISE

As for determining the *kinds* of critical questions to raise, we offer three criteria. First, we should raise critical questions that *contribute meaningfully* to the interpretation of the text before us. For example, Luke's intention "to write an orderly account" (1:3) of Christ's life and ministry, different from other accounts (1:1–2), proves the existence of "sources." Since the use of sources contributes meaningfully to our understanding of

Luke's Gospel, it seems appropriate to raise this (source-critical) issue. A sermon along these lines might stress Luke's concern for factuality, God's use of human instrumentality (sources) in revelation, and/or the zeal of the early church to preserve and to communicate the glorious events that had taken place before their eyes (1:4).

Second, we should raise only such critical questions as we can *resolve beneficially*. By "resolve beneficially" we do not mean "solve completely" or "prove beyond doubt." Instead we mean: (1) that theological imperatives should not rest on disputed questions; (2) that uncertainties should not be preached as assured results (1 Tim. 3:8); (3) that the introduction of a critical question should serve a gospel purpose; and (4) most important, that the preacher should be able to give reasons for resolving a problem in a certain way and to tell *what difference it makes*.

Consider, for example, Paul's opponents in Corinth. Were they Jewish, Jewish Christian, Jewish Gnostic, Judaizing, or something else again? The question is likely unanswerable, but it can still be "resolved beneficially." No matter who the opponents were, they had "tendencies which were leading to an inadequate view of Christianity."[86] A preacher might examine each of the hypothesized opposition groups in this light, and in doing so open up rich possibilities for exploring "inadequate views of Christianity" in contemporary culture.

Third, we should raise only such questions as we can *handle adequately* within the constraints of the sermon. If handling a critical problem requires tedious explanation, argumentation, or background discussion, the congregation may drift away, or worse, the critical "problem" may displace the Word of God.

Some Procedural Guidelines

New Testament criticism and interpretation are not ends but means to the end of preaching the whole counsel of God honestly and authoritatively. But critical study will raise critical questions. While such questions ordinarily remain in the study, informing the preacher, sometimes they demand a hearing in the pulpit. For such times, let me offer four guidelines, in the "hortatory mode."

First, consider the ability and/or desire of the congregation to handle critical questions. An urbane, thoughtful congregation might soak up what others find bewildering, irrelevant, or boring. Of course, even the most sophisticated folk may not be *biblically* literate, or they may not have a taste for critical issues—and almost nobody wants a steady diet! Above all, the preacher must never confuse scholarly interests with the spiritual needs of the congregation.

Second, question your motivation for raising critical issues. Do you want to impress your listeners, arouse their curiosity, or gab about a pet topic?

Relatedly, do you have the knowledge and skill to handle the issue honestly, accurately, and meaningfully?

Third, ask yourself—"What does the congregation really need to know and why?" We noted this briefly in the discussion of textual problems. Does raising this particular question intersect a congregational, denominational, or theological matter of significance? You might deal with Pauline authorship of the Pastorals, for example, because this question intersects a theological matter, namely, the nature and authority of Scripture. Of course, many other critical questions are simply irrelevant.

Finally, consider your preaching context. For example, generally speaking, series preaching, rather than a single sermon from an isolated text, is a more suitable format for handling historical-critical problems, especially in sermons that introduce series.

Critical study will raise tempting questions: Who wrote Hebrews? Where was Paul imprisoned when he wrote Ephesians? Which of the Synoptics came first? And dozens more—any number of which might be candidates for sermonizing. They must not find their way into a sermon, however, only because they are "tempting," but because they help us preach the gospel clearly and compellingly. Every preacher should and must be a critic, but no preacher should ever forget that critical study serves homiletics. The test for any tool of study is whether it helps us "preach . . . the unsearchable riches of Christ" (Eph 3:8).

Bibliography

Baker, D. L. *Two Testaments, One Bible.* Downers Grove, Ill.: InterVarsity, 1976.

Barr, James. *The Bible in the Modern World.* London: SCM, 1973.

Bray, Gerald. *Biblical Interpretation: Past and Present.* Downer's Grove, Ill.: InterVarsity, 1996.

Fee, Gordon D. *New Testament Exegesis.* Rev. ed. Louisville: Westminster/John Knox, 1983, 1993.

Greidanus, Sidney. *The Modern Preacher and the Ancient Text.* Grand Rapids: Eerdmans, 1988.

Kaiser, Walter C., Jr. *Toward an Exegetical Theology.* Grand Rapids: Baker, 1981.

Osborne, Grant R. *The Hermeneutical Spiral: A Comprehensive Introduction to Biblical Interpretation.* Downer's Grove, Ill.: InterVarsity, 1994.

Packer, J. I. "Preaching as Biblical Interpretation." *Inerrancy and Common Sense.* Ed. Roger Nicole and J. Ramsay Michaels. Grand Rapids: Baker, 1980.

Stott, John R. W. *Between Two Worlds.* Grand Rapids: Eerdmans, 1978.

Thiselton, Anthony. *Two Horizons.* Grand Rapids: Eerdmans, 1980.

Notes

1. Charles B. Bugg, *Preaching from the Inside Out* (Nashville: Broadman, 1992), 11.

2. Acts 3:20; 5:42; 8:5; 8:35; 9:20; 11:20; 15:21; 17:18; 19:13; 1 Corinthians 1:23; 15:12; 2 Corinthians 1:19; 4:5; 11:4; Galatians 1:16; Philippians 1:15–16; 1:18. All Scripture citations are NIV unless otherwise indicated.

3. Robert E. Van Voorst, "The Dynamic Word: A Survey and Critique of Recent Literature in Preaching and the Bible," *Reformed Review* 37 no. 1 (Autumn 1983): 1.

4. David Buttrick, "Interpretation and Preaching," *Interpretation* 35 (1981): 46.

5. Leander Keck, *The Bible in the Pulpit: The Renewal of Biblical Preaching* (Nashville: Abingdon, 1978), 22.

6. Buttrick, "Interpretation and Preaching," 46.

7. D. Martyn Lloyd-Jones, *Preaching and Preachers* (Grand Rapids: Zondervan, 1972), 53.

8. Buttrick, "Interpretation and Preaching," 12.

9. James D. Smart, *The Strange Silence of the Bible in the Church* (Philadelphia: Westminster, 1970).

10. Karl Barth, *Homiletics*, trans. Geoffrey W. Bromiley and Donald E. Daniels (Louisville: Westminster/John Knox, 1991), 17.

11. Ibid., 99.

12. Arthur Wainwright, *Beyond Biblical Criticism: Encountering Jesus in Scripture* (Atlanta: John Knox, 1982), 9.

13. Harold Lindsell, *The Bible in the Balance* (Grand Rapids: Zondervan, 1979), 275.

14. Donald Guthrie, "Biblical Authority and New Testament Scholarship," *Vox Evangelica* 16 (1986):10 (emphasis added).

15. Ibid., 20. In Guthrie's view, the results of source and form criticism are more dubious, while he allows for "some moderate use of redaction criticism" (p. 19).

16. John R. Stott, *Between Two Worlds: The Art of Preaching in the Twentieth Century* (Grand Rapids: Eerdmans, 1982). Hendrikus Boers ["Historical-Criticism Versus Prophetic Proclamation," *Harvard Theological Review* 65 (1972)] argues that, since historical-critical research and revelation are *antithetical* concepts, we can no longer evade the question "whether historical-criticism still contributes fundamentally to the strengthening of the faith, or whether it is effecting its dissolution" (p. 393). The implications for faith are not lost on Boers, but he is unwilling to abandon research: "The New Testament scholar is compelled," he concludes, "to abandon also to the 'flames of critical scrutiny' the New Testament understanding that faith is grounded in the history of Jesus as the event of salvation" (p. 414).

17. D. A. Carson, *Exegetical Fallacies* (Grand Rapids: Baker, 1984), 22.

18. The categories of problems are adapted from a helpful summary in Roy A. Harrisville and Walter Sundberg, *The Bible in Modern Culture: Theology and Historical-Critical Method from Spinoza to Käsemann* (Grand Rapids: Eerdmans, 1995), 10–12.

19. Edgar Krenz, *The Historical-Critical Method*. Guides to Biblical Scholarship (Philadelphia: Fortress, 1975), 3.

20. George Eldon Ladd, *The New Testament and Criticism* (Grand Rapids: Eerdmans, 1967), 72.

21. Ibid.

22. Sundberg, *The Bible in Modern Culture,* 1.

23. Sidney Greidanus, *The Modern Preacher and the Ancient Text: Interpreting and Preaching Biblical Literature* (Grand Rapids: Eerdmans, 1988), 24–36; also Krenz, *The Historical-Critical Method,* 55–57.

24. Greidanus, ibid., 37–47.

25. Ibid., 37 (emphasis added).

26. Ibid., 42.

27. Cf. F. F. Bruce, *The New Testament Documents: Are They Reliable?* Revised Standard ed. (Downer's Grove, Ill.: InterVarsity, 1943, 1946, 1950, 1953, 1960).

28. Bernard Ramm, *Protestant Biblical Interpretation* 3d ed. (Grand Rapids: Baker, 1970), 11.

29. Walter Kaiser, *Toward an Exegetical Theology: Biblical Exegesis for Preaching and Teaching* (Grand Rapids: Baker, 1981), 47.

30. Donald Macleod, "Preaching and Systematic Theology," in Samuel T. Logan Jr., ed., *The Preacher and Preaching: Reviving the Art in the Twentieth Century* (Phillipsburg, N.J.: Presbyterian and Reformed, 1986), 248.

31. Ian Pitt-Watson, *A Primer for Preachers* (Grand Rapids: Baker, 1986), 70.

32. Bryan Chapell, *Christ Centered Preaching: Redeeming the Expository Sermon* (Grand Rapids: Baker, 1994), 144.

33. Bruce Corley, "A Student's Primer for Exegesis," in Bruce Corley, Steve Lemke, and Grant Lovejoy, eds., *Biblical Hermeneutics: A Comprehensive Introduction to Interpreting Scripture* (Nashville: Broadman & Holman, 1996), 5.

34. Ibid., 6–7.

35. Grant R. Osborne, *The Hermeneutical Spiral: A Comprehensive Introduction to Biblical Interpretation* (Downer's Grove, Ill.: InterVarsity, 1994), 366.

36. Harold Freeman, "Biblical Criticism and Biblical Preaching," in Corley, Lemke, and Lovejoy, *Biblical Hermeneutics*, 307–17.

37. A. K. M. Adams highlights this tenuousness by reflecting on the role of higher-critical methods in the "quest" for the "historical Jesus." Because "the discipline of modern historical inquiry vigorously excludes speculation on divine agency and identity," historical reconstructions of Jesus fail to "address the pivotal questions . . . about the relation of the divine and human natures of Christ." In short, the "historians' Jesus is . . . a projection of their historical imagination." Cf. "Docetism, Käsemann, and Christology," *Scottish Journal of Theology* 49/4 (1996): 407–08. Another good example, though drawn from the Old Testament, is the historical-critical analysis of 1 Samuel 13 for preaching by Thomas Smothers ("Historical Criticism as a Tool for Proclamation: 1 Samuel 13," *Review and Expositor* 84 [Winter 1987]: 23–32). After textual, source, tradition-history, and form-critical studies, Smothers concludes that "the methods have not provided firm answers to the questions which matter most for interpretation" (p. 29). But, alas, the "questions *cannot* be answered because they involve historical reconstructions." The value of such methods, then, for preaching, is seriously limited.

38. Not surprisingly, evangelical New Testament scholars have focused a good deal of attention on redaction criticism. Cf. Grant Osborne, "The Evangelical and Redaction Criticism: Critique and Methodology," *Journal of the Evangelical Theological Society* 22 no. 4 (December 1979): 305–22. Scholars have generally given much less attention to other methods, except in textbook introductory fashion.

39. John Reumann's analysis of criticism and text transmission is helpful here. Reumann sketched out nine stages in text-tradition development subsequent to the event that gave rise to it. He then linked form, source, and redaction criticism, respectively, with the first three developmental stages. Cf. "Exegetes, Honesty and the Faith: Biblical Scholarship in Church School Theology," *Currents in Theology and Mission* 5 (February 1978): 16–32.

40. Corley, "Student's Primer for Exegesis," 7.

41. I.e., attitudes, values, perceptions, states of consciousness, and the like.

42. John P. Newport, "Contemporary Christian, Literary, and Sociological Hermeneutics," in Corley, Lemke, and Lovejoy, *Biblical Heremeneutics*, 143.

43. Ralph P. Martin, *2 Corinthians*, Word Biblical Commentary (Waco: Word, 1986), 299.

44. Ibid., 298.

45. Ibid., 299.

46. A. K. M. Adam, "Twisting to Destruction: A Memorandum on the Ethics of Interpretation," *Perspectives in Religious Studies* 23 (Summer 1996): 215–22.

47. Alasdair MacIntyre, *After Virtue,* 2d ed. (Notre Dame: University of Notre Dame, 1984) employs the term *practice* in a technical fashion. While I am not doing so here, his thinking certainly informs the discussion at this point. MacIntyre defines a *practice* as "any coherent and complex form of socially established cooperative human activity through which goals internal to that activity are realized in the course of trying to achieve those standards of excellence which are appropriate to, and partially determinative of, that form of activity with the result that human power to achieve excellence, and human conceptions of the ends and goals involved, are systematically extended" (p. 166). Thus medicine is a practice, but so is *marriage.*

48. R. B. Crotty, "Changing Fashions in Biblical Interpretation," *Australian Biblical Review* 33 (October 1985): 15.

49. The work by Walter Kaiser, *Toward an Exegetical Theology* (Grand Rapids: Baker, 1981), 69–147, is an excellent guide to these different types of analysis. Cf. also Greidanus, *The Modern Preacher*, 48–121, who discusses literary, historical, and theological interpretation.

50. Rudolf Bultmann, *History of Synoptic Tradition,* trans. John Marsh (New York: Harper, 1963).

51. Cf. Donald Guthrie, *New Testament Introduction* 3d ed. (Downers Grove, Ill.: InterVarsity, 1970), 154–55.

52. A. J. M. Wedderburn, "The Use of the Gospels in Evangelism—I," *The Evangelical Quarterly,* April-June 1977, 75–87.

53. T. E. Brinnington, "The Use of the Gospels in Evangelism—II," *The Evangelical Quarterly,* April-June 1977, 93–94.

54. Ibid., 94 (emphasis added).

55. John Broadus advocated a method of sermon preparation that developed the capacity for "logical analysis" since "few kinds of power are so valuable to [the preacher]." Cf. *On the Preparation and Delivery of Sermons,* new and rev. ed., ed. Jesse B. Weatherspoon (New York: Harper, 1870, 1898, 1926, 1944), 134.

56. See on this point Elizabeth Achtemeier, "The Artful Dialogue: Some Thoughts on the Relations of Biblical Studies and Homiletics," *Interpretation* 41 (January 1987): 21–22.

57. See especially Thomas G. Long, *Preaching and the Literary Forms of the Bible* (Philadelphia: Fortress, 1989).

58. Gerald Bray, *Biblical Interpretation: Past and Present* (Downer's Grove, Ill.: InterVarsity Press, 1996), 446–47. See also Stephen Neill, *The Interpretation of the New Testament 1861–1961* (Oxford: Oxford University Press, 1964), Cf. also an updated edition with N. T. Wright, *The Interpretation of the New Testament 1861–1986* (Oxford: Oxford University Press, 1988).

59. See the chapter by Grant Osborne in this volume.

60. Cf. Werner H. Kelber, "Redaction Criticism: On the Nature and Exposition of the Gospels," *Perspectives in Religious Studies* 6 (Spring 1979): 11. Kelber goes on to argue that, contrary to popular belief, redaction criticism is not a mere extension of form criticism, for the very reason that it presupposes a theological design that form criticism specifically denies (pp. 12–13).

61. For a helpful exposé, see D. A. Carson, "On the Legitimacy and Illegitimacy of a Literary Tool," in D. A. Carson and John D. Woodbridge, eds., *Scripture and Truth* (Grand Rapids: Zondervan, 1983), 123–37.

62. Bray, *Biblical Interpretation*, 443.

63. Grant R. Osborne, "The Evangelical and Redaction Criticism: Critique and Methodology," *Journal of the Evangelical Theological Society* 22, no. 4 (December 1979): 313.

64. Osborne, *Spiral*, 169.

65. Ibid., 170.

66. Cf. Hull, 176.

67. Kaiser, *Toward an Exegelical Theology*, 99–104.

68. Craig L. Blomberg, *Matthew,* New American Commentary (Nashville: Broadman 1992), 211.

69. Gordon D. Fee, *New Testament Exegesis*, Rev. ed. (Louisville: Westminster/John Knox, 1983, 1993), 146.

70. Ian Pitt-Watson (*A Primer for Preachers* [Grand Rapids: Baker, 1986], 70) calls series preaching "a blessed lifeline to sanity."

71. Thus Jac J. Müller, *The Epistles of Paul to the Philippians and to Philemon,* New International Commentary of the New Testament (Grand Rapids: Eerdmans, 1955), 29–121, citing Bengel's oft-quoted summary: *"Summa epistolae: guadeo, gaudete"* ("The whole of the epistle: I rejoice, you rejoice").

72. Cf. John F. Walvoord, *Philippians: Triumph in Christianity* (Chicago: Moody, 1971) Cf. Philippians 1:7, 12–13, 15–17, 20–24, 27–30, 14–17, 25–30; 3:1–2; 4:5–6, 11–14.

73. Ralph P. Martin, *Philippians,* The New Century Biblical Commentary (Grand Rapids: Eerdmans, 1976), 33.

74. Ibid., 74.

75. Philippians 1:17.

76. Martin, *Philippians,* 125–26; 3:1–2.

77. Ibid., 144.

78. Abraham J. Malherbe, "God's New Family in Thessalonica," in L. Michael White and O. Larry Yarborough, eds., *The Social World of the First Christians: Essays in Honor of Wayne A. Meeks* (Philadelphia: Fortress, 1995), 116–25.

79. Consider George E. Ladd's *A Theology of the New Testament* (Grand Rapids: Eerdmans, 1974), the organizing principle of which is the "kingdom of God." Ladd's work—tracing the "kingdom" theme through the New Testament—is highly suggestive for series preaching. Ron Nash (*Is Jesus the Only Savior?* [Grand Rapids: Zondervan, 1994]) briefly examines several passages in Acts (and other books as well) that bear on the question of Christian exclusivity. His studies could easily become a sermon series.

80. David Alan Black, *New Testament Textual Criticism: A Concise Guide* (Grand Rapids: Baker, 1994), 7.

81. J. Harold Greenlee, *Introduction to New Testament Textual Criticism*, Rev. ed. (Peabody, Mass.: Hendrickson, 1964, 1995), 6. In addition, there are some 8000 Latin manuscripts and 1,000 in other languages.

82. See the chapter in this volume by Michael Holmes.

83. Other major changes include Acts 8:37; Mark 16:9–20; John 7:53–8:11; and Matthew 6:13. Most other changes involve words or phrases.

84. Harold P. Scanlin, "Bible Translation as a Means of Communicating New Testament Textual-Criticism to the Public," *Bible Translator* 39, no. 1 (January 1988): 101–13.

85. Ibid., 113.

86. Guthrie, *Introduction*, 424.

Contributors

David Alan Black
Southeastern Baptist Theological Seminary

David Alan Black is Professor of New Testament and Greek at Southeastern Baptist Theological Seminary in Wake Forest, North Carolina. He holds the B. A. from Biola University, the M. Div. from Talbot School of Theology, and the D.Theol. from the University of Basel. He also did post-doctoral studies at Jerusalem University College in Israel. A founding editor of *Filologia Neotestamentaria* (Journal of New Testament Philology), he has contributed articles to that journal as well as to several others, including *Novum Testamentum, New Testament Studies, Biblica, Westminster Theological Journal,* and *The Bible Translator.* His other publications include *Paul, Apostle of Weakness* (Lang), *Linguistics for Students of New Testament Greek* (Baker), *Linguistics and New Testament Interpretation* (editor; B&H), *New Testament Textual Criticism* (Baker), *Scribes and Scripture: New Testament Essays in Honor of J. Harold Greenlee* (editor; Eisenbrauns), *Using New Testament Greek in Ministry* (Baker), *Learn to Read New Testament Greek* (B&H), and *The Myth of Adolescence* (Davidson Press). He also serves as the New Testament editor of the *International Standard Version* of the Bible.

Craig L. Blomberg
Denver Seminary

Craig L. Blomberg is Professor of New Testament at Denver Seminary in Denver, Colorado. He holds the B.A. from Augustana College, Illinois, the M.A. from Trinity Evangelical Divinity School, and the Ph.D. from the University of Aberdeen, Scotland. He has contributed articles to numerous books, encyclopedias and journals, including *Journal for the Study of the New Testament, Trinity Journal, Westminster Theological Journal, Perspectives in Religious Studies, Journal of the Evangelical Theological Society, Themelios, Criswell Theological Review, Catholic Biblical Quarterly, Biblical Theology Bulletin, Faith and Mission, Didaskalia, Bulletim of Biblical Research, Horizons in Biblical Theology, Stone-Campbell Journal,* and *Kairos.* His book-length publications include *Gospel Perspectives,* vol. 6 (coeditor: JSOT), *The Historical Reliability of the Gospels* (IVP), *Interpreting the Parables* (IVP), *Matthew* (Broadman), *Introduction to Biblical Interpretation* (with W. Klein and R. Hubbard; Word), *1 Corinthians* (Zondervan), *How Wide the Divide?* (with S. Robinson; IVP), *Jesus and the Gospels* (B&H), and *Neither Poverty nor Riches* (IVP). He and his wife Fran and daughters Elizabeth and Rachel live in Centennial, Colorado. He is an elder in his local Baptist church, enjoys playing the piano, and likes to travel with his family to combine ministry and tourism.

Darrell L. Bock
Dallas Theological Seminary

Darrell L. Bock is Research Professor of New Testament Studies at Dallas Theological Seminary in Dallas, Texas. His special fields of study involve hermeneutics, the use of the Old Testament in the New, Luke-Acts, the historical Jesus, and the Gospels. He is a graduate of the University of Texas (B.A.), Dallas Theological Seminary (Th.M.), and the University of Aberdeen (Ph.D.). His publications include a two volume commentary on Luke for the BECNT series (*Luke 1:1–9:50; Luke 9:51–24:53,* Baker) and *Proclamation From Prophecy and Pattern* (Sheffield). He is a cocontributor to *Progressive Dispensationalism* (Baker). He has essays in *Bibliotheca Sacra, Journal of the Evangelical Theological Society, Bulletin for Biblical Research* and *Introducing New Testament Interpretation* (Baker), *Jesus Under Fire* (Zondervan), and *Witness to the Gospel: A Theology of Acts* (Eerdmans). He is editor of *Three Views of the Millennium and Beyond* (Zondervan). He recently completed a year of post-doctoral study at the University of Tübingen as an Alexander von Humboldt scholar, where he produced a monograph on Jesus' trial entitled *Blasphemy and Exaltation in Judaism and the Final Examination of Jesus* (WUNT 2 106; Mohr-Siebeck). He is also the New Testament editor of *A Biblical Theology of the New Testament* (Moody Press). He is currently working on a life-of-Christ textbook for Baker.

Gary M. Burge
Wheaton College

Gary M. Burge is Professor of New Testament at Wheaton College and Graduate School in Wheaton, Illinois. He is a graduate of the University of California (B.A.), Fuller Theological Seminary (M.Div.), and King's College, Aberdeen University, Scotland (Ph.D.). In addition to various journal contributions, his publications include *The Anointed Community: The Holy Spirit in the Johannine Tradition* (1987), John's Gospel (1989) in The Evangelical One-Volume Commentary on the Bible [John's Gospel] (1989), *Interpreting the Gospel of John* (1992), *Who Are God's People in the Middle East?* (1993), *Commentary on the Johannine Epistles* (NIV Application Commentary, 1996), *Commentary on the Gospel of John* (NIV Application Commentary, 2000), *The Bible, the Arabs and the Jews: What Christians Are Not Being Told About Israel and the Palestinians* (2001). He also contributes regularly to practical journals designed to serve the ministry of the church: *Christianity Today, The Covenant Quarterly, The Navy Chaplain, The Reformed Journal, Touchstone,* and *Christian History*. He and his wife, Carol, have two daughters, Ashley and Grace, and live in Wheaton, Illinois.

J. Daryl Charles
Taylor University

J. Daryl Charles is associate professor of religion and philosophy at Taylor University in Upland, Indiana. His fields of research include 2 Peter and Jude, New Testament ethics, and religion and culture. He holds the B.S. degree from West Chester State University and the M.A. from Southern California College, and did his Ph.D. at Catholic University of America and Westminster Theological Seminary. Having served as a 1996–1997 affiliate fellow of the Center for the Study of American Religion, Princeton University, he also studied at the University of Siegen (Germany), where he earned a certificate in German/linguistics. His articles have appeared in theological journals including *New Testament Studies, Zeitschrift für die neutestamentliche Wissenchaft, Journal for the Study of the New Testament, Bulletin of Biblical Research, Trinity Journal, Asbury Theological Journal* and *Pro Ecclesia*. His articles on religion and culture have appeared in journals including *First Things* and *Regeneration Quarterly*. He is author of *Literary Strategy in the Epistle of Jude* (Associated University Presses), *Virtue Amidst Vice: The Catalog of Virtues in 2 Peter 1* (JSNT

Supplemental Series, Sheffield Academic Press), and *Basic Questions about Human Sexuality* (Center for Bioethics and Human Dignity/Kregel); and coauthor of *1 and 2 Peter, Jude* (BCBC series, Herald Press). He is translator of Claus Westermann's *Wurzeln der Weisheit* (Vandenhoeck & Ruprecht) into English *(Roots of Wisdom,* Westminster/John Knox Press). He contributed to volumes 3 and 4 of the InterVarsity Dictionary of the New Testament series. He is writing *Contours of Christian Ethics* (forthcoming, InterVarsity) and serves on the editorial advisory board of *Regeneration Quarterly.*

Peter H. Davids
Innsbruck, Austria

Peter H. Davids is presently an educational missionary with International Teams based in Innsbruck, Austria, teaching mainly in institutions aimed at or in Central and Eastern Europe. He was formerly Professor of New Testament Literature at Canadian Theological Seminary, Regina, Canada, and Visiting Professor of New Testament at Regent College, Vancouver, Canada. A graduate of Wheaton College, Trinity Evangelical Divinity School, and the University of Manchester (Ph.D., 1974), he has authored two commentaries on James (NIGNT, Eerdmans, and NIBC, Hendrickson) and one on 1 Peter (NICNT, Eerdmans), coauthored *Hard Sayings of the Bible* (IVP), and coedited *Dictionary of the Latter New Testament and Its Developments* (IVP). He is also the author of an internet-based correspondence course on biblical interpretation. He has lived in Innsbruck since 1999 with his wife, who is a professional counselor. Their three grown children and two grandchildren live in Canada and England.

David S. Dockery
Union University

David S. Dockery is President of Union University in Jackson, Tennessee. He holds degrees from the University of Alabama (B.S.), Grace Theological Seminary (M.Div.), Southwestern Baptist Theological Seminary (M.Div.), Texas Christian University (M.A.), and the University of Texas (Ph.D.). He is the author or editor of eighteen books, has contributed to twenty others, and published more than 150 articles and book reviews. Dockery has served as Vice President for Academic

Administration and Dean of the School of Theology at the Southern Baptist Theological Seminary. He is the general editor of the *Holman Bible Handbook* and the *Holman Concise Bible Commentary*. He also serves as the New Testament editor for the New American Commentary series. He has contributed to the *Dictionary of Jesus and the Gospels, Dictionary of Paul and His Letters, Evangelical Dictionary of Biblical Theology*, and the *New International Dictionary of Old Testament Theology*.

Brad Green
Union University

Brad Green is Assistant Professor of Christian Studies at Union University in Jackson, Tennessee. He holds degrees from the Southern Baptist Theological Seminary (M.Div.), Southwestern Baptist Theological Seminary (Th.M.), and Baylor University (Ph.D.). His reviews are published in *Evangelical Review of Theology, Trinity Journal, and Reformation and Revival Journal*. He has contributed chapters to *Theologians of the Baptist Tradition* (B&H, 2001) and *Sharping a Christian Worldview* (). His wife Dianne and their two boys make their home in Jackson, Tennessee.

George H. Guthrie
Union University

George H. Guthrie is the Benjamin W. Perry Professor of Biblical Studies and Chairman of the Department of Christian Studies at Union University in Jackson, Tennessee. He holds both the Ph.D. and the M.Div. degrees from Southwestern Baptist Theological Seminary and a Th.M. from Trinity Evangelical Divinity School. As a specialist in New Testament and Greek, he is the author of numerous articles and four books, including *The Structure of Hebrews* in E. J. Brill's *Novum Testamentum Supplements* series (published in the United States by Baker Book House), the Hebrews in the NIV Application Commentary (Zondervan), and Hebrews in the forthcoming Illustrated Backgrounds Commentary (Zondervan, forthcoming). He has participated in translation projects including the revision of The New Living Translation and serves as cochair of the Biblical Greek Language and Linguisitics Section of the Society of Biblical Literature. He is a popular preacher and conference speaker who serves the body of Christ through the ministries of teaching, writing, and preaching. He, his wife, Pat, and their two children, Joshua and Anna, live near Jackson and are members of Northbrook Church.

Michael W. Holmes
Bethel College

Michael W. Holmes is Professor of Biblical Studies and Early Christianity at Bethel College in St. Paul, Minnesota. He holds degrees from the University of California at Santa Barbara (B.A.), Trinity Evangelical Divinity School (M.A.), and Princeton Theological Seminary (Ph.D.). He has written or edited six books including *The Apostolic Fathers: Greek Texts and English Translations* (Baker, 1999), *1 and 2 Thessalonians* in the NIV Application Commentary series (Zondervan, 1998), and *The Text of the New Testament in Contemporary Research* (with Bart D. Ehrman; Eerdmans, 1995). He has authored twenty published articles or essays and over 125 book reviews. He is chair of the Society of Biblical Literature's New Testament Textual Criticism Section, editor of the New Testament in the Greek Fathers series, network editor for *Religious Studies Review*, North American editor for the International Greek New Testament Project, and executive chair of its North American Committee.

Paul N. Jackson
Union University

Paul N. Jackson is Associate Professor of Christian Studies at Union University in Jackson, Tennessee. He is author of *An Investigation of Koimaomai in the New Testament: The Concept of Eschatological Sleep* (Mellen, 1996). Jackson has published articles in the *Holman Bible Dictionary*, Bible teaching material for LifeWay Christian Resources, and numerous articles on New Testament topics for the *Biblical Illustrator*, including "The Broken Dividing Wall," "Heretic," "The Spirit World in the First Century," "The Pauline Concept of Labor," and "The Third Missionary Journey." *Southwestern Journal of Theology* published "Allegiance to Jesus from the Transfiguration to His Death in Luke's Gospel." Jackson and his wife Janet live in Humbolt, Tennessee, together with their children, Garrett, Lindsey, and Meghan.

Boyd Luter
The Criswell College

Boyd Luter is Associate Provost, Dean of Faculty, and Professor of Biblical and Theological Studies at Criswell College in Dallas, Texas. He pastored two churches in Texas and has taught at LeTourneau University, Talbot School of Theology/Biola University, Golden Gate Baptist Theological Seminary, Cedarville University, and Ashland Theological Seminary. He is a graduate of Mississippi State University (B.S.) and Dallas Theological Seminary (Th.M., Ph.D.). He has also done post-doctoral study at Jerusalem University College. He has co-authored *Disciplined Living: What the New Testament Teaches about Recovery and Discipleship* and *Women as Christ's Disciples* with Kathy McReynolds (Baker Book House). He has written commentaries for Baker's Expositor's Guide series, *Evangelical Commentary on the Bible* (Baker,) and *Holman Concise Bible Commentary* (B & H). He has contributed to projects as diverse as the *Anchor Bible Dictionary* (Doubleday), *The Complete Who's Who of the Bible* (Marshall Pickering/ Zondervan), *Dictionary of the Later New Testament and Its Developments* (IVP), *Dictionary of Paul and His Letters* (IVP), *Evangelical Dictionary of World Missions* (Baker), *Holman Bible Handbook* (Broadman & Holman), *Israel: The Land and the People* (Kregel), *Life Recovery Bible* (Tyndale) and *Nelson Study Bible* (Thomas Nelson). His articles have apeared in *Bibliotheca Sacra, Bulletin for Biblical Research, Criswell Theological Review, Decision, Journal of the Evangelical Theological Society, New Testament Studies,* and *Trinity Journal.*

Scot McKnight
North Park University

Scot McKnight is the Karl A. Olsson Professor in Religious Studies at North Park University, Chicago, Illinois. Formerly he was Associate Professor in Biblical Studies at Trinity Evangelical Divinity School. He graduated from Cornerstone College (B.A., History; 1976), Trinity Evangelical Divinity School (M.A., New Testament; 1980), and the University of Nottingham (Ph.D., 1986). He has authored *Interpreting the Synoptic Gospels* (Baker), *A Light Among the Gentiles* (Fortress), *Galatians* and *1 Peter* (NIVAC; Zondervan), *A New Vision for Israel: The Teachings of Jesus in National Context* (Eerdmans) and *The Synoptic Gospels: An Annotated Bibliography* (with M. C. Williams;

Baker). He is editor or coeditor of *Introducing New Testament Interpretation* (Baker), *The Dictionary of Jesus and the Gospels* (IVP), and the NIV Application Commentary (Zondervan). His articles and reviews have appeared in *Journal of Biblical Literature, Bulletin of Biblical Research, Catholic Biblical Quarterly, Interpretation, Word and World, Ex Auditu, Journal of the Evangelical Theological Society, Journal of Church and State, Trinity Journal,* and *Themelios.* He has as well contributed to *The Dictionary of Paul and His Letters, The Dictionary of the Later New Testament and Its Development, The Dictionary of New Testament Background, James the Just and Christian Origins* (ed. B. Chilton, C. A. Evans; Brill), *Authenticating the Words of Jesus* (ed. B. Chilton, C. A. Evans; Brill), *Evangelical Dictionary of Biblical Theology* (ed. W. A. Elwell; Baker), and *Anti-Semitism and Early Christianity* (ed. D. A. Hagner, C. A. Evans; Fortress).

M. Robert Mulholland
Asbury Theological Seminary

M. Robert Mulholland Jr. is Vice President and Chief Academic Officer at Asbury Theological Seminary, Wilmore, Kentucy. He has taught at Asbury Seminary since 1979 and has been Professor of New Testament since 1986. He is a graduate of the United States Naval Academy (B.S.), Wesley Theological Seminary (M.Div.), and Harvard Divinity School (Th.D.). He has also pursued post-doctoral studies at Duke University. His articles have appeared in *Biblical Archaeology Review, The Asbury Herald, Beacon Dictionary of Theology,* and *Christian Home.* He is also the author of *Shaped by the Word: The Power of Scripture in Spiritual Formation* (The Upper Room) and *Revelation: Holy Living in an Unholy World* (Zondervan), and *Invitation to a Journey: A Road Map to Spiritual Formation* (IVP). He is a contributor to *The Asbury Bible Commentary* (Zondervan). He is a frequent conference speaker in academic circles worldwide and is active in the United Methodist Church.

Grant R. Osborne
Trinity Evangelical Divinity School

Grant R. Osborne is Professor of New Testament at Trinity Evangelical Divinity School in Deerfield, Illinois. He holds the B.A. from

Fort Wayne Bible College, the M.A. from Trinity Evangelical Divinity School, and the Ph.D. from the University of Aberdeen. He also did post-doctoral studies at Cambridge and Marburg Universities. His articles have appeared in *Evangelical Quarterly, Semeia, Trinity Journal,* and *Westminster Theological Journal.* He has also published *The Resurrection Narratives: A Redactional Study* (Baker), *A Comprehensive Introduction to Biblical Interpretation, The Hermeneutical Spiral* (IVP), *Three Crucial Questions about the Bible* (Baker), *Handbook for Bible Study* (coauthor; Baker), *The Bible in the Churches* (coauthor; Paulist), and *Annotated Bibliography on the Bible and the Church* (Trinity). He currently serves as the editor for the IVP New Testament Commentary Series, the Life Application Commentary Series, and the Three Crucial Questions Series (Baker).

John B. Polhill
The Southern Baptist Theological Seminary

John B. Polhill is the James Buchanan Harrison Professor of New Testament Interpretation at the Southern Baptist Theological Seminary in Louisville, Kentucky. He holds the B.A. from the University of Richmond and the M.Div. and Ph.D. from the Southern Baptist Theological Seminary. He has pursued post-doctoral studies at Harvard Theological Seminary, St. Andrews University (Scotland), and Princeton Theological Seminary. He has taught New Testament at Southern Seminary since 1969. He is author of the Acts volume in the New American Commentary series (B&H, 1992) and *Paul and His Letters* (B&H, 1999). He enjoys gardening, photography, and stamp and coin collecting.

Thomas R. Schreiner
The Southern Baptist Theological Seminary

Thomas R. Schreiner is Professor of New Testament at The Southern Baptist Theological Seminary in Louisville, Kentucky, a post he has held since 1997. He has also taught New Testament at Azusa Pacific University and Bethel Theological Seminary. He received a B.S. from Western Oregon University, a M.Div. and Th.M. from Western Conservative Baptist Seminary, and a Ph.D. in New Testament from Fuller Theological Seminary. He has published numerous articles and book reviews in scholarly journals. His published books are

Interpreting the Pauline Epistles (Baker); *The Law and Its Fulfillment: A Pauline Theology of Law* (Baker); *Romans* in the BECNT series; *Women in the Church: A Fresh Analysis of 1 Timothy 2:9-15*, coedited with H. S. Baldwin and A. Köstenberger (Baker); and *Still Sovereign: Contemporary Perspectives on Election, Foreknowledge, and Grace*, coedited with B. A. Ware (Baker). Forthcoming from InterVarsity are *The Race Set Before Us: A Biblical Theology of Perseverance and Assurance*, coauthored with Ardel Caneday, and *Paul, Apostle of God's Glory in Christ: A Pauline Theology*. He is also the preaching pastor of Trinity Baptist Church in Louisville, Kentucky. He is married to Diane Elaine, and they have four children: Daniel, Patrick, John, and Anna.

Klyne Snodgrass
North Park Theological Seminary

Klyne Snodgrss is Paul W. Brandel Professor of New Testament Studies at North Park Theological Seminary in Chicago, Illinois. He holds the B.A. from Columbia Bible College, the M.Div. from Trinity Evangelical Divinity School, and the Ph.D. from the University of St. Andrews. He done post-doctoral studies at Princeton Theological Seminary, Tübingen Univeristy, and Duke University Divinity School. His articles have appeared in *New Testament Studies, Journal of Biblical Literature, Journal for the Study of the New Testament, Covenant Quarterly,* and *The Second Century.* He has also authored *The Parable of the Wicked Tenants* (J. C. B. Mohr [Siebeck]) and *Between Two Truths* (Zondervan). He is Consulting Editor for the NIV Application Commentary (Zondervan) and wrote the Ephesians volume for that series.

Robert H. Stein
The Southern Baptist Theological Seminary

Robert H. Stein is the Ernest and Mildred Hogan Professor of New Testament Interpretation at the Southern Baptist Theological Seminary in Louisville, Kentucky. He holds the B.A. from Rutgers University, the B.D. from Fuller Theological Seminary, the S.T.M. from Andover Newton Theological School, and the Ph.D. from Princeton Theological Seminary. He has also done post-doctoral studies at the University of

Heidelberg and the University of Tübingen. He has contributed articles to the *Journal of Biblical Literature, Zeitschrift für die neutesta-mentliche Wissenschaft, Novum Testamentum, Catholic Biblical Quarterly, New Testament Studies, Journal of the Evangelical Theological Society, Word & World* and to the *Dictionary of Jesus and the Gospels, Dictionary of Paul and His Letters, Harper Bible Dictionary, Anchor Bible Dictionary, The Oxford Companion to the Bible,* among others. He is the author of eleven books including *The Method and Message of Jesus' Teachings, An Introduction to the Parables of Jesus, Luke* (New American Commentary), *The Synoptic Problem, A Basic Guide to Interpreting the Bible, Jesus the Messiah.* He is presently working on a commentary on Mark for the Baker Exegetical Commentary of the New Testament. He and his wife, Joan, have three children and ten grandchildren.

C. Richard Wells
The Criswell College

C. Richard Wells is President of the Criswell College in Dallas, Texas. He holds the B.A. from Florida Southern College, the M.A. from Stetson University, the M.Min. from the Criswell College, the Ph.D. from Baylor University, and the Ph.D. from the University of North Texas. He previously taught at Beeson Divinity School in Birmingham, Alabama, and has held several pastorates. His articles and reviews have appeared in *The Indiana Baptist, Criswell Theological Review, Research on Christian Higher Education,* the *Journal of Psychology and Christianity, Journal of the Evangelical Theological Society,* and *Journal of Psychology and Theology.* He is a contributor to *Beliver's Study Bible, Holman Bible Handbook, Reclaiming the Prophetic Mantle* (Broadman), *New Testament Criticism and Preaching* (Broadman/Holman), and *The Challenge of Postmodernism.* He is coauthor with A. Boyd Luter of *Spiritual Preaching* (B&H, forthcoming).

Jeffrey A. D. Weima
Calvin Theological Seminary

Jeffrey A. D. Weima is Professor of New Testament at Calvin Theological Seminary in Grand Rapids, Michigan. He is a graduate of

Brock University (B.A.), Calvin Theological Seminary (M.Div.; Th.M.), and the University of Toronto/Toronto School of Theology (Ph.D.). He is author of *Neglected Endings: The Significance of the Pauline Letter Closings* (Sheffield: JSOT, 1994) and *An Annotated Bibliography of 1 and 2 Thessalonians* (Leiden: Brill, 1998) and is currently writing a commentary on 1 and 2 Thessalonians in the Baker Exegetical Commentary on the New Testament series. His articles and book reviews have appeared in *New Testament Studies, Novum Testamentum, Journal of Biblical Studies, Religious Studies Review, Orientalia, Calvin Theological Journal* and *Trinity Journal*. He has also contributed articles to various monographs and theological dictionaries. He is an active member in several academic societies, lectures overseas, and preaches widely in the United States and Canada.

Terry Wilder
Midwestern Baptist Theological Seminary

Terry L. Wilder is Assistant Professor of New Testament and Greek at Midwestern Baptist Theological Seminary in Kansas City, Missouri. He is a graduate of Dallas Baptist University (B.A., M.A.), Southwestern Baptist Theological Seminary (M.Div.), and the University of Aberdeen (Ph.D.). He wrote his doctoral dissertation on pseudonymity and the New Testament and has contributed articles for *Tyndale Bulletin, Biblical Illustrator*, and the revised *Holman Bible Dictionary*. He and his wife Denisse met in the Netherlands while working as volunteers for the Billy Graham Evangelistic Association's Amsterdam '86. They have two sons, Ian and Aaron, and live in Kansas City. Terry enjoys basketball, home improvement, history, and the bagpipes.

Name Index

542 Interpreting the New Testament

Scripture Index

Indexes by Adam McCollum